The Complete Archa

The Complete Archaeology of Greece

From Hunter-Gatherers to the 20th Century AD

John Bintliff

WILEY-BLACKWELL

A John Wiley & Sons, Ltd., Publication

This edition first published 2012
© 2012 John Bintliff

Blackwell Publishing was acquired by John Wiley & Sons in February 2007. Blackwell's publishing program has been merged with Wiley's global Scientific, Technical, and Medical business to form Wiley-Blackwell.

Registered Office
John Wiley & Sons, Ltd, The Atrium, Southern Gate, Chichester, West Sussex, PO19 8SQ, UK

Editorial Offices
350 Main Street, Malden, MA 02148-5020, USA
9600 Garsington Road, Oxford, OX4 2DQ, UK
The Atrium, Southern Gate, Chichester, West Sussex, PO19 8SQ, UK

For details of our global editorial offices, for customer services, and for information about how
to apply for permission to reuse the copyright material in this book, please see our website
at www.wiley.com/wiley-blackwell.

The right of John Bintliff to be identified as the author of this work has been asserted in accordance with the UK Copyright, Designs and Patents Act 1988.

Wiley also publishes its books in a variety of electronic formats. Some content that appears in print may not be available in electronic books.

Designations used by companies to distinguish their products are often claimed as trademarks. All brand names and product names used in this book are trade names, service marks, trademarks or registered trademarks of their respective owners. The publisher is not associated with any product or vendor mentioned in this book. This publication is designed to provide accurate and authoritative information in regard to the subject matter covered. It is sold on the understanding that the publisher is not engaged in rendering professional services. If professional advice or other expert assistance is required, the services of a competent professional should be sought.

Library of Congress Cataloging-in-Publication Data

Bintliff, J. L. (John L.)
   The complete archaeology of Greece : from hunter-gatherers to the 20th century AD / John Bintliff. – 1st ed.
      p.   cm.
   Includes bibliographical references and index.
   ISBN 978-1-4051-5418-5 (hardback) – ISBN 978-1-4051-5419-2 (paperback)   1. Greece–Antiquities.
2. Greece–Civilization.   3. Architecture, Ancient–Greece.   4. Art, Ancient–Greece.   5. Excavations
(Archaeology)–Greece.   I. Title.
   DF77.B626 2012
   949.5–dc23

                                        2011049091

A catalogue record for this book is available from the British Library.

Set in 10/12pt Bembo by SPi Publisher Services, Pondicherry, India

1   2012

This book is dedicated to
THE PEOPLE OF GREECE
for whom 'Philoxenia' (kindness to strangers)
has always been an essential quality
of Aegean life

Contents

Part III   The Archaeology of Medieval and post-Medieval Greece in its Historical Context

List of Figures and Tables

The author and publisher gratefully acknowledge the permission granted to reproduce the copyright material in this book

Figures

Tables

List of Color Plates

The author and publisher gratefully acknowledge the permission granted to reproduce the copyright material in this book

Acknowledgments

First and foremost to my family, Elizabeth, David, Esther, and Aileen, for suffering my mental absence of several years as I wrote this book.

Then the following helped with advice on chapters or through sending me offprints and references: Fred Aalen, Polyxena Adam-Veleni, Sue Alcock, Penelope Allison, Stelios Andreou, Pamela Armstrong, Effie Athanassopoulos, Marc Bajema, John Bennet, Leslie Beaumont, Philip Bes, Andrew Bevan, Sebastiaan Bommeljé, Joe Carter, John Casey, Bill Cavanagh, John Cherry, Jan-Paul Crielaard, Jim Crow, Jack Davis, Oliver Dickinson, Peter Doorn, Panagiotis Doukellis, Jan Driessen, Archie Dunn, Nikos Efstratiou, Harry Fokkens, Hamish Forbes, Michaelis Fotiadis, Lynn Foxhill, Kevin Greene, Catherine Grandjean, Timothy Gregory, Paul Halstead, Mogens Hansen, Alan Harvey, K.-J. Hölkeskamp, Mamoru Ikeguchi, Jorrit Kelder, Machiel Kiel, Jost Knauss, Johannes Koder, Frank Kolb, Kostas Kotsakis, Franziska Lang, Gunnar Lehmann, Quentin Letesson, Philippe Leveau, Luuk de Ligt, Peter Lock, Hans Lohmann, Nino Luraghi, Christina Marangou, Ian Morris, Joseph Maran, Peter Marzolff, Chris Mee, Maarlen Mouliou, Stelios Mouzakis, Christel Müller, Frits Naerebout, Richard Osborne, Tassos Papacostas, John Papadopoulos, Kostas Papagiannopoulos, Catherine Perlès, David Pettegrew, Jeroen Poblome, Andrew Poulter, Marcus Rautman, Reinder Reinders, Athanasios Rizakis, Wil Roebroeks, David Romano, Jim Roy, Curtis Runnels, Jerry Rutter, Erwin Sabelberg, Yannis Saitas, Guy Sanders, Paul Sant Cassia, Friedrich Sauerwein, Kostas Sbonias, Ilse Schoep, Graham Shipley, Eleni Simoni, Jean-Pierre Sodini, Natascha Sojc, Anthony Snodgrass, Tony Spawforth, Andrew Stewart, Vladimir Stissi, Lauren Talalay, Thomas Tartaron, Peter Tomkins, Vangelis Tourloukis, Dimitris and Eleni Tsougarakis, Sofia Voutsaki, Vance Watrous, Ruth Westgate, James Whitley, Eleni Zavvou.

Finally immense gratitude to Rinse Willet for many days work on the figures, to Aileen for her valiant attempts to improve its prose, and to the always encouraging Wiley-Blackwell editors Julia Kirk and Rosalie Robertson.

Introduction

This book results from my own exposure, through surface survey in many regions of Greece since the early 1970s, to the incredible richness and variety of Greek archaeology beyond the traditional foci of the Classical Greek and Bronze Ages. As a doctoral student, traveling frequently on the bus from Athens to Navplion in the Peloponnese, I was struck by the diversity of historic landscapes, monuments, and ruins which I passed through. Isolated Byzantine churches far from any village, or the crumbling Medieval castellated walls of the Acrocorinth, seemed to hint at another kind of Greek archaeology from that found in popular textbooks. Since then, so much has developed in our archaeological understanding of the whole span of Greek Prehistory and History, from the Palaeolithic to the Early Modern era, that it seemed to me timely to make a first attempt at a synthesis of the key points both for the student and for the general reader fascinated by Greece, its past, its landscape, and its people.

David Clarke, in his iconoclastic textbook for a more truly scientific "New Archaeology," *Analytical Archaeology* (1968), admitted candidly that inventing, and at the same time composing a guide to, a new form of archaeology was rash, premature, but necessary. In humility, and with a nod to this book's reviewers, I feel in the same position regarding this first book, to my knowledge, which treats "The Archaeology of Greece" quite literally. Understandably,

in the scope of 22 chapters, coverage of each phase can only paint the general picture. Period specialists might regret the inevitable superficiality, but hopefully not find erroneous oversimplification. However, my aim is to give the reader, within one volume, an understanding of the development of human society in Greece from the earliest human traces up till the early twentieth century AD. For the contemporary visitor to Greece, whether you are there for a beach-based holiday, or a cultural tour, or as a student, I would like to think that this volume can give you a basis for contextualizing your casual or detailed encounters with museums, Bronze Age palaces, Classical city walls or great intercity sanctuaries, Roman stadia, Byzantine churches, isolated Frankish towers, Ottoman mosques, and traditional villages, without forgetting those ubiquitous broken potsherds that you can find in the open fields or on the shore.

The archaeology of Greece is an ever-expanding tree but with more limited roots (MacKendrick 1962, Snodgrass 1987, McDonald and Thomas 1990, Étienne and Étienne 1992, Schnapp 1993, Morris 1994, Fitton 1996, Shanks 1997, Étienne *et al.* 2000, Whitley 2001, Morris 2004). Its foundation is the investigation of Classical Greece, emanating from Renaissance and Enlightenment scholarship during the fifteenth to eighteenth centuries AD. But precocious beginnings can be dated to Roman times, when the new rulers of the Mediterranean toured the

Aegean Sea to discover that Classical tradition of which they saw themselves as inheritors. An interest in Greek antiquity could link the intellectual Cicero, one of many members of the Roman elite who were educated in Greece, and those Roman former slaves who resettled Corinth a century after its Roman destruction in the second century BC and pillaged Classical cemeteries for items for the Italian antiquities trade. The Romanized Greek travel-writer Pausanias, in the second century AD, represents the ancient model for Baedeker's Early Modern handbook of sites worthy to be visited by foreigners, focusing on major monuments and works of art, with selective historical titbits to bring them to life (Elsner 1992, Alcock *et al.* 2001).

Ancient Greece and Rome were of fundamental importance for European national identities and a sense of special providence in the time of European world hegemony in the seventeenth to nineteenth centuries (Morris 2004), each civilization providing complementary origin myths for the assumed superior qualities of Western civilization and empires. Apart from the surviving ancient texts, objects of Greco-Roman culture were attributed the same qualities of exceptional sophistication, even as works of genius whenever there was clear artistic merit (not merely temples and sculptures, but vases with painted scenes, and coins). Greek archaeology was essentially synonymous with Classical Greece and with an approach linking ancient texts with Art History, mostly focused on large-scale works of public art or private art objects belonging to the elite of ancient society.

If this led to an emphasis on museum cases filled with fine art, a parallel tradition was rapidly evolving, topographic fieldwork. For educated people whose imagination was stirred by ancient texts describing cities, sanctuaries, and battlefields, but who were unable to travel to Greece to see what was left of these places, a small army of "Travelers" sprang up to offer the fireside reader a taste of modern and ancient Greece (Tsigakou 1981, Angelomatis-Tsougarakis 1990, Eisner 1991). Beginning as early as the fifteenth century (for example Buondelmonti), learned travelers from Western Europe voyaged in increasing numbers to Greece, especially in the nineteenth century, to compose travelogues frequently illustrated by maps and pictures.

The primary aim was to identify major towns and shrines mentioned by Classical sources, record inscriptions, and describe (often with the aim of removing them to Western Europe), works of mobile and immobile art. If the main focus remained Classical and Hellenistic Greece, minor attention was given to Roman sites, and even occasionally to Medieval and later monuments.

The scientific ethos in European scholarship, growing with increasing Enlightenment influence during the eighteenth to nineteenth centuries, led to such detailed Travelers' descriptions that only modern scholars with other aims appreciate such information. Lolling's meticulous guidebook, rejected by Baedeker, has only recently been published (1989). Today the incidental detail on Early Modern villages, and many ancient monuments now lost, make such books invaluable for long-term landscape history (Bennet *et al.* 2000, Bintliff 2007).

During the late nineteenth century, Greek archaeology's scope widened, with the discovery and then systematization of the *pre*-Classical or prehistoric eras, and a rising interest in the history and monuments of the post-Classical eras, which meant Medieval times (the Byzantine and occasionally the Crusader-Frankish periods). The polymath approach which nineteenth-century scholarship aspired to and which could still be accomplished within the limits of available information, reached its peak in Greece in the decades around 1900. For example, young scholars associated with Alan Wace could publish on prehistoric and Classical sites, Byzantine churches (Fletcher and Kitson 1895–1896), Medieval castles (Traquair 1905–1906), Crusader sculpture (Wace 1904–1905), ethnography (Wace and Thompson 1914), and even traditional Cycladic embroidery (Wace 1914). In Turkey, Heinrich Schliemann's Troy project involved the history of metallurgy, regional geomorphological developments, and local epidemiology (Aslan and Thumm 2001).

This was also a critical era in the wider development of the Science of Archaeology, and as a result we see the inception of research excavations at key Aegean sites. Naturally Greco-Roman towns and sanctuaries are the primary focus, with a secondary emphasis on major centers of the newly-discovered Bronze Age civilizations of the Minoan on Crete and the Mycenaean on the Southern Mainland. Yet the

Figure 0.1 German excavations at the Heroon in Olympia, 1880. In the foreground are Richard Borrmann
and Wilhelm Dörpfeld.
© bpk, Berlin.

open-minded scholarship of this phase allowed the
relatively unspectacular Neolithic tell (artificial settlement mound) cultures of Northern Greece to be
discovered and excavated by Tsountas (1908), whilst
another innovative Greek, Xanthoudides (1924),
brought to light the tholos-tomb culture of Crete, an
important Early Bronze Age predecessor to the
Minoan palatial societies of the later Bronze Age
periods.

Most of the twentieth century is dominated by
long-term excavation projects, usually the responsibility of one Foreign School of archaeologists. Bronze
Age Mycenae (French 2002) has been investigated
by German, British, and Greek expeditions, but
more typically the Classical sanctuaries of Delphi
(Bommelaer and Laroche 1991) and Olympia
(Kyrieleis 2002: see Figure 0.1) remain associated
with the French and German Schools. Classical
Athens' central square (the *Agora*) (Camp 1986, 2006),
and the city of Corinth (Williams and Bookidis 2003),
have been essentially American excavations. These
major projects have produced bookshelves of specialist monographs representing 100–150 years of ongoing research.

One by-product of these excavation programs has been increasing attention to all the archaeological information they offer. At first they emphasized major architecture and the finer works of mobile art. But the vast quantities of everyday household objects revealed, encouraged study in their own right. Yet till recently domestic pottery and houses were relatively neglected in Greek historical archaeology. Likewise, a traditional emphasis on Classical Greece inhibited research into Roman, Medieval, and post-Medieval times (Mouliou 1994, 2009). The Bronze Age fared better, envisaged as a uniquely "European" civilization underlying Classical Greece. Again, since Classical Greece in ancient texts was basically that of the cities of the Southern Mainland, archaeological research in Northern Greece, Crete, and the other Aegean islands was far more limited till the latter part of the twentieth century, with the exception of major Bronze Age centers, since it was recognized that in contrast the Minoan-Mycenaean (and the related Cycladic) civilizations of the Bronze Age occupied a wider zone of the Aegean.

Despite this broadening of methods and timescales which Greek archaeology adopted between the later nineteenth to mid-twentieth centuries, the special relationship to Classical texts and the History of Art led by the 1960s to an increasing "Great Divide" between developments in "mainstream" archaeology ("The New Archaeology": Greene 2002) and approaches in use in Aegean research (Renfrew 1980, Snodgrass 1985).

In the succeeding generation, there has been considerable integration into mainstream practices, yet the picture at the start of the 2000s remains patchy. Greek national archaeology and that of the Foreign Schools show a mosaic of traditions of work and interpretation. In terms of the more science-focused "New Archaeology" agenda, still only a minority of excavations in the Aegean collect environmental data or "ecofacts" (animal bones, seeds, etc.), or submit human remains for anthropological study. The commonest remnant from the Greek past, the broken potsherd, provides a similar disparity: few field projects publish domestic wares as well as the decorated table and funerary wares. Physical and chemical scientific analysis of artifacts and sites remains a rare addition to traditional forms of excavation and object study. More

radical developments are visible in the types of site being investigated. Classical rural farms and Roman villas are being excavated in increasing numbers, with Greek scholars leading the way. The excellent museum in the new Athens Airport showing the rural landscape revealed during its construction (Tsouni 2001) is symptomatic, and advertises the international quality of contemporary Greek museums. Greater engagement with the Greek and foreign public is occurring at a rapid scale, with the refurbishing of museums throughout the country and with major changes to school textbooks, in particular emphasizing local history and archaeology of all periods. An excellent model for "outreach" from a regional excavation project is offered by Kostas Kotsakis and his team on the Paliambela Project in Macedonia (Kotsakis 2007, cf. also Bintliff 2004a).

Recent interactions between mainstream archaeology and that of Greece have been more positive. Since the 1980s a significant trend in archaeology has been Post-Processualism, which forefronts approaches where Classical archaeology has long been a world leader (Shanks 1997, Morris 2004). These include an emphasis on symbolic representations (essentially artistic creations), and seeing artifacts or architecture as "texts" relatable to the written sources, lifestyles, and mentalities of past peoples.

Also from the late twentieth century new perspectives emerged with the rapid takeoff of archaeological surface survey. Aegean scholarship was always a pioneer in landscape archaeology, but the mapping of ancient sites took on new dimensions with the arrival of regional interdisciplinary survey projects. Pride of place goes to the 1960s Minnesota University extensive survey in Messenia (McDonald and Rapp 1972), followed elsewhere during the 1970s with the first intensive (field by field) surface surveys (Cherry 1983, Bintliff 1994). These latter transect blocks of countryside on foot, recording spreads of surface pottery, lithics, and building material, which mark the disturbed deposits of archaeological sites of all sizes, from a few graves, through farms and villages, to ancient cities of a square kilometer or more (Bintliff and Snodgrass 1988a, Bintliff 2000a, Alcock and Cherry 2004).

In the 1980s, mapping all visible "sites" was supplemented by "siteless" survey, in which the occurrence of pre-Modern artifacts, rather than "sites" (foci of concentrated human activity), is the primary focus. It appears that much of lowland Greece is "an artifact," since such signs of human activity are almost continuously encountered between settlements (Bintliff and Snodgrass 1988b, Bintliff and Howard 2004). Alongside mapping settlement patterns, period by period, other forms of human impact on the Greek landscape now became apparent. Although some "off-site" debris represents eroded settlements, and the scattering of finds by weather and cultivation, the denser "carpets" probably record intense land use, especially through manuring (still a controversial theory, cf. Alcock *et al.* 1994 with Snodgrass 1994).

Intensive survey from the 1970s onwards discovered that the Aegean countryside is as rich in surface sites of post-Roman as of Greco-Roman and Bronze Age date. Dealing with the surface ceramics of the post-Roman era, and exploring the rich archival resources for these 1500 years, has encouraged vigorous new research into Byzantine, Frankish-Crusader, Ottoman-Venetian, and Early Modern archaeology in Greece (Lock and Sanders 1996, Bintliff 2000b, Davies and Davis 2007).

Turning now to this volume's structure, the core is a period-based overview of material culture and society, preceded by an introduction to the Greek landscape. Where the evidence is very rich, I have split period treatment into a chapter focusing on more "functional" aspects such as demography, settlement patterns, and the forms of material culture, followed by a chapter dealing with "symbolic" or "representational" culture (the ways in which architecture and portable objects can reveal the social order or the mentalities of past societies). Summing-up each period, I have reflected on our knowledge of each era in two ways. Firstly through the approach of French historians called the *Annales* group, where we trace the interaction of processes operating at different timescales. Secondly, I offer a "reflexive" view, with my own reactions to our current "biopic" or scenario for each period.

The French historians who focused their work around the journal *Annales* (1929–present, with various forms of title), most notably Fernand Braudel and Le Roy Ladurie, developed an insightful model of analysis for past societies (Bintliff 1991, Knapp 1992,

Bintliff 2004b). They argued that History is made through a dialectic (mutual interaction) of forces. Any event is the product of short-term actions and factors (the world of *événements*) interacting with processes unfolding on a longer timescale, the medium term of several generations or centuries (the *moyenne durée*), but also with processes at a far longer timescale (the *longue durée*). The real historical outcomes are unpredictable, but through seeking to isolate both the key elements at each layer of parallel time, and their mutual interplay, the historian can come closer to comprehending why the past developed the way it appears to have done. This has been termed "postdiction" by the historian of science Stephen Jay Gould, as opposed to "prediction" (Gould 1989, cf. Bintliff 1999). Significantly, the *Annales* historians see historical processes as combining the actions and beliefs of communities and of individuals, emphasizing that History was made not just by actions and factors of production such as technology or economy, but also by ideas, by symbolic culture and ways of seeing the world (*mentalités*).

The brief injection of my own reflexive response to our current knowledge of each period of Greek archaeology, which rounds off each chapter or chapter-pair, has been encouraged by that aspect of "Post-Processual" archaeological theory which reminds us of the dialectic in which archaeologists and historians are always engaged when they encounter past societies. We cannot help but reflect on the ways a past world differs or compares to our own, and must use our embedded knowledge of the world today to comprehend past worlds. On the other hand, I am far from being a relativist. Our interpretative concepts are certainly influenced by our own lives, but we also have a wealth of anthropology and history to broaden our interpretative models of the past beyond our own meager physical experience, and when you are doing Archaeology and History honestly and attentively, the past will constantly surprise you with evidence you were not prepared for and may have difficulty in making sense of.

This volume involved very wide-ranging reading, and inevitably the time required for its authoring and production processes has meant that quite a few important new books and papers could not be studied and incorporated into the text before you. In addition there is much more detail that I gathered together which had to be left out due to constraints on this book's length. Happily the publishers Wiley-Blackwell have set up an on-line resource for purchasers of this volume, in which I have been able not only to add an extensive set of additional notes to all the chapters, but also to update the book on some key recent publications.

Color Plate 0.1 has been provided in order to orient the reader to the main provinces of Greece and the key modern and ancient centers, as well as the physical geography of the country.

Finally to help the reader navigate through the many periods of time which a complete Archaeology of Greece should encompass, there follows a basic time-chart.

General Time Chart for the Archaeology of Greece

These ranges are generalized approximations and at least from the Neolithic onwards different provinces of Greece can vary in detail from these dates. Additionally some periods still remain under controversy over their timespans, especially in the Middle and Late Bronze Age.

PALAEOLITHIC: ca. 300,000–400,000 years before present (BP) to ca. 9000 BC
EPIPALAEOLITHIC/MESOLITHIC: ca. 9000 BC to ca. 7000 BC
NEOLITHIC: ca. 7000 BC to ca. 3500/3200 BC
EARLY BRONZE AGE: ca. 3500/3200 BC to ca. 2100/1900 BC
MIDDLE BRONZE AGE: ca. 2100/1900 BC to ca. 1700 BC
LATE BRONZE AGE: ca. 1700 BC to ca. 1200/1100 BC
"DARK AGE"/EARLY IRON AGE: ca. 1200/1100 BC to ca. 800/700 BC
ARCHAIC ERA: ca. 700 BC to ca. 500 BC
CLASSICAL ERA: ca. 500 BC BC to 323 BC
EARLY HELLENISTIC PERIOD: 323 BC to ca. 200 BC
LATE HELLENISTIC TO EARLY ROMAN ERA: ca. 200 BC to ca. 200 AD

MIDDLE TO LATE ROMAN PERIOD: ca. 200 AD to ca. 650 AD
"DARK AGE" / EARLY BYZANTINE ERA: ca. 650 AD to 842 AD
MIDDLE BYZANTINE PERIOD: 842 AD to 1204 AD
LATE BYZANTINE/FRANKISH-CRUSADER ERA: 1204 AD to ca. 1400 AD
OTTOMAN PERIOD: ca. 1400 AD to 1830 AD
EARLY MODERN ERA: 1830 AD to 1950 AD

References

Alcock, S. E., J. F. Cherry, and J. L. Davis (1994). "Intensive survey, agricultural practice and the classical landscape of Greece." In I. Morris (ed.), Classical Greece. Ancient Histories and Modern Archaeologies. Cambridge: Cambridge University Press, 137–170.

Alcock, S. E., J. F. Cherry, and J. Elsner (2001). Pausanias. Travel and Memory in Roman Greece. Oxford: Oxford University Press.

Alcock, S. E. and J. F. Cherry (eds.) (2004). Side by Side Survey. Comparative Regional Study in the Mediterranean World. Oxford: Oxbow.

Angelomatis-Tsougarakis, H. (1990). The Eve of the Greek Revival. London: Routledge.

Aslan, R. and D. Thumm (2001). "Ein Traum und seine Auswirkungen." In M. Korfmann (ed.), Troia. Traum und Wirklichkeit. Stuttgart: Konrad Theiss, 323–329.

Bennet, J., J. L. Davis, and F. Zarinebaf-Shahr (2000). "Pylos Regional Archaeological Project, Part III. Sir William Gell's Itinerary in the Pylia and Regional Landscapes in the Morea in the Second Ottoman Period." Hesperia 69, 343–380.

Bintliff, J. L. (ed.) (1991). The Annales School and Archaeology. Leicester: Leicester University Press.

Bintliff, J. L. (1994). "The history of the Greek countryside: As the wave breaks, prospects for future research." In P. N. Doukellis and L. G. Mendoni (eds.), Structures rurales et sociétés antiques. Paris: Les Belles Lettres, 7–15.

Bintliff, J. L. (1999). "Structure, contingency, narrative and timelessness." In J. L. Bintliff (ed.), Structure and Contingency in the Evolution of Life, Human Evolution and Human History. London: Cassell, 132–148.

Bintliff, J. (2000a). "Beyond dots on the map: The future of artefact survey in Greece." In J. Bintliff, M. Kuna, and N. Venclova (eds.), The Future of Archaeological Field Survey in Europe. Sheffield: Sheffield Academic Press, 3–20.

Bintliff, J. (2000b). "Reconstructing the Byzantine countryside: New approaches from landscape archaeology." In

K. Blelke *et al.* (eds.), *Byzanz als Raum*. Wien: Österreichische Akademie der Wissenschaften, 37–63.

Bintliff, J. L. (2004a). "Local history and heritage management in Greece. The potential at the village level." In P. Doukellis and L. Mendoni (eds.), *Perception and Evaluation of Cultural Landscapes*. Athens: National Research Centre, 137–152.

Bintliff, J. L. (2004b). "Time, structure and agency: The Annales, emergent complexity, and archaeology." In J. L. Bintliff (ed.), *A Companion to Archaeology*. Oxford: Blackwell, 174–194.

Bintliff, J. L. (2007). "Current research on the settlement of Boeotia in the Medieval and Early Modern era: The Boeotian Village History Project." In K. Fittschen (ed.), *Historische Landeskunde und Epigraphik in Griechenland*. Münster: Scriptorium, 217–226.

Bintliff, J. L. and P. Howard (2004). "A radical rethink on approaches to surface survey and the rural landscape of Central Greece in Roman times." In F. Kolb and E. Müller-Luckner (ed.), *Chora und Polis*. München: R. Oldenbourg Verlag, 43–78.

Bintliff, J. L. and A. M. Snodgrass (1988a). "Mediterranean survey and the city." *Antiquity* 62, 57–71.

Bintliff, J. L. and A. M. Snodgrass (1988b). "Off-site pottery distributions: A regional and interregional perspective." *Current Anthropology* 29, 506–513.

Bommelaer, J.-F. and D. Laroche (1991). *Guide de Delphes*. Paris: De Boccard.

Camp, J. M. (1986). *The Athenian Agora*. London: Thames & Hudson.

Camp, J. M. (2006). "Im Zentrum der Geschichte." *Antike Welt* 37/2, 45–54.

Cherry, J. F. (1983). "Frogs round the pond: perspectives on current archaeological survey projects in the Mediterranean region." In D. R. Keller and D. W. Rupp (eds.), *Archaeological Survey in the Mediterranean Area*. Oxford: BAR Int. Series 155, 375–416.

Clarke, D. L. (1968). *Analytical Archaeology*. London: Methuen.

Davies, S. and J. L. Davis (eds.) (2007). *Between Venice and Istanbul. Colonial Landscapes in Early Modern Greece*. *Hesperia* Supplement 40. Athens: American School of Classical Studies.

Eisner, R. (1991). *Travelers to an Antique Land: The History and Literature of Travel to Greece*. Ann Arbor: University of Michigan Press.

Elsner, J. (1992). "A Greek pilgrim in the Roman world." *Past and Present* 135, 3–29.

Étienne, R. and F. Étienne (1992). *The Search for Ancient Greece*. London: Thames & Hudson.

Étienne, R., C. Müller, and F. Prost (2000). *Archéologie historique de la Grèce antique*. Paris: Ellipses.

Fitton, J. L. (1996). *The Discovery of the Greek Bronze Age*. Cambridge, MA: Harvard University Press.

Fletcher, H. M. and S. D. Kitson (1895–1896). "The churches of Melos." *Annual of the British School at Athens* 2, 155–168.

French, E. (2002). *Mycenae, Agamemnon's Capital: The Site in its Setting*. Stroud: Tempus.

Gould, S. J. (1989). *Wonderful Life*. London: Hutchinson.

Greene, K. (2002). *An Introduction to Archaeology*. London: Routledge.

Knapp, A. B. (ed.) (1992). *Archaeology, Annales, and Ethnohistory*. Cambridge: Cambridge University Press.

Kotsakis, K. (2007). "Developing educational programmes for prehistoric sites." In I. Hodder and L. Doughty (eds.), *Mediterranean Prehistoric Heritage. Training, Education and Management*. Cambridge: McDonald Institute, 105–116.

Kyrieleis, H. (ed.) (2002). *Olympia 1875–2000, 125 Jahre Deutsche Ausgrabungen*. Mainz: Philipp von Zabern.

Lock, P. and G. D. R. Sanders (eds.) (1996). *The Archaeology of Medieval Greece*. Oxford: Oxbow.

Lolling, H. G. (1989). *Reisenotizen aus Griechenland 1876 und 1877*. Berlin: Reimer Verlag.

McDonald, W. A. and G. R. Rapp (eds.) (1972). *The Minnesota Messenia Expedition. Reconstructing a Bronze Age Regional Environment*. Minneapolis: University of Minnesota Press.

McDonald, W. A. and C. G. Thomas (1990). *Progress into the Past: The Rediscovery of Mycenaean Civilization*. Bloomington: Indiana University Press.

MacKendrick, P. (1962). *The Greek Stones Speak*. London: Methuen.

Morris, I. (1994). "Archaeologies of Greece." In I. Morris (ed.), *Classical Greece. Ancient Histories and Modern Archaeologies*. Cambridge: Cambridge University Press, 8–47.

Morris, I. (2004). "Classical archaeology." In J. L. Bintliff (ed.), *A Companion to Archaeology*. Oxford: Blackwell, 253–271.

Mouliou, M. (1994). "The classical past, the modern Greeks and their national self: Projecting identity through museum exhibitions." *Museological Review* 1, 70–88.

Mouliou, M. (2009). "The concept of diachronia in the Greek archaeological museum: Reflections on current challenges." In J. Bintliff and H. Stöger (eds.), *Medieval and Post-Medieval Greece. The Corfu Papers*. Oxford: BAR Int. Series 2023, 233–241.

Renfrew, A. C. (1980). "The great tradition versus the great divide: archaeology as anthropology?" *American Journal of Archaeology* 84, 287–298.

Ross, L. (1851). *Wanderungen in Griechenland im Gefolge des Königs Otto und der Königin Amalie*. Halle: Schwetschke.

Schnapp, A. (1993). *La Conquête du passé: aux origines de l'archéologie*. Paris: Carré.

Shanks, M. (1997). *The Classical Archaeology of Greece*. London: Routledge.

Snodgrass, A. (1985). "The new archaeology and the classical archaeologist." *American Journal of Archaeology* 89, 31–37.

Snodgrass, A. (1987). *An Archaeology of Greece*. Stanford: Stanford University Press.

Snodgrass, A. (1994). "Response: the archaeological aspect." In I. Morris (ed.), *Classical Greece. Ancient Histories and Modern Archaeologies*. Cambridge: Cambridge University Press, 197–200.

Traquair, R. (1905–1906). "Laconia. I. The mediaeval fortresses." *Annual of the British School at Athens* 12, 258–276.

Tsigakou, F. M. (1981). *The Rediscovery of Greece*. London: Thames & Hudson.

Tsouni, K. (ed.) (2001). *Mesogaia*. Athens: Athens International Airport.

Tsountas, C. (1908). *Ai proistorikai akropoleis Dhiminiou kai Sesklou*. Athens: Sakellariou.

Wace, A. J. B. (1904–1905). "Laconia. V. Frankish sculptures at Parori and Geraki." *Annual of the British School at Athens* 11, 139–145.

Wace, A. J. B. (1914). *Catalogue of a Collection of Old Embroideries of the Greek Islands and Turkey*. London: Burlington Fine Arts Club.

Wace, A. J. B. and M. S. Thompson (1914). *The Nomads of the Balkans*. London: Methuen.

Whitley, J. (2001). *The Archaeology of Ancient Greece*. Cambridge: Cambridge University Press.

Williams, C. K. and N. Bookidis (eds.) (2003). *Corinth, the Centenary: 1896–1996*. Princeton: American School of Classical Studies at Athens.

Xanthoudides, S. A. (1924). *The Vaulted Tombs of the Mesara*. London: Hodder & Stoughton.

Part I

The Landscape and Aegean Prehistory

1

The Dynamic Land

Introduction

Greece is a land of contrasts (Admiralty 1944, Bintliff 1977, Higgins and Higgins 1996: and see Color Plate 0.1). Although promoted to tourists for its sandy beaches, rocky headlands, and a sea with shades of green and blue, where Aleppo pine or imported Eucalyptus offer shade, in reality the Greek Mainland peninsula, together with the great island of Crete, are dominated by other more varied landscapes. Postcard Greece is certainly characteristic of the many small and a few larger islands in the Cycladic Archipelago at the center of the Aegean Sea, the Dodecanese islands in the Southeast Aegean, and the more sporadic islands of the North Aegean, but already the larger islands off the west coast of Greece such as Ithaka, Corfu, and Kephallenia, immediately surprise the non-Mediterranean visitor with their perennial rich vegetation, both cultivated trees and Mediterranean woodlands. The Southwest Mainland is also more verdant than the better known Southeast.

The largest land area of modern Greece is formed by the north–south Mainland peninsula. At the Isthmus of Corinth this is almost cut in two, forming virtually an island of its southern section (the Peloponnese). Although in the Southeast Mainland there are almost continuous coastal regions with the classic Greek or Mediterranean landscape, not far inland one soon encounters more varied landforms,

plants, and climate, usually through ascending quickly to medium and even higher altitudes. There are coastal and inland plains in the Peloponnese and Central Greece, but their size pales before the giant alluvial and karst (rugged hard limestone) basins of the Northern Mainland, a major feature of the essentially inland region of Thessaly and the coastal hinterlands further northeast in Macedonia and Thrace. If these are on the east side of Northern Greece, the west side is dominated by great massifs of mountain and rugged hill land, even down to the sea, typical of the regions of Aetolia, Acarnania, and Epirus.

Significantly, the olive tree (Figure 1.1), flourishes on the Aegean islands, Crete, the coastal regions of the Peloponnese, the Central Greek eastern lowlands, and the Ionian Islands, but cannot prosper in the high interior Peloponnese, and in almost all the Northern Mainland. The reasons for the variety of Greek landscapes are largely summarized as *geology* and *climate*.

Geological and Geomorphological History

Although there are many areas with very old geological formations (Figure 1.2: Crystalline Rocks), the main lines of Greek topography were formed in recent geological time, resulting from that extraordinary deformation of the Earth's crust called the Alpine

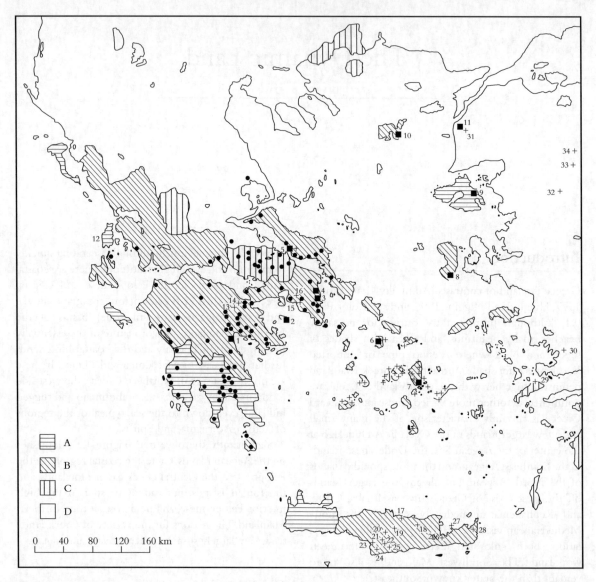

Figure 1.1 Distribution of the major modern olive-production zones with key Bronze Age sites indicated. The shading from A to C indicates decreasing olive yields, D denotes no or minimal production. Major Bronze Age sites are shown with crosses, circles, and squares.
C. Renfrew, *The Emergence of Civilization* (Study in Prehistory), London 1972, Figure 18.12. © 1972 Methuen & Co. Reproduced by permission of Taylor & Francis Books UK.

Orogeny, or mountain-building episode, which not only put in place the major Greek mountain ranges but the Alps and the Himalayas (Attenborough 1987, Higgins and Higgins 1996). In the first period of the Tertiary geological era (the Palaeogene), 40–20 million years ago, as the crustal plates which make up the basal rocks of Africa and Eurasia were crushed together, the bed of a large intervening ocean, Tethys, was compressed between their advancing masses and thrust upwards into high folds, like a carpet pushed from both ends. Those marine sediments became folded mountains of limestone (Figure 1.2: Limestone).

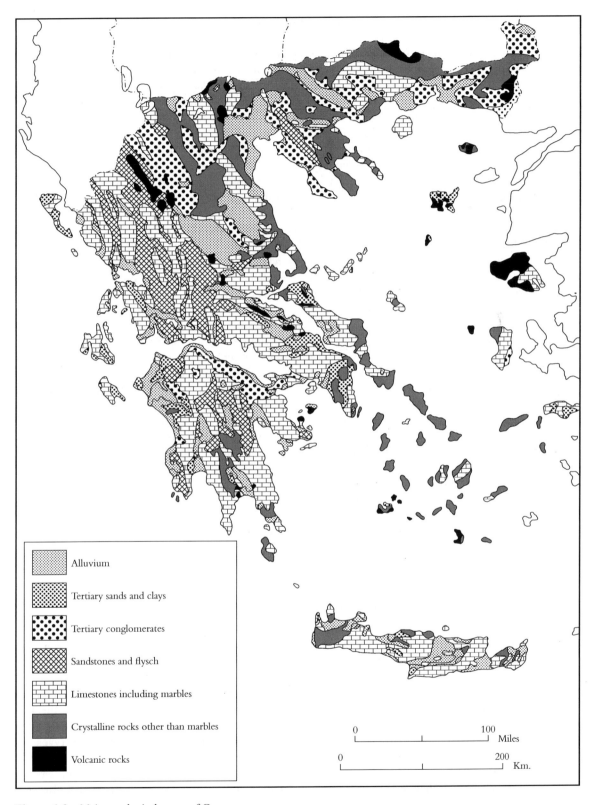

Figure 1.2 Major geological zones of Greece.

H. C. Darby *et al.*, *Naval Geographical Intelligence Handbook, Greece*, vol. 1. London: Naval Intelligence Division 1944, Figure 4.

Legend:

- Alluvium
- Tertiary sands and clays
- Tertiary conglomerates
- Sandstones and flysch
- Limestones including marbles
- Crystalline rocks other than marbles
- Volcanic rocks

0   100 Miles

0   200 Km.

This plate-tectonic compression created an arc-formed alignment of Alpine mountains and associated earthquake and volcanic belts (Figure 1.2: Volcanic Rocks), which begins as a NW-SE line for the Mainland mountain folds, then curves eastwards across the center of the Aegean Sea, as the E-W orientation of Crete illustrates, and also the associated island arc of volcanoes from Methana to Santorini, to be continued in the E-W ridges of the Western Mainland of Anatolia-Turkey (Friedrich 2000). The Ionian and Aegean seas have been formed by differential sinking of those lateral parts of the Alpine arc, creating the Aegean and Ionian Islands out of former mountain ridges, hence their often rocky appearance. But also there have been tectonic ruptures in different alignments, the most notable being that E-W downward fault which forms the Gulf of Corinth. The artificial cutting of the Corinth Canal in 1893 accomplished the removal of the remaining 8 km stretch left by Nature.

These plate-tectonic forces still operate today, since the Aegean region forms an active interface between the southerly African and northerly Eurasian blocks, and is itself an unstable agglomerate of platelets. Where zones of the Earth's crust are clashing, and ride against, or force themselves under or over each other, there are notorious secondary effects: frequent earthquakes and arcs of volcanoes set behind the active plate boundaries (Color Plate 1.1). Recurrent Greek earthquakes are a tragic reality, notably along the Gulf of Corinth, and the same zone curves into Turkey with equally dire consequences. The volcanic arc runs from the peninsula of Methana in the Eastern Peloponnese through the Cycladic islands of Melos and Santorini-Thera. A secondary arc of earthquake sensitivity runs closer to Crete and its mark punctuates that island's history and prehistory. Around 1550 years ago, a violent earthquake through the Eastern Mediterranean elevated Western Crete by up to 9 meters (Kelletat 1991), lifting Phalasarna harbor out of the ocean (Frost and Hadjidaki 1990).

The mostly limestone mountains of Mainland Greece and Crete, as young ranges, are high and vertiginous, even close to the sea. Subsequently these characteristics encouraged massive erosion, especially as sea levels rose and sank but ultimately settled at a relatively low level to these young uplands. As a result, between the limestone ridges there accumulated masses of eroded debris in shallow water, later compressed into rock itself, flysch, whose bright shades of red, purple or green enliven the lower slopes of the rather monotonously greyscale, limestone high relief of Greece (Figure 1.2: Sandstones and Flysch). For a long period in the next subphase of the Tertiary era, the Neogene, alongside these flysch accumulations, episodes of intermediate sea level highs deposited marine and freshwater sediments in the same areas of low to medium attitude terrain over large areas of Greece. These produced rocks varying with depositional context from coarse cobbly conglomerates of former torrents or beaches, through sandstones of slower river and marine currents, to fine marly clays created in still water (Figure 1.2: Tertiary Sands and Clays, Tertiary Conglomerates).

During the current geological era, the Quaternary, from two million years ago, the Earth has been largely enveloped in Ice Ages, with regular shorter punctuations of global warming called Interglacials, each sequence lasting some 100,000 years. Only in the highest Greek mountains are there signs of associated glacial activity, the Eastern Mediterranean being distant from the coldest zones further north in Eurasia. More typical for Ice Age Greece were alternate phases of cooler and wetter climate and dry to hyperarid cold climate. Especially in those Ice Age phases of minimal vegetation, arid surfaces and concentrated rainfall released immense bodies of eroded upland sediments, which emptied into the internal and coastal plains of Greece, as well as forming giant alluvial (riverborne) and colluvial (slopewash) fans radiating out from mountain and hill perimeters. We are fortunate to live in a warm Interglacial episode called the Holocene, which began at the end of the last Ice Age some 12,000 years ago. Alongside persistent plate-tectonic effects – earthquakes around Corinth, one burying the Classical city of Helike (Soter et al. 2001), earthquakes on Crete, and the Bronze Age volcanic eruption of Thera (Bruins et al. 2008) – the Greek landscape has witnessed the dense infilling of human communities to levels far beyond the low density hunter-gatherer bands which occupied it in the pre-Holocene stages of the Quaternary era or "Pleistocene" period.

The results of human impact – deforestation, erosion, mining, and the replacement of the natural plant and animal ecology with the managed crops and domestic animals of mixed-farming life – are visible everywhere, yet certainly exaggerated. Holocene erosion-deposits in valleys and plains are actually of smaller scale and extent than Ice Age predecessors. Coastal change in historic times may seem dramatic but is as much the consequence of global sea level fluctuations (a natural result of the glacial-interglacial cycle), as of human deforestation and associated soil loss in the hinterland (Bintliff 2000, 2002). (In Figure 1.2, the largest exposures of the combined Pleistocene and Holocene river and slope deposits are grouped as Alluvium.)

Globally, at the end of the last Ice Age, sea level rose rapidly from 130 meters below present, reflecting swift melting (eustatic effects) of the major ice-sheets (Roberts 1998). By mid-Holocene times, ca. 4000 BC, when the Earth's warming reached its natural Interglacial peak, sea levels were above present. Subsequently they lowered, but by some meters only. However, due to a massive and slower response of landmass readjustments to the weight of former ice-sheets, large parts of the globe saw vertical land and continental-shelf movements (isostatic effects), which have created a relative and continuing sea level rise, though again just a few meters. The Aegean is an area where such landmass sinking has occurred in recent millennia (Lambeck 1996). The Aegean scenario is: large areas of former dry land were lost to rising seas in Early to Mid-Holocene, 10,000–4000 BC, depriving human populations of major areas of hunting and gathering (Sampson 2006). Subsequently Aegean sea levels have risen slightly (around a meter per millennium), but remained within a few meters of the 4000 BC height, allowing river deposits to infill coastal bays and landlock prehistoric and historic maritime sites.

Let me try to give you the "feel" of the three-dimensional Greek landscape. From a sea dotted with islands, the rocky peaks of submerged mountains (Color Plate 1.2a), and occasional volcanoes, the Greek coastlands alternate between gently sloping plains of Holocene and Pleistocene sediments, and cliffs of soft-sediment Tertiary hill land or hard rock limestone ridges. The coastal plains and those further inland are a combination of younger, often marshy alluvial and lagoonal sediments (usually brown hues) (Color Plate 1.2b), and drier older Pleistocene alluvial and colluvial sediments (often red hues) (Color Plate

1.3a). The coastal and hinterland plains and coastal cliff-ridges rise into intermediate terrain, hill country. In the South and East of Greece this is mainly Tertiary yellowy-white marine and freshwater sediments, forming rolling, fertile agricultural land (Color Plate 1.3b), but in the Northwest Mainland hard limestones dominate the plain and valley edges, a harsh landscape suiting extensive grazing. A compensation in hard limestone zones within this hill land, including the Northwest, is exposures of flysch, which vary from fertile arable to a coarse facies prone to unstable "badland" topography. As we move upwards and further inland, our composite Greek landscape is dominated by forbidding ridges of Alpine limestone (Color Plate 1.3a), sometimes transformed by subterranean geological processes into dense marbles. Frequently at the interface between hill land and mountain altitudes occur much older rocks: tectonic folding and faulting after the Alpine mountain-building phase has tipped up the original limestone terrain, bringing to light earlier geological formations of the Palaeozoic or pre-Alpine Mesozoic eras. They were joined by post-Orogeny localized eruptive deposits. These are dense crystalline rocks such as schists, slates, and serpentines, whose bright colors and sharp edges trace the borders between the towering grey masses of limestone and the gentler hill lands of Tertiary sandstones or flysch which make up much of the Greek intermediate elevations. The intervention of such impermeable rocks even as thin bands at the foot of limestone massifs commonly forms a spring-line, neatly lying between good arable below and good grazing land above, a prime location for human settlement. The recent volcanic deposits can be fertile arable land, if sufficient rainfall frees their rich minerals to support soil development and plant growth. Finally, in some regions of Greece, mainly the Northeast Mainland, the Orogeny played a limited role, and the mountain massifs are much older dense crystalline rocks.

Climate

As with its geology, Greece does not have a single climate (Admiralty 1944, Bintliff 1977). Our image of long dry summers and mild winters with occasional rain reflects the focus of foreign visitors on the

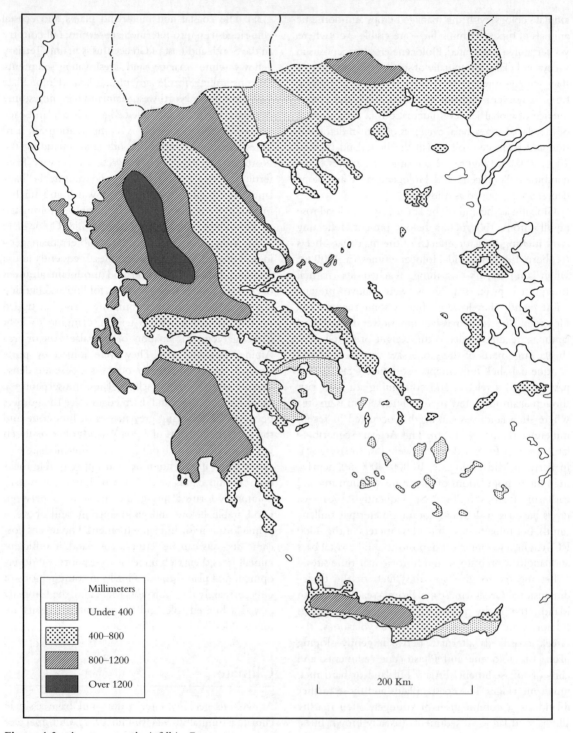

Figure 1.3   Average annual rainfall in Greece.
H. C. Darby *et al.*, *Naval Geographical Intelligence Handbook, Greece*, vol. 1. London: Naval Intelligence Division 1944, Figure 59.

Southeast Mainland, the Aegean islands, and lowland Crete, where this description is appropriate.

The two key factors in the Greek climate are the country's location within global climate belts, and the dominant lines of Greece's physical geography. Greece lies in the path of the Westerly Winds, so that autumn and spring rainfall emanates from the Atlantic, but is much less intense than in Northwest Europe. The Westerly rainbelt decreases in strength the further south and east you go in the Mediterranean. Most of Modern Greece has the same latitude as Southern Spain, Southern Italy, and Sicily, making all these regions strikingly more arid than the rest of Southern Europe. In summer the country lies within a hot dry weather system linking Southern Europe to North Africa. In winter cold weather flows from the North Balkans.

The internal physical landforms of the country also have a major effect on the distribution of rainfall, snow, and frost, and temperatures through the year. The Alpine Orogeny stamped the Mainland with mountain blocks running Northwest to Southeast. On Crete these ranges swing East-West toward Anatolia, so its high mountains form an island backbone on this alignment, but the relative depression of the Aegean Sea caused a tilting of the island, leaving its western third far more elevated. These Alpine obstacles, rising in the west and central sectors of the Greek Mainland and Crete, force the Westerly rains to deposit the major part of their load along the West face of Greece and in Western Crete, making the Eastern Mainland, the Aegean Islands, and Eastern Crete lie in rainshadow, thus restricting the available rainfall for plants and humans (Figure 1.3).

Temperature, rainfall, and frost-snow also vary according to altitude, and Greece is a land of rapid altitudinal contrasts. No part of the broadest landmass, the Northern Mainland, is more than 140 km from the sea, whilst for the Peloponnese the most inland point is 45 km distant, yet in these short spans one can move (sometimes in a few hours), from sea level to the high mountain zone. With height come lower temperatures and more snow-frost, milder summers, and more severe winters than experienced in the favored summer and winter tourist destinations of the Aegean Islands and coasts of the Southeast Mainland, but in compensation, there is less risk of drought and life-threatening heatwaves. In the drier zones of Greece drought is a constant threat to crop cultivation and animal-raising, and is frequent enough to pose an adaptive challenge for any past Greek society with a dense population and elaborate division of labor.

The powerful effects of geology and climate in creating the diverse landscapes of Greece are also dominant in the mosaic of natural and artificial vegetation belts which one meets in traveling from South to North, or East to West, and even more clearly from coast to inland mountains.

Vegetation

Climbing to higher altitudes in the Mediterranean produces effects comparable to traveling northwards toward the Arctic, passing out of Mediterranean into temperate, then continental and finally to subarctic climates (Admiralty 1944, Bintliff 1977, Rackham 1983, Kautzky 1993). Average annual temperatures decline, and although summers can be hot they are milder than in coastal lowlands; autumn, spring, and winter are colder and rainier; finally, winter frost and snow increase with height above sea level. The position of the uplands relative to rain-bearing autumn and spring Westerlies modify these effects, also true for the winter cold climate cells which derive from the Balkans. Thus when traveling west and north from the Mediterranean climate zone of the Southeast Mainland coast and its offshore islands, or merely inland and up into the hill land and then mountains, we observe a succession of natural vegetation zones which are related to the main vegetation zones of Europe from its far south to its far north.

Evergreen trees (oaks, olives) give way to mixed evergreen and deciduous trees and shrubs, then deciduous vegetation is gradually displaced by hardy coniferous trees, until finally in the highest or rockiest mountain peaks trees decline and Alpine grasses and low plants dominate. However, this is a picture of typical conditions throughout Greece in the middle of an Interglacial period, and for the Holocene this has been much modified by human impact.

Since people colonized the Greek landscape in large numbers, from the Late Neolithic (ca. 5000 BC), they have modified natural vegetation to assist their farming-herding economy, whilst from the mature

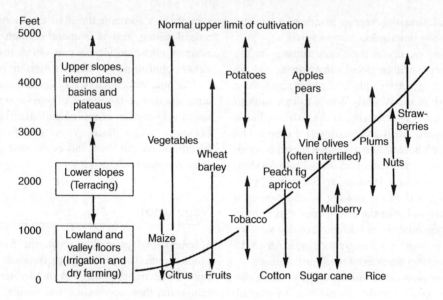

Figure 1.4   The vertical zonation of crops in the Mediterranean lands.
J. M. Houston, *The Western Mediterranean World*. London 1964, Figure 28. Courtesy of J. M. Houston.

Iron Age onwards (ca. 800 BC) intensified mining and timber extraction has increased human impact. In some regions and periods in the past, natural woodland disappeared or was reduced to a patchwork amid a landscape of fields, pastures or mere wasteland. Photographs for much of Greece from the late nineteenth to early twentieth centuries frequently portray treeless, almost lunar landscapes. Fortunately the Greek government in recent decades has implemented increasingly effective reafforestation and woodland preservation programs. Redirection of the economy away from extensive sheep and goat raising has dramatically allowed uplands to regenerate tree cover. European Union agricultural policies, and internal pressure to focus Greek farming on highly commercial forms of land use, are also creating divergent paths in the previously cultivated landscape. Open lowlands and areas with plentiful pumped irrigation water are now intensively farmed throughout the year for multiple crops. In contrast, vast areas of hill country where motor and irrigation access are restricted, and fields small, are swiftly reverting to scrubland and bushes. Areas suitable for archaeological landscape survey are increasingly confined by this polarization of land use.

However, human impact from later prehistoric times onwards has always been regionally diversified,

as the "agropastoral" (farmer–herder) economy adapted to local climate and topography (Figure 1.4). In the lowlands and hill lands, to several hundred meters above sea level, natural Mediterranean evergreen woodland, alternating with dry steppe and shrubs where stoniness or aridity prevented tree cover, has become a cultivated "woodland" of evergreen olives, figs, vines, and (after Medieval importation) citrus fruits. Natural grasses and bulbs have been replaced by the favored bread grasses wheat, barley, and the root crops beans, lentils, and melons. From the sixteenth to seventeenth centuries AD onwards, the versatile exotic maize and exotic commercial shrubs cotton and tobacco spread widely. In the cooler hill lands, fruit and nut trees, which were a natural component of the European mixed deciduous–evergreen vegetation, have been favored, such as apples, whilst the milder, wetter climate suited native vegetables and Early Modern imports such as potatoes. In the higher uplands more open landscapes due to climate, culminating in high level grass–bulb landscapes, have been drastically enhanced by human clearance (by fire, axe, and grazing) to make pasturelands, where cooler summers compared to the lowlands have encouraged specialist herders to bring seasonally transhumant domestic flocks.

Vegetation

The zonal vegetation map of Greece (Color Plate 1.4) demonstrates that topography, geology, and climate collaborate to produce a clear trend in the distribution of typical natural vegetation during a warm period such as our current Interglacial. The drier coastlands and islands, mainly in the South and especially the Southeast, display Mediterranean evergreen, drought-resistant plants. If unaffected by fire, grazing, and cultivation (a minority of the landscape!) one would find savannah or woodland composed of trees like evergreen oak, Aleppo pine, and wild olive. Moving away from the Southeast Mainland coasts and islands, north and west, higher rainfall and often higher relief support mixed Mediterranean evergreen and deciduous woodland species, deciduous oaks, beech, and chestnut. Such mixed vegetation would in the natural state typify higher land in the South and much of the lower land in the North. Within the great upland zones which constitute Mainland Greece's rugged interior, Mediterranean vegetation disappears and we find deciduous and increasingly with altitude more continental tree species, such as hardy conifers, the latter dominant as we ascend the mountains. Even without human interference there would be small zones in the uppermost mountain belts with Alpine, non-tree grassland and other low plants. Given the fact that in Greece one can move within a short distance from the dry coastland up into fringing mountains, it is often possible in many parts of Greece to walk in a day from Mediterranean evergreen brushland through deciduous, then coniferous, woodland and see ahead the bare Alpine-plant zone on the crests of the mountains.

For typical, mostly natural, tree species see Figure 1.5. In the Greek lowlands original woodland

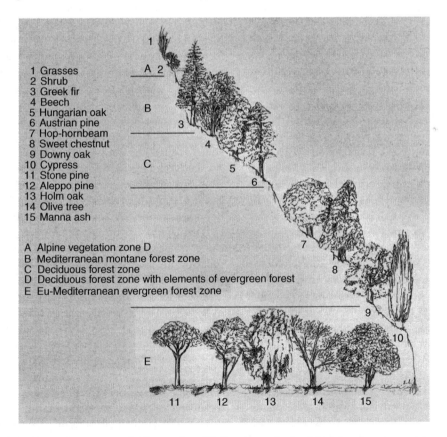

1 Grasses
2 Shrub
3 Greek fir
4 Beech
5 Hungarian oak
6 Austrian pine
7 Hop-hornbeam
8 Sweet chestnut
9 Downy oak
10 Cypress
11 Stone pine
12 Aleppo pine
13 Holm oak
14 Olive tree
15 Manna ash

A Alpine vegetation zone D
B Mediterranean montane forest zone
C Deciduous forest zone
D Deciduous forest zone with elements of evergreen forest
E Eu-Mediterranean evergreen forest zone

Figure 1.5 Vegetation sequence in Greece, from Mediterranean lowland (right) to inner mountain peaks (left). Modified from J. Kautzky, *Natuurreisgids Griekenland. Vasteland en Kuststreken*. De Bilt 1995, diagram on p. 23.

cover was first removed on a large scale by later Neolithic and Bronze Age times, and the cultivable landscape is considered to have already possessed its Early Modern appearance by Classical Greek times (Bintliff 1977, 1993): a mosaic of open land (dominated by grain crops) and cultivated olive and fig orchards and vineyards. In place of woodland, where agriculture is not found, human impact by fire and grazing, or natural climatic aridity, give rise to three levels of sub-woodland vegetation, in decreasing order of size and ground surface cover (Rackham 1983): degraded evergreen woodland becomes low shrubland ("maquis"), predominantly prickly oak bushes. More heavily degraded land, or where bare rock is very prominent, supports thin grassland mixed with spiky plants ("steppe"). Finally in the least vegetated zones, the result of maximum human impact or the dominance of bare rock, we find very low, widely-spaced "phrygana" or "garrigue" vegetation, notable for aromatic fragrances and valued by bees and humans for nourishment and cuisine respectively (sage, thyme).

Pollen analysis documents the evolution of vegetation in Greece, taken from lake and coastal corings. A prediction for a warm epoch or Interglacial, such as our Holocene period, without human interference, comes from a deep boring at Philippi in Northeast Mainland Greece which covers the last million years (Wijmstra *et al.* 1990). A warm, wet early phase, with mixed deciduous and evergreen open woodland, would by mid-interglacial in the lowlands give way to a drier Mediterranean climate, encouraging denser evergreen woodland, then be succeeded, as the era moves toward a new glacial, by a cooler and wetter climate encouraging a rise in deciduous vegetation. This reconstruction agrees with early-mid Holocene pollen cores from the drier Southern Greek climate. Here Bottema (1990) noted increasingly drier climate through the early farming eras of the later Neolithic and Bronze Age, in Middle Holocene times (more pronounced from 5000 to 4000 BC), then a postulated rise in rainfall, or aridity decline, in Late Holocene times (from the Iron Age on, ca. 1000 BC). Nonetheless, since the Middle-Late Holocene era coincides with several phases of major human impact on the landscape, through woodland clearance and the expansion of cultivated crops and managed grazing, it becomes difficult to separate out vegetational changes due to climate and those under anthropogenic (human-inspired) influence. Combinations of natural and human factors, as with soil erosion, seem preferable to comprehend Greek landscapes for these recent millennia (Rackham 1982, Atherden and Hall 1994).

From the Bronze Age till Medieval times, the natural climate seems to have been mostly warm and dry. The Mesolithic hunter-gatherers (see Time Chart in Introduction) would experience the rather different climate of the early interglacial model, whilst the Neolithic farmers would experience a transition to increasingly drier conditions. Although the Earth had probably not begun to shift definitively toward a late interglacial climate, before human-induced Global Warming overrode any natural cyclical patterns, climatologists argue that during the last 2000 years the Earth has experienced several shorter phases of wetter, colder climate. The classic example is the Little Ice Age between Late Medieval and Early Modern times (Bintliff 1982, Grove 2004). Furthermore, within the warm, dry mid-interglacial mode, and the early wetter but warm mode, climatologists have also identified large-scale episodes of intense drought, around 6200 and 2200 BC, both considered as particularly significant for the Eastern Mediterranean region (Weiss 1993, Rosen 2007).

The vegetation of the Aegean has certainly altered over the last 10,000 years, in the first place responding to global climatic changes. These changes form long-term cycles, over which are superimposed smaller interruptions. Human impact, through progressive clearance, but also cyclical, as human populations waxed and waned, are a further factor impacting on the degree of natural vegetation and its type, but we now see that visible alterations may be as much due to natural as to anthropogenic causes, most frequently it seems a combination of these.

Soils

Greece's semi-arid climate limits its soils (Figure 1.6) from developing a great depth or elaborate mature profiles. Greek soils often remain thin, accumulating slowly, and largely reflect the parent rock and sediment they develop on. Geology is therefore fundamental for soil type distribution. Thus the scattered volcanic districts are echoed by characteristic *Volcanic Soils*, mostly not too fertile as they border the dry Aegean Sea. Far commoner, hard crystalline limestone produces characteristic derived soils (*Limestone Soils*), thin and none too fertile, often patchy between rugged rock. The intermediate hill land of Greece once possessed fertile deep woodland soils, but due to human impact those parts occupied the longest, and farmed continuously, have developed thin stony soils, here mapped along with similar naturally thin soils of the interior mountains (*Stony Mountain Soils* and bare *Rock*); *Terra Rossas* and *Rendzinas* have similar properties and origins (for the former, see Color Plate 1.3a). Only in some zones do better, deeper soils survive extensively (*Brown Forest Soils* and *Mediterranean Dry Forest Soils*) (Color Plate 1.3b). Coastal plains and the drier inland basins, with alluvial and colluvial sediments, have their own fertile but sometimes marshy soils (*Alluvial*, *Marsh*, and *Meadow Soils*) (Color Plate 1.2b).

The overall picture reflects the rocky, mountainous topography of Greece, the limited expanses of rocks that make rich soil, the confined zones of plain (excepting Northern Greece), and the dry climate. Greece is not a naturally rich country for farming, reminding us why the Greeks in many eras imported food, notably grain. However, even if we assume that in regions with dense prehistoric and ancient settlement the once deeper soils have been reduced to a thinner form, due to woodland clearance and erosion, these soils can still provide plentiful harvests at subsistence level (Shiel 2000), though hardly for sustained, large-scale export of wheat, barley or vegetables. Moreover, in some areas, soil impoverishment based on a model of constant environmental decline may not hold true at all (James *et al.* 1994). In compensation, the abundant exposures of steep and rocky, thin soils in a dry climate with low frosts make ideal growing conditions for two classic Mediterranean crops, the olive and the vine, the former vital to enrich the diet, and both excellent trade crops. Even the "wasteland" of scrub and thin woodland formed till recently a sustainable, fruitful extension of food and raw materials for rural communities (Rackham 1982, Forbes 1997).

Erosion

Ever since it was commented on by the Classical philosopher Plato, the erosion of Greece and the resultant lowland sedimentation in valleys and plains was envisaged as a continuous process of landscape transformation, and condemned as negative and anthropogenic in origin (van Andel *et al.* 1986, 1990). With the advent of farming and herding commenced widespread woodland clearance, gaining momentum from prehistoric times into Greco-Roman antiquity. Soils were supposedly stripped or impoverished, sloping landscapes degraded to grazing or even rock. Ports declined as river alluvium bringing eroded debris of hinterland clearance spilled around them, creating a seawards retreating coastline. Even where sensible farmers built terraces to reduce soil loss, cycles of human depopulation apparently led to their neglect, releasing protected soil to flow into rivers.

However, the last 40 years of scientific research into Holocene geomorphology in Greece has revealed a more complex picture than that just depicted, and one where human impact is matched by natural processes (Bintliff 2000, 2002). Firstly, in parts of Greece geology or hyperarid climate restrict woodland cover. Soils here undergo natural weathering, or were always thin. Secondly, in the early Holocene, till 5000 BC, an evolving Interglacial climate stimulated more open landscapes with enhanced natural erosion. Human impact is undoubtedly registered from the later Neolithic period (ca. 5000 BC) onwards, in cycles of woodland clearance followed by regeneration, and in the high population, full land use half of each cycle, such open landscapes also favored soil erosion. But now comes a vital factor, the immediate cause of erosion, which is the weather. Studies have demonstrated that severe erosion is often linked with unusual rainstorms or other highly abnormal weather conditions. Extreme storms may occur once in a lifetime or at even longer intervals.

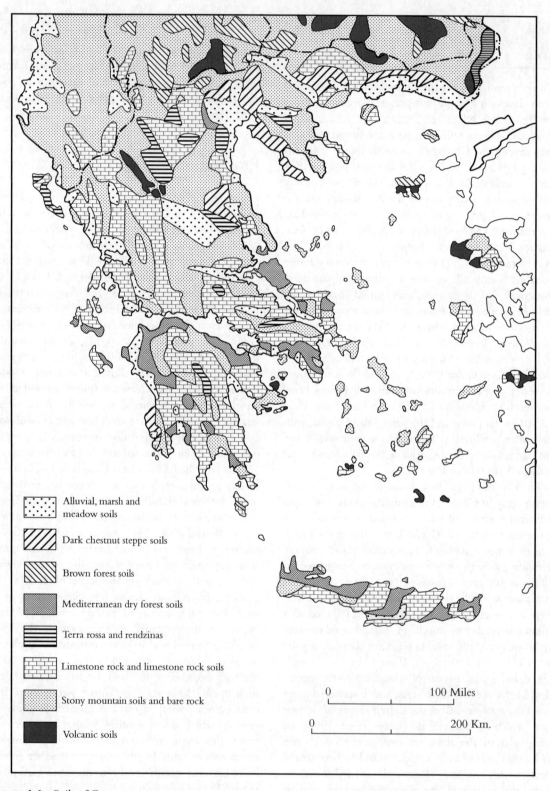

Figure 1.6 Soils of Greece.

H. C. Darby *et al.*, *Naval Geographical Intelligence Handbook, Greece*, vol. 1. London 1944, Figure 7.

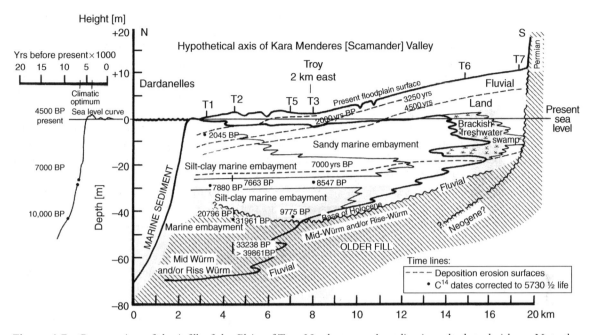

Figure 1.7 Cross-section of the infill of the Plain of Troy, Northwestern Anatolia, since the last glacial era. Note the dominance of marine deposits and of river sediments laid down in a former sea inlet almost to the innermost part of the plain, and the late and superficial progradation (advance) of the modern dry land plain alluvia.
Author after J. C. Kraft *et al.*, "Geomorphic reconstructions in the environs of ancient Troy," *Science* 209 (1980), 776–782, Figure 3. Reproduced by permission of American Association for the Advancement of Science.

Let us predict how these complex processes might register in the Greek geomorphological (land surface) record. For Early Holocene erosion processes we expect little human responsibility, then in Middle and Late Holocene times (later Greek prehistory till today), cycles of high human population would be irregularly punctuated by erosion phases, whilst even in low population phases occasional, irregular erosion episodes could appear. Most of the time, even during population climaxes, major erosion would be absent. A final qualification is required: pollen analysis shows that considerable expanses of upland Greece remained wooded, with low human populations, till the Early Modern period (Bottema 1974), chiefly in the Northern Mainland. The accumulating Holocene landscape record for Greece corresponds closely: erosion in prehistoric through ancient to Medieval times occurs as a series of irregular, short-lived episodes, set against longer periods of landscape stability marked by soil development (what is called a "punctuated

equilibrium" model). Rare phases of landscape instability, apart from Early Holocene examples, lie within periods of dense human occupation, but fail to correlate with every population climax (Pope *et al.* 2003).

Finally we must rethink our scenarios for coastline change. Firstly, it is widely forgotten that hill erosion benefits the lowlands through deposition of fertile alluvia and colluvia. Secondly, we must be critical of the view that the frequently observed advance of river deltas into the sea during historic times is clear evidence for ecological mismanagement of the hinterland of the Aegean coasts, due to human deforestation and poor soil conservation. Scientific research reveals a more complex interplay between natural Interglacial processes and human impact. Boreholes through the larger coastal plains of the Greek and Turkish Aegean coasts give comparable cross-sections, illustrating how these plains have been built up since the last glacial period (Figure 1.7). During the last Ice Age, sea levels 130 meters below present, and prolonged millennia of open landscape with highly erosive climate, produced deep slope and plain sedimentation in the coastlands and well beyond into the present marine shallows (categorized as "Older Fill" in the Figure). In the Early Holocene, swift global ice-sheet melting caused rapidly rising sea levels, outpacing the laying down of eroded sediments in river deltas, which was also drastically reduced in volume as the hinterland became increasingly wooded. Till 4000 BC the sea encroached on coastlines, and although continued natural, and human-related, erosion still brought sediments downstream, these were poured into advancing submarine bays. From this point onwards, two linked processes interacted to reverse this general trend: sea level rise globally slowed down or ceased, with subsequently only minor fluctuations in height, and human clearance from Late Neolithic times onwards became a major, if cyclical, force which exposed large hinterland terrains to potential erosion. Taken together these effects have favored coastal plains advancing on the sea. Historical references certainly match sediment cores for Aegean coastal plains (Brückner 2003, Kraft *et al.* 1977, 1980, 1987), showing dramatic gains in the land even over a few centuries during the last 2500 years. However in cross-section the depth of these historical-era natural-anthropogenic sediments is rarely great, coating a superficial skin on top of much deeper, naturally caused, delta deposits of the earlier Holocene and Ice Age millennia.

Ethnoarchaeology

The study of "traditional" Greek society as a source for reconstructing everyday life in ancient and prehistoric Greece has long been popular. When Western Travelers began to visit Greece in significant numbers, during the eighteenth and early nineteenth centuries AD, their reaction to Greek countryfolk was frequently negative (Tsigakou 1981, Angelomatis-Tsougarakis 1990). Manners, dress, houses, and education disappointed the visitor seeking the descendants of Pericles or Plato. But whereas those Travelers were educated into a colonial and imperialist condescension toward the rest of the World, by the turn of the twentieth century growing disillusionment with Western achievements encouraged intellectuals to admire a lost past of pre-capitalist, pre-industrial lifestyles. If the painter Gauguin sought this in Tahiti, others stayed at home and tapped into folk traditions within Western Europe itself (language, music, dress, folklore), a movement developing since the birth of the Romantic Movement around the start of the nineteenth century.

Now Western scholar-travelers were more inclined to cherish the characteristics of conservative society in rural Greece, previously deplored. Simple peasant life, close to an unchanging nature, its spontaneity and semi-pagan rituals, appeared preferable to Modern Life, and surely also suggested a direct insight into the world of the ordinary people of the Classical or Bronze Age landscape. This led Sir Arthur Evans for example, excavator of the Minoan palace at Knossos, to construct a Golden Age in Bronze Age Crete, which later scholarship has difficulty extricating itself from (Bintliff 1984, MacGillivray 2000). Throughout the twentieth century, observations of traditional lifeways in Greece seemed logically linked to our picture of the remoter past, and even in the 1970s and 1980s anthropologists were attached to archaeological teams (cf. Jameson 1976), not just to bring the story of a landscape into the present day, but in the expectation that traditional practices could be extrapolated to the long-term past.

A belief in direct historical continuity played a central role. Only a minority of scholars were attracted by Fallmerayer's nineteenth-century theory that Modern Greeks were largely descended from Slav colonization in post-Roman times. Most assumed that Classical Greek populations survived and dominated ethnically throughout the Medieval and Early Modern eras. The discovery in the 1950s that Late Bronze Age populations, at least on the Mainland, spoke Greek, allowed Greek ethnicity to extend even further back. Renfrew's hypothesis (1987) that the most significant populating of the Aegean occurred with Neolithic farming colonization around 7000 BC, would envisage ancestral Greeks in parts of the country from an astonishingly early date. With such an embedded ethnicity, and the concept that "traditional" Greek countryfolk in the Early Modern period possessed limited horizons, focused on their village and a nearby market town, could one not reasonably suppose that the practices of farming, house-building, social behavior, and ritual could have changed little over the centuries or even millennia?

However, during the late twentieth century, Post-Colonial thinking (Said 1980), and a growing interest in globalization, led historians and anthropologists to question how untouched and authentic "traditional" societies could be. Almost none was remote enough to escape significant impact from the expansion of colonialism and capitalism. For Greece, Halstead (1987, 2006) challenged the assumption that lifeways had changed little since the Bronze Age.

On my own Boeotia Project, cultural anthropologist Cliff Slaughter radically deconstructed the "traditional" nature of life in the villages where our fieldwork was based (Slaughter and Kasimis 1986). Although the Askra villagers are notorious today as in the poet Hesiod's lifetime in the same valley community (ca. 700 BC), for legal disputes about estate boundaries, ties between antiquity and the present day remain limited and superficial. Farmers depart at dawn for scattered smallholdings, but village incomes chiefly derive from factory work, intensive irrigation using deep machine-pump wells, massive low-interest bank loans, and income earned abroad. It is noteworthy that most Boeotian villagers are descendants of Albanian colonization in the fourteenth and fifteenth centuries AD (Kiel 1997, Bintliff 1995, 2003), and conversations amongst the oldest residents are in Greek laced with this "Arvanitic" dialect, which most rural Boeotians used as their primary tongue into the early twentieth century.

This questioning of "tradition" has nonetheless produced positive effects. Observations from Early Modern Greece can still provide a series of possible ways of life, against which the empirical data for a particular period of antiquity or prehistory can be compared or indeed contrasted (Efstratiou 2007). This is currently the basis for global ethnoarchaeology and experimental archaeology. A common way of managing field crops, such as alternate fallow years, might have been practiced at certain stages of population density in the past, especially when the appropriate technology had become available, but for the same reasons would be unlikely in other periods. Likewise the well-known large-scale transhumance of sheep, goats, and cattle (seasonal long-distance movement of herds especially between uplands and lowlands), a familiar practice in many parts of the Mainland and Crete, developed in the post-Medieval era in intimate relation to proto-capitalist and later capitalist markets for textile manufacture, and to modern forms of communication enabling long-distance trade in pastoral products. It becomes necessary to account for alternative economic circumstances in earlier periods (such as palace economies), which could have stimulated and supported such an elaborate lifeway in the remoter past, rather than assume, as was the case up to the 1980s, that Aegean transhumance was an unchanging feature of rural life ever since prehistory.

On this historically-contextualized basis, Greek ethnoarchaeology has entered a new phase of indispensable insight-production for researchers into the pre-Modern eras. At the same time, it has given more depth to our understanding of the specific nature of the Early Modern period itself, which has till recently been characterized as an unchanging society representing ancient lifeways rapidly pulled into Western modernity.

References

Admiralty (1944). *Greece*. 3 vols. London: HMSO, Naval Intelligence Division.

Angelomatis-Tsougarakis, H. (1990). *The Eve of the Greek Revival*. London: Routledge.

Atherden, M. A. and J. A. Hall (1994). "Holocene pollen diagrams from Greece." *Historical Biology* 9, 117–130.

Attenborough, D. (1987). *The First Eden*. London: BBC Books.

Bintliff, J. L. (1977). *Natural Environment and Human Settlement in Prehistoric Greece*. 2 vols. Oxford: BAR Supplementary Series 28.

Bintliff, J. L. (1982). "Palaeoclimatic modelling of environmental changes in the East Mediterranean region since the last glaciation." In J. Bintliff and W. van Zeist (eds.), *Palaeoclimates, Palaeoenvironments and Human Communities in the Eastern Mediterranean*. Oxford: BAR Int. Series 133, 485–530.

Bintliff, J. L. (1984). "Structuralism and myth in Minoan Studies." *Antiquity* 58, 33–38.

Bintliff, J. (1993). "Forest cover, agricultural intensity and population density in Roman imperial Boeotia, central Greece." In B. Frenzel (ed.), *Evaluation of Land Surfaces Cleared from Forests in the Mediterranean Region During the Time of the Roman Empire*. Stuttgart: Fischer Verlag, 133–143.

Bintliff, J. L. (1995). "The two transitions: Current research on the origins of the traditional village in Central Greece." In J. L. Bintliff and H. Hamerow (eds.), *Europe Between Late Antiquity and the Middle Ages. Recent Archaeological and Historical Research in Western and Southern Europe.* Oxford: BAR Int. Series 617, 111–130.

Bintliff, J. (2000). "Landscape change in Classical Greece: A review." In F. Vermeulen and M.D. Dapper (eds.), *Geoarchaeology of the Landscapes of Classical Antiquity.* Leuven: Peeters, 49–70.

Bintliff, J. (2002). "Time, process and catastrophism in the study of Mediterranean alluvial history: a review." *World Archaeology* 33, 417–435.

Bintliff, J. (2003). "The ethnoarchaeology of a 'passive' ethnicity: The Arvanites of Central Greece." In K. S. Brown and Y. Hamilakis (eds.), *The Usable Past. Greek Metahistories.* Lanham/Boulder: Lexington Books, 129–144.

Bottema, S. (1974). *Late Quaternary Vegetation History of Northwestern Greece.* Groningen: Rijksuniversiteit te Groningen.

Bottema, S. (1990). "Holocene environment of the Southern Argolid: A pollen core from Kiladha Bay." In T. J. Wilkinson and S. Duhon (eds.), *Francthi Paralia. The Sediments, Stratigraphy, and Offshore Investigations.* Bloomington: Indiana University Press, 117–138.

Brückner, H. (2003). "Delta evolution and culture-aspects of geoarchaeological research in Miletos and Priene." In G. A. Wagner, E. Pernicka, and H.-P. Uerpmann (eds.), *Troia and the Troad.* Heidelberg: Springer, 121–144.

Bruins, H. J. *et al.* (2008). "Geoarchaeological tsunami deposits at Palaikastro (Crete) and the Late Minoan 1A eruption of Santorini." *Journal of Archaeological Science* 35, 191–212.

Efstratiou, N. (2007). "Neolithic households in Greece. The contribution of ethnoarchaeology." In R.C. Westgate, N. Fisher, and J. Whitley (eds.), *Building Communities: House, Settlement and Society in the Aegean and Beyond.* London: British School at Athens, 29–39.

Forbes, H. (1997). "A 'waste' of resources: Aspects of landscape exploitation in lowland Greek agriculture." In P. N. Kardulias and M.T. Shutes (eds.), *Aegean Strategies. Studies of Culture and Environment on the European Fringe.* Lanham: Rowman & Littlefield, 187–213.

Friedrich, W. (2000). *Fire in the Sea.* Cambridge: Cambridge University Press.

Frost, F. J. and E. Hadjidaki (1990). "Excavations at the harbor of Phalasarna in Crete: The 1988 season." *Hesperia* 59, 513–527.

Grove, J. M. (2004). *Little Ice Ages: Ancient and Modern.* London: Routledge.

Halstead, P. (1987). "Traditional and ancient rural economy in Mediterranean Europe: Plus ça change?" *Journal of Hellenic Studies* 107, 77–87.

Halstead, P. (2006). "Sheep in the garden: The integration of crop and livestock husbandry in early farming regimes of Greece and Southern Europe." In D. Serjeantson and D. Field (eds.), *Animals in the Neolithic of Britain and Europe.* Oxford: Oxbow, 42–55.

Higgins, M. and R. Higgins (1996). *A Geological Companion to Greece and the Aegean.* London: Duckworth.

James, P. A., C. B. Mee, and G. J. Taylor (1994). "Soil erosion and the archaeological landscape of Methana, Greece." *Journal of Field Archaeology* 21, 395–416.

Jameson, M. H. (ed.) (1976). "A Greek countryside: Reports from the Argolid Exploration Project." *Expedition* 19(1), 2–49.

Kautzky, J. (1993). *Reiseführer Natur. Griechenland – Festland und Küste.* München: BLV.

Kelletat, D. (1991). "The 1550 BP tectonic event in the Eastern Mediterranean as a basis for assessing the intensity of shore processes." *Zeitschrift für Geomorphologie,* Supplement 81, 181–194.

Kiel, M. (1997). "The rise and decline of Turkish Boeotia, 15th–19th century." In J. L. Bintliff (ed.), *Recent Developments in the History and Archaeology of Central Greece.* Oxford: BAR Int. Series 666, 315–358.

Kraft, J. C., S. Aschenbrenner, and G. Rapp (1977). "Palaeogeographic reconstructions of coastal Aegean archaeological sites." *Science* 195, 941–947.

Kraft, J. C., I. Kayan, and O. Erol (1980). "Geomorphic reconstructions in the environs of ancient Troy." *Science* 209, 776–782.

Kraft, J. C. *et al.* (1987). "The pass at Thermopylae, Greece." *Journal of Field Archaeology* 14, 181–198.

Lambeck, K. (1996). "Sea-level change and shore-line evolution in Aegean Greece since Upper Palaeolithic time." *Antiquity* 70, 588–611.

MacGillivray, A. (2000). *Minotaur: Sir Arthur Evans and the Archaeology of the Minoan Myth.* London: Jonathan Cape.

Pope, R. J. J., K. N. Wilkinson, and A. C. Millington (2003). "Human and climatic impact on late Quaternary deposition in the Sparta Basin Piedmont: Evidence from alluvial fan systems." *Geoarchaeology* 18(7), 685–724.

Rackham, O. (1982). "Land-use and the native vegetation of Greece." In M. Bell and S. Limbrey (eds.), *Archaeological Aspects of Woodland Ecology.* Oxford: BAR Int. Series 146, 177–198.

Rackham, O. (1983). "Observations on the historical ecology of Boeotia." *Annual of the British School at Athens* 78, 291–351.

Renfrew, A. C. (1987). *Archaeology and Language: The Puzzle of Indo-European Origins.* London: Jonathan Cape.

Roberts, N. (1998). *The Holocene. An Environmental History.* Oxford: Blackwell.

Rosen, A. M. (2007). *Civilizing Climate*. Lanham: AltaMira.

Said, E. W. (1980). *Orientalism*. London: Routledge.

Sampson, A. (ed.) (2006). *The Prehistory of the Aegean Basin*. Athens: Atrapos.

Shiel, R. S. (2000). "Refuting the land degradation myth for Boeotia." In G. Bailey, R. Charles, and N. Winder (eds.), *Human Ecodynamics*. Oxford: Oxbow, 55–62.

Slaughter, C. and C. Kasimis (1986). "Some social-anthropological aspects of Boeotian rural society: A field report." *Byzantine and Modern Greek Studies* 10, 103–159.

Soter, S. *et al.* (2001). "Environmental analysis of cores from the Helike Delta, Gulf of Corinth, Greece." *Journal of Coastal Research* 17, 95–106.

Tsigakou, F. M. (1981). *The Rediscovery of Greece*. London: Thames & Hudson.

van Andel, T. H., C. N. Runnels, and K. O. Pope (1986). "Five thousand years of land use and abuse in the Southern Argolid, Greece." *Hesperia* 55(1), 103–128.

van Andel, T. H., E. Zangger, and A. Demitrack (1990). "Land use and soil erosion in prehistoric and historical Greece." *Journal of Field Archaeology* 17, 379–396.

Weiss, H. (1993). "The genesis and collapse of third millennium North Mesopotamian civilization." *Science* 261, 995–1004.

Wijmstra, T. A., R. Young, and H. J. L. Witte (1990). "An evaluation of the climatic conditions during the Late Quaternary in northern Greece by means of multivariate analysis of palynological data and comparison with recent phytosociological and climatic data." *Geologie en Mijnbouw* 69, 243–251.

Further Reading

Renfrew, A. C. (1972). *The Emergence of Civilisation. The Cyclades and the Aegean in the Third Millennium BC*. London: Methuen.

Warren, P. (1975). *The Aegean Civilizations*. London: Elsevier.

2

Hunter-Gatherers

The Palaeolithic and Epipalaeolithic in Greece

The Wider Framework

It is helpful to summarize the narrative that relates to the early colonization of Greece by human populations still in the hunter-gather mode of life (Gowlett 1999, 2004). Human beings arose in sub-Saharan Africa 5–8 million years ago (mya), as several species within the hominin genus of *Australopithecus*, and by 2.7 mya had developed a stone tool tradition of Oldowan (chopper-flake) type. Around then a more advanced human genus, *Homo* (with various species, notably *habilis*), arose also in Africa, but soon afterwards groups of this hominid spread to Eurasia ("Out of Africa 1"). The next significant development was the appearance of a new *Homo* species, *erectus*, but this may have developed outside of Africa and recolonized that continent as well as the rest of the Old World ("Out of Asia"?) (Dennell and Roebroeks 2005, Kohn 2006). It is present in Georgia by 1.8 mya, and by 1 mya occupied a vast area from Spain to China. A major technological advance occurred ca. 1.6 mya with the development and variable diffusion of the Acheulean stone tool industry (typified by handaxes).

By 300–250 thousand years ago (kya) a yet more advanced group of hominid species had emerged within the genus *Homo*, *Homo neanderthalensis*, associated with a stone-tool industry known as the Levallois-Mousterian (typified by broad flakes derived from prepared "tortoise-shell" cores). Probably,

though, these earliest Neanderthals were diverging from *Homo erectus* from 600–500 kya, possibly independently at various points of the Old World. Around 200 kya our own species, *Homo sapiens*, appears as a distinct descendant out of *neanderthalensis*, arguably an African evolutionary development which then retraces the original human spread (thus "Out of Africa 2") through the entire Old World, before colonizing the New World. But *sapiens* expands into Europe and the Middle East at the expense of *neanderthalensis*. Both species possessed advanced adaptive skills and intelligence, and an elaborate cultural repertoire (formal burials for example), and coped with extreme environments (especially the cold northern latitudes of Eurasia).

In Europe the interaction between human colonization and the diffusion of new technologies is complex (Roebroeks 2001, 2003). *Homo erectus* is found at Europe's periphery, in Georgia (1.8 mya) and Spain (800 kya), but the associated lithic traditions are contested by researchers. Possibly *erectus* used a wide range of tool types, deposited in different combinations at different parts of sites and at diverse sites, probably including the Acheulean tradition from an early date. However, major colonization of Italy, and north of the mountain barriers of the Pyrenees, Alps, and Balkan massifs into continental and temperate Europe, only really takes off into a permanent and widespread presence ca. 600–500 kya, associated probably with

The Complete Archaeology of Greece: From Hunter-Gatherers to the 20th Century AD, First Edition. John Bintliff.
© 2012 John Bintliff. Published 2012 by Blackwell Publishing Ltd.

earliest *neanderthalensis*. Maybe the preceding *habilis* incursions from "Out of Africa 1" into the Middle East, and those subsequent and more significant incursions for Europe by *erectus* ("Out of Asia?"), were not lasting occupations.

This takeoff of significant human diffusion through Europe around 500 kya still displays a diverse culture, with varying proportions of handaxes and chopper-flake industries at individual sites. Nonetheless, the emergence of Neanderthal Man, and the changed scale of human spread over Europe, seem to be fundamentally related: the association emphasizes greater brain-size, increased socialization, and a more pronounced division of gender tasks between cooperating male large-game hunters, and female gatherers and small-game hunters. A focus on hunting larger game may have brought evolutionary selection for bands practicing cooperation in food- and information-sharing, indicating the likelihood that although social groups (bands) might be small for parts of the year, we would also expect to find sites where larger human groups socialized. As part of this new form of human society, language may have arisen.

Although the origin of our own species (*sapiens*) is controversial, most scholars believe that *Homo sapiens* arose in Africa, and broke out into Eurasia around 100 kya, to compete with and finally displace all other human species ("Out of Africa 2"). Probably from within *sapiens* populations a new stone tool technology arose by 50 kya to replace the Levallois-Mousterian of the later Neanderthals (Upper Palaeolithic types: a blade industry from prismatic cores, elaborate bone and antler work, also varied forms of art and personal decoration). In Europe, Neanderthals were alone till the arrival of *sapiens* bearing the new Upper Palaeolithic tools and wider cultural package from around 45 kya. Between then and 25 kya Modern Humans expanded through Europe and the Neanderthals became extinct. However recent reconstructions of the Neanderthal genome from skeletal material show that during this process, significant interbreeding with *sapiens* must have occurred, since modern human populations retain a distinctive if minor genetic inheritance from *neanderthalensis* (Green *et al.* 2010).

Almost all of the period when Modern Humans were a distinct new species globally coincided with the last Glacial era, which witnessed cycles of variable climate between 100 kya to 12 kya, but reached a climax of cold and arid conditions ca. 20 kya. *Homo sapiens*, with its unique new adaptive intelligence and associated technology and cultural behaviors, seems to have reacted to the Glacial climax and the subsequent dramatic global rewarming and vegetation recovery, that marked the onset of our current Interglacial warm era (the Holocene, 12 kya to present), by elaborating new forms of resource exploitation: a wider use of wild foods (including marine fish and shellfish) (Broad-Spectrum hunter-gathering) and in places an intensive manipulation of wild plant and animal resources (wild cereals and sheep/goat in the Levant, wild cattle in North Africa). In most places there developed at this same final Glacial to early Interglacial (Holocene) time, new stone industries, called Epipalaeolithic or Mesolithic, associated with these complex economic practices (and in Europe and the Levant including small blades mounted in sets as elaborate hunting or harvesting tools). From these adaptive innovations there arose by the early Holocene in widely dispersed regions of the Old and New World, independently, the vital advance of the domestication of plants and animals, which we associate with the Neolithic farming "revolution" (Louwe Kooijmans 1998).

The Hunter-Gatherers of Greece

What might we expect to find in Greece for the immense timespan during which hunter-gatherers lived in Europe? Actually little to nothing, when we consider the geological processes which have destroyed or hidden the record of hundreds of thousands of years of human presence in Greece (Runnels 1995, Bailey *et al.* 1999, Perlès 2000, Galanidou and Perlès 2003).

However, if Europe was first colonized by *Homo erectus* 1–2 mya, with a likely entry-point through the Balkans, Greece could have seen human occupation during this period. A very early appearance might associate hominids with a chopper-flake industry, preceding the spread 1.5 mya onwards of the more elaborate Acheulean handaxe industries. But no Greek findspots are this early, or belong to a completely pre-Acheulean tradition. The oldest human activity appears to include handaxes, although no extensive site of this "technocomplex" (a toolkit used by many human groups rather than a culture associated with one) has been identified. Instead isolated finds at widespread points of the country, in outcrops of ancient landsurfaces, attest to derivative forms of Acheulean Lower (older) Palaeolithic culture throughout the Greek lowlands. These early handaxes seem late varieties. A "technocomplex" of varying chopper-flake and handaxe forms is likely to be characteristic of European early human settlement sites. Actually two of the best described early Greek sites may reflect such a mixed culture, although their dates are more appropriate for the Middle Palaeolithic. Kokkinopilos in Epirus has a handaxe in a stratigraphy around 150–200 kya, whilst Rodia in Thessaly is a chopper-and-flake industry with perhaps the limited presence of handaxes, ca. 200–400 kya. Secure radiometric dates (absolute dates from physics) for the Greek Palaeolithic only begin around 100 kya.

In 2008–2009 a team led by Curtis Runnels of Boston University, the Plakias Mesolithic Survey on Crete, made unexpected Palaeolithic discoveries in southern coastal Crete (Strasser *et al.* 2010). At 11 localities stone tool (lithic) scatters were found in geological contexts indicating an age of 130 kya or older, and belonging to forms typical for late Lower Palaeolithic (Acheulean handaxes and cleavers) and Middle Palaeolithic industries. The significance of this for maritime travel at such a remote period is remarkable, given the lack of known land-bridges between Crete and the Greek Mainland or the Cyclades even in times of low sea level in the Glacial eras.

From this stage of human occupation in Europe, the wider site evidence from the long duration of the Middle Palaeolithic (ca. 300–35 kya), allows reconstruction of the lifeways of Greece's oldest occupants. Based on the European record, and its general agreement with the Greek material, Middle Palaeolithic hominids in Greece (Neanderthal Man), foraged in small groups, irregularly merging into larger social gatherings (up to about 150 individuals) at times of richest resource profusion. Rather than remaining in one location they ranged over a large annual territory, to coincide with the seasonal appearance of herds of animals or stocks of edible plants in particular areas of the regional landscape, as well as to visit geological outcrops to obtain raw material for tools. Sourcing

the lithics in use has shown that band movements of this kind could extend 100 km.

If there had been later Lower Palaeolithic human colonizers of Greece, they were probably already very early Neanderthals. This distinct species, *Homo neanderthalensis*, competed successfully in the Levant with expanding fully modern *Homo sapiens* from around 100 kya, and then unsuccessfully in Europe after 45 kya, but through interbreeding did contribute to the latter's genetic make-up. Greece's first human remains, like its oldest well-dated open air lithic sites, appear to be early Middle Palaeolithic, and come from the Petralona Cave in Northern Greece, probably ca. 300 kya; they may indeed be Neanderthal Man.

It was these later Neanderthal populations in Europe who adopted new technologies which were diffusing through the Old World, significantly expanding stone toolkits beyond handaxes and chopper-flake tools, into more complex tool manufacturing and tool diversity. Around 300 kya, these new forms of stone-tool preparation appear, distinctive for the Middle Palaeolithic era and known collectively as the Levallois-Mousterian tradition. Manufacturing techniques include specially prepared cores with tortoise-shell shaped platforms from which radial flakes are struck. This technology, especially suited for making hafted implements, only appears sporadically in the early Middle Palaeolithic in Greece. More elaborate toolkits known as the mature Mousterian tradition appear in Greece from around 150 kya. A type-site is the cave of Asprochaliko in Epirus, where the oldest excavated levels are ca. 100 kya. Nearby at Kokkinopilos, ancient sediments called Red Beds, which also produced some of the few even earlier Acheulean handaxes, gave finds of open-air Mousterian activity from 150 kya onwards. Mousterian populations on this evidence were till recently argued to have favored the wetter, more varied landscapes of Northwestern Mainland Greece during the final period of the last Interglacial and the first half of the last Ice Age, their sites only appearing in the drier East and South after 55 kya. However, a series of new sites has shifted our focus toward the latter regions, cave sites in the arid and rocky Mani peninsula in the Southern Mainland, Kalamakia and Lakonis, and the most recent finds from the south coast of Crete (Strasser *et al.* 2010). In particular, Lakonis has dense occupation layers dated

Figure 2.1 Peneios River open valley terraces, Thessaly, with archaeologists recording lithic finds from Palaeolithic hunter-gatherer activity.
Courtesy of Curtis Runnels.

between 100 and 40 kya, including a Neanderthal tooth (Panagopoulou *et al.* 2004).

Fieldwork in the plains of Thessaly (East-Central Greece) offers insights into how Middle Palaeolithic communities used the landscape (Runnels 1989, Runnels and van Andel 1993). Tectonic sinking of these plains has caused gradual lowering of river levels, achieved by their cutting down through much older deposits, but luckily the rivers remained in similar locations. Very ancient river terraces and banks are thus exposed, places where hunters camped, prepared tools and cut up their prey, those animals being attracted to the rivers for water and grazing. Series of such activity foci have been mapped from eroding ancient river-terraces west of the modern town of Larisa. However, these stone tools and animal bones are not found in their original place (*in situ*), but were reworked by changing river channels. Yet geomorphological and stratigraphic study confirms that these remains lie close to the original places of hunters' activity. The great grassy plains of Thessaly with their large, permanent rivers would have attracted considerable herds of game, a resource underpinning

the economic and social structure of Middle Palaeolithic hominids.

The oldest of the Thessalian early Middle Palaeolithic river-gravel findspots is at Rodia (ca. 400–200 kya), and may form part of the European-wide flexible cultural tradition tying together use of handaxes and chopper-flakes. After a long absence of human activity, a new colonization of this landscape is evidenced by numerous late Middle Palaeolithic or mature Mousterian sites, datable after 60 kya.

Figure 2.1 shows how the Peneios river passes through the Thessalian Plain. Animals moving along the river could be ambushed by hunters and it is in the relict gravel banks and flood deposits eroding by the present riverbank that archaeologists can discover stone tools used by these foragers and the bones of contemporary animals grazing and seeking water.

Increasing evidence identifies locations preferred by Neanderthal hunter-gatherers in choosing where to camp, temporarily or for longer periods, within a seasonal round of several sites (Papagianni 2000). Riversides and coastal marshes and estuaries are selected, whilst the many Middle Palaeolithic sites in

Northwest Greece associated with "terra rossa" sediments termed "Red Beds" were formerly seasonal lakes and marshes, where sediments accumulated during the Pleistocene within limestone (karst) depressions possessing underground drainage. Also favored are locations where the movements of game herds could be monitored without disturbing them, such as rockshelters high above passes and narrow valleys (for example Asprochaliko). Papagianni suggests that in the rich hunter-gatherer environment of the Epiros lowlands, base camps for longer residence lay a day's travel apart (around 30 km), between which occur many smaller lithic sites, evidence of short-lived hunting, gathering or raw material procurement activities. Strontium isotopes from a Neanderthal tooth from Lakonis (see below) suggest that this individual probably foraged over a landscape, at least at some period of its life, at least 20 km from the cave where the body was found (Richards *et al.* 2008).

The Thessaly Mousterian assemblages are late enough to contain possible borrowing from the yet more advanced stone industry, the Aurignacian, which replaces them throughout Europe during the second half of the last Glacial period. This early form of Upper Palaeolithic culture is associated however with the spread of our own species, anatomically modern humans, *Homo sapiens*. Modern humans with Upper Palaeolithic culture probably colonized the Balkans from the Middle East and the Black Sea steppes around 45–30 kya. By 30 kya Neanderthals and the Mousterian have died out throughout Europe, so that Upper Palaeolithic modern humans and their novel toolkits are now the only people and culture throughout the subcontinent.

There is lively debate on the interactions between European Neanderthal and incoming *Homo sapiens* populations, both in terms of physical contact and mixing of cultural traditions. The open-air riverside sites of Middle Palaeolithic hunters in Thessaly occasionally include Upper Palaeolithic tools, but since these deposits are reworked by the river and represent accumulations from many encampments, it is impossible to exclude mixing of older and younger assemblages. Indeed, the cave of Theopetra in Thessaly, probably one base in a seasonal round of camps including open-air river sites, was formerly suggested to show a transitional lithic assemblage between Middle and Upper Palaeolithic, but now thermoluminescence dates (TL) indicate the likelihood that these deposits are also artificially mixed together (Valladas *et al.* 2007).

In contrast, Lakonis cave in the Southern Mainland, on the Mani peninsula (Panagopoulou *et al.* 2004) offers evidence for Neanderthal populations adopting Upper Palaeolithic tool-types without a break in occupation. Absolute dates (from physical science) and stratigraphy suggest continuity of population and occupation from a dominant Middle to a dominant Upper Palaeolithic assemblage. A Neanderthal tooth from this transitional era confirms the likely acculturation due to contact with Modern Humans. The latest genetic evidence for interbreeding between Neanderthals and Modern Humans agrees very well with these cultural interchanges.

However, this particular period coincided with the worst climate in Europe for more than 100,000 years, the Ice Age climax, 30–20 kya, causing human populations to gather in the far south of the subcontinent to find warmth to survive in, and a sufficient density of animals and plants to live off. Even in Southern Europe only some regions fulfilled these needs, and here Jochim (1987) argues that the close packing of refugee hunter-gatherer groups may have stimulated unparalleled symbolic activity (cave art and mobile art objects). The classic refuges are Southwest France and the Spanish coastal Pyrenees, where less severe climate was linked to proximity to the Atlantic. Greece was not overall such a favored ecological zone during the height of the Glacial, and evidence for early Upper Palaeolithic populations is very slight, notably when compared to Middle Palaeolithic activity. Hyperaridity was the limiting factor. Symptomatic is the virtual absence of open-air sites from the early Upper Palaeolithic, contrasted to the frequency of Middle Palaeolithic examples in regions such as Epirus, Thessaly, and the Western Peloponnese. The exceptional discovery of Lakonis and other recent sites in the coastal South Peloponnese may argue that these environments, as other Mediterranean peninsulas, encouraged refuge occupation: they offered milder temperatures and adjacent extensive coastal plains (now submerged by sea level rises), with marshy river deltas backed by hills with open scrubby vegetation. Larger game recovered from the Lakonis domestic debris include wild cattle, pig, and deer.

After the cold, arid maximum around 18 kya, the final Glacial sees warmth returning to Greece, but more tardily increased moisture. Upper Palaeolithic activity becomes visible again, including the expansion of hunting sites into the now more attractive high uplands, still open and with milder climates (for example in Epirus). A reorientation of hunter-gatherer annual ranges (seasonal movements) and economic strategies occurred. In Thessaly the riverine campsites of the Plain are not in significant use in Upper Palaeolithic or Mesolithic times, although seasonal cave use at long-used locations persists. The raw materials in use for tool-making at Theopetra Cave now shift from local stone, suiting a confined regional annual round, to significant amounts of long-distance imports. This change could reflect expanding trade networks, but in the context of the contemporary evidence for the colonization of the Pindus Mountains by summer hunting bands and the disappearance of the Plain camps, might rather point to lowland foragers now themselves expanding their annual seasonal movements into the uplands, as the lowlands gradually became wooded and less attractive to game herds throughout the year.

A key site for Upper Palaeolithic occupation, although never permanent through the year, is the Franchthi Cave (see Text Box) in the Northeast Peloponnese, a coastal limestone peninsula bordering Koilada Bay. Here there was also Middle Palaeolithic occupation, and a very significant occupation in the Early Holocene (Postglacial) period, when human activity in Greece as a whole has proved difficult to identify. Perlès argues that human use of this spacious, well-located shelter varied from regular seasonal occupation for a variety of hunter-gatherer activities, to sporadic and highly specialized foraging for short periods, so that it was always just one of a series of camps utilized discontinuously for some 100,000 years. Nonetheless, the innovative excavation methods and large scientific staff brought together by Tom Jacobsen has produced one of our best insights into the different ways foragers in Greece could use the same landscape (Jacobsen 1987–2010; Perlès 1999, 2001).

Until recently Franchthi Cave was the only site where the transition from Late Glacial to Early Holocene could be observed. However in Thessaly we now possess the major findspot of Theopetra Cave

was occupied from Middle Palaeolithic to Late Neolithic times, including the period lacking in the Thessalian river camps, the transition from Upper Palaeolithic to early Holocene Mesolithic (Kyparissi-Apostolika 1999, Panagopoulou 1999). Other recent Mesolithic discoveries (Figure 2.2), are Klisoura Cave (Northeast Peloponnese) and the Cave of Cyclope (Sporades Islands).

Theopetra cave lies in limestone hills marking the edge of the western plain of Thessaly and the start of the Pindus Mountains, which here divide West and East Greece. The oldest layers belong to the older Middle Palaeolithic, perhaps even earlier. However the dominant Middle Palaeolithic occupation is a late phase of that tradition, contemporary to the open-air camps studied by previous teams in Thessaly, and belongs to the middle of the Last Glacial (ca. 50–30 kya). Environmental studies portray the Plain as a steppe and the hills and mountains with limited deciduous and more pine woodland: bear and deer are hunted, and probably gathering of edible steppe grasses and legumes occurred. There follows an Upper Palaeolithic occupation from 38 kya till 25,300 BP, when as elsewhere in Greece, the peak cold and aridity of the Glacial caused abandonment; vegetation seems to have been negligible. Reoccupation by late Upper Palaeolithic foragers, 15–11 kya, was followed by an Early Holocene Mesolithic phase dated 10–8 kya. Whereas the warming climate in the former, final Glacial times caused pine and steppe to expand, low moisture still kept this Tardiglacial period very arid. But with the advent of the Early Holocene and the Mesolithic occupation, both high altitude pine and lower altitude oak expanded considerably. The game brought back to the cave, wild goat or chamois (a form of ibex), deer, wild cattle and pig, hare, and birds, and the plants gathered (grasses and legumes), became more plentiful as climate improved from Late Upper Palaeolithic into Mesolithic times, but increasing afforestation encouraged seasonal use of the adjacent uplands.

Like Franchthi, the Theopetra Mesolithic stone-tool assemblage does not resemble adaptive technologies found elsewhere across Europe in response to the spread of modern climate and vegetation, suggesting that Greek landscapes posed particular requirements for survival, and also that the country became isolated from wider cultural developments. There are better

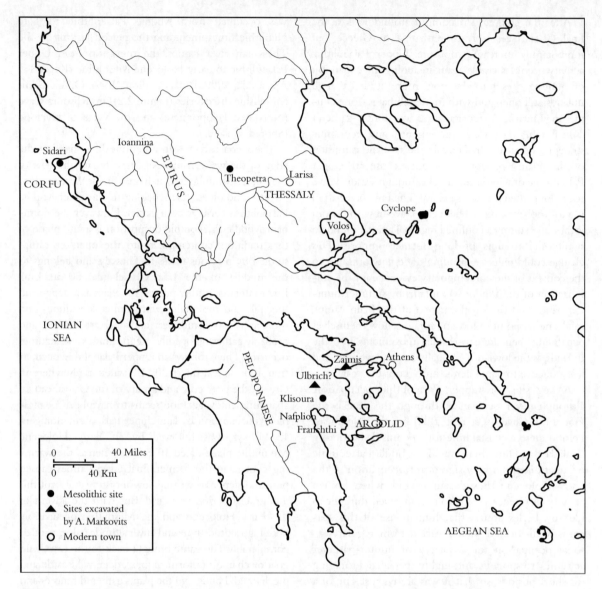

Figure 2.2 Key Mesolithic sites in Greece.
N. Galanidou and C. Perlès (eds.), *The Greek Mesolithic. Problems and Perspectives.* London 2003, Figure 1.1.

parallels, however, over an intermediate geographical scale (Tourloukis and Palli 2009). As in the Balkans as a whole, "Mesolithic" or "Epipalaeolithic" industries tend to replace blades with flake tools.

The long use of the site reflects its very favorable location for exploiting a series of terrain-types, where varied food sources could be tapped. It

remains uncertain if Theopetra was a permanent base-camp, rather than a seasonal camp in an annual range incorporating numerous other locations, as has been argued for Franchthi. Significantly, in the Middle Palaeolithic occupation layers, the raw material for stone tools came predominantly from within a 10 km radius; this is a maximum predicted site

The Franchthi Cave

Franchthi Cave is a large rockshelter in a dry, scrub- and cultivation-covered region, now on the sea and even in the peak of Last Glacial low sea levels, never more than 5 km distant. Throughout the Upper and Final Palaeolithic and early Holocene cave occupation, lower marine levels created a plain with a river beside and ahead of the cave, making it much more attractive to occupy than its present barren headland location washed by the sea.

The Upper Palaeolithic occupation has a first phase when the regional environment was dry and cold steppe vegetation, since at this time, ca. 30–17 kya, the Last Glacial was reaching its maximum severity. Hunting groups utilizing Franchthi as temporary residence pursued deer and wild horse or ass (the lithic assemblage is predominantly the type called backed-bladelets, used mounted in wood for hunting projectiles), and their sporadic, short-lived occupation left thin debris. After an abandonment of the site for several millennia, doubtless a response to the Glacial climax, reoccupation around 13 kya is different enough to justify the term Tardiglacial (Late Glacial), whilst changes in culture and economy anticipate those seen elsewhere in Europe where they accompany a new form of life, the Mesolithic.

The stone tool assemblage now diversifies along with far more rubbish build-up, indicating longer use and more varied activities at Franchthi. Wild cattle and goat join the game hunted, and collected seeds include wild vegetables and wild cereals. Furthermore, shellfish and fish are added to the diet. Perlès categorizes these changes ca. 13–10kya as the creation of a "broad-spectrum economy," where in contrast to earlier phases of use at Franchthi, whole domestic units of men, women, and children spent long periods annually living in and in front of the cave, occupied with a wide range of subsistence strategies. Undoubtedly these transformations reflect rising temperatures and moisture as the Glacial waned and global climates were transformed into the current Interglacial, the Holocene, but also to the specific way these changes

affected a site near the coast. A milder climate created a richer Mediterranean scrub-savannah landscape, stimulating more varied if less concentrated game, and edible plants, whilst rising sea levels brought more accessible seafood. During this phase an exotic raw material is used for tool preparation: obsidian from the distant Cycladic island of Melos. I suggested many years ago (Bintliff 1977) that the development of fishing may have stimulated the discovery of the rich Melos obsidian outcrops, as well as the means for its transport to the Mainland, since traditional fishermen have ranged over the same wide territories following the seasonal appearances of great shoals of the same species (notably the giant tuna). As however the first appearance of obsidian predates at this site the evidence for special tools for marine hunting and great amounts of fish-bone, perhaps Franchthi began as a consumer of other Tardiglacial fishing forays into the Cyclades.

Around 10 kya, Franchthi enters its Mesolithic phase, and exhibits two contrasted ways that hunter-gatherers adapted to a climate comparable to today, if perhaps drier. The Lower (older) Mesolithic shows an economy specialized in plant foods and shellfish, with little land game or fish. Stone tools are limited and unsophisticated, largely used for reed- and wood-working. The contemporary dry plant cover supported a low density of game, but this favored legumes and edible wild cereals. Remarkably, this scanty occupation is associated with a cemetery, possibly including collective burials (Cullen 1995). In hunter-gatherer societies in the Tardiglacial and Mesolithic of the Near East and Europe the appearance of formal burial areas seems to mark highly productive foraging at certain locations, often based on a rich resource such as marine, estuarine or lake fauna and flora. Here the ancestors might be placed to signify the centrality of the site for a particular band, and as a territorial claim to its use. Since Franchthi remained just one of a seasonal range of foraging sites, it probably did form a ritual focus in a more varied set of camps, whose totality might have created this kind of stability. Till very recently, such a network eluded discovery (see below).

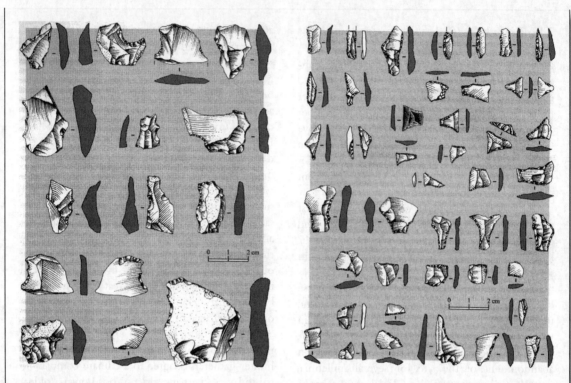

Figure 2.3   Upper Mesolithic stone-tool assemblage from Franchthi Cave. Most of the small tools or microliths (right) are related to fishing: tools for preparing nets and traps for the capture of fish and then their processing for eating and storage. Shellfish collection and processing would also benefit from some of these small tools but also from some larger tools (left). The curved trapezoidal arrows however (upper right) could also be used for the land game, red deer and boar, identified in the Cave deposits. Many of the larger cutting and scraping tools (left) would be useful for processing land animals. Plant remains include wild fruits, nuts, and cereals, but no specific tools can yet be associated with these.
C. Perlès, *The Early Neolithic in Greece*. Cambridge University Press 2001, Figures 2.4 and 2.5.

Even scantier activity marks the late ninth millennium BP (before present), Final Mesolithic, but the intervening Upper Mesolithic, earlier ninth millennium, sees the cave occupants take up sea-fishing, especially tuna, as their dominant activity, with supplementary hunting and plant collection. The tools (Figure 2.3) are largely for catching and processing marine fish. This use of Franchthi was highly seasonal, since fish such as tuna appear at limited times in varied parts of the Aegean coasts, although in impressive shoals.

territory for a hunter-gatherer settlement, although as noted, perhaps other local sites were in use seasonally. In contrast, as noted earlier in this chapter, the Final Palaeolithic and Mesolithic evidence for long-distance stone imports may show a greatly enlarged yearly territory of exploitation.

The Cyclope Cave on the island of Youra in the Sporades lies east of Thessaly and has revealed a long

Mesolithic use ca. 8700–7000 BC (Sampson 2006). During the peak of the preceding Ice Age these islands were linked to the Mainland owing to low sea levels, but in this Early Holocene period a smaller channel than today existed, although the import of obsidian from the Cycladic island of Melos to Franchthi Cave before this phase already evidences that adequate boat technology was available in Mesolithic Greece. The economy reflects a "broad spectrum" expansion from traditional Palaeolithic larger game, since fishing (including large species such as tuna), shellfishing, and land mollusc collecting are central sources of nourishment, alongside birds. It is suggested that fish were smoked and dried, whilst the species caught required both open-sea and coastal fishing. The suggestion that the site was used by migratory ("transmerant") fishermen reinforces the model I proposed for fishing and exotic imports into the final Palaeolithic and Mesolithic at Franchthi.

Another near-Mainland island, Kythnos, in the western Cyclades, has an open settlement with traces of round houses and formal burials of Mesolithic age, and seems to belong to the same expansive Broad-Spectrum economy (Sampson 2006). Significantly, intensive use of marine resources is a Mediterranean trend from the final Glacial and earliest Holocene: on the coasts of Mount Carmel open-air "fishing villages" are known, now submerged by rising sea levels (Galili et al. 2002), developing from around 10,000 BP. Also intensive use of marine and freshwater resources is a shared concern with the rest of early Holocene Europe, both in site locations, fauna, and tool specializations (Tourloukis and Palli 2009).

There had been a window of opportunity in the final Glacial and earliest Holocene periods (see Klithi Cave Box below), which had allowed a burst of human exploitation in the high mountains of Greece: there was a warmer climate but still insufficient rainfall to promote the recovery of woodland (afforestation), which would progressively close down open-country hunting and plant-gathering. But now in the mature Holocene such afforestation did occur. Partial compensation came from better stream flow through the year, and the expansion of lake and marsh environments, which offered alternative food sources. Human groups also made increased exploitation of the sea for fish, shellfish, and marine mammals. However, claims for incipient domestication of the key species of domestic animals and plants, such as wheat and barley, sheep and goats, at sites such as Theopetra and the Cyclope Cave, are suspected by most specialists to be intrusions into Mesolithic layers from later activity at these sites, or in the case of Franchthi (where at an early stage of the excavations a similar local development was voiced), to contacts with contemporary immigrant farming groups in the region.

The mature Early Holocene environment, then, offered much compensation for the loss of large coastal plains now submerged below rising sea levels, and of the previous dry steppe climate with limited woodland supporting game herds but limited plants. In its place came far more running freshwater, with marshes, lakes, varied forms of woodland, and a wider fauna and flora. Replacing a lifestyle of wide-ranging hunter-gatherers of the Palaeolithic phases, Mesolithic foragers could find more localized niches with a mosaic of resources. Our expectation might well be then for favored locations in such a landscape to encourage dense pockets of population. The formal burials in Franchthi Cave in theory seem to suggest that its occupants were indeed part of such a local network of regionally dense hunter-gatherers. As Cullen (1995) comments: "At Franchthi, the concern to preserve the bones of the deceased within the living space may signal an emphasis on the continuity and definition of the social group, a possibility supported by the coinciding appearance of personal ornaments and ochre." They would have been supported, according to the reconstruction of resources exploited by the Franchthi foragers of this period, by a diet of deer and wild pig, land and marine molluscs, fish, nuts, legumes, and wild cereals.

Fulfilling these expectations, a recent field survey in the coastal region west of Franchthi (Runnels et al. 2005) has documented exactly such a dense network of Mesolithic sites (Figure 2.4). Interestingly, Runnels' success where almost all previous researchers had failed, in showing that Greece did not lack a flourishing Mesolithic population, lay in his reverting to traditional forms of landscape research for hunter-gatherer sites, whilst retaining some state-of-the-art

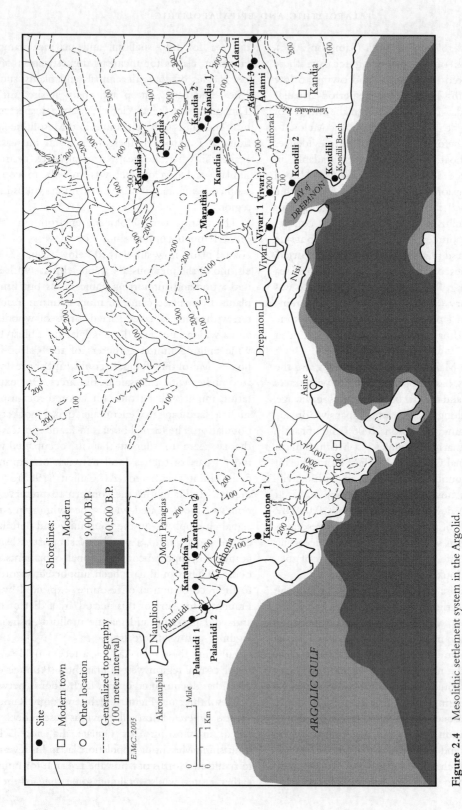

Figure 2.4 Mesolithic settlement system in the Argolid.

C. Runnels et al., "A Mesolithic landscape in Greece: Testing a site-location model in the Argolid at Kandia." *Journal of Mediterranean Archaeology* 18 (2005), 259–285, Figure 2.

theory. Whilst intensive survey without prior selection of terrain has proven largely unsuccessful in documenting significant lithic findspots for Holocene foragers, seemingly supporting the traditional view of a real poverty of sites and minimal populations, Runnels targeted microlandscapes (small districts) which should in terms of human ecology have offered the ideal locations for contemporary hunter-gatherers. These were minor coastal plains, with springs and streams, marshland and backing hills, in which a similar wide range of land and sea resources would be easily accessible. Fifteen Mesolithic sites were found by scouring the slopes below caves suitable for occupation and in adjacent landscapes (two were in fact open-air sites). Two caves had sufficient debris to suggest lengthy residential use as "base-camps," whilst the remainder might have been part of a mobile strategy of camping temporarily at a series of locations.

Runnels and colleagues have now had equal success applying the same targeted survey in finding the first clear evidence for Mesolithic communities on Crete, where the same locational preferences by the coast were revealed (Strasser *et al.* 2010).

Equally surprising have been the results of recent surface survey in a very different physical environment, the high mountains of Mainland Greece. An international team is investigating how ancient was the traditional use of summer seasonal pastureland in the high mountain plateaux that form the watershed zone in Northern Greece between the western lowlands of Epirus and those on the east in Macedonia and Epiros (Efstratiou *et al.* 2006). At this altitude, 1400–1900 meters above sea level, lie flysch (limestone erosion sediment) basins between rugged limestone, offering excellent summer grazing, whereas in winter they are harsh, inhospitable landscapes, forcing grazing animals to retreat to warmer lower altitudes (or as today to be kept in stalls and given supplementary fodder). The survey team discovered more than 90 open-air lithic findspots, documenting repeated and significant use of these high mountains. The earlier findspots are Middle Palaeolithic, and would suit milder intervals during the earlier phases of the last Glacial, whilst limited Upper Palaeolithic finds agrees with the most severe climate inhibiting regular use.

At the end of the Glacial and in the earliest Holocene, hunters returned with the warming climate, following their quarry of large herds of game, just as we shall see in the uplands of Epirus at the Klithi and Kastritsa rockshelters. However, the inexorable extension of pine and fir forests made such seasonal upland hunting increasingly impractical without woodland clearance.

The Lifeworld of Hunter-Gatherers in Greece

In future chapters we shall explore the potential of archaeology, and ultimately historical texts as well, to reveal how the peoples of Greece expressed their concepts of society, nature, and religion. In the absence of abundant art, or elaborate ritual, the longest period of Greece's human occupation, Palaeolithic to Mesolithic, poses almost insuperable problems for such an approach. Within Palaeolithic studies, much discussion has occurred as to why only certain regions of European hunter-gatherer settlement are associated with most of its art (such as Southwest France and Pyrenean Spain). One theory, which associates elaborate symbolic representation with enhanced social territoriality in areas relatively heavily populated due to their richer resources in times of severe climate ("refugia," Jochim 1987), might be relevant, since Greece's Upper Palaeolithic occupation (the period of maximum artistic production elsewhere), appears still to be low density. Curtis Runnels' optimistic conclusion that his recent discoveries suggest high levels of Mesolithic population in favored districts of Greece, might predict evidence for increased symbolic territoriality. The burials of Franchthi fit, as does the rise of body-ornament using shell-beads and probably body-ochre.

In the Klithi Cave Box we summarize how one major specialist in this phase of Greek archaeology has offered us both a realistic attempt to maximize our insights into economic and social life, and a personal philosophical viewpoint on what can and cannot be achieved in terms of the mentalities of Greece's remote hunter-gatherer world (Bailey 1997).

The Klithi Cave: Landscapes of Hunter-Gatherers (Figure 2.5)

Klithi is a cave in an upland valley of Epirus, Northwestern Greece. Hunters used it primarily in the Tardiglacial (final Glacial) era, 16,500–13,000 BP. These 4000 years fell between the maximum cold peak ca. 20,000 BP and rapid warming and afforestation which occurred after the cave's abandonment. Game caught was open rugged landscape fauna, ibex and chamois, comprising 99 percent of the animal bones. The main activity carried out from Klithi was killing these animals and converting their carcasses into food, artifacts, and clothing. Plants were insignificant in the diet, but in contrast, to the west down in the extensive coastal lowlands, with more woodland and water, flora would have been high in the food supply. The on-site manufacture of tools suits the tasks outlined well. The site itself and its territory calculated using the method of Catchment Analysis (local resource mapping) pioneered by the founder of this project in the 1960s, Eric Higgs, suggest that 5–10 people, less likely 10–20 people, used the cave together. A key factor is length of stay in these uplands (the winter months must be ruled out), so that the lower estimate would fit a stay of 6–9 months, the upper of 3–6 months. There are hints these are families, not a male hunting group. The ideal time to be in these mountains would be spring and autumn when animal herds moved to higher and lower ground, respectively, with the seasons. Nonetheless, resources for hunter-gatherers were always more plentiful in the western lowlands, allowing larger human populations to remain there the whole year, but that landscape is much less explored archaeologically. However the sites that are known there are indeed more plentiful and larger. The model proposed is that most Epirus Upper Palaeolithic hunters stayed in the lowlands (for the permanently resident game and good flora), while a minority of humans plus large numbers of mobile game (deer and horse) transhumed in the warmer half of the year into the eastern uplands to take advantage of seasonal grazing (though ibex and chamois, the key species exploited at Klithi, are hardy enough to remain in the uplands all year). The seasonal moves allowed both humans and animals to maintain higher regional populations. Other Upper Palaeolithic sites in the Epirus mountains show different specializations and different time uses (see Figure 2.5). The site of Kastritsa, by a mountain lake, is larger and more elaborate than Klithi, and may have formed a summer agglomeration focus for many hunting groups.

After the period of use of Klithi conditions became less favorable for different reasons: trees spread rapidly as the Glacial era faded and the animals hunted moved further up the mountains to find their open habitat. The Mesolithic hunters of the next stage may have focused more on woodland game in the lowlands.

In the 1960s, this project's founder, Eric Higgs, proposed a model of Late Glacial transhumant hunters which he derived from the recent pastoralists (specialist herders) of this region, the Sarakatsani. The main sites located, Asprochaliko, Kastritsa, and Klithi were identified as staging posts in winter-summer movements of hunters following migrant game such as deer and horse. Although some aspects are now disproved, since these sites are not contemporary and have different animal specializations, the general principle survives. Upland Eastern Epirus in the Late Glacial was exploited seasonally from the western lowlands. The human carrying capacity of Eastern Epirus was some 100, but linked seasonally with the west allowed the combined region to nourish 500–1000 hunter-gatherers. Yet most animals and people probably stayed the whole year in the western lowlands. The entire region is large enough for an effective human mating network (for genetic health, calculated at 500 people or more, based on the theories of Wobst 1974).

The oldest upland site, Asprochaliko, is utilized ca. 26,000 BP, then after abandonment marking the climax Glacial millennia, Kastritsa and Klithi higher up come into deployment for the Glacial end phase. This suggests progressive penetration of the mountains as climate eases, succeeded by

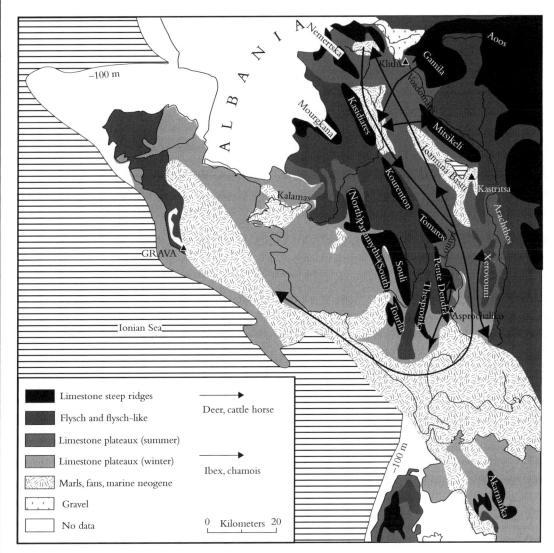

Figure 2.5 The setting of the Klithi Cave and other sites in the Epirus upland and lowland region with likely seasonal moves of game animals. Arrowed routes between uplands and lowlands mark migrations of deer, cattle and horse. Routes purely within the uplands those of ibex and chamois. Low glacial sea levels made Corfu island part of the mainland.

G. Bailey (ed.), *Klithi: Palaeolithic Settlement and Quaternary Landscapes in Northwest Greece*, vol. 2. Cambridge University Press 1997, Figure 30.25.

contraction as the Glacial ends and woodland closes pastures. The Catchment Analysis of all three upland sites shows that they are positioned to watch, without disturbing, herds of game, in a series of basins controlled by strong topographic features, especially as animals move from one natural grazing area to another. Selection of particular species to hunt can be seen in the different fauna at these caves and from their diversity of lithic tools. Close links between hunting behavior and the local environmental potential, revealed through site Catchment Analysis, suggest that this is less "environmental determinism" than the results of humans calculating logical means to combine a knowledge of the terrain with the types and frequencies of suitable game.

Over the years, Higgs' use of analogy for the transhumant migration model has been criticized, on the basis that the recent Sarakatsani herders are specialists brought into being by large urban markets and even capitalist commercial systems, making a Palaeolithic parallel implausible. However, exhaustive archaeological analysis concludes that the use of Klithi and other sites is based on seasonal hunting.

An additional causative element for Late Glacial mountain exploration was rising sea level, which occurred after the climax cold period. At this time there is generally an occupational gap in sites in Greece. This seems in part due to loss of the coastal plains with their fresh water, animals, and plants, where contemporary human and animal groups would have been clustered. Generally these lost zones of settlement and exploitation are invisible to us as they are submerged by a sea level rise of 100–130 meters. After the cold climax these landscapes began to vanish to warming seas, whereas the inland mountains became temporarily more hospitable, hence stimulating their increasing, if, seasonal use. Subsequently, as the warming trends became combined with greater rainfall, the Epirus uplands became far less exploitable, as noted earlier: only a fleeting sporadic use of the Megalakkos shelter near Klithi suggests some use of the now wooded mountains of Eastern Epirus. In compensation, the fast recovery of sea levels close to present have allowed the preservation on the modern shore of later Mesolithic coastal camps, such as Sidari on Corfu with shell middens.

Bailey concludes the Klithi monograph with some intriguing thoughts about the nature of history. If there is a long-term narrative of repeated transhumant life in the region for human groups, the project director is keen to avoid determinism, with humans as robots driven by the nature of the landscape. But at the same time he expresses skepticism toward the focus in contemporary Archaeological Theory on individual human beings, who decide almost on a daily basis how they will control their world and fate. Rather he sees in the Epirus story a co-adaptation of society, climate, fauna, and flora, with the central connecting thread being mobility. For him we are not dealing with "disembodied actors engaged in purely cerebral or symbolic exercises" – a clear attack on the more extreme, anti-ecology wing of current archaeological theorists known as the "Post-Processual" theorists.

The chronological coarseness of data in the Late Glacial, and the surviving samples which focus on more long-lived occupations, mean that application of such currently popular anthropological approaches of a "Post-Modern" kind are in any case infeasible: the individual is not findable. At Klithi the smallest unit of observation is 500 years and that site is part of a system of sites whose total span of use is 100,000 years. This is a landscape dominated by processes too slow for human perception to have comprehended in a single lifetime. No existing archaeological or anthropological theory is ready to deal with this, so it is better for archaeologists to create useful theory to relate to the realities of the data. This study as a whole prefers to take a view where landscapes, plant, animals, and humans evolve together and in constant close relationship. Here events and persons are relevant only in terms of the creation of higher-level entities and behaviors at the group or landscape level and over persistent periods longer than the normal perception of a single person. Acceptance of this philosophy of the past would lead us to rethink both that past and ourselves, allowing us to learn openly from our data rather than be forced endlessly to repeat dogmas derived from preconceived ideologies and philosophies.

I found this synthesis controversial but rather convincing.

An Annaliste Integration of Processes at Different Timescales

Bailey's reflections on the Palaeolithic of Epirus have already raised the central issues when we try to portray and unravel that interplay of lives and eras, homes and entire landscapes, which lies at the heart of the project of the Annales School of French historians. That was to capture analytically as well as empathetically (involving our emotional engagement), how the past was created and yet experienced by contemporaries. Our time resolution for this chapter is coarse, which allows us an extremely long-term perspective (the *longue durée*) during which various species of hominid spread and perhaps retreated from Greece, and over which traditions of tool-making persisted for unimaginable periods of time with minimal change, whilst their replacement by more complex assemblages was equally spread over eras encompassing untold human generations. Our insight into ways of life (the Annalistes' *modes de vie*) has even less sense of time about it: based on ethnography, hunter-gatherers are believed to have followed seasonal rounds over larger or smaller annual territories, responding to shorter and longer-term changes to local ecology, notably the drastic alternations caused by the Ice Age cycles. Even when, in the final phases of hunter-gatherer lifestyles in Greece, symbolic representations might be expected from evidence in other parts of Europe, the Aegean offers little beyond some hints of body ornament. This artistic poverty has been explained through the harsher conditions of subsistence in the region and low absolute population densities.

One ray of light occurs to illuminate life at shorter timescales, the rare finds of deliberate burials, especially the cemetery at the Franchthi Cave. With modern techniques to study diet and disease, and the movements of individuals, it becomes possible to see one human life, at least in its cumulative imprint on that person's physical body (Bintliff 1989). Already some intriguing insights are emerging, and we can expect more as science increases the range and sophistication of its applications to "the biography of the body." The discovery of Middle Palaeolithic human footprints in the Theopetra Cave (Karkanas *et al.* 1999) is another tantalizing if unique contact with

moments in time and specific individuals. Isotope analysis will also reveal the long-term movements of individuals. But otherwise the Aegean era of hunter-gatherer life, more than 99 percent of human occupation, suits those like Bailey with a Darwinian, ecological perspective, but frustrates anyone who would wish to see, if not the experience of life in the short term of a human life (the world of *événements*), yet at least the fluctuations of human behavior in the medium term of a few hundreds of years (the *moyenne durée*). Is it really the case that landscape exploitation did not experience less continuity within a given ecology, and witness more experimentation by human groups? Is our model of effectively static lifestyles and an invisible, and by implication, non-existent symbolic life correct, or merely the product of the sparseness of the evidence? In other parts of Europe, extremely detailed study of our chief data, stone-tool assemblages, has attempted to use these products of human skill to access individuality and diversity, as well as a sense of aesthetics, and perhaps such approaches in the future will take us further into the world of lived experience amongst Greek foragers.

A Personal View

The world of Palaeolithic studies is very specialized and not for the romantic archaeologist. Where I see Aegean hunter-gatherers come to life, in the absence of an Aegean cave art, is through their movements in the landscape. To understand, as we saw for Franchthi and Klithi, the careful modes of adaptation to the varied terrains of Greece, including their altering form in successive warm and cold, open and wooded, manifestations, gives one a pathway into hunter-gatherer life which has an immediacy sparking one's imagination. To stand at a cave-mouth and be able to tie the views in all directions, with a well-supported model of how that "taskscape" was exploited by the cave's forager occupants, gives one the ability to "people" the Greek landscape for an era for which other forms of reconstruction remain still beyond our capabilities.

This specific route to the past did not come to me immediately, when my first enthusiasm for Archaeology arose as a teenager. Then it was very concrete things, Roman coins, villa mosaics, and vivid reconstruction drawings of past lifestyles by gifted artists such as Alan Sorrell, which fed my fascination. However, in 1967, I was drawn to watch a black-and-white documentary on BBC television, offering a new perspective on early human life in Greece. Puzzlement followed: much of the program consisted of a bulky, mature, balding figure in shorts, sitting on a rock, expounding his philosophy of the past, with occasional glimpses of students sieving soil, and flocks of goats moving across the landscape. Not, I thought, what I expected Archaeology to be, and beyond my comprehension. In fact this was Eric Higgs, explaining an entirely new way of approaching the Human Past, and illustrating this from his current project in Epirus (Higgs 1967). Watching the same program was another schoolboy, Geoff Bailey, a little older than me, and he *did* understand what was new and exciting about the arrival of the new science of Human Ecology into Archaeology. He wrote to Higgs and joined the Epirus project before going to Cambridge University (where I met him and was later myself to become unavoidably under the spell of Higgsian ecological ideas). After Higgs died it was Bailey who took the Epirus Project to its conclusion and pulled all the threads of almost 40 years research into an outstanding two-volume edited work.

References

Bailey, G. N. (ed.) (1997). *Klithi: Palaeolithic Settlement and Quaternary Landscapes in Northwest Greece*. 2 vols. Cambridge: McDonald Institute for Archaeological Research.

Bailey, G. N. *et al.* (eds.) (1999). *The Palaeolithic Archaeology of Greece and Adjacent Areas*. London: The British School at Athens.

Bintliff, J. L. (1977). *Natural Environment and Human Settlement in Prehistoric Greece*. Oxford: BAR Supplementary Series 28.

Bintliff, J. L. (1989). "Cemetery populations, carrying capacities and the individual in history." In C. A. Roberts, F. Lee, and J. L. Bintliff (eds.), *Burial Archaeology*. Oxford: BAR Brit. Series 211, 85–104.

Cullen, T. (1995). "Mesolithic mortuary ritual at Franchthi Cave, Greece." *Antiquity* 69, 270–289.

Dennell, R. W. and W. Roebroeks (2005). "An Asian perspective on early human dispersal from Africa." *Nature* 438, 1099–1104.

Efstratiou, N. *et al.* (2006). "Prehistoric exploitation of Grevena highland zones: hunters and herders along the Pindus chain of western Macedonia (Greece)." *World Archaeology* 38, 415–435.

Galanidou, N. and C. Perlès (eds.) (2003). *The Greek Mesolithic. Problems and Perspectives*. London: The British School at Athens.

Galili, E. *et al.* (2002). "The emergence and dispersion of the Eastern Mediterranean fishing village: Evidence from submerged Neolithic settlements off the Carmel coast, Israel." *Journal of Mediterranean Archaeology* 15, 167–198.

Gowlett, J. A. J. (1999). "The Lower and Middle Palaeolithic, transition problems and hominid species: Greece in broader perspective." In Bailey *et al.* 1999, 43–58.

Gowlett, J. A. J. (2004). "Chronology and the human narrative." In J. Bintliff (ed.), *A Companion to Archaeology*. Oxford: Blackwell, 206–234.

Green, R. E. *et al.* (2010). "A draft sequence of the Neandertal genome." *Science* 328, 710–722.

Higgs, E. S. (1967). "Greece and Paleolithic man." *The Listener* 77, 425–427.

Jacobsen, T. W. (ed.) (1987–2010). *Excavations at Franchthi Cave, Greece*. Vols. 1–14. Bloomington: University of Indiana Press.

Jochim, M. (1987). "Late Pleistocene refugia in Europe." In O. Soffer (ed.), *The Pleistocene Old World*. New York: Plenum, 317–331.

Karkanas, P. *et al.* (1999). "Mineral assemblages in Theopetra, Greece: A framework for understanding diagenesis in a prehistoric cave." *Journal of Archaeological Science* 26, 1171–1180.

Kohn, M. (2006). "Made in Savannahstan." *New Scientist* (1 July), 34–39.

Kyparissi-Apostolika, N. (1999). "The Palaeolithic deposits of Theopetra Cave in Thessaly (Greece)." In Bailey *et al.* 1999, 232–239.

Louwe Kooijmans, L. (1998). *Between Geleen and Banpo. The Agricultural Transformation of Prehistoric Society, 9000–4000 BC*. Amsterdam: Archaeology Centre, Amsterdam University.

Panagopoulou, E. (1999). "The Theopetra Middle Palaeolithic assemblages: Their relevance to the Middle Palaeolithic of Greece and adjacent areas." In Bailey *et al.* 1999, 252–265.

Panagopoulou, E. *et al.* (2004). "Late Pleistocene archaeological and fossil human evidence from Lakonis Cave, Southern Greece." *Journal of Field Archaeology* 29(3/4), 323–349.

Papagianni, D. (2000). *Middle Palaeolithic Occupation and Technology in Northwestern Greece. The Evidence from Open-Air Sites*. Oxford: BAR Int. Series 882.

Perlès, C. (1999). "Long-term perspectives on the occupation of the Franchthi Cave: Continuity and discontinuity." In Bailey *et al.* 1999, 311–318.

Perlès, C. (2000). "Greece, 30–20,000 bp." In W. Roebroeks *et al.* (eds.), *Hunters of the Golden Age.* Leiden: University of Leiden, 375–397.

Perlès, C. (2001). *The Early Neolithic in Greece.* Cambridge: Cambridge University Press.

Richards, M. *et al.* (2008). "Strontium isotope evidence of Neanderthal mobility at the site of Lakonis, Greece using laser-ablation PIMMS." *Journal of Archaeological Science* 35, 1251–1256.

Roebroeks, W. (2001). "Hominid behaviour and the earliest occupation of Europe: An exploration." *Journal of Human Evolution* 41, 437–461.

Roebroeks, W. (2003). "Landscape learning and the earliest peopling of Europe." In M. Rockman and J. Steele (eds.), *Colonization of Unfamiliar Landscapes. The Archaeology of Adaptation.* London: Routledge, 99–115.

Runnels, C. (1989). "Greece before the Greeks." *Archaeology* 42(2), 43–47.

Runnels, C. (1995). "Review of Aegean Prehistory IV: The Stone Age of Greece from the Palaeolithic to the advent of the Neolithic." *American Journal of Archaeology* 99, 699–728.

Runnels, C. and T. H. van Andel (1993). "The Lower and Middle Palaeolithic of Thessaly, Greece." *Journal of Field Archaeology* 20, 299–317.

Runnels, C. and T. H. van Andel (1999). "The Palaeolithic in Larisa, Thessaly." In Bailey *et al.* 1999, 215–220.

Runnels, C. *et al.* (2005). "A Mesolithic landscape in Greece: Testing a site-location model in the Argolid at Kandia." *Journal of Mediterranean Archaeology* 18, 259–285.

Sampson, A. (ed.) (2006). *The Prehistory of the Aegean Basin.* Athens: Atrapos.

Strasser, T. F. *et al.* (2010). "Stone Age seafaring in the Mediterranean. Evidence from the Plakias region for Lower Palaeolithic and Mesolithic habitation of Crete." *Hesperia* 79, 145–190.

Tourloukis, E. and O. Palli (2009). "The first Mesolithic site of Thesprotia." In B. Forsen (ed.), *Thesprotia Expedition I. Towards a Regional History.* Athens: Papers and Monographs from the Finnish Institute at Athens XV, 25–38.

Valladas, H. *et al.* (2007). "TL age-estimates for the Middle Paleolithic layers at Theopetra cave (Greece)." *Quaternary Geochronology* 2, 303–308.

Wobst, H. M. (1974). "Boundary conditions for Paleolithic social systems." *American Antiquity* 39, 147–178.

3

Early Farming Communities
Neolithic Greece

Chronology

(In calibrated Carbon 14 dates, that is including corrections to direct dates to allow for atmospheric carbon fluctuations)

Primary phase of Greek Neolithic or First Farmers, the so-called Preceramic, begins ca. 7000 BC

Early Neolithic (EN, ceramics in general use) begins ca. 6500 BC

Middle Neolithic (MN) begins ca. 5800 BC

Early phase of Late Neolithic (LN) begins ca. 5300 BC

Later LN begins ca. 4800 BC

Final Neolithic (FN) begins ca. 4500 BC

Early Bronze Age (EBA) begins ca. 3200 BC

Introduction

In the days of the Travelers and topographers, until the late nineteenth century AD Greece's past was confined to Classical (Greek and Roman) antiquities and the monuments of Byzantium. But subsequently, the establishment of a long prehistory for Europe (Greene 2002) encouraged archaeologists working in Greece to search for *its* prehistoric record. Rapidly the standard subdivisions were recognized: Palaeolithic and Mesolithic (early and later hunter-gatherers), Neolithic (first farmer and herder societies), Bronze Age (mature farmer-herder societies with copper then bronze metallurgy), and Early and Later Iron Age (most recent prehistoric then protohistoric societies, iron-using, on the edge of and then in the first period of historical records). The Aegean was immediately envisaged as promising for prehistoric research, firstly because it bordered the Middle East, considered a major source of European cultural development from the Neolithic onwards, and secondly because ancient

The Complete Archaeology of Greece: From Hunter-Gatherers to the 20th Century AD, First Edition. John Bintliff.
© 2012 John Bintliff. Published 2012 by Blackwell Publishing Ltd.

Greek mythology suggested a rich pre-Classical society, with layers of legendary events stretching into a remote past.

Alongside the discovery at this time of Bronze Age palace civilizations on the Mainland (the Mycenaean), Crete (the Minoan), and the small towns of the Cyclades (Cycladic), the most numerous prehistoric earthworks attracting late nineteenth and early twentieth-century fieldworkers were the habitation mounds ("tells," "magoulas," or "toumbas") which dotted the great, fertile plains and low hill lands of Northeast Greece. Those in Macedonia and Thrace were still in the Ottoman Empire till 1913 and 1920, respectively, so at first research by Greek and foreign archaeologists focused on the Plains of Thessaly. The former regions opened up to serious investigation only when they became part of the Greek state. Thus it was that the great Greek pioneer Tsountas, and the British team of Wace and Thompson, in Thessaly, subsequently the British scholar Heurtley in Macedonia, revealed that the dominant period when these tell-villages were occupied was that of a spectacular Greek Neolithic, with rich architecture, decorated ceramics, and figurines.

The culture–history sequence

Neolithic society represents a remarkable rupture in human occupation of the Aegean. In contrast to the highly localized but scanty remains of mobile hunter-gatherer bands which characterize the Palaeolithic and Mesolithic eras, Neolithic communities seem from the first to have lived (at least for the most part) in permanent villages, with an economy of domestic plants and animals. The roots of that economy and the accompanying material culture lie within older Neolithic communities of the Near East, and it is generally, but not universally, accepted that this whole way of life was introduced to Greece by human colonization out of Anatolia (Asian Turkey) and the Levant (the Eastern Mediterranean coastal countries) (Perlès 2001, Efstratiou 2007; opposed by Kotsakis 2001, 2006a).

The early excavators were already interested in tracing social and economic developments across the Neolithic. Signs of increasing political complexity and technological progress have always been central to archaeologists seeking the origins of modern society through a series of critical developmental stages, beginning in the remote past (Bintliff 1984). The "Neolithic Revolution" in the Aegean showed one such critical discontinuity compared to preceding foraging peoples. Then, excavated Neolithic tell sites generated evidence for subsequent social evolution, since the sites of Middle Neolithic (MN) Sesklo and Late Neolithic (LN) Dhimini appeared to demonstrate the rise of social stratification and intercommunity warfare, together with the production of elaborate, and traded, fine pottery products. These aspects were highlighted in the 1970s by Theochares, an authority on Thessalian prehistory (1973).

Contemporaneously, John Evans' (1971) exploratory trenches beneath the Minoan Bronze Age palace at Knossos on Crete, revealed a very early colonizing village of farmers at the site. More importantly, this village grew progressively across the long Neolithic era, until, on the threshold of the Early Bronze Age, its size could justify the term "town" (several thousand inhabitants). Might all these unfolding developments of prehistoric Greek society offer insights into the creation of Europe's first civilizations, the Minoan and Mycenaean, within the subsequent Bronze Age period in the Aegean?

Origins of the Greek Neolithic

The Mesolithic contribution

Till the 1980s, it was orthodoxy that Europe received knowledge of domestic plants and animals from the Near East, in almost all regions through the arrival of immigrant settlers from Anatolia and the Levant and their direct European descendants. Radiocarbon dates showed a progressive diffusion of agropastoralism (farming and herding) and associated culture (ceramics, village life, new forms of lithic tools) from Southeast to Northwest Europe, agreeing with an expanding colonist settlement from that direction (Clark 1965) (Figure 3.1). Only in the outer margins of Europe was there evidence for indigenous hunter-gatherers moving gradually toward the Neolithic way of life, but this could be accounted for by acculturation (educative culture contact) through association with adjacent settlers of Near Eastern origin. The

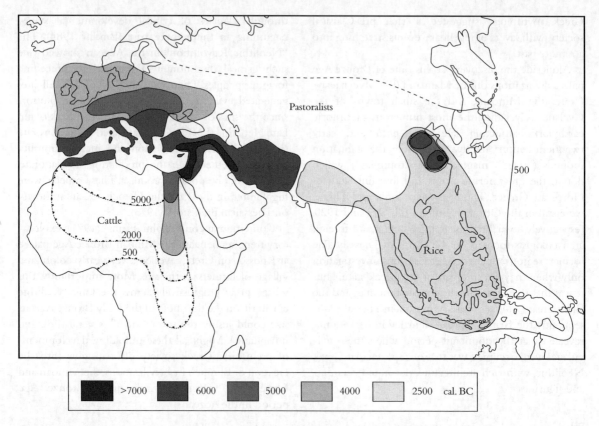

Pastoralists

500

5000

Cattle

2000

500

Rice

| | >7000 | | 6000 | | 5000 | | 4000 | | 2500 | cal. BC |

Figure 3.1   The spread of Neolithic farming and herding during the Holocene (our current Interglacial, ca. 10,000 BP [before present] till now). Dates are in years BC.
L. Louwe Kooijmans, *Between Geleen and Banpo. The Agricultural Transformation of Prehistoric Society, 9000–4000 BC.* Amsterdam, Archaeology Centre, Amsterdam University 1998, Figure 2.

most recent data confirm this general model (Ammerman and Cavalli-Sforza 1984, Gkiasta *et al.* 2003, Colledge *et al.* 2004).

Nonetheless, Greece might tell a different story. Its lowlands possessed natural semi-open vegetation, wild forms of the Neolithic cereals, pulses, and legumes, and indeed these were intentionally collected by its hunter-gatherers. Wild forms of cattle, goat, and pig were native to the fauna. Aegean Late Glacial and Early Holocene foragers were adopting a Broad Spectrum economy (see Chapter 2), which in the contemporary Near East was a major factor in the development of the agropastoral (farmer-herder) economy in several regions independently. Even if the domestication of plants and animals spread from the Near East to the Aegean, perhaps it was through contacts between early

farmers in the former region and indigenous hunter-gatherers, "acculturation," rather than via immigration from the East (Kotsakis 2001). The precocious maritime travel demonstrated by the provision of Cycladic obsidian into Mainland forager sites as early as the Upper Palaeolithic, as I suggested a generation ago (Bintliff 1977), perhaps in connection with seasonal pursuit of fish shoals ("transmerance"), might have stimulated knowledge exchange into Greek societies already adapted to more intensive forms of plant and animal exploitation (Sampson 2006).

Perlès' (2001) counter-arguments on this issue were persuasive. The Mesolithic evidence, when she wrote, indicated sparse populations exploiting dispersed resources of low energy yield. The conditions else-where (dense packing of increasingly sedentarized foragers in high-quality resource localities), that allowed hunter-gatherers to move to a productive Neolithic economy, seemed lacking in Greece. Early Neolithic settlements, excepting a few special cases, lack underlying Mesolithic occupation, and that handful are more plausibly evidence for acculturation of foragers by nearby Neolithic colonists (e.g., the Franchthi Cave, and Sidari on Corfu). The great island of Crete appeared devoid of human occupation till the full Neolithic package arrived, unavoidably externally colonized. Nonetheless, the rapid disappearance of hunter-gathering sites (hunting is a very minor component of the Early Neolithic economy) surely resulted from conversion of indigenous foragers to the agropastoral lifeway, particularly through intermarriage. Significantly, Mesolithic technology and other aspects of material culture are absent from the standard Neolithic assemblage (collection of everyday objects), underlying the domination of the new culture and economy. However, some reverse acculturation would be expected. The high level of use by Neolithic communities throughout Eastern and Southern Greece of Melian obsidian plausibly reflects local knowledge transfer to the colonizers, whilst Perlès speculates that the specialist task of visiting the largely unpopulated Cyclades for this raw material remained with the descendants of indigenous foragers within the new mixed population.

We have extensive knowledge of Neolithic and Early Bronze Age (EBA) boats. Models from various Greek sites and surviving freshwater boat outlines from Macedonian lake deposits can be combined with EBA iconography on pottery. A range of boat types, but all sail-less, can be reconstructed (Broodbank 2000, Marangou 2001a). Tree dugouts, hide-coated light wood structures, and reed bases, all seem likely boat varieties. In 1988 an experimental sailing from Central Greece to Melos in a flat, lake-reed craft with a cypress frame showed the feasibility of such an extended journey.

The recent Mesolithic survey by Runnels et al. in the Argolid peninsula (2005), nonetheless, challenges the perception of low-density Mesolithic populations, struggling to survive in unfavorable mid-Holocene landscapes (Kotsakis 2006a). At least in favored localities (niches) with a variety of rich plant and animal food, relatively dense networks of temporary and permanent settlement or camp sites may have existed. On the other hand, the fact that very extensive parts of Greece do not offer such rich environments prevents us from generalizing from the sheltered coastal bays of the Argolid to repopulate the rest of the country to the same density of hunter-gatherers. Nonetheless, warning us not to underestimate the complexity of Greece's broad-spectrum foraging populations is the discovery at Maroula (island of Kythnos), of a Mesolithic settlement with round houses and formal burials (Sampson 2006). Most recently, Runnels has repeated his success in a targeted survey in likely ecologies for Mesolithic lifestyles on Crete, discovering a score of Mesolithic findspots on the southwest coast (Strasser et al. 2010). Despite all this, the very weak contribution of Mesolithic culture to the succeeding Neolithic, and its strongly exotic elements, would seem to leave the balance of evidence in support of Perlès' position, where genuine colonization is the dominant factor in the spread of the Neolithic throughout Greece.

Near Eastern roots

The vast majority of Early Neolithic sites present a homogenous culture, quite different from preceding Mesolithic assemblages (Perlès 2005). Only immigrants could have brought the range of skills on display: farming, herding, building, stone polishing, pressure flaking, and spinning. Chronology and cultural similarities lead to the inevitable conclusion of Near Eastern colonization. Even the potential for local domestication of many Neolithic plants and animals represents unfulfilled opportunities: Upper Palaeolithic and Mesolithic exploitation in Greece remains at gathering and hunting rather than showing progressive domestication. DNA study confirms this, showing that the domesticated species of Europe are predominantly descended from Near Eastern rather than local breeding stocks (Bollongino and Burger 2007, Brown et al. 2009, Tresset and Vigne 2007). Equally significant is the genetic evidence suggesting that Southeastern Europe has been predominantly peopled from the Near East, with increasing contributions from indigenous populations the further west through Europe one travels (Bentley et al. 2003).

Yet, there is no total match for the Early Greek Neolithic with any particular Near Eastern region, leading to the inference that there were multiple founder groups from different parts of the Near East. Plausible overland connections are claimed between Northern Greece and Northern Anatolia (Asian Turkey), and by sea between Crete, Cyprus, and the Levant (Perlès 2005, Efstratiou 2005), and most recently across the Aegean from Anatolia (Ammerman *et al.* 2008).

The timescale of supposed colonization fits neatly into major developments within the Near Eastern Neolithic (Efstratiou 2005, 2007). Although the Greek Early Neolithic (EN) horizon is seventh millennium BC, if we allow for its earlier origin in the Levant and Anatolia, its source cultures should be eighth millennium BC. The complex of related Neolithic groups at this time in those neighboring regions are known as the Pre-Pottery Neolithic B (PPNB). Cauvin (1994) characterizes this as the "great exodus," when farmers expanded from a nuclear zone for early farming in the "Fertile Crescent" into Central Anatolia, the Near Eastern semi-deserts, and the temperate Mediterranean zone. This dispersal coincides with the development of second-generation cereals (for example the more advanced hexaploid wheat), the domestication of pulses (legumes such as beans and peas), and the full package of early domestic animals, especially cattle. The fact that at some Greek sites pottery use in the oldest EN levels is confined to figurines and ornaments, is consistent with the same limited use in the oldest Neolithic cultures of the regions of the Near East and on Cyprus considered ancestral to the Greek Neolithic (the Preceramic Neolithic group).

Settlement Patterns

The overall settlement picture

The overall distribution of Neolithic settlements discovered so far in Greece suggests a major role for geographical factors in the spread of early farming communities (Perlès 2001). Topography, climate, and soils favored dense but isolated clusters of settlements in certain regions, with a much thinner cover elsewhere. This argues for a preference amongst early farmers in the landscapes of Greece to occupy areas most comparable to those where the domestication of

plants and animals was first accomplished (a semi-arid climate, open woodland). It excludes the cooler, wetter uplands of West and Central Greece, the arid Southeast Mainland and Cycladic Islands, and points to the intermediate geographical zone of the plains and hills of Central and Northeast Greece. The great lowlands of Thessaly, Macedonia, and Thrace unsurprisingly reveal unparalleled densities of early farming sites, whilst the rest of Mainland Greece has hitherto given more dispersed, lower-density Neolithic settlement patterns, and finally the Cyclades have virtually no settlement until the Final Neolithic period. These generalizations are especially pronounced for the Early and Middle Neolithic, since in later Neolithic times economic developments encouraged population expansion in the rest of Greece, including smaller Aegean islands.

Till these later Neolithic phases, farming was carried out by hand, using hoes and spades. This is very time-consuming, and hard to accomplish if soils are dry for much of the year. Johnson (1996) and Perlès (2001) draw a clear contrast, based on Sherratt's earlier models (1980, 1981), between Northern plains such as the Thessalian, where rainfall was adequate for dry-farming with such technology, and the Southern Mainland, especially the Peloponnese, where village locations were usually constrained to limited sectors of the landscape where well-watered fertile soils occurred near springs, lakes, or marshes. Hence the latter villages were few and far between, creating social conditions opposite to those of densely-settled Thessaly and similar plains further north. Perhaps also, the uneven spread of such desirable resources led in Southeastern Greece to more dispersed and smaller-scale forms of settlement: individual family farms or kin-group hamlets, rather than nucleated (population-concentrating) tell-villages which so far dominate settlement forms in the Plains of Thessaly and beyond.

In the Late and Final Neolithic the basic conditions of the agropastoral life altered fundamentally. Sherratt (1981) argued for a second vital diffusion of agricultural skills at this time (broadly the fifth and fourth millennia BC). In his "Secondary Products Revolution" (2PR), he suggested that two critical improvements to farming and herding arose in the Near East and spread through contact, relatively rapidly, across Europe.

Firstly, a simple "ard" or scratch plough, drawn by cattle, enabled farmers to prepare their fields faster and hence over a larger area, thus making far more use of drier soils even where high water tables were not available (cf. Halstead 1995b). Outside of those lowlands where rainfall had always been high enough to pose few problems for hoes and spades, this innovation allowed farmers in more arid landscapes to move out of the areas they had been restricted to, the semi-wetland sectors, and open up cultivation on the good but hitherto too dry soils lying between rivers, springs, and lakes, the so-called "interfluves."

Secondly there developed a wider use of domestic animals beyond their meat-value, chiefly for wool and dairy products (milk, cheese, yoghurts, etc.). The domestic economy was thereby boosted, as was the value of specializing in larger-scale herding, encouraging settlement in less agriculturally-favorable landscape sectors which were more ideal for grazing, particularly on a seasonal basis (transhumance). In many parts of Greece and the wider Mediterranean, strong seasonal contrasts between hot summer lowlands and cooler uplands, or cold and snowy winter uplands and warmer lowlands, have given rise to seasonal migrations of domestic animals and their herders, well attested since the first historical records. The projection of recent Mediterranean transhumance into the ancient and prehistoric eras has nonetheless been challenged, since arguably Early Modern specialist pastoralism is closely tied to commercial economies and factory production (see Chapters 1 and 2) (Lewthwaite 1981, Halstead 1987, 1996). It now appears, however, that the archaeological evidence does support the development of long-distance pastoral transhumance, especially into the high Greek mountains, from exactly this period onwards, the Late Neolithic (Efstratiou *et al.* 2006), underlining the radical economic changes identified by Sherratt.

Although often criticized, the accumulating empirical evidence in the Near East and Europe remains largely supportive of the Sherratt model. In particular, a radical rise in settlement numbers and an expansion into new sectors of the landscape appear to be striking features of later Neolithic Europe as a whole, not least in Greece. In the Aegean this is the time of the first large-scale colonization of the Cyclades (Davis 1992), and of a clear expansion of population in the Southern

Mainland, on Crete (Branigan 1999), and even in long and densely settled more northerly plains such as in Thessaly (Demoule and Perlès 1993), as well as into the uplands throughout the Greek Mainland.

However, the latest research offers a more complex chronology for the "2PR." Sherratt's dating utilized pictures and texts from the oldest urban societies in Mesopotamia, clearly showing all the components of his agropastoral changes, together with rare but controversial use of artifacts from the rest of the Near East and Europe (animal models, "cheese-strainer" pots, etc.), and changes in the age-structure of domestic animals excavated in settlement contexts (seen as probably indicating the balance of meat production versus a greater emphasis on dairy and textile products). More recently an independent approach has been developed, involving direct analysis of the residues of pottery vessel contents to detect the distinctive traces of milk products (Evershed *et al.* 2008). A large-scale study of early pottery from a wide range of sites has given clear results for the timing and scale of early dairy production from Britain through to the Near East, revising the details of Sherratt's chronology.

If cattle, sheep, goats, and pig were domesticated by the eighth millennium BC in the Near East, at the start of the Neolithic era, already by the later seventh millennium the knowledge of dairying was visible from the Balkans across Anatolia to the rest of the Near East, within the oldest Neolithic cultures. On the other hand, the actual practice remained small-scale at this time, with the notable exception of Northwest Turkey, where from the seventh to sixth millennia BC it was significant. In Romania dairying rose to prominence by 5000 BC, and once the Neolithic had spread to Britain dairying rapidly grew in importance after 4000 BC. The exceptional early foci are associated with a local emphasis on cattle-rearing, suggesting that the first development of dairying was with cows rather than sheep and goats. In line with this more regionally diversified picture for the spread of dairying, faunal analysis of domestic animals at various places in Neolithic Europe, including Knossos (Isaakidou 2006), indicates knowledge, but limited use, of dairying and animal traction (for ploughs or carts) in the earlier Neolithic, preceding widespread, large-scale shifts to these strategies in Final Neolithic and Bronze Age times. Thus despite the apparent contradiction from the new scientific evidence to the Sherratt model, its main lines seem intact (cf. Halstead 2006b), in that the general use of dairy products probably impacts on the Near East and Europe in the fourth to third millennia BC as he suggested, at a time when the animal bone and artifactual data still seem to support a similar large-scale adoption of the animal-drawn ard-plough.

Settlement form

The known Neolithic settlements of Greece are dominated by the nucleated tell-village, with dispersed farms and hamlets of non-tell type clearly in a minority. Yet new research suggests that the balance requires significant adjustment. Tells are highly visible and hence became an early focus for archaeologists, whilst "flat sites" require more intensive surface survey, a methodology of recent application and one so far used in just a few Greek landscapes. Site survey is also revealing a greater density of Neolithic settlements outside of the well-known concentrations in Thessaly, Macedonia, and Thrace. Such methods, combined with rescue and research excavations by Greek archaeologists, have now identified flat sites amidst the tell landscapes themselves, including Thessaly. In South-Central Greece, around ancient Tanagra city (Bintliff *et al.* 2006), a complex, probably pre-plough non-tell Neolithic settlement pattern can be reconstructed, composed of nucleated hamlets or villages based on the most fertile expanses of high water table soils, around which a series of small rural sites line the river valley soils up to several kilometers away. The fact that such nucleated settlements in Southern Greece are rarely tells, probably reflects a much lower use of mudbrick and a more mobile settlement network than in the Northern plain tell societies, rather than indicating a less long-lived occupation of such landscapes.

General characteristics of tells

These artificial mounds represent villages with prolonged occupation and the dominance of mudbrick architecture, where over centuries or even millennia new houses are built upon the remains of older and accumulated domestic debris, constantly elevating the village mound. The plains of East Central and Northeast Greece have revealed through extensive survey remarkable numbers of such early farming settlements (Figure 3.6). The density of such small villages is unusual in Europe and high productivity was needed to sustain them, whilst social conflicts were clearly avoided. How these special landscapes were managed for high, sustainable productivity can be modeled, but more problematic is how such community packing avoided destructive inter-settlement warfare. The fixity of the tell domestic base, creating a radial zone of exploitation of the surrounding countryside in the direction of neighboring villages, and a vertical build-up of successive settlements on top of the original foundation, is contrasted to another form of settlement, commoner outside of the tell landscapes, where flat settlements may have been occupied over shorter periods as a result of regular relocation of the houses and fields of a community. One might expect that the confined tell territory led to a scarcity of building space in the village, whilst the larger occupation area and more extensive land use of flat sites might display open village plans with more scope for gardens, working areas, and stock enclosures.

Tells and their settlement plan

Interestingly, tells in Neolithic Greece and related cultures of the North Balkans share many features as regards village layout. Since in the Near East tells were a regular aspect of early farming societies, this form of village life and its associated worldview were also already present in ancestral communities. The striking feature is the ordered nature of living space, a design reinforced by generational replacement of houses on top of, or close to, earlier houses (Chapman 1994). Houses, and structures for storage, workshops or ritual, were separated by narrow lanes, often sharing the same orientation. Seemingly due to the high value of land around the village for subsistence, tells did not expand outwards to allow open space for that variety of inter-house activities which we are familiar with from Early Modern European village-plans: large open areas for communal gatherings of a social, political or ritual nature, household gardens, and stock enclosures.

Chapman argues convincingly that the tell is a powerful ancestral space, a social landmark with a cumulative place-value achieved through long-term

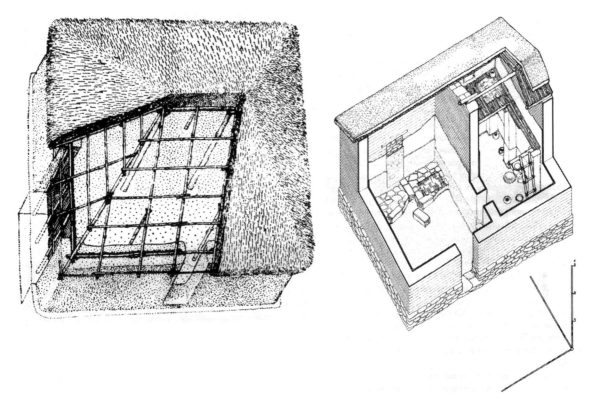

Figure 3.2 Early Neolithic house from Nea Nikomedeia (left) and Middle Neolithic house from Sesklo acropolis (right). D. R. Theochares, *Neolithikos politismos. Suntomi episkopisi tis neolithikis ston helladiko choro.* Athens 1993, Figures 19 and 48.

community participation, a "habitus" (or traditional way of life, following Bourdieu) of stability. Replacing houses or even whole village-plans on the literal lines of older structures enforced conservatism, and perhaps an atmosphere of unchanging or cyclical time for tell societies. The increasing elevation of tells, usually set against flat plains, over time, emphasized the continuity between people and place. Elites seem normally absent within these small settlements (for exceptions see below), suggesting that the social structure was organized around families and larger kin-groups (lineages). The visual focus in tells is the individual domestic house, generally on a scale suitable for a large nuclear family. Appropriately, excavated tell houses, generally rectangular, rarely show differences from house to house or complex internal spaces. Figure 3.2 contrasts the simple, organic construction huts of Early Neolithic Nea Nikomedeia with a more elaborate Middle Neolithic house from the Sesklo

acropolis; the latter highlights the rare exceptions to this rule.

Halstead (1999b) stresses that the tell is focused on the individual household, usually discretely placed from its neighbors, with a general (but not complete) absence of community spaces (perhaps most village-level social and ritual events took place outside the tell). In stark contrast to Chapman's communal model of the tell, Halstead prefers a small-scale society composed of competing households.

Halstead's viewpoint (modified more recently, see below) has the distinct advantage in offering a potential origin for the postulated, if very localised, development in mature to later Neolithic times of higher-status individuals or families. And yet Chapman's emphasis on these communities as consciously nucleated societies cannot be neglected. If competitive households were central, a more efficient settlement pattern would have dispersed family farms across the tell's territory, which was small enough for most farms to have been intervisible and to enable social gatherings to occur with little effort at some central point, while offering ideal least-effort access to the family estate.

This is the appropriate moment to introduce a set of linked models, offering fundamental insights into Neolithic Greek societies, but also into later prehistoric and historic societies in Greece (following Text Box). Their suitability is so striking that at the time of my own application of these ideas in the late 1990s for both early farming societies and also for later periods (Bintliff 1999a), some of the same concepts were being explored for Neolithic Greece by Paul Halstead and Catherine Perlès.

Fissive and Corporate Communities

Anthropologists studying recent pre-Industrial societies have identified a cross-cultural tendency for human settlements without social classes to break up or undergo "fission" when they reach around 200–300 individuals (Figure 3.3). Below this figure, a "face-to-face" community exists, where everyone knows everyone else at a personal level. Beyond 150 people, this social bonding becomes difficult to sustain, encouraging conflicts and factions, which disrupt the traditional resolution of intracommunal tensions through personal contacts. At this point a common solution is for part of the growing village to break off and found a daughter settlement, often nearby.

If larger nucleated communities succeed in arising, three alternative mechanisms seem to account for almost all examples. The simplest, potentially operating even in Palaeolithic and Mesolithic times, would limit such large gatherings of people to seasonal camps, where many smaller bands agglomerated (gathered together) at times of peak animal or plant availability, to collaborate in great animal drives and exchange marriage partners, exotic raw materials or symbolic ornaments. The second mechanism is to subdivide the growing village into semi-autonomous neighborhoods, each of which stayed within the bounds of face-to-face population size. At a primary level households belonged to a largely self-managed social unit, the neighborhood, then at a secondary level there existed social institutions linking these units into the village as a whole. The third mechanism is that of a vertical rather than horizontal division of the village: management devolves on a social elite,

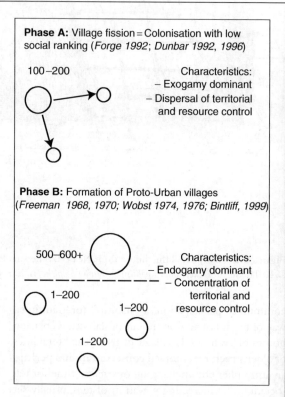

Figure 3.3 The author's model for fissive and corporate community settlement systems.
J. L. Bintliff, "Emergent complexity in settlement systems and urban transformations." In U. Fellmeth *et al.* (eds.), *Historische Geographie der Alten Welt. Festgabe für Eckart Olshausen.* Georg Olms Verlag, Hildesheim 2007, 43–82, Figure 7.

whose influence reduces but need not abolish the role of the household and neighborhood in social relations. This elite might be one or more powerful households, or merely a council of the senior male heads of households or lineages. Renfrew's pioneer application (1973) of ethnographic parallels highlighted two forms of elite power which might have occurred in later prehistoric Europe: a "Big Man" system, where an elite family or lineage might dominate a community on the basis of acquired status, wealth or social power (being effective warleaders, or ritual specialists, having large economic surpluses, or controlling extensive social networks); and a "Chiefdom" model, where status arises from inherited positions in a dynastic elite lineage or family. As to why larger communities might arise, Wobst (1974) has argued that a healthy human population can only escape the long-term dangers of inbreeding if it reaches 500–600 people. In face-to-face societies this has to be met through constant exchange of marriage partners with several other nearby small communities, making the alternative, an expansion to a large village, more attractive in this respect. Before knowledge of genetics, the harsh experience of genetic mutations and accumulating levels of disease appear to have led through Darwinian adaptation to a worldwide cultural behavior in which small communities have out-married to survive in the long term.

Returning to "face-to-face" society, physical anthropologist Robin Dunbar (1996) introduced additional arguments. Taking monkeys, apes, different early hominid types, and modern humans, he compared for each group that part of the brain associated with socialization, against their characteristic group size. Dunbar calculated a group size of around 150 people as the upper capacity of advanced humans to socialize effectively with.

Our prediction for global social organization, based on these complementary insights, would be that the simplicity and efficiency of the face-to-face organization would favor cooperating units of less than 200 people at innumerable times and places in world prehistory and history. Such indeed proves to be the case, even with historic state societies, since many pre-Industrial and particularly pre-centralized states allowed rural communities wide scope for self-management in communal affairs. It is surely not coincidental that estimated population sizes for early farming villages of the Near East and the Balkans are typically 50–200 (Redman 1978, Chapman 1989), although there were rare larger settlements, some even of town-like character like Chatal Hüyük. Thus early farming communities over this very large region plausibly evidence a social organization in which face-to-face relations are central, encouraging daughter settlement creation whenever settlement growth threatened internal cohesion. Since Near Eastern population densities appear to have been usually well below the sustaining capacity of the landscape, the spread of farming settlers which brought colonists to Europe might have been significantly linked to fissioning rather than resource pressures.

However, if a settlement grows beyond the face-to-face parameters, to achieve 500–600 inhabitants or more, not only would there need to be novel mechanisms for the peaceful coordination of such communities (the commonest ways were outlined above), but "emergent complexity" (Bentley and Maschner 2003) occurs, where wholly new socio-political dimensions to such a society become apparent, as explained in a subsequent section.

Greek Neolithic villages appear to fit our predictions for face-to-face societies with a broadly egalitarian ethos, with very few (but important) exceptions. Thus for our best-researched landscape, the tell villages in Thessaly, Halstead (1994, 1999b) suggests that small tells probably housed 40–80 people, large ones 120–240. On the other hand, Nea Nikomedeia in Macedonia, a tell where extensive excavation has taken place, is claimed by Pyke and Yiouni (1996) to have had even in EN times a population of 500–700 inhabitants. However just 12 percent of the site was dug, and Halstead (1981) downscales this estimation for the 2.4 ha tell site by arguing that many of the houses were not contemporary, and also that only a

Figure 3.4   Reconstruction of the Upper Town at Sesklo. D. R. Theochares, *Neolithikos politismos. Suntomi episkopisi tis neolithikis ston helladiko choro.* Athens 1993, Figure 43.

minority of the site was built over, leading to a recalculation of 120–240 inhabitants. Perlès (1999, 2001) has her own formula for relating settlement size to population, but still concludes for Thessalian tells that 100–300 occupants suits all but a few sites.

This analysis favors a position on tell social organization intermediate between Chapman and Halstead: the typical village was normally an effective, small-scale community based on interfamilial cooperation, but households remained independent and distinct units.

Complex tell societies

Exceptional amongst hundreds of tells mapped or excavated for Neolithic Greece are a small number where special features point to significant changes to the face-to-face model. Amongst the earliest tells excavated were Sesklo and Dhimini in Eastern Thessaly (Tsountas 1908), and their unusual character has led to re-excavations and re-studies of the material.

Middle Neolithic Sesklo (Figure 3.4, reconstruction of the Upper Town) is a giant site, comprising a large lower town and a small upper town ("acropolis") (Kotsakis 2006b). The Upper Town (Sesklo A), is less than 1 ha, but including the Lower Town (Sesklo B) brings the total settlement to more than 13 ha. The walled "acropolis" boasts far more substantial houses than the more extensive Lower Town. If the entire site was completely occupied by domestic structures, then the population, after Theochares, could have reached 3000 inhabitants. The excavated part of Late Neolithic (LN) Dhimini (Figure 3.5, plan and reconstruction) is notable for the architecture of its central complex. This consists of a series of concentric, if low, walls, with limited space between them, rather few potential living structures fitted amidst these wall circuits, then in the more extensive innermost enclosure a large structure of "megaron" form. The latter is a design with a long popularity into the Bronze Age and Early Iron Age in Greece, comprising a rectangular house subdivided into a sequence of porch, main room, and an optional extra, smaller room at the rear. LN Sesklo

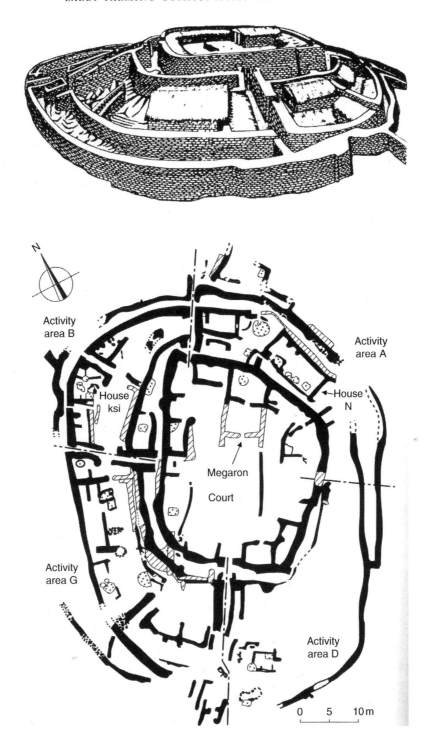

Figure 3.5 Plan of excavated areas at Dhimini and reconstruction drawing.
D. Preziosi and L. A. Hitchcock, *Aegean Art and Architecture*. Oxford University Press 1999, Figures 7 and 8.

significantly also has a large megaron form in the center of what by that phase is claimed to have become an otherwise small settlement on the acropolis.

Tsountas (1908) considered Dhimini as a princely seat, with a ruler's megaron residence protected by concentric three-meter high walls. The social gulf to peasants and retainers was marked by the simple house structures between these walls. Hourmouziadis' re-excavations (1979) made clear that the concentric walls were never lofty, strategic barriers (probably one meter high), representing rather a combination of ter-races on the hill to form construction and working zones, and internal divisions of the site to demarcate social or economic sectors. Hourmouziadis hypothe-sized a first phase for the site with a set of cooperating households, succeeded by the emergence of a domi-nant elite, signified by the central megaron. However, the area excavated and reproduced as this plan perhaps represents just 10 percent of the entire settlement, with traces of simple dwellings outside the dug zone, so it is premature to draw conclusions on the overall organization of the site (Preziosi and Hitchcock 1999). If the lower settlement around the dug mound was as extensive as thus implied, LN Dhimini would form a closer parallel to MN Sesklo.

The significantly unequal size of houses between upper and lower town at MN Sesklo, followed in the LN at both Sesklo and Dhimini by the evidence for a centrally-located complex structure of megaron form, encourage the claim that social stratification (a formal class division) has emerged at these sites. MN Sesklo is certainly larger and more architecturally diversified than the typical Neolithic village, and our demographic theories outlined above would predict communal inte-gration through horizontal or vertical divisions within its society. Sesklo's small-scale MN "acropolis" com-pared to its Lower Town, then the LN megaron foci at both sites (more likely to be domestic than temples), arguably present settlements dominated physically and politically by leading families. Strikingly at Sesklo, the LN reoccupation seems to go a step further, with just an area of 0.4 ha on the acropolis in use, taken up by the large megaron building and some associated build-ings, and fortified (Demoule and Perlès 1993).

Boundary walls and ditches may also reflect social divisions in tell sites. They enclose some EN and MN villages: occasionally a drainage function appears

possible, whilst their slight nature argues against a defen-sive purpose. Perhaps they commonly acted symboli-cally to demarcate the community (Demoule and Perlès 1993). At MN Sesklo the acropolis has a delim-iting wall to the Lower Town, also perhaps a social rather than military boundary. Additionally, Sesklo's MN architecture (Kotsakis 1999, 2006b), exhibits striking differences between the "acropolis" buildings and those in the more extensive Lower Town: the Upper Town has a typical tell plan, with distinct houses rebuilt on the same location, creating a deep stratigraphy, whilst in the Lower Town houses shift around the site over time and there is little continuity at any point, and even empty sectors. Moreover the Lower Town houses form blocks with party walls to households. LN Dhimini also appears in some respects to resemble the supposed elite sector at MN Sesklo.

Returning to our earlier discussion, we saw that villages rising above the figure of around 150 people resolve social tensions through either horizontal sub-divisions (for example neighborhood semi-autonomy), or vertical subdivisions (the emergence of a governing minority, household or lineage heads, Big Men or Chiefs). At Sesklo, even after downscaling population in the Lower Town (Kotsakis 1999) to allow for its discontinuous occupation, the likely total MN popu-lation could be above face-to-face society levels. The evidence for spatial divisions and a higher status sector in the Acropolis meets our predictions. The transfor-mation by the LN era at Sesklo, with a similar form of "elite" centralized plan at nearby LN Dhimini, into a complex focused on a putative dominant large residential structure, may more obviously mark a formal class structure, and by implication a smaller controlling group. At LN Sesklo, however, dependent peasants must be sought in adjacent settlements.

As previously mentioned, Wobst (1974, 1976) has suggested that prehistoric societies had to unite two adaptive concepts to flourish: the fitting of population density to available resources and technology, and marriage exchange within a demographic group large enough to prevent damaging inbreeding. For hunter-gatherers in Palaeolithic-Mesolithic Greece, overall densities seem to have been low (but probably in localized clusters), so that seasonal, multi-band gather-ings and perhaps individual mobility across bands were essential to maintain a healthy gene pool.

Intriguingly, Wobst's calculations favored a minimal breeding network of 500–600 people. If most early farming villages remained in the comfortable margins of 150±100 people, then a typical tell village needed regular marriage exchanges with several neighboring settlements. With tells in the great plains of Northern Greece a half hour apart, this posed no difficulty.

Social anthropologists have documented in many diverse societies that when a village reaches a population of around 500, it often appears to alter its sociopolitical and economic behavior, giving rise to a "corporate community" (Bintliff 1999a). Arising from an agglomeration of independent households vying for status, and with strong links to surrounding villages, such novel communities begin to act more like towns or tiny states, centralizing much decision-making and creating stronger barriers to free movement of people and products toward its neighboring settlements. The key factor fostering this transformation is a realignment in marriage customs. Whereas a face-to-face community sends many of its men or women to neighboring communities in return for incoming marriage partners (exogamy), once a village rises to a population at or beyond the level of Wobst's breeding network (500–600 people), it can largely provide its own marriage requirements (endogamy) (see Figure 3.3, Phase B). Now in most rural communities recorded by ethnographers and historians, exogamy is associated with movement of rights over land and/or livestock (bridewealth). The village does not control its own resources, since families in adjacent villages acquire rights over land and the products of land. But when a largely endogamous regime appears, the community can dispose of its resources as it wishes. Since breaching the 200–300 population level normally requires internal political changes, i.e., the family loses power to representatives of neighborhoods (horizontal subdivision) or to elites (vertical subdivision), there can arise a potent metamorphosis in community social organization. The leading members of the enlarged society begin to dispose of communal resources for the benefit of the village as a whole, or even to the personal advantage of its most influential families. The reduced importance of good neighborly relations with adjacent communities can enhance the potential for conflict over territory and other resources.

Increased signs of warfare and the erection of defenses might be observed. Such processes could account for the frequency in many global cultures at diverse periods of a proliferation of small city-states, generally in regular competition or warfare with each other.

I believe that these linked models help us to comprehend the processes at work behind the elite-focused large villages or towns at MN-LN Sesklo and Dhimini, an increase in the fortification of settlements in general during the later Greek Neolithic, and perhaps most significantly, why most scholars see the relentless expansion of the EN village at Knossos on Crete, from an estimated 0.3 ha at its foundation (a few score people?) to 3–5 ha (500–700 people?) by Final Neolithic times (Evans 1971), as a key to its Bronze Age transformation into a palace and city-state center. Sadly the destruction of almost all the remains of the intervening Early Bronze Age settlement at Knossos, as a result of the construction of the First Palace in its final phase, was so severe that we cannot clearly trace the later stages of this process, and too little is known of the Neolithic settlement tested in limited places below the Palace. Yet it is reasonable to suggest that here we are observing the evolution of another corporate community, with a predominance of endogamy, as the social basis for the later emergence of the Knossos state. Whether community expansion was achieved through elaborate cooperation between a number of internal neighborhood communities, as now appears likely for Chatal Hüyük, or through the rise of a political minority controlling communal affairs, awaits future research. But it is surely remarkable that the other great Minoan palace at Phaistos likewise appears to grow from a major Neolithic settlement of 5.6 ha in size, also potentially a "town-like" agglomeration (Watrous 1994).

Defensive settlements of Final Neolithic times

In recent years, a series of defended hamlets and villages from Southern Mainland Greece, and now the Cyclades, point to conflicts as populations expanded out into a wider range of landscape forms under the influence of plough agriculture, and the widespread adoption of secondary products from domestic animals which encouraged more intensive pastoralism.

Some half dozen small fortified settlements in Attica, for example, have now been discovered (Lohmann *et al.* 2002). Finds of this date from more elaborate Early Bronze Age walled-and-towered sites in the Corinth region might suggest that they also could originate in this period (Tartaron *et al.* 2006). On the island of Andros the site of Strophilos has recently revealed an extensive wall, whilst associated rock-carvings of longboats could hint that piracy was already a possible threat to the pioneer early farmer-herder colonizers of the Cyclades (Renfrew 2004).

A case study: Neolithic Thessaly

The only region where we have plentiful information concerning Neolithic lifeways on a large scale is Thessaly, in Northern Greece (Perlès 2001, Nanoglou 2001, Halstead 2006a).

Demographic considerations

Even in the Early Neolithic the density of tell villages is surprising, with some 120 sites recorded for the whole of Thessaly, whilst roughly as many are known in the succeeding Middle Neolithic. With such numbers, intervillage distances were generally small and each had close neighbors. If the midpoints between villages are likely territorial borders, making contiguous cells from these (Thiessen polygons) is informative (Figure 3.6). With the exception of certain districts (notably the southeastern part of the Eastern Plain), the villages are dispersed rather regularly across the landscape, with an average of 2.5 km distance between them. This allows Perlès to reconstruct a typical village territory as having 450 ha of exploitable fields.

Perlès adopts the social fission model for the origins of this dense network, and on the basis of demographic models used by Ammermann and Cavalli-Sforza (1984) for the dynamics of Neolithic population growth, she points out that theoretically all the Early Neolithic villages in the Eastern Plain and Central Hill Land could have originated in a single pioneer colonizing village, by the process of continual social fission, within a relatively short period of time.

Tell site locations

The density of Thessalian Neolithic tells encourages investigation of which locational considerations affected settlement distribution. Halstead (1994) argued that tells were unevenly spread, clustering where they could exploit several different micro-environments; this reflected a farming economy preferring security to poor yields in just one environment (buffering). In contrast van Andel and Runnels (1995), whilst agreeing that sites cluster, claimed that tells were placed primarily to access land with a high water table (wet bottomlands, valley floodplains), so that spring rain would bring natural irrigation to the soils (a great advantage for hoe cultivators). Perlès' (2001) reanalysis with a larger database prompts revision. The majority of the tells are closely clustered, but their distribution spreads regularly across different environments with little respect for their boundaries. Indeed in Eastern Thessaly almost half the sites do not lie on the Plain at all but in the central Revenia hill land.

Sherratt's thesis (1980), supported by recent analyses from Johnson (1996), and our own fieldwork in Central Greece (Bintliff *et al.* 2006), was that Neolithic farmers in the Balkans, till near the end of that long period, preferred naturally moist, high watertable soils to aid hand cultivation. Thessalian farmers' lack of restricted preferences to site location comes as a surprise. However, there are neglected sectors of Eastern Thessaly where probably the land *was* too arid or heavy for hoe cultivation (the limited settlement in the south part of the Eastern Plain seems to fit this explanation), whilst the central hills show a division into densely occupied and almost empty areas, which could reflect the operation of the same limiting factors. Secondly, regional rainfall is high compared to Southern Greece, creating large zones where even hoe cultivation would be assisted by adequately rainfed soils. In contrast, the much more arid climate of Southern Greece appears to be associated with a Neolithic settlement pattern which is much lower in density and usually takes the form of linear rather than two-dimensional lattice networks. I consider that this contrast does emanate from drier soils in general further south, constraining early farmers to follow spring-lines and alluvial valleys or the edges of lakes and marshes. Thirdly, the small size of Thessalian tell territories (average radius is 1.25 km), meant that farming was almost at one's door, allowing extremely intensive land use.

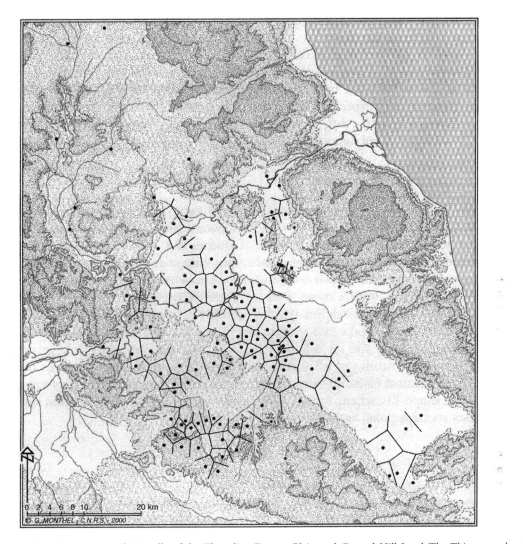

Figure 3.6 Distribution map of EN tells of the Thessalian Eastern Plain and Central Hill Land. The Thiessen polygon analysis suggests territory packing.
C. Perlès, *The Early Neolithic in Greece*. Cambridge University Press 2001, Figure 7.9.

This last distance conforms with mathematical precision to a predictive model (Bintliff 1999a) which was developed to suit the progressive colonization of a fertile landscape on the basis of a fissioning process. The cross-cultural study of agropastoral nucleated settlements, particularly that form of territorial investigation called Catchment Analysis (Vita-Finzi and Higgs 1970) has prompted the suggestion that such communities tend to restrict their exploited territory to a maximum radius of about 1 hour or 5 km in flat terrain (due to the "friction of distance" which progressively reduces effective labor on one's estate as daily journeys to remoter plots consume more and more time). However, in periods of population growth, with a variety of crops and animals, favorable climate and a reasonably effective technology, and when the settlement is small, the area needed to sustain the village with enough annual surplus for buffering against bad years can be considerably smaller.

Let us create a model which begins with one pioneer colonizing village, and then through an initial social fission from this one outwards, plant a series of similar villages, each with a maximal 5 km radius of territory. Then let such villages send out daughter offshoot villages to infill the land between the first generation. Later the network fissions again and another set of offspring villages are inserted into the interstices of the existing network, and so on until it would be likely that any further subdivision of the territories would create settlement hinterlands too small for economic viability. We should note that a perfect infill at geometrically accurate smaller and smaller radii might only be achievable in an ideal landscape (called "isotropic" by geographers), where resource potential was the same in all directions and did not prevent internal colonization from occupying any point on the landscape. In purely theoretical terms the successive generations of settlements in an isotropic landscape would have territorial radii of 5, 5, 3.5, 2.5, and 1.72 km. A village territory of around 1 km or less would usually not be viable under dry-farming conditions, if it was more than a small number of families in size.

Investigation of a series of prehistoric and historical case-studies, using this model, has found remarkable agreement with a recurrence of the radii predicted. Given that much of Eastern Thessaly has been well argued to conform to an isotropic surface, with social fissioning as the main stimulus to settlement colonization, we might expect that the outcome of a long process of infill could stabilize in the range of one of the predicted radii. The average of 1.25 km for Thessaly is close enough to our expected endpoint of territory shrinkage (>1 to <2 km radius) to suggest that the network probably began at a thinner density in the range of 2–3 or 3–4 km radius territories, but continual social fission reached the maximum permissible to sustain communities in the 100–300 population range. However, since colonizing villages would rapidly have settled into face-to-face levels, ideally of 150 inhabitants or less, tells may from a very early stage already have had territories with a closer packing, perhaps half-an-hour or 2–3 km radius, reduced to half that dimension as regional populations rose.

On the basis of the small average territory associated with each tell, Perlès calculates that the average cultivable sector of 450 ha was adequate to feed a mixed-farming community of some 200 people, with fallowing, crop rotation, cereals, and pulses, supplemented by sheep and goat. Moreover, the high density of communities in Thessaly created a remarkable clustering of people, animals, and demands for raw materials, with a potential for social interactions and also for social conflicts, which Perlès argues must have fostered a very different kind of socio-economic adaptation than that in the low density, dispersed populations of Southern Greece.

The landscapes of Southern Greece appear to have been much less favorable to hoe-cultivators than Thessaly, with the result that known sites are discontinuous and tend to be confined to locations with high water table soils. Johnson (1996) argued therefore that clusters of settlements could not have built up through radial fission. This creates a problem through the need for such small communities to participate in mating networks of 500–600 people or more, raising wider issues of how these apparently isolated Neolithic settlements of Southern Greece arose and interacted. But is our knowledge of the Neolithic outside of Thessaly adequate for such a judgment? Perlès comments that the map of Southern Neolithic sites is surprisingly thin even if we take high water table locations as far more discontinuous than in the North; there are too many potential districts for early farmers which lack known sites. One obvious difference is the high visibility of Thessalian tells, compared to that for site types which seem to have predominated in the South. Although there *are* Neolithic tells there (famously Lerna in the Peloponnese, and Knossos below the later palace), the accumulating evidence from modern intensive field survey suggests that flat sites, whose existence requires careful scrutiny of individual fields for surface scatters of flintwork and potsherds, are the norm. The limited districts so far subjected to intensive survey in Southern Greece restricts our knowledge of these rare and low-visibility surface sites. Indeed, new evidence suggests that flat settlements may have made up a significant proportion of early farming sites even in the tell landscapes of Northern Greece, but till recently these remained unknown there too, because of their low visibility in contrast to the tells.

Flat sites and other parts of Greece

The discovery that flat settlement sites were a significant alternative to tells in the Greek Neolithic landscape is recent, although there is a similar dualism in early North Balkan farming communities. Intensive survey followed by test trenching, and rescue excavations (Andreou and Kotsakis 1994, Kotsakis 1999), have registered increasing numbers of flat sites, often 6–20 ha but in some cases as much as 50–100 ha, dramatically contrasted to the typical Thessalian tell of 1–3 ha. However, excavations consistently show such sizes as illusory, since house clusters are scattered over the site with wide spaces between, whilst dwellings were of short duration because the inhabitants shifted house location around the total occupied area (as with most flat sites known in the Balkans). Halstead (1999b) suggests that the contemporary population of tells and flat sites was closely comparable, from around 60 to 200–300 inhabitants. The absence of rebuilding prevented a deep stratigraphy of older house foundations and rubbish, so that flat site levels are thin and discontinuous across these sites, and no tell mound betrays their presence in the countryside.

Chapman (1994), for North Balkan examples, hypothesizes that shifting house locations might be to avoid pollution from the dead buried in and around older houses, but the lack of such a practice in Greek tells, where the rare burials tend to be off the tell, or in flat sites, scattered around their surfaces, seems to go against this view. More functional arguments seem relevant. In the Hungarian Plain, flat sites line elevated linear river levees (river overflow sediments) above wet bottomlands; houses are abandoned and relocated further along the levee every few generations, ultimately creating linear smeared settlements of considerable size. In the Langhadas Basin of Greek Macedonia, survey and excavation (Andreou and Kotsakis 1994) demonstrate that flat sites follow patches of highly fertile soil, and are made up of an accumulation of shifting houses and fields (probably fertilized from deliberate spreading of household rubbish onto the cultivation zone). Here the Macedonian flat sites can be directly contrasted with adjacent tells: the latter's location allows radial land use on easily worked soils, so that continuity and nucleation of the community is possible. In contrast the flat sites, even

if their overall population was similar, appear to "burn up" a small part of the land and then move on to a fresher patch of high-quality soil. It is unclear whether this latter method of land use is conditioned by irregular strips of soil which cannot sustain a nucleated community or long cultivation, or reflects another form of social organization. However, excavated houses on flat sites compare in scale but not form to examples from tells, and the burial of bodies dispersed across the former is interpreted as emphasizing the entire community of scattered households, reminiscent of the supposed communal spirit of tell societies.

Intensive survey in South-Central Greece, across the ancient city of Tanagra and for several kilometers around (Bintliff et al. 2006), has identified a Neolithic settlement system with two components: a nucleated hamlet at the later city site, and then farms or small hamlets lining the banks of a major river and its small tributary streams. A possible ritual or burial focus was also discovered atop a precipitous hilltop 3 km south of the city. The critical resource is a largely lost floodplain of moist fertile soil which once covered the floor of the river and its sidestreams (whose surviving edges are now the "Middle Terrace"), emphasizing the preference for high water table soils in the drier southern half of Greece. Elsewhere in Boeotia, nucleated sites of a tell or semi-tell character are known beside river bottomlands (Thespiae, Chaeronea). One can compare this complementarity with that in the Langhadas Basin in Macedonia. The Nemea Survey in the Peloponnese (Cherry et al. 1988), also discovered Neolithic settlements in a small district and of varying sizes, with one MN example at 4 ha, others much smaller. One suspects that the dispersed nature of suitable farming land encouraged networks of larger and smaller sites at Nemea as at Tanagra, and in ideal ecology even tells.

If Southern Mainland settlements were more scattered than Northern Greece, creating a sustainable population there in the Neolithic may have been problematic. One solution was intermarriage within and between clusters of nucleated and dispersed sites, as discovered at Tanagra and Nemea. Another could be heightened nucleation, so that the required social group for biological reproduction resided in a single large village, although smaller-scale out-marriage would be needed to ensure long-term biological fitness and cooperation in trade systems. Kouphovouno is a large (4 ha) MN flat settlement near Sparta in the Peloponnese (Cavanagh 2004), and if completely occupied, conceivably housed 500 or so inhabitants, the minimum number for a largely self-sufficient community. Nonetheless since most lithic tools were made in exotic obsidian from the Cyclades (Cavanagh *et al.* 2001), this village was well integrated into regional exchange systems and not isolated from other communities.

Our best known flat site is Makriyalos in Macedonia (Pappa and Besios 1999, Kotsakis 2007). Only a small sector of this 50 ha site has so far been excavated, but there are two occupation zones used at different points of the LN period, both demarcated by ditches defining zones of shifting habitation. Although houses are insubstantial, the communal effort of the ditches points to inter-house collaboration, and burials in the ditches (and in a large pit) and not with houses, seem also to emphasize a sense of community. The suggestion that some animal bone and pottery debris might indicate large-scale community feasting reinforces this reconstruction.

As we have seen, the exact forms which Mesolithic-Neolithic interaction took in Greece remain unclear. It is possible that more aspects than we expect were adopted from forager lifestyles into the dominant new farmer-herder lifeway, whereas we tend still to see one-way traffic with a Near Eastern origin. So also with settlement systems. As the scope for dispersed, shifting Neolithic households increases, to set against the exotic settled tell village, we can note that in Europe as a whole, broad-spectrum foragers of the Holocene created series of sites along favored niches such as river valleys, visited repeatedly over hundreds or even a thousand years (Ellis *et al.* 2003). The similarities to the use of Neolithic flat sites and small site networks is striking, even if the economic base had changed decisively.

Long-term change in Neolithic village societies

Some scholars believe that within the immensely long Neolithic era in Greece we can observe directional change. Moreover, the transformations involved appear to pave the way for the much more complex societies of the Aegean Bronze Age. In a more nuanced

model to his earlier reconstructions, Halstead (2006a, cf. also Halstead 1995a) notes firstly, that on many settlements a contrast exists between early house and site plans, where cooking facilities lie in open ground outside and between homes (stage 1), and later plans, where enclosures shield off groups of houses with associated open-air working areas from each other (stage 2), or individual houses enclose their own cooking zones (stage 3). For Halstead (based on Thessaly sites, confirmed for Knossos by Tomkins 2004), the early villages (EN-MN) shared food and did not conceal their subsistence resources, whilst later villages (LN-EBA) witnessed a new ethos of privacy rather than community. Moreover EN-MN homes seem to have inadequate storage for a year's household needs, suggesting that families may have depended on supplements such as the rotating obligation for a family to slaughter stock and distribute it around the community (animal bones support the possible operation of this practice). Possibly the main stores were communal and, lying peripheral to villages, may have so far escaped observation. Indeed, in the earliest period at Knossos, there is a large grain cache at the site's edge, associated with a timber building (Tomkins 2004). In LN times deep storage pits ("bothroi") are commonly dug both within homes and outside them, and at the same time the ceramic assemblage expands to include large storage jars. Further confirmation comes from ceramic and stone-tool (lithic) production, for the idea of a growing emphasis on distinct families in a settlement, over an early communitarian ethos. Pottery is argued to have developed from a high-quality product emanating from group activity in EN-MN (excepting some high-quality trade wares), to a family or clan-based lower-quality product in LN-FN. Likewise in lithic tool production, more household involvement is suggested in LN, compared to EN-MN when it is suggested that visiting specialists catered for high-quality artifacts to be supplied to the whole settlement (Demoule and Perlès 1993). Finally, EN-MN house models emphasize the external form or roof, whereas LN examples are more usually house interiors, sometimes including figurines, seeming to refocus attention to individual families and away from the anonymous replicated house which is the building block of the entire settlement (Nanoglou 2001, 2005).

Halstead believes this evolution was the inevitable result of tension within the Neolithic village between the economic interests of the household and of the community, a conflict ultimately won by the family at the expense of shared resources and values. This explanation is reasonable, but raises difficulties. If such tension characterized the entire Neolithic, why, a tiny few villages excepted, did it take thousands of years to bring about the LN changes described? Rather than see the late transformations as inevitable, we might rather agree with Perlès (2001) that the remarkable thing is the immense timescale over which these communities appear to have remained socially and economically stable and egalitarian.

If we still accept that these changes are widespread and critical, perhaps then a "punctuated equilibrium" model (sudden major changes interrupting lengthy periods of stability) is preferable to a gradual, deterministic approach (i.e., change was inherent in the system). Surely significantly, the shift from "sharing to hoarding" and other signs of households refocusing away from the community, is manifested most strongly for the Late and Final Neolithic, when it appears likely that the main impact of Sherratt's key economic changes were spreading throughout Greece. Did the effect of ploughs, and textile and dairy product innovations, destabilize the cooperative agricultural economics of the Neolithic village, providing the means for households to erect more autonomous food production and consumption practices?

The Agropastoral Economy

A striking argument for a Neolithic colonization of Greece is the very limited use of wild plants and animals in the seed and bone samples recovered from settlements. The basis of the diet was cereals, together with pulses (beans, peas, vetch, and lentils) (Demoule and Perlès 1993, Halstead 1999b, 2006a–b), a combination which catered for humans, and, via stubble grazing and fallow for stock, as well as through a postulated crop rotation, helped the intensively hand-cultivated soils to recover nutrients (Kroll 1981). As for domestic herds, in the lowland sites which dominate our economic remains, sheep and goat are primary, cattle rarer, which suits the climate and the

absence till the later Neolithic of the wider value of cattle beyond meat, that is for diary products and the pulling of ploughs and wagons.

Neolithic villagers could not have managed their major domestic animals at the level of the household alone (Halstead 1992). A viable breeding population requires at least 20 cattle, 100 pigs, and several hundred sheep. Inter-household exchange was fundamental, and together with the use of domestic animals as a food buffer against failures in the dominant cereal and pulse economy, could lead to stock becoming a form of capital. Again following Halstead, when in LN and later times households turned to more competitive surplus accumulation, the formation of village elite families could thus have been stimulated. Although all this is plausible, there is an alternative (Perlès 2001), the herding and breeding of village stock as a collective, where individuals or a few families take responsibility for moving herds to water and pasture on a daily basis.

The impact of Sherratt's Secondary Products Revolution ("2PR") and the diffusion of Plough Traction, which seem to have risen to prominence by the Late to Final Neolithic, would have boosted the Greek Neolithic economy to a very significant extent. Cattle statistics at LN Makriyalos suggest their breeding for secondary products (Collins and Halstead in Halstead 1999a), and faunal analysis from LN Knossos may evidence plough traction and textile production (Isaakidou 2006, Tomkins 2004, Halstead 2006a). Perhaps the clearest evidence is the expansion of settlement out of the favored regions and districts of the earlier Neolithic into more upland areas and onto the dry islands of the Aegean, that marks the Greek later Neolithic. The added value of stock in the Secondary Products economy, and the greater ease of cultivating dry soils with the animal-drawn scratch-plough (ard) allowed population to colonize areas previously neglected. Particularly the Southern Greek Mainland and the Aegean islands, which were less ideal for dense agropastoral settlement under the previous regime of higher rainfall or wetland hand-cultivation, now opened up for permanent settlement.

As already noted, the origins of traditional pastoral (domestic herd) transhumance in Greece have stimulated controversy. The critique of applying ethnographic models to pre-capitalist times highlighted the market orientation of recent transhumance (Halstead 1987, Lewthwaite 1981). The first step to rehabilitate elements of the model came with the recognition that stock-keeping on a much larger scale than the household or village might have been organized in previous complex societies, such as Classical, Imperial Athens (Hodkinson 1990), or in the palace-states of Bronze Age Crete (Halstead 1999c). This has been supported by archival sources and the existence of archaeological sites in the Greek uplands which can only have been seasonally visited (e.g., Final Neolithic sites in the Sfakia Mountains, Western Crete). Halstead, initially critical of the continuity model, has reinstated it for palatial Crete, and now acknowledges the possibility of transhumance developing in LN Neolithic Greece following the introduction of the 2PR, also confirmed by the Grevena Pindos survey (Efstratiou et al. 2006). High levels of cave use in the Greek LN could support a rise in pastoralism, although they are also taken into use now for burial and ritual (Demoule and Perlès 1993). But as Halstead demonstrates convincingly (1987, 1996), a village economy based on domestic animals alone, particularly in Greece, is hardly viable (unless grain and other crops were exchanged on a large scale), so that even upland settlements where grazing was especially favorable should be supplemented by complementary farmland there or elsewhere. Indeed locational studies throughout Greek later prehistory and history support this observation, with permanent settlements favoring a mixed economy even in the Greek uplands (Bintliff 1997, Wallace 2003).

Worth emphasizing from the Thessalian Neolithic is the great occupational duration of most tells and their close packing. This shows undeniably that their economy was extremely successful (Perlès 2001), further supported by the ability of their occupants to obtain large amounts of external lithic imports, for which agricultural and pastoral surpluses were the most likely product for reciprocal exchange. Since the theory of "bad year economics" (Halstead and O'Shea 1989) for rural societies suggests that regional crises from drought or crop/animal diseases tend to afflict whole districts, extra-regional socio-economic networks beyond Thessaly may have been important to buffer its villages from such occasional disasters, whereby food could be imported from unaffected

regions; here the evidence discussed below for exchange systems could offer some support for this resource being tappable.

In addition to transhumance, the role of migratory fishermen deserves some discussion, for which I coined the term "transmerance" (Bintliff 1977). The association between obsidian from the island of Melos and evidence for fish catches, beginning with the final Palaeolithic and running through the Mesolithic and Neolithic in Greece, is patchy but suggestive. Thirty years ago I used ethnographic and historic records to suggest that early marine travel, especially coastal moves and island-hopping, may have been perfected by fishermen traveling from one point to another where regular or seasonal catches of fish (both inshore and open-water) could be encountered. This theory has received extensive criticism (Stratouli 1996) as well as support. Some key sites fit very well, such as the type-site for the Final Neolithic (FN) colonizing culture of Saliagos in the Cyclades, with its massive fish and shellfish remains and a central role for stone points which could be harpoons (Evans and Renfrew 1968). Yet, another site of this culture, also in a prime position to carry out sailing and fishing, Phtelia, reveals no significant fish remains (Sampson 2006). On the other hand, Mesolithic and EN colonization of the Sporades islands does reveal a special interest in fishing and shellfish, including open-water species (Sampson 2006). Even large urban sites such as EBA Phylakopi on Melos, fronting a bay which is one of the finest for fishing on the island, provided no significant fish remains in its faunal finds from excavation, although there are iconographic depictions of fishing from the town.

Critics have apparently misunderstood "transmerance." Saliagos is a full Neolithic economy, where fish and shellfish were accompanied by a range of domestic plants and animals. The ethnohistoric evidence makes clear that fish usually forms a high-quality food supplement to other basic foods, as well as being a resource best caught in the summer months, off-season for foraging or crop-cultivation. Most skeptics of prehistoric fishing in Greece rely on the demonstrable fact that fulltime subsistence is highly unlikely from such a resource. Although fish and shellfish were thus always a minor element in Mesolithic-Neolithic diet, this does not mean that their exploitation might not have been organized and extensive, encouraging seasonal travel beyond normal exploitation territories. A second critique is that fish would not have been a very valuable resource until methods of preservation were perfected. In fact on the Sporades there is evidence that fish were dried and salted in late Mesolithic-Neolithic times (Sampson 2006). Finally, the survival of fish debris may pose problems for the archaeologist, and I am not convinced that "absence of evidence means evidence of absence."

Craft Production, Exchange, and Neolithic Material Culture

The prehistorian Gordon Childe developed a highly influential model for European Social Evolution (1951), in which early Neolithic farmers produced almost all their own artifacts, with exchange of raw materials and finished products being of minor importance. Momentous changes occurred with the Bronze Age, when metal artifacts created the need for long-distance bulk trade and enhanced craft specialization at the regional and interregional scale; thus arose a class of merchants and professional artisans above the peasantry, and also an aristocratic class whose power was buttressed by controlling the traders and manufacturers of the age. The Greek Neolithic is one of the best-researched areas in Europe to re-examine Childe's theory.

Ceramics

Greek Early and Middle Neolithic pottery is peculiar in its limited role within everyday activity (Vitelli 1995). The shapes are simple and denote their function for serving and consuming food and drink. Reconstructed numbers of whole pots suggest that production was very low and a family's cupboard of ceramics remarkably sparse. Coarse and plain wares for storage or cooking are extremely rare. In the Late Neolithic the latter groups rise in proportion, and by the Final Neolithic they have expanded to service all a family's needs in food storage, processing, serving, and consumption. Other features fit this picture. Traces of burning on EN-MN pot exteriors are absent, so food was cooked directly over a fire or boiled in organic containers with heated stones, not in cookpots. The dominance of small, round-based bowls of a nice appearance (burnishing, slip, occasionally painted red-brown) highlights pots as the chief focus of meals, emphasizing their social significance (communal kin-group dining, inter-household social events, and perhaps special feasts). Although such tableware was probably made by a village specialist over a limited period each year, using a basic technology, it is very well made and survives surprisingly well, far better than the coarser wares which dominate the FN assemblage.

Tomkins (*pers. comm.*) believes that EN ceramics are imitations ("skeuomorphs") of organic containers in wood and leather. This reminds us that the dominance of eating and drinking forms in EN-MN pottery probably conceals a wider range of vessels which do not survive the Greek climate, although very rare traces of these are claimed, as at Tsangli in Thessaly (Tomkins 2004). Storage and even cooking are possible in organic containers. As for the scale of potential loss, Coles (2001) estimates from the full organic assemblages recovered in waterlogged sites in Northern and Central Europe that contemporary dry land settlements might only preserve some 5 percent of portable material culture. Greece would have less woodland but plenty of domestic animals (so skin might be preferred rather than wooden containers), thus we could reasonably assume a substantial missing component of non-pottery household containers. A more challenging point of Tomkins is that since we know neither the EN-MN nor Late Mesolithic types of organic containers, it cannot be ruled out that Greek EN pots were copying traditional vessels used by indigenous Greek foragers rather than shapes derived from the Near East.

For the Greek Mainland, most ceramics seem to have been made for local use during the EN-MN eras, rather than for inter-settlement pottery exchange. However, already during MN and especially in LN, the situation becomes transformed. More elaborately decorated tablewares develop, for example MN Sesklo Ware with red-brown geometric designs on a white background and LN Dhimini Ware with polychrome designs, both in Thessaly, which are linked to a growing network of exchange within each region and sometimes further afield (Figure 3.7). These later wares were perhaps produced to enhance wider social

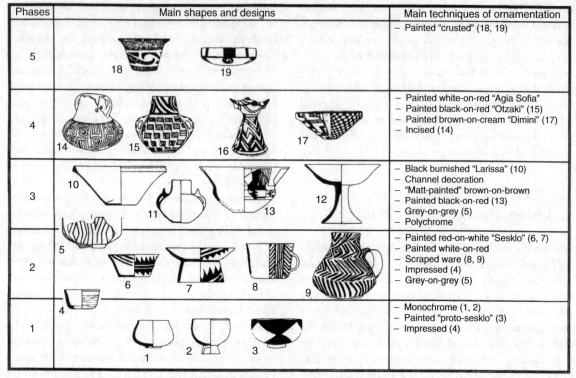

Phases	Main shapes and designs	Main techniques of ornamentation
5	18 19	– Painted "crusted" (18, 19)
4	14 15 16 17	– Painted white-on-red "Agia Sofia" – Painted black-on-red "Otzaki" (15) – Painted brown-on-cream "Dimini" (17) – Incised (14)
3	10 11 13 12	– Black burnished "Larissa" (10) – Channel decoration – "Matt-painted" brown-on-brown – Painted black-on-red (13) – Grey-on-grey (5) – Polychrome
2	5 6 7 8 9	– Painted red-on-white "Sesklo" (6, 7) – Painted white-on-red – Scraped ware (8, 9) – Impressed (4) – Grey-on-grey (5)
1	4 1 2 3	– Monochrome (1, 2) – Painted "proto-sesklo" (3) – Impressed (4)

Typochronology of the Thessalian Neolithic ceramics. (1–3, 6–8, 13, 15) Otzaki; (5) Plateia Magoula Zarkou; (10, 12) Arapi; (14) Dimini; (17) Sesklo; (18, 19) Rachmani. Not to scale.

Figure 3.7 Characteristic tableware pottery forms from the Neolithic sequence of Thessaly. Phase 1=EN, 2=MN, 3–4=early then late LN, 5=FN. Note that in the last three phases a wide range of undecorated domestic and cookwares are in use, not shown here.
J.-P. Demoule and C. Perlès, "The Greek Neolithic: A new review." *Journal of World Prehistory* 7/4 (1993), 355–416, Figure 8. London: Springer Verlag.

networks under the encouragement of a local Big Man or chieftain, such as indeed are inferred at contemporary Sesklo and Dhimini (Demoule and Perlès 1993). In contrast to such local and Northerly variants which may have been used in competitive intervillage exchanges, the uniformity of a style such as MN Urfirnis Ware with patterned burnish popular in the Southern Mainland may reflect the need to create large-scale social bonding between a thin and scattered population (Perlès and Vitelli 1994). In the FN however, distinct regional products decline and once again broad similarities link much of Greece's ceramics, suggesting wide sharing of styles but a return to the dominance of localized production and

consumption. The precise meaning of this long cycle remains to be fully explained.

One attractive interpretation of the high visibility and food consumption function of most Greek Neolithic pottery is that it served an important role in community integration, not just linking families within a settlement (tell or flat) but probably functioning in feasts bringing more than one community together. As we have seen, there would have been a critical need for smoothing the exchange of marriage partners and limiting intervillage violence over disputed land rights.

However, studies of EN-MN ceramics on Crete have been interpreted as giving a contrasted picture

(Tomkins 2004). Rather than small-scale localized production, more than half the pottery at Knossos was made from raw materials of "non-local" provenance. Most of these "exotic clay" pots are from material in the range 7–30 km distant, with a small percentage from some 70 km away, or even from outside Crete. On the other hand, the ethnographic record (Morris and Woodward 2005) shows that potters in a settlement may travel up to 10 km to add special tempering material to their clay (some two hours on foot), so it is quite possible that the vast majority of Knossos pottery was made by its own specialists within a day-return, leaving a very small component of genuine long-distance imports. If Knossos was in touch with a distant region, perhaps this had more to do with intermarriage, with few available partner settlements close to Knossos. In favor of a social rather than economic explanation is the fact that the pots are very uniform in appearance, so that "exotic" pieces would not be apparent to the users (unless they came with distinct contents). As was observed on the Southern Mainland, the apparently low population of earlier Neolithic Crete may have encouraged wide social links to ensure social and biological reproduction, the shared styles evidencing ties with distant communities.

Lithics

Very few localities in a rocky, mountainous country such as Greece lacked local hard rocks with a crystalline structure suitable for making stone tools: their varied types served the equivalent of modern knives, drills, chisels, razors, and bullets. Neolithic lithic assemblages are less varied than Palaeolithic and Mesolithic (Figure 3.8), as the economy was far less wide-ranging. Blades knapped (struck off) from cores dominated, followed by scrapers and borers, with a low production of arrow-points for hunting or human conflict (they are trapeze-shaped in earlier, then lozenge-shaped in later Neolithic times). Types conform to Near Eastern parallels, and only the arrow forms may indicate influence from indigenous hunter-gatherers.

Surprisingly, study of stone sources utilized in Greece (Torrence 1986; Perlès 1989, 2001) shows that the majority of lithics were nonetheless made from exotic imported material (Figure 3.9), with local sources neglected unless "next door" to a site, or where the settlement was particularly remote from wider contacts. The leading provenance are obsidian quarries on the Cycladic island of Melos (and more limited use of Giali sources): this black-grey volcanic glass with remarkable sharpness properties was probably spread as prepared cores to its consuming villages, where it was reduced to blades and other tool-types. Even Northern Mainland Greek sites may still contain up to 80 percent of their lithics from Melos. Another, less common source was fine honey flint from Northwest Greece, but this traveled as ready blades and was not worked in receiving villages. As well as these hard stones for cutting and scraping, andesite (from Aegina and nearby) was exchanged to make grinding stones, and Naxos emery (a rock like sandpaper) for shaping and polishing stone bowls and axes.

Torrence (1986) studied the open-air obsidian quarries on Melos. The evidence at the extraction and working areas, and study of various Mainland assemblages, convinced her that distant communities traveled themselves to the island, where a single voyage sufficed to obtain more than a year's supply. Perlès (1989, 2001) agrees with this "direct procurement" model for the Greek LN and FN, at least for villages of Eastern Greece and the islands, but communities further away would have more likely relied on intermediaries for their lithic supplies. As for the EN and MN, careful study leads Perlès to the conclusion that communities throughout Greece were almost entirely reliant on circulating traders, who visited the sources, prepared cores or blades, then went from village to village with their wares. Even there, the skill deployed in manufacturing tools on-site suggests a professional rather than local craftsperson, so probably traders also made the tools to order. The logic of proposing middlemen follows from the calculation that an entire village's needs could be met by less than 1 kg of obsidian a year. In the rarer dispersal of honey flint from Epirus, the already-prepared blades probably circulated over the Mainland through a combination of traveling traders and "down-the-line" trade (Renfrew 1975), that is, passed from village to village.

Remarkably, Melos was only permanently settled, along with most other Cycladic islands, in the LN–FN period, making it clear that no community seized the advantage of monopolizing access, or living entirely on the obsidian trade. This surely indicates, as would

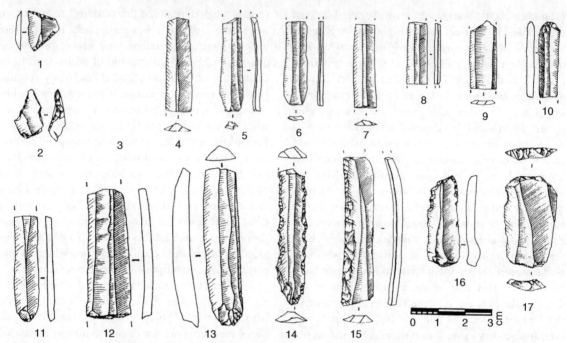

Chipped stone tools. (1) Franchthi, EN, Jasper; (2) Franchthi, EN, flint; (10) Franchthi, EN, obsidian; (16) Franchthi, LN, obsidian; (18–20) Franchthi, EN, honey-flint; (22) Franchthi, MN, honey-flint; (23) Franchthi, LN, flint; (24) Franchthi, FN, jasper; (26) Franchthi, MN, honey-flint; (11), (13) Argissa, "preceramic Neolithic," obsidian; (12) Argissa, "preceramic Neolithic," honey-flint; (3–9) Tharounia, LN/FN, obsidian; (14), (15) Tharounia, LN/FN, obsidian; (17) Tharounia, LN/FN, obsidian; (21) Tharounia, LN/FN, jasper; (25) Throunia, LN/FN, obsidian.

Figure 3.8   Characteristic stone tools of the Greek Neolithic.
J.-P. Demoule and C. Perlès, "The Greek Neolithic: A new review." *Journal of World Prehistory* 7/4 (1993), 355–416, Figure 6. London: Springer Verlag.

be expected given the flimsy nature of Neolithic boats (see Chapters 2 and 4) and the off-season of bad conditions for Aegean sailing in the winter months, that obsidian trade was a seasonal activity, probably carried out by maritime communities in the summer months when their own crops needed little intensive work. Any neglect of their own farming economy might be made up through obtaining, in return for their lithic trade items, local surpluses of grain or animal products. Indeed it is difficult to think what else the dense tell-villages of Thessaly could have given in exchange, *but* farming products. In Greece as late as the early twentieth century, before motor access connected every village to the wider world, tinkers circulated widely with pottery and metalwork, also carrying out specialist craftwork as well.

Melos obsidian was first obtained by hunter-gatherers in the late Upper Palaeolithic, possibly connected with the activity of migratory fishermen. Perhaps descendants of these pioneers, foragers who became farmers, were key players in the Neolithic trade in obsidian, honey flint, and other exotics such as jasper. Indeed it is probably no coincidence that the first culture to colonize the Cyclades has a mixed-farming economy in which specialist fishing is a characteristic feature (Evans and Renfrew 1968, Bintliff 1977). On the other hand, the putative Near Eastern colonizing farmers themselves had become deeply involved with long-distance exchange for obsidian from Near Eastern sources before their spread to Greece, so a reliance on exotic supplies is not so surprising for the Greek Neolithic.

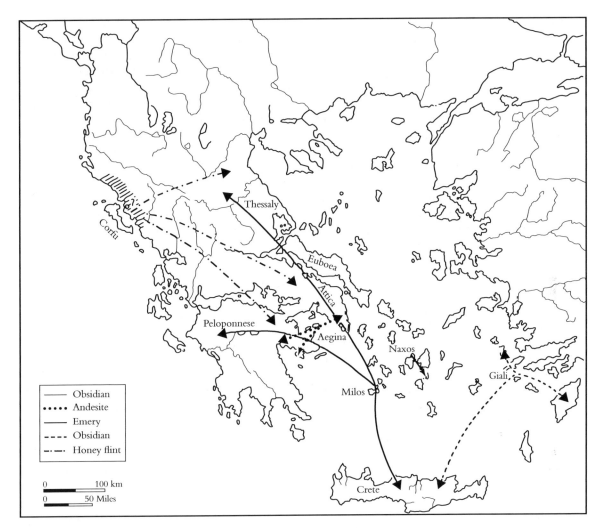

Figure 3.9 The spread of exotic lithic raw materials (obsidian, andesite and honey flint) and the location of the emery source on Naxos. C. Perlès, "Systems of exchange and organization of production in Neolithic Greece." *Journal of Mediterranean Archaeology* 5 (1992), 115–164, Figure 1.

The Neolithic in Europe was distinguished by nineteenth-century archaeologists as the "New Stone Age," not on the basis of changes in chipped stone tools, but on the accompanying polished stone artifacts such as axes, adzes, and hammers (and in later Neolithic times warlike versions of such shapes). Some of these in Greece utilize exotic rock (e.g., green-stones). In line with the vigorous expansion of settlement which occurred in LN-FN Greece, the axes of EN-MN are small and seem suited for light carpentry or bone and skin processing, whilst in LN-FN large

axes appear widely, appropriate for major woodland clearance (Perlès 2001). Even more specialized was the source of good millstones, usually volcanic rocks which were gritty but very hard and dense (Runnels 1985). A major source was andesite from old volcanic rocks in the Saronic Gulf (especially on Aegina). For these "macrolithic" artifacts a combination of modes for distribution are likely: specialist traders, down-the-line exchange, and direct procurement. Finally Neolithic settlements procured special hard stones and exotic shells for making ornaments and seals (perhaps for body decoration). These are rare and probably usually came through down-the-line exchanges.

Metals

From the LN and more so from the FN the first metal artifacts, of copper, appear, but are so rare that one cannot talk about a Copper Age. If the LN pieces in copper are perhaps traded from outside Greece, the FN objects, now in precious metal as well (gold and silver), probably mark the beginnings of Aegean production at such sources as the Cycladic island of Siphnos and the Lavrion mines in Attica. Ornaments and daggers are the forms desired, perhaps both of them more for display than function.

Neolithic trade mechanisms

In the EN and MN, pottery and lithics have contrasted production systems (Perlès 2001). Ceramics were special household artifacts, rarely and very well made, but typically produced at long intervals within each community. Lithics were usually obtained from far away by specialists who either brought them to the village and then worked them there, removing surplus raw material, or sent them on long exchange-chains across the settled landscape; but they were sufficient for each village and utilized in a range of everyday functional tasks. A third procurement system brought rarer stone and shell, perhaps by a combination of mechanisms. From the MN and more clearly in LN, pottery seems to have been exchanged over a district as a function of social and political networking, or even, with a few of the finest tablewares, for trade.

In the LN–FN period, increased seafaring encouraged more communities to procure their own lithic materials. The FN particularly coincided with a great settlement explosion all over Greece, most clearly in the colonization of the smaller Aegean islands, enhancing direct procurement and exchange of exotic materials. The increased role of the Cyclades, supplying obsidian, millstones, marble, and metals, may even have been an important factor in its settlement (Davis 1992). Yet the fact remains that the major island settlements in this and subsequent periods never appear to be located so as to dominate or prosper from such resources, which suggests that trade control was not

the incentive (contrary to Runnels and van Andel 1988). Easier direct access to island raw materials was nonetheless desirable and clearly taken advantage of, and in the EBA it is the Cyclades which is clearly the hub of Greek exchange systems. Perlès (2001) wonders if the greater subsistence viability of the Southern Mainland and islands due to the Secondary Products and Plough "revolutions" might have had a negative effect on the supposed reciprocal trade between lithic merchants and the food surpluses of the Northern plains of Greece, helping to account for the limited socio-political developments in Thessaly, Macedonia, and Thrace in the Bronze Age, whilst civilization emerged in the South Aegean.

Social Relations

Settlement evidence

What we have learnt so far, is that almost all Neolithic settlements in Greece appear to be small, probably confined by face-to-face social controls. Social fission encouraged radial colonization of the most fertile landscapes, but more linear or patchy expansion in regions less suitable for the technology and economy of the EN–MN phases. Although stable location tells and shifting flat sites represent alternative modes of settlement and land use, they have a similar range of crops and animals, whilst larger flat sites have comparable population estimates to tells. A third settlement mode combines the two, with a focal tell or flat site with longer use surrounded by less fixed farm or hamlet sites. All these forms generally needed to exchange marriage partners with comparable settlements or settlement clusters, to create a healthy gene pool. The lack of clearly defensive walls and ditches until occasional MN examples and then commoner LN occurrences, suggests that settlements achieved the peaceful intercommunity relations needed both for exogamy and for the flows of imports and visiting specialists testified to in the lithic record. The limited role of ceramics in EN and still to a large extent in MN times, focused on communal eating and drinking, has plausibly been seen as a mechanism through which households within nucleated settlements, and neighboring communities, renewed good social ties. But if social fission was the dominant means of settlement colonization, then one's neighbors were often relatives, and even if not originally, the multi-community breeding group soon created kinship webs through constant exogamy.

The plans of nucleated settlements, tell and flat, are seen as emphasizing the competitive household, a model reinforced if we add satellite farms in some neighborhoods (neglected since their detection requires unusually fine-focus surface survey). But how did nucleated sites, and the satellite networks around nucleated settlements, achieve social integration? In the Neolithic Near East, one or more larger or other-wise special houses are claimed as facilities where many households met for social and ritual activities. Such features are hard to identify in the excavated plans for Neolithic Greece. One exception is the "shrine" at EN Nea Nikomedeia (Pyke and Yiouni 1996), a central larger structure with unusual finds, including fine exotic axes. However Halstead (1995a) wonders if this is a precocious example of a household with special status, controlling the exchange of imports, and thus a first link in his evolutionary model which accounts for the less controversial elite enclosures in Sesklo, or at Dhimini, in MN and LN Thessaly. At MN Sesklo there might be a communal structure on the acropolis and another in the Lower Town, distinctive through pos-sessing three entry doors, if small (Nanoglou 2001). EN-MN house models include several examples with four doors, again perhaps for public use.

The narrow built-up spaces of tells suggest that normally important village-wide or intervillage social events took place extramurally, but the large flat sites would have ideal spaces between their loose networks of houses, and indeed it is at one, Makriyalos, that the excavators found feasting debris (Pappa and Besios 1999). In the nucleation–satellite form of settlement, we have suggested for Central and Southern Greece that the larger focal site might be a social center for outlying farms and hamlets rather than a locus of dis-trict power, essential to the social and economic reproduction of such a network. In contrast, the latter (power focus) interpretation better suits MN Sesklo. This seems large enough to have formed an endoga-mous society, and here Kotsakis has argued (1999) that the supposed elite enclosure of the acropolis, with its

tell-like permanent dwellings, is surrounded by a very extensive Lower Town of shifting flat-site type; here the relationship of satellite settlement to the fixed tell nucleation might be one of subordination.

Rarely in MN and more commonly in LN times, appear two surely linked phenomena: possible defen-sive features and elite residences or enclosures. Contemporaneously, the restricted role for ceramics opens up progressively to cover the full range of household needs, suggesting a decline in the centrality of communal dining. Some fine wares which are exchanged around wide areas have even been claimed to show the economic reach of influential chieftains or Big Men, while their distribution within MN Sesklo suggests privileged access for the occupants of the elite enclosure over those in the Lower Town. The advent of the great "2PR" transformation in the agropastoral economy which occurred most likely in LN and FN times must have stimulated major changes in the socio-political sphere, and one wonders if all these trends are not linked in a highly causative fashion.

The surprise, difficult to assimilate into our social reconstructions, is the case made by Perlès with regard to chipped stone and macrolithic tools, for an early division of labor, on the scale of Neolithic Greece as a whole, into consumer rural settlements on the one hand, and mobile procurers, distributors, and on-site artifact makers on the other. The best clue to the ori-gins of such a system, she hypothesizes, lies in the evi-dence from the Final Palaeolithic for the start of such economic specialization, suggesting that acculturated foragers were the principal community who devel-oped this way of life. In any case, these specialists probably worked seasonally so as to be able still to maintain their own subsistence economy.

Burial evidence

Archaeologists generally view the form and elabora-tion of mortuary rituals as highly insightful for shed-ding light on the social relations of the living (Parker Pearson 1999). In an excellent synthesis of the burial record for prehistoric Greece, Cavanagh and Mee (1998) highlight the extraordinary rarity of Neolithic mortuary evidence. Demoule and Perlès (1993) link Greek customs to those general in the contemporary North Balkans: a very low visibility of the dead in EN and MN, a lack of defined cemeteries or funerary monuments, small numbers of burials inside the village ("intramural"), usually under house floors, and no emphasis on status. Only by the FN is there a general shift, with community cemeteries appearing outside the settlement (such as at Kephala on the Cycladic island of Kea), a practice normal for the subsequent Early Bronze Age in most of Greece. Over the same LN-FN period, the wider use of caves includes many functioning as burial locations.

In the early farming era of the Near East, burial beneath the house is often read as stressing the importance of the family, or perhaps a larger kin group. Their occurrence would suit the view that tell villages in Greece are amalgamations of competing families. Yet a central problem lies in what is *not* visible to us, raising the point made at the start of this section on the obscuring as well as illuminating potential of the mortuary sphere. The number of intramural burials is very low, and where palaeodemographic studies are available women and children are emphasized. The vast majority of the village dead are simply missing. It is more likely that the minority placed in the houses are the exceptions to customary ritual, than that these are the key individuals in the social world (Perlès 2001). Perhaps the nature of their death, or their passing away at a certain stage of the family or house-construction cycle, marked them out for exclusion from normal community practice. And what might the latter have been?

One idea is that the dead were normally disposed of outside the tell. A chance discovery at Souphli tell in Thessaly has indeed revealed an extramural cremation cemetery. Further support comes from the extended settlement at the giant flat site of Makriyalos in Macedonia (Kotsakis 1999; Pappa and Besios1999), where the excavated settlement includes ditches and open spaces between house clusters. In the ditches parts of human bodies have been recovered, which Kotsakis interprets as a sign that the dead are merged into the soil of the whole community rather than isolated as house burials or into a communal burial-place. These new results may weaken the supposed opposition between tell individualism and the supposed more communal extended sites, since the Souphli cemetery, if other examples emerge, surely anticipates the FN-EBA extramural cemeteries, generally seen as reflecting village solidarity.

Neolithic Symbolic Behavior and Material Culture

In the Near Eastern Neolithic, symbolic aspects of material culture in architectural forms and their decoration, and in portable artifacts, are central to community life. But in the derivative Neolithic Balkans, including Greece, we see a stripped-down symbolic culture. Buildings which could have served as ritual are rare and not undisputed in function, such as the EN "shrine" in a central location at Nea Nikomedeia, larger than typical houses and containing outstanding traded stone axes, unused lithic blades, a collection of small figurines, and other unusual objects of clay. It could have held 16 people, but whether a temple, village elders' house or chieftain's residence remains debatable (Marangou 2001b).

The Balkan Neolithic shares with the Near East (Nandris 1970) a recurrent series of small items in clay or hard stone, presumed non-functional and of symbolic or ornamental purpose: stamps which could have decorated textiles or the body, plugs perhaps for ears or noses, and other small objects. Although Perlès (2001) candidly finds these hard to interpret and rather uninteresting, ethnohistory suggests that village communities, especially close-packed with much social interaction, develop recognizable dress and body ornamentation to mark village and even kin-group affiliation, something well documented in the Mediterranean for several centuries before the present (Broufas and Raftis 1993, Congedo 2001) and which deserves more attention for much earlier periods.

Figurines

The artifact type with most potential for reading symbolic aspects of Neolithic material culture is the clay, or rarely stone, figurine. These represent animals, usually domestic, and humans, predominantly female, and are relatively abundant in the Greek (and Balkan) Neolithic, with clear Near Eastern parallels. However, little can be said with confidence about their meaning in any of these contexts. The natural tendency has been to read the female class (Figure 3.10) either as a goddess or a series of goddesses, or as ancestors (in a female-oriented kinship system or matriliny), or,

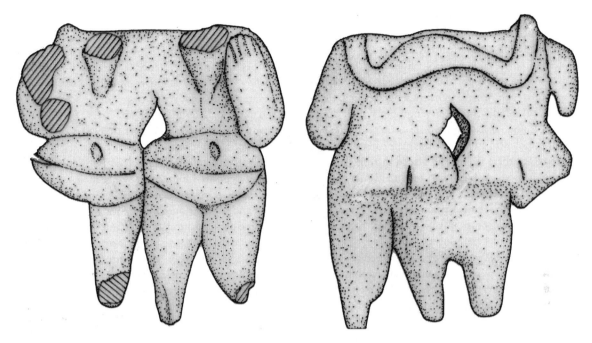

Figure 3.10 Middle Neolithic double figurine from Thessaly. Drawing by Professor Lauren Talalay, University of Michigan.

given the ample proportions of most, as symbolic representations of (female or general) fertility, which can then be extended to animals whose fertility is also welcome. Alternative theories are toys, or educational devices for women's *rites de passage* (the passing of key life-stages: puberty, marriage, birthing). Most economically, some suggest that figurines served all these roles. Preziosi and Hitchcock (1999) note that at Late Neolithic Dhimini, figurines of women occur amongst the lesser structures for storage and adjacent living spaces. This link to storage they relate to fertility and a female role in the domestication and management of food, connecting these ideas to Hodder's (1990) theory of Neolithic gendered domestic space: the home or *domus* of women and the natural extra-settlement world, the *agrios*, or wild space of men.

The association of women, food production, and storage is thus identified as a gendered socio-ritual concept, combining nourishment and productivity. Here figurines represent sacred and secular in the household and are found embedded in its everyday life (combining a fertility goddess and the special roles of human females). One figurine from FN Pefkakia

contained several sorts of grains, whilst the common "coffee-bean" form given to eyes might also refer to seeds (Marangou 2001b). But most recently several commentators suggest that the meaning of figurines depended more on their context, such as their deployment in different phases of human life or in the circulation of the objects themselves.

It is very unhelpful that their occurrence in Greek Neolithic burials is little known about, due to the poverty of such contexts, since the successor figurines from the FN-EBA in Southern Greece occur frequently in formal cemeteries, and are then considered as likely to have religious associations. Nonetheless the limited range of types and their widespread occurrence indicate that the meanings they conveyed were probably shared across the Greek, North Balkan, and maybe Near Eastern Neolithic, which, if they were ritual meanings, might open up the worldview of these innumerable rural communities. Indeed this potential was taken up in a charismatic way by Marija Gimbutas (1991), who argued that the early farming world of the Near East and Balkans was strikingly different in its global outlook from the metal-using societies which succeeded it. For her, this long and geographically vast world was a peaceful one focused on female values and female divinities, to be violently destroyed, at the end of the Neolithic and during the Copper Age, through the incursions out of the Eurasian steppe of patriarchal, warrior semi-nomads, bringing the Indo-European languages which dominate in Europe today and a male-centered value system of violence and supreme male divinities. The timescale of these events she placed during the third millennium BC. When first published during the 1960s, these theories were received with extreme skepticism by the scholarly community, as a revival of the nineteenth-century imaginary social evolutionary ladder. From the 1970s onwards, however, the rise of Feminism in the Western world found her concept of a primeval society run by women and imbued with "female values" a fascinating tool with which to combat the very real, traditional male assumption of an eternal female inferiority. She was fêted in Feminist literature and the media, notably in the United States. Even if her invasion theories and the concept of rule by women (matriarchy) are not currently accepted on the basis of the now available evidence, some (including male) scholars have nonetheless defended the possibility of at least a female-centered mentality in the European Neolithic (Sherratt 1984; see also Talalay 1994, Meskell 1995).

We can go somewhat further with the figurines by introducing additional empirical evidence. Firstly, recent excavations in the Near East have found Neolithic villages with figurines and architectural representations dominated by males, for example Göbekli Tepe and Nevali Çori in Turkey (Hauptmann 1999), challenging a unitary emphasis on female ritual power. Secondly, the earlier Greek human figurines are schematic, and only gradually become more naturalistic and clearly predominantly female. Thirdly, Talalay (1994) and Perlès (2001) associate the fact that the majority of figurines come from Northern Greek tells with the greater need for them there in ritual behaviors assisting peaceful relations within those densely settled regions. This might perhaps be research bias, since the Southern Greek Neolithic is still poorly recovered and often known from surface finds rather than excavations. In my own fieldwork region of Boeotia, South-Central Greece, the small hamlet of

Thespiae Magoula (a low tell) is several kilometers from the next nucleated Neolithic village, yet its rich surface finds include numerous figurines. Perhaps it is safer to suggest that in general, North and South, the figurines may have been part of rituals assisting intra- and inter-settlement social cohesion.

So far, a cult significance for Greek figurines still remains somewhat speculative. Indeed in by far the commonest domestic context of discovery, figurines are found broken and dispersed around settlements in rubbish deposits, hinting that when their use-life was over, they lost any special value they might have possessed and joined household debris. Whilst this could reinforce the educational or toy function, it might also indicate that they acted in practical rituals, which once finished, or when the figurine was accidentally damaged, removed their usefulness.

Marangou (1996) combines evidence from Greece and the North Balkans in an intriguing explanation for the figurines' popularity. Although she considers that the artifacts had multiple roles even in one community, she takes some fortunate contexts where figurines appear in groups as the key to one major role. She argues that in some Balkan Neolithic settlements, figurines, model clay furniture, and animals could be assembled in one building within the community into a dramatic scenario, where they formed an attention-focusing device for community religion (for this important concept in identifying a ritual context see Renfrew 1985). After the ceremony, the set was dispersed into separate households, perhaps as a related symbolic activity linking families to the community, and to allow individual models to act as "apotropaic" (warding off evil) devices to protect or bless the household or its goods. They could also be stored in house models. Hearths, ovens, storage areas, and generally settlement domestic debris, seem typical contexts for Neolithic figurines, whilst their female dominance emphasizes a focal role for women and the home in their symbolism (Marangou 2001b).

Another intelligent attempt at penetrating the mental world of Neolithic Greece comes from Talalay (2004) in her study of "head cult." In common with Near Eastern Neolithic societies, there are numerous instances in the Aegean where disembodied skulls have been placed under house floors, or visibly in yards, a structure or cave. This would have made heads part of "the visual vocabulary of the living." She links this to figurines, some of which have detachable and hence perhaps exchangeable heads, while others seem to have "mask" heads. The head as the center of human awareness as well as visual identity might have appeared a rich "text" to be used in performances by the living (ceremonial masks?), and through placing of the disembodied skull to symbolize past and present social roles and identities, all in the context of the enhancement of social cohesion.

General Considerations for Neolithic Greece

As the archaeological record stands, this long era of three to four thousand years is remarkable for the rare, and generally late, evidence for social hierarchy. The emphasis on the domestic household and then to a lesser extent on the rural community is still central, even where, in the dense tell networks of the plains of Northern Greece, such settlements are packed within sight of each other in all directions. The late spread of fortifications appears to signal the success with which these early farmers managed their social relations, and Perlès rightly highlights the artifactual evidence which shows both vigorous exchange in raw materials and prepared tools, and suggestions of an important role for communal feasting, as likely means through which harmonious and mutually beneficial interactions were maintained. We have also argued that the social fission and face-to-face models are dominant in community organization, so that rare exceptions such as Sesklo or Knossos represent isolated examples where more internalized, more endogamous, and more complex societies arose, meriting the term "proto-city state" in my model of the "corporate community." Taken together, the limited and usually late cases of unusual sites where an elite and/or a proto-city state can be argued for, still provide a potential springboard for more widespread signs of similar complex societies in the succeeding EBA.

The evidence continues to link social and political transformations over time, at least in some areas, with the introduction out of the Near East of Sherratt's Secondary Products and Traction Plough Revolutions. Alongside the great expansion in areas occupied and

sites known for LN–FN due to these innovations, they must also have enhanced the economic surplus potential of most communities, surely an added stimulus for the sustenance of social elites and larger nucleated communities. Nonetheless, despite being able to isolate tendencies which could be laying the social and economic foundations of the "High Cultures" of the EBA, the vast majority of settlements in Neolithic Greece give a very different picture, of small-scale peaceful villages (nucleated, dispersed or in combinations), achieving a remarkably successful economic balance with their technology and environment over very long periods, and participating in long-distance exchanges on a totally unexpected scale. Even if these settlements were full of competing families, very rarely indeed does it appear that individual kin-groups achieved dominance. The persistence of the face-to-face community of itself speaks for the normal operation of an egalitarian society, excepting precisely the rare, much larger settlements. Thus one is tempted to agree with Catherine Perlès, that the Greek Neolithic is "a foreign country" far removed from our historical parallels of the European peasantry.

An Annaliste Perspective on the Integration of Different Timescales

The overwhelming impression one obtains from this review of the Greek Neolithic is that of a very static society, with change registered in limited places over some 4000 years of farming life. This is in the Annales long term, and could be associated with a similarly static worldview tied to a fixed economic and social pattern. The model of Halstead, where competition between households led to the emergence over the Neolithic as a whole of elite village/town families, is problematic when viewed at such a timescale. Why did this not occur faster and more generally? An even longer perspective, also a *longue durée*, is opened up if we consider the spread of mixed farming into Greece as the ultimate outgrowth of the diversification and specialization of the final phase of hunter-gatherer lifestyles, the Broad Spectrum Economy, stimulated by the unique combination at the end of the last Glacial of truly Modern Humans (*Homo sapiens*) adapting to dramatic ecological changes. Scope for the medium, and short term, and the individual, still focus around exceptional sites such as Sesklo, Dhimini, and Knossos, and here much still remains controversial about these potential "chieftain centers" or "town-like agglomerations." Their "historical" trajectories are still to be unraveled. Since in any case the Thessalian complex tell sites do not appear to be central to the rise of the subsequent Early Bronze Age "High Cultures" of Southern Greece, only Knossos being arguably a locus for the elaboration of long-term political complexity, the rarity of complex settlements in the Greek Neolithic is reinforced. At the present, Perlès' emphasis on the overwhelming sense of stability, to the point of a static society, is attractive, where a sense of time might have been limited, centering around a mentality of peaceable agricultural preoccupations, and directly reminiscent of Ladurie's concept of "motionless time" (1974; Bintliff 1999b, 2004). But then Perlès also persuasively argues for a remarkable degree of human mobility and economic complexity in the large-scale exchange systems for essential lithic materials. In comparison to Neolithic excavations in Northwest Europe, where in Germany and the Netherlands large-area settlement analysis and highly refined chronologies allow scholars to follow individual generations of early farming families as they abandon one house and build its successor (Lüning 2005, cf. Bintliff 2003), opening up the possibility of the world of individuals and events, this perspective is not yet with us in Greece, but it surely will soon come. At that point some better understanding of the fluctuations in people's lives over time and space should emerge, to confirm or challenge the current appearance of relative "immobility" for the Greek Neolithic.

A Personal View

As just described, Neolithic Greece does seem "a foreign country" far removed from our expectations from Early Modern rural societies. But I am not so sure. What is striking about the Early Modern peasantry, and those elsewhere in the records of ethnohistory, is that some of the key processes we have identified for the Neolithic – face-to-face size limits, then the breakthrough from these restrictions which creates the corporate, more endogamous and socially

complex corporate community – can also be found in these recent societies (Bintliff 1999a), even when they exist within a state. Gimbutas's theory of a Neolithic worldview in which "female" values were unusually privileged, and women's status high, is attractive, and is in no way contradicted by the evidence from Greece and the Balkans, but it is still unclear how one could get closer to demonstrating it more conclusively. I also feel that we know too little about the Neolithic outside of the tell heartlands of Thessaly and Macedonia, especially concerning how the Southern Mainland settlement system operated, and whether isolated developments toward more complex political organization were also occurring there. If my concept of the "hidden prehistoric landscape" of Greece (Bintliff et al. 1999) is correct (but some specialists disagree with this, cf. Davis 2004) then we are just at the beginning of understanding the non-tell societies.

References

Ammerman, A. J. and L. L. Cavalli-Sforza (1984). *The Neolithic Transition and the Genetics of Populations in Europe.* Princeton: Princeton University Press.

Ammerman, A. J. et al. (2008). "Finding the early Neolithic in Aegean Thrace: The use of cores." *Antiquity* 82, 139–150.

Andreou, S. and K. Kotsakis (1994). "Prehistoric rural communities in perspective: The Langadas survey project." In P.N. Doukellis and L.G. Mendoni (eds.), *Structures rurales et sociétés antiques.* Paris: Les Belles Lettres, 17–25.

Bentley, R. A. and H. D. G. Maschner (eds.) (2003). *Complex Systems and Archaeology.* Salt Lake City: University of Utah Press.

Bentley, R. A. et al. (2003). "The Neolithic transition in Europe: Comparing broad scale genetic and local scale isotopic evidence." *Antiquity* 77, 63–65.

Bintliff, J. L. (1977). *Natural Environment and Human Settlement in Prehistoric Greece.* 2 vols. Oxford: BAR Supplementary Series 28.

Bintliff, J. L. (1984). "Introduction: Archaeology and theories of social evolution." In J. Bintliff (ed.), *European Social Evolution. Archaeological Perspectives.* Bradford: Bradford University Research Ltd, 13–39.

Bintliff, J. L. (1997). "Regional survey, demography, and the rise of complex societies in the Ancient Aegean: Core–periphery, Neo-Malthusian, and other interpretive models." *Journal of Field Archaeology* 24, 1–38.

Bintliff, J. (1999a). "Settlement and territory." In G. Barker (ed.), *The Routledge Companion Encyclopedia of Archaeology*. London: Routledge, 505–545.

Bintliff, J. (1999b). "Structure, contingency, narrative and timelessness." In J. L. Bintliff (ed.), *Structure and Contingency in the Evolution of Life, Human Evolution and Human History*. London: Cassell, 132–148.

Bintliff, J. L. (2003). "Settlement patterns and landscapes." In P. Bogucki and P. Crabtree (eds.), *The Encyclopedia of the Barbarian World*. New York: Charles Scribner/Gale, 55–64.

Bintliff, J. (2004). "Time, structure and agency: The Annales, emergent complexity, and archaeology." In J. Bintliff (ed.), *A Companion to Archaeology*. London and New York: Blackwell, 174–194.

Bintliff, J. L. *et al.* (2006). "Landscape and early farming settlement dynamics in Central Greece." *Geoarchaeology* 21(7), 665–674.

Bintliff, J. L., P. Howard, and A. M. Snodgrass (1999). "The hidden landscape of prehistoric Greece." *Journal of Mediterranean Archaeology* 12, 139–168.

Bollongino, R. and J. Burger (2007). "Neolithic cattle domestication as seen from ancient DNA." *Proceedings of the British Academy* 144, 165–187.

Branigan, K. (1999). "Late Neolithic colonization of the uplands of Eastern Crete." In P. Halstead (ed.), *Neolithic Society in Greece*. Sheffield: Sheffield Academic Press, 57–65.

Broodbank, C. (2000). *An Island Archaeology of the Early Cyclades*. Cambridge: Cambridge University Press.

Broufas, C. and A. Raftis (1993). *40 Greek Costumes from the Dora Stratou Theatre Collection*. Athens: Dora Stratou Theatre.

Brown, T. A. *et al.* (2009). "The complex origins of domesticated crops in the Fertile Crescent." *Trends in Ecology and Evolution* 24(2), 103–109.

Cauvin, J. (1994). *Naissance des divinités, naissance de l'agriculture. La Révolution des symboles au Néolithique*. Paris: CNRS.

Cavanagh, W. (2004). "WYSIWYG: Settlement and territoriality in Southern Greece during the Early and Middle Neolithic periods." *Journal of Mediterranean Archaeology* 17, 165–189.

Cavanagh, W. and C. Mee (1998). *A Private Place: Death in Prehistoric Greece*. Lund: Paul Astrom.

Cavanagh, W., C. Mee, and J. Renard (2001). "Kouphovouno." *Bulletin de Correspondance Hellénique* 125, 645–648.

Chapman, J. C. (1989). "The early Balkan village." *Varia Archaeologica Hungarica* II, 33–53.

Chapman, J. (1994). "The origins of farming in South East Europe." *Préhistoire Européenne* 6, 133–156.

Cherry, J. F. *et al.* (1988). "Archaeological survey in an artifact-rich landscape: A Middle Neolithic example from Nemea, Greece." *American Journal of Archaeology* 92, 159–176.

Childe, V. G. (1951). *Social Evolution*. London: Watts and Co.

Clark, J. G. D. (1965). "Radiocarbon dating and the spread of the farming economy." *Antiquity* 39, 45–48.

Coles, J. (2001). "Energetic activities of commoners." *Proceedings of the Prehistoric Society* 67, 19–48.

Colledge, S., J. Conolly, and S. Shennan (2004). "Archaeobotanical evidence for the spread of farming in the Eastern Mediterranean." *Current Anthropology* 45 (Supplement), 35–58.

Congedo, M. (ed.) (2001). *Il costume popolare pugliese*. Lecce: Municipality of Lecce.

Davis, J. (1992). "Review of Aegean Prehistory I: The islands of the Aegean." *American Journal of Archaeology* 96, 692–756.

Davis, J. L. (2004). "Are the landscapes of Greek Prehistory hidden? A comparative approach." In S. E. Alcock and J. F. Cherry (eds.), *Side-by-Side Survey. Comparative Regional Studies in the Mediterranean World*. Oxford: Oxbow Books, 22–35.

Demoule, J.-P. and C. Perlès (1993). "The Greek Neolithic: A new review." *Journal of World Prehistory* 7(4), 355–416.

Dunbar, R. (1996). *Grooming, Gossip and the Evolution of Language*. London: Faber & Faber.

Efstratiou, N. (2005). "Tracing the story of the first farmers in Greece – A long and winding road." In C. Lichter (ed.), *How Did Farming Reach Europe?* Istanbul: Deutsches Archäologisches Institut, BYZAS 2, 143–153.

Efstratiou, N. (2007). "The beginning of the Neolithic in Greece – Probing the limits of a 'grand' narrative." In S. Antoniadou and A. Pace (eds.), *Mediterranean Crossroads*. Athens: Pierides Foundation, 124–138.

Efstratiou, N. *et al.* (2006). "Prehistoric exploitation of Grevena highland zones: Hunters and herders along the Pindus chain of Western Macedonia (Greece)." *World Archaeology* 38, 415–435.

Ellis, C. J. *et al.* (2003). "An early Mesolithic seasonal hunting site in the Kennet Valley, Southern England." *Proceedings of the Prehistoric Society* 69, 107–135.

Evans, J. D. (1971). "Neolithic Knossos: The growth of a settlement." *Proceedings of the Prehistoric Society* 37(II), 95–117.

Evans, J. D. and A. C. Renfrew (1968). *Excavations at Saliagos near Antiparos*. London: British School at Athens, Supplementary Volume 5.

Evershed, R. *et al.* (2008). "Earliest date for milk use in the Near East and southeastern Europe linked to cattle herding." *Nature* 455(7212), 528–531.

Gimbutas, M. (1991). *The Civilization of the Goddess*. San Francisco: Harper.

Gkiasta, M. *et al.* (2003). "Neolithic transition in Europe: The radiocarbon record revisited." *Antiquity* 77, 45–62.

Greene, K. (2002). *An Introduction to Archaeology*. London: Routledge.

Halstead, P. (1981). "Counting sheep in Neolithic and Bronze Age Greece." In I. Hodder, G. Isaac, and N. Hammond (eds.), *Patterns of the Past: Studies in Honour of David Clarke*. Cambridge: Cambridge University Press, 307–339.

Halstead, P. (1987). "Traditional and ancient rural economy in Mediterranean Europe: Plus ça change?" *Journal of Hellenic Studies* 107, 77–87.

Halstead, P. (1992). "From reciprocity to redistribution: Modelling the exchange of livestock in Neolithic Greece." *Anthropozoologica* 16, 19–30.

Halstead, P. (1994). "The north–south divide: Regional pathways to complexity in prehistoric Greece." In C. Mathers and S. Stoddart (eds.), *Development and Decline in the Mediterranean Bronze Age*. Sheffield: J. R. Collis Publications, 195–219.

Halstead, P. (1995a). "From sharing to hoarding: The Neolithic foundations of Aegean Bronze Age society?" In R. Laffineur and W.-D. Niemeier (eds.), *Politeia. Society and State in the Aegean Bronze Age*. Liège: Université de Liège, Aegaeum 12.

Halstead, P. (1995b). "Plough and power: The economic and social significance of cultivation with the ox-drawn ard in the Mediterranean." *Bulletin of Sumerian Agriculture* 8, 11–22.

Halstead, P. (1996). "Pastoralism or household herding? Problems of scale and specialization in early Greek animal husbandry." *World Archaeology* 28, 20–42.

Halstead, P. (ed.) (1999a). *Neolithic Society in Greece*. Sheffield: Sheffield Academic Press.

Halstead, P. (1999b). "Neighbours from hell? The household in Neolithic Greece." In P. Halstead (ed.), *Neolithic Society in Greece*. Sheffield: Sheffield Academic Press, 77–95.

Halstead, P. (1999c). "Missing sheep: On the meaning and wider significance of 0 in Knossos sheep records." *Annual of the British School at Athens* 94, 145–166.

Halstead, P. (2006a). *What's Ours Is Mine? Village and Household in Early Farming Society in Greece*. Amsterdam: Stichting Nederlands Museum voor Anthropologie en Praehistorie.

Halstead, P. (2006b). "Sheep in the garden: The integration of crop and livestock husbandry in early farming regimes of Greece and Southern Europe." In D. Serjeantson and D. Field (eds.), *Animals in the Neolithic of Britain and Europe*. Oxford: Oxbow, 42–55.

Halstead, P. and J. O'Shea (eds.) (1989). *Bad Year Economics. Cultural Responses to Risk and Uncertainty*. Cambridge: Cambridge University Press.

Hauptmann, H. (1999). "The Urfa region." In M. Özdogan (ed.), *Neolithic in Turkey*. Istanbul: Arkeoloji ve Sanat Yayinlari, 39–55, 65–86.

Hodder, I. (1990). *The Domestication of Europe*. London: Blackwell.

Hodkinson, S. (1990). "Politics as a determinant of pastoralism: The case of Southern Greece, ca. 800–300 B.C." *Rivista di Studi Liguri* 56, 139–163.

Hourmouziadis, G. (1979). *To Neolithiko Dhimini*. Volos: Society of Thessalian Studies.

Isaakidou, V. (2006). "Ploughing with cows: Knossos and the secondary products revolution." In D. Serjeantson and D. Field (eds.), *Animals in the Neolithic of Britain and Europe*. Oxford: Oxbow Books, 95–112.

Johnson, M. (1996). "Water, animals and agricultural technology: A study of settlement patterns and economic change in Neolithic Southern Greece." *Oxford Journal of Archaeology* 15, 267–295.

Kotsakis, K. (1999). "What tells can tell: Social space and settlement in the Greek Neolithic." In P. Halstead (ed.), *Neolithic Society in Greece*. Sheffield: Sheffield Academic Press, 66–76.

Kotsakis, K. (2001). "Mesolithic to Neolithic in Greece. Continuity, discontinuity or change of course?" *Documenta Praehistorica* 28, 68–73.

Kotsakis, K. (2006a). "A bridge too far: essentialist concepts in Greek archaeology." In S. Antoniadou and A. Pace (eds.), *Mediterranean Crossroads*. Athens: Pierides Foundation, 107–119.

Kotsakis, K. (2006b). "Settlement of discord: Sesklo and the emerging household." In N. Tasic and C. Grozdanov (eds.), *Homage to Milutin Garasanin*. Belgrade: Serbian Academy of Sciences and Arts, 207–220.

Kotsakis, K. (2007). "Pottery, cuisine and community in the Neolithic of North Greece." In C. Mee and J. Renard (eds.), *Cooking Up the Past*. Oxford: Oxbow Books, 225–246.

Kroll, H. (1981). "Thessalische Kulturpflanzen." *Zeitschrift für Archäologie* 15, 97–103.

Ladurie, E. L. R. (1974). "L'Histoire immobile." *Annales, Économies, Sociétés* 29, 673–692.

Lewthwaite, J. G. (1981). "Plains tails from the hills: Transhumance in Mediterranean archaeology." In A. Sheridan and G. Bailey (eds.), *Economic Archaeology*. Oxford: BAR Int. Series 96, 57–66.

Lohmann, H., G. Weisgerber, and G. Kalaitzoglou (2002). "Ein endneolithische Wehrdorf auf dem Megalo Rimbari (Attika) und verwandte Anlagen." *Boreas* 25, 1–48.

Lüning, J. (2005). "Bandkeramische Hofplätze und die absolute Chronologie der Bandkeramik." In J. Lüning, C. Frirdich, and A. Zimmermann (eds.), *Die Bandkeramik in 21. Jahrhundert*. Rahden: Leidorf, 49–74.

Marangou, C. (1996). "Assembling, displaying, and dissembling Neolithic and Eneolithic figurines and models." *Journal of European Archaeology* 4, 177–202.

Marangou, C. (2001a). "Neolithic watercraft: Evidence from Northern Greek wetlands." In B.A. Purdy (ed.), *Enduring Records. The Environmental and Cultural Heritage of Wetlands*. Oxford: Oxbow Books.

Marangou, C. (2001b). "Sacred or secular places and the ambiguous evidence of prehistoric ritual." In P. F. Biehl, F. Bertemes, and H. Meller, *The Archaeology of Cult and Religion*. Budapest: Archaeolingua, 139–160.

Meskell, L. (1995). "Goddesses, Gimbutas and 'New Age' archaeology." *Antiquity* 69, 74–86.

Morris, E. L. and A. Woodward (2005). "Ceramic petrology and prehistoric pottery in the UK." *Proceedings of the Prehistoric Society* 69, 279–303.

Nandris, J. (1970). "The development and relationships of the earlier Greek Neolithic." *Man* 5, 192–213.

Nanoglou, S. (2001). "Social and monumental space in Neolithic Thessaly, Greece." *European Journal of Archaeology* 4, 303–322.

Nanoglou, S. (2005). "Subjectivity and material culture in Thessaly, Greece: The case of Neolithic anthropomorphic imagery." *Cambridge Archaeological Journal* 15, 141–156.

Papathanassopoulos, G. A. (ed.) (1996). *Neolithic Culture in Greece*. Athens: Goulandris Foundation.

Pappa, M. and M. Besios (1999). "The Makriyalos Project: Rescue excavations at the Neolithic site of Makriyalos, Pieria, Northern Greece." In P. Halstead (ed.), *Neolithic Society in Greece*. Sheffield: Sheffield Academic Press, 108–120.

Parker Pearson, M. (1999). *The Archaeology of Death and Burial*. Stroud: Sutton.

Perlès, C. (1989). *From Stone Procurement to Neolithic Society in Greece*. Bloomington: Indiana University Press.

Perlès, C. (1999). "The distribution of magoules in Eastern Thessaly." In P. Halstead (ed.), *Neolithic Society in Greece*. Sheffield: Sheffield Academic Press, 42–56.

Perlès, C. (2001). *The Early Neolithic in Greece*. Cambridge: Cambridge University Press.

Perlès, C. (2005). "From the Near East to Greece: Let's reverse the focus. Cultural elements that didn't transfer." In C. Lichter (ed.), *How Did Farming Reach Europe?* Istanbul: Deutsches Archäologisches Institut, BYZAS 2, 275–290.

Perlès, C. and K. D. Vitelli (1994). "Technologie et fonction des premières productions céramiques de Grèce." In Anon. (ed.), *Terre Cuite et Société*. Juan-les-Pins: Éditions APDCA, 225–242.

Preziosi, D. and L. A. Hitchcock (1999). *Aegean Art and Architecture*. Oxford: Oxford University Press.

Pyke, G. and P. Yiouni (1996). *The Excavation of an Early Neolithic Village in Northern Greece 1964–1981. The Excavation and the Ceramic Assemblage*. London: British School at Athens, Supplementary Volume 25.

Redman, C. L. (1978). *The Rise of Civilization*. San Francisco: W. H. Freeman & Co.

Renfrew, C. (1973). *Before Civilization*. London: Jonathan Cape.

Renfrew, C. (1975). "Trade as action at a distance: Questions of integration and communication." In J. A. Sabloff and C. C. Lamberg-Karlovsky (eds.), *Ancient Civilisation and Trade*. Albuquerque: University of New Mexico Press, 3–59.

Renfrew, C. (1985). *The Archaeology of Cult: The Sanctuary at Phylakopi*. London: British School at Athens.

Renfrew, C. (2004). "Rethinking the emergence." In J. C. Barrett and P. Halstead (eds.), *The Emergence of Civilisation Revisited*. Oxford: Oxbow Books, 257–274.

Runnels, C. (1985). "Trade and demand for millstones in Southern Greece in the Neolithic and the Early Bronze Age." In A.B. Knapp and T. Stech (eds.), *Prehistoric Production and Exchange. The Aegean and Eastern Mediterranean*. Los Angeles: Institute of Archaeology, University of California, 30–43.

Runnels, C. and T. H. van Andel (1988). "Trade and the origins of agriculture." *Journal of Mediterranean Archaeology* 1, 83–109.

Runnels, C. et al. (2005). "A Mesolithic landscape in Greece: Testing a site-location model in the Argolid at Kandia." *Journal of Mediterranean Archaeology* 18, 259–285.

Sampson, A. (ed.) (2006). *The Prehistory of the Aegean Basin*. Athens: Atrapos.

Sherratt, A. (1980). "Water, soil and seasonality in early cereal cultivation." *World Archaeology* 11, 313–330.

Sherratt, A. (1981). "Plough and pastoralism: Aspects of the secondary products revolution." In I. Hodder, G. Isaac, and N. Hammond (eds.), *Pattern of the Past. Studies in Honour of David Clarke*. Cambridge: Cambridge University Press, 261–305.

Sherratt, A. (1984). "Social evolution: Europe in the later Neolithic and Copper Ages." In J. L. Bintliff (ed.), *European Social Evolution. Archaeological Perspectives*. Bradford: Bradford University Research Ltd, 123–134.

Stratouli, G. (1996). "Die Fischerei in der Ägäis während des Neolithikums. Zur Technik und zum potientellen Ertrag." *Prähistorische Zeitschrift* 71, 1–27.

Talalay, L. E. (1994). "A feminist boomerang: The Great Goddess of Greek prehistory." *Gender and History* 6(2), 165–183.

Talalay, L. E. (2004). "Heady business: Skulls, heads, and decapitation in Neolithic Anatolia and Greece." *Journal of Mediterranean Archaeology* 17, 139–163.

Tartaron, T. F., D. J. Pullen, and J. S. Noller (2006). "*Rillenkarren* at Vayia: Geomorphology and a new class of

Early Bronze Age fortified settlement in Southern Greece." *Antiquity* 80, 145–160.

Theochares, D. R. (ed.) (1973). *Neolithic Greece*. Athens: National Bank of Greece.

Tomkins, P. (2004). "Filling in the Neolithic background: Social life and social transformation in the Aegean before the Bronze Age." In J. C. Barrett and P. Halstead (eds.), *The Emergence of Civilisation Revisited*. Oxford: Oxbow Press, 38–63.

Torrence, R. (1986). *Production and Exchange of Stone Tools. Prehistoric Obsidian in the Aegean*. Cambridge: Cambridge University Press.

Tresset, A. and J.-D. Vigne (2007). "Substitution of species, techniques and symbols." *Proceedings of the British Academy* 144, 189–210.

Tsountas, C. (1908). *Ai proistorikai akropoleis Dhiminiou kai Sesklou*. Athens: Sakellariou.

van Andel, T. H. and C. N. Runnels (1995). "The earliest farmers in Europe." *Antiquity* 69, 481–500.

Vita-Finzi, C. and E. S. Higgs (1970). "Prehistoric economy in the Mt. Carmel area of Palestine: Site catchment analysis." *Proceedings of the Prehistoric Society* 36, 1–37.

Vitelli, K. D. (1995). "Pots, potters and the shaping of Greek Neolithic society." In W. K. Barnett and J. W. Hoopes (eds.), *The Emergence of Pottery: Technology and Innovation in Ancient Societies*. Washington, DC: Smithsonian Institution Press.

Wallace, S. A. (2003). "The changing role of herding in the Early Iron Age of Crete: Some implications of settlement shift for economy." *American Journal of Archaeology* 107, 601–627.

Watrous, L. V. (1994). "Review of Aegean Prehistory III: Crete from Earliest Prehistory through the Protopalatial Period." *American Journal of Archaeology* 98, 695–753.

Wobst, H. M. (1974). "Boundary conditions for Paleolithic social systems." *American Antiquity* 39, 147–178.

Wobst, H. M. (1976). "Locational relationships in Palaeolithic society." *Journal of Human Evolution* 5, 49–58.

Further Reading

Alram-Stern, E. (ed.) (1996). *Die Ägäische Frühzeit. 1. Band. Das Neolithikum in Griechenland*. Wien: Österreichischen Akademie der Wissenschaften.

Andreou, S., M. Fotiadis, and K. Kotsakis (1996). "Review of Aegean Prehistory V: The Neolithic and Bronze Age of northern Greece." *American Journal of Archaeology* 100, 537–597.

Barrett, J. C. and P. Halstead (eds.) (2004). *The Emergence of Civilisation Revisited*. Oxford: Oxbow Books.

Gimbutas, M. (1989). *The Language of the Goddess*. London: Thames & Hudson.

Louwe Kooijmans, L. (1998). *Between Geleen and Banpo. The Agricultural Transformation of Prehistoric Society, 9000–4000BC*. Amsterdam: Archaeology Centre, Amsterdam University.

Perlès, C. (1994). "Les débuts du Néolithique en Grèce." *La Recherche* 266, 642–649.

4

Complex Cultures of the Early Bronze Age

Introduction

This period lasting from ca. 3500/3200 to ca. 2000/1900 BC is widely considered as the birth phase of Aegean civilization (general reading: Shelmerdine 2008, Cline 2010, Mee 2011). Colin Renfrew (1972, 1973), highlighted the "high cultures" of the Early Bronze Age (EBA) as preparatory to the true civilizations which followed in Middle and Late Bronze Age times (MBA, LBA). Key indicators of transformation were: the rise of a more productive agricultural economy in the Southern Mainland and the islands, based on the "Mediterranean triad" of cereals, olive oil (see Figure 1.1), and wine ("polyculture"); the impact of bronze metallurgy; the appearance of "central places" dominating local settlement clusters; and by the end of the period, the localized appearance of nucleated, town-like settlements with elaborate fortifications. He considered the associated cultures of the EBA as intermediate between the tribal, egalitarian or Big Man societies of the Neolithic, and the state forms of the later palace civilizations: "High Cultures" in which chiefdoms might have arisen in key places.

Previous scenarios emphasized migrations or invasions, or strong imitation of Near Eastern societies, as critical to the appearance of Minoan and Mycenaean civilizations. Renfrew envisaged those palace societies as the logical outcome of *internal* developments which had commenced during later Neolithic times and accelerated in the EBA. He still conceded that diffusion from the Near East and the North Balkans was an essential component: metallurgy was introduced from the precocious copper- then bronze-using societies to the north of Greece, and from Northwest Anatolia; the cultivation of the olive was a diffusion of know-how (but the tree was local) from the Levant, that of the grape vine probably from Northern Greece or adjacent areas in the South Balkans. Most importantly, the remarkable EBA developments in political organization and proto-urbanism were confined to Southern Mainland Greece and the Aegean islands, indicating apparent stagnation in political complexity within Northern Greece after the Final Neolithic.

As this tendency toward regionalization of culture and socio-political trajectories becomes increasingly pronounced during the course of the EBA, we shall follow custom and treat the key regions of the Aegean separately: the Southern Mainland EBA/EH (Early Helladic Culture), the Cretan EBA/EM (Early Minoan Culture), the EBA/EC on the Cycladic and North Aegean Islands (the Early Cycladic and related culture further north in the Aegean Sea), and finally the EBA in the Northern Mainland.

The Early Bronze Age Mainland: The Early Helladic Culture

Population

EH sites are the commonest prehistoric sites found on the Southern Mainland, pointing to a major rise in population. Some caution is required however. The vast majority of sites are small, farms or hamlets, and in contrast to the larger size and greater continuity of Neolithic tells, frequently have shorter lives. A community at the scale of a Neolithic tell, if dispersed, shifting location regularly, might create a much greater site density without increasing total population. On the other hand, EH sites are far denser than the hitherto recognized flat (and occasional tell) sites of the Neolithic in Southern Greece, suggesting colonization of entire districts. Moreover, small Bronze Age sites, especially of the LN-FN and EH1 periods, are hard to recognize on the surface, and are probably massively underrepresented even in the recent results of intensive field survey, a phenomenon I characterize as a "Hidden Landscape" (Bintliff *et al.* 1999, anticipated by Rutter 1993; *contra* Davis 2004). For EH sites as a whole, nonetheless, including those of village type, and allowing for considerable underrepresentation of the ubiquitous farms/hamlets, the elevated numbers and wider dispersal should still reflect significant population rise.

In detail, EH sites are mostly dated to the "climax" phase, EH2. Whereas the low record for EH1 may be due to difficulties in pinpointing distinctive artifacts from site survey for this phase, the decline in EH3 is linked to evidence for widespread destructions in this timespan throughout the Aegean and further afield, causing a discontinuity in cultural development to the Middle Bronze Age (Rutter 1993).

The Economy

The EH period brings further confirmation of local achievement of Sherratt's Secondary Products (2PR) and plough "revolutions" (see Chapter 3), including a figurine seemingly of two yoked oxen (Pullen 1992). Implementing these technological advances would increase population and the geographical scale

Figure 4.1   Olive and wine presses from the rural mansion of Vathypetro, Late Minoan Crete.
Photos J. Lesley Fitton.

and density of mixed farming settlement; this can be seen in all regions of the EBA Aegean. Renfrew's (1972) thesis that olives and wine now played a significant economic role remains contested (see Figure 4.1). Halstead (2004), regretting the limited botanical and press evidence for the period, comments that the situation "is at least compatible" with the view that oil and wine in the Greek Bronze Age were cultivated only on a small scale and consumption was more or less restricted to prestige or ritual contexts (Runnels and Hansen 1986, Hansen 1988, Hamilakis 1996).

Yet with insufficient information, dismissal of the polyculture thesis appears premature. Actually the dominant tree in wood charcoal from settlement deposits on the Cycladic island of Thera is the olive, already from the EBA as well as in MBA–LBA contexts, whilst LBA occupation levels provide finds of domestic olives and vine-cultivation. Asouti (2003) concludes that these data support the significance of polyculture from the Aegean EBA onwards. On Crete, the EBA Myrtos village gave rare evidence for press equipment, together with other evidence for wine and olive oil production, and since a mere 10–15 families are considered to occupy the site, it is hard to deny that one or both of the new crops occupied a standard role in the domestic economy here. By implication why should this not be valid more generally in Bronze Age Greece? Further support on Crete comes from the Chamalevri and Trypeti settlements (Fitton 2002). On the Cyclades many sites, including small settlements, provide pots with impressions of vine-leaves on their bases. A novel scientific aid is chemical analysis of residues from pots used for storage and consumption, which confirm wine storage in large jars from Myrtos, whilst goblets and conical cups from later Aegean Bronze Age contexts evidence wine, beer, and mead, perhaps mixed in a "cocktail" (Pain 1999). Finally, in a restudy of the pithos (large storage vessel) burials of EH Levkas (Ionian Islands), Kilian-Dirlmeier (2005) notes that everyday household pots were employed, of which a number show fittings for emptying liquids out of them. Two varieties for near-base liquid-pouring are registered, and these are known from other EBA Aegean sites. Ethnohistorical comparisons suggest they stored wine and olive oil, respectively, and indeed a "wine" pithos type from the Aghios Kosmas site contained grape pips. Moreover it should be pointed out that household production of wine and oil is likely to be so small-scale that it probably dispensed with stone presses (Mattingly 1988), so that restricted archaeological press finds do not reflect frequency of production.

The popularity of drinking and pouring vessels throughout the EBA and later BA phases has been interpreted as a generalized high consumption of wine (Renfrew 1972, 2004), and since cups and pourers are common at small rural sites, clearly social drinking was not restricted to elites. The find contexts of such pots indicate that wine-drinking was probably also a religious and funerary accompaniment at all social levels.

Thus despite criticism, accumulating evidence from many different sources appears to confirm Renfrew's theory that a major element in the EBA and later economy of Bronze Age Southern Greece was polyculture of cereals, pulses, olives, and wine, at all social levels. These discoveries are not surprising, since in Palestine large-scale olive gathering is documented from the Pottery Neolithic of the sixth millennium BC, and its cultivation from the Copper Age around 4000 BC (Galili et al. 1997).

Whilst traditional Mediterranean farmers often maintain small areas of vines and olives for personal consumption, production beyond family subsistence could have occurred if peasants owed tribute to emergent central places during the Bronze Age, where such storable "cash crops" (produce for sale or tax) were probably required items.

Why were these now "traditional" Mediterranean crops so significant to the rise of complex societies? Olive trees were, with vines, wild plants of the Balkans, but only with human manipulation could their fruit become a major product. Olives provide wood for construction and foliage for animal fodder, fires, and ovens, whilst the oil is a lamp-filler and highly nutritious food, as well as a lubricant for body-cleansing and perfuming. Wine has a secondary advantage of providing safer refreshment than water in large settlements, but its prime use was as a delightful beverage to accompany social meals and festivities, a sphere of great importance already within Neolithic Greece. What enhanced both novelties immeasurably was their storability and transportability. Grain and other grass and root species were hard to store efficiently over a number of years, and the same was true of meat products. In contrast, olive oil and wine could be kept for years, and easily carried long distances in sealed ceramic containers. These properties meant that bad years could be compensated for by storage over several, and also that surpluses could be exchanged over increasing distances for exotic imports, or delivered as taxes to distant state authorities.

Copper metallurgy certainly involved an increasing demand in all areas of Greece for that ore, rarely locally available, whilst the subsequent spread of bronze-working required the alloys arsenic or tin; in parallel a rise in more ornamental-symbolic objects brought demand for silver and gold. Whilst some ores were not far to import (silver and gold from Cycladic Siphnos, copper from the Cycladic island of Kythnos, copper and silver from the Lavrion district near Athens), others were much more exotic, especially tin (no Aegean sources). However, widespread exchange of lithic material was well established in the Neolithic, with roots in Palaeolithic-Mesolithic Greece, encouraging Runnels and van Andel (1988) to claim an early emphasis on Aegean commercialism. Other scholars prefer to explain the distribution of exotic lithics and metals through innumerable small-scale local exchanges, gift-exchange, and the collection of raw materials during seasonal fishing and herding trips or through direct procurement in intentional expeditions from village to quarry, for both. On the one hand, Perlès' argument for a class of at least seasonal long-distance traders in Neolithic times makes the "commercial" case more plausible. On the other, it is surely significant that the metal and lithic sources did not encourage the emergence of major controlling communities in their vicinity, taking advantage of such widespread demand. The Aegean appears to have learnt its copper then bronze, as well as gold and silver metallurgy, through contacts to more advanced metal-producing societies in the North Balkans and the Near East, but as Nakou (1995) points out, its impact is more striking owing to the widespread deposition of metal objects in the innumerable EBA graves, following a long Neolithic era when burials are hardly recovered. But additionally, since weapons are a major grave-gift (of which 70 percent are daggers), we can see that the Aegean shares in a common trend throughout Europe at this time to emphasize male warrior status as opposed to the clearer female emphasis of that preceding period, creating a strong social pressure rather than merely functional value for the spread of early metallurgy (although this is present too).

Ceramic analysis in the Peloponnese demonstrates that tableware, despite its simplicity, was exchanged locally between EH communities, although the receiving sites made similar products. Some of this pot circulation might reflect social rather than economic networks, as in Neolithic Greece (Rutter 1993). However at the EH Aghia Irini settlement on adjacent Kea island (Davis 1992), up to 30 percent of ceramics was imported from elsewhere in the Western Cyclades, favoring commercial exchange. Moreover, the diffusion from Anatolia of the potter's wheel for making ceramics during the EB2–3 era, throughout the Aegean, alerts us to a deep penetration of intra- and extra-Aegean contacts, even if the mechanisms remain unclear. Cretan evidence (see below) also indicates commercial ceramic exchange over significant distances.

Brody (in *Horizon*) has recently underlined the revolutionary importance of the evidence for the spread of donkeys in the EBA Aegean for facilitating trade and agricultural transport. He even suggests that important innovations such as the spread of metallurgy and of the needed ores to the Aegean was probably mostly by donkey-caravans overland rather than by the simple longboats available in EBA times, until the arrival of the sailing ship at the end of the period.

Settlements

Several researchers identify a "settlement hierarchy" for well studied districts of the Southern Mainland, at least in the EH2 climax phase (Rutter 1993, Cosmopoulos 1998). Certain sites are arguably organizational nuclei ("central places") for surrounding settlements, based on greater size and/or special buildings of some architectural pretension. In the ideal case of a very elaborate power structure, more than two steps in the settlement hierarchy can be seen, with authority descending over several levels of increasingly subordinate settlements. Amongst specialists, Pullen and Mee see only two authority levels for the Peloponnese, Runnels (Figure 4.2) three, and Kilian-Dirlmeier four. Interestingly Konsola finds little evidence for hierarchies in the bracketing phases EH1 and 3.

Some of the reasons given for "central-place" status could be challenged. Differences in land potential, or in the local history of a village, might create smaller and larger neighboring communities, without implying political dominance. On the other hand, large sites surrounded by several smaller ones may exercise "social power," a pathway to possible emergence at a later date of small statelets. Secondly, where surface pottery is the evidence for site extent, and when

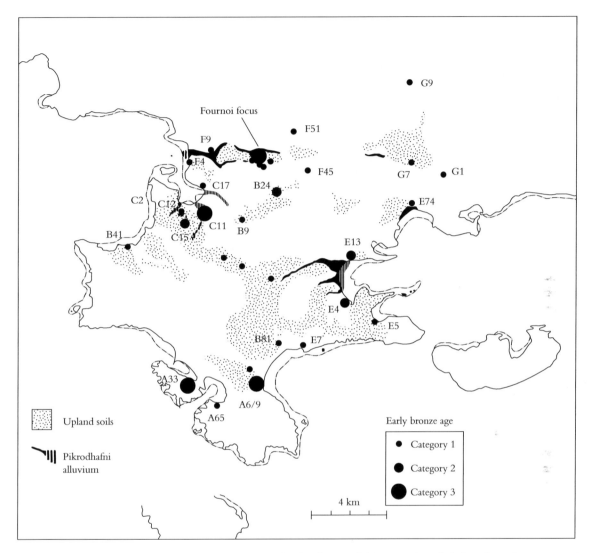

Figure 4.2 Proposed Early Helladic settlement hierarchy for the Argolid Survey: size of circle reflects site extent and implied political status.
M. H. Jameson *et al.* (eds.), *A Greek Countryside. The Southern Argolid from Prehistory to the Present Day.* Stanford 1994, Figure 6.9. © 1994 Board of Trustees of the Leland Stanford Jr. University.

ceramic dating is no finer than several centuries, or even a thousand years (as with the EH subphases or the period as a whole, respectively), horizontal shifting of houses could create archaeological sites several times the settlement's real extent at any one point in time (Andreou *et al.* 1996). These difficulties apply to the example shown in Figure 4.2 from the Argolid, with its three levels of settlement hierarchy based primarily on the extent of surface pottery-scatters. A third argument, that larger sites have more lithics, or other finds with a wider variety of types, need not be inconsistent with a longer use or larger population, rather than "power."

Convincing evidence for special status are remarkable architectural complexes absent in typical rural settlements. Attention has rightly focused on the

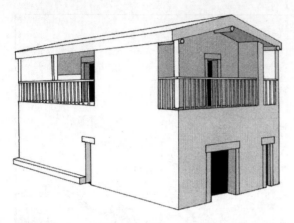

Figure 4.3 Monumental structure ("House of the Tiles") at Lerna.
D. Preziosi and L. A. Hitchcock, *Aegean Art and Architecture.* Oxford University Press 1999, Figure 17.

"Corridor Houses" and a few other monumental constructions. The type-site is the House of the Tiles at Lerna in the Argolid Gulf (Figure 4.3). Subsequently more than 20 buildings of this type have been proposed from the Mainland (Rutter 1993, Shaw 2007). Probably such communal buildings were a long-lived focus for their sites, as consecutive rebuildings are claimed for Lerna, nearby Tsoungiza, Kolonna on Aegina island, and Akovitika in the Southwestern Peloponnese (Shaw 1987). Their plan is a large, two-storied, free-standing rectangular building consisting of a linear series of halls with corridors running parallel on the long sides of the structure, and built of mudbrick on stone foundations. Another distinctive feature is a roof of stone or ceramic tiles. In some cases and just in some of their phases, these buildings are within fortified enclosures (Lerna, Thebes, perhaps Kolonna). As for other monumental EH structures, a mysterious round building at the large settlement at Tiryns across the Gulf of Argos from Lerna might be a communal granary, although it has recently been interpreted as a monumental meeting-place (Marzolff 2004).

The idea that such buildings housed an elite administration not merely for their own surrounding settlement, but also for subordinate rural sites in their district, arose from the discovery at the Lerna House of the Tiles and its predecessor, Building BG, of stamped clay sealings, apparently once attached to containers stored in the building, and similar shapes

used to ornament a monumental terracotta hearth. This is so reminiscent of more complex tribute recording within the later Middle to Late Bronze Age Aegean palaces, and the storage systems of Near Eastern states already during the EBA, that a similar interpretation for Lerna is logical. Arguably, tribute of rural products was conveyed to this House, where it was sealed and marked with a particular set of symbols defining its source and perhaps future destination. The archive room, where also ceramic sets perhaps for communal feasting and ritual were stored, interestingly was only accessible from outside the building, where a bench may have allowed "clients" to wait formal reception. Renfrew envisaged these EH sites as proto-state, proto-urban, High Culture centers on the way toward the Aegean's first palaces in the early MBA, to follow not too long afterwards (1972, 1973). Because the construction techniques are the same as normal houses elsewhere in EH sites, and the Corridor House and its material culture cannot be paralleled in the Near East, these "central places" are generally considered as internal developments on the Greek Mainland.

However, it is far more problematic to suppose that seals and sealings were independently invented in the Aegean, when their use was already so common in the Levant, while seals themselves were being imported into contemporary EBA Crete from the Levant and from Egypt. Recent discoveries of sealings from the contemporary Cyclades (Renfrew 2004), and widespread seal-use in EM Crete, point to a wider proto-bureaucracy. However the remarkable fact that the same seal was used to decorate pithoi at Lerna and other regional sites such as Zygouries and Tiryns could also equally mark traveling craftsmen.

An alternative idea on the significance of the Corridor House is as district cult foci or centers for formal social gatherings of corporate groups (kin groups or clans), for which contributory surpluses were required, instead of assuming that they were centers for a dominant secular elite (Joffe 2004). These structures contain domestic debris (Shaw 1987), whilst at Lerna the larger of the typical central two rooms on the ground floor, provided with a hearth, decoration, and multiple entrances, suggests a social gathering-place for large numbers of people (Peperaki 2004). In contrast, the separate and indirect access to an upper floor, and its very existence as an elaborate complex construction, might serve a select group of users or occupants for that level, favoring an elite function or perhaps a restricted ritual audience. The veranda running around this upper floor underlines its special character. Shaw (2007) assigns the ground floor a public and storage/administrative role, the upper as possibly an elite residence. He has added to these interpretations the observation that several Corridor Houses have paved areas adjacent to them, where social groups may have gathered for public activities; maybe the Corridor Houses were a later outgrowth from such open-air meeting-places.

Significantly, "mansion-like" enclosed sites, with bastioned walls, are a contemporary development in the North Aegean at the settlement of Troy II in North-West Turkey (Preziosi and Hitchcock 1999). Here a fortified inner acropolis with two formal entry gates from a Lower Town comprises one large and four smaller houses of "megaron" plan (sequent access chambers), reasonably interpreted as elite dwellings (Korfmann *et al.* 2001). Similar phenomena occur at several islands of the Eastern and Northeastern Aegean, and elsewhere in West Turkey (Liman Tepe).

Konsola (1984) characterizes typical EH settlements as showing communal planning. Houses are similar, with several rooms usually on a single axis, and are generally on the same alignment. Whether linked into blocks, or freestanding, the dwellings are packed close, with well-made paths linking the different sectors of the community, sometimes paved and even, rarely, with street drains. Direct access to the street without intervening yards emphasizes communal interaction. Fortifications are common, which combined with the lack of squares or wide streets, might point to inter-community conflicts. EH Kolonna on Aegina not only has a notably formal settlement plan with regular house-blocks and radial paths, but since more than one potential "mansion" has been identified here, may show an overall guiding authority at work.

However in reality, field survey shows that the commonest EH site-type was a dispersed small settlement of one or several families at the most. Yet when we consider that the individual lifespans of such rural sites are likely to be very limited compared to that of villages, it is probable that at any one time most people were in nucleations. Nonetheless for the EBA Mainland only Tiryns, at 6 ha, and perhaps Thebes, might claim a possible population at "proto-city state" level, where 500–600 people can create a largely endogamous, inwardly-focused society (see Chapter 3). Other sites, even where major buildings are known, seem to be smaller villages or are amalgamations of small sites.

Burials

Archaeologists often find more diversity in burials than in the abodes of the living, so that a rising social and political complexity in the Mainland EH culture might be echoed in cemeteries. Unfortunately the key period EH2, although its tombs are numerous compared to the almost invisible burials of EH1 and 3, reveals little richness or elaboration. Exceptions are Mainland imitations of, or maybe settlers from, the contemporary Early Cycladic culture (such as the east coastal, Cycladic-oriented cemeteries in Boeotia and Attica). The commonest grave-form is a stone cist for individuals, with limited gifts seemingly of a personal nature. In dramatic contrast are the rich EH2 tumulus "R" graves of the island of Levkas, Western Greece (Renfrew 1972, Branigan 1975, Kilian-Dirlmeier 2005), although their local origins or detailed settlement context remain unclear (Figure 4.4).

Kilian-Dirlmeier's exhaustive analysis clarifies this remarkable cemetery. Thirty-three tumuli have been excavated of a possible total of 50. The mounds are stone heaps with stone ring walls, with mostly a prominent central burial associated with secondary burials both within and around the mound. Burial forms and body treatment vary, although most central burials are in storage jars (pithoi). The living population at any one time represented was around 20, suggesting an exclusive minority, buried apart. Social symbolism is also marked in the gifts, with men and women distinguished by weapons and jewelry respectively. Also within the cemetery, internal stratification seems indicated. Central graves (14) have two wealth classes, secondary burials (32) have few or no gifts (pottery replaces a virtual absence of precious metal or imports). An elite with their followers or extended clan is postulated for this three-level social symbolism, whilst a fourth level is implied by the likelihood of non-monumental graves elsewhere in the region for a peasant class.

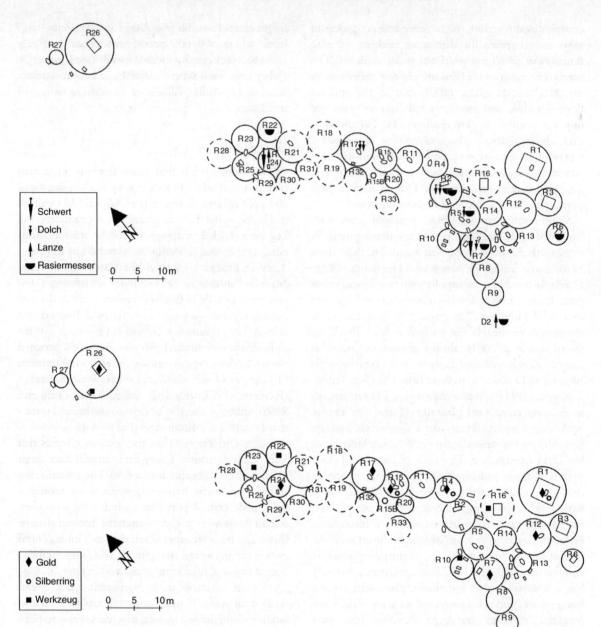

Figure 4.4 (Upper) Male status graves with weapons (Schwert = sword, Dolch = dagger, Lanze = lance, and Rasiermesser = razor-knives) in the EH2 R Grave tumuli at Nidri, Levkas. (Lower) Precious metal in the same graves (Silber = silver, Werkzeug = symbolic craft-tools).
I. Kilian-Dirlmeier, *Die Bronzezeitlichen Gräber bei Nidri auf Leukas*. Bonn 2005, Abb. 95–96. Courtesy of Römisch-Germanischen Zentralmuseums Mainz.

What was the source of power on Levkas, without mineral resources, and with unexceptional agricultural potential? The imported bronze, gold, and silver found in the richer burials, in material and in style, link this community to the Cyclades and other parts of the Aegean. Levkas' location on Greece's western periphery might make it a stopping-off point for trade between Italy and the Adriatic coasts, and Greece and further east. Perhaps elites on the island offered merchants a harbor, food, and ship-repair possibilities, and security from piracy. In return came prestige objects and materials. Given the limited range and seaworthiness of EBA boats, however (see below), voyages from the Aegean would have been a series of innumerable short trips and stopovers on beaches, requiring almost as many such local negotiations (cf. Maran 2007). And a significant western trade-network has yet to be demonstrated. Additionally, the Prestige-Goods Model deployed by Kilian-Dirlmeier, famously applied to the rich tumulus graves of the Western Hallstatt Culture (Frankenstein and Rowlands 1978), has frequently been criticized. Its essence is a model where the control of foreign high-status imports is used by local leading families to achieve and sustain power over their communities. It usually fails to consider that local elites may have risen to power before external contacts blossomed, which they then exploit to acquire prestigious imported luxuries (Bintliff 1984).

Intriguingly, Dörpfeld found a defense wall for a contemporary harbor settlement near the R Graves, allowing Kilian-Dirlmeier to argue for "a defended settlement and rich graves in Nidri Bay," potentially providing closer parallels to contemporary Aegean island towns.

EH2 tumulus burials appear very rarely in other peripheral parts of Greece, but subsequently monumental tumuli occur in EH3 at wider points of the Mainland. Some are burials, others ritual mounds (the ruins of the Lerna House of the Tiles are enclosed underneath an artificial mound) (Forsen 1992). The increasing importance of burial- and other artificial-mounds shows important continuity into the following Middle Helladic culture, where it is a common monument for containing single and collective burials.

Burial archaeology theory suggests that signaling elite status through rich or prominent burials may be exceptional, depending on the local or temporary necessity of emphasizing political realities. The highly visible Levkas graves need not imply that other EBA Aegean societies with little burial ranking *lacked* social divisions. A small but significant number of child burials with prestige gifts could mark a family's status in other ways in several Aegean contexts (Marangou 1991), whilst a number of gold and silver prestige vessels from Mainland Greece and adjacent Cycladic islands with EH culture, but without find context, could have come from lost burials (Kilian-Dirlmeier 2005). Additionally, as noted earlier, the prominence of male warrior statuses in Aegean burials points to competition and conflict in EBA society, confirmed by numerous fortifications in EH, EM, and EC cultures.

The EH3 crisis?

Lerna, till recently, was the key site for demonstrating disruption of Southern Mainland life on a massive scale at the border of the flourishing EH2 and the scanty evidence from EH3. Lerna's fire destruction and the disappearance of innumerable other EH2 sites signal a violent end to the climax High Culture and its Corridor House centers. Some scholars suggest foreign invaders, perhaps the arrival of Indo-European language speakers (the first "Greeks") from the North Balkans or Anatolia, although innovations in culture are most obvious from the start of the Mainland MBA (Middle Helladic culture). Despite justifiable critique of this overall reconstruction (Rutter 1993), parts remain plausible. The settlement evidence supports violent catastrophe in the later part of EH, followed by dramatic depopulation. The sluggish MH recovery confirms the deepness of this crisis. Of course, troubled times might clear the countryside of exposed small sites (most EH2 settlements are farms or hamlets) into refuge nucleations, but the rarity of such latter sites and their generally hamlet or village scale underline the case for wholesale depopulation over most of the Southern Mainland.

Importantly, however, a single late EH2 disaster has been disproved. Stratigraphic (excavation records) and ceramic analyses, the work of Forsen (1992) and Rutter (1993), make clear that settlement destructions occurred at several points within the EH2 and EH3 periods, usually in different places at differing times, even for intervisible sites (Lerna and Tiryns). Cultural changes, notably in ceramic types, were gradual. Perhaps, it is now argued, these were more the result of the diffusion of new styles at varying times into each region, rather than providing us with a map of invaders bearing a uniform new culture with them. Renfrew's (1987) thesis that Indo-European speakers arrived with the Neolithic colonization of Greece appears more plausible than a late EBA colonization of the country from the Black Sea steppes (cf. Bentley *et al.* 2002).

We seem without an explanation for the demographic collapse that occurs over later EH2 and in EH3, with lasting effects well into MH, although almost all excavated sites suffered violent human destruction, even if at varying times. Widespread, serious, and prolonged conflicts seem the most plausible scenario, but precise causes for this are unclear.

On the Mainland, there is evidence from the Argolid and Attica for a phase of significant landscape change, arguably caused by soil erosion between late EH and early MH times (van Andel *et al.* 1986, Paepe *et al.* 1987, Zangger 1994, Bintliff 2000). The lack of fine dating makes it unclear if a potentially serious transformation in agricultural land occurred during the height of the flourishing EH2 and hence was perhaps one element in the decline, or if it happened in EH3/early MH and was the result of abandoned land being washed away in the absence of terrace maintenance (thus a *consequence* of decline).

I have argued that the timing of erosion episodes in Greece may owe more to a coincidence of open, largely treeless landscapes and extreme weather events or phases. Even if the EH countryside was widely cleared for farming and grazing, erosion was not therefore inevitable, but significantly dependent on the vagaries of climate. In fact there *are* extraordinary, hard to dismiss cultural and environmental coincidences between the environmental sequence in the Aegean over this period and events in the Eastern Mediterranean. Egyptian Nile flood levels (Bell 1971) and Syrian and Israeli geomorphical (sedimentary) evidence (Weiss *et al.* 1993, Rosen 1995, 2007) have identified a period of some length (100–200 years?) around 2200 BC, of severe climatic fluctuation typified by drought, involved in the temporary collapse of the Egyptian state and the decline of many settlements in the Levant. Independent earth-science climatic data confirm a major arid period (Wossink 2009).

This field is moving swiftly, so that a provisional suggestion for the occurrence of observed erosional sediments in Greece might be due to a convergence of several factors. One was sea level dynamics (Shriner and Murray 2003), another climatic fluctuations. A third is the existence of a largely open landscape cleared by LN-EH farmers and herders, which encouraged the surface flow of rain and the washing away of soil deposits in the hinterland into coastal streams and slope wash. Since for the Argos Plain, a case-study landscape, the result was a very large expanse of new fertile soil, one must now doubt that the alluviation was itself a major disaster.

Summary

Colin Renfrew's long-established view that the EH Southern Mainland nourished a more complex society than that of the Neolithic, remains the likeliest reconstruction, although primarily still centering on the special character of the Corridor Houses and the unique sealed storage facilities at Lerna. Chieftain levels of social organization are harder to demonstrate (except for Levkas), and alternative reasons for the appearance of "central places" are equally supportable. The cycle of population rise then fall across EH suggests a florescence slow to achieve and declining over a longish period, although there are doubts about the reality of an almost invisible EH1, if we follow the theory of a "hidden landscape."

Early Minoan Crete

Introduction

The major site of Knossos in North-Central Crete is a focus of attention owing to its gradual expansion in settlement size over the many millennia of Neolithic occupation (Evans 1971, Katsianis 2004, Tomkins 2004). By the Final Neolithic it was perhaps 3–5 ha, as was the settlement underlying another later palace, that of Phaistos in South-Central Crete (Watrous 1994). If these areas were fully settled, on most formulas calculating population from domestic space they would form potential proto-urban "corporate communities" able to exist largely on endogamy (intra-community marriage). If our somewhat speculative scenario is correct, a process of internal development in Neolithic Crete witnessed the emergence of a small number of these focal settlements of unusual population size and internal political structure, which elsewhere and in other periods can be associated with the rise of "city-states" (Bintliff 1999). Since current theory favors a city-state model for the various regional palace centers of the Middle to Late Bronze Age on Crete, the Neolithic background could conceivably provide a key to the rise of Europe's first civilization, that of Minoan Crete. Our previously presented model would predict for such a society a necessary horizontal or vertical political coordination. Sadly too little is known till the mature EM period of the architecture of the intriguing settlement beneath the Knossos palace, apart from houses which shared with the Mainland a trend toward greater "privatization" (Tomkins 2004).

It is striking that Crete, after its initial farming settlement, remains largely isolated in material culture from other cultures of the Aegean and from the Near East, till the Late Neolithic. Then, and during the EBA, considerable raw materials were imported (metals, obsidian, and marble) alongside cultural tastes from the wider Aegean (metals, obsidian, and marble) and limited artifacts from the Early Cycladic culture (EC).

Settlement

Very few EN-MN settlements are known, then site numbers rise dramatically in LN-FN, followed by further population growth in EM1–2 (Watrous 1994). Earlier Neolithic settlement is implausibly thin, and one suspects a "hidden landscape" of small (and perhaps several larger) sites awaiting ultra-intensive survey. Ceramic imports provenanced scientifically to siteless regions confirm this (Tomkins 2004). Nonetheless, the later Neolithic site proliferation probably reflects a *relative* explosion across the island (Branigan 1999). Despite earlier scholarly tendencies to explain significant changes in Minoan culture through migrations into the island, after the initial colonization there is little and disputed evidence until

Late Minoan 2 for any widespread immigration. The FN-EM2 population takeoff probably represents instead the local impact of the Secondary Products and Plough revolutions. Nonetheless, a good case exists for a small Cycladic colony on the north coast of Crete in EM times at Aghia Photia, whilst Cretans themselves colonized Kythera island, off the south coast of the Mainland, in EM2.

By EM1 Cretan settlement is extensive enough to clearly show that it includes numerous small rural sites and hamlets, alongside a class of large, town-like communities (developing from those few known by LN). To call this a settlement hierarchy implies a pyramid of regional control more surely evidenced for subsequent palatial Crete. It is too simple merely to equate larger versus smaller settlements, with dominant and subordinate communities. Nonetheless it is plausible that Knossos, Phaistos, and other extra-large settlements exercised strong influence on their districts, if not further afield, even by the Final Neolithic, possessing unparalleled economic surpluses, unusual population resources, and exchange potential compared to all other settlements. I have suggested that their probable "corporate" community structure represents incipient city-states.

In discussions of the several excavated EM2 hamlets, the search for progressive social evolution has encouraged scholars to find intermediate steps between the typical largely autonomous and egalitarian villages of the Greek Neolithic, and the hierarchical palace civilizations of the Middle to Late Bronze Age: elite residences evidencing a chieftain stage would suit the prediction very nicely. For "linear progress" in social evolution to operate in the Aegean, the flame of High Culture should survive on EM Crete, since the promising Corridor Houses of the EH Mainland disappear a long time before the MH societies which follow them locally show any signs of emergent civilization. This is the context for older claims that some EM2 hamlets were chieftains' residences, or specialist villages in an elaborate economy.

Myrtos-Fournou Korifi (Warren 1972) on the south coast of Crete possessed an outer wall and tower, and its village inhabitants were originally claimed to have produced textiles on an industrial scale (Warren 1968). Reanalysis by Whitelaw (1983) downscaled the community to 5–6 households with a broad economy:

a prosperous, largely self-sufficient hamlet. The individual household units were also autonomous economically. However Tenwolde's (1992) reanalysis of the ceramic assemblage showed that the "household" room clusters differed in economic tasks: storage, cooking, lithic stores, textile production, pot production, were in separate sectors of the hamlet. A cooperative society of 50–75 people was reconstructed. This division of labor may indicate incipient role specialization in Myrtos, anticipating the subsequent organization of space in palace sites, where activities are also localized. The abundance of vessels for processing, storage, and consumption of liquids seems excessive for self-sufficiency, and taken with the evidence for wine and olive production, and wool specialization, supports an interpretation that the community was marketing or otherwise supplying surpluses to other communities or even proto-palaces (see below). Myrtos also evidences early use of sealings, probably symptomatic of a more elaborate economy than egalitarian household production. Since up to half of Myrtos' pottery was also imported, the economic complexity of such small rural sites cannot be underestimated (Watrous 1994, Schoep and Knappett 2004).

Reinterpretation of the village site of Vasiliki in East-Central Crete focuses on an EM2 architectural complex, the "House on the Hill." Traditionally seen as a Chieftain's Residence, re-excavation has deconstructed this into several houses within a rural hamlet (Zois 1976). These, like at Myrtos nearby, were built up piecemeal as conjoined structures, maybe for related families. The hamlet of Trypiti in the same region, with neat house plans lining a central street, also does not diverge from the communal planning typical for Mainland Neolithic villages. But once again, even in such a minor community as Vasiliki, there have been observed some anticipations of settlement design typical of the later palaces (Preziosi and Hitchcock 1999): an evolving integrated plan and a paved western court associated with careful construction of the west face of one part of the complex. Taken with the inferences from Myrtos for suprahousehold complexity, it seems that patterns of social, economic, and ritual behavior at the hamlet level may be small-scale parallels for the grander designs of contemporary emergent and future palatial "central places." In the same way, as we shall see later, claims for

Early Minoan peak sanctuaries may provide a religious geography onto which a grander series of shrines in palatial times could have arisen.

Till recently, the small towns at Knossos and Phaistos and other settlements at later palatial sites were considered to lack signs in EM of architectural elaboration. Nothing like a Mainland Corridor House was known: instead, fragments of modest houses. However there was virtual ignorance of the layout of both sites, since only little windows could be explored beneath the overlying palaces, whilst the construction of the great palaces had dug away most of the immediately preceding levels.

All this has radically altered over the last two decades (Driessen 2007, Schoep 2007). Firstly we should note that in his classic work on the Minoan palaces, Graham (1962) had emphasized their distinctiveness from Near Eastern models, being composed of blocks arranged around a large open, central rectangular court. The traditional date for the construction of the First Palaces is early Middle Bronze Age, Middle Minoan 1B (ca. 1900 BC). However a French team led by Pelon has restudied the development of the Malia palace, in northeast coastal Crete, and not only backdated the First Palace to the EM3-MM1A period, but beneath this has reconstructed a major building of EM2 date associated with open spaces and a seal impression. They argue that this could form a simplified earlier version of a "palace" block bordered already by the familiar west and central courts (see Figure 5.7). Although the Malia EM2 complex is built of foundations of small stones below a mudbrick superstructure and possesses small internal rooms, it remains a more monumental structure than contemporary houses. At EM Knossos likewise it is now suggested that there was a similar monumental complex beneath parts of the later palace, with sealings which might indicate early administrative activity, whilst there are similar hints for Phaistos and the far eastern Cretan palace-site of Zakro of an EM early "courtyard complex." The associated argument now current, that the First Palaces of MM times were also less elaborate than the Second Palaces, allows us to see a long stepwise evolution of the palace plan, which has usually been taken to reflect their final form from the first.

Malia always challenged prevailing views on the Minoan palaces and their relations with surrounding towns, since the district called "Quartier Mu" in the settlement surrounding the palace revealed impressive MM mansions associated with "palatial" activities: major craft production, administration, and public foci. It now seems likely that such elaborate private town houses also commence earlier than formerly believed, judging by EM monumental buildings now identified in the towns of Palaikastro, Tylissos, and Mochlos, where true palaces will not arise later (Schoep and Knappett 2004). It has also been shown that elaborate features that are first found in the palace architecture of the mature Minoan palaces, make their first appearance not in the earliest true palaces, but in such town mansions during the early palatial period. All this alerts us to the existence of a long evolution of monumental architecture on Minoan Crete, in which major buildings lying outside the palaces as well as in non-palatial settlements are as important as the new evidence of the EM proto-palaces or "court-complexes" under the palaces.

What are the implications for social change? Pelon considered the proto-palace at EM2 Malia to have housed an early ruler, whilst members of the royal family or an associated elite class might have occupied the town mansions. Other scholars, however, offer a radical deconstruction of the traditional concept of the Minoan palace in both its new proto-form of EM2 and its First Palace form in MM1–2 (or EM3 on for Malia) (Driessen 2007, Schoep 2007). For these authors, based on a reanalysis of the excavation data, the key element in the Minoan "palace" was the Central Court, a place of communal ceremony for surrounding populations. Initially only parts of its rim were taken up with monumental blocks of rooms, allowing easy public access to the court. The associated buildings, rather than being storehouses and accommodation for a residential regional elite, were primarily for caching ceramics and foodstuffs required for ceremonial feasting and associated rituals. An external West Court served for other formal communal activities. There was competition for control over these "court-complexes" between a number of leading families in the large surrounding town. This model would predict that non-palatial towns might also possess at an early stage the residences of leading families. In fact, such monumental buildings from EM2 onwards have been interpreted in this way.

Day and Wilson (2002), expanding on a theory of Arthur Evans, offer an additional source of "social power." By Early Minoan times, the 7 meter high tell mound of Neolithic Knossos might have possessed sacred associations from its mythical founder-status as one of the first settlements in Crete, stimulating its development as a regional "ceremonial center." Special EM dump deposits in and around the later palace represent communal feasting, distinct from the domestic assemblages recognized elsewhere at EM Knossos. These festival clearance-deposits are composed of large numbers of pots for serving and consuming food and drink. Similar deposits have been recorded at Malia (Driessen 2007).

However, Day and Wilson's assumption that emerging elites at Knossos were organizing these ritual banquets runs ahead of the evidence, and one might question their conclusion that "whether the nature of the ceremonies described are labelled as religious, or not, matters little." If we are correct in seeing later Neolithic Knossos, and Phaistos, as proto-city state corporate communities with a need for integrated socialization events, then communal feasts would be likely outcomes of such ceremonies. At Phaistos, the FN settlement is already notable for its rich ceramic assemblages in which drinking vessels are unusually prominent, leading Relaki (2004) to hypothesize that such large sites acted as foci for surrounding smaller settlements to participate in ceremonial feasting. EM Phaistos possesses similar assemblages. Purely religious interpretations, or a pronounced elite basis, do not follow automatically from this background. We saw in Chapter 3 that communal food stores at Knossos date back to the earlier Neolithic community. Although Driessen (2007) links the later EM development of courts at villages such as Vasiliki, and outside the communal EM stone "tholos" tombs, to the appearance of the first court-complexes at later palatial sites, this also warns us that we are observing a far broader phenomenon than elite emergence, indicating increasingly formal community socialization events.

The economy

The Kavousi survey in Eastern Crete (Haggis 2002) shows an expansion of the settlement system from Early Minoan into the "First Palace" (MM1–2) period, both in areas exploited and site density, although there is no obvious regional palace in this area till later, in Late Minoan times, at Gournia. Till then, the centralized control of large regions from palaces is probably not relevant to many areas such as Kavousi, remote from an early Middle Minoan, or even "pre-palatial" Early Minoan, power center. A major reorganization of the Kavousi landscape occurs in Second Palace, LM times, suggesting pressure for commercial or tax-driven surplus production, arguably from a controlling palace. However, I am not so persuaded that the less dramatic landscape infill over the EM-MM eras, based on intensification of traditional agriculture, is "auto-consumption" (consumed by the producers alone) without reference to exchange and regional interactions. Traditional Greek farming has also rested on a similar broad-spectrum mix of crops and animals to that suggested now for Kavousi. This ensured that peasants grew most of their needs but also produced sufficient marketable surpluses to purchase necessary items as well as minor luxuries in regional market centers, and pay taxes when required.

We earlier mentioned EM Crete imports of metal and hard stone. Although Cretan copper was formerly considered a potential early source, analyses now demonstrate that the sources used were those dominating the Southern Mainland and the Cyclades: Lavrion in Attica and several Cycladic islands for copper as well as precious metal (Davis 1992, Rutter 1993). Also striking are recent analyses of ceramic production. Large regions of EM Crete share stylistic similarities in pottery shapes and decoration, considered as cultural borrowing. However Wilson *et al.* (1999) have demonstrated that EM Knossos in North-Central Crete was receiving pottery from the Mesara region in Southern Crete in quantity, whilst the Mesara obtained pottery from Eastern Crete. The social and economic framework for these exchanges remains unclear, and they need not imply incipient civilization, if we recall the ceramic exchange already shown for Neolithic Knossos and the remarkable Aegean-wide Neolithic exchange systems for stone-tools.

The site of Poros, on the closest coastline to Knossos (Wilson and Day 2000, Day and Wilson 2002, Day *et al.* in *Horizon*), is a port community with more extensive Cycladic links at this period than inland Knossos, which it might be thought to have served. Here large-scale working of imported island obsidian may be a key source for already prepared lithics exported to the rest of Crete. Likewise metal-working here from imported ores and a wide range of ceramic imports all indicate a "gateway community" which is as much concerned with consuming its own privileged access products from abroad as exporting them elsewhere within Crete. In Eastern Crete, the coastal settlement at Mochlos, with notable Aegean trade evidence and local production of stone vases and gold jewelry, may play a similar role. Here tomb variation in architectural complexity and gift-wealth, and similar contrasts between houses in the domestic area, have been interpreted as indicating a class of status families (Fitton 2002; Soles 1978, 1992). More dramatic claims are made for the Eastern Crete coastal site of Aghia Photia (Betancourt in *Horizon*) with a large EBA cemetery. Here the ceramics are 90 percent Cycladic alongside rare EM vessels, and it is widely agreed that this is a genuine Cycladic colony acting as a "gateway community" through which there diffused through Crete items such as figurines, copper ore and metal prototypes, obsidian, and ceramics. The stimulus role all these coastal "gateways" played in the increasing elaboration of EM society is currently being stressed.

As for external trade with the contemporary Eastern Mediterranean kingdoms and small city-states, current opinion sees this occurring on a regular basis, but probably in a "down-the-line" mode, in which Eastern merchant ships followed an anti-clockwise route from Egypt round to the Aegean, with many ports of call in between. Local elites acquired exotica for display purposes, such as Egyptian stone vases (Bevan 2004). Nonetheless we should not underestimate the range of powerful stimuli given to EM society, and to a lesser extent to EH and EC communities, by these persistent low-level contacts to a wider and more developed world. The development of property-marking and administration using seal-stones and sealings, as well as increasing skills in monumental architecture and craft production, clearly show Near Eastern influence. When in final EM, merchant sailboats are adopted in the Eastern Mediterranean and their technology diffuses to the Aegean to replace the local rowed longboats, Greece's peripheral position to the "core" advanced societies to its east becomes far more integrated into international economic and political relations. This is a phenomenon which plays a vital role in the construction of the true First Palaces and the local adoption of other innovations such as written archives and wheel-made ceramics (Schoep 2007).

Many authors rightly stress the significance for social and economic evolution of the use of seals and sealings. From EM2 onwards there is clear evidence for the widespread marking of containers, either directly with seals or through attached seal-stamped "nodules," and not only in the "proto-palace" courtyard complexes, but also in private houses (Schoep and Knappett 2004). Since this practice was adopted from Near Eastern state-societies, and is of little value in a village of egalitarian farmers, one should infer a generalized involvement of large numbers of EM Cretans in formal transactions of surplus agricultural products and manufactured or mined objects beyond the household economy. These could have been circulating in purely commercial networks, or to support religious or social networks. Confirmation comes through the widespread exchange of ceramics and clear evidence for craft specialization in the production of sealstones, bronze-work, and stone vases.

Burial and society

The mortuary sphere has been a major focus for our understanding of Early Minoan society, particularly since one tradition has a monumentality which stimulated early distribution maps and excavations. The stone beehive (tholos) tomb, essentially South Cretan, begins in EM, continues into MM, and still sees occasional use in LM. Xanthoudides produced an excellent study of these above-ground stone communal tombs of the Mesara Plain and surrounding hill-country as early as 1924. Excavations have continued ever since, whilst research on their location, demography, ritual, and social context have made them one of our best understood prehistoric Aegean monuments. Branigan's work since the 1970s is an outstanding contribution (Branigan 1993).

The tholos (Figure 4.5) is a circular burial chamber with thick stone foundations and lower courses, often

possessing rectangular antechambers. Roofs were stone slabs in some, but perhaps not all, cases. Burial was the primary function, and body-counts run to hundreds of individuals. Tholoi are usually isolated, but a significant minority appear in small clusters. The social group represented was originally envisaged as a rural village, with all community members being deposited. The Western Mesara Survey's discovery of a flat cemetery however warns us that tholoi were not the only burial locale (Relaki 2004). A major breakthrough for tholos studies came from the Agiofarango Survey (see Box).

Locational analysis of Minoan tholoi shows that they are rarely placed in eye-catching positions, but all were probably associated with a nearby settlement (Branigan 1998). The Agiofarango Survey indicates that these range from farms or hamlets to true village sites. An east-facing tomb door predominates (facing the life-giving sun?), but so is an avoidance of intervisibility to the domestic site (the living can see the house of the dead but the dead are prevented from "looking back"). Significantly, a minority of burials were loaded with stones or other obstacles as if to prevent a ghostly mobility, whilst even when one looks into tomb entrances there is usually a blocking wall from the main burial chamber preventing a direct sightline from outside.

The basic tholos burial rites created in EM still dominate through into their continued use and new constructions in the Palace eras (Murphy 1998): at first the dead were placed as inhumations carefully in the reopenable main chamber or the antechambers, with gifts and ceramics for death rituals. At a later point, perhaps when new burials were brought, the previous inhumation was pushed aside to join the disarticulated bone piles of the ancestors, whilst some body parts were removed, and sometimes skulls were left. Ethnoarchaeology (using anthropological accounts to suggest interpretations of archaeological data), including traditional Greek rural practices, suggests that the first stage of care treats the newly deceased as in a "liminal" (borderline) relationship between the living and the dead, still an individual, followed by a second stage in which he/she is merged into an undifferentiated ancestral "body."

Three kinds of additional ritual activity are associated with tholoi. Firstly, at a burial, mourners

Restored view and plan of the tomb at Apesokari, overlooking the Mesara plain

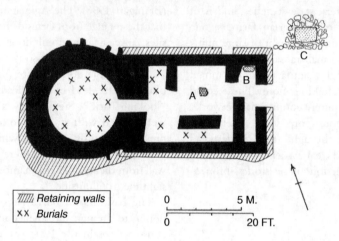

⊞ Retaining walls
xx Burials

0   5 M.

0   20 FT.

Figure 4.5   A Mesara communal tomb or tholos, Early and Middle Minoan. Whether the stone roof was a corbelled dome, or flat, is still disputed.
S. Hood, *The Minoans. Crete in the Bronze Age*. London 1971, Figure 127. Reconstruction drawn by Martin E. Weaver. Plan drawn by Patricia Clarke.

apparently poured libations and consumed liquids within the tomb confines, and subsequently revisited the tomb for similar "feasts of the dead," to judge by broken libation-vessels and cups outside the tholos. At a later stage such rituals became elaborate enough to cause the common construction of paved forecourts. Scholars speculate that these were "theaters" for more general ritual performances in which the cycle of death and birth of families, but also of the natural world, could be the subject. Were ritual dances a major component? A circular "dance floor" at the Palace of Knossos has been identified and linked to Greek

myths connecting Cretan dancing with such religious beliefs (Warren 1984).

Debate continues on the evidence for social divisions in the EM tholoi. They are better built than private domestic buildings, and clusters are seen by some as places of greater importance. But I have suggested (see Text Box) that multiple tholoi probably reflect the size of the associated settlement rather than political rank. More promising for social inferences are the gifts deposited. Especially from EM2 onwards, sealstones and metal daggers are common, and these are not everyday objects. Seals seem to mark

The Agiofarango Survey

This pioneer total fieldwalking survey of a 7 km long valley between limestone ridges (Blackman and Branigan 1977) aimed to uncover the Minoan countryside in unprecedented detail. My own contribution was to analyze prehistoric land use and social structure (Bintliff 1977a, Bintliff in Blackman and Branigan 1977).

The Minoan landscape consisted of settlements, tholos tombs, and putative peak sanctuaries (Figure 4.6). Domestic sites were small-scale, each denoting a farm or two; the one exception in the center of the valley was probably a hamlet or small village. Surface finds indicated that the dispersed farms and the nucleated site were largely contemporary, a pattern similar to that we have postulated for the Neolithic-EH of Southern Mainland Greece. The tholoi were surprisingly numerous for such a small district, and whilst two were on the edge of the hamlet, the rest were scattered regularly down the narrow valley. The peak sanctuaries were

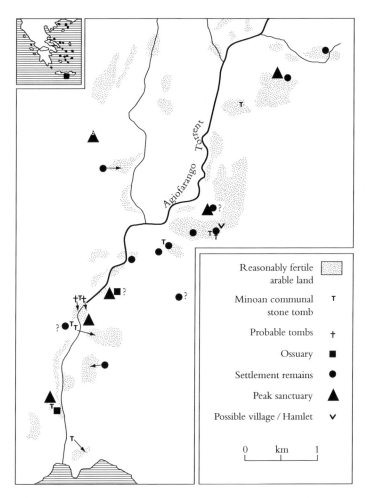

Figure 4.6 The Agiofarango Valley in Minoan times.
J. L. Bintliff, *Natural Environment and Human Settlement in Prehistoric Greece*. Oxford British Archaeological Reports 1977, Chapter 8, Figure 9.

a controversial identification, especially as some started in EM, since the site type was considered to commence from early palatial (MM) times. However, recent evidence elsewhere confirms such sanctuaries from EM2 times onwards, including perhaps what later became a major "state" peak shrine for the Knossos palace at Mount Iuktas (Day and Wilson 2002, Fitton 2002). Also novel was the discovery that the Agiofarango examples were on small rocky eminences rising out of the valley floor, whereas peak sanctuaries had previously been identified on prominent hill or mountain tops. Nonetheless, their unusual finds, and the physical unsuitability as occupation sites, together with the absence of tomb structures, made Blackman and Branigan's interpretation the most likely.

Although in the 1970s farming had virtually ceased in the surveyed sector of the valley, I was able to map a series of discontinuous blocks of land suitable for cultivation (Figure 4.6, and see Bintliff 1977b), revealing that the dispersed Minoan farms and tholoi marked associated scattered landholdings belonging to discrete social groups who mostly lived and buried by these fertile patches. The limited areas of land, and the closeness of these dispersed locations, indicated small units of people, probably one to a few families. The double

tholoi at the hamlet was appropriate for a larger social group. To test this hypothesis independently, I examined estimates for body counts amongst the dug Mesara region tholoi, and taking the length of tomb use into account, confirmed that the typical tomb-using group was just a few families.

If the mini-peak sanctuaries are correctly identified, the Minoan population of the valley inhabited a small nucleation and a series of satellite farms, distributed following the patches of cultivable land, and accompanied by similarly dispersed small (family?) shrines. Including the upper valley not surveyed at that time, the total Minoan population was probably well within the scale of a face-to-face community (less than 200 people) and would necessarily have practiced exogamous marriages with nearby social groups at the same demographic scale. The Agiofarango settlement pattern does not evidence elite groups, although the burial finds from the Mesara regional tholoi when taken as a whole may suggest that a minority of the dead with richer gifts possessed higher status in their associated rural communities. However, heads of small kin groups or families more successful in their crop and animal production ("Big Men"), could have received more valuable burial-gifts, without this implying a local elite class.

personal identity and perhaps private property rights, whilst metal was imported and weapon display could be as much for social power as everyday function. Careful excavations of tholoi have been rare, problematizing comparison of gifts to the number of dead. Whitelaw (1983), assuming that daggers marked male family heads, was led to argue that tholoi were for single families. However, comparing body numbers to how long the tomb was in use indicates that rarely one, but more commonly several, families were responsible (Bintliff 1977a). Branigan (1993) reanalyzed the occurrence of gifts and concluded that two to three and rarely one family was typical for the burying group. The frequency of daggers then marks just selected males in a social group larger than the head of each nuclear family. Karytinos (1998) and Maggidis

(1998) suggest that in well-excavated tomb contexts seals also occur too rarely for individual family use, and rather seem to be used by a minority, arguably higher-status group.

Branigan (1993), Murphy (1998), and Karytinos (1998) feel that in the final stages of the pre-Palatial era (EM3-MM1A) tholos and other built tombs elsewhere in Crete were being used by a rising social elite to legitimate their power, providing a platform for the following emergence of palace-states. Some multiple-tomb sites (e.g., Arkhanes) became theaters of kin-group competition and display in tomb dimensions and gifts, whilst single tomb locations remained in the previous mode of egalitarian rurality. Likewise, Sbonias (1999) used late EM and pre-Palatial MM1A sealstone types and distributions to identify a small

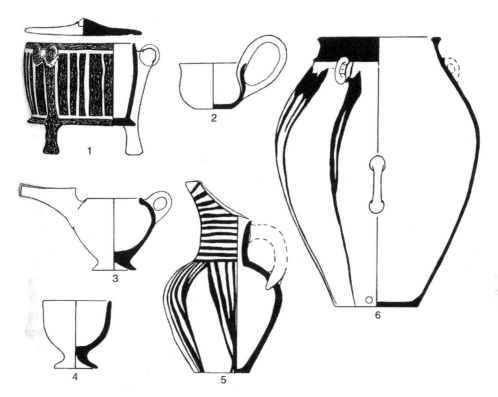

Figure 4.7   Selected Early Minoan wares, emphasizing the significance of drinking sets.
K. Branigan (ed.), *Cemetery and Society in the Aegean Bronze Age.* Sheffield 1998, Figures 1.5 and 8.1. Reproduced by permission of Continuum International Publishing Group.

number of larger settlements with an emergent elite, amidst an undifferentiated sea of villages and farms lacking social classes.

The non-tholos rectangular tombs of Central and Eastern Crete are relevant to this debate. Here, communal tombs are also characteristic for EM, although these are square or rectangular complexes of one to three rooms. Gifts and practices seem nonetheless comparable to the tholoi of South-Central Crete. Yet at Mochlos and Gournia the more modest tombs were placed in less prominent locations in the cemetery, and are poorer in finds. The more prominent and monumental house-tombs are associated with gifts of silver and gold cups and other precious finds, whilst such tombs have built terraces, shrines, and elaborate paved piazzas (Soles 1978, 1992; Whitelaw 2004).

As in EN-MN Greece, there is striking use of elaborately formed and decorated ceramics suitable for

social dining and drinking in EM Crete (Figure 4.7). Apart from ceremonial deposits around and inside communal tombs, sets of appropriate wares also occur in clusters in settlement sites, especially the large "town-like" centers which will transform into "palaces" across or at the end of this period. These special deposits are taken by some to signify large-scale community feasting, perhaps reflecting the emergence of controlling families in the larger sites, coordinating ritual ceremonies and the display and consumption of surplus agricultural products (Driessen 2007).

Nonetheless, some scholars remain skeptical about the complexity of EM society. Watrous (1994) found no convincing evidence for a ranked society on Crete before the appearance of the First Palaces in MM1B, rejecting the emergent elite thesis of Branigan, Soles, and subsequently Driessen and Schoep. This creates difficulties in accounting for the implied scenario of an immediately-subsequent, rapid, and widespread rise of palace-states. Moreover most authorities reject older theories of the arrival of new peoples or an elite at the end of EM, or a wave of civilizational "know-how" from Egypt or the Levant, which would set up these palaces from nothing. What is decisive for me is the likelihood that by the end of the Neolithic some later palace locations were large, even town-like communities, arguably complex corporate communities comparable to emergent city-states. On both these grounds, and the accumulating stratigraphic evidence from Driessen and Schoep, I prefer the view that during EM some larger settlements were theaters of political evolution ("court-complexes"), where leading families dominated large nucleated populations, whilst these centers already played a controlling role over surrounding rural communities. Following Sbonias, sealstones may have been an important part of status rivalry through the manipulation of food and craft surpluses. The fact that EM tombs do not clearly reflect all this need not surprise us when we learn that even during the First and Second Palace periods only one or two tombs can be claimed as symbolizing elite status.

Further symbolic culture in EM Crete

One of the most intriguing objects from the village of Fournoi Korifi is a vessel in the form of a woman, nicknamed the "Goddess of Myrtos." Its location was in the main room of a house, near a bench interpreted as an altar, suggesting a shrine. An adjacent storeroom contained a large collection of small fine ware vases and capacious storage jars. The presence of the female image in this context could confirm the association already suggested for Neolithic female figurines, between the home, fertility, and the nourishing and protection of human, animal, and crop reproduction (Preziosi and Hitchcock 1999).

The Early Minoan 3 crisis

Another, startling, fact in the puzzle of palatial origins is the apparent disasters of EM3 across the island (Watrous 1994). Surveys show a general pattern of the desertion of numerous settlements after EM2, then an MM1 resettlement of the landscape. This is supported

from excavations, where the end of EM2 sees destruction and abandonment of many sites. At the major settlement of Knossos, where EM3 has been identified, it cannot be securely tied to a phase of human occupation. At Vasiliki, after fire-destruction at the end of EM2, just a small area contains meager EM3 finds.

We have reviewed the evidence for, and explanations of, a similar catastrophe on the late EH Mainland. Also on Crete a combination of warfare and ecological stress might be invoked. The evidence, unusual for Bronze Age Crete, for defended sites or defenses at otherwise open settlements in the period EM3-MM1 (Aghia Photia, Malia, Gournia) (Fitton 2002), surely marks unparalleled threats to Minoan society. Watrous (*pers. comm.*) believes that the practice of frequently merging EM3-MM1 ceramics to a single period may conceal greater discontinuities, and hypothesizes that a wave of new settlement locations in Eastern Crete might represent additional colonizers from the Cyclades.

Early Cycladic Culture

Introduction: The character of the Cyclades in later prehistory

The Bronze Age of the Central Aegean islands attracted attention from the nineteenth century. Small cist-grave cemeteries furnished with unique stone vessels, attractive ceramics, and strange stone figurines revealed a distinctive prehistoric Cycladic culture. Renfrew uncovered the later Neolithic colonizers of the Cyclades through excavations at Saliagos (Evans and Renfrew 1968), and systematized and reinterpreted the succeeding Early, Middle, and Late Cycladic Bronze Age phases (EC, MC, and LC) (Renfrew 1972). He subsequently used the important results of his excavations at the MC-LC town of Phylakopi on Melos to shed deeper light into the archaeology of this and the other islands (Renfrew and Wagstaff 1982). Further landmarks were his monograph on the LC shrine at Phylakopi (Renfrew 1985) and another on EC figurines (Renfrew 1991). On the island of Kea, American excavations at Kephala (Coleman 1977) and Aghia Irini (published as the *Keos* monographs), and field survey in the hinterland of the

Classical city of Koressia (Cherry *et al.* 1991), deepened knowledge of the Cycladic LN-BA. Spectacular Greek excavations at the "Pompeii of the Aegean" by Marinatos and Doumas, the MC-LC town of Akrotiri on the island of Santorini-Thera, have revealed intensive interactions between Cycladic societies and Minoan Crete (Forsyth 1999). Davis (1992) and Broodbank (2000) have provided novel insights into the social dynamics and maritime interactions of the islands with each other and with surrounding larger land masses (the Mainland and Crete).

The Cyclades have also been a magnet for holiday-makers from cooler climates since popular tourism swept across them in the later nineteenth century. Limited agricultural resources, an arid climate, and predominantly rocky environments have encouraged the perception that traditional island life before mech-anization had probably changed little from prehistory. Nowadays the Cyclades are sustained primarily from outside, through tourist income or European Community and Greek state subsidies, but visitors could imagine that in pre-Modern times each island was largely self-sufficient, often focused on a single central harbor-town, balancing mixed farming with fishing, but exploiting close inter-island and island to Mainland distances to indulge in circular trade. Renfrew and Wagstaff (1982), and Cherry (1990) in wider studies of the colonization and early develop-ment of these and other Mediterranean islands, identified islands such as the Cyclades as ideal "labora-tories" for studying social change, based on a predominance of isolation punctuated by episodes of external intervention.

Broodbank (2000) however, noting that the density of the Cycladic islands is without Mediterranean par-allel, with total intervisibility (cf. Chapman 1990), challenges the assumption of each island as a bounded community. He convincingly demonstrates that Cycladic culture has always been a community of inter-island links, with regular if less intense interac-tions to both adjacent east and west Mainlands.

What is the significance of the EBA era on the Cyclades (EC) in itself, and as a precursor of the fol-lowing MC-LC eras? Actually in none of these peri-ods do we find palaces or indubitable states emerging locally. Even by the Late Bronze Age, the scarce signs of archives in the form of tablets, and the one or two

residences of possible state officials, appear in contexts of external domination, or at least overwhelming influence, from the Minoan and then Mycenaean states on the periphery of the Cyclades (Renfrew and Wagstaff 1982, Davis 1992). What *can* however be seen are island towns, and although the first of these only appear at the very end of the EC period, there are earlier fortified villages which some see as their beginning.

The first settlement

A limited settlement of near-Mainland islands in Mesolithic and EN-MN times was followed by a wider occupation of the Cyclades as part of the expansive colonization throughout Greece during the LN-FN periods (ca. 5200–3200 BC). Significantly, although the advent of ard ploughs and pastoral sec-ondary products provided key stimuli for occupying the generally less attractive agricultural environments of the Cyclades, the first sites show a strong locational interest in deep fish-rich bays, particularly in the first clear culture, that of Saliagos. Crops and domestic ani-mals formed the economic foundations, but marine resources were probably a significant buffer against seasonal food shortages as well as a common food supplement. Since boats till the late EBA were beached not anchored, deep bays suggest wider resources than mere storm shelter. That marine food acted as a useful dietary supplement at certain times of the year, if not being consumed alongside more regu-lar food staples, is confirmed by the dietary analysis of human bones from the EC site of Daskaleio (Broodbank 2000).

The Saliagos culture

The known LN Saliagos settlements are estimated at 70–150 inhabitants each, appropriate to face-to-face communities stabilized by social fission. Succeeding FN villages of 50–150 occupants had a similar econ-omy. However, for viable demography, several of these settlements must have combined in exogamous mar-riage networks. We must imagine the venues of social gatherings either circulating around the component villages, or at a communal location, much as tradi-tional Mediterranean villagers visit each other's annual festivals. The long existence of seaworthy boats made such meetings possible, especially in summer, when little farming activity occurred and when seas were calmest.

Final Neolithic

Nonetheless, the discovery of double fortification walls, one bastioned, at the FN site of Strophilos on Andros (Televantou in *Horizon*), associated with rock-carvings of longboats, may indicate how quickly settlement and marine mobility may have led to raiding and less positive intercommunity interactions. It is surely no coincidence that this period sees the creation of fortified sites on the nearby Mainland and Crete.

The EC1 Grotta Pelos culture (ca. 3200–2800 BC)

This first Early Cycladic phase sees a dramatic rise in site numbers, yet these are usually small, apparently representing dispersed farmsteads of 1–2 families (Bintliff 1977a). Many are close to small dispersed cemeteries of individual stone cist (box) graves, where burial numbers would also be appropriate for a few families over several generations, whilst the dead reflect all ages and both genders. In many respects this landscape recalls the EM Agiofarango, except that Minoan tholoi are reusable communal tombs representing centuries of use.

Cherry (1979) observed acutely that the new density of EC farms was misleading. Since the EC period as a whole was very long, whilst a typical small site was in use for just a generation or two, only a handful of known sites could have been in contemporary use. EC farmers presumably exploited estates for a limited period, then shifted to another patch of fertile land. Given the arid climate, rocky soil, and low numbers of stock providing farmland manure, this is a sensible adaptation for keeping soils fertile after intensive use, but only feasible when population is low and land is plentiful. Renfrew (1972) calculated a Neolithic Cycladic population of 3000, and for EC more than 34,000, but Cherry downscaled this to just a few thousand for EC times (1979, Wagstaff and Cherry 1982). Broodbank (2000) notes that EM

Knossos, estimated at 1290–1940 occupants, was not far below the entire Early Cycladic island population.

Despite the evidence of a distinct link between communities and land use possibilities, and a low population, artifacts show that exchange systems around the Cyclades were expanding in types and quantity. Marble vessels are a notable feature, and closed pottery shapes could have been used to contain traded materials. Yet the social needs of these dispersed, low-density societies were the same as before, and we would expect that several islands must have engaged in regular communal activities for marriage exchange, festivities which would have offered a prime opportunity for ritualized or purely functional trade. I still consider it possible that migratory fishing was another medium for inter-island contacts. Again as Broodbank rightly adds, small islands must always have depended on other larger ones to stay viable demographically.

Sites which might have served for integrative festivals, and other social and economic interactions, are still hard to demonstrate, however, and even the typical face-to-face village of the LN-FN was largely replaced by the small EC farm. One suggested locale is the Zas Cave on Naxos, where possible ritual deposits go back into LN-FN times. The existence there of accompanying domestic debris would strengthen rather than weaken the idea of a communal festival focus. Another element worth introducing is the symbolic culture now becoming more elaborate after simple beginnings in the Cycladic LN-FN. Figurines begin in the latter period but now become common, and are claimed to show distinct personal features, whilst also being mostly female. Perhaps linked with these is the fact that burials show diversity in gifts. Broodbank (2000) suggests that these aspects of symbolic culture and death ritual might reflect the importance of women marrying into other communities and bringing necessary fertility to small population groups, together with a recognition of individuals as nodes in social interactions which were vital to hold this dispersed society together.

In contrast to Neolithic Thessaly then, where Perlès sees symbolic culture as soothing friction in a very densely populated settlement system, we here see it serving to stimulate *closer* interaction in a very low-density settlement system. The appearance of

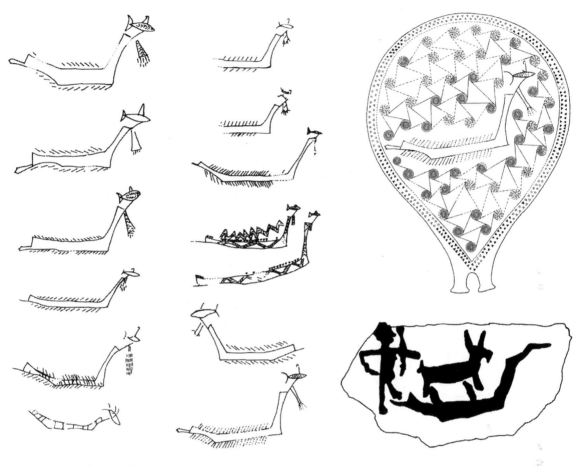

Figure 4.8 Early Cycladic boats.
C. Broodbank, *An Island Archaeology of the Early Cyclades.* © Cambridge University Press 2000, Figure 23.

fortifications at various stages from the FN to late EC in the islands may however indicate that raiding occurred too, an alternative way to obtain tradable items and wives. Indeed the impressively fortified if small settlements of Strofilas and Markiani, established in FN and EC1 respectively, can be linked to the better-known EC2–3 walled villages to suggest that the whole EC era saw a constant awareness of warfare (Renfrew, Introduction in *Horizon*).

Boats

What kind of boats were in use? Thorough recent research by McGeehan Liritizis (1988) and Broodbank (2000) enlightens us. Sadly, the EBA "shipwreck" from Dokos is not certainly a ship and anyway lacks a hull, whilst lead boat models could be recent forgeries. Securer evidence comes instead from depictions on Cycladic pottery (Figure 4.8). Two boat types are proposed, both longboats: a small and large boat, the latter being rowed by up to 25 oarsmen. The images prevent us seeing if the hull was a tree dugout or a clinker (constructed from overlapping planks); the former is possible for the small shape, but might be difficult for the larger. A notable feature is a high stern sometimes decorated with a large fish. Only at the end of the EC do we see Aegean depictions of sails and a deep hull, marking the diffusion of a more advanced ship-type from the Eastern Mediterranean.

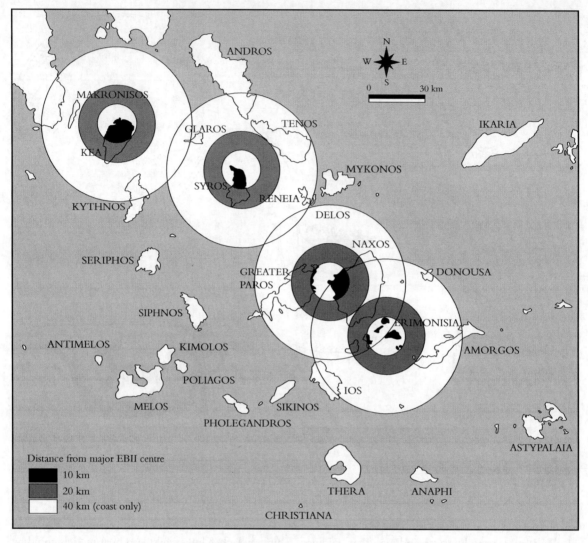

Figure 4.9   Travel ranges in the Early Cycladic Aegean from major island foci. The chief centers indicated, north to south, are Aghia Irini (Kea), Chalandriani (Syros), Grotta Aplomata (Naxos), and Daskaleio (Keros).
C. Broodbank, *An Island Archaeology of the Early Cyclades*. © Cambridge University Press 2000, Figure 85.

Since EC communities were small, manning the larger boat was a community effort of considerable risk. Broodbank believes this occurred for war, trading, ceremonies, and in general for long-range voyaging, leaving the small version for day-to-day fishing, local social visits, and carrying stock to dispersed grazing land. Even the larger boat however, with its shallow draft, could not have moved significant cargoes, although both types allowed easy beaching

almost anywhere, rather than requiring protected anchorages.

Based on experimental archaeology on such sailless boats and ethnographic records of island mobility patterns, Broodbank estimates that the small boats could travel 20 km per day, or a 10 km return trip, the larger 40–50 km per day, or a 20+ km return trip (Figure 4.9). Mapping the first range shows that the smaller boats could travel locally around specific islands on a day-return basis, and reach a neighboring island in a day. The second range, plotted around the larger settlements which appear in EC2, creates day-return visits to one or more neighboring islands; but within a single day-long journey large blocks of the Cyclades are generally neatly focused on access to or from a single larger settlement, hinting that everyone was probably in reach of a larger population center. This two-level network of communications surely suggests how these generally dispersed and low-density populations formed social interactions at different temporal and demographic scales. Although larger sites appear absent in the west, similar radial networks presumably operated there too, either from undiscovered examples, or from islands settled by dispersed settlements. Since socio-demographic factors required communal gatherings of the inhabitants of dispersed island farmsteads, even if at open countryside festivities, such foci need not be large settlements as in the eastern islands. Indeed one possible non-residential ceremonial center has been identified in mature EC times (see below).

The EC2 period: The Keros-Syros culture

In this central, most flourishing era an "International Spirit" was created, which spread outwards to Crete and the Eastern Greek Mainland in cultural influence and imitation (Renfrew 1972). The cultural assemblage (Figure 4.10) includes the "sauceboats" (in pottery, occasionally metal), pedestal-based collared jars, "frying pans," metal weapons and jewelry, and the bulk of the famous figurines.

Site numbers rise further, but remain predominantly dispersed farms and small-group cemeteries. However some previous farms grow into villages, and additional population nucleations appear. The larger sites are nonetheless rarely more than a hectare in size, the key ones being Aghia Irini (Kea), Chalandriani-Kastro (Syros), Grotta Aplomata (Naxos), and Skarkos (Ios). Daskaleio-Kavos (Keros) is also extensive, but of disputed function. Estimated populations for these "centers," 150–250 people, retains them in a "face-to-face" mode, requiring exogamy for long-term survival. Like the EH Mainland, dependence on a penumbra of small farms or neighboring villages was

necessary for social reproduction. Given the likelihood that the small farms recorded were rarely contemporary, indicating low population densities, a wide social interaction sphere is indicated to bring families regularly together, reinforcing the importance of maritime travel.

However on the rim of the Cyclades there are important exceptions to these generalizations, but on other Aegean islands. The most striking is the site of Manika (Sampson 2006), on Evvoia, a large island virtually part of the Eastern Mainland, where mixed Helladic and Cycladic (and in EH3 also Anatolian) cultural features appear. This remarkable settlement at its maximum covers 50–80 ha, although it is unclear how large the domestic zone was at any one time. It was a planned town with streets, regular house orientation, and fortifications, perhaps throughout the Early Bronze Age. The site of Kolonna on the island of Aegina is similarly placed between the Mainland and the Cyclades, but despite a size befitting a small village, its town-like plan and suspected political organization are also surprisingly complex. Further afield, in the North Aegean, the islands of Lemnos and Chios possess nucleated sites (Poliochni and Thermi respectively), small it seems and also of face-to-face scale (Davis 1992), although likewise surprisingly complex socially, since they are argued to exhibit resident elites (Kouka 2002). Significantly, these can be compared with the nearby Troad region of mainland Northwest Anatolia, where Early Bronze 2 Troy (Korfmann et al. 2001, Bintliff 2002) possesses a walled acropolis (Upper Town) with plausible "elite" mansions as well as a defended Lower Town. However in this case Troy II is 9 ha, probably a demographically self-sufficient proto-urban agglomeration or proto-city state.

Taken together, the Mainland Early Helladic Corridor Houses, Anatolian Troy, the Northeast Aegean fortified villages, and perhaps also Manika, may well evidence complex societies, either organized by an elite, or at least achieving corporate, proto-city state form. On Crete, despite the valid deconstruction of special status for certain rural architectural complexes, we have also seen that it is likely that proto-city state corporate communities existed in Early Minoan times at key later palace sites such as Knossos, Malia, and Phaistos, plausibly also with a controlling

Figure 4.10 Typical ceramic and metal pot forms of Early Cycladic 2.
C. Broodbank, *An Island Archaeology of the Early Cyclades*. © Cambridge University Press 2000, Figure 60.

elite class. In contrast, the Early Cycladic cultures of the Cyclades merely evidence face-to-face villages, something extremely common in earlier Neolithic Greece, although the contemporary burial evidence (see below) points to community leaders. Is it because of the complexity of essential maritime networks, and the strong suggestions for intercommunal warfare,

that such small EC communities nonetheless supported elite families?

The known Early Cycladic nucleated settlements possessed clear advantages for social and economic interaction and their members must have cooperated in maritime activity (a 25-man longboat would have to be supported by a minimum total community of

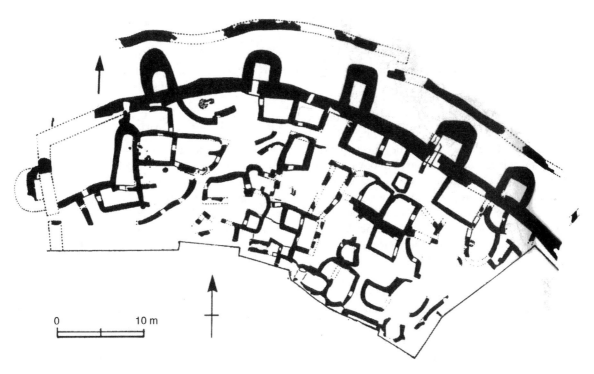

Figure 4.11 The fortified enclosure site at Chalandriani, Syros.
O. Dickinson, *The Aegean Bronze Age*. © Cambridge University Press 1994, Figure 4.5.

around 125 when we include their wives and children). Nonetheless it is puzzling that they are still too small (150–250 estimated) and had to intermarry with a wider social group of some 500 people for long-term reproduction. Broodbank (2000) is aware of this, and the map reproduced in Figure 4.9 of day-voyages in longboats radiating out from the known EC2 villages covers at least all of the Eastern Cyclades. But it is unclear if even these "small worlds," in which all the associated small and larger islands in each identified cluster might meet at a fixed point for festivals, contained 500 people. If these clusters needed to exchange partners *between* each other, the map reveals that this either required journeys of two days, or, perhaps more likely, a location at the joint border of two clusters might have acted as a meeting-point. Maybe an anomaly on this map gives a clue in this direction: there is a major overlap between the Naxos-centered radius and that placed around Daskaleio-Kavos on Keros to its south in the Eriminisia islands. This might support the view of some scholars that Daskaleio was

not a permanent settlement at all, but a ceremonial meeting-place, since it lies at the rim of the Naxos cluster and could have allowed the populations of two clusters to interact.

Chalandriani-Kastri (Syros) and Daskaleio-Kavos (Keros)

At Chalandriani (Figure 4.11) a nucleated 1 ha EC2 settlement is associated with several cemeteries, but relocates in later EC2 to an adjacent hilltop with bastioned drystone walls. Broodbank (2000) on site area suggested 100–300 inhabitants, but Hekman's exhaustive (2003) analysis of the cemeteries lowers this to 75–100.

The Daskaleio-Kavos complex of findspots supports varied interpretations. The latest research identifies a fortified settlement on Daskaleio island of EC2 date (which with lower EBA sea levels was joined to the mainland), and on the adjacent main Keros island at Kavos another, open settlement of the same period, a metallurgical area, and a "Special Deposit" of EC1–3 age (Renfrew and Sotirakopoulou in *Horizon*). Doumas (1972) proposed Kavos as a burial zone for a mobile trading group, with the dead being conveyed here. Renfrew (1991) compared it to the Classical role of the islet of Delos in the center of the Cyclades, as a pan-Cycladic sanctuary with many ritual deposits. We observed earlier (Figure 4.9), that its longboat radius is not discrete but overlaps with another; its marginal location could have acted as a border meeting-place for the inhabitants of the Grotta Aplomata "small world" *and* that which should exist for the Southern Cyclades. If Kavos and Daskaleio are permanent settlements, their surface area implies 100–150 people each. Like Chalandriani, external partnerships for social reproduction still seem necessary, even if the two sites are contemporary. Renfrew's recent project at the "Special Deposit" has not confirmed its regional "sanctuary role," and the degree of robbing cannot rule out that it was originally a rich cemetery. Nonetheless there does seem to be unparalleled ceremonial deposition of hundreds of already-broken figurines, marble bowls, and ceramics, as well as local-ized parts of human bodies, which might still indicate some remarkable religious significance to the locality, although how far this extended beyond the island of Keros remains unclear.

The finds from these two important sites, and from other villages, are more numerous and varied than from typical EC2 farm sites, showing greater exchange activity in marble, metal, or pottery. However, a settle-ment 30 to 40 times the size of a family farm would naturally exhibit extraordinary artifact densities and a wider spectrum of types, not only due to sampling problems, but also because such nucleations were also magnets for social interactions between near and dis-tant communities. To propose that there was a political hierarchy of central places and subordinate farms requires better arguments than these alone, especially as the scale of these nucleations is clearly that of villages not town or even proto-town. Thus the importance of recent discoveries of late EC2 clay sealings from the Cave of Zas (Naxos) and the small (if fortified) settlement of Markiani (Amorgos) (Marangou in *Horizon*), suggesting links with the Lerna sealings and the common use of seals in later EM Crete. Although inadequate to demonstrate a redistributive, centralized economy, they suggest far more than simple household organization of products, bringing the Cyclades into the orbit of early systems of property marking and perhaps organized distribu-tion of goods, which might indeed reflect Early Cycladic class distinctions (Renfrew 2004).

The islands of the Northeast Aegean

The EC Cyclades till recently lacked possible elite residences to match their occasional wealthy burials, whilst larger sites merely indicate communal cooper-ation and warfare. Recent discoveries of larger build-ings are still not clearly elite homes. Clearer social classes are recognizable in the Northeastern Aegean islands and adjacent Anatolian Mainland. Preziosi and Hitchcock (1999) compare EH Corridor Houses with the "mansion-like" enclosed site, with bastioned walls, at the settlement of Troy II, where a fortified inner acropolis with formal entry gates leads to one large and four smaller "megaron" houses (a plan with sequent access chambers), plausibly elite dwellings (Korfmann *et al.* 2001). Detailed study of EBA "towns" on the islands of Lemnos, Lesbos, Samos, and Chios (Kouka 2002) argues that alongside communal facili-ties and infrastructural provision (town planning, a coherent street system, defensive walls, public store-houses and water control, and possible meeting-houses), a resident elite group are strongly indicated (a dominant house or walled-off complex associated with metalworking, and by the presence of prestige goods and hoards as well as sealing practices).

Metallurgy and other trade items

Cycladic marble is a famous resource, and was already widely exploited in this period, but the sources of contemporary Aegean metals have required scientific analyses to trace exchange routes. The island of Siphnos produced silver, gold, lead, and possibly cop-per, and Kythnos copper, whilst the Mainland region of Attica, within easy communication for the Cyclades, and including sites with a strong Cycladic cultural content, produced silver, lead, and copper. Remarkably the island population centers do not coincide with lithic or metal sources (Nakou 1995), suggesting that population nucleation may reflect land use and demography, and positioning in relation to maritime social networks, rather than trade and industry. Larger settlements may also signify the "historical" achievements of particular social groups. The continuing wide spread of Cycladic obsidian throughout the Aegean raises issues of who was responsible and how much organization was involved. Carter (1998) notes that key larger sites on the coasts of the Mainland and Northern Crete have more Cycladic obsidian than some of the Cycladic islands, and on Crete it is often obtained for burial gifts and prestige more than for everyday use. The founding of small-scale Cycladic colonies in such areas has been proposed, and may indicate opportunistic trading ventures, for which the Neolithic model of Perlès (see Chapter 3) provides an older foundation.

Cycladic ceramics were exchanged between the islands but also with the Greek Mainland, and such products were also copied locally beyond the Cyclades. Taken with the other evidence for widespread circulation of lithic tool material, metals, grinding-stone, marble, and perhaps wine to Crete, this has encouraged several scholars to envisage the Cycladic economy as driven by manufacturing and trade (e.g., Marthari in *Horizon*). Without underestimating the vigorous exchanges now documented, one must beware of incorporating modern economics into ancient and prehistoric societies, since this tends to ignore other mechanisms of a more social and cultural nature. Moreover the existence of a class of very small settlements entirely dependent on trade for food seems an unlikely scenario for this era, prompting the proposal that communities might rather have supplemented agricultural and fishing activities with local and long-distance exchanges.

Social structure

Renfrew (1972) portrayed the Early Bronze Age as transitional between the relatively egalitarian village societies of the Neolithic and the highly hierarchical state societies of the Middle and Late Bronze Age, a Chieftain society. Yet the Cyclades offer ambiguous evidence. Larger sites with a wider variety and number of trade goods, as well as weaponry in some graves, and individual burials with more than average gifts in larger cemeteries, need not imply permanent Chieftains. These larger sites, though sometimes

fortified, are villages, with populations probably within face-to-face parameters. Richer graves could be older males of more prominent families, key nodes in small scale kin-based societies, rather than an aristocracy. Broodbank (2000) sees them as "Big Men," persons of temporary community status based on individual achievement in social or economic affairs. However Hekman (2003), analyzing the Chalandriani cemetery, offers a convincing argument for both "clan" groups and a communal leading family (see below).

The larger longboats required a major part or even the majority of village males, indicating a communal decision to undertake voyaging for the benefit of the village. Inter-island raiding might explain the defenses of several sites, with metal, other trade items, and women as booty. The defended FN site of Strophilos could mark an early start to piracy. However, given the demographic dependence of even larger villages on other settlements, such aggression might have been against more distant settlements, pooling warriors from a larger village and its surrounding farms and hamlets to attack the next "small world" of like type. A failed raid, or a shipwreck during exchange ceremonies, would have been catastrophic to the community left behind. Broodbank rightly suggests that longboat trips gave rise to songs and poems of the deeds of the ancestors, whilst the boats themselves, requiring communal effort, were probably surrounded by ritual.

Were the village sites foci of economic power? Through their likely domination of exchange networks they plausibly tied the smaller sites around them to their populations, whilst it was probably these larger communities that organized longboat construction and voyaging. These links can explain the spread of similar styles of decorated pottery, both copies and real exports. One area where recent research shows promising insights into social organization is the recognition of one substantial building in several settlements, although these are variously interpreted as sanctuaries (Strofilas), chief's houses (Ftelia), and Cycladic parallels to administrative-central storage structures of the Mainland Corridor House type (Koukounaries, on which see Katsarou-Tzevelaki and Schilardi in *Horizon*).

Burials in the EC are cist graves for individuals or rarely for several presumed family members, usually with limited, probably personal objects as gifts. The small size of most cemeteries, their wide dispersal over the islands, and their normal use-life of a few generations, marked the land and probably homes of rural families. Exceptions, such as the 1000 or more burials associated with the village of Chalandriani on Syros, given the timescale of the settlement complex and cemetery, of some 400–600 years, offer a remarkable chance to probe deeper into EC society (Hekman 2003). The early EC2 settlement, ca 1 ha, probably lies under modern Chalandriani village, succeeded in late EC2 by a smaller fortified settlement at Kastri to the north. The associated cemetery lies between them. The graves are almost entirely individual drystone built tombs with small corbelled roofs, facing east and down to the sea and a small bay. Is this alignment, like Cretan tholos tombs, facing the life-giving sun but away from the sight of the living? Hekman prefers a prosaic explanation, the dominant sloping topography. Many excavations cumulatively indicate some 1000 original tombs, but this when spread over time reduces to a living population of 75–100 people, or 10–14 nuclear families.

The minority of graves with usable records can on statistical analysis of their contents be split roughly equally between what appear to be female and male graves (Clusters 1 and 3), and apart from the likely absence of infants, seem to contain the entire community. The female graves have a round plan, bowls, jars, pans, stone tools, palettes, bone tubes for pigment, and pigment itself. Male graves are rectangular in form and contain cups, metal tools, and specific ornaments. Cluster 2 graves are both male and female but are distinctive through kits argued to be for tattooing, perhaps signaling an age group. Within the cemetery are five spatially-discrete groups of tombs, argued to be small kin groups of 2–3 families each (thus hardly "boat communities," as almost the entire settlement's adult males would be needed to man the larger longboats). As for wealth variations, 75 percent of recorded grave contents have just 0–3 items, whilst 25 percent contain two-thirds of all gifts. In the well-published sample, two burials represented a tiny elite class with far higher assemblages (17 and 29 pieces respectively). Hekman argues persuasively that the 25 percent wealthier graves were heads of families, both male and female, whilst the richest exceptional burials in the sample are representative of single community leaders, perhaps for each generation of use of the site. It is notable that "wealth" was shown less by exclusive access to special artifacts but rather through the number of items (which might reflect accumulated property but also grave-gifts from a larger number of mourners).

If the entire community could man 2–3 small boats or a single longboat, the role of the community leader could be closely tied to expeditions to other islands for socialization, exchange, and perhaps raiding. This agrees with the analysis noted earlier for Levkas by Kilian-Dirlmeier (2005), who suggests that the EBA Aegean was a mosaic of different levels of social complexity. She argues that maritime activity was a suitable nexus in which certain families might have developed higher status in the community through the successful organization of high-risk but high-profit expeditions. This seems plausible to account for the rare appearance of very rich graves in such small communities.

Other interaction spheres

As we have already observed, the Cyclades interact at a lesser scale with other cultural networks linked by proximity and the sea (Broodbank 2000). In the Northeast Aegean the town at Troy shows strong connections to the island walled settlements on Lemnos and Lesbos. Advanced bronze metallurgy occurs, and in late EB2 these products and skills spread into the Aegean metal zone dominated by the Cycladic culture. In the Southeast Mainland and the adjacent islands of Euboea and Kea, a network of big coastal EB2 villages has been recognized (Aghia Irini, Aghios Kosmas, Askitario, and Raphina), along with several sites dominated by the seemingly giant settlement at Manika. Worth noting is their mixed Helladic and Cycladic culture. Possible Cycladic settlement on northern coastal Crete is matched by Cretan colonization of Kythera island off the southeast Peloponnese (Zapheiropoulou in *Horizon*).

Late EC2 and EC3

We have already seen that the final phase of the Aegean Early Bronze Age witnesses widespread cultural dislocation and destructions. Thus signs of change in late EC2 are of interest. The spread of Northeastern Aegean metallurgy is associated with Anatolian pottery styles which indicate new forms of food and drink consumption and the gradual introduction of wheel-thrown technology for making ceramics to supplement continued handmade production. On the other hand, the increase in fortifications around the larger Cycladic villages in this Kastri subphase has been connected to these novelties, to suggest an invasion or migration into Southern Greece by people from the North Aegean or adjacent Mainlands.

Careful evaluations (Davis 1992, Rutter 1993) play down the implications of these new cultural influences in ceramics and metal, whilst the increase in fortifications follows earlier EH2 walls on the Mainland and in the Northeast Aegean, and growing evidence for Cycladic fortifications from FN through to EC2. Migrations are thus seen skeptically. Since there are certainly serious human destructions throughout the EB3 Aegean, one should be cautious in denying that cultural redirections and increased signs of intercommunity warfare in the *preceding* late EC2 period might not shed light on this.

The EBA 3 period (ca. 2200–2000 BC) is one of dramatic changes. For EC3 the poverty of data reflects large-scale abandonments of major and small sites, and at certain settlements clear further destructions, with as much as a 150–200 year gap possible before reoccupation or resettlement occurs (Rutter 1993). We earlier introduced the various theories for this catastrophe, but in reviewing the Cyclades Davis and Rutter are skeptical of most explanations:

1. The "Coming of the Greeks" theory is difficult to reconcile with the cultural changes noted, and is not necessarily required by the linguistic evidence.
2. Sherratt and Sherratt's proposition (1993) of an Aegean destabilized by being drawn into larger commercial and political spheres emanating from the advanced states of the Eastern Mediterranean is problematic, since Aegean involvement in such spheres is slight until the developed Middle Bronze Age.
3. Widespread soil erosion has ambivalent chronology and effects (negative and positive), although

possible ties with a contemporary phase of prolonged Eastern Mediterranean drought coincident with EB3 could just conceivably have triggered major social breakdown.

All these theories, whether individual or combined, need to account for both the apparent disappearance and at times destruction of large numbers of Early Bronze Age sites, and then at the same time for exceptional settlements which survive the EB3 era. One example of the latter is the important site at Kolonna (Aegina island), a bridge between the South Mainland and the Cyclades, where, despite a destruction episode in late EH3, the site's occupation runs through both EH2 and EH3 and on into a major urban phase during the Middle Bronze Age (Davis 1992; Rutter 1993; Gauss and Smetana in *Horizon*).

The symbolic culture of Early Cycladic society

Figurines

Easily the most famous images of Greek prehistory are the marble figurines from the Cycladic Early Bronze Age, whose modern replicas are a standard item in tourist souvenir shops throughout Modern Greece. It is strange for us to discover, as Colin Renfrew reminds us in his classic study of these sculptures (1991), that when these works of art first came to public notice in the late nineteenth century, they were considered primitive and clumsy. However shortly afterwards, when the Modern Art movement in Western Europe turned to a similar simplification, these marble figurines were reassessed as the masterpieces of Bronze Age Henry Moores. As Renfrew goes on to elaborate in his monograph, the figurines are only a part of a culture in which many other objects were made with great care and skill, such as marble vessels and ceramics (see Figure 4.10), and with all such media we need to question if the artisans and users of all these, to our eyes, remarkably attractive objects, saw them as "art" at all. Unfortunately, although the statues range in size from some 10cm to human life-size, so few have been recovered from their original context of deposition rather than via the antiquities market, that there is no clear guide to their function. Clearly many if not most come from burials (Gill and

Chippindale (1993) estimate 72 percent of the 1600 documented), but this does not imply that they were made purely for accompanying the dead, and even if this were so, their symbolic meaning in a grave could have varied. Recent excavations at Kavos on the island of Keros by Renfrew (Whitley 2007, Renfrew in *Horizon*) appear to have confirmed his theory that it formed a Cycladic focus for ritual, where very large numbers of broken figurines were brought here to be deposited in a ceremonial context.

The very beginning of generalized settlement on the Cyclades, with the Late Neolithic Saliagos culture, is already associated with marble figurines (Figure 4.12) but they belong to the Neolithic Greek and Near Eastern style. In the following Final Neolithic, at Kephala on Kea, both ceramic figurines and marble vessels show the development of characteristic Early Cycladic styles, and the formal cemetery here also introduces the Cycladic form of burials. However the florescence of Cycladic Bronze Age art, as the chart indicates, is in the EC1–2 periods of the third millennium BC (Grotta-Pelos and Keros-Syros phases).

The commonest figurine appears on analysis to be female, with folded arms, and naked, with a highly schematic appearance. It appears throughout the islands and on their margins, such as parts of the Eastern Greek Mainland and in Early Minoan Crete. Much less common are other types of figurine, including some males, and these can be portrayed in more varied poses, such as the best-known examples of the figurines as a whole, the musicians (playing the harp and flute), but also rare armed men. Since the musicians are the most striking, compared to the enigmatic "folded-arm" variety, there remains an element of doubt if such role-playing objects are all originals rather than modern "fakes," as it is still impossible to date stone objects of this type (although happily at least one harp-player is securely tied to an Early Bronze Age context).

In terms of their conditions of production, workshops have not yet been discovered. Getz-Preziosi (1987) has deployed an art historian's approach of trying to recognize distinctive schools of "master craftsmen" on style details, but this is controversial. Perhaps more significant is the realization, from the minute study of the corpus of figurines, that nearly all seem to have been painted. Although the aim was to highlight

detail, the effect dramatically alters their appearance, with hair and eye color and painted designs on the face (resembling warpaint or tattoos rather than makeup, to my eyes). It can be suggested that the canonical "undifferentiated human," till recently forming the accepted reading of the figurines, now appears to be a distinctive individual, very much affecting the possible meaning of such objects.

Hekman's (2003) analysis of gift associations in the large cemetery at Chalandriani found a strong grouping of some graves which possessed equipment for body decoration. On ethnographic analogy he suggested that adults and juveniles on the brink of adulthood may have been tattooed. However, here figurines were associated with male heads of households.

What more can be said about use? In general the figurines cannot stand upright, so that they might have been held or placed recumbent; this could indicate a ritual activity and suitability for tomb deposition respectively, or both. Graves are undoubtedly the final depositional context for the majority, and it is suggested that the finer pieces may have been made as grave-goods. But they also occur in settlements. The fact that the objects are broken or repaired when put in burials could imply that they had a role in the lifetime of the deceased or their social group, maybe in a cult context, and then were sealed with the body of someone closely tied to their former use. This might be linked to a concept that they represent real people or ancestors. On the other hand, whereas these smaller objects may be associated with group representations, even when focusing on particular individuals of significance within the group (living or ancestors), the largest figurines, which cannot fit into a typical EC cist (stone box) grave, and are unfortunately not yet linked to a known archaeological context, would more likely have been placed in a formal ritual context, which we might think of as a shrine. In the Middle and Late Bronze Ages of the Cyclades, shrines have indeed been excavated with terracotta figurines inside them, some up to life-size (Davis 1992), although by then the figure styles are from Minoan Crete and the Mycenaean Mainland rather than in a Cycladic tradition. Renfrew's hypothesis that the site of Daskaleio-Kavos could have been such an inter-island ritual center is now supported by his recent fieldwork there. Large numbers of deliberately broken

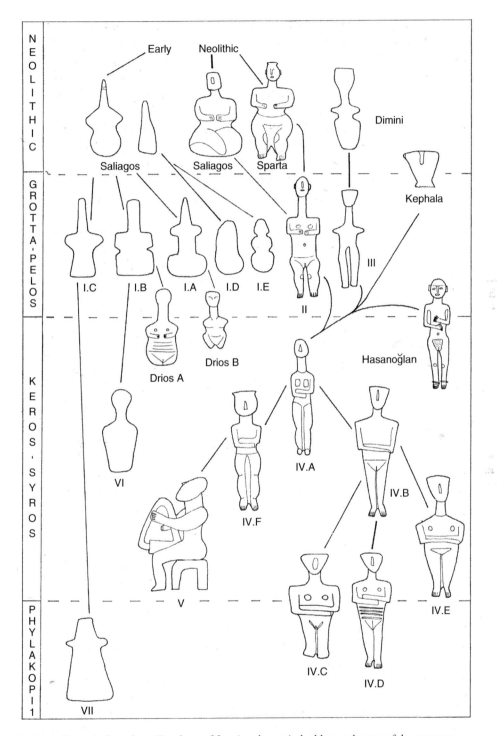

Figure 4.12 Cycladic symbolic culture. Typology of figurines by period, oldest at the top of the sequence.
C. Renfrew, *The Emergence of Civilization* (Study in Prehistory). London 1972, Figure 11.8. © 1972 Methuen & Co. Reproduced by permission of Taylor & Francis Books UK.

figurines and marble vessels were deposited, it seems from many different locations, where the figurines were "destroyed" before being brought to this cult locality. In contrast to their deposition in someone's burial, does this mark an alternative "resting-place" for the personalities they represented in life?

Despite the fact that a fine example of such a figurine might command up to a million dollars in the high-art saleroom today, and that since the early twentieth century these objects have been treasured for their classic purity of idealized human form, we clearly need to discard these and many other preconceptions in order to begin to comprehend this art in its *original* context. Experimental archaeology has shown that making such objects did not require immense skill or time, so that the character of island society as we have reconstructed it earlier in this chapter, one of a network of villages and hamlets, poses no difficulty for the production of these items. That same society, with the constant requirement for social interactions within and between the Cycladic islands, seems also to harmonize with the discovery of the personalization of the figurines. The recent emphasis on the importance of dress and body paint fits in well with recent insights into burial gifts with their jewelry, tweezers (for depilation?), and the possible use of obsidian blades for body ornamentation. The well-made ceramics and stone vessels, particularly special forms such as the "sauceboats" (Figure 4.10) seem to reflect a special attention to social drinking and dining. A recent suggestion that the flat ceramic vessels popularly called "frying-pans" were used to mix cosmetics, remains in the same sphere of interpretation, as would the thought that water poured into their rimmed surface could form a simple mirror.

All these aspects could be bound up with the "social" presentation of the body, to situate all these aspects of Cycladic material culture into a mentality highlighting group interactions. In this context, one reasonable hypothesis would suggest that Cycladic figurines could represent both real people, as nodes of social interaction, and divine forces as nodes of society's ritual interaction. In the absence of a system of genuinely large communities acting as a focus for individual islands, or as centers for a much larger scale of sociability between several islands, we may be seeing instead an exaggerated emphasis on chains of smaller-scale interactions: these would revolve around communal meals, voyages, marriages, burials, festivals, and acts of group worship, materialized for us in the rich and attractive Cycladic symbolic culture of the pre-urban phases of the Bronze Age.

The Early Bronze Age in Northern Greece

The archaeology of "the other Greece" is gradually rising in favor amongst researchers, strongly aided by vigorous archaeology departments in the provinces of Northern Greece, innovative work by the local Archaeological Services, and a growing number of international field projects (see Andreou *et al.* 1996, Andreou 2001). It is still difficult to gain a full picture of Bronze Age developments in this large region, however, and one suspects many surprises are in store when ongoing research becomes accessible through international publications.

As occurs also in later Bronze Age times, the coastal zone of Thessaly near modern Volos has revealed sites with strong exchange connections to the South Aegean and interesting features pointing to more complex social organization. Pevkakia is a promontory once flanked by two bays, with a circuit wall and an area of ca. 2 ha, where excavations have shown large buildings at different phases of the EBA. Nearby Petromagoula also has a circuit wall. However further evidence that might suggest a political or settlement hierarchy is lacking. Inland, the very dense Thessalian Neolithic tell societies undergo radical settlement discontinuity to the EBA. Large-scale abandonments are followed by relocations, and initially a drop in site numbers, recovering only in later Bronze Age times. The smaller sites of the Neolithic are widely replaced by rarer larger tells, although these are best evidenced in Middle to Late Bronze Age times. A wider use of the landscape is associated with a broadening of the economy, and one can suspect that much of the locational and economic shifts are connected to the full adoption of the plough, animal traction, and the Secondary Products Revolution. Some argue that because painted wares decline in the Bronze Age and households make their storage and workplaces more private, there has occurred a process of disruption of

Neolithic communal dining and social interaction, emphasizing competitive families. Nonetheless signs of the rise of an elite are lacking away from the coast, whether in houses, art or burial. Within Thessaly and to a small extent with other Aegean regions, exchanges of pottery continue, but their significance is unclear.

In Macedonia, the western regions also see expansion of site locations from Neolithic into the Bronze Age, attributed partly to the same economic developments as in Thessaly. Additionally, since increasingly hilltop locations are favored, the role of intercommunity warfare has been raised, and perhaps also the appearance of some minor district centers. Although clear evidence for the latter is lacking, local researchers now question whether Northern Greece need any more be assumed to stagnate into undefended village life in the EBA whilst the South develops successive civilizations. In central Macedonia a similar discontinuity in settlements is observed to that in Thessaly, with widespread abandonments and relocations between Neolithic and EBA times, plus site number reductions. However this is followed by a settlement recovery in the later Bronze Age, and we can still see an overall wider use of the landscape over time. Only in the later Bronze Age are there clear signs of an emergent settlement hierarchy. In eastern Macedonia and Thrace, a broadly similar sequence of large-scale settlement transformations seems indicated.

In Northwestern Mainland Greece (Tartaron 2004), ongoing survey and excavation projects promise to revolutionize our knowledge of the Bronze Age, so the traditional assumption of minimal development may need serious revision, something not unexpected when we consider the isolated elaborate burials already discussed from offshore Levkas island.

The Early Bronze Age: An Annaliste Perspective

This long and eventful phase of Greek Prehistory offers suitable evidence for processes at all three of the classic "Braudelian" timescales. On the one hand, in the long-term evolution of Greek society, the Early Bronze Age appears to be a pivotal era in which the creation of political classes and regional foci of economic and social power occurs in many, but perhaps just a minority, of the regions of Southern Greece (Kilian-Dirlmeier 2005). Despite critique of Renfrew's arguments for this view, the evidence in total seems to me more in harmony with this scenario, than that of purely egalitarian villages. The apparent lack of such developments in Northern Greece remains enigmatic, especially as further north in the Balkans there are also increasing signs of complex regional changes focusing on major settlements during the EBA (Harding 2000). According to Renfrew, the chief stimuli for the Aegean "high cultures" of EH, EM, and EC were a combination of the economic boost provided by the cultivation and storage of olive oil and wine, and the drive to increased trade promoted by the spread of bronze metallurgy (also associated with increased warfare). We have also noted the increasing effect of the likely widespread adoption of plough traction and the use of secondary products from domestic animals. All these elements involved diffusion into Greece of economic practices out of adjacent lands.

In the latter context, we should not underestimate the influence of more complex societies on Aegean developments (Anatolian, Levantine (Syro-Palestine), and Egyptian), attested by the Aegean adoption of seals and sealing, new forms of ceramics and by the end of the EBA new ceramic technologies, and other craft skills in stone and metalworking. The exact significance of the Aegean's "periphery" relations to these societies remains to be further elucidated, but this is an important issue if we accept that the EBA is in many respects a more elaborate world than that of the Neolithic. However, the fact that throughout Europe this period witnesses the clear appearance of individual male status linked with symbols of war, whether in burial or in public art (Shennan 1993), demonstrates that the novelties of Aegean polyculture and limited Near Eastern contacts can only be a partial explanation. Perhaps greater weight should be sought in more indirect but wider ranging economic changes, notably the diffusion of the plough, secondary products, and metallurgy.

On the medium term of one or more centuries, a greater abundance of data and refined chronologies allow us to obtain an increasingly nuanced picture of variety between each major phase of the EBA, with now sub-phases being highlighted as historically significant (for example the Kastri phase of late EC2). Nonetheless, a cyclical pattern dominates all three major regions in focus, EH, EM, and EC, with signs of a developmental rise, climax, and decline associated with the three subsequent phases of EB1, 2, and 3 in each area. This suggests that below the "big picture" of the long term, the era has its own internal dynamic of increasing then decreasing complexity. As this pattern is very common in archaeological sequences, and we shall indeed see such a cyclicity repeated throughout the later periods of Greek prehistory and history, some comment now seems appropriate (see Bintliff 1997a for a wider discussion).

If we observe the development of rural or urban settlements in any part of the Mediterranean world, and at any period since the Neolithic commenced locally, comparable phenomena appear: the rise and fall of rural settlement numbers, and of the size and number of nucleated settlements. This can be associated with pre-state, as well as state and imperial political organizations. Explanations have included overpopulation and land degradation, climate fluctuations, the instability of complex social and political systems, a collapse due to internal warfare or invasion/ migration from beyond the region, and the ebb and flow of long-distance commercial networks. Sometimes combinations of these factors have been invoked, and indeed current thinking would argue that human societies are complex and adaptive enough to require more than monocausal (single factor) explanations to account for major regressions in demography and social and economic complexity.

In the specific case of the EBA Aegean, the signs are there, in later EB2 and more clearly in EB3, of several of the above elements – warfare, climate, landscape change. Some would add migration, and long-distance commerce (core–periphery dependency effects involving the Near East as a dominant economy impacting on a less developed Aegean periphery). Closer resolution awaits future research results, which I suspect will not be long in coming.

Finally the short term in the Annaliste's analytical framework. At a site such as Lerna, one feels very close to specific historical individuals and events, as one assumes that particular group-leaders are instituting a district-wide system of economic control and supervising the construction of impressive focal buildings.

At Knossos, the suggestion of communal feasts in EM, giving the future palace site the role of a regional ceremonial-center, and even the first elaborate buildings at this and other later "palace" sites, provide a similar impression. Meanwhile Broodbank's evocation of longboat crews sailing adventurously between the Cyclades in EC, to trade, raid, establish marriage ties, and share in inter-island rituals, brings individual events and people into a sharp focus, a process now harmonizing with the new more personalized reading of contemporary figurines.

The Early Bronze Age: A Personal View

There is no doubt that the Early Bronze Age is currently one of the most dynamic research foci in Greek Archaeology. There are many ongoing projects whose results will keep this field creative and insightful for the foreseeable future, and this has a much wider relevance, if we agree with the view that the era is fundamental in the establishment of the palace civilizations which will follow in the Middle and Late Bronze Age. Can I feel a personal contact with any of the three regional societies we have highlighted? Only with the Early Cycladic world, where Renfrew and others analyzing its symbolic culture, and Broodbank's innovative research on inter-island voyaging, have brought the prospect of a deeper empathy with this culture, reminiscent of the German historian von Ranke's evocation of a History "wie es eigentlich gewesen" ("How it really was").

References

Andreou, S. (2001). "Exploring the patterns of power in the Bronze Age settlements of Northern Greece." In K. Branigan (ed.), *Urbanism in the Aegean Bronze Age.* Sheffield: Sheffield Academic Press, 160–173.

Andreou, S., M. Fotiadis, and K. Kotsakis (1996). "Review of Aegean Prehistory V: The Neolithic and Bronze Age of northern Greece." *American Journal of Archaeology* 100, 537–597.

Asouti, E. (2003). "Wood charcoal from Santorini (Thera): New evidence for climate, vegetation and timber imports in the Aegean Bronze Age." *Antiquity* 77, 471–484.

Bell, B. (1971). "The Dark Ages in ancient history: I. The first Dark Age in Egypt." *American Journal of Archaeology* 75, 223–269.

Bentley, R. A. *et al.* (2002). "Prehistoric migration in Europe: Strontium isotope analysis of Early Neolithic skeletons." *Current Anthropology* 43, 799–804.

Bevan, A. (2004). "Emerging civilized values? The consumption and imitation of Egyptian stone vessels in EMII–MM1 Crete and its wider Eastern Mediterranean context." In J. C. Barrett and P. Halstead (eds.), *The Emergence of Civilisation Revisited*. Oxford: Oxbow Books, 107–126.

Bintliff, J. L. (1977a). *Natural Environment and Human Settlement in Prehistoric Greece*. 2 vols. Oxford: BAR Supplementary Series 28.

Bintliff, J. L. (1977b). "New approaches to human geography. Prehistoric Greece: A case study." In F. Carter (ed.), *An Historical Geography of the Balkans*. London: Academic Press, 59–114.

Bintliff, J. L. (1984). "Introduction: Archaeology and theories of social evolution." In J. Bintliff (ed.), *European Social Evolution*. Bradford: Bradford University Research Ltd, 13–39.

Bintliff, J. L. (1997). "Regional survey, demography, and the rise of complex societies in the Ancient Aegean: Core–periphery, Neo-Malthusian, and other interpretive models." *Journal of Field Archaeology* 24, 1–38.

Bintliff, J. (1999). "Settlement and territory." In G. Barker (ed.), *The Routledge Companion Encyclopedia of Archaeology*. London: Routledge, 505–545.

Bintliff, J. (2000). "Landscape change in Classical Greece: A review." In F. Vermeulen and M.D. Dapper (eds.), *Geoarchaeology of the Landscapes of Classical Antiquity*. Leuven: Peeters, 49–70.

Bintliff, J. (2002). "Rethinking early Mediterranean urbanism." In R. Aslan *et al.* (eds.), *Mauerschau. Festschrift für Manfred Korfmann*. Vol. 1. Tübingen: Bernhard Albert Greiner, 153–177.

Bintliff, J. L., P. Howard, and A. M. Snodgrass (1999). "The hidden landscape of prehistoric Greece." *Journal of Mediterranean Archaeology* 12, 139–168.

Blackman, D. and K. Branigan (eds.) (1977). "An archaeological survey of the lower catchment of the Ayiofarango valley." *Annual of the British School at Athens* 72, 13–84.

Branigan, K. (1975). "The round graves of Levkas reconsidered." *Annual of the British School at Athens* 70, 37–49.

Branigan, K. (1993). *Dancing with Death. Life and Death in Southern Crete c.3000–2000 B.C.* Amsterdam: Hakkert.

Branigan, K. (1998). "The nearness of you: Proximity and distance in Early Minoan funerary behaviour." In K. Branigan (ed.), *Cemetery and Society in the Aegean Bronze Age*. Sheffield: Sheffield Academic Press, 13–26.

Branigan, K. (1999). "Late Neolithic colonization of the uplands of Eastern Crete." In P. Halstead (ed.), *Neolithic Society in Greece*. Sheffield: Sheffield Academic Press, 57–65.

Broodbank, C. (2000). *An Island Archaeology of the Early Cyclades*. Cambridge: Cambridge University Press.

Carter, T. (1998). "Reverberations of the international spirit: Thoughts upon 'Cycladica' in the Mesara." In K. Branigan (ed.), *Cemetery and Society in the Aegean Bronze Age*. Sheffield: Sheffield Academic Press, 59–77.

Chapman, R. (1990). *Emerging Complexity. The Later Prehistory of South-East Spain, Iberia and the West Mediterranean*. Cambridge: Cambridge University Press.

Cherry, J. F. (1979). "Four problems in Cycladic prehistory." In J. Davis and J. F. Cherry (eds.), *Papers in Cycladic Prehistory*. Los Angeles: University of California, 22–47.

Cherry, J. (1990). "The first colonization of the Mediterranean Islands: A review of recent research." *Journal of Mediterranean Archaeology* 3, 145–221.

Cherry, J. F., J. C. Davis, and E. Mantzourani (eds.) (1991). *Landscape Archaeology as Long-Term History: Northern Keos in the Cycladic Islands*. Los Angeles: Institute of Archaeology, University of California.

Cline, E. H. (ed.) (2010). *Oxford Handbook of the Bronze Age Aegean*. Oxford: Oxford University Press.

Coleman, J. E. (1977). *Kephala: A Late Neolithic Settlement and Cemetery*. Princeton: American School of Classical Studies at Athens.

Cosmopoulos, M. B. (1998). "Le Bronze Ancien 2 en Argolide: Habitat, urbanisation, population." In A. Pariente and G. Touchais (eds.), *Argos et l'Argolide. Topographie et urbanisme. Bulletin de Correspondance Hellénique*, Supplementary Volume, 41–56.

Davis, J. (1992). "Review of Aegean Prehistory I: The islands of the Aegean." *American Journal of Archaeology* 96, 692–756.

Davis, J. L. (2004). "Are the landscapes of Greek Prehistory hidden? A comparative approach." In S. E. Alcock and J. F. Cherry (eds.), *Side-by-Side Survey. Comparative Regional Studies in the Mediterranean World*. Oxford: Oxbow Books, 22–35.

Day, P. M. and D. E. Wilson (2002). "Landscapes of memory, craft and power in prepalatial and protopalatial Knossos." In Y. Hamilakis (ed.), *Labyrinth Revisited. Rethinking 'Minoan' Archaeology*. Oxford: Oxbow Books, 143–166.

Doumas, C. (1972). "Notes on Cycladic architecture." *Archaeologischer Anzeiger* 87, 151–170.

Driessen, J. (2007). "IIB or not IIB: On the beginnings of Minoan monumental building." In J. Bretschneider, J. Driessen, and K. van Lerberghe (eds.), *Power and

Architecture. Monumental Public Architecture in the Bronze Age Near East and Aegean. Leuven: Peeters, 73–92.

Evans, J. D. (1971). "Neolithic Knossos: The growth of a settlement." *Proceedings of the Prehistoric Society* 37(2), 95–117.

Evans, J. D. and A. C. Renfrew (1968). *Excavations at Saliagos near Antiparos.* London: British School at Athens, Supplementary Volume 5.

Fitton, J. L. (2002). *The Minoans.* London: The British Museum Press.

Forsen, J. (1992). *The Twilight of the Early Helladics.* Jonsered: Paul Åström.

Forsyth, P. Y. (1999). *Thera in the Bronze Age.* New York: P. Lang.

Frankenstein, S. and M. J. Rowlands (1978). "The internal structure and regional context of early iron age society in south-western Germany." *Bulletin of the Institute of Archaeology* 15, 73–112.

Galili, E. *et al.* (1997). "Evidence for earliest olive-oil production in submerged settlements off the Carmel coast, Israel." *Journal of Archaeological Science* 24, 1141–1150.

Getz-Preziosi, P. (1987). *Sculptors of the Cyclades: Individual and Tradition in the Third Millennium BC.* Ann Arbor: University of Michigan Press.

Gill, D. W. and C. Chippindale (1993). "Material and intellectual consequences of esteem for Cycladic figures." *American Journal of Archaeology* 97, 601–659.

Graham, J. W. (1962). *The Palaces of Crete.* Princeton: Princeton University Press.

Haggis, D. C. (2002). "Integration and complexity in the late Prepalatial period: A view from the countryside in Eastern Crete." In Y. Hamilakis (ed.), *Labyrinth Revisited. Rethinking 'Minoan' Archaeology.* Oxford: Oxbow Books, 142.

Halstead, P. (2004). "Life after Mediterranean polyculture: The subsistence subsystem and the emergence of civilisation revisited." In J. C. Barrett and P. Halstead (eds.), *The Emergence of Civilisation Revisited.* Oxford: Oxbow Books, 189–206.

Hamilakis, Y. (1996). "Wine, oil and the dialectics of power in bronze age Crete: A review of the evidence." *Oxford Journal of Archaeology* 15, 1–32.

Hansen, J. M. (1988). "Agriculture in the prehistoric Aegean: Data versus speculation." *American Journal of Archaeology* 92, 39–52.

Harding, A. (2000). *European Societies in the Bronze Age.* Cambridge: Cambridge University Press.

Hekman, J. J. (2003). "The Early Bronze Age cemetery at Chalandriani on Syros (Cyclades, Greece)." PhD thesis, Institute of Archaeology, University of Groningen.

Horizon = Brodie, N. *et al.* (eds.) (2008). *Horizon. A Colloquium on the Prehistory of the Cyclades.* Cambridge: McDonald Institute Monographs.

Joffe, A. H. (2004). "Athens and Jerusalem in the Third Millennium: Culture, comparison, and the evolution of social complexity." *Journal of Mediterranean Archaeology* 17, 247–267.

Karytinos, A. (1998). "Sealstones in cemeteries: A display of social status?" In K. Branigan (ed.), *Cemetery and Society in the Aegean Bronze Age.* Sheffield: Sheffield Academic Press, 78–86.

Katsianis, M. (2004). "Stratigraphic modelling of multi-period sites using GIS: The case of Neolithic and Early Bronze Age Knossos." In Stadtarchäologie Wien (ed.), *Enter the Past: The E-way into the Four Dimensions of Cultural Heritage.* Oxford: BAR Int. Series 1227, 304–307.

Kilian-Dirlmeier, I. (2005). *Die Bronzezeitlichen Gräber bei Nidri auf Leukas.* Bonn: Rudolf Habelt Verlag.

Konsola, D. (1984). "Beobachtungen zur Wegenetz in Frühhelladischen Siedlungen." *Archäologischer Anzeiger,* 197–210.

Korfmann, M. *et al.* (eds.) (2001). *Troia. Traum und Wirklichkeit.* Stuttgart: Theiss Verlag.

Kouka, O. (2002). *Siedlungsorganisation in der Nord- und Ostägäis während der Frühbronzezeit (3. Jt. v. Chr.).* Rahden: Marie Leindorf Verlag.

McGeehan Liritzis, V. (1988). "Seafaring, craft and cultural contact in the Aegean during the 3rd millennium BC." *International Journal of Nautical Archaeology* 17, 237–256.

Maggidis, C. (1998). "From polis to necropolis: Social ranking from architectural and mortuary evidence in the Minoan cemetery at Phournoi, Archanes." In K. Branigan (ed.), *Cemetery and Society in the Aegean Bronze Age.* Sheffield: Sheffield Academic Press, 87–102.

Maran, J. (2007). "Seaborne contacts between the Aegean, the Balkans and the Central Mediterranean in the 3rd millennium BC: The unfolding of the Mediterranean world." In I. Galanaki *et al.* (eds.), *Between the Aegean and Baltic Seas.* Liège: Université de Liège, 3–21.

Marangou, C. (1991). "Social differentiation in the Early Bronze Age miniature metal tools and child burials." *Journal of Mediterranean Studies* 1, 211–225.

Marzolff, P. (2004). "Das Zweifache Rätsel Tiryns." In E.-L. Schwandner and K. Rheidt (eds.), *Macht der Architektur – Architektur der Macht.* Mainz: Philipp von Zabern, 79–91.

Mattingly, D. J. (1988). "Olea mediterranea?" *Journal of Roman Archaeology* 1, 153–161.

Mee, C. (ed.) (2011). *Greek Archaeology: A Thematic Approach.* Oxford / New York: Wiley-Blackwell.

Murphy, J. M. (1998). "Ideologies, rites and rituals: A view of Prepalatial Minoan tholoi." In K. Branigan (ed.), *Cemetery and Society in the Aegean Bronze Age.* Sheffield: Sheffield Academic Press, 27–40.

Nakou, G. (1995). "The cutting edge: A new look at early Aegean metallurgy." *Journal of Mediterranean Archaeology* 8, 1–32.

Paepe, R., M. E. Hatziotis, and E. Van Overloop (1987). "Anthropogenic sediments and the dating of climate and its periodicities in historical Greece." *Striae* 26, 31–34.

Pain, S. (1999). "Grog of the Greeks." *New Scientist* 27, 54–57.

Peperaki, O. (2004). "The House of the Tiles at Lerna: Dimensions of 'social complexity'." In J. C. Barrett and P. Halstead (eds.), *The Emergence of Civilisation Revisited*. Oxford: Oxbow Books, 214–231.

Preziosi, D. and L. A. Hitchcock (1999). *Aegean Art and Architecture*. Oxford: Oxford University Press.

Pullen, D. J. (1992). "Ox and plow in the Early Bronze Age Aegean." *American Journal of Archaeology* 96, 45–54.

Relaki, M. (2004). "Constructing a region: The contested landscapes of Prepalatial Mesara." In J. C. Barrett and P. Halstead (eds.), *The Emergence of Civilisation Revisited*. Oxford: Oxbow Books, 170–188.

Renfrew, A. C. (1972). *The Emergence of Civilisation. The Cyclades and the Aegean in the Third Millennium BC* London: Methuen.

Renfrew, A. C. (1973). *Before Civilization*. London: Jonathan Cape.

Renfrew, C. (1985). *The Archaeology of Cult: The Sanctuary at Phylakopi*. London: British School at Athens.

Renfrew, A. C. (1987). *Archaeology and Language: The Puzzle of Indo-European Origins*. London: Jonathan Cape.

Renfrew, C. (1991). *The Cycladic Spirit*. London: Thames & Hudson.

Renfrew, C. (2004). "Rethinking the emergence." In J. C. Barrett and P. Halstead (eds.), *The Emergence of Civilisation Revisited*. Oxford: Oxbow Books, 257–274.

Renfrew, C. and M. Wagstaff (eds.) (1982). *An Island Polity. The Archaeology of Exploitation in Melos*. Cambridge: Cambridge University Press.

Rosen, A. M. (1995). "The social response to environmental change in Early Bronze Age Canaan." *Journal of Anthropological Archaeology* 14, 26–44.

Rosen, A. M. (2007). *Civilizing Climate*. Lanham: AltaMira.

Runnels, C. and J. M. Hansen (1986). "The olive in the prehistoric Aegean: The evidence for domestication in the Early Bronze Age." *Oxford Journal of Archaeology* 5, 299–308.

Runnels, C. and T. H. van Andel (1988). "Trade and the origins of agriculture." *Journal of Mediterranean Archaeology* 1, 83–109.

Rutter, J. B. (1993). "Review of Aegean Prehistory II: The Prepalatial Bronze Age of the Southern and Central Greek Mainland." *American Journal of Archaeology* 97, 745–797.

Sampson, A. (ed.) (2006). *The Prehistory of the Aegean Basin*. Athens: Atrapos.

Sbonias, K. (1999). "Social development, management of production, and symbolic representation in Prepalatial Crete." In A. Chaniotis (ed.), *From Minoan Farmers to Roman Traders*. Stuttgart: Franz Steiner Verlag, 25–51.

Schoep, I. (2007). "Architecture and power: The origins of Minoan 'palatial architecture'." In J. Bretschneider, J. Driessen, and K. van Lerberghe (eds.), *Power and Architecture. Monumental Public Architecture in the Bronze Age Near East and Aegean*. Leuven: Peeters, 213–236.

Schoep, I. and C. Knappett (2004). "Dual emergence: Evolving heterarchy, exploding hierarchy." In J. C. Barrett and P. Halstead (eds.), *The Emergence of Civilisation Revisited*. Oxford: Oxbow, 21–37.

Shaw, J. H. (1987). "The Early Helladic II corridor house." *American Journal of Archaeology* 91, 59–79.

Shaw, J. H. (2007). "Sequencing the EHII 'corridor houses'." *Annual of the British School at Athens* 102, 137–151.

Shelmerdine, C. W. (ed.) (2008). *The Cambridge Companion to the Aegean Bronze Age*. Cambridge: Cambridge University Press.

Shennan, S. J. (1993). "Settlement and social change in Central Europe, 3500–1500 BC." *Journal of World Prehistory* 7, 121–161.

Sherratt, A. and S. Sherratt (1993). "What would a Bronze-Age world system look like? Relations between temperate Europe and the Mediterranean in later prehistory." *Journal of European Archaeology* 1, 1–57.

Shriner, C. M. and H. H. Murray (2003). "The application of clay mineralogical analysis to the reconstruction of a Greek Bronze Age coastal environment." In E. Dominguez, C. Mas, and F. Cravero (eds.), *Proceedings of the 12th International Clay Conference*. Amsterdam: Elsevier, 163–170.

Soles, J. S. (1978). "Mochlos." *Expedition* 20(2), 5–15.

Soles, J. S. (1992). *The Prepalatial Cemeteries at Mochlos and Gournia and the House Tombs of Bronze Age Crete*. Princeton: American School of Classical Studies at Athens, *Hesperia* Supplement 24.

Tartaron, T. F. (2004). *Bronze Age Landscape and Society in Southern Epirus*. Oxford: BAR Int. Series 1290.

Tenwolde, C. (1992). "Myrtos revisited. The role of relative function ceramic typologies in Bronze Age settlement analysis." *Oxford Journal of Archaeology* 11, 1–24.

Tomkins, P. (2004). "Filling in the Neolithic background: Social life and social transformation in the Aegean before the Bronze Age." In J. C. Barrett and P. Halstead (eds.), *The Emergence of Civilisation Revisited*. Oxford: Oxbow Press, 38–63.

Van Andel, T. H., C. N. Runnels, and K. O. Pope (1986). "Five thousand years of land use and abuse in the Southern Argolid, Greece." *Hesperia* 55, 103–128.

Wagstaff, M. and J. Cherry (1982). "Settlement and population change." In A.C. Renfrew and M. Wagstaff (eds.), *An Island Polity. The Archaeology of Exploitation in Melos*. Cambridge: Cambridge University Press, 136–155.

Warren, P. M. (1968). "A textile town – 4500 years ago?" *Illustrated London News* (17 February), 25–27.

Warren, P. M. (1972). *Myrtos. An Early Bronze Age Settlement in Crete*. London: British School at Athens.

Warren, P. M. (1984). "Circular platforms at Minoan Knossos." *Annual of the British School at Athens* 79, 307–323.

Watrous, L. V. (1994). "Review of Aegean Prehistory III: Crete from earliest prehistory through the Protopalatial Period." *American Journal of Archaeology* 98, 695–753.

Weiss, H. *et al.* (1993). "The genesis and collapse of Third Millennium urbanization and state formation." *Science* 261, 995–1004.

Whitelaw, T. (1983). "The settlement at Fournou Korifi, Myrtos and aspects of Early Minoan social organization." In O. Krzyszkowska and L. Nixon (eds.), *Minoan Society*. Bristol: Bristol Classical Press, 323–340.

Whitelaw, T. (2004). "Alternative pathways to complexity in the South Aegean." In J. C. Barrett and P. Halstead (eds.), *The Emergence of Civilisation Revisited*. Oxford: Oxbow Books, 232–256.

Whitley, J. *et al.* (eds.) (2007). *Archaeological Reports for 2006–7*. London: British School at Athens.

Wilson, D. E. and P. M. Day (2000). "EM1 chronology and social practice: Pottery from the early palace tests at Knossos." *Annual of the British School at Athens* 95, 21–63.

Wilson, D. E., P. M. Day, and L. Joyner (1999). "EM IIB ware groups at Knossos: The 1907–1908 South Front tests." *Annual of the British School at Athens* 94, 1–62.

Wossink, A. (2009). *Challenging Climate Change. Competition and Cooperation among Pastoralists and Agriculturalists in Northern Mesopotamia (c. 3000–1600 BC)*. Leiden: Sidestone Press.

Xanthoudides, S. A. (1924). *The Vaulted Tombs of the Mesara*. London: Hodder & Stoughton.

Zangger, E. (1994). "Landscape changes around Tiryns during the Bronze Age." *American Journal of Archaeology* 98, 189–212.

Zois, A. A. (1976). *Vasiliki*. Vol. 1. Athens: The Archaeological Society.

Further Reading

Branigan, K. (ed.) (1998). *Cemetery and Society in the Aegean Bronze Age*. Sheffield: Sheffield Academic Press.

Butzer, K. W. (1976). *Early Hydraulic Civilization in Egypt*. Chicago: University of Chicago Press.

Cavanagh, W. and C. Mee (1998). *A Private Place: Death in Prehistoric Greece*. Lund: Paul Astrom.

Cherry, J. F. *et al.* (1988). "Archaeological survey in an artifact-rich landscape: A Middle Neolithic example from Nemea, Greece." *American Journal of Archaeology* 92, 159–176.

Dickinson, O. T. P. K. (1994). *The Aegean Bronze Age*. Cambridge: Cambridge University Press.

Efstratiou, N. (2005). "Tracing the story of the first farmers in Greece – A long and winding road." In C. Lichter (ed.), *How Did Farming Reach Europe?* Istanbul: Deutsches Archäologisches Institut, BYZAS 2, 143–153.

Hamilakis, Y. (1998). "Eating the dead: Mortuary feasting and the politics of memory in the Aegean Bronze Age societies." In K. Branigan (ed.), *Cemetery and Society in the Aegean Bronze Age*. Sheffield: Sheffield Academic Press, 115–132.

Isaakidou, V. (2006). "Ploughing with cows: Knossos and the secondary products revolution." In D. Serjeantson and D. Field (eds.), *Animals in the Neolithic of Britain and Europe*. Oxford: Oxbow Books, 95–112.

5

The Middle to Early Late Bronze Age on Crete

The Minoan Civilization

Introduction

Minoan civilization arises from a prolonged social and economic development on Crete, in which Knossos and Phaistos, two major Middle Bronze Age palaces, had already appeared earlier as exceptional settlements within their regions (North-Central and South-Central Crete, respectively). Despite the disruptions in the Aegean and Near East which threw late Early Minoan society into disorder, Crete is one region where recovery during the early centuries of the MBA is not only strong but leaps into a higher level of political complexity. This is seen in the construction or better elaboration of great architectural complexes, the "palatial" centers across the island. (For general reading see Shelmerdine 2008, Cline 2010, Mee 2011.)

Aegean integration into an Eastern Mediterranean world system?

The second millennium BC sees Aegean societies for the first time becoming vigorously active in the much older Eastern Mediterranean trading and political systems. Over time, in the MBA and LBA, aspects of at least the exchange network spread to parts of the Central Mediterranean too. These phenomena are tied to a debate on the significance of the societal transformations involved (Sherratt and Sherratt 1993). The central concepts are Core–Periphery and World Systems Theory, and both originate in historical and economic models for the relations in Early Modern times between Western colonial and imperial states, and the Second and Third World peoples. *Core–Periphery* focuses on the usually dominant role of a region or state with advanced technology or economic systems in relation to a region or state at a lower level of political or economic complexity: influences from the core encourage internal transformations in the periphery. *World Systems* theory (Wallerstein 1974) models complex societies as different networks of interaction, or world systems: a world empire is a political unity of diverse regions or peoples, yet in pre-Modern times usually constitutes a series of local economies which fail to unify into a single efficient flow of goods and services. A world economy on the other hand achieves the latter aim with a well-lubricated and open flow of products and personnel, but for Wallerstein this only expanded to fill and then exceed the space of world empires in the post-Medieval period, with the unique spread of global capitalism and colonialism. Many archaeologists disagree with Wallerstein and suggest that ancient and even prehistoric exchange systems may have formed world economies, including within the Mediterranean.

The Complete Archaeology of Greece: From Hunter-Gatherers to the 20th Century AD, First Edition. John Bintliff.
© 2012 John Bintliff. Published 2012 by Blackwell Publishing Ltd.

Around 2000 BC, social and economic relations within the Aegean are clearly transformed. Renfrew (1972) embedded this development into the longer-term rise of complex societies *within* the Aegean, emphasizing the increasing rate of change in the EBA. Nonetheless, he admitted that some key elements have been introduced from outside, for example the spread by colonizing Neolithic groups of mixed farming, then the FN-EBA adoption, through indirect diffusion, of olive and vine cultivation and metallurgy, all from the Near East, Anatolia or the North Balkans. In contrast the Sherratts emphasize a far more radical, deliberately engineered reorientation of Aegean societies, when the region shifts from a predominantly internal exchange system to an economy locked into strong trade systems already in action throughout the Eastern Mediterranean since the EBA. For them, this begins by EB2 in Greece, when the region is a "periphery," already significantly affected by the "core" of state societies in the Levant-Anatolia. With the MBA rise of Minoan palatial states, Crete emerges as a new core, creating its own periphery, the Cycladic and Mainland cultures of MC and subsequently LH respectively.

Chronological context and periodization

Minoan civilization has two flourishing eras, the First and Second Palace periods. The transition from EM was not smooth. EM3 saw widespread destructions and site desertions, and although MM1 marks resettlement and expansion of existing sites, this phase has short-lived fortifications at several of them (Knossos, Malia, Vasilike, Gournia) and curious small defensive complexes at Chamaizi and Aghia Photia (Watrous 1994, Fitton 2002).

The Old Palaces begin around 2000 BC. After several centuries there is an island-wide catastrophe which destroys the palaces, probably a particularly violent earthquake to which Crete is prone (although a few scholars have raised an alternative explanation, internal warfare). However almost immediately most palaces are rebuilt along very similar lines, and the resultant Second Palace period is even more complex and sophisticated. Another island-wide destruction that occurs at the end of the LBA1 phase (LM1B), and which brings all the palaces except Knossos out of effective use, is placed here around 1550 BC as a choice amongst widely differing dates. This is not now considered to be the direct result of a somewhat earlier (LM1A) giant volcanic eruption on the nearby island of Thera in the Cyclades. In the following, rather misleadingly-named Postpalatial era, Knossos was certainly functioning as a great palace, maybe ruling over much of Crete, in place of the defunct regional palaces it survived. It was also very possibly under the control of a new power, the Mainland Mycenaeans, rather than the Cretan elites (or corporate communities, see below), who had been responsible for the rise and management of the network of large and small palaces dominating Minoan Crete in the preceding eras of the First and Second Palaces.

The final destruction and abandonment of that LM2–3 survivor, the "Palace of Minos" at Knossos, has several possible dates, from 1375 down to 1250 BC. If the Postpalatial period coincides in a causal way with the fast rise of the militaristic Mycenaean civilization, opting for the latest date for the fall of Knossos places that palace's final violent destruction in the same time frame as the equally violent fall of the Mainland Mycenaean palaces themselves. Since this wave of destructions in the late thirteenth to early twelfth century BC is also visible in the adjacent Near

---

Minoan Palace Civilization

Early court-centered complexes ca. 2500–2100/2000 BC: Early Minoan 2 to Middle Minoan 1A

First/Old Palace period ca. 2100/2000–1750 BC: Middle Minoan 1B–2

Second/New Palace period ca. 1750–1550 BC: Middle Minoan 3 to Late Minoan 1

Postpalatial period (Knossos excepted) ca. 1550–1250 BC: Late Minoan 2–3

East (with the fall of the great civilization of the Hittites in Anatolia for example), wider forces seem to have been at work. If, however, we opt for the earlier dates for the fall of Knossos, in LM3A in the early fourteenth century, then a collapse of Mycenaean control *within* Crete is a better explanation, perhaps due to a successful indigenous uprising.

Landscape Archaeology and Population, and the Rural Economy

Minoan Crete is remarkable for the density of its remains. Elsewhere in Greece it was the "New Wave" of intensive regional surface survey since the 1970s which revealed the staggering density of archaeological sites in the Greek landscape (Cherry 1983, Bintliff 1994). But for Crete, Pendlebury's prewar (1939) maps of Minoan Bronze Age sites, then as now, amaze with their hundreds of findspots. Caution is required however. Pendlebury mapped almost every place where a Minoan sherd popped up during his travels over the entire island (mainly on foot!) (Gkiasta 2008). There is also reason to believe that the high quality of Minoan ceramics, already from EM times, allowed them to survive and be recognized in the plough soil much better than the coarser wares which often make up the bulk of the site assemblages on the Bronze Age Mainland and Islands (Bintliff *et al.* 1999, Bevan 2002, Bintliff 2002, Watrous *et al.* 2004), making site discovery perhaps many times easier for Crete. Recent high-quality intensive surveys allow a more realistic and nuanced view of the infill of the prehistoric Cretan landscape.

Figure 5.1 illustrates the increasing settlement density for the district of Vrokastro (Eastern Crete) (Hayden *et al.* 1992). The Second Palace era exhibits climax levels of population and land use, not to be repeated until Roman Imperial times on the island. Elements accounting for this growth include the long-term impact of the introduction of ploughs drawn by oxen, the use of secondary products from domestic animals (Isaakidou 2006), the development of olive and vine production, and the mutual feedback between growing urban populations' demand for

surpluses and the levels of production achieved by rural villages. Additional boosts to the Cretan rural economy came from agricultural terracing and water control dams. The former at the Minoan settlement of Pseira are argued to be of palatial age (French 1991), where the terraces' soil chemistry, associated with abundant household pottery fragments, suggests that agricultural productivity was increased by using manure from settlement waste products (Palmer 1995). Such a density of Middle Bronze Age rural settlement is absent from the contemporary Cyclades and Southern Mainland. Significantly, on the island of Kythera off the south coast of the Mainland, and on the heavily Minoan-influenced Cycladic island of Thera, we find a similar settlement pattern, pointing to the export of a specific approach to land-use (Bevan 2002, Forsyth 1999).

Till recently, on analogy with the subsequent, better-documented Mycenaean palace societies, it was argued that Minoan elites controlled the total production of Crete, whether in food staples or manufactured products. Palaces in both civilizations manipulated surpluses for their personnel's needs, for foreign exchange, and to alleviate shortages: a "redistribution" system (Renfrew 1972). The immense areas devoted to bulk storage of varied goods within the palaces, and the generalized use of archives and seals, which were linked both in location and in the images on them with numbered goods, seemed to agree. This scenario has undergone radical revision. The Mycenaean texts have now been shown to differ in significant ways from the archaeological evidence for the economy (Halstead 1992), suggesting that a public economy was at least evenly matched in production by a flourishing private economy, although there were essential exchanges of labor and products between them.

For the Minoan palaces, an additional if controversial argument has reconceptualized these architectural complexes as "ceremonial-centers," dedicated to large-scale ritual feasting, at least in their early "courtyard complex" form during the Early Minoan Pre-Palatial and the Middle Minoan First Palace eras (Schoep 2010). Much of the stored equipment and foodstuffs within these complexes might have served to support communal rituals for their associated town and wider rural populations. Nonetheless, in the Second Palace period, especially after the

Figure 5.1   The Vrokastro Survey in Eastern Crete shows the progressive infill of the Cretan landscape between the Final Neolithic and First Palace period (above) and the Second Palace period (facing page).
J.B. Hayden, J. A. Moody, and O. Rackham, "The Vrokastro Survey Project, 1986–1989. Research design and preliminary results." *Hesperia* 61/3 (1992), 293–353, Figures 16 and 17. Reproduced by permission of American School of Classical Studies at Athens © 1992.

traumatic effects of the Thera volcanic eruption in LM1A, it is conceded that the palaces may have become increasingly shut off from the general public and undergone conversion to an activity sphere for a limited elite sector and its officials and servants, perhaps involving actual residence within them of a part of this class. This would conform more closely to the traditional "dynastic palace" model which the pioneer excavator of Knossos Arthur Evans proposed (Evans 1921–1935).

Figure 5.1 *(Cont'd).*

Haggis (2002) uses regional survey innovatively to place these dynamics in the palaces in parallel with changes in the countryside. In the Kavousi district of Eastern Crete he records rural settlement intensifying between the Pre-Palatial and First Palace periods; he reconstructs a preference for areas suited to mixed cropping using spring-fed gardens alongside dry-farming (rain-fed), and village-based pastoralism. However for Second Palace times, a significant reloca-

tion of sites into the lowlands, and to places with easy access to the coast and road systems, together with population nucleation into larger rural sites, mark a new emphasis: he sees this as large-scale irrigated specialist farming, whilst the older, traditional settlements in the hill country become nucleated into "estate centers." The first mode sees rural populations produce small surpluses for intervillage exchange, focusing on broad mixed economies at the individual settlement level, and where distant "courtyard complex/palace" centers played no real role. In the second mode, palatial intervention shifts the dominant locally-based consumption into a production for state-controlled manipulation of specialized crop surpluses. Also in the Malia Survey (Müller 1996) and the Mesara Survey (Watrous *et al.* 2004) the later Palatial sites are fewer but larger, perhaps indicating greater outside control of production.

Some doubts remain: the evidence for large-scale irrigation is lacking. Alternatively the shift to the lowland plains might represent a redirection toward cereal monocropping, although this would still work with his model. More unclear is why Haggis sees this gearing-up to a market economy as unstable. If we look at the increasing size and complexity of the dominant towns in Minoan Crete, at the postulated rising intervention into rural areas symbolized by the widespread creation of the so-called Second Palace "villas" and additional small palaces, and at changes in remoter village societies which Haggis himself documents, we could see all this as a more positive development, with the integration of the island's resources from local to interregional exchange.

Much depends on whether benefits flowed back to rural settlements, and how far they could cover their own food needs as well as obtain necessary manufactured items and minor luxuries. Two contrasted models from later Greek history spring to mind: the late Ottoman *çiftlik* estates, where serfs lived in relative poverty whilst producing cash crops for the market, and the early Ottoman and Early Modern Greek villages, where adequate self-sufficiency in most agricultural products was balanced by specialization in certain crops for the market to pay taxes and buy consumer goods. In the Minoan case, the "market" may have been in part "tax" levied by the authorities at the major or minor palace centers, but part, it is now generally agreed, was available for the peasants' own private exchanges. A sample of Minoan population has been examined from burials, and combined with chemical analyses of pottery contents and the evidence of plant and animal remains (ecofacts), has prompted a provisional conclusion that the Minoans in general had a good diet and low disease rates, whilst rich *and* poor consumed meals high in protein from meat and pulses (Smith 1999).

Palace Design

From the first discovery of the Minoan civilization through Sir Arthur Evans' excavations at Knossos (Evans 1921–1935), the most striking aspect, and certainly its dominant feature also in Bronze Age times, is the Minoan palace (Figure 5.2). The similarity of plans for these major complexes was early apparent. Graham's (1962) architectural and functional analysis showed that the architects must have formed a school, either migrating around Crete from palace to palace, or sharing design templates, to explain why discrete parts of these complexes are found in most examples, often in related position (cf. Letesson and Vansteenhuyse 2006).

Shortly after the uncovering of the Knossos palace, similar complexes were discovered at Phaistos and Malia. It seemed reasonable to associate these with control of state territories for their regions, respectively North-Central, South, and East-Central Crete. In the postwar decades, further research revealed additional palatial centers controlling areas arguably beyond the reach of the larger foci. Kato Zakro, in the extreme east of the island, is matched by a probable palatial focus for the far west of Crete, at Khania. But in recent years many new sites have produced architectural complexes linking them to the "palace phenomenon," some near known "palatial centers."

For some scholars, the proliferation of "central places" brings into question the accepted concept that Crete was divided into large states centered on dynastic palaces. This feeds into the radical rethinking of the nature of the Minoan "palace" and of its controlling elite. For example, how should we interpret settlements such as the small town of Gournia which incorporates an administrative complex (Figure 5.3) showing clear design parallels to the larger palaces? Furthermore, during the Second Palace era rural mansions (villas?) appear, although most seem now to be linked to a larger settlement in their vicinity. An additional complication is that although it is customary to record an increase in the number of "palaces" in Second Palace times, current research indicates that many of these may possess a First Palace and even perhaps a "Pre-Palatial" predecessor, even if these public complexes seem far less elaborate (Fitton 2002, Driessen 2007, Schoep 2010).

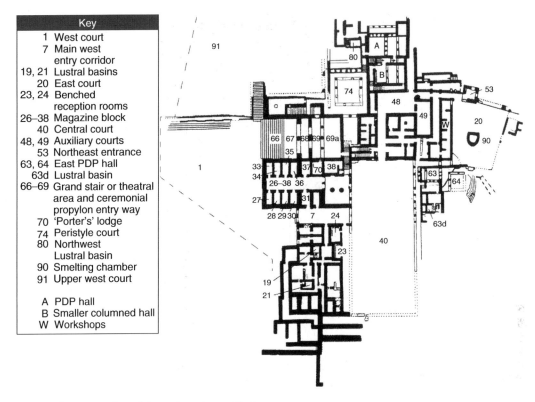

Key

1	West court
7	Main west entry corridor
19, 21	Lustral basins
20	East court
23, 24	Benched reception rooms
26–38	Magazine block
40	Central court
48, 49	Auxiliary courts
53	Northeast entrance
63, 64	East PDP hall
63d	Lustral basin
66–69	Grand stair or theatral area and ceremonial propylon entry way
70	'Porter's' lodge
74	Peristyle court
80	Northwest Lustral basin
90	Smelting chamber
91	Upper west court
A	PDP hall
B	Smaller columned hall
W	Workshops

Figure 5.2   The mature plan of the major palace at Phaistos.
D. Preziosi and L. A. Hitchcock, *Aegean Art and Architecture*. © Oxford University Press 1999, Figure 62.

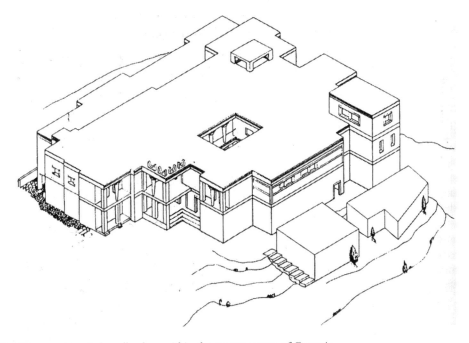

Figure 5.3   The reconstructed small palace within the country town of Gournia.
J. L. Fitton, *Minoans. Peoples of the Past*. London 2002, Figure 54.

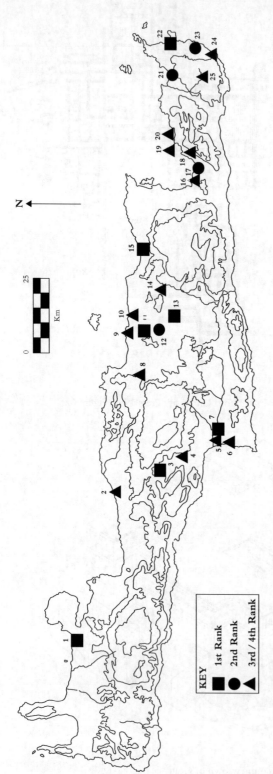

Figure 3.1 The location of certain and probable Minoan towns.

KEY

■ 1st Rank
● 2nd Rank
▲ 3rd / 4th Rank

1. Khania
2. Khamalevri
3. Monastiraki
4. Apodhoulou
5. Ayia Triadha
6. Kommos
7. Phaistos
8. Tylissos
9. Poros

10. Amnisos
11. Knossos
12. Arkhanes
13. Galatas
14. Kastelli Pediadha
15. Malia
16. Priniatiko Pyrgos
17. Gournia

18. Plakoures
19. Pseira
20. Mochlos
21. Petras
22. Palaikastro
23. Zakros
24. Xerokampos
25. Katelionas

Figure 5.4 A possible settlement hierarchy in Palatial Crete. The following centers are suggested to have possessed palaces, large or small, in the First and/or Second Palace period: Khania, Monastiraki, Phaistos, Knossos, Arkhanes, Galatas, Malia, Gournia, Petras, Zakro. E. Adams, "Social strategies and spatial dynamics in Neopalatial Crete: An analysis of the North-Central area." *American Journal of Archaeology* 110 (2006), 1–36. Reproduced by permission of Archaeological Institute of America (Boston).

Table 5.1 Hypothetical food-sustaining radii for Bronze and Iron Age towns in the dry-farming Mediterranean.

Town area	Population	BA food needs	IA food needs	BA sustaining radius	IA sustaining radius	5 km radius + 1/3 beyond
4–5 ha	480–1500	864–2700 ha	346–1060 ha	2,4–4,2 km	1,5–2,6 km	BA within 5 km★★ IA within 5 km★★
12–14 ha	1440–4200	2592–7560 ha	1037–3024 ha	4,1–6,9 km	2,6–4,4 km	BA 6,6 km★ IA within 5 km★★
20 ha	2400–6000	4320–10,800 ha	1728–4320 ha	5,2–8,3 km	3,3–5,2 km	BA 9,7 km★ IA within 5 km★★
30 ha	3600–9000	6480–16,200 ha	2592–6480 ha	6,4–10,2 km	4,1–6,4 km	BA 12,4 km★ IA 6.1 km★
80 ha	9600–24000	17,280–43,200 ha	6912–17,280 ha	10,5–16,6 km	6,6–10,5 km	BA 23 km IA 14 km★
150 ha	18,000–45,000	32,400–81,000 ha	12,960–32,400 ha	14,4–22,7 km	9,1–14,4 km	BA 32 km IA 20 km

★★ = core access zone   ★ = market return zone

Why did scholars assume from an early stage of research that the larger palaces (Figure 5.4) were centers of kingdoms for sizeable parts of Crete? Greek myths of King Minos of Knossos encouraged Evans to tie his Bronze Age palace to such a society, but he and later scholars also saw in the palatial plans evidence for such a political system. Only a powerful centralized organization could seemingly have constructed these complexes. Then their massive storage provision, apparently for agricultural taxes from subordinate peasants, taken with clay archive tablets showing accounts of foodstuffs and equipment, all indicated an elite deriving its incomes from large regions. From this it was easy to identify particular spacious, well-appointed rooms as suites for the King and Queen, especially as one at Knossos indeed possessed a built throne. Finally, similarities between the palace designs and those of contemporary Near Eastern small states clinched the interpretation. The only disputes over this scenario were whether the dominant role of women in palatial art could indicate a female power base equal or even superior to that of a male, and whether (as Evans opined), Cretan states were theocracies ruled by "god-kings and -queens."

Often forgotten is that Minoan "palaces" are all embedded within larger, urban settlements. And regardless of whether or not we accept these centers as possessing larger or smaller states under their domination, one can draw tentative conclusions from estimates of their total urban areas. Knossos, the most extensive, is 25–40 ha in the First and 75–100 ha in the Second Palace era. Malia is 50 ha at maximum, and a recent "palatial town" at Galatas is 25 ha (Adams 2006). I recently (2002) calculated the scale of territory required to sustain the food supply of such Bronze Age towns, allowing for some food production by urban dwellers themselves, and for rural satellite settlements needing to balance their own food needs against providing surpluses for the town population. I deliberately left out import of food from distant regions, in order to provide a "base-level" estimate of the scale of supporting catchment required if a town was to rely essentially on its own hinterland.

From Table 5.1, I hypothesize that these three towns had, from largest to smallest, between 9000 and 30,000 inhabitants (Knossos), 6000–15,000 (Malia), and 3000–7500 (Galatas). If we took the median of these figures, the food supply "catchment" needs are: a 22 km radius territory (Knossos); 16 km radius (Malia); and 10 km radius (Galatas). Re-examining the map of centers on Crete in Figure 5.4 allows that such a range is reasonable for Galatas, although it overlaps with possible resource areas required by Archanes, which some see as a semi-autonomous center. Malia however would need a major zone East-West along the coast, and parts of its rugged hinterland (as long ago postulated by Van Effenterre 1963). Knossos would require dominant control over food surpluses from most of North-Central Crete, the very region traditionally associated with its "state."

Central Courts and the evolution of the "Palatial Complexes"

Compared to contemporary Near Eastern, and later Mainland Mycenaean palaces, Minoan palatial complexes have a unique feature dominating their layout, the large open space or Central Court. Pedestrian circulation in Mycenaean palaces culminates in the internal audience-space or Megaron, but equivalent routeways through Cretan palaces lead to rectangular courts. A large architectural complex in a semi-arid part of Southern Europe naturally benefits from an open area to allow light, breeze, and internal circulation into surrounding rooms, whilst Mediterranean life traditionally has adapted itself to being largely open-air. It is not therefore essential to assume a symbolic or ideological role to this large space. On the other hand, palatial civilization was a complex organization, with we can reasonably assume a hierarchy of personnel: from the occupants of remote peasant holdings, through what we can suspect was a large group of servants or slaves participating in communal activities in and around the palaces, followed by a widespread and numerous class of artisans, then on into a class of administrators of religion, the army and politics.

The theatrical potential of a large interior space for holding public events, in order to represent and reproduce this complex society, cannot be underestimated. Significantly, Central Courts by the Second Palace era are deliberately hard to access from outside the palaces. Some contemporary crowd scenes in frescoes and engraved gems probably show social, political, and religious activities in the Central Court, perhaps for an exclusive audience of the privileged castes within later palace society. These are complemented by crowds portrayed in the *outer* courts, where "town and

palace" may have met (Figures 5.5 and 5.6 for the West Court and Central Court respectively). However, despite the trend to restrict access to central courts from the surrounding town and countryside, calculations for the Knossos Central Court would allow more than 5000 standing participants (perhaps one quarter of the settlement of Knossos) in group ceremonials (Driessen 2003).

The alignment of these great courts to regional natural highpoints where peak sanctuaries or sacred caves existed, reinforces Evans' intuition that Minoan civilization was permeated by religious ceremony and institutions. The use of space in the final form of the palaces does appear comparable to a Medieval monastery (Bintliff 1977b). In place of the Abbey church and Abbot's residence stood the Central Court and the elaborate reception rooms of Minoan palaces.

In the preceding chapter we noted that recent research at several palaces reconstructs large architectural clusters bordering early forms of Central Court by the mature EM period, associated with ceramic evidence for communal feasting. In the final EM and early MM or First Palace period, it is suggested that the "palaces" remained discontinuous blocks of rooms facing onto a Central Court, facilitating access from the wider landscape (Figure 5.7). Such open ceremonial centers acted as integrative foci for their hinterlands. Driessen (2007) notes that in these early palaces, raised walks running through the West (outer) Court but also coming from other directions, created formal processional routes leading into the communal ceremonial space of the Central Court and other circulation areas of these complexes. Since this model is linked to skepticism regarding a residential elite, at least until very late in the Second Palace era, Driessen and Schoep prefer the term "court-complexes" in place of the tendentious label "palace" till that era. Significantly, in the mature palaces these routes were not generally maintained, as access grew more exclusive.

With the rebuilding of the Second Palaces, a gradual process of enclosure of the Central Court occurs, leading by its final subphase (LM1B) to measures to restrict "public" access to palatial complexes. Contact with regional populations was increasingly mediated through the external courts, especially the West Court, during this Second Palace period. In parallel,

Figure 5.5 Knossos palatial fresco taken to represent public ceremonies in the outer West Court.
J. Driessen, "The King Must Die: Some Observations on the Use of Minoan Court Compounds." In J. Driessen, *et al.* (eds.),
Monuments of Minos, Austin: University of Texas at Austin Press, 2002, 1–14. Courtesy of J. Driessen.

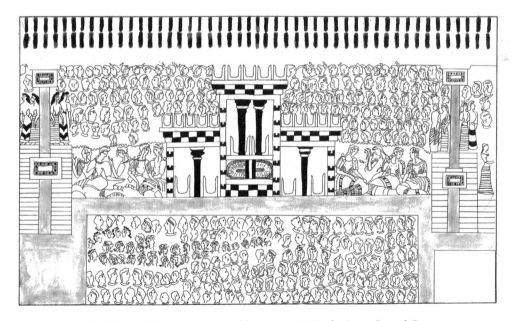

Figure 5.6 Knossos palatial fresco taken to represent public ceremonies in the inner Central Court.
J. Driessen, "The King Must Die: Some Observations on the Use of Minoan Court Compounds." In Driessen, Laffineur,
Schoep eds., *Monuments of Minos*, Austin: University of Texas at Austin Press, 2002, 1–14. Courtesy of J. Driessen.

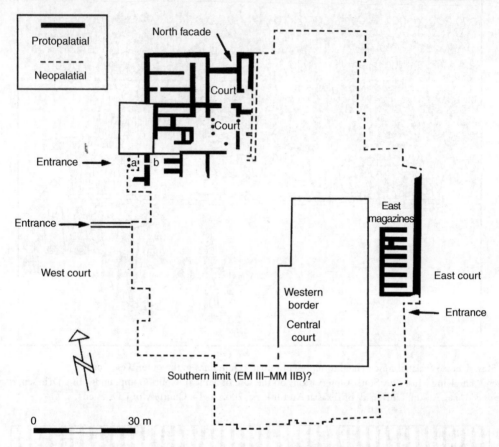

Figure 5.7   The early First Palace (Protopalatial) court-complex at Malia set against its New Palace (Neopalatial) successor. I. Schoep, "Looking beyond the First Palaces: Elites and the agency of power in EMIII-MMII Crete." *American Journal of Archaeology* 110 (2006), 37–64, Figure 3. Reproduced by permission of Archaeological Institute of America (Boston).

a wide power-base (heterarchy) is currently suggested to give way to a narrower political elite, who may indeed have taken up residence in the ceremonial centers by LM1B, converting them into the residential palaces of the traditional model. In tune with these changes, the rare signs of individual status in iconography and burial, and the probable first layout of the Knossos Throne Room, seem to belong to these later phases (Second Palace era and especially the final LM1 period).

Who lived in the Minoan Palaces?

The roots of this controversy run deep, as even contemporaries of Arthur Evans criticized his tendency to construct scenarios and chief actors from the mute evidence of the Knossos Palace ruins (Bintliff 1984). Evans, influenced by Greek myths of prehistoric Crete with its King Minos, gifted architect Daidalos, and a fleet dominating the Aegean (the Minoan "thalassocracy"), reasonably assumed that Cretan palaces were ruled by Kings and Queens. Generations of scholars since have largely agreed, not least because the later Mainland palaces of the Mycenaean civilization, indelibly influenced by Crete, have yet stronger architectural and additional archival reasons for Kingship (plus the more precise legends of ruling dynasties in later Greek epics).

Finely furnished Knossos rooms became the "King's" or "Queen's" apartments, benefiting from

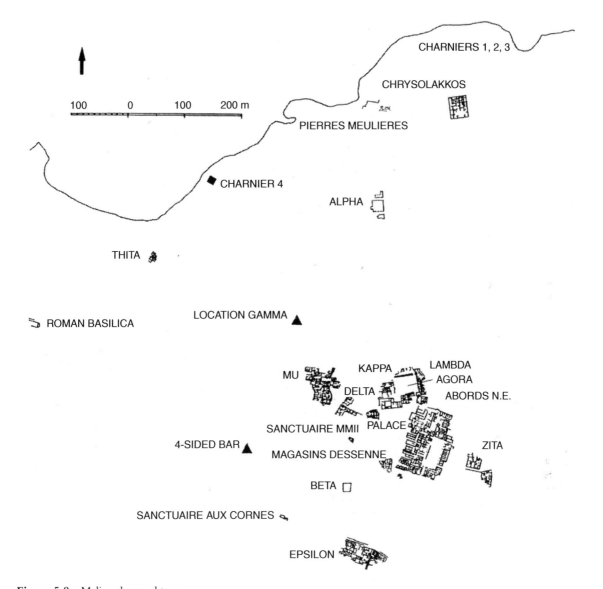

Figure 5.8 Malia palace and town.
I. Schoep, "Social and political organization on Crete in the Proto-Palatial Period: The case of Middle Minoan II Malia."
Journal of Mediterranean Archaeology 15 (2002), 101–132, Figure 1.

luxuries such as flushed toilets. Yet curiously the palace frescoes and mobile art were remarkably free of individuals shown wielding authority over others. There *is* a throne in Knossos, usually dated to the supposed Mycenaean takeover of the palace during LM2, but recently scholars have suggested that it was installed in the final Second Palace era (the troubled LM1B phase after Thera erupted) (cf. Shaw 1993). Even here though, our natural tendency to identify a "royal seat" must be set against the possibility of a priest or priestess officiating at a major communal ritual, perhaps representing or impersonating a divinity. If anything, the remarkable emphasis on women in Minoan frescoes, although chiefly in ritual scenes or symbols, could be read as privileging a female role in power relations.

There is growing evidence for alternative locations where power might have resided, outside of the palaces and their fine apartments. At Malia (Figure 5.8) excavators have identified a series of prestigious house blocks in its extramural town, whilst Evans had discovered large mansions around the Knossos Palace (such as the South House). Balanced against the (contested) royalty surrounded by their supposed "court" in the palaces, might there not have been a class of merchants or major landowners dominating their adjacent towns?

Driessen and Schoep take this argument a radical step further. The palaces are famous for the giant storage facilities for dry and wet measures, and great quantities of tableware such as drinking cups. Yet there is a surprising poverty of the normal debris of domestic residential life, as if the main activity in the palaces was ceremonial, especially large-scale feasting. Given the absence of clear evidence for domestic quarters within the palaces, they wonder if virtually nobody lived continuously in them, at least until the Second Palace era and especially its final LM1B phase (only Knossos and perhaps Khania continue later). Were they essentially ceremonial centers for residents of the associated towns and sectors of the regional population? Was there no single dynastic ruler occupying each palace, and did perhaps the various elite families in the surrounding mansions share or dispute control over the ceremonial life of the palaces (a "heterarchy" rather than "hierarchy")? This challenging rethink nonetheless allows for both the plan and role of the palaces to alter over time. In particular, in the course of the Second Palace era, one elite group may have succeeded in taking control of the Knossos Palace and assuming a more regal residential presence there. The Thera volcanic catastrophe could have enhanced factional politics in the direction of dictatorship. Some see these tensions as linked to the subsequent arrival of the Mycenaeans (LM2), who were perhaps invited by, or took advantage of, factional interests within Minoan society.

The best evidence for "decentered" palatial towns comes from Malia (Fitton 2002, Schoep 2002). French scholars have long argued for public functions and important families being based in the extra-palatial settlement. Its "political center" links a square ("Agora") with a pillared crypt, the latter perhaps a council chamber with storage facilities. In the Mu Quarter, mansions such as A, B, and E share "palatial" features, many of which appear to predate and hence form a model for later adoption in the Second Palaces (Schoep 2010). Characteristic elaborate ashlar (cut-block) masonry for external walls and a special group of rooms often associated with "state functions" (a pair of rooms separated by movable doors in the "pillar and pier" arrangement, associated with a sunken basin for ritual, the "lustral basin"), appear first in these large town houses during First Palace times, then become typical for the palaces in the Second Palace era. Significantly, Quarter Mu becomes disused in the latter phase, hinting that its role in the town and state's administration had been absorbed into the palace itself. The hypothesized public assembly area and council chamber also go out of use in this Second Palace period. The wide range of workshops in the town and a Linear A tablet which lists 7000 sheep all add up to a challenge to the model of centralized palace control of both town and surrounding region.

Minoan palace society, with its reluctance to portray individuals in political roles, communicates other aspects as central to Minoan society: cult and ceremonies. Yet there *are* a handful of scenes which have reasonably been taken to display power roles, such as the Chieftain's Cup (Figure 5.9), or the Master of the City.

The repetitive formal gesture of the staff-bearing man in these two scenes plausibly demonstrates authority, over a soldier and a Minoan town respectively. Driessen emphasizes the attribution of all such images of power to the late Second Palace era, especially LM1B (Driessen 2003). Perhaps more indicative of an influential elite in earlier centuries is the status of certain groups of women in palatial art. In both of the Knossos frescoes which have been interpreted as public ceremonies, a group of individualized seated women are in the forefront, behind which a mass of men is portrayed at a much smaller scale (Figures 5.5 and 5.6).

Figure 5.9 Carved serpentine cup, known as the Chieftain's Cup, found at the Minoan site of Ayia Triada on Crete.
© Roger Wood/CORBIS.

Relations Between "Palatial Centers": Toward a More Historical and Regional Perspective

Cherry (1986) found the evidence ambiguous as to whether palatial Crete formed a series of autonomous polities centered on the larger and perhaps smaller palaces, or at some point, if not usually, it was dominated by the largest example at Knossos. Greek legend suited the latter, with King Minos ruler of Crete from Knossos, although his brother Rhadamanthys controlled another great palatial center in Phaistos, and a third brother Sarpedon might be associated with Malia ("Milatos"). The associated legends of a Mainland Mycenaean intervention (Theseus raiding the island, then at the later time of the Trojan War Crete being ruled by Mycenaeans (Hooker 1969)), focused again on Knossos. Is there firmer evidence for either hypothesis, or indeed for a recent third suggestion, that for most of the "palace" era, contiguous large territorial states did not actually exist?

For the widely-accepted Mycenaean occupation from LM2, there is strong reason to assume that Knossos controlled Central and Western Crete, but this is irrelevant to a possible fragmentation of power in the preceding Minoan era. The Linear A archives of the latter period are only marginally understood, and thus indications of political boundaries are lacking. However since Cherry's publication, a new generation of researchers has again brought provocative evidence into consideration (Driessen and MacDonald 1997, Driessen *et al.* 2002).

Painstaking reworking of older excavations has allowed Driessen and his colleagues to propose a new picture of the history of the Minoan palaces, swinging the argument in favor of an alternation between their autonomy and Knossian dominance. Disruption of palace life by earthquakes or side-effects of the Thera eruption might cause individual palaces to cease functioning as state centers, whilst others might take over control of regions lacking an effective palace (merely to fill a vacuum or perhaps opportunistically through military action). Despite cultural uniformities across Crete, and virtually absent fortifications, this scenario envisages competitive states seeking to expand control over their neighbors. Palatial Linear A archives are only fragmentarily readable, and military equipment is almost never portrayed, but weapons known from graves could have been as much for use *within* Crete as abroad in military ventures. The late MM2 catastrophe which destroyed the First Palaces, usually attributed to a massive island-wide earthquake, might, some now speculate, have been due to war (Cadogan 2004), and in any case, the subsequent failure to rebuild the Phaistos palace to its former grandeur, coupled with the development of the "mansions" nearby at Aghia Triadha (La Rosa 1985), could indicate a Knossos coup over its southern rival. Another theory is that the later catastrophic destructions in LM1B, leaving all palaces destroyed apart from Knossos (and perhaps Khania) by LM2, could have been the work of Knossos militarism, which nonetheless somehow opened the way for the introduction of a Mycenaean administration at Knossos. On the other hand, Knossos in LM1B has been described as "ruined" or at least in much diminished use (Adams 2004).

Here we suffer, as with the later Mycenaean civilization, from the almost certain fact that the political and diplomatic palatial correspondence was on perishable paper or vellum sheets of animal hide. Their existence is detectable from impressions on the undersides of sealings. Matching seal designs do however demonstrate a nexus of correspondence in LM1B between the major and minor centers of Kato Zakro, Aghia Triadha, Gournia, and Sklavokampos, with the hypothesis that the source of the missives was Knossos (Betts 2000). Sealings from Thera in LM1A may be part of the same web of diplomacy or economy. All this might support the theory of Knossian expansionism in the Second Palace era, especially after the LM1A Thera eruption. Although recent fresco discoveries at Avaris in Egypt (see below), are believed to represent an exceptional pictorial link to Crete, the diplomatic relations implied by the hypothesis that they represent a marriage between Minoan and Egyptian dynasties, serve to remind us that missing and crucial contemporary historical evidence may well appear in the near future and cause us to rethink our established theories.

As increasing numbers of small palaces are discovered, other doubts are being raised. Is a political geography of a few large states centered on the largest palatial towns too simplistic? Were lesser palaces autonomous? Were regions remote from known palaces also outside their control, at least till Second Palace times (as Haggis (2002) argues for the Kavousi district)? Kommos, a port-town at the coastal end of the Mesara Plain, was the main maritime outlet for the Palace of Phaistos, but the excavators (Shaw and Shaw 1993, Shaw 2006) having identified a "palace-like" courtyard complex and a plausible mansion for a controlling residential elite, query whether Kommos was a direct dependency of Phaistos in MM-LM1 times (and later under the Mycenaean domination of Crete, of Knossos), or a semi-independent town, at least in the Minoan palace eras.

Till recently the accepted view pictured a revolutionary transformation with the start of the MM period: a society where humble villagers had previously directed their architectural pretensions into communal stone tombs was catalyzed into erecting a few vast architectural splendors, the First Palaces, for a meteorically-rising group of regional dynasties. When just a few centers were known, it was natural to assume that they carved Crete into respective spheres of control. The formal similarity between the Minoan palace archives in Linear A and those of the subsequent Mycenaean Linear B variety obscured possible differences between their administrative systems; this was especially likely when one of the largest archives came from Mycenaean Knossos, and evidenced a very wide sphere of economic influence to almost all parts of Crete.

Current rethinking reflects the discovery that "court-centered complexes" appear at staggered intervals across Crete, with precocious examples during EM times, others only in the First or Second Palace phases. Whilst "functionalist" scholars of the 1970s and 1980s, such as Renfrew, Cherry, Halstead, and the author, had believed that major palaces had virtually totalitarian control over the population and resources in their regions, scholars now ask if smaller centers were necessarily subordinate to larger centers or to each other. This is a natural consequence of the shift from a "ruler-centered," to a "ceremonial-center" view of "court-complexes." If palaces acted as foci for different groups of regional populations to congregate, for various religious ceremonies, then lesser foci and larger could coexist without power inequalities.

Finally there has been a growing interest in the homes of ordinary Minoans, and how their architecture relates to more grandiose private and public buildings. Innovative research (Letesson 2007) shows that beneath an apparently diverse set of plans there are underlying generating principles in the design of Minoan buildings. Moreover, between the earlier and later palace eras both everyday domestic homes and the status architecture of palaces and mansions show the same tendencies: increasing the number of rooms into which the built environment is divided, and making human movement around these constructed spaces more indirect. This has been recognized cross-culturally as a symptom of increasing complexity in social structures.

The Minoans Abroad

Evans saw the inspiration for the rise of Minoan civilization in early contacts with more advanced cultures of the Near East, particularly Egypt and the Levant

(Syro–Palestine). As a "Secondary Civilization" the Minoans spread the seed to the Mainland, stimulating the subsequent birth of Mycenaean civilization. Apart from diplomacy, trade was taken as key for the incorporation of the Aegean into the intense political and economic exchanges of the "*koine*" (cultural commonwealth) of Near Eastern states. Despite a trend during the 1970s and 1980s to privilege internal developments in the origins of Aegean civilization (Renfrew 1973), since then scholarly interest has revived in considering interregional ties as a vital factor in Aegean social developments. The popularity of World System and Core–Periphery theories (Kardulias 1999) has encouraged many Aegean prehistorians to conceptualize the rise and functioning of Minoan-Mycenaean state systems as fundamentally due to their interlocking into Near Eastern "world economies" (cf. Sherratt and Sherratt 1993, Sjöberg 2004, *Rethinking* 2007).

Viewing the EBA Aegean as already embedded in these networks, however, fits poorly with the evidence. Admittedly Mesopotamian trade systems in the EBA do penetrate Eastern Anatolia, and it is possible to suggest that the spread of states and towns through Anatolia in the third millennium and their mutual trade not only may have been affected by this, but also that limbs of these exchange relations may have entered the EBA Aegean. Nonetheless the artifactual evidence and the likely depth of such networks in stimulating Aegean transformation seem feeble. Direct imports from the Levant or Egypt even to Crete are scant, "exotic knick-knacks" (Renfrew). Watrous (1994) even redates most of these imports into the palatial period, whilst EB2 objects leaving the Aegean are virtually nil. For the "Secondary Civilization" school, however, it is the Middle Minoan (MBA) appearance of the First Palaces that securely places Crete as a new "core" of civilization.

I would favor an intermediate view between the World System proponents and those favoring an essentially internal social development for Crete, by acknowledging that there is already from the EBA, and then increasingly onwards, continuous evidence for important external contacts which do change Aegean cultures. Yet this is better seen as indirect diffusion and freelance trade, without a political or economic strategy in terms of a core–periphery or world system dimension. Mobile craftsmen and independent traders, perhaps moving stepwise around well-established maritime circuits, seem better able to explain our evidence, than state-sponsored political and commercial expeditions emanating from the small and large states of the Levant, Anatolia, and Egypt. Thus the Neolithic colonization out of the Near East in general, followed in later Neolithic times by the Secondary Products Revolution, do not lead to lasting links back to the Near East. The Final Neolithic spread of copper, then EBA arsenic-bronze and tin-bronze metallurgy, chiefly from the direction of the North Balkans and Northwest Anatolia, can be accommodated into the less grandiose model outlined above. The same can be said for the EBA spread of vine and olive cultivation from the North Aegean and the Levant, even the spread of new social drinking customs with related tableware in late EB2 out of Western Anatolia into the Aegean (Davis 1992, Rutter 1993); equally for the late EBA diffusion of wheel-made pottery and the use of sealings. Broodbank (2000) has added a perhaps equally vital change between EBA and MBA in the Aegean, the arrival of the boat with sails to replace the sail-less oared long-boat, which would surely have revolutionized the size, transport capacity, and speed of boats and their ability to cross the open sea on long voyages. The origin of this technology was clearly Eastern Mediterranean.

Thus the EBA Aegean was in regular relations with Anatolia and the Levant, in ways which in combination profoundly altered life by the beginning of the MM era. Such contacts, even if the creation of entrepreneurial merchants and mobile craftspeople, rather than powerful rulers in the East, nonetheless allowed knowledge to enter the Aegean. Till recently this knowledge was believed to include the importation at the start of the First Palace era of both the idea, and the practical plan, of palaces with literate bureaucracies. In the light of the piecemeal evolution of court-complexes from early in EM, then the prior use of key "palatial" architectural features in town mansions of the First Palace period before their adoption in "palaces" of the Second Palace period, this scenario has had to be modified. Schoep and Driessen suggest that elite families resident in surrounding town houses controlled ceremonies in the locally-evolved court complexes, drawing on their traditional power as ritual leaders of their communities. In the MM era these elites then came to emulate Near Eastern urban elite lifestyles and economic management practices: they introduced more sophisticated architecture, literacy and archives, a vast increase in the production of prestige objects for use in communal ceremonies and the homes of the upper classes, and the adoption of motifs and materials representative of the exotic world of developed states in the Eastern Mediterranean.

Nonetheless, none of this confirms the "world economy" model, where Minoan Crete would have been dependent on Eastern commerce during the MM–LM "palatial eras." Minoan trade to the Levant and Egypt appears remarkably slight, as befits the sporadic and insignificant textual hints in those societies regarding what are taken to be Minoans or Aegean peoples. Although the Minoans certainly derived raw materials and finished objects from the same areas, these are numerically small compared to regional production. One notable exception is copper from Cyprus, an island which by the end of the Bronze Age has become as much an Aegean as a Levantine culture, perhaps as a result (Voskos and Knapp 2008). I see no evidence that the Minoan economy was dominated by production for external trade; it is probable that the bulk of island production in food, ceramics, and textiles supplied its own inhabitants. Judging from the similarities of Linear A to B archives, monitoring this island production was an obsessive aim of the Minoan elite, who needed to take maximum advantage of significant parts of it for the smooth support of the "palatial establishment," and the personal wealth and prestige of those who occupied town mansions and country villas.

Thus by definition, these Aegean civilizations were small "world empires" and not segments of larger "world economies." This does not however rule out the likely powerful effects of a systematic participation by both societies in trade, as well as political dealings, with state societies in the MBA–LBA Eastern Mediterranean, which may well have affected central aspects of Minoan and Mycenaean civilization.

An unexpected twist to this debate arose with the discovery in an Egyptian palace in the Nile Delta (modern el-Dab'a, ancient Avaris), of Pharaonic state apartments incorporating frescoes of indubitably Minoan character and likely craftsmanship (Bietak 1995, 2000). The excavator proposes that this very

unusual close link to Crete reflects a royal marriage with a Minoan princess. It has also been argued that Minoan artists were sent to decorate palaces at Tell Alalakh, Tell Kabri, and at Qatna in the Levant during the same Second Palace era (Negbi et al. 1994).

The situation regarding Minoan involvement in the Aegean is very different. As Warren and Schofield have persuasively argued, Minoan influence is highly visible and increases in depth and range over time from the First to the Second Palace period (Warren 1975, Warren in Bintliff 1977c, Warren 1984; Schofield 1982). Already during EM times Minoans colonized the island of Kythera, whilst during MM and even more clearly in early LM there is an inner ring of Cycladic islands, closest to Crete, with strong Minoan acculturation, or even some colonial presence, such as Thera and Melos, together with points on the Southwestern Anatolian coast (especially Miletos) (Davis 1992). This passes into strong trade influence in the more distant Cycladic islands and on the Aegean coasts of Southern Mainland Greece. Inland, and north of Central Greece, Minoan contacts decline rapidly. Lively debate on the political context of these rings of influence continues, particularly regarding the reality or otherwise behind Greek legends of a Minoan seaborne empire ("thalassocracy"). Most scholars reject this militaristic scenario, but we need to be just as cautious of accepting the pervasive myth (that Evans created) of a Golden Age of Minoan peacefulness. Minoan art portrays sieges and naval warfare, whilst the highly "Minoanized" island of Thera provides explicit scenes of maritime and land warfare, echoed in iconography from the island of Aegina (Rutter 1993). Aegina is part of the Minoan cultural sphere, as well as nourishing a local elite (Felten et al. 2004).

It is certainly no coincidence that the development of Mainland culture in the early Middle Bronze Age (Middle Helladic culture) is sluggish in comparison to contemporary First Palace Crete, but as the Minoan wave of influence deepens at the end of that period and into the beginning of the Late Bronze Age (locally MH3–LH1), the age of the Second Palaces, a dramatic change manifests itself, particularly at the key sites of Mycenae and Pylos in the Peloponnese. At the former, the rapid development of prestigious elite burials in the Shaft Graves A and B portends the emergence of Mycenaean civilization, and these graves are filled with spectacular gifts generally accepted as of Minoan origin or fabricated by Minoan craft specialists. At Pylos the earliest palace is now reconstructed as a replica of a Minoan open "court-complex" with other imitative architectural details (Nelson 2007). There can be little doubt that the rise of the Mycenaeans was intimately connected to the stimulus of Minoan cultural, and arguably economic and political, expansion.

I suspect then that the Minoan economy and its foreign policy were geared in the first place to island production and consumption, and then in second place to supplying necessary exports for obtaining exotic raw materials and prestige goods. This did not inhibit Crete developing a strong sphere of economic and political influence in the South Aegean region (the Cycladic and adjacent islands and the Mainland of Greece). Crete appears to play a dominant role in brokering exchanges between the Near East and the rest of the Aegean, and this may explain why in the rare Egyptian references to the Aegean world, Crete appears as representative for the "Keftiu" (probably Aegean people). But significantly, Late Bronze Age shipwrecks such as Uluburun and Gelidonya give the impression of freelance merchants carrying mixed-origin cargoes along routes filled with numerous exchange points (Negbi *et al.* 1994) rather than state-financed trading missions.

The End of the New Palaces

The violent catastrophe which destroys the Second Palaces in LM1 remains highly controversial. Till recently some scholars favored an earthquake. Many more looked to the giant and well-documented volcanic eruption during this ceramic phase on the island of Thera (just 60 km from Crete), potentially assaulting the Minoans with tidal waves and a poisonous ash-fall (see following Text Box). In the 1930s, however, Arthur Evans had to contest vigorously a theory of Mycenaean specialists Blegen and Wace, that the Second Palaces were destroyed by invading Mycenaeans who then occupied Knossos. This was the only palace then known to remain in significant use in the "Post-Palatial" LM2–3 period, and it was claimed that "occupied Knossos" ran the island as a Mycenaean state. Greek myth perhaps preserved a

memory, in the Theseus and the Minotaur legend, of a dramatic Mycenaean intervention in Minoan palatial civilization. The decipherment by Ventris in 1953 of the Linear B script in which Mycenaean palace archives were written, identifying it as Greek, offered dramatic support for Blegen and Wace, as the Knossos tablets from this final "Post-Palatial" period were in Linear B, rather than the different language of Linear A as used in the earlier Minoan culture palaces.

Surprisingly, the subsequent and final destruction of Minoan palatial organization, with the ultimate torching of the Knossos palace, is of unclear date. Most argue that the end came with a Mycenaean withdrawal from Crete, or a local revolt leading to the same result, implying that a new Mainland regime was installed at Knossos after the end of the Second Palaces in LM2 ca. 1550 BC, which subsequently collapsed ca. 1375 BC (LM3A). Others believe that the Knossos palace survived into the thirteenth century BC, when the Mainland Mycenaean palaces themselves were burnt down, and thus its fate might be part of wider catastrophic events (civil wars, external raiders or invaders).

Writing and Administration

Evans' interest in prehistoric inscribed clay tablets and gems sourced to Crete stimulated the first major palace excavations, and the tablet archives certainly form a key source of information regarding Aegean Bronze Age palatial life, but sadly not yet for the First and Second Palaces of Crete. The reason was appreciated from the first, that the Cretan tablets fall into two main groups, both deploying a syllabic script, Linear A and B, with a small number in another writing style (the pictographic).

Linear A archives (Figure 5.10) are in an unknown language and were produced by the Minoan culture. Very similar in signs and form are Linear B archives, but these are written in an early form of Greek, hence can be translated; they were produced by Mycenaean states on the Mainland, and for the Mycenaean administration of "Post-Palatial" LM2–3 Crete, based at the Palace of Knossos and at Khania. Nonetheless, the similar format of these records, and a wide overlap in signs (allowing names to be read), suggest strongly that

Santorini–Thera and the Destruction of Minoan Crete

Marinatos (1939) suggested that the Greek myth of Atlantis, where as reported by Plato a great island civilization vanished underwater in a giant catastrophe, was a memory of a great eruption on the Cycladic island of Thera in LM1. Minoan Crete, close neighbor to Thera, was devastated by tsunamis (tidal waves) and a poisonous ash-fall, whilst associated earth tremors might have caused violent fires in the palaces. Following this natural catastrophe, the Mainland Mycenaeans invaded Crete, either taking advantage of its political collapse, or being responsible themselves for the fire-destruction of the palaces.

Marinatos' and subsequently Doumas' excavations at the town of Akrotiri on Thera (see Chapter 6), buried under the volcanic eruption, ultimately ran into a central contradiction in this scenario. The style of Minoan pottery imported and imitated on Thera at the time of its abandonment, very shortly before the eruption, is LM1A, whilst that in use on Crete at the time of the destruction of the Minoan palaces is LM1B; this should separate these disasters by at least 50 years, maybe much longer. A related problem is the date of the eruption, because cross-dating of artifacts from excavated levels in Minoan, Egyptian, and Levantine sequences, tied to dates inferred from Egyptian historical texts, indicates a lower date, ca. 1450 BC (some 100–200 years later), than the balance of so-called absolute dates from Aegean C14 samples. A recent series of high-resolution C14 dates from Crete and Santorini (Bruins *et al.* 2008) places the LM1A volcanic catastrophe around 1628 BC, perhaps bringing the chronology debate to an end. This creates a satisfactory timescale to allow later phases to unfold. A date in the sixteenth century BC for the main phase of LM1B now seems correct. Finally, new associations between LM1 and a seventeenth-century date in the Levant allow better synchronisms with Near Eastern chronologies.

However, Marinatos' concept that the Thera explosion destabilized Minoan civilization has not disappeared. Although scientific study has shown that the claim that the ash-fall was thick enough on the soils of Crete to bring agricultural disaster cannot be sustained, the hypothesis of a giant tsunami devastating Minoan harbor-towns has been revived from the coastal town of Palaikastro (Eastern Crete) (Bruins *et al.* 2008). Here extensive traces have been claimed for a 9-meter high tidal wave, associated with LM1A artifacts, and fragments from the ash-fall. Although one of the excavators, MacGillivray, agrees that a significant period elapsed before the subsequent fall of the Cretan palaces, he believes that the immense psychological trauma occasioned by this and similar effects elsewhere in coastal Crete broke the cohesion of the palatial system and laid the island open to external conquest. However co-director Driessen thinks the sediments concerned are local flashflood deposits (*pers. comm.*) and prefers the idea that a widespread crisis occurred in the religious system sustaining Minoan society, since the cataclysmic natural disaster on Thera might have brought into question the ability of the Minoan population and especially their community leaders to negotiate prosperity with the gods (Driessen 2001).

Driessen and Macdonald (1997) have suggested that the consequent destabilization of the palatial political system paved the way for a Mycenaean coup at the end of LM1B. They speculate that the eruption traumatized parts of Minoan society, allowing one family to assume control of the Knossos palace, reflected in changed iconography and ground-plans (and the throne room?). Perhaps also in LM1B the new centralized power at Knossos attacked other palaces, a conflict in which the Mainland power of the new Mycenaean states became involved, ultimately precipitating the destruction of all but Knossos at the end of 1B and the assumption of control over most of the island by Mycenaeans, who were ruling from Knossos by LMII.

Figure 5.10 Clay archive records in Minoan Linear A script.
P. M. Warren, *The Making of the Past. The Aegean Civilizations.* Ekdotiki Athenon SA, Athens 1975, 37. Heraklion Museum, Crete. Photo: Ekdotiki Athenon, Athens.

regarding internal and external politics, so significant to our understanding of the Bronze Age civilizations of the contemporary Near East, where such letters were preserved on clay tablets or even stone.

In terms of the traditional "royal dynastic palace" model for Minoan Crete, these elaborate and widespread recording systems seem appropriate for a centralized bureaucracy keeping a close control over the island out of the major palatial centers. For the revisionary "court-complex, heterarchic" model, it is argued that these records were primarily concerned with the semi-communal organization of products necessary for the all-important religious rituals and feasts held at the numerous "palatial" foci across the island. In addition, since they occur in non-palace, private contexts, they could also have monitored the production and marketing of surpluses from the agricultural estates of the wealthier landowners and the marketing of local private workshops for ceramics, metal, and stone vessels.

Pottery Styles

Minoan ceramics are finely crafted and already from the EM period highly decorated, with certain styles exported from their production districts to other parts of Crete. These characteristics expand in the "palatial" eras to even more diverse products, of which the fine wares with their successive styles remain the basis for chronology, whilst the fast-wheel improves quality from MM1 onwards (Figure 5.11). It has been assumed that the great and lesser palaces were the main craft production centers of the island, as well as being the prime consumers of the highest-quality wares, such as the eggshell-thin Kamares style. However, scientific analysis (Day and Wilson 2002) suggests that much of the ceramics found in major palatial centers was imported from elsewhere, including regions believed to have their focus on other centers. Although craft production has been demonstrated within the towns surrounding the palaces (notably at Malia), and on a small scale even within the court-complexes themselves, there is evidence for much of the island's artisans operating in a private capacity and located in adjacent or distant towns and villages (such as the LM1B industrial community on the coast opposite the islet of Mochlos). The discovery that the ceramic trade is no

the untranslated A series is broadly comparable to B. Moreover, the numerical system in Linear A is also understood, and occasional pictograms provide rare detail of what is being counted. It is thus inferred that the Minoan, as the Mycenaean, tablets existed to document the income and outgoings of the palaces' central administration, in aspects such as agricultural and craft production, and the provision of ritual. Although the specific script is not derivable from earlier, Near Eastern state systems, the idea of developing such clay archives was clearly adopted from Near Eastern administrative practices, from whence also some aspects of mature palatial architecture are likely to have been copied.

Apart from archive tablets, inscribed clay discs (roundels) and nodules were attached to objects or containers, inscriptions were painted on pots, and most tantalizingly, clay sealings occur, whose folds betray that they once wrapped parchment letters. Nearly all these stamped and inscribed objects appear to be associated with controlling the storage and movement of products, probably both public and private, and their occurrence in the Aegean islands under strong Minoan influence has variously been seen as proof of resident merchants or colonial officials. The lost letters surely account for the absence in both Minoan and Mycenaean civilizations of that correspondence

Figure 5.11   Typical painted fine wares of First Palace date.
O. Dickinson, *The Aegean Bronze Age.* © Cambridge University Press 1994, Figure 5.8.

longer essentially the output of "palace industry" is less surprising when we recall the widespread exchange of pottery not only in EM but also Neolithic Crete.

Other Products

The centralized organization underlying the construction and functioning of the court-complexes and later palaces, and the demand created by their associated towns, required surplus food to support differentiation of labor, whilst creating a large market for manufactures. This stimulated an increasingly dense rural population, whilst vital urban–rural interactions were serviced through the construction of roads, at least in the most highly developed districts around the great "palaces."

Cretan mobile artifacts in stone, metal, and precious stones today grace museum cases throughout the island, combining beauty, mysterious iconography, and technical sophistication. Most famous are the figure-decorated sealstones, requiring the use of a magnifier by the artist. These were already in general use in pre-Palatial times (probably to define ownership, power, and the administration of storage, but perhaps for a social group as much as for individuals). The time-consuming products of stone bowl workshops are derived from Egyptian prototypes, whilst delicate gold jewelry demonstrates elaborate smithing skills. And with such expensive luxury items, many for special display-use, it is logical that workshops were placed in the palaces themselves, as well as adjacent in their surrounding towns.

Highly significant are specialist workshops associated with larger town mansions in the First Palace period town of Malia. It is suggested that wealthy and powerful families resident in these houses employed craftsmen to create objects for their own use, to attach clients to themselves through gifts, and to increase their influence through trade contacts within and outside Crete. In the "heterarchy" model, a class of such magnates shared or disputed control of the ritual activities in the "court-complexes"/early palaces from their urban power-bases.

Burial Archaeology

Current thinking considers Early Minoan tholos tombs and related house tombs (which continued in use during the earlier Middle Minoan First Palace era, but decline or cease in Second Palatial times) as primary foci of kin-group and communal ritual in the vicinity of settlements. These religious ceremonies are believed to have commemorated the individual dead and collective ancestors, but also marked the seasons, and the fertility of crops and humans. A growing representation of leading families in the course of EM has been suggested for grander or more prominent tombs and prestigious gifts (e.g., at Archanes and Mochlos), as well as through the use of seals found in the tombs. In late EM and MM individuals in general are further highlighted through the spread of burial in clay coffins (*larnakes*) and giant storage jars (pithoi), collective burial declining progressively through the First and Second Palace periods. However, the burial record for these later eras is inadequately researched. Exceptional complex architectural mausolea such as the Temple and Royal Tombs at Knossos, and rich graves at the Knossian port of Poros (including LM1A-B warrior graves), are significantly late, Second Palace, and probably from its final disrupted LM1 period, during which the effects of the Thera eruption may have led to major shifts toward the more prominent role for an elite and more pronounced militarism in Minoan society (Fitton 2002). A rare earlier exception is the MM1–2, First Palace burial building at Chrysolakkos outside the town of Malia, usually considered a rich elite necropolis, but not without controversy (Driessen 2007). But this is not isolated within the First Palace era: at Arkhanes the traditional tholos tomb is now being developed into a clearly status-enhancing grandeur (Schoep and Knappett 2004), while Mochlos has elite burial evidence (Schoep 2006). In the "dynastic" model Chrysolakkos was considered a "royal" burial complex, whereas in the new "heterarchic" approach it is suggested that Malia town possessed neighborhoods with their own leading families, and for each a separate town-periphery cemetery existed on the edge of town. Nonetheless, the rarity of elaborate tombs in Palatial times confirms the "low profile" of Minoan social elites in conspicuous arenas of display such as death ritual and commemoration, a considerable contrast with the later Mycenaean civilization or the contemporary Near East.

Paved areas outside collective EM-MM tombs are interpreted as ritual plazas and also "dancing-floors." A plausible link ties these small-group arenas to their counterparts which are attested by mature EM times and on into MM, the Central and West Courts in the major settlement and palace complexes, where public events took place, plausibly of a social, political, and religious character. That minor EM settlements such as Vasiliki and Fournou Korifi already during the "early court-complex phase" added plazas to their community design, seems equally significant. The idea that a nested set of rituals, involving increasingly large populations and human catchments, took place in such plazas, finds its possible correspondence in a hierarchy of formal sanctuaries.

Minoan Religion: Plazas, Temples, Peak Sanctuaries, and Sacred Caves

The formal paved courts within the "palaces" (Central Court), and one or more on its exterior (generally a West Court), are believed to have formed "theaters" for key public events of a politico-religious character. Over time, as the "palaces" become more enclosed and less accessible, the roles of internal and external courts may have altered considerably. The West Court, arguably particularly important for ceremonies linking the town and those elite groups believed to have controlled the rituals of the "palace complexes" and of the Central Court, has a carefully-enhanced outer face of the "palace" fronting it, with fine-cut ashlar work. The insets along this façade may indicate important upper-floor windows, and some suggest that elite members formally presented themselves at these apertures ("windows of appearance") to the assembled populace, perhaps in conscious imitation of Egyptian royal practices. This could have been a sign of real power or some sacred theater.

However both academic and popular imagination has long speculated whether the Central Court was the locus of a different, more intriguing activity, bull-leaping (Color Plate 5.1). This dangerous "sport" or "ritual" is so frequently portrayed that it assuredly played a major part in the Minoan mental world. Young men, and quite possibly women, grasped a charging bull's horns, somersaulted onto its back, then somersaulted off, to be caught by a companion on the ground. Like all recent Mediterranean bull-sports, deadly accidents could occur, and indeed there are scenes of such a kind. But is such an athletic feat even possible? Some expert bull-fighters say absolutely not. A recent video on YouTube does though show an athlete somersaulting over a charging bull, but not via a first leap onto its back. Furthermore Graham (1962), in his notable study of palatial architecture, suggested that the Central Court design could be matched in particular portrayals of the "sport," and indeed has claimed to have found traces of possible "safety-barriers" around the Knossos example. There is also the unlikely coincidence that later Greek myth, in its tale of Theseus accompanying a regular tribute of Mainland youths to the palace of King Minos at Knossos, informs us that they were to be sacrificed to the bull-monster the Minotaur. Cretan palatial art uses bulls and bull-horns as a regular emblem, both for prestigious artifacts and as architectural decoration. Finally, scholars have frequently drawn links between the earth-shaking powers attributed to the later god Poseidon and the permanent threat and frequent visitation of earthquakes on Crete; perhaps in Minoan Crete, this supernatural force requiring appeasement had metamorphosed into a giant bull beneath the earth tossing the island with its horns. In combination, a reasonable argument can be made that the immense and potentially violent power of bulls was the basis for a form of cult-propitiation in palatial times.

However, does Minoan art portray a Minoan legend, or a real event whose public performance and real-world fatalities, like contemporary Spanish and French bull-sports, created a propitiatory or merely cathartic theater of the conflict between humans, death, and dangerous subterranean forces? Personally I believe that bull-leaping took place, especially given the recurrent detailed and varied depictions (not least the accidents). How to accommodate the skeptics of its feasibility? Sherratt (1995) has emphasized the significance of narcotic consumption in Eastern Mediterranean Bronze Age societies, with clear evidence in Minoan art. Were the bulls drugged so that they were dangerous, but slower and less deadly, so that bull-leaping was usually successfully accomplished? This recently became less hypothetical, since

doping tests are now applied at premier Spanish bull-fights to counter allegations that bulls have been drugged to make the matador's job easier.

We have so far mentioned public events which often (always?) included a ritual element (I share the opinion that Minoan society was diffused with religion). Formal evidence for cult includes structures interpreted as shrines and representations on frescoes, gems or in figurine form which are with variable degrees of confidence taken to relate to supernatural beings or events.

Surprisingly small structures, for example facing onto the Central Court, are reasonably interpreted as palace shrines, whilst larger complexes such as at Archanes near Knossos (Sakellarakis and Sapouna-Sakellaraki 1991) are likewise clearly temples. The cult paraphernalia and similarities to artistic scenes combining such structures with supernatural activity form convincing evidence. Much less clear are the possible readings of images on wall-paintings and in mobile art. In the illustrated gems (Figure 5.12a–b) a female figure hovers in the air above ecstatic worshippers, and a seated woman receives gift-bearing females "in state" in an open-air context (note the opium poppies and the double-axe, the latter a recurrent motif in Minoan art and argued to have a central ritual role). Scholars are at odds if these are goddess-scenes, or priestesses and followers in activities of a ritual hallucinogenic nature. The figurines of women are also variously seen as priestess (or) worshipper (or) goddess images, while the occurrence on some of them of snakes also favors a religious context.

Unequivocal evidence for religious activity, if of an extreme form and unparalleled context, comes from the temple complex of Arkhanes Anemospelia. The excavators suggest that a young man was being sacrificed on an altar slab by a woman and an older man when a great earthquake brought the structure down, sealing the entire scene. It is proposed that the event was propitiatory against the quake after pre-shocks warned of its imminence.

Peak sanctuaries and rarer sacred caves found throughout the island have pre-First Palace era origins as places of local worship. The larger class of peak sanctuary is generally defined by an enclosure wall (in Classical Greek called a *temenos*) with an open-air

Figure 5.12a Scene on Isopata engraved ring gem showing ritual dancing in a natural setting with a small floating figure. Drawn by V.-P. Herva after Platon and Pini 1984: no. 51, from V.-P. Herva, "Flower lovers, after all? Rethinking religion and human-environment relations in Minoan Crete." *World Archaeology* 38 (2006), 590, Figure 2.

Figure 5.12b Engraved ring gem. Offerings to a seated female figure before a mystical tree. Clyde E. Keeler, *Apples of Immortality from the Kuna Tree of Life*. New York 1961/Hathi Trust Digital Library.

altar, sometimes a roofed storeroom, and gifts by worshippers, particularly clay but sometimes also metal figures. These could be seen as reflecting various desired relationships with divine powers: human figures as worshippers, human body-parts to seek healing, and animals to promote their fertility (Fitton 2002).

I have argued (Bintliff 1977a–b) that a sacred landscape of local cult centers was already widespread in EM Crete, linking dispersed farms and villages into district community cult practices. Their number rises dramatically in the "Palace" periods, and I proposed that the "court-complex" elites used local cult foci as a grassroots basis to tie ideologies of family, clan, and district community into regional or even island-wide systems of belief. This could support the "palace" foci through creating physical links between worship at peak and cave sites at different geographical levels and for different combinations of population. I drew on an insightful ethnographic analogy (Vogt 1968) which described hierarchies of ritual practice in traditional Mexican society, in which processional ceremonies unite household groups at hamlet shrines, then groups of households visit district shrines, and finally representatives of whole regions process to prominent mountain shrines. This pattern of increasing physical integration creates a ritual cohesion, and at the same time a hierarchy of social statuses can be made visible when we see who are the key players and organizers of ritual at each spatial and social level. In the same way, local Minoan groups may have worshiped at dispersed rural shrines, then representatives from a whole district could have processed to ritual performances at focal peak sanctuaries or sacred caves, finally selected participants from a whole region (maybe the entire zone centering on each palace), might have processed to certain key sanctuaries. Amongst the latter we can surely rank those rituals taking place in the outer and inner courts of the palaces themselves.

As for Minoan divinities, Dickinson (1994) wisely warns against traditional assumptions of a unitary Minoan pantheon (fixed group of gods or goddesses), as well as a dominant Great Goddess. It is more likely that the current trend to see regionalism in Crete should lead us to expect diverse local cults, and this suits the variety of offerings found archaeologically.

Strengths and Weaknesses of the New Model for Minoan "Court-Complex" Society

No-one has defended the propositions that the First and Second Palaces and the Second Palace era rural mansions were occupied by peasants, or that the system was run by middle-class artisans and traders, on a communitarian basis. Yet the exact form of the managerial elite is surprisingly difficult to capture from the archaeological or iconographic evidence. This is not helped by the fact that Linear A archives are only translatable to the level of names and pictograms, and seem mostly to relate to records of storerooms.

Minoan civilization is traditionally depicted as an exception amongst ancient civilizations, for its virtual absence of evidence (archaeological, architectural, and iconographic) for a powerful (if not oppressive) elite,

for the minimal emphasis on warfare, and an unusual bias in art on females in significant social roles. Mycenaean Mainland Greece seems its direct opposite, except for the role of women, who also in art and burial were given status (though not on a scale comparable to Minoan Crete). Greek myth portrayed otherwise: King Minos of Knossos, in a tradition plausibly Bronze Age in origin, possessed a seaborne empire, extracted tribute from the Aegean peoples, and sacrificed annual victims from these subjects to his Minotaur monster. This monster dwelt in the Labyrinth, probably a memory of the "labyrinthine" passages and rooms of the giant palace-complex with its double-axe or *labrys* symbols.

The Minoan world as a "Golden Age" of peaceful innocence was the creation, appropriately, of the civilization's discoverer Arthur Evans (Bintliff 1984; MacGillivray 2000). He felt ill at ease in the late Victorian and Edwardian world, seeking something better and more idealistic, which he found, or rather created, out of the remains he excavated in Knossos. He was indeed right in noting the virtual absence of fortifications around the palaces, although there are watchtowers along roads, and whilst access to the palaces is carefully controlled and difficult, this only appears in the *later* phases of these complexes.

We have in this chapter outlined persuasive reinterpretations of the origins, development, and functioning of the Minoan "court complex" societies. These theories have powerful attractions and even to skeptics of such revisionism serve to remind us that Evans' picture rested on little archaeological evidence. Are there problems in turn with the new historical narrative?

Firstly, it is difficult to envisage how the palaces, both in their (new) EM "Pre-Palatial" and in their mature First and Second Palace form, could have been constructed, and evolved, to a broadly similar plan, across the island, by a series of infighting families each based in their own mansions across the towns of Crete. Moreover, in contrast to the situation at MM Malia where town mansions are identified as elite private homes, at Knossos the LM1A mansions around the Palace lack storage facilities and normal domestic equipment: instead, their ritual or ceremonial functions are clear. Warren (2004) believes they were supported by "the Palace establishment" economically, and this fits better with the traditional view that this series of mansions were residences of people responsible for major functions *within* the palace. But proponents of the new models could reasonably respond that this First to Second Palace era contrast (MM Malia compared with LM1 Knossos) can just as well agree with a gradual shift of power from a controlling elite who may initially have occupied independent mansions in the towns around the "palaces," to an elite controlled from *within* the palace.

Secondly, the existence of bureaucracies, itemizing it seems the same kind of detailed production and consumption of food and artifacts across wide territories as in the comparable and readable Mycenaean archives, also fits poorly with a group of competitive families disputing power. To whom were the scribes answerable? The parallels which are now drawn to Mesoamerican ceremonial centers highlight common features with Minoan palaces. These include an overriding emphasis on ritual spaces and large storage zones which were necessary in regional foci where rituals were performed that integrated whole regions, as well as a town plan with scattered elite palaces (Driessen 2007). But these parallels do not emphasize sufficiently other typical Mesoamerican features such as dynastic rulers, regular warfare between states, and the systematic control and display of violence to underpin elite power. One might speculatively wonder if the bloodthirsty ball-game ubiquitous in pre-Columbian states of Mesoamerica has its reflection in the bull-leaping sport.

Thirdly, it is difficult to imagine that the survival of the "palatial" system over some 1000 years, and its deep impact on the Aegean islands and the Mainland (with some likely colonial foundations, Kythera, Miletus, and perhaps on southerly Cycladic islands such as Thera), could have been accomplished without the realization of the standard definition of the state – its monopoly on the use of force within its domain. Recent thinking on Minoan palatial political "history" reinforces the view that Minoan neglect of the iconography (artistic representation) of power and militarism sprang from a deeper control of the island's population, and did not reflect political relations on the ground. Nonetheless it is striking that Linear A tablets are almost completely lacking in picture-symbols for weapons, armor, and chariots, unlike those

from Mycenaean Linear B archives. On the other hand the oldest (EM3-MM1) "palace" at Malia possesses a suite of reception rooms opening onto the West Court, in which two ceremonial swords were found. Driessen (in Laffineur 1999) admits these prestige weapons "imply the use of force in the establishment of relations and a warlike mentality."

A fourth query concerns elite residences. The fact that MM townhouses and Second Palace "villas" possess major storage areas, evidence of craft specialists, "state rooms" and ritual activity, and sometimes Linear A documents, is open to various interpretations. These building complexes could, as traditionally assumed, be merely extramural extensions of the palaces, residences of members of the controlling elite, state officials. But alternatively, they might belong to independent merchants and major landowners. In complex state societies such as Medieval Europe, the Ottoman Empire, and pre-Modern Japan and China, the elite class is a very broad one, with intermarriage bonding together innumerable powerful families, within which different individuals can possess a share of the power structure and construct and own their own urban and rural mansions, despite being ultimately, at least nominally, subordinate to a single ruler. In Renaissance Florence, the Medici dynasty controlled the city for long periods from their town and country houses, only at a late stage moving into the Town Hall (the Palazzo Vecchio) and converting it into a ducal palace. It would seem more reasonable to create a less unstable form of elite than so far envisaged in the "heterarchic model," to accommodate the issues raised above regarding military, bureaucratic, and architectural planning within Minoan society.

All this need not prevent the adoption of the main lines of the revisionist model: in EM-MM times Minoan society was coordinated by a class of linked powerful families, dwelling in mansions within smaller and larger settlements across the island, and perhaps, or perhaps not, in apartments within the "court-complexes" themselves. A major function of this class, along with its personal aggrandizement within its community through land ownership, control of craft production, and special access to interregional and international trade, was the management of ceremonial centers or "court-complexes/palaces." Over time, notably in the late Second Palace era, the most dominant families may have distanced themselves from the wider elite, and made palaces more "remote" in their religious and political activities from popular participation. In keeping with this, controlling dynasts now commissioned prominent art and tombs of a more individualistic nature. Personally I am inclined to envisage a more "hierarchical" than "heterarchical" Minoan society, based on the relative stability and flourishing of the palace era. The mansions would then be signs of a broad elite occupying public and private roles in tandem or cooperation. Whether the dominant family dwelt in the "palace" at all, or only later, or usually in a town mansion, may be less important than the current view that till late on "court-complexes" were theaters for ritual and political integration. Nonetheless, elite solidarity regarding control over internal law and order and external aggression or defense, appears an essential requirement.

Our data currently available cannot yet resolve these possibilities into a single narrative, but we can be confident that the ongoing meticulous reworking of the accumulated excavation data, enriched by ever-improving scientific techniques for the dating of finds, by dietary and environmental reconstructions, the search for family relationships (DNA tests of burials), and more open theoretical debate, will take us to solutions in the near future.

Aspects of Symbolic Culture

We have seen several ways in which art sheds light on Minoan society: the elevated status of women, at least the upper class; the importance of religion and general ritual in public life; and the late chronology for most representations of individuals, especially in assumed stances of power, agreeing with a gradual tendency over time for more visible, if not more actual, exercise of personal power within the court-complexes. If Knossos in MM3B is the first phase of the Second Palace, some suggest we call its later LM1A phase the Frescoed Palace, whilst Driessen even suggests that ruler images on all art forms are from its final LM1B phase.

Some scholars link the image on a sealstone, the "Mother of the Mountains," of a "powerful female" flanked by lions, to the flanking griffins in the Knossos Throne Room, as part of a symbolism relating to a Minoan goddess "mistress of animals," who was perhaps role-played by a priestess on the throne. The association there with a sunken stepped depression or "lustral chamber" introduces a general set of associations with many similar elaborate room complexes, of which one of the most informative is that in the heavily "Minoanized" town of Akrotiri on Thera; there frescoes are claimed to show initiation rites, including one for pubescent girls (Preziosi and Hitchcock 1999, see Chapter 6).

Also noteworthy in Minoan art are representational conventions, potentially a pathway for accessing Cretan mentalities. Uncontroversial is the pale color for women in frescoes, compared to brown-skinned adult males, a distinction common in many other cultures, where it is associated with the desirability (if not always reality) that upper-class women should remain indoors whilst men are active in the outside world of production and war. That adolescent males can be portrayed in intermediate shades may reflect Minoan emphases on age grades and associated initiation rituals.

Further connections have been drawn between age, gender, and status in Minoan art through utilizing distinctions in hairstyles (Davis 1986, Koehl 1986). Group scenes also deploy dress to differentiate elaborately-clothed individuals from those with far simpler, even clearly "rustic" wear (Barber 1991). German (2005) argues that most Minoan figure-scenes represent young men and women, many of higher status. Predominantly they are shown dancing and bull-leaping, which in palatial architectural surroundings may show ceremonies of passing to adulthood. For German, these representations are created for palace elites rather than the masses. However, many societies (for example Archaic and Classical Athens) represented their citizens in idealized form as youthful and bodily perfect to symbolize inner virtues, whilst little suggests that bull-leapers are an aristocratic caste. But her idea that these key "performances" portray Minoans passing into adult membership of the community seems insightful.

Shaw (1993) notes that Minoan art till the late Second Palace era emphasizes impressionistic combinations of the real and surreal, in which nature and especially flowers are central components. People collect and present flowers and we see orgiastic behavior of both sexes toward trees and stones. Arthur Evans had suggested a form of worship oriented to natural objects, and Herva (2006) reinforces these ideas with a general thesis that the art represents such animistic cults rather than anthropoid (human-like) divinities.

Also striking are the recurrent, stereotyped gestures of the rare figures found on wall-paintings and the commoner figures on seal stones and in portable figurines of clay or bronze. Verlinden (1984) classified hand and arm gestures into six types: amongst the most recurrent and clearest in context are one where the hand is placed to the forehead ("Minoan salute"), seen as a mark of respect to elite or supernatural individuals, and two others interpreted as postures of power, where the individual has hands on hips or folded across the chest.

The remarkable complexity and richness of Minoan "palatial" ceramics has likewise encouraged interpretation. The famous polychrome "Kamares" fine ware was probably highly decorated and widely distributed for use in communal feasting, but might (as provocatively argued for Classical Greek decorated wares) be imitating more valuable metal vessels (Schoep 2010).

The Minoan Civilization: An Annaliste Perspective

During a medium-term cycle (*moyenne durée*) of 600 years, or in the new scenario, a *longue durée* of 1000 years, a remarkable "palace"-based civilization flourished on Crete, with an undeniable organizational and cultural homogeneity. A parallel with later Greek city-states is helpful: they were continually fighting each other, but shared a religious pantheon and a common *mentalité* or way of seeing the world, and tended to build similar domestic and public architecture. Arguably the short-term history of each "palace" was of a world of political events and personalities, focused on competition between particular families for control over people and resources, power, and wealth. But beneath this there must have existed deeper, more long-lasting structural principles which gave rise to and helped maintain this first European civilization.

Currently this foundation is sought in communal ritual, associated from Early Minoan times onwards with feasting within the proto-palaces, the open-access "court-complexes." This can harmonize well with my older view of the Early Minoan development of a Sacred Geography across the Cretan landscape and the later "palace" as akin to a great Medieval monastery (Bintliff 1977a–b). In sacred geographies settled and unsettled places in the landscape are given cultural meaning through ritual ceremonies or processions, or through associations with mythical and religious concepts, rather than through economic and political connections.

Some see the slow elaboration of settlements during the long Greek Neolithic era as preparing the way for the rise of "central places," which become commoner by EBA times. Within larger settlements, the dynamics of "corporate communities" may increase intercommunity competition at the same time as a more intense internalized political structure, leading to "city-state" forms of community. Stimuli which "feed" the energy within such systems, such as the adoption of the plough and Secondary Products, Mediterranean polyculture (olive and wine cultivation) and bronze metallurgy, or the arrival of sailing-ships, continually enhanced the size and power of pioneer "city-states" emerging from the later Neolithic corporate communities. If a more communal and ritual emphasis is now prevalent for comprehending the ethos of the First and Second Palaces, then this longer-term viewpoint from Late Neolithic times, some 2500 years or so, becomes a significant but more complex developmental trend.

The suggested existence of more competitive or heterarchical social structures within the EM and First Palace corporate communities at the larger centers, could be seen as creating the potential for the observed tendency during the Second Palace era (especially after the Thera eruption), for a genuine dominant political elite to emerge. In the medium term, the suggestions of interstate warfare or absorption and a possible expansionism out of Knossos hint at varied local histories for each major region and for each political center of Crete, which then can include the short-term historical events which may have brought Mycenaean conquerors or allies to the island, achieving what finally looks like a partial conquest.

A Personal View

The Minoans are being transformed before our eyes, looking more divided and aggressive. Changes at the level of individual settlements counterbalance the cultural uniformity which strikes us at a general level. There are still mysteries: was there a calculating secular elite or set of competing families in each center, or alternatively was the entire system more religious, where political roles emerged through elite dominance of priestly/priestess functions? How many centers and their associated regions were there on Crete at any time? Current thinking makes a stimulating comparison to the political situation in Hellenistic Crete some 1500 years later, when large and small polities created alliances or fought wars of expansion between each other. And yet the extreme rarity of fortifications, or scenes of militarism, and of warrior graves, surely limits the scope for warring Minoan states. One is most struck by the prominent role of formal dress, hairstyles, gestures, age- and gender-identifiers in Cretan art, together with indications of a prevailing religiosity. Perhaps the next stage of scholarship should build on the stimulating "ceremonial center," "courtyard-complex" theories to model testable forms of "sacred states" and their possible interactions within the isle of Crete during Minoan times.

References

Adams, E. (2004). "Power relations in Minoan palatial towns: An analysis of Neopalatial Knossos and Mallia." *Journal of Mediterranean Archaeology* 17, 191–222.

Adams, E. (2006). "Social strategies and spatial dynamics in Neopalatial Crete: An analysis of the North-Central area." *American Journal of Archaeology* 110, 1–36.

Barber, E. (1991). *Prehistoric Textiles: The Development of Cloth in the Neolithic and Bronze Ages with Special Reference to the Aegean*. Princeton: Princeton University Press.

Betts, J. H. (2000). Review. *Journal of Hellenic Studies* 120, 189–90.

Bevan, A. (2002). "The rural landscape of Neopalatial Kythera: A GIS perspective." *Journal of Mediterranean Archaeology* 15, 217–256.

Bietak, M. (1995). *Avaris: The Capital of the Hyksos*. London: British Museum Press.

Bietak, M. (2000). "Rich beyond the dreams of Avaris: Tell el-Daba and the Aegean world – a guide for the perplexed: a response to Eric H. Cline." *Annual of the British School at Athens* 95, 187–205.

Bintliff, J. L. (1977a). *Natural Environment and Human Settlement in Prehistoric Greece*. 2 vols. Oxford: BAR Supplementary Series 28.

Bintliff, J. L. (1977b). "New approaches to human geography. Prehistoric Greece: A case study." In F. Carter (ed.), *An Historical Geography of the Balkans*. London: Academic Press, 59–114.

Bintliff, J. L. (1977c). *Mycenaean Geography*. Cambridge: The British Association for Mycenaean Studies.

Bintliff, J. L. (1984). "Structuralism and myth in Minoan Studies." *Antiquity* 58, 33–38.

Bintliff, J. L. (1994). "The history of the Greek countryside: As the wave breaks, prospects for future research." In P.N. Doukellis and L.G. Mendoni (eds.), *Structures rurales et sociétés antiques*. Paris: Les Belles Lettres, 7–15.

Bintliff, J. (2002). "Rethinking early Mediterranean urbanism." In R. Aslan *et al.* (eds.), *Mauerschau. Festschrift für Manfred Korfmann*. Vol. 1. Tübingen: Bernhard Albert Greiner, 153–177.

Bintliff, J. L., P. Howard, and A. M. Snodgrass (1999). "The hidden landscape of prehistoric Greece." *Journal of Mediterranean Archaeology* 12, 139–168.

Broodbank, C. (2000). *An Island Archaeology of the Early Cyclades*. Cambridge: Cambridge University Press.

Bruins, H. J. *et al.* (2008). "Geoarchaeological tsunami deposits at Palaikoastro (Crete) and the Late Minoan IA eruption of Santorini." *Journal of Archaeological Science* 35, 191–212.

Cadogan, G. (2004). "Minoans emerging." *Antiquity* 78, 923–926.

Cherry, J. F. (1983). "Frogs round the pond: Perspectives on current archaeological survey projects in the Mediterranean region." In D. R. Keller and D. W. Rupp (eds.), *Archaeological Survey in the Mediterranean Area*. Oxford: BAR Int. Series 155, 375–416.

Cherry, J. (1986). "Polities and palaces: Some problems in Minoan state formation." In A. C. Renfrew and J. Cherry (eds.), *Peer Polity Interaction and Socio-Political Change*. Cambridge: Cambridge University Press, 19–45.

Cline, E. H. (ed.) (2010). *Oxford Handbook of the Bronze Age Aegean*. Oxford: Oxford University Press.

Davis, E. (1986). "Youth and age in the Thera Frescoes." *American Journal of Archaeology* 90, 399–406.

Davis, J. (1992). "Review of Aegean Prehistory I: The islands of the Aegean." *American Journal of Archaeology* 96, 692–756.

Day, P. M. and D. E. Wilson (2002). "Landscapes of memory, craft and power in prepalatial and protopalatial Knossos."

In Y. Hamilakis (ed.), *Labyrinth Revisited. Rethinking 'Minoan' Archaeology*. Oxford: Oxbow Books, 143–166.

Dickinson, O. T. P. K. (1994). "Comments on a popular model of Minoan religion." *Oxford Journal of Archaeology* 13, 173–184.

Driessen, J. (2001). "Crisis cults on Minoan Crete." *Aegaeum* 22, 361–369.

Driessen, J. (2003). "The court compounds of Minoan Crete: Royal palaces or ceremonial centres?" *Athena Review* 3, 57–61.

Driessen, J. (2007). "IIB or not IIB: On the beginnings of Minoan monumental building." In J. Bretschneider, J. Driessen, and K. van Lerberghe (eds.), *Power and Architecture. Monumental Public Architecture in the Bronze Age Near East and Aegean*. Leuven: Peeters, 73–92.

Driessen, J. and C. Macdonald (1997). *The Troubled Island. Minoan Crete Before and After the Santorini Eruption*. Liège: University of Liège.

Driessen, J., I. Schoep, and R. Laffineur (eds.) (2002). *Monuments of Minos. Rethinking the Minoan Palaces*. Liège: Universite de Liège.

Evans, A. (1921–1935). *The Palace of Minos*. London: Macmillan.

Felten, F. *et al.* (2004). "Aegina-Kolonna 2003." *Jahreshefte des Österreichischen Archäologischen Institutes in Wien* 73, 97–128.

Fitton, J. L. (2002). *The Minoans*. London: British Museum Press.

Forsyth, P.Y. (1999). *Thera in the Bronze Age*. New York: P. Lang.

French, E. (1991). "Archaeology in Greece 1990–91." *Archaeological Reports* 37, 3–78.

German, S. C. (2005). *Performance, Power and the Art of the Aegean Bronze Age*. Oxford: BAR Int. Series 1346.

Gkiasta, M. (2008). *The Historiography of Landscape Research on Crete*. Leiden: Archaeological Studies from Leiden University (ASLU) 16.

Graham, J. W. (1962). *The Palaces of Crete*. Princeton: Princeton University Press.

Haggis, D. C. (2002). "Integration and complexity in the late prepalatial period: A view from the countryside in Eastern Crete." In Y. Hamilakis (ed.), *Labyrinth Revisited. Rethinking 'Minoan' Archaeology*. Oxford: Oxbow Books, 120–142.

Halstead, P. (1992). "The Mycenaean palatial economy: Making the most of the gaps in the evidence." *Proceedings of the Cambridge Philological Society* 38, 57–86.

Hayden, B. J. *et al.* (1992). "The Vrokastro Survey Project, 1986–1989: Research design and preliminary results." *Hesperia* 61, 293–353.

Herva, V.-P. (2006). "Flower lovers, after all? Rethinking religion and human-environment relations in Minoan Crete." *World Archaeology* 38, 586–598.

Hooker, J. T. (1969). "Homer and Late Minoan Crete." *Journal of Hellenic Studies* 89, 60–71.

Isaakidou, V. (2006). "Ploughing with cows: Knossos and the secondary products revolution." In D. Serjeantson and D. Field (eds.), *Animals in the Neolithic of Britain and Europe*. Oxford: Oxbow Books, 95–112.

Kardulias, P. N. (ed.) (1999). *World-Systems Theory in Practice*. New York: Rowman & Littlefield.

Koehl, R. (1986). "The chieftain cup and a Minoan rite of passage." *Journal of Hellenic Studies* 106, 99–110.

La Rosa, V. (1985). "Preliminary considerations on the problem of the relationship between Phaistos and Hagia Triadha." *Scripta Mediterranea* 6, 45–54.

Laffineur, R. (ed.) (1999). *Polemos. Le Contexte guerrier en Égée à l'Âge du Bronze*. Liège: University of Liège.

Letesson, Q. (2007). "Du phénotype au génotype: analyse de la syntaxe spatiale en architecture minoenne (MM IIB-MR 1A)." Université Louvain-la-Neuve, PhD thesis.

Letesson, Q. and K. Vansteenhuyse (2006). "Toward an archaeology of perception: 'Looking' at the Minoan palaces." *Journal of Mediterranean Archaeology* 19, 91–119.

MacGillivray, A. (2000). *Minotaur: Sir Arthur Evans and the Archaeology of the Minoan Myth*. London: Jonathan Cape.

Marinatos, S. (1939). "The volcanic destruction of Minoan Crete." *Antiquity* 13, 69–96.

Mee, C. (ed.) (2011). *Greek Archaeology: A Thematic Approach*. Oxford: Wiley-Blackwell.

Müller, S. (1996). "Malia. Prospection archéologique de la plaine de Malia." *Bulletin de Correspondance Hellénique* 120, 921–928.

Negbi, O. *et al.* (1994). "The Libyan landscape from Thera: A review of Aegean enterprises overseas in the Late Minoan 1A period." *Journal of Mediterranean Archaeology* 7, 73–112.

Nelson, M. C. (2007). "Pylos, block masonry and monumental architecture in the Late Bronze Age Peloponnese." In J. Bretschneider, J. Driessen, and K. van Lerberghe (eds.), *Power and Architecture*. Leuven: Peeters, 143–159.

Palmer, D. (1995). "Minoan farmers were muckspreaders." *New Scientist* (29 April), 16.

Pendlebury, J. D. S. (1939). *The Archaeology of Crete. An Introduction*. London: Methuen.

Preziosi, D. and L. A. Hitchcock (1999). *Aegean Art and Architecture*. Oxford: Oxford University Press.

Renfrew, A. C. (1972). *The Emergence of Civilisation. The Cyclades and the Aegean in the Third Millennium B.C.* London: Methuen.

Renfrew, A. C. (1973). *Before Civilization*. London: Jonathan Cape.

Renfrew, C. (1996). "Kings, tree rings and the Old World." *Nature* 381, 733–734.

Rethinking = Galaty, M. L. and W. A. Parkinson (eds.) (2007). *Rethinking Mycenaean Palaces II.* Los Angeles: Cotsen Institute of Archaeology, University of California.

Rutter, J. B. (1993). "Review of Aegean Prehistory II: The Prepalatial Bronze Age of the Southern and Central Greek Mainland." *American Journal of Archaeology* 97, 745–797.

Sakellarakis, Y. and E. Sapouna-Sakellaraki (1991). *Archanes.* Athens: Ekdotike Athinon.

Schoep, I. (2002). "Social and political organization on Crete in the Proto-Palatial Period: The case of Middle Minoan II Malia." *Journal of Mediterranean Archaeology* 15, 101–132.

Schoep, I. (2006). "Looking beyond the First Palaces: Elites and the agency of power in EMIII-MMII Crete." *American Journal of Archaeology* 110, 37–64.

Schoep, I. (2007). "Architecture and power: The origins of Minoan 'palatial architecture'." In J. Bretschneider, J. Driessen, and K. van Lerberghe (eds.), *Power and Architecture. Monumental Public Architecture in the Bronze Age Near East and Aegean.* Leuven: Peeters, 213–236.

Schoep, I. (2010). "Making elites: Political economy and elite culture(s) in Middle Minoan Crete." In D. J. Pullen (ed.), *Political Economies of the Aegean Bronze Age.* Oxford: Oxbow, 66–85.

Schoep, I. and C. Knappett (2004). "Dual emergence: Evolving heterarchy, exploding hierarchy." In J. C. Barrett and P. Halstead (eds.), *The Emergence of Civilisation Revisited.* Oxford: Oxbow, 21–37.

Schofield, E. V. (1982). "The western Cyclades and Crete: A 'special relationship'." *Oxford Journal of Archaeology* 1, 9–26.

Shaw, J. W. (2006). *Kommos: A Minoan Harbor Town and Greek Sanctuary in Southern Crete.* Princeton: American School of Classical Studies at Athens.

Shaw, J. W. and M. C. Shaw (1993). "Excavations at Kommos (Crete) during 1986–1992." *Hesperia* 62(2), 129–190.

Shaw, M. C. (1993). "The Aegean garden." *American Journal of Archaeology* 97, 661–685.

Shelmerdine, C. W. (ed.) (2008). *The Cambridge Companion to the Aegean Bronze Age.* Cambridge: Cambridge University Press.

Sherratt, A. (1995). "Alcohol and its alternatives: Symbol and substances in pre-industrial cultures." In J. Goodman, P. E. Lovejoy, and A. Sherratt (eds.), *Consuming Habits: Drugs in History and Anthropology.* London: Routledge, 11–46.

Sherratt, S. and A. Sherratt (1993). "The growth of the Mediterranean economy in the early first millennium BC." *World Archaeology* 24(3), 361–378.

Sjöberg, B. L. (2004). *Asine and the Argolid in the Late Helladic III Period. A Socio-economic Study.* Oxford: BAR Int. Series 1225.

Smith, H. (1999). "Stuff of dreams and Minoan mealtimes." *The Guardian* (14 October).

Van Effenterre, H. (1963). *Fouilles exécutées à Mallia. Étude du site.* Paris: Études crétoises 13.

Verlinden, C. (1984). *Les Statuettes anthropomorphiques crétoises en bronze et en plomb.* Louvain: Archaeologia Transatlantica IV.

Vogt, E. (1968). "Some aspects of Zinacantan settlement patterns and ceremonial organization." In K. C. Chang (ed.), *Settlement Archaeology.* Palo Alto: National Press Books, 154–173.

Voskos, I. and A. B. Knapp (2008). "Cyprus at the end of the Late Bronze Age: Crisis and colonization or continuity and hybridization?" *American Journal of Archaeology* 112, 659–684.

Wallerstein, I. (1974). *The Modern World-System. Capitalist Agriculture and the Origins of the European World Economy in the Sixteenth Century.* London: Academic Press.

Warren, P. (1975). *The Aegean Civilisations.* London: Phaidon.

Warren, P. (1984). "The place of Crete in the thalassocracy of Minos." In R. Hägg and N. Marinatos (eds.), *The Minoan Thalassocracy. Myth and Reality.* Stockholm: Skrifter utgivna av Svenska Institutet i Athen XXXII, 39–44.

Warren, P. M. (2004). "Review of Mountjoy *et al.* Knossos: The South House." *Antiquaries Journal* 84, 438–439.

Watrous, L. V. (1994). "Review of Aegean Prehistory III: Crete from Earliest Prehistory through the Protopalatial Period." *American Journal of Archaeology* 98, 695–753.

Watrous, L. V., D. Hadzi-Vallianou, and H. Blitzer (2004). *The Plain of Phaistos. Cycles of Social Complexity in the Mesara Region of Crete.* Los Angeles: Cotsen Institute of Archaeology, UCLA.

Further Reading

Bintliff, J. *et al.* (2002). "Classical farms, hidden prehistoric landscapes and Greek rural survey: A response and an update." *Journal of Mediterranean Archaeology* 15, 259–265.

Dickinson, O. T. P. K. (1994). *The Aegean Bronze Age.* Cambridge: Cambridge University Press.

Rehak, P. and J. G. Younger (1998). "Review of Aegean Prehistory VII: Neopalatial, Final Palatial and Postpalatial Crete." *American Journal of Archaeology* 102, 91–173.

Schoep, I. (2004). "Assessing the role of architecture in conspicuous consumption in the Middle Minoan I-II periods." *Oxford Journal of Archaeology* 23, 243–269.

6

The Middle to Early Late Bronze Age on the Cyclades and the Mainland

> ## Chronology
>
> Middle Cycladic / Middle Helladic: ca. 2000/1900 to ca. 1800/1700 BC
>
> Late Cycladic 1 / Late Helladic 1: ca. 1800/1700 to ca. 1500 BC
>
> Late Cycladic 2 / Late Helladic 2: ca. 1500 to ca. 1400 BC
>
> (General reading for this period: Shelmerdine 2008, Cline 2010, Philippa-Touchais *et al.* 2010, Mee 2011)

The Cycladic Middle to Late Bronze Age

Introduction

Since Scholes' (1956) pioneering research the main focus in the Middle to Late Bronze Age of the Cyclades has been on the rise of island towns on a larger scale than the villages (sometimes fortified) of the Early Cycladic (EC) period. Renfrew's re-excavation of Phylakopi, one such town on Melos, led to a wide-ranging investigation of the vulnerability of islands to incorporation by surrounding larger-scale state systems (Renfrew and Wagstaff 1982). The evidence for dominant Minoan influence on some, and later of a dominant Mycenaean influence on most if not all of the Cyclades, has fed discussions on the intervention

of these sequent civilizations on Middle Cycladic (MC) and Late Cycladic (LC) life.

The island towns

The final stage of EC, EC3, around 2200–1900 BC, is as elsewhere in the Aegean a phase of general disruption. The island towns emerge from this, usually one per island, although occasionally multiple nucleated foci exist, for example on Naxos (admittedly the largest, most fertile island) (Figure 6.1). But is this not a revival of the walled settlements of the EC? What *is* actually novel? Firstly, there are more, and regular, nucleated settlements. At the same time the culture of MC immediately shows the curious interplay of a lively regional cultural assemblage continually interpenetrated by novel Minoan artifacts and styles,

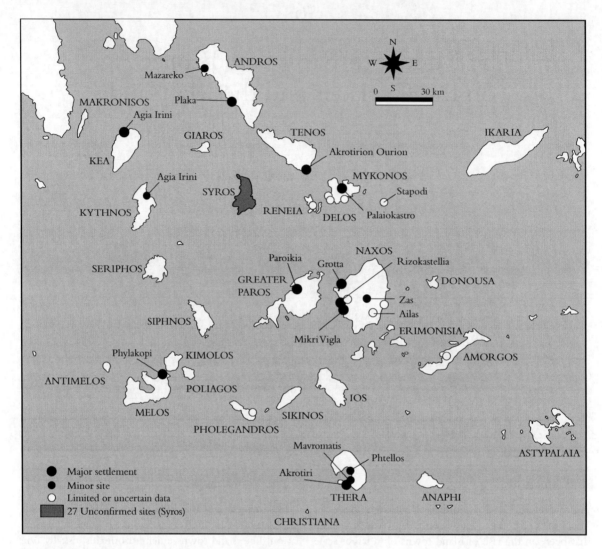

Figure 6.1 Major and minor settlements on the Middle Cycladic Cyclades.
C. Broodbank, *An Island Archaeology of the Early Cyclades.* © Cambridge University Press 2000, Figure 109.

emanating from the recently-arisen "palatial" societies of Crete. Does in fact the emergence of the island towns at the same time as the arrival of significant palatial cultural elements point to linked phenomena, with "urbanization" at least on a small scale also a product of Minoan social, political, or even perhaps military intervention?

My own view differs, and builds on fundamental theories presented in earlier chapters regarding the contrast between settlement systems where communities fission when they exceed some 150–200 inhabitants, and those which reach 500 persons or more, when we see the "emergence" of corporate self-focused "proto-state" communities. This has already led us to underline the necessity of district networks linking the dispersed rural farms and hamlets of the EC era, at times certainly requiring inter-island marriages.

This scenario from the anthropology of Early Modern communities is certainly a vital key to the later development in the Aegean of the "Normal

Polis" or city-state of 500–3000 or so inhabitants, and indeed of small city-state landscapes in many other historic contexts, but it also seems appropriate to the noteworthy appearance of a network of dispersed "towns" in the MC era of the Aegean. The island of Melos is perhaps an ideal case-study: in the EC it shows only a plethora of dispersed farms and perhaps one or two hamlets (Bintliff 1977b, Renfrew and Wagstaff 1982) associated with localized zones of fertile land. Almost no dispersed rural sites are known in MC and LC, although we must be cautious since archaeological survey of the island only covered 20 percent of the island's surface. For the new walled town at Phylakopi in MC-LC (Figure 6.2) Renfrew's and my own estimates suggest a population between 1000 and more than 2000 (my own proposal took account of the need to suppose only some structures were homes and that a significant area has been lost to the sea). This would be well above the threshold of demographic self-sufficiency, thus allowing endogamy (in-marriage) rather than exogamy (out-marriage) for the creation of new households, in contrast to what had previously been necessary on the island.

The corporate community in recent history and ethnography takes on a new character: we witness more communal management of the inhabitants and their property, an increased symbolic life arising out of more intense internally focused communication, and often hostility to neighbors, expressed in violence and defense works or competitive public structures. In other words the village emerges into a village-state, with a town-like culture overlying a village culture. I suspect that several MC and LC towns were transformed into tiny city-states. The preceding nucleations are all clearly below the threshold for such developments. This marks a deeper contrast than at first apparent when we note the similar defense walls and the integrated street and house block plans of the few EC villages sometimes considered as "towns" in the literature.

But why did these changes happen now? We know that the phenomenon developed out of a prolonged period of disruption (EC3). Moreover the emergence of a number of genuine towns (and hypothetically city-states) on some islands coincided with the transformation of marine navigation from paddle-dugouts

to larger sailing boats. The first sailing-ship images appear on seals from Crete in the EM3-MM1A period, while pottery from Phylakopi in MC seems to show the new vessels. Moreover the inception of MC closely parallels the major elaboration of the Minoan court-complexes into "palaces" and an immediate expansion of Minoan cultural products into the South Aegean region (Minoan ceramics appear there from MM1B).

Not to be forgotten is that this process of town emergence had already occurred by the Late Neolithic at Knossos and probably Phaistos on Crete, and was present in all likelihood at the isolated major island settlement at Manika in the EC and transitional EC-MC era. All but Phaistos are adjacent to the Cyclades. Some synergy between internal changes after a period of stress, external stimuli in terms of that navigation so critical to island life, and finally the appearance of "palatial" societies to the south, seems an appropriate basis for deeper explanations. But I suspect the critical factor may well be the movement of rural population into towns and the creation, perhaps as a result, of emergent state properties. Since Minoan settlements always included towns, villages, and farmsteads from EM onwards, the general implosion of population into the MC towns now is something seemingly specific to the Cyclades and this reinforces our suggestion of an internal settlement system change. As Chaos Theory (Bentley and Maschner 2003) nonetheless reminds us, similar pressures may result in radically divergent outcomes, if initial states of the object under study differ even in small ways: did the general final EBA crises have different impacts on societies in Crete, the Cyclades, and the Mainland because of their varied nature? Certainly the subsequent regional societies are drastically contrasted in the MM, MC, and MH periods, as we have already noted for Crete and will later note for the Mainland.

Phylakopi

Recent excavation and reworking of older finds suggest that Phylakopi underwent a progressive process of internal transformation during MC and early LC times (Whitelaw 2005). The town expands physically across these phases, becoming walled in mature MC (City 2). At this time an unparalleled Minoan-style

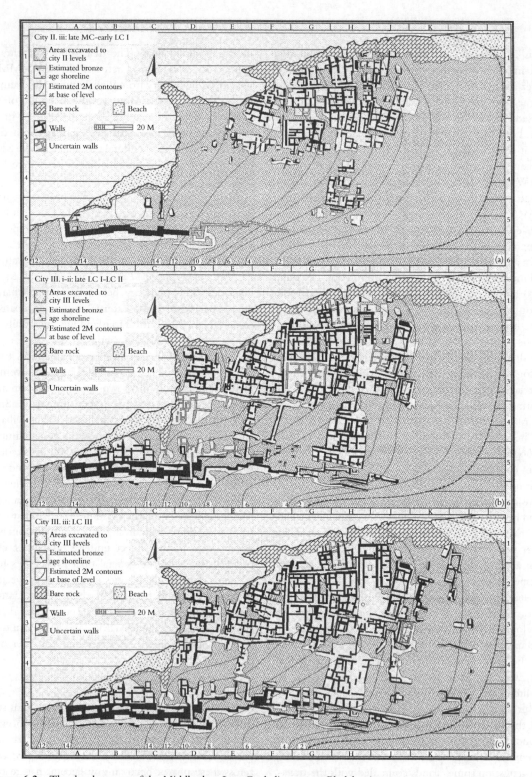

Figure 6.2 The development of the Middle then Late Cycladic town at Phylakopi.
T. Whitelaw, "A tale of three cities: Chronology and Minoisation at Phylakopi in Melos." In A. Dakouri-Hild and S. Sherratt (eds.), *Autochthon. Papers Presented to O. T. P. K. Dickinson.* Oxford 2005, 37–69, Figure 1.

monumental complex, that of the Pillar Rooms, is seen as an elite residence. This is replaced by another such mansion in LC1 in a different part of the town. Yet the town's burials, in collective rock-cut tombs or as jar inhumations under houses, appear more suited to an emphasis on egalitarian families. On the other hand despite the rise of true palaces in contemporary Crete, burials there rarely display a social elite, either in the traditional collective tholos burial or the new custom of more individualizing jar/coffin graves. The large size of the site, and the apparent nucleation of almost the entire Melos island population into it, signals a major change from the small fortified villages of the EC. Was the management of the town, of necessity beyond face-to-face relationships, carried out by a minority of family heads, amongst whom over time there arose an individual prominent clan providing community leaders (a Big Man society)? We might recall the recent analysis (Hekman 2003) of the cemetery at the fortified EC2 village at Chalandriani, where a broad minority of wealthier graves, formerly seen as an elite, are now considered to be heads of families, but also where one or two exceptional burials could mark a "mayor."

The Minoan impact

There remains lively discussion of the precise manner in which the palace societies on Crete affected island life in MC and early LC times. Few today would support a literal interpretation of later Greek traditions of a Minoan thalassocracy or maritime empire (Hagg and Marinatos 1984), but simple trade and cultural borrowing also seem too limited for some aspects of the evidence for a dominant Minoan influence, or "Minoanization."

Minoan cultural impact is especially notable on the islands of Melos, Thera, and Kea, and indeed Davis (1979) proposed a Western String theory, in which Minoan economic and political influence spread along this westerly group of the Cyclades to exploit commercial potential, especially the copper and silver at Lavrion on the east coast of Attica (the earlier use of Cycladic metal sources declined owing to their limited potential). For Broodbank (2000), the diffusion of sailboats into the Aegean allowed such wideranging trade to occur over long distances, by making

obsolete for such purposes the slow step-like canoe communication which had previously dominated to the advantage of smaller island communities. Subsequently Minoan influence would spread also to the Eastern Aegean islands, and by early LC the Dodecanese group (Southeast Aegean) would see a growth of new settlements with strong Minoan links (Davis 1992) (Figure 6.3).

Nonetheless the visible nature of Minoan influence is predominantly cultural, essentially technological innovations and style imitations. There is an emphasis on pottery for drinking and pouring, suggesting a particular tie to the Minoan culture of socialization. Significantly, with the exception of localities of the Aegean where Minoan colonies are very likely (the island of Kythera off the south coast of the Peloponnese, or the settlement at Miletos on the west coast of Turkey), the commonest material culture in the Cyclades is still locally produced: these Middle to Late Cycladic objects include delightful and distinctive decorated ceramics. The spread of the latter around the islands testifies to flourishing internal exchange, with "duck vases" possibly used to transport olive oil (Broodbank 2000).

On the other hand, contemporary with the Second Palace era on Crete, the rise of new and larger settlements in the Late Cycladic Dodecanese islands of the Southeast Aegean is associated, in contrast, with an almost entirely Minoan culture. Some would see this as purposeful large-scale Minoan colonization. For the Cyclades themselves there is a lively debate about further possible Minoan colonies now at the sites of Akrotiri on Thera and Aghia Irini on Kea, with some scholars suggesting that, at the least, Minoans held political control over these towns or town-like settlements. A different view is taken by Davis and Gorogianni (in Brodie et al. 2008), who argue that the intense economic and cultural exchange sphere projected into the South Aegean by Second Palace Crete encouraged local elites on the islands to competitive emulation, with Minoan fashions being "the cultural language of power that Aegean communities co-opted to serve their symbolic and economic needs" (340). They see the impact of these interactions as explaining the creation of elite mansions during the high watermark of Minoan influence at Aghia Irini, Phylakopi, and Akrotiri, where the mobilization of

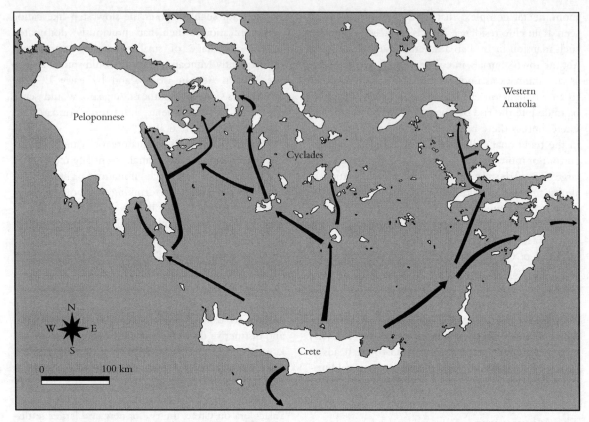

Figure 6.3 Minoan cultural radiations.
C. Broodbank, *An Island Archaeology of the Early Cyclades*. © Cambridge University Press 2000, Figure 121.

contacts to Crete could have been focused. On the other hand more basic changes support the arrival of Minoan craftsmen and perhaps scribes: these include the adoption of Minoan weaving technology and weighing systems, the shift to wheel-made pottery production, and evidence for the local use of Minoan Linear A accounting procedures (Karnava in Brodie *et al.* 2008). Many specialists consider these to indicate a deeper penetration of Cycladic society by the Minoans.

Perhaps we are still too attracted by Evans' peaceful ritualized Minoans to envisage them as pursuing aggressive foreign policies, but then we need to ask who is waging war on whom on the Akrotiri Ship Fresco (see below), in scenes on ceramics from Aegina, and on the MM3 Siege Mosaic from Knossos?

Aghia Irini, Kea
If Kephala is the best-known Neolithic settlement on Kea, its replacement as the main nucleated community on the island during the Bronze Age is Aghia Irini, which has been thoroughly published in a series of *Keos* monographs and thus provides exceptional insights into proto-urban life in the Cyclades (for the M–LBA phases see Davis 1986; Overbeck and Crego, and Mountjoy in Brodie *et al.* 2008). Perhaps owing to its near-Mainland location, Kea everyday material culture is Helladic (Early to Late) rather than Cycladic. The settlement is however revealing for other aspects of Cycladic development. In the EH, regional survey (Cherry *et al.* 1991) suggests that alongside the usual scattered farms on the island, there was a clear concentration of population at the nucleation of Aghia Irini. Was this already large enough for "corporate"

(city-state) status? At less than 1 hectare (Dickinson 1994) it seems not, warning us not to overestimate the autonomous "town-like" role which some such centers are often given. However, this development is interrupted in a microcosm of the wider Cycladic trajectory, as Aghia Irini is abandoned in the troubled era of final EH and early MH, and is then resettled as an impressively defended and more complex (but still small) island focal nucleation.

The potential to see this settlement's rise as a purely independent phenomenon is complicated by a parallel process of increasing Minoanization of the community during the course of MH and into early LH, with as elsewhere the adoption of Minoan pottery techniques, weights and measures, and even the finding of a Linear A tablet. The most striking discovery is a temple with at least 30 almost life-size terracotta statues in Minoan forms. Wall-painting fragments are also of Minoan style and are in addition comparable to those from Thera, with marine and town scenes. With parallels to other grand houses, such as the West House in Akrotiri on Thera and the Pillar Rooms and later mansion at Phylakopi, House A of LC1 date in Aghia Irini is suggested to be an elite mansion which might have held goods for commerce with Crete, suitably linked to the presence of sealings and Linear A documents at the site. However, during the preceding MC period Minoan influence remains subordinate to cultural and exchange links to the MH Mainland and the other Cycladic islands. It is really only in LC1 that Minoan influence becomes more intense, significantly during the climax of Second Palace society's impact on the South Aegean, and it is now that the Minoan-style mansion is in use. As on Crete, there is a general destruction of the site in LH2/LM1B which may well reflect Mycenaean aggression, but it is swiftly rebuilt as a town, within the now dominant cultural sphere of the Mainland.

Thera-Santorini and Akrotiri
The dramatic volcanic island of Santorini-Thera is as famous today for its "Bronze Age Pompeii" as till recently for its picturesque island town and villages (Doumas 1983, 1991; Forsyth 1999, Palyvou 2005). But the early LC town at the site of Akrotiri (see following Text Box), buried by the greatest recent

eruption, has a long development going back to the Late Neolithic, when a hamlet already occupied the same location. This is just 25 m above sea level by a harbor on the south coast of the island, where the oldest volcanic rocks provided the best agricultural land. By EC a larger settlement was accompanied by smaller domestic sites elsewhere on Thera, but during MC Akrotiri itself began to expand toward the imposing size it had reached at the time of the early LC eruption which caused the island's abandonment. It is not yet clear what the rest of Thera's settlements comprised in MC, although a number of sites have been recorded. For the following LC era it has been noted that the complementing of the town at Akrotiri with villages and farms across the island is in contrast to other Cycladic islands such as Melos or Kea with little outside their nucleated island towns, and is more reminiscent of the Minoan palatial landscape. This last feature has been used to support the idea that Thera was a political dependency or part-colony of Crete, rather than merely an indigenous settlement with much cultural influence from the Minoan "palace" societies a mere 60 km distant to the south. However, recent trials into town levels of MC date show that Akrotiri was already an extensive complex settlement with only limited Minoan contacts and a rich iconographic style on its ceramics comparable to that later made famous from its LC1 frescoes. These new discoveries support similar evidence from Phylakopi and Aghia Irini for a major Cycladic "urban revolution," which only subsequently became increasingly attracted into the Minoan economic, cultural, and political sphere of influence (Renfrew's Introduction, and Nikolakopoulou and Papaghiannopoulou in Brodie *et al.* 2008).

Till recently it was believed that the Late Bronze Age Thera eruption took place out of a circular island dominated by a central volcanic peak. Its unparalleled violence blew the mountain away, leaving a giant sea-filled caldera (remnant hollow), with the former mountain rim surviving as the modern arc-shaped island (Figure 6.4). The archaeological discoveries at Akrotiri have stimulated a series of geological and other scientific research programs on the island, leading to a very different picture for its development (Friedrich 2000). Until a couple of million years ago Thera was non-volcanic, then it began an irregular

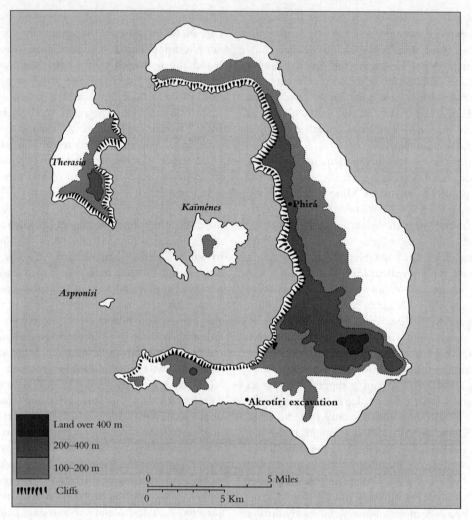

Figure 6.4   The present–day outline of Thera island with the location of the Bronze Age town at Akrotiri. J. Chadwick, *The Mycenaean World*. Cambridge 1976, Figure 4.

cycle of volcanism. By the time of the Akrotiri town, Thera consisted most probably of two (north and south) bays filling old calderas, separated by a small island, and almost encircled by narrow, rugged, and infertile northern and central landmasses. Only to the south lay a wider land area, the Akrotiri peninsula, with a good water supply and fertile soil, and thus it is in the latter area that almost all Bronze Age settlements have been located.

Even so there has been debate on the carrying capacity (supportable human population) of the pre-eruption island for feeding its population. The island's natural vegetation, probably depicted on Akrotiri frescoes, and also analyzed from wood remains, was probably always limited, due to natural aridity and soil conditions. Cultivated olives and figs were however plentiful, judging from the same botanical remains (Birtachi *et al*. in Brodie *et al*. 2008).

Akrotiri Town

Although little more than one hectare of the settlement has been excavated, estimates based on tests below the thick layer of ash from the LC eruption suggest that the total site may have been 10 (or even 20) ha. A population of several thousand people would be appropriate, based on ethnoarchaeological parallels, and one may rank this as a significant town in Bronze Age terms. In the area cleared so far, houses which can be multi-storey are separated by narrow streets with widenings comparable to small squares. Houses vary in scale and elaboration of furnishings. The town plan is less regular than that of the larger Cretan settlements, and compares better to other Cycladic nucleated communities, whilst the house architecture is a clear combination of local and Minoan traditions: the method of construction is local, but other clearly exotic internal and external features confirm that by LC1, Thera was the most Minoanized island (lustral basins, light-wells, horns of consecration).

Most attention has been drawn to the remarkable frescoes, which are a combination of Minoan style and a distinct Theran (and Cycladic) aspect (Preziosi and Hitchcock 1999, Morgan 2005, Papaghiannopoulou in Brodie *et al.* 2008). The famous Miniature Fresco on a marine theme is historically significant (Color Plate 6.1), since it may relate to the role of the island in international affairs. A great fleet, a sea battle, a town siege, and indications of elite individuals are packed into an intriguing fresco running around the walls of a room of the West House, arguably a building of a semi-public character, conceivably the mansion of a resident elite. Unsurprisingly, the detailed interpretation remains disputed. One can hope that further investigations at Akrotiri might illuminate the island's contemporary politics, with perhaps the Therans (and allies – other Cycladic islands or the Minoans?) in control of a fleet which acted over a wide radius and could raid towns elsewhere. Some see this as a scene confirming the Minoan thalassocracy, others suggest it shows scenes from an epic poem, in which case it might be entirely imaginary, or at least only semi-historical.

Only two large houses have been fully excavated at Akrotiri, Xeste 3, considered to be a major ritual focus for rites of passage involving adolescent girls and youths, and the West House, suggested to be an elite mansion in LC1 which could have been a focus for international contacts as well as a textile processing center (Davis and Gorogianni, and Karnava in Brodie *et al.* 2008). Linear A inscriptions made on Thera record quantities of sheep, textiles and olive oil as part of a local administrative system, but it remains unclear if these deal with goods for internal island use or export and import records to the wider world.

The Xeste 3 house (Palyvou 2005, Morgan 2005, Vlachopoulos in Brodie *et al.* 2008), is three storeys high, with 15 rooms on each of its main floors, and is exceptional so far in its architectural grandeur and the density and complexity of its wall-paintings. Whilst specific Minoan elements are striking in this LC1 complex, such as a lustral basin, grand staircase, and pillar-and-door partitions (*polythyra*), the art combines locally evolved figured and nature styles and images with Minoan influences. The surviving eastern rooms seem public and ceremonial, the western service and/or domestic in function. Alongside scenes of bull capture and animal sacrifice appear a possible procession of status individuals bringing offerings to a "goddess," and separately gendered scenes interpreted as rites of initiation to adulthood, maybe also for elite family members. It is difficult to challenge the identification of an awesome seated female in rich plant and animal associations, to whom young girls bring flowers, and who is accompanied by a tame griffin, as other than "Potnia" or a central nature-fertility goddess, whose role is commonly seen as central to Minoan religion.

The role of the island

Current thinking is moving to a model for Akrotiri in its Late Cycladic Aegean context where Middle Cycladic traders in flourishing Cycladic towns had become incorporated as junior partners into a more extended and influential Minoan-based sphere of influence, both commercial and military. The Classical historian Thucydides' legend of the Minoan seaborne empire could begin to gain credence as reflecting at least some historic foundations. The scenes of warfare have also been linked to legends about piracy in the context of the thalassocracy myth. Most scholars have speculated that a Minoan presence on the most "Minoanized" islands may have involved resident merchants, and just possibly officials if there were formal political ties to Cretan "palaces." The exchange contacts that finds on the Cyclades show to the East Mediterranean do seem to flow via Crete, supporting the idea of a junior partner role in Minoan trade expansion overseas. The strong continuity of Cycladic material culture is nonetheless noteworthy: Marthari (cited in Forsyth 1999) has estimated that on Thera 90 percent of the ceramics at this period remain locally manufactured. Even the famous frescoes have been seen more recently as made by local craftsmen adapting Minoan traditions to their own purposes. As with the island centers at Aghia Irini and Phylakopi, perhaps it is now too simplistic to see such island towns purely as bases for international merchants (Doumas 1991; an Early Modern parallel being Ermoupoli on nineteenth-century Syros). A more plausible explanation might combine the nucleation of island populations supported largely by a highly intensive use of local resources, an island-based commercial sector and perhaps one able to launch maritime raiding expeditions, and a growing partnership with the far greater resources of Minoan Crete.

Chronology

As for the giant Thera eruption of LM1A date, the current evidence argues strongly for a date of 1628 BC (see Chapter 5, Thera Text Box). A recent study of imports to "Minoanized" Kea and Melos (Mountjoy and Ponting 2000) indicates that Minoan pottery is replaced by Mycenaean between LM1A and B, supporting a collapse of Minoan cultural preeminence on the Cyclades following the eruption. Worth noting is

that the same study downplays the scale of imports at either period, favoring "trade" rather than colonies.

The Middle Helladic and Early Late Helladic Periods on the Mainland

Introduction

The discovery of the Middle Helladic (MH) culture has built up gradually, since Schliemann during his excavations at Orchomenos in Central Greece in the late nineteenth century identified an unusual dark and heavily burnished ware, which he named after the legendary ruler at Orchomenos as Minyan Ware (Figure 6.5). Later, painted ceramics were also assigned to this era, termed Matt-Painted Ware. The pottery seemed dull and lifeless compared to contemporary pottery designs in Middle Minoan and Middle Cycladic societies.

Although simple and conservative (Rutter 2007), MH ceramics show a shift over time from a dominance of dark-burnished wares in varied colors, to paler forms such as Yellow Minyan, and this leads through further development and outside influences

Figure 6.5 Middle Helladic gray Minyan ware goblet. © Trustees of the British Museum.

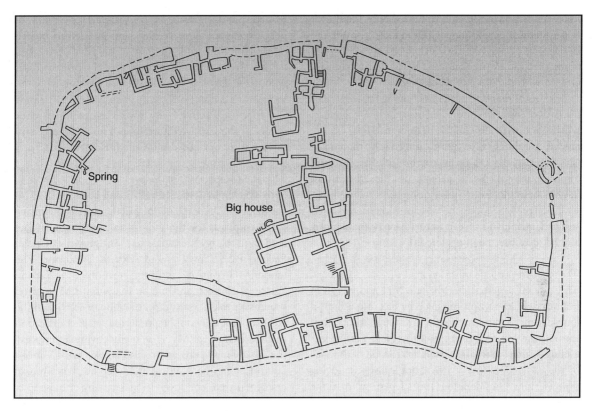

Figure 6.6   Middle Helladic village at Malthi, Peloponnese.
E. Vermeule, *Greece in the Bronze Age*. Chicago 1964, Figure 14.

(adding lustrous paint) into Late Helladic or Mycenaean ceramics. In keeping with this negative comparison to Crete and the islands, settlement evidence showed the disappearance of elaborate architecture such as the "mansions" of the Mainland EH culture. Extensive survey already showed that compared to EH, site numbers in MH sank almost everywhere (McDonald and Rapp 1972; Renfrew 1972a–b; Bintliff 1977b), and they did not increase significantly when intensive survey improved our resolution of the evidence for smaller and less conspicuous sites. The type-site became a hilltop village in Messenia (Southwest Peloponnese), Malthi, published in the 1930s by Valmin (1938), which had a possible chief's house in its center and peasant houses dispersed elsewhere inside its primitive fortification wall (Figure 6.6). The unimpressive construction and scale of Malthi's buildings signaled a decline in culture and at most the existence of petty chieftains with very localized author-

ity. In burials, the period is generally typified by pit and cist graves with a poverty of gifts, although it has gradually become accepted that in later MH the spread of earthen grave mounds containing multiple burials, followed by even more dramatic changes involving "shaft" graves and the first stone and earth tumuli (tholoi) with often rich gifts, signify a very different and swiftly emerging complex society (Voutsaki 1998).

Explanations for these changes have tended to adopt a narrative history approach in various forms, aiming to link changing patterns in material life with historical events and personalities. Firstly, the catastrophic destructions in EH2–3, paralleled as we have seen throughout the Aegean, are believed to have had far more severe effects on the Mainland, inhibiting recovery for several centuries, but for unclear reasons. Attempts to link these disasters (or alternatively the late MH appearance of elite graves) to the arrival in Greece of Indo-European speakers, are less popular today than previously, and I find Colin Renfrew's (1987) radical rethinking of this question, from the archaeological and linguistic data, persuasive. He proposes that the Greek language arrived in Mainland Greece with the Neolithic colonizers.

In a similar fashion, in later MH times, the reversal of the signs of material culture decline and then stagnation which appeared to have hitherto dominated the era, has tended to be viewed in historical terms. At the end of MH (MHIII) the sudden appearance of elaborate built tombs, such as Shaft Graves in the Northeast Peloponnese and tholoi in the Southwest Peloponnese, with rich prestige goods and warrior equipment, is seen as too dramatic, and special factors have been adduced. Several ideas have been explored (Dickinson 1977):

The international trade crossroads model

This model suggested that the late MH and early LH Mainlanders rose to prominence by creating a hub of long-distance trade networks running throughout Europe, the Mediterranean, and the Near East. It was Colin Renfrew who made a telling critique of this idea by the early 1970s (1968, 1973), not least by removing from serious consideration the suggestion that the great concentric monument of Stonehenge in England was a gift by Mycenaean (LH) architects for access to the tin resources of Cornwall. Simple archaeological considerations and a revised chronology based on calibrated C14 dates make this impossible. Likewise in a thorough examination of the evidence for, and nature of, exchange systems between late Middle Helladic and Late Helladic Greece and the rest of Europe, Anthony Harding (1984) reduced this network to a multiplicity of indirect links, without any vital significance to the origins and development of more complex societies in late MH and LH Mainland Greece.

The mercenary / pirate model

It would be a circumstance with many ancient and later historical parallels, to find a politically undeveloped society on the fringes of the civilized world using its warlike culture to gain wealth from the latter by either raiding or mercenary service. There is however no evidence so far in contemporary Near Eastern texts for Aegean forces, and this appears otherwise very hard to prove. In favor of the idea nonetheless, one can point to artistic representations in Cycladic,

Minoan, and later in Mycenaean art of scenes of marine warfare, land warfare, and attacks on coastal cities. Moreover, some of these scenes have been taken to show non-Aegean settings. These representations seem to make clear that the Aegean was probably the location of raiding or open war in MBA-LBA times, and that such activity also took Aegean forces elsewhere in the East Mediterranean. Hints of mercenary service in Egypt can also be cited (Kelder 2010).

The Minoan sphere of influence

Peter Warren in particular (1975, and in Bintliff 1977a) has made a coherent case for placing the main explanatory emphasis for the radical transformation of late MH and early LH societies, on growing Cretan Second Palace involvement with the Mainland. The end of MH coincides with the creation of the Second Palaces on Crete, and in the following LM1 period there is a peak of expansion of Minoan activity in the Aegean. Not only do the prestigious artifacts placed in the Shaft Graves at Mycenae include Minoan imports, but locally made objects are also infused with Minoan culture. It has been normally accepted that Minoan craftsmen were employed to make many of these gifts, even if they can be shown to have responded to distinctive local tastes (for example in the recurrent emphasis on hunting and war). The positive effect of Minoan intervention in Mainland societies was to stimulate the emergence of regional centers of dynastic elite power. Unfortunately this led to the consequence that at the end of LM1B most scholars believe that the ungrateful early Mycenaean leaders attacked Crete, destroyed almost all its palatial centers, and ruled the island from Knossos (recalled in a garbled way in the later legend of Theseus and the Minotaur).

If MH society was ranked in some way, leading families would still probably have relied on land and stock for distinction, but in its final Shaft Grave subphase the availability of portable wealth may have dramatically diversified the means of economic and political power (Betancourt 2007). Indeed throughout much of Europe (Shennan 1993, Kristiansen 2001) a simple chiefdom society proliferates in the second millennium BC, linking elite warfare and expanding trade systems, and allowing regional hierarchies of centers and dynasties to emerge at varying times and places. However, the distinctive emphasis on masculine warrior lifestyles, seeming to set the final MH and then true Mycenaean LH apart from the Minoans, is not unparalleled in later Second Palace society on Crete (Kilian-Dirlmeier 1986), where a new iconography of male power, and the warrior graves at Poros (see Chapters 5 and 7), mark a novel direction at a period of critical influence on the Mainland.

Developments in Middle Helladic Messenia

Since construction of Mycenaean palaces and towns is a late phenomenon in the development of that Mainland civilization, the development of Mycenaean life from its MH beginnings must rely on transformations in rural settlements and burial traditions. Surprisingly some of the best evidence for that preceding phase comes from a peripheral region, Messenia. Although this remote province of the Southwest Peloponnese was long neglected by archaeologists owing to its limited Classical monuments, its potential as a major Bronze Age focus was signaled in Homeric legend, where King Nestor ruled at his palace at Pylos. In the 1930s the American scholar Carl Blegen succeeded in identifying this palace on the hill of Epano Englianos, in fertile rolling plateau land some kilometers from the coast, and excavated it in 1939 and then from 1952 to 1958. One of the most important finds from this palace was a rich archive in Mycenaean Linear B script, opening up a continuous research program into the organization of the Pylian state (McDonald and Rapp 1972, Chadwick 1976, Shelmerdine 1997). In the 1960s Richard Hope-Simpson and William McDonald conducted a pioneer large-scale regional field survey in Messenia, under the umbrella of the University of Minnesota, precisely with the idea of providing the settlement evidence to match the textual information for the state (McDonald and Rapp 1972). The monograph of this project remains a classic for regional archaeology, and for Mycenaean studies it succeeded in identifying the major centers and the general spread of settlement in Middle to Late Bronze Age Messenia, allowing informed insights into the genesis and then internal organization of a Mycenaean state centered on the palace at Pylos.

In the 1990s a new, intensive survey project was inaugurated in the Pylos palace region (Davis *et al.* 1997, Davis 1998, ongoing reports in *Hesperia*). As regards the Bronze Age there were three major aims: firstly to discover what differences intensive survey would make to our knowledge of the development of settlement before and contemporary to the rise of the Pylos palace; secondly to clarify the size and development of the extra-palatial settlement or "town" around the excavated palace; and thirdly, to synthesize the combined evidence from burial monuments (tumuli, tholos tombs), the origin and development of the palace, and changes in the regional settlement system, in order to reconstruct the historical processes behind the creation of the Mycenaean state in Messenia.

The Middle Helladic and Early Late Helladic mounded burials

Although there are several burial modes on the Mainland in MH, including intramural (within settlement) pithoi (giant storage-jars) and intra- and extramural cist (stone box) graves, particular attention has been focused on earthen mounds, often containing multiple graves of the same type as in non-mound contexts, and becoming common from MH1 (Kilian-Dirlmeier 2005). Whereas the settlement-based burials have been seen as representative of small domestic groups and their ancestors, the tumuli have been suggested to indicate low-level social elites within MH settlements. Through this interpretation the otherwise extremely limited evidence for status groups in settlements and the other burial forms can be contrasted to such widespread signs of a dispersed class of local clan-heads or Big-Men (if not chieftains). Such tumuli are especially frequent in Messenia province and it is here that a transformation in their construction appears first and perhaps originates, when a false-vaulted stone chamber and connected entrance passageway is inserted into some tumuli, creating the Mycenaean tholos tomb, the characteristic monument for Late Helladic elite burials. Hood's (1960) suggestion that this emulates traditional Minoan stone tholos tomb construction, much criticized, has recently received new life from a reinterpretation of the earliest Pylos palace plan as of Minoan inspiration (see below).

In 1977 I suggested that the pattern of tholoi and associated tumuli in Messenia appeared to show small scale territoriality (marking of political units) (Bintliff 1977b), suitable for elites at the individual village level. This would support the concept that from late MH, when the more complex tholoi monuments are first constructed, into the early part of LH (after which their number decreases very sharply), power was practiced widely in Messenia. This period preceded the construction of the first palace at Pylos and could point to the importance in this early phase of Mycenaean development of multiple local elites in the organization of society. In mature LH times throughout Mycenaean Greece tholos tombs become far rarer, whilst appearing to dominate wider districts, and are argued to be reserved for the upper echelons of a hierarchical power structure within palace-based "polities" (states).

Subsequently Voutsaki, in studies of tumulus and tholos distributions on the Mainland, has argued for a more dramatic emergence of power in Messenia (Voutsaki 1995, 1998). She prefers to envisage the MH tumuli of Messenia as for all classes of the population. However their density, at least as so far known, would seem to require that only representative members of society were interred within them, with the remainder, perhaps the majority, of other bodies being placed in intramural or extramural flat graves. Nonetheless, so little has been excavated of Messenian MH settlements that it is far too early to generalize on the prevalence of flat graves (Bennet and Galanakis 2005). She nonetheless agrees with wider opinion that the late MH creation of the mounded stone-built tholos chamber creates a form of burial for local elites. We might note too that the older mounds could be used for consecutive burials and hence might already signify clan or dynastic groups, as opposed to adding graves to an undifferentiated communal flat cemetery. The tholos tomb even more clearly symbolizes dynastic attention, as its entry corridor and door not only made subsequent interment simple, but allowed ceremonial visits to the ancestors in a suitably theatrical architectural context.

Recently the Pylos Project team have considered the development of several settlements around the Pylos palace in order to contextualize the rise of the later palace community in terms of competitive local elites (Bennet 1999). This includes links between the erection of regional tumuli and later tholoi. It is not clear however if the clustering of villages and dispersed monumental tombs at and near the later palace must indicate rival elites vying to take control of the central homeland of the later Pylos state. Alternatively we could be seeing related elite families with discrete residential bases, within which a political hierarchy emerges to control the first palace in LH3A (the mature LBA). Interestingly, the concept of a cluster of local leading families around an emergent palatial center, creating its eventual managerial base, is reminiscent of recent "heterarchical" rethinking of the organization of Minoan palaces (see Chapter 5).

Nelson's reworking of the original excavation records for Pylos palace (Nelson 2007, Rutter 2005), postulates an early mansion for LH1–2 associated with a gated defense wall, followed by the first palace in LH3A with a strongly Minoan design. These significant buildings agree with the Pylos site surface survey which shows a contemporary outer settlement which is precociously extensive for its region.

So far the reader can get the impression that the Mainland Middle Bronze Age is viewed less as a period in itself, than as a phase of lost achievement (the disappearance of the EH complex sites), delaying the reappearance of yet greater achievement (the following rise of the LH Mycenaean civilization). Let us instead try to give MH a significance and structure in its own right, perhaps thereby helping us understand better the otherwise still rather inexplicable swift changes in the final centuries of that era.

The Middle Bronze Age from the surface survey record

The traditional way of seeing the development of prehistoric farming settlements in Mainland Greece has been in social evolutionary terms, as expounded by Colin Renfrew, where the seemingly inevitable rise of Aegean palatial society suffers a local setback during Middle Bronze Age times. Renfrew also used extensive survey data to identify settlement decline in this Middle Helladic era (cf. Renfrew 1972a, 1972b).

Since that time, through intensive surface survey, we have gained a whole series of regional settlement histories. It is revealing to re-analyze the Neolithic to

Mycenaean settlement patterns of Southern Mainland Greece in order to clarify the place of the MH era within its development. During the Neolithic and the Early Helladic eras the range of settlement sizes and the variety of their spatial grouping is rather comparable. Small villages of 1–2 ha or less are typical, separated in fertile areas by a few kilometers, and south of Thessaly, often associated with dispersed farm/hamlet sites. Occasionally, a village may achieve 4–5 ha or more, whilst also rarely, small or large nucleations can evidence signs of special monumental buildings of a public or maybe elite character.

In the following Middle Helladic period, the overall impression is of similarity to these earlier periods, in that the key element is a chain of nucleated villages or hamlets separated by a few kilometers, although a thinning out in landscape cover can be argued in most regions. The striking difference is the loss of most smaller rural sites. This confirms that Middle Helladic settlement patterns and population show strong reduction of occupation, rather than (as I once opined), merely show a process of population nucleation following the abandonment of the many small dispersed settlements of the Early Helladic era. With the Late Helladic comes a fuller network of villages and a minor recovery of smaller rural sites, but in the focus on small population foci the overall picture remains similar to earlier periods, apart from the emergence of rare palaces and other high-ranking central places. We could take as an example for these later periods the Methana Survey (Mee and Forbes 1997). Early Helladic settlement consists of four villages a few kilometers apart, and numerous dispersed hamlets and farms, followed in Middle and Late Helladic times with three of these villages surviving as hamlets or villages, and a slight number of lesser Mycenaean (LH) rural sites.

Let us approach these settlement pattern similarities from the viewpoint of the Social Landscape. Here we shall return to two familiar models (Bintliff 1999; see Chapter 3). Firstly, a settlement of 150 or less people is the ideal, with growing social tensions at 200–300. Typical Neolithic and Bronze Age Mainland nucleated settlements are 1–2,5 ha, representing something like 100–300 inhabitants. We can hypothesize that a major factor in Mainland settlement systems, from Neolithic through to Middle Helladic

times, was social pressure, to stay small to sustain an easily managed community life. But this demands local networks of village intermarriage to reach a viable 500 to 600-plus demographic pool. What follows from this model is that we should no longer focus on the individual settlement in later Greek prehistory, but must assume that nearly all sites were systematically tied into local social networks of marriage exchange. Given the extreme rarity of Mainland settlements, up to and including the Middle Helladic, which exceeded the parameters of face-to-face community size, we now realize that the Mainland was a mosaic of overlapping clusters of socially integrated villages, the spatial scale of which south of Thessaly was maybe 5–15 kilometers radius around any participating settlement. Traditional Palestinian villages provide good examples of such local networks (Lehmann 2004).

Our second model is that of arenas of Social Power. Anthropology also allows another important generalization concerning district marriage networks. If resources and technology permit, a community can solve its marriage needs through expanding to a size where it is predominantly endogamous. This also brings advantages and disadvantages. On the positive side, maintaining perfect relations with the neighbors is no longer a priority, and previous dowry arrangements could be replaced by the community assuming control of almost all its resources for itself. Indeed it is precisely in such settlements, larger than 500 or so inhabitants, that cross-cultural research has documented the emergence of town-like political behaviors. The implication is that later prehistoric Mainland communities of some 4–5 ha or more (generally seen as at or over the 500–600 inhabitant threshold), might be considered to have begun to develop political behaviors of an incipient city-state character. On the pre-Mycenaean Southern Mainland, on estimated settlement area, such proto city-state communities may be represented by the settlements at Early Bronze Age Tiryns and Middle Helladic Argos, and Fournoi in the Argolid in EH and MH times. Their potential populations could be close to demographic self-sufficiency, or at least in Lehmann's model, represent dominant partners in district marriage networks.

What is the significance for neighboring settlements of the metamorphosis of a face-to-face village into a proto city-state? Well, such village-states are rarely *totally* endogamous, and Cosmopoulos' (1998) figures for the size of EH Mainland settlements suggest that most potential examples are not yet autonomous demographically. Yet the swollen village-town dominates local politics by its demography, economic resources, and availability of excess marriage partners. Lehmann has modeled such marriage networks for site-clusters in Early Iron Age Palestine to demonstrate how districts dominated by single large settlements could have focused social interactions, claiming that this is one means through which such communities achieved political and economic preeminence.

Now a vital piece of the jigsaw: such enlarged communities need to be held together socially either through horizontal political subdivisions, for example clans, or through the existence of dominant families. We must expect therefore that Neolithic to Middle Helladic settlements of 4–5 ha or more would be run on a different social basis than the face-to-face villages of 100–300 people that were the norm throughout. In the case of MH Argos (Touchais 1998) and EH–MH Fournoi (Jameson *et al.* 1994), both in the Northeastern Peloponnese, the suggestion of multiple hamlets meets one of these alternatives.

Thus from the beginning of farming settlement in Greece, nearly all individual communities were part of local clusters with intense social bonds. The potential for one member of a cluster to achieve enhanced status is always present. Nevertheless this was generally inhibited throughout the Neolithic and most of the Bronze Age by the preferred aim of face-to-face political organization within each settlement, and the necessity in the case of expansion toward proto city-state size for an elaborate internal system of social control to be put in place: either a set of semi-autonomous quarters within the enlarged community, or the emergence of a minority ruling elite.

In the particular case of Middle Helladic settlement systems, we continue to see the emphasis of preceding periods on regularly spaced villages, mostly small, very rarely of "city-state" potential. The vast majority required several social partners for their reproduction and hence were set in clusters allowing significant scope for economic and political interaction. The changing fortunes of individual members must in part be linked to the dynamics of each cluster and of cluster-to-cluster interactions, including perhaps diversion of smaller settlements from the influence of one dominant village to that of another. A rare emergent super-village – for example the key MH sites of Argos and Mycenae – could exploit its advantages over its neighbors and presumably enhance its own leading families over theirs. Nonetheless, regional politics is not enough: I also agree with Wright (2004) that in Early and Middle Helladic times, enhanced participation by one member settlement in external political, military or economic contacts (see below) could elevate its regional status so as to reorientate the allegiances of minor sites into its social "field of gravity." Indeed it seems likely that the sudden rise within the Plain of Argos in the relative status of Mycenae over Argos during the late MH period must be explained through these kinds of political shifts within local settlement networks, which have become entangled into increasing interactions with external societies and events in the wider Aegean world.

We might conclude that from the start of the Neolithic the emergence of more complex societies was always a possible outcome. The necessity for district social clusters, given the rareness of communities large enough to be self-sufficient "small worlds" or achieved city-states, created creative social "arenas." These greatly facilitated a number of key potential developments: the mobilization of manpower for military purposes, of agricultural and other surpluses for economic purposes, and of participants for large-scale cult activities. In this model we may identify one of the mechanisms through which Bronze Age territorial states were formed. Essentially, breaking free of face-to-face limitations was of course a critical step toward state-formation, when individual nucleations emerged as district super-villages, out of interrelated village clusters.

The Argos Plain and Mycenae

As just introduced, the other key area for observing critical change in MH society is the opposing corner of the Peloponnese to Messenia (Northeast rather than Southwest): the region of the Plain of Argos and its surrounding hill land. Here the later MH era sees a revival of recorded settlements and evidence for a hierarchy of smaller and larger communities, with the probability that the latter are also centers of political power. The later palatial site of Mycenae is a settlement of minor significance until this late phase, in contrast to a clearly extensive and important focus through the era at the more central location of Argos, which is a large, multifocal community with a series of tumuli. Quite suddenly, however, the balance of power shifts, and within the very large but undistinguished MH cemetery at Mycenae, which as elsewhere mixes domestic areas with burial-clusters (French and Shelton 2005), a dramatic new form of burial appears, the Shaft Grave, beginning in late MH and continuing in construction into early LH.

The Mycenae Shaft Graves, their outstandingly rich contents, and historical significance have been central to discussion of the rise of Mycenaean civilization ever since Heinrich Schliemann uncovered the first cluster, Shaft Grave Circle A, in the 1870s. In the 1950s a Circle B was revealed by the Greek archaeologist Mylonas (see Text Box).

But we need to return to our earlier question: How did late MH/early LH Mycenae gain such wealth and justify its claims to importance?

Shaft Grave Circles A and B at Mycenae

They are termed circles as both were defined in Mycenaean times by enclosures, to make clear the distinctive groupings of elite dead, whilst the A circle was subsequently re-enclosed in even more monumental form into a grand theatrical arena. The accumulated evidence from the two series of Shaft Graves demonstrates the rapid growth in wealth and status of the men and women interred in these deep pits, which contained single or multiple burials. In contrast to the poverty of grave goods from preceding phases of MH, the Shaft Grave period sees extraordinary grave gifts piled into the shafts, making novel statements about the international contacts of the elite at Mycenae. They had relatively swiftly gained the ability to access large amounts of precious metal, long-distance prestige goods (faience, amber), and the services of exceptionally skilled craftsmen (argued to have been Minoan) (Dickinson 1977). Above some of the tombs were stone stelae (tombstones) inscribed with heroic scenes.

The central issues concerning our understanding of the Mycenae Shaft Graves seem to be:

1. How can we explain the dramatic appearance of such wealth, and the evidence for elite families, at a previously low-status site?
2. How does this abrupt emergence of a new regional power at Mycenae create the basis for the subsequent establishment there of the great fortified palatial center in late LH times?

3. How do the two Circles relate to each other? and
4. What is the relationship between the Shaft Grave phenomenon at Mycenae and the tumulus-tholos developments in Messenia, which occur at a comparable historical moment?

Some of these questions are easier to propose answers to than others. Shaft Grave Circles A and B overlap, but B begins earlier and A lasts longer. Moreover it is only Circle A which is much later given the exceptional privilege of causing the LH3 circuit wall of the Mycenae citadel to bulge out so as to enclose it, leaving Circle B beyond the walls, at risk of pillage. This sequence suggests that the circles are for two distinct lineages, of which the slightly younger, represented in A, eclipses the dynasty of B by later LH times. Thus it is only A which would eventually become a showpiece of multi-generational dynastic power beside the main entrance gate to the citadel (the famous Lion Gate) as one enters it. It was already argued by Schliemann that the Mycenaean creation of a special enclosure for Shaft Graves A was to make a theater for public ceremonies of a dynastic character (Cavanagh 2001).

Recent analysis of the dress codes and gifts with the dead of both circles has also brought valuable insights. Kilian-Dirlmeier (1986) makes an excellent case for the gradual elaboration over time of a distinct prestigious dress code for the elite from the oldest to youngest graves, notably the warrior males (Figure 6.7), but also the highly ornamented

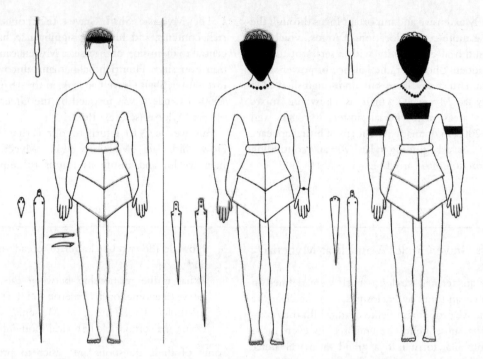

Figure 6.7   From left to right, development over time of male dress and gifts in the Shaft Graves. Areas shaded black are in gold.

I. Kilian-Dirlmeier, "Beobachtungen zu den Schachtgräbern von Mykenai." *Jahrbuch des Römisch-Germanischen Zentralmuseums Mainz* 33 (1986), 159–198, Figures 14–16. Courtesy of Römisch-Germanischen Zentralmuseums Mainz.

and richly gifted females. The increasing symbolic pretensions shown by the elaboration of tombs and of the dress worn by the elite burials are reasonably seen as representing the growing pretensions of this novel center of wealth. Its leading families, in what had been hitherto a minor MH settlement, now appear to aspire to the status of major players in the politics, not only of the immediate Argos Plain, but in a wider sphere, including relations with the Minoan palaces. Nonetheless, Shaft Graves have been found elsewhere, also with wealth and status objects, although not in such remarkable quantities. Although Mycenae remains outstanding at this moment in time, competition in the display of elite status will spread to numerous other Mainland centers in early LH, when tholos tombs become the standard means of advertising who are the families in power in most regions.

Confirmation for the new political status of the settlement at Mycenae comes later, when over LH2–3 an unparalleled series of tholos tombs at the site is eventually accompanied by the construction of a fortified palace center with a large extramural community. At that stage it is reasonable to link these observed developments with the legendary status of Mycenae as the center of the most powerful Mycenaean state. Such a position naturally took some time to achieve, and the Shaft Graves (pretentious burials but for a non-palatial settlement), would suit our expectation of a prolonged developmental phase in Mycenae's rise to preeminence, or at least to a "first among equals" status with the other great

Mainland Mycenaean centers such as Pylos and Thebes which were emerging at the same time.

Recent survey in the inland valley of Nemea, lying to the north between the Plain of Argos and the Corinth coastal region, has offered further insight. Cherry and Davis (2001) note the surprisingly low population evidenced here in MH and early LH times, then a sharp rise in the mature to late LH period. They pick up on a point I made many years ago (Bintliff 1977b) that so far the rich hill land of Corinth lacks a major Mycenaean center, perhaps indicating that Mycenae's state territory may have first expanded northwards toward the Gulf of Corinth, before absorbing rival centers in its own Plain of Argos, such as Argos, Dendra-Midea, and Tiryns.

The large quantities of weaponry, coupled with the warrior iconography which the Shaft Graves as well as later art of the Mycenaean states provide, offer a plausible explanation for the increasing role of the Mycenaean elite – aggressive and successful warfare. But how did this work? Did the hypothesized enlargement of the Mycenaean state, first north and then south, occur through attacks and threats? Possibly. But how did the Shaft Grave elites gain their wealth and warrior concept? Till recently it seemed difficult to derive this from Minoan culture, despite the well-attested Minoan influence in the technology and raw materials of the grave goods. Yet the recent evidence of rich warrior-graves at Second Palace period Poros near Knossos could provide wider evidence for increasing militarism in all parts of the Aegean (Kilian-Dirlmeier 1986, Driessen and Langohr 2007). Maybe we are seeking explanations which the archaeological timescale cannot yet accommodate. Earlier, we touched on the idea that ambitious warlike males from Mycenae, a backwater village in the earlier MH period, traveled abroad (especially in the quarreling world of the East Mediterranean), and served as mercenaries, gaining unparalleled military skills and much wealth. In the light of recent evidence from the Anatolian Hittite imperial archives (Korfmann et al. 2001), Mycenaean expeditions into Western Anatolian native states are more than a possibility. Could the Mycenaean warrior elite, like the Normans of the early Medieval world in the Atlantic coasts and the Mediterranean, have set themselves up as lords of small and later

larger "conquest states"? Such events could be rapid and difficult to trace in our sources, historical or archaeological. The world of Braudel's short term, or événements, has always to be allowed for, even if the longer-term impact of unique historical events tends to involve social and economic constraints and possibilities which operate in a more measurable framework for the archaeologist.

We have already discussed the rise of Mycenae to become the apparently richest and most monumental center in the Plain of Argos by the LH3 period. But how sure are we that Mycenae ultimately *controlled* the contemporary rival Mycenaean centers of the Argive Plain? Legend can of course be misleading, and we require objective support. The Linear B archive finds are rare in the region, and the palace at Mycenae is poorly preserved. The case is not so secure for total control of the Plain: was the great fortified palatial center of Tiryns in its south and on the coast an autonomous state, or merely the maritime face of the Mycenaean kingdom, where a relative of the king held control?

Can the tholos tombs enlighten us? Voutsaki (1995, 1998) identifies a cycle of pretentious burials at Mycenae itself, and a response from neighboring centers in the region. Whilst in late MH/early LH the Shaft Graves have no parallel in their wealth and warrior symbolism in the Plain of Argos, suggesting a statement of intent by the elite of Mycenae to be preeminent, by LH2 when the Argos Plain elite adopt the Messenian form of prestigious burial – the tholos – Mycenae's tholos tombs are matched by several elsewhere in the region, perhaps signaling competition for power and status. In LH3, however, Mycenae continues to build multiple tholoi, including the grandest in the region (Figure 6.8), and most if not all other centers cease their construction or use. It could be argued that Mycenae had by now achieved regional dominance, allowing it to restrict such burial to the aristocracy within its own state apparatus. It is also conceivable that the leaders of the other major centers of the Plain were now secondary figures below the king of Mycenae, and were required to signify this through construction of their tombs at Mycenae itself.

Comparable developments are occurring elsewhere, such as at the later Mycenaean palace-center of

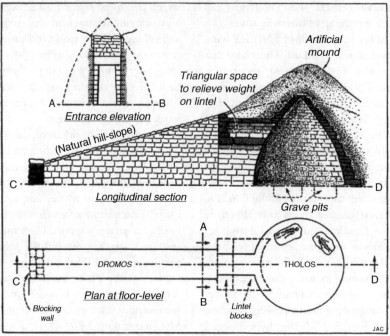

Tholos tomb, section and plan (after Wace and Stubbings)

Figure 6.8   Plan of the late "Treasury of Atreus" tholos at Mycenae. W. Taylour, *The Myceneans*. London 1966, Figure 43.

Thebes in Central Greece (Dakouri-Hild 2010). In the MH era its size expands to 20 ha, although like other large settlements such as Argos, it appears to be constituted of mixed clusters of domestic and burial deposits, perhaps on a dispersed plan. During the transitional MH-LH era there are several large stone-built or rock-hewn tombs resembling Shaft Graves, and the giant cist grave on the Ampheion hill may have contained precious gifts. Elite tombs at Thebes include weapons, horse remains, and boars' tusk helmet-fittings. Likewise the important cluster of Mycenaean centers in coastal Thessaly, eventually crystallizing into the palace-state based at Iolkos-Dimini, seems to develop out of a rich MH settlement background (Adrimi-Sismani 2007).

So far we have sought to comprehend the spectacular rise of Mycenae in terms of regional competition, relations with all-powerful Minoan Crete on the Aegean level, and perhaps some extra-Aegean

(particularly West Anatolian) military adventures. But recently another, unexpected focus has appeared on the scene, much closer to home, the settlement of Kolonna on the island of Aegina between Attica and the Northeast Peloponnese. The EBA township here was highly unusual, in that although it shared in the general destructions of EB2–3, it was rapidly reconstructed, becoming an even more substantial planned community with massive fortifications, even to rival its contemporary Troy City VI in Northwest Anatolia in the MBA and early LBA (Walter and Weisshaar 1993). Excavations evidence craft specialization and exchange on a significant scale, whilst the community's characteristic ceramics ("Gold mica ware") are found over a wide area of the Mainland and islands (Rutter 1993). In the late MH phase a rich Shaft Grave was deposited and to the same period may belong a very large, monumental building in the center of the settlement (Felten *et al.* 2004). Intriguingly there are even scenes on Aeginetan pottery of shiploads of warriors. It would not be unreasonable to suppose that Aegina was a significant player in the politics, warfare, and trade of these dynamic final MH and early LH centuries between 1700 and 1400 BC.

However, a cautionary note is required: Kolonna, like the similar off-Mainland walled settlement of Aghia Irini on Kea island, is remarkably small: both are estimated to be less than 1 ha (Dickinson 1994). Compared to the 10–20 ha estimated for LC Akrotiri town on Thera, and the much larger major towns of Second Palace Crete, how much economic, political, and military power can we imagine emanating from communities of say a couple of hundred people (of whom a mere fifth were likely to be adult males)? In neither case is there evidence for a large rural population to add to these small island foci. On present evidence we might only imagine these small centers as part of a mosaic of very small polities, who would require mutual alliances and probably association with Minoan initiatives to achieve much on a South Aegean scale (a case reasonably made for Akrotiri). On a lesser scale, the closeness of the developing Mainland to a flourishing Cycladic culture cannot be ignored: local MH ceramic traditions and the whole tradition of Matt-Painted wares within that culture are substantially influenced by MC pottery, alongside the better-known role that Minoan styles played in the birth of Mycenaean ceramics at a later point in early LH.

Frustratingly, little evidence survives of the building complexes of early Mycenaean times which underlay the later LH3 palaces. It was thus generally assumed that emergent elites invested chiefly in display burials rather than prestige residences, until the Mycenaean takeover of Crete in LH2 inspired Mainland imitations of Minoan palaces. Claims for earlier LH mansions at Tiryns and Mycenae are based on disputed architectural evidence (Fitzsimons 2007), although the rather stronger recent evidence for an LH1–2 mansion at Pylos makes them more plausible. In Laconia however the two sequent mansions at the Menelaion site of LH2 and LH3A date do seem like small-scale precursors of the later palaces in plan, but lack the fine decoration (Rutter 2005). The design of these early mansions appears to form an elaboration of normal house architecture of MH, notably the megaron plan, a building with a set of rooms in succession. This

brings into stark contrast the fact that the oldest so far reconstructed Mycenaean palace, that of LH3A Pylos, nonetheless incorporates a clearly Minoan design.

Greece beyond the Mycenaean heartlands

The growing evidence from Northeastern Greece has been summarized and interpreted by Andreou et al. (1996) and Andreou (2001). The Bronze Age in Macedonia and Thrace is not static stagnation whilst the South takes off into complexity, yet society till the end of the era follows an alternative model, one of small-scale settlement networks, as if resisting the palatial urbanization and hierarchy of the Mycenaean world. The focus is the large or small village, yet their numbers rise steadily over this period, and by the early Late Bronze Age some of these may form foci for surrounding smaller communities (such as Assiros with its intriguing centralized storage complex). In the late LBA-Early Iron Age there is evidence for the increasing elaboration of these district central places, perhaps forming the core of small regional polities with defense walls and prestige artifacts for their elites. Thessaloniki-Toumba is a giant example (Figure 6.9).

Yet although contacts to MH and LH societies in the South are clear, imports are small-scale and seem to be used to enhance internal processes of increasing social differentiation. In keeping with this, the plans of these settlements, although suggesting co-residential groups larger than nuclear families, have not revealed mansion-like residences for a controlling family. If there really were small statelets, such political power seems to rest more in the domination by widely spaced larger centers in fertile locations, over smaller satellite communities in less favored sectors of the landscape, a model we have already explored for the contemporary Southern Mainland in this chapter.

Middle Helladic and Early Late Helladic art

The lack of figurative art till the end of MH seems to reflect a society with limited social competition, where kinship was the basis for social differences. In the final phase (MH3) this all seems to change toward an emphasis on personal and family status rising above the mass of the population. This is symbolically

Figure 6.9   The great settlement mound or Toumba at Thessaloniki. Author.

expressed in the spread of much more elaborate graves which exhibit prestigious gifts and elite dress codes for a minority (Voutsaki 1998). Art is also deployed to signal this transformation. The stone grave-pillars above some of the Mycenae Shaft Graves may look very primitive compared to Minoan-Cycladic art, lacking landscape elements in favor of outline figures in heroic postures, but Betancourt (2007) considers it more likely they were originally covered with plaster and/or painted. The heroic emphasis is also found in the special gifts in the tombs themselves. An inlaid dagger represents warriors hunting a lion with spears and shields, rather than at a safer distance with chariots and arrows. The gold face-masks of some Shaft Grave males might well be portraits, telling us how important individual elite members were to the rise of Mycenae (Preziosi and Hitchcock 1999). Laffineur (2007), essentially having to rely on tomb finds, summarizes early Mycenaean art at Mycenae and elsewhere as dominated by an imagery of male aggression: hunting and fighting, expressing the superiority of a military upper class. Even the widespread imagery on early Mycenaean ceramics, that seems instead to deal with concepts of regeneration and rebirth, may not be unconnected to concepts of dynastic power succession as well as personal ideas of the afterlife.

An Annaliste Perspective

The Cycladic and Mainland Middle Bronze Ages offer a classic laboratory for an Annaliste approach, and we have already begun to draw out the parallel processes operating at different timescales, as well as the importance of reconstructing ways of life and thinking, *modes de vie* and *mentalités*. In the short term, the world of events (*événements*), the impact of the Thera eruption seems potentially cataclysmic, with long-term consequences for Minoan civilization. But why not also for the adjacent coastlands of the Mainland? Catastrophes and other less dramatic events are correctly envisaged, in Annaliste Structural History, as dependent for their power on their context, and this includes the long-term trajectory of the society on which they impinge. Indeed in the case of Crete, Driessen and colleagues suggest that the underpinning of Minoan palatial culture by religious conviction may have opened up internal chaos when "the gods" struck their "chosen people," or at the least their likely protégés the Theran polity, even if physical disaster on Crete may have been grossly exaggerated. Another short-term element is the rapid appearance of spectacular elite graves at Mainland Mycenae, and here we have argued that unique historical personalities and events are required to account for this phenomenon occurring at a hitherto unimportant settlement on the margins of the fertile Argos Plain. Again emphasizing the importance of the short term, the hard-to-trace regional politics in which this seemingly upstart power competed successfully with older centers such as Argos, and rivals at Tiryns or nearby Midea, cannot have been a foregone conclusion. On the other hand, this can also serve to remind us that the potential of short-lived events and individual ambitions for changing the course of history depends on suitable conditions, and these can only be understood through studying a wider context in time and space.

This brings us to the medium term. Archaeologists, like art historians, recognize cyclical eras of a few hundred years, characterized by a style or way of life, and here we can also find in the MBA a certain middle-term (*moyenne durée*) structure: the flourishing nucleated foci of the Cyclades, some we suggest evolving into city-state form in this era, on the one hand, and then the very different village-based networks we have reconstructed on the Mainland on the other, with their petty chiefs and occasional proto-states constituted of village and chieftain clusters.

For the long term, one cannot deny the possibility that the "emergent complexity" which corporate communities of 500–600 people give rise to, has an inbuilt tendency toward city-state formation. In turn, intercommunity interaction and competition between such nucleations (what Renfrew (Renfrew and Cherry 1986) has dubbed "peer-polity interaction") can open up strong tendencies toward territorial (multi-center) states. That Knossos could well have been on this trajectory by the end of the Neolithic, whilst becoming the most lasting and spectacular of the Minoan palatial foci, suits this scenario. On the Mainland, Paul Halstead (2006) has argued that family competition in village societies may likewise contain the recurrent potential for the rise of dominant lineages, whose intercommunity political, military, and economic networking creates a certain opportunity for the emergence of settlements with regional preeminence. This is certainly relevant to the creation of a suitable background in MH for the development of a small number of district centers during its duration, out of which rather swiftly, at the end of that era, expanding political systems begin to carve the landscape into a mosaic of mini-states, the foundation of the LH Mycenaean palatial system.

A Personal View

It is tempting to see the MC island towns as similar to their modern physical counterparts. Today most Cycladic isles have a single dominant town, often the major port. These picturesque agglomerations of flat-roofed and whitewashed houses summon up a feeling of communities to a significant extent set apart from the world. On the island of Melos the contraction of the dispersed settlement of EC into the single great town of Phylakopi may have led to something of this mentality, although just as modern island towns, these MC towns were constantly interacting with each other, and with the Minoan palaces, as well as with the coasts of the Mainland. As yet perhaps the Cyclades were not dominated by outside powers, maintaining significant vigor in their portable art, and even into the following LC era, in their wall-paintings.

As for Mainland society, I suspect that research will continue to find more complexity within MH, tracing those lively intercommunity social networks which I have posited. The rise of Mycenae however, still seems a kind of supernova, something to do with certain "adventurers," warriors for sure, who defeated improbable odds to establish a great state from humble beginnings.

References

Adrimi-Sismani, V. (2007). "Mycenaean northern borders revisited: New evidence from Thessaly." In M. Galaty and W. Parkinson (eds.), *Rethinking Mycenaean Palaces II*. Los Angeles: Cotsen Institute of Archaeology, University of California, 159–177.

Andreou, S. (2001). "Exploring the patterns of power in the Bronze Age settlements of Northern Greece." In K. Branigan (ed.), *Urbanism in the Aegean Bronze Age*. Sheffield: Sheffield Academic Press, 160–173.

Andreou, S., M. Fotiadis, and K. Kotsakis (1996). "Review of Aegean Prehistory V: The Neolithic and Bronze Age of northern Greece." *American Journal of Archaeology* 100, 537–597.

Bennet, J. (1999). "Pylos. The expansion of a Mycenaean palatial centre." In M. Galaty and W. Parkinson (eds.), *Rethinking Mycenaean Palaces*. Los Angeles: Cotsen Institute of Archaeology, University of California, 9–18.

Bennet, J. and I. Galanakis (2005). "Parallels and contrasts : Early Mycenaean mortuary traditions in Messenia and Laconia." In A. Dakouri-Hild and S. Sherratt (eds.), *Autochthon. Papers Presented to O. T. P. K. Dickinson*. Oxford: Archaeopress, 144–155.

Bentley, R. A. and H. D. G. Maschner (eds.) (2003). *Complex Systems and Archaeology*. Salt Lake City: University of Utah Press.

Betancourt, P. P. (2007). *Introduction to Aegean Art*. Philadelphia: Instap Academic Press.

Bintliff, J. L. (1977a). *Mycenaean Geography*. Cambridge: The British Association for Mycenaean Studies.

Bintliff, J. L. (1977b). *Natural Environment and Human Settlement in Prehistoric Greece*. Oxford: BAR Supplementary Series 28.

Bintliff, J. (1999). "Settlement and territory." In G. Barker (ed.), *The Routledge Companion Encyclopedia of Archaeology*. London: Routledge, 505–545.

Brodie, N. *et al.* (eds.) (2008). *Horizon. A Colloquium on the Prehistory of the Cyclades*. Cambridge: McDonald Institute Monographs.

Broodbank, C. (2000). *An Island Archaeology of the Early Cyclades*. Cambridge: Cambridge University Press.

Cavanagh, W. (2001). "Empty space? Courts and squares in Mycenaean towns." In K. Branigan (ed.), *Urbanism in the Aegean Bronze Age*. Sheffield: Sheffield Academic Press, 119–134.

Chadwick, J. (1976). *The Mycenaean World*. Cambridge: Cambridge University Press.

Cherry, J. and J. Davis (2001). " 'Under the sceptre of Agamemnon': the view from the hinterlands of Mycenae." In K. Branigan (ed.), *Urbanism in the Aegean Bronze Age*. Sheffield: Sheffield Academic Press, 141–159.

Cherry, J. F., J. C. Davis, and E. Mantzourani (1991). *Landscape Archaeology as Long-Term History: Northern Keos in the Cycladic Islands*. Los Angeles: Institute of Archaeology, University of California.

Cline, E. H. (ed.) (2010). *Oxford Handbook of the Bronze Age Aegean*. Oxford: Oxford University Press.

Cosmopoulos, M. B. (1998). "Le Bronze Ancien 2 en Argolide." In A. Pariente and G. Touchais (eds.), *Argos et l'Argolide. Topographie et urbanisme. Bulletin de Correspondance Hellénique*, Supplementary Volume, 41–56.

Dakouri-Hild, A. (2010). "Thebes." In E. H. Cline (ed.), *Oxford Companion to the Aegean Bronze Age*. Oxford: Oxford University Press, 690–711.

Davis, J. L. (1979). "Minos and Dexithea: Crete and the Cyclades in the Later Bronze Age." In J. L. Davis and J. F. Cherry (eds.), *Papers in Cycladic Prehistory*. Los Angeles: Institute of Archaeology, University of California, 143–157.

Davis, J. L. (1986). *Keos 5. Ayia Irini: Period V*. Mainz: Philipp von Zabern.

Davis, J. L. (1992). "Review of Aegean Prehistory I: The islands of the Aegean." *American Journal of Archaeology* 96, 692–756.

Davis, J. L. *et al.* (1997). "The Pylos Regional Archaeological Project. Part I: Overview and the archaeological survey." *Hesperia* 66, 391–494.

Davis, J. L. (ed.) (1998). *Sandy Pylos*. Austin: University of Texas Press.

Dickinson, O. (1977). *The Origins of Mycenaean Civilisation*. Göteborg: Paul Åström Verlag.

Dickinson, O. (1994). *The Aegean Bronze Age*. Cambridge: Cambridge University Press.

Doumas, C. G. (1991). "High art from the time of Abraham." *Biblical Archaeology Review* 17, 40–51.

Doumas, C. G. (1983). *Thera. Pompeii of the Ancient Aegean*. London: Thames & Hudson.

Driessen, J. and C. Langohr (2007). "Rallying round a 'Minoan' Past: The legitimation of power at Knossos during the Late Bronze Age." In M. Galaty and W. Parkinson (eds.), *Rethinking Mycenaean Palaces II*. Los Angeles: Cotsen Institute of Archaeology, University of California at Los Angeles, 178–189.

Felten, F. *et al.* (2004). "Aegina-Kolonna 2003." *Jahreshefte des Österreichischen Archäologischen Institutes in Wien* 73, 97–128.

Fitzsimons, R. (2007). "Architecture and power in the Bronze Age Argolid." In J. Bretschneider, J. Driessen, and K. van Lerberghe (eds.), *Power and Architecture*. Leuven: Peeters, 93–115.

Forsyth, P. Y. (1999). *Thera in the Bronze Age*. New York: P. Lang.

French, E. and K. Shelton (2005). "Early palatial Mycenae." In A. Dakouri-Hild and S. Sherratt (eds.), *Autochthon. Papers Presented to O. T. P. K. Dickinson*. Oxford: Archaeopress, 175–184.

Friedrich, W. (2000). *Fire in the Sea*. Cambridge: Cambridge University Press.

Hägg, R. and N. Marinatos (eds.) (1984). *The Minoan Thalassocracy. Myth and Reality*. Stockholm: Swedish Institute of Archaeology at Athens.

Halstead, P. (2006). *What's Ours Is Mine? Village and Household in Early Farming Society in Greece*. Amsterdam: Archaeologisch Centrum, Amsterdam University.

Harding, A. (1984). *The Mycenaeans and Europe*. London: Academic Press.

Hekman, J. J. (2003). "The Early Bronze Age cemetery at Chalandriani on Syros (Cyclades, Greece)." PhD thesis, University of Groningen, Institute of Archaeology.

Hood, S. (1960). "Tholos tombs of the Aegean." *Antiquity* 35, 166–176.

Jameson, M. H., C. N. Runnels, and T. H. Van Andel (1994). *A Greek Countryside. The Southern Argolid from Prehistory to the Present Day.* Stanford: Stanford University Press.

Kelder, J. M. (2010). "The Egyptian interest in Mycenaean Greece." *Jaarbericht Ex Oriente Lux* 42, 125–140.

Kilian-Dirlmeier, I. (1986). "Beobachtungen zu den Schachtgräbern von Mykenai." *Jahrbuch des Zentralmuseums Mainz* 33, 159–198.

Kilian-Dirlmeier, I. (2005). *Die Bronzezeitlichen Gräber bei Nidri auf Leukas.* Bonn: Rudolf Habelt Verlag.

Korfmann, M. *et al.* (eds.) (2001). *Troia. Traum und Wirklichkeit.* Stuttgart: Theiss Verlag.

Kristiansen, K. (2001). "Rulers and warriors. Symbolic transmission and social transformation in Bronze Age Europe." In J. Haas (ed.), *From Leaders to Rulers.* New York: Kluwer Academic Press, 85–104.

Laffineur, R. (2007). "Building for ruling. Architecture and power at Mycenae." In J. Bretschneider, J. Driessen, and K. van Lerberghe (eds.), *Power and Architecture.* Leuven: Peeters, 117–127.

Lehmann, G. (2004). "Reconstructing the social landscape of early Israel: Rural marriage alliances in the central hill country." *Tel Aviv* 31, 141–193.

McDonald, W. A. and G. R. Rapp (eds.) (1972). *The Minnesota Messenia Expedition. Reconstructing a Bronze Age Regional Environment.* Minneapolis: University of Minnesota Press.

Mee, C. (ed.) (2011). *Greek Archaeology: A Thematic Approach.* Oxford: Wiley-Blackwell.

Mee, C. and H. Forbes (eds.) (1997). *A Rough and Rocky Place. The Landscape and Settlement History of the Methana Peninsula, Greece.* Liverpool: Liverpool University Press.

Morgan, L. (ed.) (2005). *Aegean Wall Painting. A Tribute to Mark Cameron.* London: British School at Athens Studies 13.

Mountjoy, P. and M. J. Ponting (2000). "The Minoan thalassocracy reconsidered." *Annual of the British School at Athens* 95, 141–184.

Nelson, M. C. (2007). "Pylos, block masonry and monumental architecture in the Late Bronze Age Peloponnese." In J. Bretschneider, J. Driessen, and K. van Lerberghe (eds.), *Power and Architecture.* Leuven: Peeters, 143–159.

Palyvou, C. (2005). *Akrotiri Thera. An Architecture of Affluence 3,500 Years Old.* Philadelphia: Instap Academic Press.

Philippa-Touchais, A. *et al.* (2010). *Mesohelladika: la Grèce continentale au Bronze Moyen.* Athens: École française d'Athènes, BCH Supplement 52.

Preziosi, D. and L. A. Hitchcock (1999). *Aegean Art and Architecture.* Oxford: Oxford University Press.

Renfrew, A. C. (1968). "Wessex without Mycenae." *Annual of the British School at Athens* 63, 277–285.

Renfrew, A. C. (1972a). "Patterns of population growth in the prehistoric Aegean." In P. J. Ucko, R. Tringham, and G. W. Dimbleby (eds.), *Man, Settlement and Urbanism.* London: Duckworth, 383–399.

Renfrew, A. C. (1972b). *The Emergence of Civilization.* London: Methuen.

Renfrew, A. C. (1973). *Before Civilization.* London: Jonathan Cape.

Renfrew, A. C. (1987). *Archaeology and Language: The Puzzle of Indo-European Origins.* London: Jonathan Cape.

Renfrew, C. and J. F. Cherry (eds.) (1986). *Peer Polity Interaction and Socio-Political Change.* Cambridge: Cambridge University Press.

Renfrew, C. and M. Wagstaff (eds.) (1982). *An Island Polity. The Archaeology of Exploitation in Melos.* Cambridge: Cambridge University Press.

Rutter, J. B. (1993). "Review of Aegean Prehistory II: The Prepalatial Bronze Age of the Southern and Central Greek Mainland." *American Journal of Archaeology* 97, 745–797.

Rutter, J. B. (2005). "Southern triangles revisited: Lakonia, Messenia, and Crete in the 14th–12th centuries BC." In J. Moody and A. L. D'Agata (eds.), *Ariadne's Threads: Connections Between Crete and the Greek Mainland in the Postpalatial Period.* Athens: Italian Archaeological School in Athens, 17–64.

Rutter, J. B. (2007). "Reconceptualizing the Middle Helladic 'type site' from a ceramic perspective: is 'bigger' really 'better'?" In F. Felten *et al.* (eds.), *Middle Helladic Pottery and Synchronisms.* Wien: Österreichischen Akademie der Wissenschaften, 35–44.

Scholes, K. (1956). "The Cyclades in the Later Bronze Age: A synopsis." *Annual of the British School at Athens* 51, 9–40.

Shelmerdine, C. W. (1997). "Review of Aegean Prehistory VI: The palatial Bronze Age of the Southern and Central Greek Mainland." *American Journal of Archaeology* 101, 537–585.

Shelmerdine, C. W. (ed.) (2008). *The Cambridge Companion to the Aegean Bronze Age.* Cambridge: Cambridge University Press.

Shennan, S. J. (1993). "Settlement and social change in Central Europe, 3500–1500 BC." *Journal of World Prehistory* 7, 121–161.

Touchais, G. (1998). "Argos à l'époque mésohelladique: Un habitat ou des habitats." In A. Pariente and G. Touchais (eds.), *Argos et l'Argolide. Topographie et urbanisme. Bulletin de Correspondance Hellénique*, Supplementary Volume, 71–84.

Valmin, N. (1938). *The Swedish Messenia Expedition*. Lund: CWK Gleerup.

Voutsaki, S. (1995). "Social and political processes in the Mycenaean Argolid: The evidence from the mortuary practices." In R. Laffineur and W.-D. Niemeier (eds.), *Politeia. Society and State in the Aegean Bronze Age*. Liege: Aegaeum 12, 55–66.

Voutsaki, S. (1998). "Mortuary evidence, symbolic meanings and social change: A comparison between Messenia and the Argolid in the Mycenean period." In K. Branigan (ed.), *Cemetery and Society in the Aegean Bronze Age*. Sheffield: Sheffield Academic Press, 41–58.

Walter, H. and H.-J. Weisshaar (1993). "Alt-Ägina. Die prähistorische Innenstadt westlich des Apollontempels." *Archäologischer Anzeiger*, 293–297.

Warren, P. (1975) *The Aegaean Civilisations*. London: Phaidon.

Whitelaw, T. (2005). "A tale of three cities: Chronology and Minoanisation at Phylakopi in Melos." In A. Dakouri-Hild and S. Sherratt (eds.), *Autochthon. Papers Presented to O. T. P. K. Dickinson*. Oxford: Archaeopress, 37–69.

Wright, J. C. (2004). "Comparative settlement patterns during the Bronze Age in the northeastern Peloponnese." In S. E. Alcock and J. F. Cherry (eds.), *Side-by-Side Survey. Comparative Regional Studies in the Mediterranean World*. Oxford: Oxbow, 114–131.

Further Reading

Bintliff, J. L., P. Howard, and A. M. Snodgrass (1999). "The hidden landscape of prehistoric Greece." *Journal of Mediterranean Archaeology* 12, 139–168.

Bintliff, J. L. *et al.* (2002). "Classical farms, hidden prehistoric landscapes and Greek rural survey: A response and an update." *Journal of Mediterranean Archaeology* 15, 259–265.

Bruins, H. J. *et al.* (2008). "Geoarchaeological tsunami deposits at Palaikastro (Crete) and the Late Minoan 1A eruption of Santorini." *Journal of Archaeological Science* 35, 191–212.

Kirsten, E. (1956). *Die Griechische Polis als historisch-geographisches Problem des Mittelmeerraumes*. Bonn: Colloquium Geographicum 5.

Ruschenbusch, E. (1985). "Die Zahl der griechischen Staaten und Arealgrösse und Bürgerzahl der 'Normalpolis'." *Zeitschrift für Papyrologie und Epigraphie* 59, 253–263.

Spencer, N. (1995). "Heroic time: Monuments and the past in Messenia, southwest Greece." *Oxford Journal of Archaeology* 14, 277–292.

Voutsaki, S. (1999). "Mortuary display, prestige and identity in the Shaft Grave era." In Anon., *Eliten in der Bronzezeit*. Mainz: Monographien des Römisch-Germanischen Zentralmuseums 43, 103–117.

Watrous, L. V. (1994). "Review of Aegean Prehistory III: Crete from Earliest Prehistory through the Protopalatial Period." *American Journal of Archaeology* 98, 695–753.

7

The Mature Late Bronze Age on the Mainland and in the Wider Aegean

The Mycenaean Civilization

Historical Development: The Mature Civilization and Its Collapse

The rise of Mycenae and its wider civilization (general reading: Shelmerdine 2008, Cline 2010, Mee 2011) is not only marked in the development of the elite tholos tomb in Messenia, but more dramatically in the Shaft Graves of Mycenae itself. These phenomena span final MH and early Late Helladic (LH1), ca. 1800–1500 BC. LH begins with a new ceramic style, heavily influenced by Minoan Crete, for example in the introduction of a lustrous iron-rich paint, new firing technique, and scenic elements (Betancourt 2007), and it also remains characteristic for Mycenaean culture on the Mainland and abroad in its subsequent evolution (LH1–3, Submycenaean) (Figure 7.1).

Mycenaean civilization proceeds toward full complexity at a slowish pace. In LH1–2 (ca. 1800/1700–1500/1400 BC) tholos tombs spread around the Mainland, forming power statements by local chiefs and princes. Did a tholos mark autonomy or could satellite chiefs deploy the same elite burial form as a superior lord? This makes it difficult to envisage how many chiefdoms or states were in the process of forming, and what role precocious centers such as Mycenae already exercised over their immediate regions. These prestigious monuments are commoner than the later major settlements during the LH3 climax Mycenaean state development (ca. 1400–1250/1200 BC), whilst a clear settlement hierarchy is also still lacking.

Meanwhile dramatic events outside the Mainland surely impacted on Mycenaean development. The Thera eruption was (probably) in the 1620s BC, while not many generations later the Minoan palaces

Figure 7.1 Mycenaean krater (LH3) depicting an octopus, from Ialysos (modern Trianda), Rhodes, Aegean Sea, h. 41 cm. © Trustees of the British Museum.

(excepting Knossos) were violently destroyed by fire. Even Knossos was drastically altered in its subsequent, more limited use (although still a major administrative center) in LM2, whilst only small areas in other palaces were reoccupied and not for any revival of their palatial system (except perhaps for Khania). There is widespread consensus that the Thera explosion destabilized but did not break Minoan power. The latter occurred subsequently, following most scholars, as the result of an invasion of Crete by Mainland Mycenaeans. In any case by LM2/ LH2 it seems probable that the Mycenaeans were ruling most of Crete from Knossos, as well as through secondary centers elsewhere (for example at the former West Cretan palatial center at Khania). We must acknowledge that a minority of scholars, significantly Minoan specialists, maintain that a Minoan elite was still in charge at Knossos but ruled with Mycenaean support. This has recently been supported by Strontium analysis of bone (Nafplioti 2008) suggesting that "Mycenaean-style" tombs actually contain local Minoan populations, although this study is problematic.

To capitalize on the great agricultural and labor wealth of the Minoan civilization, its new Mycenaean rulers adapted the Linear A script for writing their own language, an early form of Greek, into Linear B. The rich Knossos archive from the occupation era is a remarkable source for understanding economic organization in Mycenaean Crete, which some see as the most powerful Mycenaean state in LM2/early LM3 (Rutter 2006). In Eastern Crete many believe a series of independent Minoan "statelets" arose from the ruins of the LM1B destructions (Nodarou 2007). The language change and details of the records are in fact the most convincing evidence for Mainland occupation of Crete.

Knossos suffered catastrophic destruction in LH3, the scholarly majority favoring the end of the last palace in LH3A1 during the fourteenth century BC. In the absence of further evidence, explanations include a native uprising expelling the invaders but unable to revive the Minoan palatial system, or alternatively, some internal conflicts between the Mycenaeans themselves which resulted in their abandoning the island.

Recent work on Kythera island off the Southern Peloponnese, a Minoan colony, suggests its absorption into the Mycenaean state of Pylos after the Mycenaean takeover on Crete (Broodbank *et al.* 2005). The islands of the Cyclades see their ceramic imports from Crete replaced by Mainland items after the Thera eruption, then increasing Mycenaean influence, usually seen as leading to a political takeover, which some argue to have involved military conquest.

It is certainly striking that Mainland life jumps into new formats in line with these events abroad. Just as the Messenian tholoi and Mycenae Shaft Graves appear at a time of immense Minoan influence on the South Aegean under the Second Palaces, so the takeover of Crete (ca. 1500) is followed in LH2 by the first architectural complexes on the Mainland anticipating the later palaces, such as the Mansion at the Menelaion near Sparta. At Pylos recent study has shown the existence also of a mansion complex in LH2, perhaps even traces of an LH1 predecessor. Some hundred years later, during early LH3 (fourteenth century BC), substantial palaces were erected at a series of Mainland centers, some clearly state capitals (Mycenae, Pylos, Thebes), some with the first Linear B archives, at a

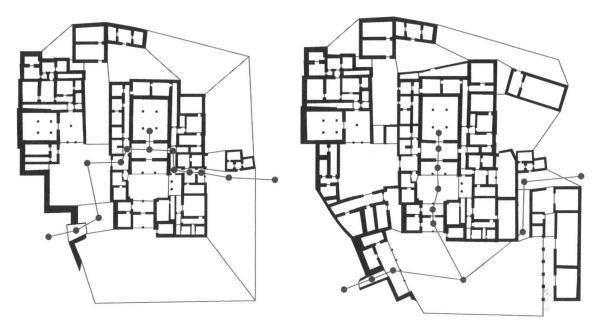

1. Shortest routes of access to the throne room 6 in topological terms in the earlier building state, dating to around 1300 B.C.

2. Shortest routes of access to the throne room 6 in topological terms in the later building state, dating to around 1200 B.C.

Figure 7.2 The earliest clear palace plan at Pylos, LH3A period (left) shows some resemblance to a Minoan "court-complex," whilst the later palace, LH3B period (right) has more controlled access and is less permeable to the public. U. Thaler, "Constructing and reconstructing power." In J. Maran *et al.* (eds.), *Constructing Power: Architecture, Ideology and Social Practice.* Hamburg 2006, 93–116, Tafel 16, 1–2.

time when Mycenaean experience of running the vast economy of Crete had been achieved. Notably at Pylos the first palace of LH3A does not simply elaborate on the LH2 Mainland design seen at the Menelaion but adds an unparalleled Minoan influence, consisting of three blocks around a large open court (Nelson 2007). However in the LH3B reconstruction of this plan, a typical Mainland palatial design is reinstated, conforming to the norm at the other Mycenaean palatial centers (Figure 7.2).

Coincident with the rise of Mycenaean palaces and formal territorial states in regions like the Plain of Argos, is a decline in the numbers and spread of elite tholoi, but Mycenae remains a location for multiple such monuments. This has been seen (Voutsaki 1995) as a centralization of power, either restricting the rights to monumental tombs to a few centers, or obliging satellite rulers to locate their tombs at the state capital.

In contrast to Crete, with its long-lived proto- and full "Palace" eras (ca. 2500–1500 BC), the splendor of the Mainland palaces was short-lived. Already by LH3A (fourteenth century BC) massive defensive walls arise around key centers, extended or multiplied in the thirteenth century (LH3B). A heightened alert seems to explain the addition in final 3B of hidden passages to underground springs at Mycenae, Tiryns, and the Athens Acropolis. Destruction already hits some centers at the end of 3B1, and all centers by the end of 3B2. The final formal Mycenaean ceramic phase of early LH3C, in the twelfth century BC, does see occupation continuing at quite a few palatial-towns, but at a much reduced scale of culture and complexity. It is apparent that state-level political and economic organization was no longer functioning at a significant regional scale. This phase and the succeeding twilight culture of the eleventh century BC in late LH3C (in some areas only, called Submycenaean), see massive abandonment of Mycenaean sites, radical depopulation at the few that do survive, and clearly the collapse of that civilization.

The End of Mycenaean Civilization

As for the causes of the fall of the Mycenaean world, no firm answers have been forthcoming, despite continual attempts at explanations (Shelmerdine 1997, Dickinson 2006). At the major centers of Mycenae, Tiryns, and Midea in the Argos Plain, at Athens, and at the Central Greek foci of Thebes and Gla, during the mid to late phases of the climax Mycenaean era of LH3B, we witness the erection of enlarged fortifications and at some centers secret water-supply tunnels, associated with multiple destruction events. But many of these mentioned centers go on into the final LH phase of 3C, if significantly without evidence for any palatial administration. It is therefore problematic when one of the older excavators of Mycenae described it as experiencing in 3C "its last century of greatness" (Mylonas 1968). Exceptionally, the Tiryns Lower Citadel continues in occupation through 3C into Submycenaean times, and its Lower Town expands not only significantly but as a well-planned urban extension (elevating the settlement to perhaps 45 ha). Some see a lone attempt here to revive a minor state during 3C. Midea sees occupation and remodeling of the settlement in 3C. Athens' continuity through Submycenaean and beyond is taken to confirm Classical Athens' tradition of its resistance to outside conquest. In contrast, many other sites are abandoned in late 3B or early 3C, with or without destruction. Suiting the idea of people fleeing to refuge centers, some sites grow or arise in 3C (Perati in Attica, and a large cluster in the Northwest Peloponnese). It is generally accepted that by 3C the palatial system has collapsed even if many centers survive in use. A poignant bowl from Mycenae of 3C date could even depict one of its last contingents of troops heading out to confront its unknown nemesis, with soldiers carrying lunch-bags hanging on their spears.

Later Greek tradition recognized an age of disturbance after the Age of Heroes and the time of the Trojan War, with invasions, migrations, but nonetheless no mention of "foreign" attack. Legend suggests that the warfare was occasioned by internal strife and one particular group of Greek-speakers, the Dorians. What caused these civil wars and migrations is left rather unclear, and although legend describes dynastic power struggles, archaeology shows that no-one was "the winner," and it is hard to accept competition between elites where every palace is destroyed.

Surely relevant are wider disturbances during the period of Mycenaean collapse: the almost contemporary violent downfall of the Anatolian civilization of the Hittites, and the attacks on Egypt and the Levant by a coalition called the "Sea Peoples." If the Hittites succumbed to Anatolian enemies, the Sea Peoples may have arisen from opportunistic raiders or displaced groups gathered from a surprisingly wide region including the Central Mediterranean, the Aegean, and Cyprus.

Environmental factors have been linked with the end of the Mycenaean powers and related crises in the East Mediterranean. There is still a lack of convincing evidence for dramatic climatic change for this era. Earthquakes do seem to be proven for some Mycenaean centers during 3B, but are a regular phenomenon in the Aegean, and without ancillary crippling disasters are implausible as a cause of lasting civilizational collapse.

Other theories include changes in warfare, allowing "barbarians" to challenge Aegean and other East Mediterranean states (Drews 1993), which has not convinced most specialists, and the detection of alien invaders in Greece through a characteristic handmade burnished ware – likewise unlikely to be a "smoking gun" for the Mycenaean collapse (Rutter et al. 2007). One thing is sure, that military attack is the central direct agent for the violent Mycenaean fall. The increasing defense measures and multiple fire destructions, plus the absence of rebuilding of palaces and other indications of state organization, most suit human violence aimed at the nerve-centers of the Mycenaean states. The subsequent legends and archaeological evidence for migrations and abandonments could reflect major conflicts ranging widely over the Mainland and islands. Ingenious attempts to find signs of crisis in the Linear B archives (Chadwick 1976) lack conviction, but admittedly the political archives have never been located at any palatial site, in contrast to the economic records.

It is still too soon to choose a best-fit scenario for the Mycenaean collapse, but some key elements can be suggested. Inter-elite warfare is problematic as no center benefits. Large-scale immigrant invasion fails to convince since the succeeding culture develops out of Mycenaean. If civil war swept through the Mycenaean states, eliminating the royal palatial elites, ethnohistoric parallels could explain much of the puzzling post-palatial political landscape. With the destruction of large unitary states, did temporary warlords, perhaps directing those attacks, create an unstable mosaic of feuding statelets? Many scholars consider the complex palatial civilization as unpopular in its tax load or labor demands from the middle and lower classes, envisaging massive popular uprisings against the top level of the hierarchy, which does explain the total disappearance of all the palaces. However, current thinking on the Mycenaean economy has balanced private against public in such a way as to undermine such a model, whilst surveys generally do not support overpopulation and high levels of land use driven by palatial pressure to extract ever-greater surpluses. Finally, recently the idea has developed that Mycenaean palaces were dependent on international trade to support their power, so that the decline of exchange systems in the thirteenth and twelfth centuries due to military disruption in the Eastern Mediterranean brought collapse to all the Aegean palaces. Since expert analyses of ceramics and other materials find Mycenaean exports abroad as small-scale, and it has yet to be demonstrated that the palaces were primarily (as claimed) maintained by prestige craftwork ("wealth finance") as opposed to the much more plausible support for their personnel through a tax on food, textile production ("staple finance"), and the right to labor-services, I don't see this model as realistic.

With the collapse of "the monopoly of power" which is a key definition of "the state," ordinary folk may have concentrated in fortified or remote refuge settlements, and (as we see in war-torn parts of Africa today), migrate *en masse* to safe territories. Early Iron Age populations in Southern Greece appear much reduced from a peak in the Late Bronze Age. We can consider direct casualties in the razing of larger and small Mycenaean centers, then indirect fatalities from the collapse of the redistributive economy formerly radiating from the state, and finally food shortages with the abandonment of settlements and cultivated land, or the burning or expropriation of food stores by competing war-bands.

Archaeology can highlight processes operating over several centuries, but can rarely pinpoint events within a single decade (the *histoire événementielle* of the Annales School). As with the rise of Mycenae, I am tempted to conclude that some of the critical moves in the military and political history of this period are as yet undetectable with any clarity at the archaeological timescale. Were it not for the historically-recorded Egyptian victories over the Sea Peoples, we would not have an inkling of such dramatic international processes during this era.

The Mycenaean Settlement System

From the 1960s, extensive survey and inferences from the palace archives demonstrated that Mycenaean civilization was organized around a settlement hierarchy. Below the palaces were lesser fortified centers of population and power, then unfortified villages, followed by hamlets and farmsteads. There were also strategic forts on high places, such as around Lake Copais in Central Greece. Palatial centers were few, each dominating large territories. The late construction of the palaces and even later great walling programs around the *acropoleis* (upper towns) of their associated communities indicated a long period of gradual centralization of power. As discussed earlier, the early to middle Middle Helladic period offers a picture of numerous villages (with a few small towns), providing the political base for one or several leading families (marked by tumuli). This is succeeded in late MH/early LH by an Early Mycenaean era in which larger territorial states vied for power (marked by tholos tombs or Shaft Graves), thence leading into the consolidation of even larger major states ruled from walled palatial centers. The archival evidence from the kingdom of Pylos for some twelve regions, split between two halves of the state, plausibly reflects earlier independent districts, progressively absorbed by the expanding state (Chadwick 1976, Bintliff 1977b–c). In the Plain of

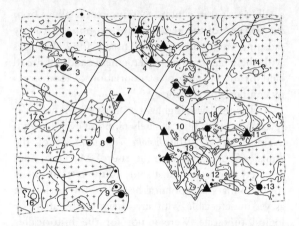

Figure 7.3 A first attempt to model the settlement hierarchy for the Mycenaean Plain of Argos: primary, secondary, and tertiary settlements are shown as triangles then larger and smaller circles.
J. L. Bintliff, *Natural Environment and Human Settlement in Prehistoric Greece*. Oxford 1977, Appendix A, Figure 1a.

Argos, settlement analysis (Figure 7.3) also suggests that a mosaic of statelets may have become fused over time into a unitary Mycenaean state emerging from Mycenae itself in the northernmost corner (No. 1). Mycenae could have become the paramount center in a four-tier settlement hierarchy, or alternatively remained the "first amongst equals" with possible rivals at Tiryns (No. 10) and Midea (No. 6). Marzolff (2004) has recently updated the map of major and minor centers for this region.

Intensive surveys in Mycenae's hinterland (the Nemea and Berbati Valleys) (Wells and Runnels 1996, Cherry and Davis 2001) show a late infill of their Mycenaean landscapes, argued to be a response to political and economic intervention from the expanding Mycenae state. This raises the potential to detect the hand of History behind our use of rather general models of the rise of civilization as resulting from population growth and the rise of a settlement hierarchy.

On Crete, accepting the mainstream theory of a Mycenaean domination based in Knossos for the LH2–3 era, despite the razing of the other palaces at the start of this period, the new state seems to have taken the inevitable decision to use traditional regional centers (but usually not their former palaces) as secondary bases for its administration. The vast scale of crops and animals documented by Knossos scribes, and place-names, seem to indicate that the state was involved with a major degree of control across some two-thirds of Crete (Killen in *Rethinking* 2007).

Recently much debate has rightly tested the strength of evidence for our understanding of Mycenaean politics and economy (see *Rethinking* 2007). One revisionist school is unsure if the major centers were really state capitals, preferring multiple competing centers (chiefly for the crowded Argos Plain), or alternatively envisages palaces as having a small role in their regions, with most economic activity under the "private" control of local elites, sanctuaries, and village communities (the "*damos*" or people). Others take a completely opposite stance, and view references from the Anatolian Hittite Empire archives to negotiating with the Great King of the *Ahhiyawa* (Achaeans or Mycenaeans) as evidence for an empire in which the separate palaces owed allegiance to a super-king, although dispute revolves around Mycenae or Thebes as his base. For the first scenario, the Plain of Argos has little to help us reconstruct its politics from the Linear B archives, but at least a high status for Tiryns compared with Mycenae seems necessary from the archaeology. Where the texts are richer a much clearer situation emerges, supporting the traditional view. The organization of the states of Pylos and Knossos appears to depict very large realms under a high degree of control and exploitation, whilst the recent Thebes records and the role of its rival Orchomenos in the drainage of Lake Copais and the construction of a giant satellite administrative center within it, appear to indicate the same for Central Greece. The archaeology of these centers would suit their preeminence in their supposed state-territories. As for a super-king, in the absence of Mycenaean diplomatic records we can add little regarding this scenario, but an alternative solution is the model presented in the poems of Homer, where King Agamemnon of Mycenae is the "first among equals" in the legendary coalition of Greeks against Troy. This might encourage foreign states to assume a single ruler.

Intensive and extensive archaeological surveys are now plentiful enough to allow a provisional estimate of the scale of population and land use in Mycenaean

Greece. This has not been attempted, although it would shed light on the theory that palatial demands on crop surpluses could have threatened economic and social stability and assisted the fall of the Mycenaean states. In the Argos Plain the density of major centers does seem to be accompanied by very high population density, based on burial evidence (Bintliff 1989), but other provinces seem not to be densely settled in the countryside, for example Boeotia (Bintliff *et al.* 2007). There is growing evidence for an out-of-phase rise of human settlement by region, responding to varied local and external stimuli (Bintliff 2005), and this does challenge any idea of a general ecological collapse or economic revolt against palatial extortion leading to the fall of the civilization. Nonetheless, it is clear that the hierarchy of Mycenaean settlements required a solid body of regular secondary sites in each state-territory, something confirmed by the Linear B records where most economic activities were dispersed in the latter. Such lesser settlements will have been local foci from later MH times, and under the influence of flourishing conditions assumed for the mature Mycenaean period they should have grown in size and prosperity. We know too little of such sites, but Tsoungiza in the Nemea district, which climaxes in LH3B at some 7,5 ha, provides a precious insight into neglected lower levels of the settlement system (Shelmerdine 1997). The apparent lack of villas, a form of local administration on Second Palace era Crete (Bennet 1988), could indicate a more embedded economy focused on existing nucleated settlements.

Beyond the Mycenaean heartlands of the Southern Aegean, developments in Northern Greece are a useful counter to explanations coined purely from the southern civilizational perspective (Andreou *et al.* 1996, Andreou 2001, Bommeljé 2005). During the later Bronze Age there is evidence for both population rise and wider use of many landscapes in Aetolia, Epirus, Macedonia, and Thrace, during which networks of larger villages or even small urban sites emerged as likely "central-places" with economic, social, and arguably political influence on limited zones of satellite settlements in their districts.

But even within the Southern Mainland there are regions whose Mycenaean settlement patterns are very unclear, leaving open whether these were districts where less complex networks of fortified sites and villages prevailed, or alternatively where minor states await discovery.

Towns and Palaces

Two aspects of Mycenaean centers remain poorly known. The first is the reason for the delay between the rise of elite burials at the MH-LH transition, and the first definite construction phases of the palace complexes, securely dated from the fourteenth century (early LH3A). The second is, to what extent were the major fortified acropoleis surrounded by towns, and were these large or small? For the first question, there are several sites where elite residences are evidenced or claimed from LH2, such as the Menelaion near Sparta (Rutter 2005), and an LH1–2 mansion (?) at Pylos (Nelson 2007). Warren's theory that the delayed appearance of full palaces is a consequence of the Mycenaean takeover of Minoan civilization around 1500 BC remains a powerful explanation for this uneven development of the Southern Mainland over time.

For query two, Mycenaean Lower Towns are becoming better known. LH3B Tiryns possesses a surrounding settlement of 25 ha. Extensive survey of the Lower Town outside the Mycenae citadel suggests an extent of 30 ha (although dispersed cemeteries might reduce the settled area). Intensive survey around the Pylos palace indicates a surrounding town also of at least 15–30 ha. On a comparative scale, these central-places appear to be modest, but consistent with the scale of their inferred territorial states. They compare well to the size of city-state foci in the Early and Middle Bronze Age Levant, and to the lesser palatial centers of Minoan Crete (Bintliff 2002).

Nonetheless, the internal planning and range of house types in Lower Towns remain largely unknown. Clusters of tombs in the Mycenae Lower Town might represent dispersed house-zones rather than a monolithic block of residences. Darcque has recently argued (2005) that the excavated houses closest to the Citadel are all extensions of the palace-complex, rather than representing the houses, workshops or stores of independent merchants and craftsmen.

Our understanding of the internal plans of the Citadels has advanced through studying access routes

Figure 7.4　The palace at Pylos in LH3B: the Great Megaron reconstructed.
Watercolor by Piet de Jong, digitally edited by Craig Mauzy. Courtesy of Department of Classics, University of Cincinnati.

and functional differentiation (Cavanagh 2001, Mühlenbruch 2003, Thaler 2006; cf. Figure 7.2). Mycenaean palaces focus on a modest-sized "Great Court" which faces onto a special large building, the Great Megaron (Figure 7.4). From the main entrance to the Citadel, the way to this heart leads through a series of gates or doors and passageways, and is complex and indirect. On the route from the entrance of the Citadel to the core of the palatial complex would be placed the archive rooms, storehouses for oil, wine, and grain, and perhaps residential areas for members of the elite. At Pylos this last role has been argued for the Southwest Building, which has its own court (left of the Great Megaron on the plan in Figure 7.2), but other scholars suggest this open area was for social feasting.

How influential in this design was Minoan palatial architecture? Only the first Pylos palace is a court-centered plan, succeeded by this more characteristic Mainland layout, although the later Minoan palaces also made access to the center of the complex tortuous. Taking the normal late Mycenaean palace as described above for our comparison, the Minoan Central Court is far grander than the Great Court, and considered as a "theatrical zone" where major events were staged, initially for the general populace but later more for the elite. Views and alignments to distant landmarks, some of ritual significance, are also a feature on Crete. Yet although Mycenaean Great Courts are smaller in scale, and lack distant views, it is probable that major events also occurred within them, whilst the upper floors around and above them might have functioned as spectator areas. The visual focus on the Megaron, the seat of power, is a striking contrast to Minoan architecture. Mycenaean art represents processions, and there is speculation that at Mycenae and Tiryns the elite may have used the Citadel entrance route directed to the Great Court for formal movements, perhaps leading into sacrifices in the

Great Megaron porch and within the inner hall of the Megaron itself, for which there is some evidence. Other details of Mycenaean palatial architecture nonetheless show clear Minoan influences, such as light wells (unroofed internal rooms to introduce sunlight) and *polythyra* (folding doors).

At the same time, possible parallels in Near Eastern states can be cited, for example the palace of the city-state of Ugarit, where we find a similar access route, archive location and a court associated with a great hall. However one clear contrast between the Levant and Minoan-Mycenaean palatial-citadel plans is the low profile and limited scale of formal shrines in the latter (notably the excavated tiny Mycenae ritual complex). This has been taken to suggest that both of the Aegean civilizations may have tied ritual to secular power, so that "public spaces" could have been also places for religious ceremonies.

Apart from the focal Great Megaron, agreed to be the audience hall of the state ruler (throne emplacements are reconstructed at Pylos and Tiryns), several palace plans have additional megaron-style complexes, seen as possible residences or reception halls for other members of the elite.

Construction Works of Monumental Scale

Fortifications

In Antiquity, the great circuit walls of large stones around the Mainland Bronze Age citadels such as Mycenae encouraged the belief that they were built by Giants (*Cyclopes*) rather than men, hence the style of construction is still termed Cyclopaean (Figure 7.5). Similar fortifications have been found on strategic hilltops as military posts. Very large, lightly-shaped limestone rocks are piled carefully into walls, with an infill of small stones in the interstices. The walls are often built in sections whose ends are marked by a pronounced projecting facet, either reflecting work teams or an adaptation to earthquakes. Only the weakest and also the most public parts of the circuits, the great and lesser gates, are constructed with evenly-cut blocks, usually of immense proportions. The main entrance is via a ramp for chariots and large groups of

people, but generally this is slanted so that those ascending to the gate are exposed to missile attack from the walls and gate towers on their shield-less right side. The main phase of circuit construction, together with outlying forts, is the last century of palatial power, the thirteenth century BC (LH3B). Late in 3B, extra defensive measures were taken at several centers. The great citadel at Thebes, the Cadmeia, dominated by possibly two successive palaces, may have been fortified earlier, in 3A, as were some other major foci. At Pylos, a basic fortification around the area of the later palace may have existed in late MH/early LH but was not renewed when the palace was built.

Two aspects of Mycenaean citadel fortification have been focused on, probably complementary rather than exclusive explanations for their purpose. The first, and traditional, attributes to the Mycenaeans, in contrast to the Minoans, a bellicose mentality. It is still the case that Minoan centers have little or no defenses, and the deliberately difficult access from their towns to the inner palace seems more designed to filter out the ordinary people and strangers from the operational zone of the elite than to repel invading armies, and in any case appears to be very late. But why then does it take so long, from the first signs of a warrior elite in the Shaft Graves and elsewhere in the early Mycenaean world, to several hundred years later, for great circuit walls to be erected? The second theory answers this by emphasizing the walling as a symbol of power and prestige rather than primarily a functional necessity. But this view also comes up against the time factor, why so late? It is difficult to avoid making a link between the short life of the circuits, the swift addition of features without display value such as the underground water access, and the rising wave of destructions, as a sequence of historic significance in which perception of immense threat, an increase in that threat, and the fulfillment of a feared catastrophe chain together into a narrative.

This need not remove the factor of prestige. The enormous labor required to create these circuits, and their overwhelming power even today, must have been equally intended to intimidate rivals and enemies, as to form a genuine refuge for the elite. In previous Mycenaean centuries, conflicts were expected to be settled in the open battlefield, but in late Mycenaean

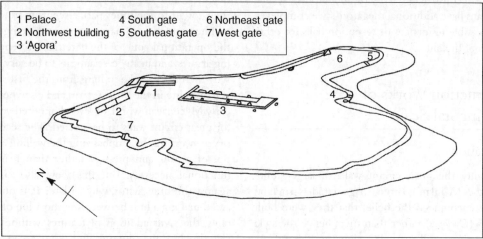

Figure 7.5   View and partial plan of Mycenaean fortress at Gla, Central Greece.
Photo R. V. Schoder, SJ, © 1989 Loyola University of Chicago. Plan from R.V. Schoder, SJ, *Ancient Greece from the Air*. London: Thames and Hudson 1974, 79.

times, sieges were clearly anticipated and Minoan-Mycenaean-Cycladic art has quite a few siege scenes depicted in various media. The functional success of the larger circuit walls is also an issue, such as at Gla where the entire island perimeter of around 3 km was fortified, requiring a very large force to defend.

Drainage works

Not far to the north of the great fortified rock of the Tiryns Citadel, in the southeast Plain of Argos, a wide torrent is blocked by a great dam of earth faced with large stone blocks, clearly of Mycenaean construction. Examination of the dam reveals that the seasonal torrent has been diverted from its westward natural course, so as to run into an entirely artificial course, cut for this purpose in the Pleistocene sediments of the Plain, through which its flow was fed into a more southerly streambed. The reason appears to have been a perceived threat to Tiryns from storm floods (Bintliff 1977c). Zangger (1994) found evidence in the Lower Town of Tiryns for vast flashflood sediments, dated around the end of the LH3B or the peak Mycenaean period, which had stimulated this large-scale engineering work. But this is just one and not the greatest example of Mycenaean water management systems, and it seems likely that many more will be discovered when landscape research looks beyond the palace centers. The evaluation of recent claims for the construction of a giant artificial harbor serving the palace of Pylos in the Southwest Peloponnese (Zangger et al. 1997) await detailed publication.

So far the most remarkable well-published example of Mycenaean large-scale engineering lies far to the north, in the former Lake Copais basin of Boeotia, Central Greece (see following Text Box).

Lake Copais

In Greco-Roman times we know that this great natural karst (porous limestone) depression lake, some 200 km² at its seasonal maximum, was beyond contemporary attempts to drain or even regularly control, with just marginal side-basins kept periodically dry enough for cultivation. A successful drainage in the late nineteenth century AD by French and British engineers brought a surprise, however, when the dry lake-bed revealed a systematic network of dams of clearly great antiquity, in part centering on a hitherto unknown Mycenaean fortress on an island in the north-east of the lake, called Gla (Figure 7.5). The hypothesis that the Mycenaeans had succeeded in draining all or a major part of Copais, perhaps from the mysterious new center at Gla, was rapidly formulated as excavations at Gla achieved enigmatic and rather limited results within the clearly Cyclopaean walls that encompassed the entire (3 km) island cliff perimeter. Sporadic excavations and studies of the lake dams continued throughout the first half of the twentieth century, but it was only in the period from the 1980s to the turn of the millennium that large-scale modern excavation at Gla by Iakovidis (1998, 2001), matched with a high-quality technical survey of the drainage evidence throughout Copais by a German hydro-geological and archaeological team (Knauss 1987, Kalcyck and Knauss 1989), gave us detailed understanding of Gla in its total physical context.

It is now clear that the Mycenaeans had built a vast single or double-dyked canal along the northern lakeside, and possibly a second along the south and east lakesides, so as to divert the inflowing water from outside the basin around the lake periphery and onwards into the subterranean limestone sinkholes (natural underground drainage caves) on its northeasternmost borders. A large lake remnant in the Melas sub-basin near Orchomenos was left as an overflow reservoir. These measures secured a huge area of drained lake for seasonal cultivation. The dams were vast affairs with the outer faces sheathed in well-fitted stone, while the inner body, some 30 meters broad, consisted of packed earth. The estimated length of the dams today is around 200 km. Large blocks of lake-bed were also dyked to create farmland permanently free from water (polders).

Around Gla island the dams run toward the fortress and would have allowed chariots to reach it. As for the fortress itself, the recent excavations confirmed previous puzzling impressions of a largely empty enceinte with little domestic debris. No town or even extensive palatial complex appeared. Rather, in the center of the island, a large enclosed, flattish area contained a series of warehouses, especially for storing grain, together with accommodation and workshops, whilst on the highest point a paired set of identical monumental buildings with an L-shaped design have been interpreted by Iakovidis as the residences of the garrison commander and the controller of stored crop surpluses, respectively, these being the main if not sole functions of the island.

If Gla was not itself a town or state center, but a military stronghold linked to massive crop-storage, regional logic makes clear that its controlling focus lay in the nearest major Mycenaean center, the site of Orchomenos, in the northwest of the lake borders. The precious resources which Gla protected were firstly, the bountiful crops which came from the spectacular drainage of the fertile and untouched lake clays, with their high water table even in midsummer, and secondly, the highly vulnerable drainage system itself. In legend, Orchomenos was the great rival of the other key Mycenaean center of Boeotia, Thebes, which had its own rich landscape in the plains and plateaus which directly border it to its north and south respectively. Perhaps not coincidentally, myth also records that the Theban hero Heracles unleashed a great flood against its enemy.

Roads

As with Minoan Crete, there is clear evidence that in some districts the Mycenaeans managed routes through terracing, stream-control, and small bridges. Dating such features is not always easy, and most claimed roads do not have secure Mycenaean chronology (Cavanagh 2001). In Greece today rural transport largely follows dirt-tracks and this must have been the case in the Bronze Age, leaving no real trace of their early use today. The widespread use of chariots is clear from the considerable numbers listed in the archives, but it seems they were not deployed directly in warfare as in the contemporary Near East, but as taxis in and out of combat, and more normally for elite travel and communication between centers (Littauer and Crouwel 1996).

Burials

Burial customs are one of the best researched forms of evidence for Mycenaean culture (for an excellent overview see Cavanagh and Mee 1998). The origins of the Mycenaean states have been investigated through grave elaboration, since little is known of the architecture of contemporary settlements, although this is believed to be unsophisticated until LH2. The tholos tomb (Figure 6.8) is plausibly the prerogative of elite families, although over time it becomes exclusive to the uppermost princely dynasties, as we progress from the MH3 examples within their putative origin in Messenia (Southwest Peloponnese), through to the latest palatial series of LH3B, with an unparalleled concentration at Mycenae. Voutsaki (1998) suggests that the greater numbers from Messenia reflect a wider social use there in final MH/early LH, whereas following the diffusion of the form to the key region of the Argolid and elsewhere in LH1–2, it was designated as more exclusive to an upper class. However, this regional contrast could also mark the increasing centralization of power over time, from numerous local chiefs or Big Men, toward a formal series of regional leaders with defined roles within the palace organization (as the later Linear B archives suggest). That process of hierarchization may also have moved at different rates regionally, with Pylos perhaps assuming regional dominance at a slower rate than Mycenae, where the Shaft Graves might already be taken as a claim to future supremacy.

Indeed at the time of those latter fabulous burials, nothing comparable can be seen at contemporary cemeteries elsewhere in the Plain of Argos (such as at Lerna, Asine, and especially the key MH focus of Argos), and by LH1 these potentially rival centers fade out of competition at the same time as Mycenae adopts the new tholos prestige burial form. However, other significant centers in Mycenae's region will adopt tholoi, for example Tiryns and Berbati. Might this indicate that after Mycenae had "seen off" potential rivals in the west and southeast Plain, it found itself competing with nearer neighbors to its immediate south, in the eastern Plain? Was there then a period in Early Mycenaean times when Mycenae was the first amongst equals, until the Late Mycenaean era sees a cessation of tholos construction outside of that center, when it seems Mycenae's preeminence appropriated the tholos as an almost exclusive attribute? Or do we read too much into burial symbolism, as achieved power, when it might have been competitive display between several dynasties in the Argos region? Only in the last centuries of palatial power, LH3, could we say that the virtual restriction of tholos construction to Mycenae in the Plain of Argos should indicate the supremacy of the Mycenae dynasty. Perhaps conclusive is the parallel evidence from Messenia, where a similar wide use of tholoi leads by LH3B to their restriction to the palace of Pylos.

If tholos tombs are complex to read as documents of changing political relationships over time within the separate regions of the Peloponnese, the nature of status burials becomes even less certain elsewhere in the Southern Mainland. In Attica the plausible case for a fortified palatial center on the Athenian Acropolis remains unaccompanied by a royal tomb, whilst the tholoi in other districts of Attica might argue for competing assertive elites. In Boeotia, the palatial center at Thebes ignores the tholos form, but its legendary rival Orchomenos, with the only regional tholos (the Treasury of Minyas) seems to be marking its distinctiveness through imitating the prestige tombs at distant Mycenae.

The commonest Mycenaean burial tradition is however that of chamber-tomb cemeteries (Figure 7.6). Like tholoi, the burial chamber is preceded by an entrance way (*dromos*), with either of these being sealed so as to allow reuse. This strongly emphasizes the importance of kin-group continuity in Mycenaean society. The shape of chamber tombs could represent an emulation of the tholos at lesser cost in time, labor, and materials, although the social composition of those buried within them is less clear. An older view considered these tombs as designed for a middle class, with the lower class disposed of in cist graves, earth tombs or even discarded into rubbish deposits. Current views prefer to see the majority of non-elite members being interred in chamber tombs. Calculations I have carried out on the recorded chamber tomb burials indicate a relatively high population for the Mycenaean Plain of Argos (Bintliff 1989) and since then their number has risen through

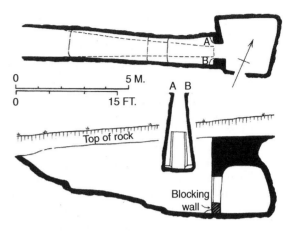

Figure 7.6 Mycenaean-style chamber tomb construction. S. Hood, *The Minoans. Crete in the Bronze Age.* Thames and Hudson, London 1971, Figure 29. Drawn by Patricia Clarke.

additional discoveries. This supports the current orthodoxy. Consequently the least sophisticated of body disposal methods just noted may represent a small minority excluded from "normal burial rights" for various reasons. On the other hand, although occasionally chamber tombs have revealed rich burials, or those with elaborate dress (including the famous Dendra warrior with full body-armor), analytical study (Kilian-Dirlmeier 1986) confirms that even the finest chamber-tomb assemblages do not compete with either the older Mycenae Shaft Grave elite graves or the rare surviving objects from the later tholos tombs of the Peloponnese. In a contrasting trend to the increase in the status of tholos burial over time, chamber tombs after LH2 show a decrease in wealth.

In a detailed investigation of Argolid chamber tomb cemeteries, Mee and Cavanagh (1990) tested a number of propositions.

1. Are the finest tombs nearest the citadel or main settlement area of Mycenaean centers? This might indicate that this was a sign of higher status in the community. It appears not. Are even the oldest there, from which later tombs spread out to a greater distance? The implication would again be that it was desirable to bury the dead close to the living. Again the answer seems to be no.

2. Are there rich and poor cemetery areas? If we look, for example, at the extended cemetery clusters around Mycenae and classify the tombs into four wealth classes on their finds, once again we receive a negative answer. This result and that to question 1 point to an alternative structuring principle, in which the dominating concept in chamber-tomb cemeteries was the discrete cluster of burials, each of which focused on a powerful elite group and also contained its client families, although these social units seem to be small.

3. The analysis also produced an unexpected trend: there *is* a correlation of early graves being wealthier than later graves. Mee and Cavanagh link this to the changing status of burial forms over time. If tholoi are reserved for the aristocracy, then in Early Mycenaean times "archaic" cist and pit graves (a heritage from MH village tradition), or no formal burial at all, might mark the poorest peasantry, leaving the dominant chamber tomb to a middle class. In mature-late Mycenaean times the "archaic" grave forms fade out and a great rise in the numbers of dead in chamber tombs could mark their use by the middle *and* lower classes (hence perhaps creating an average decline in the level of wealth in graves), at the same time as tholoi become exclusive to the inner circle of aristocrats around the dynastic princely family.

However, settlement studies indicate a substantial population rise in LH3 times, suggesting an additional or alternative explanation for an increase in chamber tombs. Their decreasing wealth might reveal an intriguing gulf emerging between the power and lifestyle of the palatial elite (in terms of tholos splendor and the construction of the palace complexes), and the vast mass of the people, maybe some support for theories that the collapse of Mycenaean civilization followed a mass rising by an oppressed majority.

Religion

Mycenaean cult-buildings (Shelmerdine 1997) surprise us by their small size. They have been identified at palatial and other urban sites, such as Mycenae (three linked structures), and the "Mycenaeanized"

town at Phylakopi on the island of Melos (two structures). In these complexes raised platforms serve for libations and offerings and also for display of idiosyncratic figurines (male, female, and animals, including snakes). These shrines are interpreted as serving several deities. Finally a cult place on the peninsula of Methana (Aghios Konstantinos) has yielded a large collection of cattle figurines and those of chariots and helmeted riders, perhaps reflecting the symbols of wealth and military prowess familiar to a "heroic" hierarchical society. These small and not very accessible ritual buildings are unsuitable for large-scale communal worship, although their cult paraphernalia might be taken elsewhere for more public ceremonies. One such context could be open-air shrines, such as the hilltop above the Classical sanctuary at Epidauros, where animal sacrifice is associated with figurines. The central fresco in the Mycenaean Cult Center raises questions: two imposing women face each other, one with a great sword, the other with a staff, whilst small floating figures hover beside them. Has the clear centrality in Minoan ritual scenes for female participants and "divinities" been transferred to Mycenaean cult?

The standardized, most popular Mycenaean figurines are frequently found in tombs. In settlements they can be associated with doors and hearths, and especially where these contexts involve cups and cooking-pots could mark popular, non-elite worship. Do these Phi- and Pi-shaped idols represent a powerful Minoan-Mycenaean fertility Mother-Goddess? Other figurines, found in varied contexts, are hard to interpret. Some, such as the ugly "grotesques," may be worshippers with offerings for the divinities, whilst others (domestic animals, warriors) might symbolize the desire for supernatural blessing on fertility, wealth, and warrior virtues.

It has recently been suspected that religion played a more central and public role in the Mycenaean state than the evidence just summarized allows. The prominence of a cult center called Pakijana in the Pylos archives, distant from the palace, may indicate extensive undiscovered ritual complexes in the Mycenaean world, paralleled by Minoan sites such as Archanes. Moreover the frequency in Linear B texts of religious events has encouraged scholars to reconsider the palatial contexts themselves. Could the central hall (megaron) and its porch, as well as the court facing its entrance, have functioned on certain occasions as the scene for ritual involving the dynastic elite? Some fresco fragments may portray formal processions where state ceremonial plausibly incorporated a ritual dimension. Particular attention is given to a fresco from the Pylos megaron, where a formal feast with men drinking at tables, a throne, a bard with a lyre, and a trussed bull, may show events in the megaron itself, where feasting, music and poetry, and even animal sacrifice seem associated. Additionally, the Linear B texts suggest that religious institutions were involved in significant agricultural and craft production, whilst palatial secular activities often also had associated shrines (Lupack in *Rethinking* 2007).

The remarkable painted stone and terracotta coffins (*larnakes*) from Tanagra in Central Greece and from Mycenaean Crete not only shed light on funerary ceremonies, and later rituals to the dead, but perhaps on beliefs in the afterlife. The LM3A Aghia Triada coffin appears to represent a procession toward the tomb of, and sacrifice in honor of, a person who is shown wraith-like beside their monument (Betancourt 2007). The form of the procession and some of the objects being brought to the deceased, such as a boat-model, have been taken by some as a sign of Egyptian influence, representing the voyage of the soul. Gallou (2005) assembles some fragmentary evidence from iconography and Linear B that there may have been other religious processions involving the carrying of cult images. It is suggested that formal group rituals took place in relation to the ancestors in the entrances to tholoi, larger chamber tombs, and in the "theatrical area" constructed over the Shaft Grave Circle A at Mycenae (Gallou 2005).

Pots and Trade

As well as providing for regional needs, Mycenaean pottery workshops throughout Southern Greece have been shown to export across regions. Unfortunately references to potters in Linear B texts are very rare and the degree of centralized control versus independent non-palatial workshops is disputed. Scientific analyses of "stirrup-jars" has shown for example that West and Central Crete sent shipments of these oil-containers to several regions of the Mainland during the Mycenaean occupation (Shelmerdine 1997).

Mycenaean societies required significant imports of metal for making bronze tools, with copper largely supplied from Attic Lavrion and Cyprus, and tin from an unknown source outside the Aegean (Gale and Stos-Gale 2008). Alongside bronze, which was in use widely across classes, the Mycenaean elite deployed prestigious exotic stones, ivory, and precious metal for display and conspicuous consumption in everyday life and burial. What did Mycenaean communities offer in return for such imports? Greece had little to give except staples such as grain, oil, and wine, and only in the latter two could it perhaps have competed with local products in the Eastern Mediterranean civilizations where most of its trade seems to have been focused. The absence of references in palatial archives to trade of course need not imply its insignificance, as we also lack the foreign affairs archives which must once have existed. On the other hand, textual reference to, or iconographic depictions of, Aegean trade objects are extremely rare in the Near East, and this supports the view that Aegean exports were of minor value there compared to other trade partners.

Archaeology is very helpful because Mycenaean ceramics are distinctive and occur widely in the East and less commonly in the Central Mediterranean (Figure 7.7). Some are containers, others table-wares or those suitable for religious use, so that analytical study of Mycenaean pottery abroad is a crucial guide to the nature of Aegean exchange with other regions. Van Wijngaarden (2002) has shown that the distribution of such wares in the Near East is commonest in port towns, where it may have been dispersed amongst all social classes, whilst inland it tends to be linked with local elites acquiring it as mildly prestigious ware, either for its contents (stirrup-jars for wine or oil), or as table- and cult-ware. Since both wine and oil were available in the East from regional production too, it is likely that additional factors (for example perfumed oil, or the Aegean wine being in exotic and attractive containers with matching cups) gave added value to Mycenaean products. His second key point is the very low presence numerically of such imports, supporting the evidence already cited from texts and art that

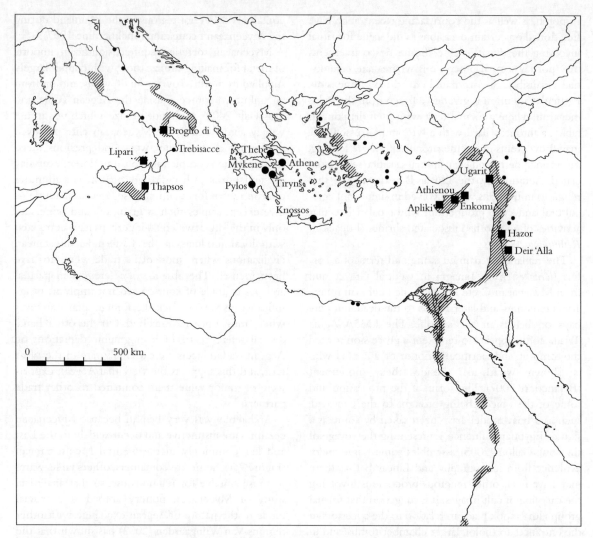

Figure 7.7   Mycenaean ceramic findspots abroad. Shaded areas and black squares mark areas and settlements with important concentrations, isolated dots mark small findspots. Black circles denote key Mycenaean centers in the Aegean homeland.
G.-J. van Wijngaarden, *Use and Appreciation of Mycenaean Pottery in the Levant, Cyprus and Italy*. Amsterdam 2002, Figure 2.

Mycenaean trade was of minor importance in the overall Near East economy.

In contrast to the Levantine (Syro-Palestinian) trade, where the existence of complex societies with their own vigorous regional exchanges inhibited the scope for Aegean products, which were anyway locally available, Mycenaean interactions with Italy seem more significant (van Wijngaarden 2002). This is unsurprising, since the local pre-state communities lacked wine and olive oil production, or the kind of maritime exchange levels common in the Aegean and further east. From around the inception of Mycenaean culture ca. 1600 BC, individual fortified settlements in Southern Italy show signs of "emergent complexity," evidencing more elaborate social and political systems and contacts with Aegean state societies, an interaction which notably increases by the time of the Mycenaean florescence ca. 1300 BC. Both imports and more commonly local imitations of Mycenaean wares occur. Their main function seems to have been for elite dining, suggesting that rising local aristocratic families adopted aspects of palatial lifestyle from the Aegean to enhance their distinctiveness from commoners. Aegean influence was sufficient to give rise to the local cultivation of olives for oil production, probably leading to regional circulation of this valuable material for food and body-care. Kelder (2009) has recently suggested that an abrupt rise in Mycenaean ceramics in Egypt from the fourteenth century might be associated not only with the import of products such as perfumed oil but also with the introduction of olive plantations.

Linear B

Arthur Evans was first led to the Minoan palace at Knossos by the appearance in antiquities markets of inscribed artifacts in a lost script and language. Knossos and most other major Minoan and Mycenaean centers have yielded considerable numbers of tablets and other inscribed objects, in two major scripts and an early pictographic form, and it was Evans who labeled the two commonest writing systems Linear A and B. Comparison of the findspots suggests the more limited use to which Mycenaean Linear B was put on Crete and the Mainland, in contrast to Minoan Linear A. Evans compared the documents to those from contemporary Near Eastern civilizations and interpreted them as palace archives. In the 1950s Linear B surprisingly was deciphered as an early form of Greek, and it is believed to have been developed by the Mycenaeans from Linear A in order to write that language, whereas Linear A defies translation hitherto and is clearly the script of the records of the earlier Minoan civilization. The great resemblances in the organization of the documents (mostly inscribed clay tablets), the use of recognizable pictograms in both alongside the normal sound-based (syllabic) script, and the comprehensibility of the system of numbers deployed in both scripts, all make it clear that the dominant function and contents of both sets of records is the same: an administrative accounting of products and services within the control and wider concern of the palace bureaucracy.

Renfrew (1972) linked these records to his view that the Minoan-Mycenaean palaces were essentially sustained by regional production in staple food and clothing, whilst exotic imports required for functional or prestige artifacts (metal, ivory, specialist stones) were traded into the palaces in return for exported staples (essentially regional surpluses in grain, wine, olive oil, and textiles under their direct control). Imported raw materials were directed toward specialist workshops in palatial towns or major centers elsewhere in the kingdom. The palaces were seen as redistributive economies, collecting regional staple surpluses as tax, then giving these out to feed the staff and state officials residing at diverse points of the kingdom (elite officials, soldiers, craftspeople) and likewise exchanging them for imports as required.

Since the decipherment of Linear B, intensive analysis of the growing archives of the Mycenaean states has increasingly modified this view of what they represent and in turn how the palatial organization functioned (Halstead 1992 and 1999, Shelmerdine 1997, Killen in *Rethinking* 2007). Analysis of place-names in the Pylos and Knossos records shows the palaces being especially busy with areas nearby and less concerned with distant regions. This incompleteness fits an archaeological observation, that the tablets largely ignore products well-attested in excavations: cereals means essentially wheat in the archives, but the probably commoner barley only appears dominant in archaeological contexts. Pulses (peas, beans, lentils, etc.) are also neglected in the archives, as is pottery production. It looks as if the palaces had a selective interest in close monitoring of parts of the total economy, in which case the rest is left to private production. Support is claimed from the abundant information for sheep-rearing in the Mycenaean Knossos archives. Some 100,000 sheep are indicated, requiring an area estimated at 25–35 percent of the entire island's grazing land; however, these archives are full of references to "owners," especially at greater distances from the center.

Putting this together (Figure 7.8) leads Halstead to argue that the palaces operated a dual economy rather than acting as single economic nodes for their states. They owned farming estates and herds of animals in their own districts, and probably employed private labor at busy times of the year to operate these resources. A very large part of the palaces' income in foodstuffs and textiles (the key products) was left to private individuals and communities, from whose sur-

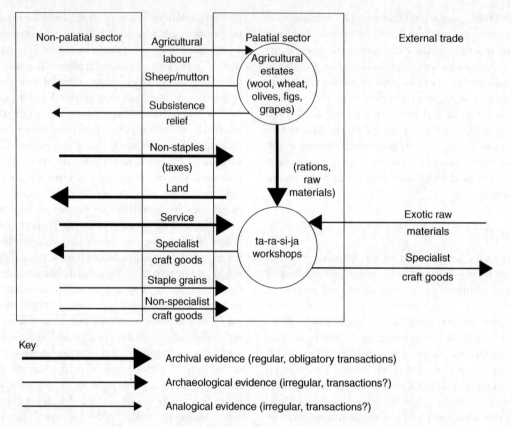

Figure 7.8 Halstead's model for the Mycenaean palatial economy.
P. Halstead, "The Mycenaean palatial economy: Making the most of the gaps in the evidence." *Proceedings of the Cambridge Philological Society* 38 (1992), 57–86, Figure 4. © Cambridge University Press.

pluses the center extracted important shares, in order to support its own personnel and to exchange them for necessary imports of raw materials and finished goods. Likewise although the palaces obtained materials for artifact production (for example metal goods), and supplied workshops in diverse locations, it also relied on private workshops for important artifacts, presumably utilizing its control over surpluses of staples as well as imports to sustain their requirements in food and raw materials. Naturally if there was a distant high-quality resource, then the palace may have intervened directly, as must be the case with the very large quantity of cereals which the Knossos palace scribes itemized from the production of the vast Mesara Plain (formerly controlled by the Minoan palace of Phaistos on the other side of the island).

More radical ideas have recently been proposed. Some now suggest that a primary aim of the Mycenaean palatial elites was to mobilize surpluses from the towns and villages of the kingdom in order to deploy them in international trade networks (Galaty and Parkinson in *Rethinking* 2007, Sjöberg 2004). This model resembles the modern economy of the relevant Greek regions, where a major part of agricultural production and the animal stock or plants maintained for textile production are carried out as commercial farming, chiefly aimed at interregional or international markets.

Actually whilst all scholars agree that the need to import metal, and prestigious materials or objects, can only have been met by reciprocal exchange with Aegean products, the scale of this has generally been questioned. Mycenaean ceramic containers abroad support the impression of limited activity, whilst Linear B does not indicate products assigned for places beyond the Aegean. The dominant theme of the archives is monitoring regional production, whether public or private, and a selected manipulation of these resources to achieve palatial aims (rations to palatial dependants of all kinds, and then presumably, but not mentioned, sufficient for negotiating for imports). It still seems to me most probable that the bulk of the kingdom's production in plant, animal, and craft products was consumed within that region, and produced on private or communal land for private and state use. In second place came the production from the palace's own, or its officials', estates and workshops, mainly designed for consumption by all levels of state officials. In third place in order of scale I believe comes what the palace and probably also private merchants gathered from surplus regional production for use in foreign exchange. Killen's robust defense (in *Rethinking* 2007) of palatial domination in the overall management of regional economies seems to me convincing.

A missing aspect of most discussions is to relate the static archives, mostly from the final year of the Mycenaean states, to the way those polities had emerged. The rather confusing mixture of public and private, shown especially in the roles of the so-called "collectors," might indicate that pre-palatial local elites were coopted into the emerging states in return for reciprocal obligations and benefits. Major owners or controllers of land and stock, as well as official personnel, were perhaps confirmed in such rights by the palace in return for "collector" roles in the levying of tax and labor duty from districts in which these elites had responsibility. Similar arrangements may have been made by the palace with other important regional institutions such as major sanctuaries (Lupack 2006) and the councils of local free communities (the "*damos*" or people).

Finally there is growing interest in palatial studies in the practice of feasting as a form of power creation and reproduction (Wright 2004). We noted earlier how rethinking of the architecture and role of the Minoan "palaces" has emphasized the function of storerooms and tableware for social dining; the same aspect is increasingly arising in the context of the social interactions through which Mycenaean elites may have structured displays of, and claims to, power. Thus the 25,000 male sheep withdrawn from the total flock resource of the Mycenaean Knossos state might have been destined for major feasts at central and provincial locations (Halstead 1999).

However, there remains still too little known about the mechanisms of surplus collection in these recent studies: was there "tax" on production, did peasants owe labor services to the state, and how far did the mass of the population obtain staples and artifactual goods by market purchase or via the state? Were palace stores largely enormous pantries for parties, rather than for rations to state employees and for reserves against regional famine? We also always need to be cautious on the grounds of our lost records of foreign affairs and trade, which were presumably on material other than clay tablets. It is not unreasonable to suggest that other aspects of the internal organization of the Mycenaean states, including further economic management, also remain missing.

Greece and the Aegean Beyond the Palaces

In Chapter 6 we briefly summarized the main trends in Macedonia and Thrace for growing settlement complexity across the Bronze Age, without reaching the level of territorial states. But the localized rise of small polities (statelets) is likely by this LBA period (Andreou 2001). Similar developments may be occurring in Northwest Greece in lowland Epirus (Tartaron 2004).

Troy

In the northwest coastal corner of Anatolia the site of Bronze Age Troy now appears very likely to have formed the capital of the small state of Wilusa mentioned in the Late Bronze Age archives of the imperial state of the Hittites further east (Korfmann *et al.* 2001, Latacz 2004). That the legendary "siege" by Achaeans (Mycenaeans) rests on some real events may be confirmed less by the several archaeologically-attested destructions of Troy from uncertain causes in this general period, than by Hittite records which indicate

Mycenaean military aggression and political interference with this and other minor states of Western Anatolia.

Mycenaean Art

Mycenaean art shows a complex mixture of its own iconographic agenda and the deployment of Minoan elements in old and new contexts. We have already examined examples relating to religious activity of a public and personal nature, and the early Shaft Grave art.

The Lion Gate, which forms the display entry to the Mycenae citadel, has a pair of rampant lions (?) either side of a Minoan column, their feet on altars, and their faces facing out to visitors (Preziosi and Hitchcock 1999). The missing heads on the Lion Gate, presumed in plaster, wood or a different stone, are not securely lions (Betancourt 2007), but might be birds of prey or mythical griffins, which appear in the same posture and setting in Minoan and Mycenaean art. We remain impressed by the Lion Gate as we approach Mycenae, even in its damaged form, retaining its ability to awe us into knowledge that we are entering an enclosed center of power. This "antithetical" setting of great animals not only recurs in the lions and griffins backing the throne in the Pylos palace, but is common in Minoan art in a religious rather than political form. The Knossos throne room is a complex case, since the similar accompanying art (paired griffins flanking the throne) may back a secular Minoan and/or Mycenaean ruler, or religious official (perhaps female). The least disputed interpretation is that the beasts are associated with divine *and* secular power in all these cases.

Apart from the existence of Mycenaean art in obvious places where art could underline power or ritual, the site of Gla challenges the conception of Mycenaeans as a warrior society contrasted with the more sensitive and playful Minoans. Frescoes were identified in almost all the buildings of this very "functional" series of administrative and storage structures, even the granaries, puzzling even to the excavator (Iakovidis 1998, 2001), and are of peaceful images (e.g., dolphins). It does seem likely that our traditional contrast between the Minoan worldview and that of the Mycenaeans, as displayed in art, is too superficial, and perhaps there was more homogeneity than

allowed for. Thus at a minor Mycenaean settlement in Central Greece, by the modern village of Tanagra, around 50 terracotta mold-made coffins have been excavated from extensive cemeteries, showing strong Cretan cultural influences. Images are of funeral scenes, hunting, bull-leaping, and plausibly aspects of the spirit-world (Dakouri-Hild 2010).

Further insights have been derived from the analysis of the frescoes from the palace at Pylos (Davis and Bennet 1999). Scenes of warfare in the "combat frieze" may belong to the first phase of the final LH3B palace, when the incorporation of the outer provinces had recently been achieved, perhaps through military aggression. These warfare scenes are in the Southwest Building, which some see as the residence of the *Lawagetas*, war-leader and/or crown prince of the kingdom (Palaima 2000). The Great Megaron friezes with peaceful heraldry, feasting, and sacrifice would be later, celebrating the pomp and ceremony of the mature state. It is impossible when considering reconstructions of these Pylos feasting images, with tables of men holding cups aloft and a bard with a harp, not to recall the much later epics of Homer (probably active around 700 BC), where an elite warrior society with its kings feast in halls to the accompaniment of tales of their ancestors and living "heroes." Few doubt that the Homeric poems of Troy and Odysseus' wanderings represent a cumulative amalgam of stories and images deriving from a continuous elaboration of oral poetic recitation, beginning in the Mycenaean age, if not in the preceding Middle Bronze Age, right down to Homer's own time (Sherratt 1990, Morris and Powell 1997).

Nonetheless, there are limits to a simple "Homeric warrior elite" gloss on Mycenaean society. Whilst it is true that the Mycenaeans favored heroic scenes of the hunt or war, whereas Minoan art has far fewer examples of such scenes and they are not so prominently displayed, the Mainlanders followed their predecessors in generally (but not entirely) rejecting the contemporary Near Eastern norm where art was used to show personal power (Betancourt 2007). No kings or war-leaders stride larger than life across Mycenaean palace walls.

The commonest Mycenaean art is of course on the plentiful ceramics. Betancourt (2007) perceptively comments that the naturalistic, swirling, busy animal, human, and plant forms of Minoan and Cycladic art are adopted by Mycenaean potters, only to become "domesticated" and then increasingly schematized into unrealistic abstractions. The process is well shown by the "stiff" LH3 octopus (Figure 7.1) and the typical mature Mycenaean style on kylix-cups with their almost entirely abstract squids.

The Mycenaean Era: An Annales Perspective

It still seems supportable to claim that in the *long term*, the definitive emergence of the Mycenaean civilization by 1400 BC represents a civilizational climax to a progressive development on the Mainland from simple early farming villages ca. 7000 BC. The emergence of politically stratified villages or those with a putative "city-state character" in later Neolithic Greece is followed by the EH corridor houses with their associations of local organization and administration. Despite apparent devolution of socio-political and economic complexity in MH, the LH period exhibits a revived growth of elaborate social hierarchies and central-places, with complex division of labor and intensive administrative procedures for states of some size. Scholars have identified an accumulation of innovations and stimuli which are relevant to this trajectory: metallurgy, polyculture, advanced sailing-ships, increased incorporation into the economic and political world of the Near Eastern states, as well as the potential over millennia for status rivalry between families within rural communities to develop into ranking of wealth and influence.

Yet the rise of Mycenaean states cannot be explained merely through such contributory or even necessary preconditions. Some regions of the Southern Mainland do not (at least yet) exhibit state formation and major centers (the Corinthia and Achaea for example), and the fact that Mycenaean achievements appear to focus on particular settlements which are not always those with more natural advantages to become the seats of power, also requires that we call upon the other levels of Annaliste time-perspective.

The *medium term* of several centuries finds the Mycenaean era conform to a standard timescale for the cyclical growth and decline of state systems; from ca. 1600–1200 BC comes an oft-identified wave of emergence, climax, and collapse. Admittedly the pre-

cise reasons for the rise of powerful states from around 1700 BC, as well as the forces which destroyed Mycenaean states by 1200 BC, are disputed, although we should bear in mind the long-term tendency just identified, which in Complexity Theory terms was a civilizational structure waiting for the right conditions to emerge. Chaos-Complexity Theory is an approach widely used in several scientific disciplines, in which highly elaborate structures can "emerge" out of innumerable diverse components into repetitive and relatively stable structures (attractors), yet at the same time a small yet critical change in a minor element can destabilize such structures and project them into new formations (the "butterfly effect") (Bentley and Maschner 2003, Bintliff 2007). A medium-term perspective is in any case more about recognizing the generic character of the cyclical rise and fall of certain complex forms of society, and we can discuss this for the Mycenaeans without resolving the details of those processes that lit up and then destroyed their civilization. One is struck by the early phase marked by display burials, only much later followed by monumental power centers and elaborate state administration. Then rapidly, massive defensive systems are put in place, before a growing series of destructions takes the civilization apart step by step. Here the attractiveness of Peter Warren's outsider perspective (Warren 1975, and in Bintliff 1977b) is clear: the early, unparalleled Mycenaean prestigious burials occur at a peak of Minoan cultural and political impact on the Mainland, the Second Palace era, whilst closer at hand the Kolonna center on the island of Aegina is flourishing (putatively a significant maritime player too). Voutsaki has suggested that the Mainland chieftain families are both stimulated by, and also wish to assert themselves against, these well-established and influential outsider societies. For Warren, the erection of the Mycenaean palaces from around 1400 BC follows the takeover of Crete by Mainlanders, and their adoption of the archival and other administrative habits of the Minoans, as well as their creation at Knossos, the grandest Cretan palace, of a new Mycenaean state.

The coincidence of the ca. 400-year time-span for the Mycenaean rise and fall with other Aegean cultural climaxes of earlier and later times, points to a degree of inherent instability in these phenomena, an element of Complexity Theory allowing us to link the Mycenaean cycle with other global early civilizations in a stimulating way. Of course our current uncertainty as to the key elements in the initiation and collapse of Mycenaean state-societies hinders closer parallels at the medium-term perspective.

Another element of the Annales approach may also be relevant: the *mentalité* (ways of seeing the world) of this culture. It remains attractive to associate the civilization with the "heroic" values of Homeric poetry, even though the final version of these tales postdates the LBA by some 500 years and certainly incorporates much intervening and indeed earlier lifestyles and culture. This aristocratic machismo and militaristic ethos does suit distinctive aspects of Mycenaean art, burial symbolism, the emphasis on fortifications, and increasingly the Hittite records when they refer to the constant aggression of the "Achaeans."

The Annales *short term* brings us directly to processes which could be hidden by the absence of local political texts, and perhaps might mislead us into giving credence to every relevant Greek myth in our search for some historical events and personalities. Nonetheless some progress is possible even at the level of generational history. All scholars agree that the displacement of the natural center of the Argive Plain at Argos, at the end of MH, by a place previously of no importance, Mycenae, signifies a claim to importance by local elite families which can only be due to some unique and short-lived historical events involving a few individuals. Service as mercenaries or raiders abroad is an attractive theory, or some regional power-game in which the elite at Mycenae gained an early lead and were able slowly to consolidate into a lasting preeminence. Perhaps the current physical anthropological research, including DNA tests, of the high-status burials in the Argive Plain may shed insights into inter-settlement family dynamics. One suspects that short-lived events and the role of individuals were indeed crucial in the power-game as to which centers grew to the top level in the later settlement hierarchy. Even the success of the rise of Mainland civilization in the wider Aegean world and beyond may owe much to chance events and personalities, especially as regards potential rivals for power in the Aegean such as the Minoan palace-states, island statelets on Aegina, Melos, and Thera, as well as the more distant expansive empires such as the Hittites in Asia Minor.

In the same way, the general collapse of the Mycenaean states during the thirteenth century was not necessarily inevitable: if it was the result of internal conflicts then the probability of one center emerging as a survivor and victor would seem a far likelier outcome than the mutual destruction of all the competing forces. Some would use this argument to support an external enemy, such as the elusive Sea Peoples, or the even more elusive Dorians. Or perhaps the collapse of all centers of power would suit a popular rising throughout the Mycenaean world, leaving merely local chieftains (called in the subsequent period the *basileus* class), still in power. I confess to finding inadequacies in all these scenarios to account for the absolute disappearance of all central power, except the most traditional of all, the external or peripheral invasion theory. If a powerful group of tribes without an equivalent complex political hierarchy overwhelmed Southern "palatial" Greece, it would produce exactly the effect we seem to observe in subsequent centuries. We would need to assume that these arrivals absorbed local material culture and contributed very little of their own to subsequent societies. The result would be the disappearance of the entire palace-society way of life and its replacement by a less complex social system, with nonetheless the survival of important memories of former days which could remain embedded in the conquered indigenous and soon assimilated conquering populations. The Slav and Albanian settlements of the Early and Final Medieval eras, respectively (see later Chapters), seem to represent appropriate models for such colonizing groups. Countering criticism of the poverty of material-culture traces for non-Aegean invaders, one might adopt the suggestion of destruction by groups on the margins of the Mycenaean palatial states, within the borders of Modern Greece.

The Mycenaeans: A Personal View

The Mycenaean powers arise meteorically out of the relative obscurity of the Mainland Middle Bronze Age, if we take the spectacular dynastic Shaft Graves as their official debut on the stage of history. In contrast the MC island townships, which we have likened to Classical city-states, and the mature Minoan palaces of LM, possess a gradual evolutionary trajectory out of earlier developments in their regions. Nonetheless, the achievement of urban, bureaucratic, state societies on the Mainland is also the product of development over a period of 300 years after the first Shaft Grave and the first tholoi in Messenia. One wonders if ambitious local chiefdoms required time to grow into domesticated civilization, doubtless through interaction with the dominant Aegean civilization on Crete, but maybe through contacts with the coherent island statelets of the MC/early LC Cyclades and on nearby Aegina island. And yet even when these palatial states are in place, much remains unclear. For example how was the regional landscape organized politically? My own spatial analysis of territoriality revealed that larger and small Mycenaean centers have discrete and largely self-sufficient landscapes to control and draw resources from. We can assume that larger centers dominated lesser settlements closest to them, but how do we adjudge the power relations between adjacent major, fortified towns such as Mycenae, Midea, and Tiryns? This problem has led some researchers to a "feudal" model of elite interrelations, where dominant lords achieved temporary allegiance from potential rivals through marriage, confirming their rights to resources, and cooperative military expeditions, thus allowing moderate assertions of regional power to coexist at multiple centers. This model is attractive, probably too seductively, since it reappears in the Homeric poems, which convey in corrupted and garbled form some elements of Mycenaean society (Sherratt 1990). The emotional feelings generated today by the physical appearance of Mycenaean citadels, and their art, also mesh with advances in our knowledge of the Mycenaeans abroad, to suggest that a central element in this society's ethos may nonetheless have been "heroic" values driving the behavior of the elite into raids and wars within and beyond the Aegean. A necessary balance to this stereotype however meets us the moment we are confronted with the painstaking bureaucracy of the palace scribes, the immense peaceful achievements of large-scale drainage projects, and finally (surely the clinching argument), the dramatic rise and spread of agricultural populations across the Southern Mainland landscape.

References

Andreou, S. (2001). "Exploring the patterns of power in the Bronze Age settlements of Northern Greece." In K. Branigan (ed.), *Urbanism in the Aegean Bronze Age.* Sheffield: Sheffield Academic Press, 160–173.

Andreou, S., M. Fotiadis, and K. Kotsakis (1996). "Review of Aegean Prehistory V: The Neolithic and Bronze Age of northern Greece." *American Journal of Archaeology* 100, 537–597.

Bennet, J. (1988). " 'Outside in the distance': Problems in understanding the economic geography of Mycenaean palatial territories." In J.-P. Olivier and T. G. Palaima (eds.), *Texts, Tablets and Scribes. Studies in Mycenaean Epigraphy and Economy.* Salamanca: *Minos* Supplement 10, 19–41.

Bentley, R. A. and H. D. G. Maschner (eds.) (2003). *Complex Systems and Archaeology.* Salt Lake City: University of Utah Press.

Betancourt, P. P. (2007). *Introduction to Aegean Art.* Philadelphia: Instap Academic Press.

Bintliff, J. L. (1977a). "New approaches to human geography. Prehistoric Greece: A case study." In F. Carter (ed.), *An Historical Geography of the Balkans.* London: Academic Press, 59–114.

Bintliff, J. L. (ed.) (1977b). *Mycenaean Geography.* Cambridge: The British Association for Mycenaean Studies.

Bintliff, J. L. (1977c). *Natural Environment and Human Settlement in Prehistoric Greece.* 2 vols. Oxford: BAR Supplementary Series 28.

Bintliff, J. L. (1989). "Cemetery populations, carrying capacities and the individual in history." In C.A. Roberts, F. Lee, and J. L. Bintliff (eds.), *Burial Archaeology.* Oxford: BAR British Series 211, 85–104.

Bintliff, J. (2002). "Rethinking early Mediterranean urbanism." In R. Aslan *et al.* (eds.), *Mauerschau. Festschrift für Manfred Korfmann.* Vol. 1. Tübingen: Bernhard Albert Greiner, 153–177.

Bintliff, J. L. (2005). "Parallels and contrasts in the settlement patterns of prehistoric Greece." In A. Dakouri-Hild and S. Sherratt (eds.), *Autochthon. Papers Presented to O. T. P. K. Dickinson.* Oxford: Archaeopress, 17–23.

Bintliff, J. L. (2007). "Emergent complexity in settlement systems and urban transformations." In U. Fellmeth, P. Guyot, and H. Sonnabend (eds.), *Historische Geographie der Alten Welt. Grundlagen, Erträge, Perspektiven. Festgabe für Eckart Olshausen.* Hildesheim: Georg Olms Verlag, 43–82.

Bintliff, J. L., P. Howard, and A. Snodgrass (eds.) (2007). *Testing the Hinterland: The Work of the Boeotia Survey (1989–1991) in the Southern Approaches to the City of Thespiai.* Cambridge: McDonald Institute.

Bommeljé, L. S. (2005). "The Aetolia Survey." In G.-J. van Wijngaarden (ed.), *On Site: Dutch Archaeologists in Greece.* Athens: Motibo, 32–45.

Broodbank, C., E. Kiriatzi, and J. B. Rutter (2005). "From Pharaoh's feet to the slave-women of Pylos? The history and cultural dynamics of Kythera in the Third Palace period." In A. Dakouri-Hild and S. Sherratt (eds.), *Autochthon. Papers Presented to O.T.P.K. Dickinson.* Oxford: Archaeopress, 70–96.

Cavanagh, W. (2001) "Empty space? Courts and squares in Mycenaean towns." In K. Branigan (ed.), *Urbanism in the Aegean Bronze Age.* Sheffield: Sheffield Academic Press, 119–134.

Cavanagh, W. and C. Mee (1998). *A Private Place: Death in Prehistoric Greece.* Lund: Paul Aström.

Chadwick, J. (1976). *The Mycenaean World.* Cambridge: Cambridge University Press.

Cherry, J. F. and J. L. Davis (2001). " 'Under the Sceptre of Agamemnon': The view from the hinterlands of Mycenae." In K. Branigan (ed.), *Urbanism in the Aegean Bronze Age.* Sheffield: Sheffield Academic Press, 141–159.

Cline, E. H. (ed.) (2010). *Oxford Handbook of the Bronze Age Aegean.* Oxford: Oxford University Press.

Dakouri-Hild, A. (2010). "Boeotia." In E. H. Cline (ed.), *Oxford Handbook of the Bronze Age Aegean.* Oxford: Oxford University Press, 614–630.

Darcque, P. (2005). "Mycènes: une ville ou un palais?" In I. Bradfer-Burdet, B. Detournay, and R. Laffineur (eds.), *Kris Technitis. L'Artisan crétois.* Liège: Aegaeum 26, 51–61.

Davis, J. L. and J. Bennet (1999). "Making Mycenaeans: Warfare, territorial expansion, and representations of the other in the Pylian kingdom." In R. Laffineur (ed.), *Polemos.* Liège: Aegaeum 19, 109–120.

Dickinson, O. T. P. K. (2006). *The Aegean from Bronze Age to Iron Age.* London: Routledge.

Drews, R. (1993). *The End of the Bronze Age.* Princeton: Princeton University Press.

Gale, N. H. and Z. A. Stos-Gale (2008). "Changing patterns in prehistoric Cycladic metallurgy." In N. Brodie *et al.* (eds.), *Horizon. A Colloquium on the Prehistory of the Cyclades.* Cambridge: McDonald Institute, 387–408.

Gallou, C. (2005). *The Mycenaean Cult of the Dead.* Oxford: BAR Int. Series1372.

Halstead, P. (1992). "The Mycenaean palatial economy: Making the most of the gaps in the evidence." *Proceedings of the Cambridge Philological Society* 38, 57–86.

Halstead, P. (1999). "Missing sheep: On the meaning and wider significance of 0 in Knossos sheep records." *Annual of the British School at Athens* 94, 145–166.

Iakovidis, S. (1998). *Glas II. I Anaskafi 1981–1991.* Athens: Archaiologiki Etaireia.

Iakovidis, S. (2001). *Gla and the Kopais in the 13th Century B.C.* Athens: Library of the Archaeological Society at Athens 221.

Kalcyck, H.-J. and J. Knauss (1989). "The Munich Kopais-Project." In J. M. Fossey (ed.), *Boeotia Antiqua 1.* Amsterdam: J.C. Gieben, 56–71.

Kelder, J. M. (2009). "Royal gift exchange between Mycenae and Egypt: Olives as 'greeting gifts' in the Late Bronze Age Eastern Mediterranean." *American Journal of Archaeology* 113, 339–352.

Kilian-Dirlmeier, I. (1986). "Beobachtungen zu den Schacht-gräbern von Mykenai und zu den Schmuckbeigaben mykenischer Männergräber." *Jahrbuch des Römisch-Germanisch Zentralmuseums Mainz* 33, 159–198.

Knauss, J. (1987). *Die Melioration des Kopaisbeckens durch die Minyer im 2. Jt. v. Chr. Kopais 2.* München: Technische Universität München.

Korfmann, M. *et al.* (eds.) (2001). *Troia. Traum und Wirklichkeit.* Stuttgart: Theiss Verlag.

Latacz, J. (2004). *Troy and Homer.* Oxford: Oxford University Press.

Littauer, M. A. and J. H. Crouwel (1996). "Robert Drews and the role of chariotry in Bronze Age Greece." *Oxford Journal of Archaeology* 15, 297–305.

Lupack, S. (2006). "Deities and religious personnel as collectors." In M. Perna (ed.), *Fiscality in Mycenaean and Near Eastern Archives.* Paris: De Boccard, 89–108.

Marzolff, P. (2004). "Das zweifache Rätsel Tiryns." In E.-L. Schwandner and K. Rheidt (eds.), *Macht der Architektur – Architektur der Macht.* Mainz: Philipp von Zabern, 79–91.

Mee, C. (ed.) (2011). *Greek Archaeology: A Thematic Approach.* Oxford: Wiley-Blackwell.

Mee, C. and Cavanagh, W. (1990) "The spatial distribution of Mycenaean tombs." *Annual of the British School at Athens* 85, 225–243.

Morris, I. and B. Powell (1997). *A New Companion to Homer.* Leiden: Brill.

Mühlenbruch, T. (2003). "Zu vorderorientalischen Parallelen der mykenischen Palastarchitektur." *Archäologisches Korrespondenzblatt* 33, 479–491.

Mylonas, G. (1968). *Mycenae's Last Century of Greatness.* Sydney: Sydney University Press.

Nafplioti, A. (2008). "Mycenaean political domination of Knossos following the Late Minoan IB destructions on Crete: Negative evidence from strontium isotope ratio analysis (87Sr/86Sr)." *Journal of Archaeological Science* 35, 2307–2317.

Nelson, M. C. (2007). "Pylos, block masonry and monumental architecture in the Late Bronze Age Peloponnese." In J. Bretschneider, J. Driessen, and K. van Lerberghe (eds.), *Power and Architecture.* Leuven: Peeters, 143–159.

Nodarou, E. (2007). "Exploring patterns of intra regional pottery distribution in Late Minoan IIIA-B East Crete." In S. Y. Waksman (ed.), *Archaeometric and Archaeological Approaches to Ceramics*. Oxford: BAR Int. Series 1691, 75–83.

Palaima, T. G. (2000). "Wannabe wanaks' power rise." *Times Higher Education Supplement* (9 June), 31.

Preziosi, D. and L. A. Hitchcock (1999). *Aegean Art and Architecture*. Oxford: Oxford University Press.

Renfrew, C. (1972). *The Emergence of Civilization*. London: Methuen.

Rethinking = Galaty, M. L. and W. A. Parkinson (eds.) (2007). *Rethinking Mycenaean Palaces II*. Los Angeles: Cotsen Institute of Archaeology, University of California.

Rutter, J. B. (2005). "Southern triangles revisited: Lakonia, Messenia, and Crete in the 14th – 12th centuries BC." In J. Moody and A.L. D'Agata (eds.), *Ariadne's Threads: Connections Between Crete and the Greek Mainland in the Postpalatial Period*. Athens: Italian Archaeological School in Athens, 17–64.

Rutter, J. B. (2006). "Southwestern Anatolian pottery from Late Minoan Crete: Evidence for direct contacts between Arzawa and Keftiu?" In M.H. Wiener *et al.* (eds.), *Pottery and Society*. Boston: Archaeological Institute of America, 138–153.

Rutter, J. B. *et al.* (2007). "Report on the final general discussion." In S. Deger-Jakotzky and M. Zavadil (eds.), *LH III C Chronology and Synchronisms II*. Wien: Österreichischen Akademie der Wissenschaften, 345–356.

Shelmerdine, C. W. (1997). "Review of Aegean Prehistory VI: The palatial Bronze Age of the Southern and Central Greek Mainland." *American Journal of Archaeology* 101, 537–585.

Shelmerdine, C. W. (ed.) (2008). *The Cambridge Companion to the Aegean Bronze Age*. Cambridge: Cambridge University Press.

Sherratt, S. (1990). " 'Reading the texts': Archaeology and the Homeric question." *Antiquity* 64, 807–824.

Sjöberg, B. L. (2004). *Asine and the Argolid in the Late Helladic III Period*. Oxford: BAR Int. Series 1225.

Tartaron, T. F. (2004). *Bronze Age Landscape and Society in Southern Epirus*. Oxford: BAR Int. Series 1290.

Thaler, U. (2006). "Constructing and reconstructing power." In J. Maran *et al.* (eds.), *Constructing Power: Architecture, Ideology and Social Practice*. Hamburg: Lit Verlag, 93–116.

Uchitel, A. (1988). "Charioteers of Knossos." *Minos* 23, 47–58.

Van Wijngaarden, G.-J. (2002). *Use and Appreciation of Mycenaean Pottery in the Levant, Cyprus and Italy*. Amsterdam: Amsterdam University Press.

Voutsaki, S. (1995) "Social and political processes in the Mycenaean Argolid: The evidence from the mortuary practices." In R. Laffineur and W.-D. Niemeier (eds.), *Politeia. Society and State in the Aegean Bronze Age*. Liège: Aegeum 12, 55–66.

Voutsaki, S. (1998). "Mortuary evidence, symbolic meanings and social change: A comparison between Messenia and the Argolid in the Mycenean period." In K. Branigan (ed.), *Cemetery and Society in the Aegean Bronze Age*. Sheffield: Sheffield Academic Press, 41–58.

Warren, P. (1975). *The Aegean Civilizations*. London: Phaidon.

Wells, B. and C. Runnels (eds.) (1996). *The Berbati-Limnes Archaeological Survey 1988–1990*. Jonsered: Paul Aströms Forlag.

Wright, J. C. (ed.) (2004). *The Mycenaean Feast*. Princeton: American School of Classical Studies at Athens.

Zangger, E. (1994). "Landscape changes around Tiryns during the Bronze Age." *American Journal of Archaeology* 98, 189–212.

Zangger, E. *et al.* (1997). "The Pylos Regional Archaeological Project, Part II. Landscape evolution and site preservation." *Hesperia* 68(4), 548–641.

Further Reading

Bennet, J. (1999). "The Mycenaean conceptualization of space or Pylian geography (… yet again!)." In S. Deger-Jakotzky, S. Hiller, and O. Panagl (eds.), *Floreant Studia Mycenaea*. Wien: Österreichischen Akademie der Wissenschaften, 131–157.

Dakouri-Hild, A. and S. Sherratt (eds.) (2005). *Autochthon. Papers Presented to O. T. P. K. Dickinson*. Oxford: Archaeopress.

McDonald, W. A. and G. R. Rapp (eds.) (1972). *The Minnesota Messenia Expedition. Reconstructing a Bronze Age Regional Environment*. Minneapolis: University of Minnesota Press.

Websites: aegeanet.html; dartmouth.edu/~classics/faculty/rutter.html; classics.uc.edu/nestor

Part II

The Archaeology of Classical, Hellenistic, and Roman Greece in its Longer-term Context

8

The Greek Early Iron Age and the Concept of a "Dark Age"

Phases of the "Dark Age" or Early Iron Age

Late Helladic 3C Early to Middle: late thirteenth to twelfth century BC

Late LH3C/Submycenaean: ca. 1100–1050 BC

Protogeometric (PG): ca. 1050–900 BC

Early to Middle Geometric (EG/MG): ninth century BC

Late Geometric (LG): eighth century BC

(General reading for this period: Dickinson 2006, Mee 2011)

Introduction

In the late thirteenth to early twelfth centuries BC, as we saw in the preceding chapter, the Bronze Age palace civilization of Aegean Greece went down in flames. Though strongly fortified, the urban centers of small Mycenaean states in Southern Mainland Greece, together with centers on Crete and lesser Aegean islands, suffered violent destruction, unraveling complex political and economic structures. Although the attackers' origin is unknown, and other factors may have intervened at least locally (earthquakes, climatic downturns), it must be significant that the Aegean collapse occurred amidst equal unrest throughout the Eastern Mediterranean: the Hittite civilization in

Anatolia is destroyed, whilst in Egypt and the Levant armies of seaborne raiders of diverse backgrounds ("Sea Peoples") sack towns and threaten the great power of Pharaonic Egypt, and settle as founders of Philistine city-states in Palestine. In the following century (LH3C) many centers continue, others are already abandoned, but none have functioning palaces. At just a few sites (notably Tiryns: Maran and Papadimitriou 2006, Dickinson 2006), attempts may have been made, none ultimately successful, to revive some semblance of kingship.

Current scholarship is nonetheless skeptical regarding waves of invaders penetrating Greece from outside the Aegean to perpetrate the assassination of the Mycenaean kingdoms, although alternative scenarios

Figure 8.1 Characteristic fine ware, early Iron Age (Protogeometric style), a grave assemblage from the Kerameikos cemetery in Athens.
© Trustees of the British Museum.

of internal civil wars, or a peasants' uprising, remain mere hypotheses, with only later Greek legend to suggest the former (Dickinson 2006). The succeeding archaeological assemblages of the terminal Bronze Age and Early Iron Age (Figure 8.1) seem firmly rooted in Mycenaean, or on Crete Minoan, Bronze Age traditions, so putative invaders moved on or were rapidly absorbed into local cultures. In any case, the disruption associated with the violent end to the Mycenaean world was awesome enough to plunge the Aegean into what has customarily been described as a "Dark Age," lasting from ca. 1100 to 800 BC (LH3C/Submycenaean to Middle Geometric).

Since this "Dark Age" is more half-light than blackness, we prefer Early Iron Age (EIA) (Dickinson 2006), although iron in everyday use spreads only

gradually (Snodgrass 1989), if nonetheless standard for functional tools and weapons after the start of the Protogeometric phase ca. 1050 BC. Iron technology may have diffused from Cyprus, and perhaps through elite exchange links, as early finds are often swords in warrior graves (Crielaard 1998). Still, no-one disputes that "history" leaves us, with the extinction of literacy for four centuries. As Snodgrass (1980) pointed out, striking signs of "deskilling" characterize this period: elaborate architectural complexes disappear, we find highly impoverished assemblages of metal, the virtual absence of human representations, a dramatic fall in the number of dated occupation sites, very reduced evidence for foreign exchange compared with the preceding period, and no sign of political centers of a state-like character dominating larger regions. Whatever the reasons for the end of the palace states, the reduction in social, economic, and artistic complexity was not only severe but persistent for many generations.

Why did recovery take so long? The evidence in this Early Iron Age (EIA) era of large-scale population movements around the Aegean is relevant. Although reconstructed from the later distribution of ancient Greek dialects, legends, and recorded history, plus some archaeology, it seems that during this long, disturbed period few parts of the Aegean world did not become involved in folk movements. Some scholars compare these migrations to the later, historically-attested colonization by Aegean Greeks throughout the Mediterranean and Black Sea in the final Early Iron Age, the Archaic, and early Classical centuries (750–400 BC) (Osborne 1996), but the latter generally occurred in times of elaborate state organization.

Why would whole communities abandon their homelands and risk all to settle far away, especially when organized authority had collapsed violently? I suspect endemic insecurity was indeed decisive. In our present-day world, civil wars, starvation or drought constantly displace entire communities, particularly to escape arbitrary violence associated with the breakdown of law and order. One might tentatively suggest that violent attacks on the Mycenaean state centers by forces internal to Greece (possibly including speakers of the later Dorian dialects), with or without assistance from maritime raiders (Sea

Peoples), caused their definitive removal, ushering in a long period of insecurity which effectively blocked the reconstitution of regional states, and the rule of law, for several centuries. However recent scholarly opinion rejects the traditional, part-legendary model, where the destroyers of the Mycenaean states and the fleeing populations of those kingdoms can already in the EIA be identified firmly with the speakers of the major regional Greek dialects as they are first well attested in the sixth century BC (Hall 1997). An earlier emphasis on cultural novelties in the post-palatial EIA, such as dress-pins, cist-graves, cremation burial, new weapon types, seen hopefully as the "smoking gun" of invaders and then settlers who laid the palaces to ruin, is now generally (but not universally) explained as gradual introductions, often anticipated on a small scale in the late palatial period, but essentially marking the cultural dislocation and reorientations by surviving populations (Dickinson 2006).

Curiously, Classical Greek historians of events between the Age of the Heroes (a legendary era rooted in memories of the Minoan-Mycenaean Bronze Age), and their own era, were unaware of any "Dark Age." The world of the legendary leaders at palace centers like Thebes or Mycenae is certainly portrayed in its final phase as riven by warfare, assassination, and internal migrations, but is conceived as giving rise directly to the elite-dominated world of early historic Greece, from ca. 700 BC (the Archaic era), with its kings or aristocrats (*basileis*) claiming heroic progenitors for their dynasties. This has seemed difficult to accommodate with the archaeological picture just described, with 300–500 years of apparent reversion to a thin scatter of short-lived rural hamlets, with narrow horizons, and limited evidence for economic specialization or social stratification. The statistics of Early Iron Age cemeteries also till recently suggested tiny, dispersed communities appropriate to such limited achievements (Snodgrass 1977, 1980).

Light Reappears in the "Dark Age"

The first sign that the "Dark Age" was merely dim came with the spectacular discoveries in 1981 at Lefkandi, on a small coastal peninsula called Xeropolis on the island of Euboea near Athens in Southern

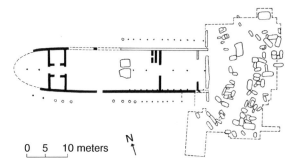

Figure 8.2 Lefkandi elite mansion and/or cult burial structure, ca. 1000 BC, with subsequent cemetery to its east. A. Snodgrass, *An Archaeology of Greece. The Present State and Future Scope of a Discipline.* Stanford 1987, Figure 54. Reproduced by permission of University of California Press Books.

Greece (Popham *et al.* 1982, *Lefkandi I–III*). Like Nichoria in Messenia (see below, McDonald *et al.* 1983) the EIA community seems to consist of a collection of households, dispersed across the hills of Xeropolis and adjacent Toumba (Morris 2000). At the latter a rich cemetery grew up around a monumental tumulus. Under the mound, at a surprisingly early date of ca. 1000 BC, the supposed nadir of Greek culture, was found an impressive apsidal (one end curved) building over 40 meters long, with dressed stone foundations but mudbrick, wood, and thatch superstructure (Figure 8.2). Beneath the floor were pits with a male and female elite burial together with four horse graves, the male with warrior accoutrements (iron sword and spears) cremated and deposited in a bronze urn, the female alongside as an inhumation. The bronze cremation urn is an eastern import, whilst the female burial is rich in gold. Current opinion sees the great house ("Heroon") as representing a chieftain's residence or a tomb-shrine imitating such (Whitley 1991, 2001, Pakkanen and Pakkanen 2000). The gifts from the later community cemetery that grew up beside it indicate exchange with more advanced East Mediterranean EIA city-states and with Egypt, perhaps brought by Phoenician traders to the Aegean (their presence is known also at the port of Kommos on the south coast of Crete at this time (Shaw 2006)). Appropriately, Euboean ceramics are widely distributed around the Levant during the tenth to eighth centuries BC, although recent scholarship is less inclined to see enterprising Aegean merchants at work, than Levantine merchants bringing and taking away products from Greece. Others, however, see the coastline settlements along the protected Gulf of Euboea as a major area where populations and exchange flourished with only minor disruption from the early post-palatial era into the dawn of historic times (Snodgrass 1994, Papadopoulos 1996, Crielaard 1998, 2006). Problematically, however, Snodgrass (1983) had calculated from the size and duration of Lefkandi's cemetery that the population was a small hamlet, hard to see as a viable basis for a district chiefdom.

The key to this discrepancy followed soon after. Ian Morris (1987) showed that the demographic evidence from EIA cemeteries (settlements being rarely excavated) was completely misleading. Through analysis of the structure of Athenian cemeteries, and their age, sex, and wealth patterning, he argued that whilst the transitional era between the Mycenaean era and the EIA, the Late LH3C/Submycenaean, saw whole communities buried in cemeteries, with the inception of the EIA (Protogeometric period, ca. 1050 BC), formal cemetery burial became reserved for a social elite (later called the *agathoi* or "the Good"). This privileging remains in force in the subsequent Early to Middle Geometric period, but then in the Late Geometric (eighth century BC) there is a dramatic return to social inclusiveness. Effectively this cycle mimics an *apparent* demographic collapse for the main era of the EIA, bracketed by much higher populations. Reconstituting a significant "invisible" population (later termed the *kakoi* or "the Bad"), reduces our previous image of extraordinary depopulation, and equally important, such power over burial privileges implies the survival of at least a district elite society throughout the whole EIA. The Lefkandi house, and possible similar structures elsewhere in Greece (Morris 2000), fall exactly into place. The Lefkandi chief would have been associated with a reasonable support population, and we can see the impressive residence from which the community was kept under elite sway. There is a growing feeling (Dickinson 2006), that Lefkandi was no "one-off" special site, and as our knowledge of rural settlement in the EIA improves, we may expect many more examples of

small centers of power and exchange. Nonetheless, settlement research (see below) makes clear that there still occurred a major overall drop in population between Mycenaean and Archaic times.

Morris (2000) has elaborated on this research by dividing the post-palatial era into a series of key social stages. In the twelfth century Mycenaean society survived in fragmentary form, but with the birth of the EIA from around 1050 BC (Protogeometric era) a new social framework was put in place by individual, or groups of, elite families (later known as *basileis*) with the support of a yeoman middle class (making up the other and larger part of the free population or *agathoi*). Together these groups controlled a perhaps equally large body of serfs (the *kakoi*). From the start of the Geometric era (ca. 900 BC), there is an increase in exchange with the Eastern Mediterranean, if never large-scale, and on Crete particularly early Near Eastern cultural influences anticipate the more general "Orientalizing" turn that typifies the subsequent early Archaic era for the rest of the Aegean. In the Late Geometric era or eighth century BC rising wealth, increased international exchanges, and expanding populations led to internal pressures which polarized attitudes within the upper two dominant classes. One faction, the "elitist," favored retaining traditional hierarchy, emphasizing the heroic status of the aristocrats and their external contacts, the latter being a combination of gift-exchanges and more commercial ties within their regions and abroad. The other, the "middling" mentality, often expressed in later Classical city-states as the basis for their moderate forms of democracy, seems to have wished to level class into a single citizen community, inclusive of the serf population. It emphasized the value of local agriculture and pastoralism as well as a desire to internalize social life within the focus of an exclusive city-state. Morris proposes that we can link the rising conflicts between these solutions to the pressures of change in Late Geometric and Archaic times, with fluctuations in burial privileges and varying investment in the arts and public constructions, and they also emerge clearly in the poetry and semi-historic accounts of these centuries. The end result of the polarized programs for social development led to some half of Greek cities in Classical times possessing a moderate democracy, where the EIA serfs were replaced by slaves or paid labor from the poorer classes, while the other half retained a form of serfdom (Thessaly, Sparta-Messenia, much of Crete) or excluded their free lower class from full citizenship.

Landscape and Settlement from Early Iron Age to Archaic Times

In the Late Geometric (eighth century BC), and the following Archaic periods (seventh to sixth centuries BC), the archaeological evidence expands immensely, and historical sources mark the return of literacy, allowing us to reconstruct the main features of an Aegean political map. We shall be suggesting (see below) that the preceding EIA landscape had been characterized by innumerable small-scale communities and rare dispersed towns, organized by Big Men, village and district chiefs or councils of elders, and, some hypothesize, the occasional Paramount Chief with wider, regional control. By the Archaic period we have emerged into a very different world. In the South and Central Aegean the city-state (*polis*) now dominates, a town supported by its agricultural hinterland (*chora*). Its government is shared between an aristocratic elite or dominant dynasty and a much broader group of citizens, together incorporating some half of the non-slave adult male population. Elsewhere, chiefly the northern half of the Mainland, the *ethnos* dominates, sometimes translated as a "tribal" state. Here the political unit is based on one or more peoples or *ethne*. Its government is more varied, including dynastic kingship (arguably arising from occasional paramount chiefs of the EIA), such as in Macedonia and Epirus, as well as federations of peoples and city-states, such as in Boeotia and Thessaly. To confuse matters, within the Southern Mainland the expansive state of Sparta was a city-state, but run by two royal dynasties and a council of elders who shared power with a large citizen body of middle-class males (*Spartiates*). However, throughout Greece by the end of Archaic times, whether in *polis* or *ethnos* areas, population is concentrated (or is evolving into this pattern), in regularly spaced towns,

usually modest in size, rarely much larger, forming "central-place" foci for generally small districts (again rarely whole regions), and generally incorporating dependent villages and farms.

To understand this long-term transformation we shall next investigate the archaeological evidence for changes in town and country, for both the period of this chapter and the Archaic era of the following chapter. If we focus first on the surface survey record for Central and Southern Greece, there has been recently a great improvement in data quality for the period from Geometric through Archaic times. Almost two generations ago the Messenia Project, covering a Peloponnesian province 3800 km² in size (McDonald and Rapp 1972) was only able through extensive survey to record a relatively few locations as occupied in this time-period. In contrast, the current intensive resurvey of one small part of this province, around Pylos (the PRAP Project) has detected dense distributions of rural site and offsite finds for the Geometric-Archaic era (Alcock *et al.* 2005). Turning to the rise of towns, already during the 1980s the Boeotia Project had used the total survey of ancient city areas to map the growth of entire towns during this era (Bintliff and Snodgrass 1988). Snodgrass (1991) used such data to contrast two forms of urban development over our period: at Haliartos, from a single Geometric core-community on the acropolis, the settlement explodes over the whole city area during Archaic times, whereas the much larger city of Thespiae originates from several dispersed hamlets in Geometric times, fusing subsequently into a giant Archaic town.

As a result of this increased body of data, are we now able to see realistic evolving landscapes and townscapes for the period from the Dark Ages to the Archaic? Let us start with the countryside as a whole. All are agreed that the Late Bronze Age concluded with a disastrous collapse of towns and complex political centers, and major depopulation of the countryside, although not as severe as the older interpretations of the cemeteries had suggested. A prolonged phase of reduced size, and number, of settlements in PG and MG times was followed in the LG and Archaic centuries by an accelerating trend of demographic expansion. The central theme of the latter periods is "colonizing the landscape." Regional survey teams have considered three possible models for this sequence:

1. Major continuity of the Mycenaean landscape, with variable levels of reduction in the number, size, and population of sites. No published survey project has opted for this, but I shall later advocate something comparable.
2. Virtual emptying of most landscapes, with repopulation from rare points of EIA refuges only during Late Geometric times (suggested by the Melos, Berbati Valley, Southern Argolid, and current Pylos surveys). The model, however, sits uneasily with the data.
3. Similar to 2 but with limited activity until the next, Archaic era, or even till early Classical repopulation (suggested by the Kea, Nemea, Methana, Atene, and South Euboea surveys).

Quite apart from these models emerging from regional landscape surveys, the previous record of excavations has created its own narratives of recolonization:

1. Discussion has focused on famous Classical sites with evidence for significant EIA *and* early historic communities (Athens, Argos, Thebes, Knossos). These are identified as large EIA population refuges, from which the surrounding regions could have been repopulated (such as Attica from Athens) and even whole abandoned areas resettled (such as Melos and Kea islands). If these large settlements had preserved complex social and political arrangements, a similar stratified society could have later diffused from them into the colonized landscape, suiting the evidence for the continuity of elite power structures throughout the Dark Age (Morris 1987).
2. Excavation of discontinuously occupied smaller but also nucleated refuge settlements of the "Dark Age" such as Zagora, or Lefkandi, also suggests a likely association with a "Chieftain" society, but these are seen as "failed *poleis*" (proto-city states) which do not survive competition with other emergent centers so as to last into historical times.

Comparing the intensive (and extensive) survey picture just outlined for town and country, with the excavation record, raises difficult questions, suggesting that we have not yet got things right. Firstly, does the evidence support rural recolonization over time from refuge towns or refuge regions? Most if not all areas of the Aegean have widespread findspots yielding slight archaeological traces of PG and Geometric activity from excavation, casual finds, survey, or even clear occupation and burial sites, as well as the expected ubiquitous Archaic sites. The scattered finds are explained as "pastoral activity" or "visits" from a few larger "refuge" foci. Compounding the problem, intensive survey maps often classify sites with just one or two sherds collected for a particular period as non-permanent activity, ignoring sampling problems. A second difficulty is "scale of observation." Melos is seemingly deserted (Renfrew and Wagstaff 1982), apart from tiny activity at Melos city, until rural repopulation in late Geometric times. The Methana peninsula (Mee and Forbes 1997) is a similar-sized region with likewise thin EIA pottery finds, but these come from *several* settlement foci; yet the survey's narrative repeats the story from Melos, of isolated small-scale occupation followed by major recovery by Classical times. These two regions were surveyed at quite different levels of intensity (Methana is later and far more thorough): is the divergence in their settlement history real, or the product of contrasted methodologies?

We really need a stricter "source criticism" (*Quellenkritik*) of our survey record and how narratives have been created from it. What do the dots on maps (sites, offsite finds) mean? Another fundamental issue is: how well do we understand Iron Age to Archaic ceramics? Richard Catling confesses for Laconia (in Cavanagh *et al.* 1996) to "the lack of knowledge we possess regarding all but the decorated wares from Dark Ages through Classical in that region," and an "ignorance … virtually complete" of domestic wares. My own experience suggests that in cultivated surface soils even decorated pre-Classical wares easily lose surface paint and become assigned to the vaguely dated Archaic to Hellenistic or Geometric to Hellenistic classes. Moreover, on long-occupied sites where later periods produce more and wider spreads of surface pottery, chances are remote for finding such early fragments under occupational overlay and numerically swamping Classical material. These limits to ceramic analysis are powerfully demonstrated by the Phlius urban survey (Alcock 1991). Tiny amounts of definitely-dated sherds, and of "possible" sherds, from a single period, contrast with the mass of finds from "overlaps," sherds only dated to several *possible* periods. This problem especially targets the Geometric era, and is little better for the Archaic period.

To pottery-dating problems can be added factors of sampling and taphonomy (the way finds are buried or disturbed). Inadequate attention has been paid to the biases introduced from these aspects of survey. For example the Phlius urban survey maps showing finds of the Geometric and Archaic eras, show tiny numbers of dated sherds and enigmatic dispersal patterns: are there several small sites, or a large, poorly-sampled and thin, but ubiquitous nucleation? On the Kea Survey, the urban survey of Koressia exhibited the same patchiness of finds (Cherry *et al.* 1991), but this is surely linked to the fact that only about 100 well-dated sherds were collected from this 30 ha town for all its phases. For the Kea *rural* survey, perhaps the extreme rarity of PG and Geometric finds really reflects minimal countryside occupation, yet a claimed Archaic rural site expansion also rests on very slight finds (sometimes one sherd from a site).

Given that Kea rural sites have usually only small collections of dated finds, one wonders whether the presence or absence of a Geometric or Archaic sherd is reliable evidence for a site's foundation, or the result of chance finds from a largely "hidden landscape" (Bintliff *et al.* 1999). On the Atene survey (Lohmann 1993), occasional Archaic sherds on Classical farmsites are interpreted reasonably as evidence for a pre-Classical beginning for many. At our "komopolis" (large village) site of Askra in Boeotia (Bintliff and Snodgrass 1988), where Hesiod, at the transition from Late Geometric to early Archaic, wrote his poem *Works and Days*, our total survey (fortunately for us!) confirmed that archaeologically there was indeed a settlement from PG and Geometric times there for him to have lived in. Yet sherd numbers for these phases were extremely low even in our large collection (2175 collected in total for all periods from the site, just

one being definitely PG!) and it is unclear how we read their findspots in terms of the site shape. Was Geometric occupation a single or multiple foci plan?

Larger site collections are really needed, carefully located on grids, to allow firmer inferences on the early history of Classical sites. An example is an estate center in the countryside of ancient Thespiae (Bintliff *et al.* 2007). Site LSE1 (Figure 11.2) has a sizeable sherd collection (577) and the gridded collection revealed a large Classical to Early Hellenistic farmstead, yet there was also sufficient if rare Geometric-Archaic and Archaic pottery (ca. 35 sherds) to indicate earlier, smaller-scale occupation.

"Source-criticism" raises serious doubts about empty Dark Age landscapes. The ubiquitous scanty finds of PG and Geometric pottery mark a general survival of life, admittedly less people and less sites but still more than acknowledged, probably in all Aegean landscapes. The taphonomic, sample, and ceramic recognition problems predictably create such a vestigial record.

One final aspect of deconstruction can be swiftly dealt with, the theory that EIA societies "reverted" to pastoralism, or even nomadic pastoralism, until the Late Geometric population-boom caused a revival of large-scale agriculture (Snodgrass 1980). Both the "ecofacts" (bones and seeds from excavation) (Dickinson 2006), site locations (Wallace 2003), and an improved understanding of pastoral societies from ethnography (Halstead 1996) rule out this view: EIA Greeks were essentially farmers.

The origins of the Polis and the evolution of a settlement hierarchy

Let me construct a revised model for these developments from my own survey region, Boeotia. In the Geometric period both intensive and extensive survey suggest that the *majority* of people were living in a network of smaller and larger nucleated communities dispersed regularly across the landscape, and usually on sites which later, in Archaic to Classical times, appear as hamlets and small to large towns. By Archaic times (Figure 8.3, Upper) the region is probably divided into a modular series of nucleations each dominating comparable areas, often equivalent to some 2–3 km radius territory. I term these competing

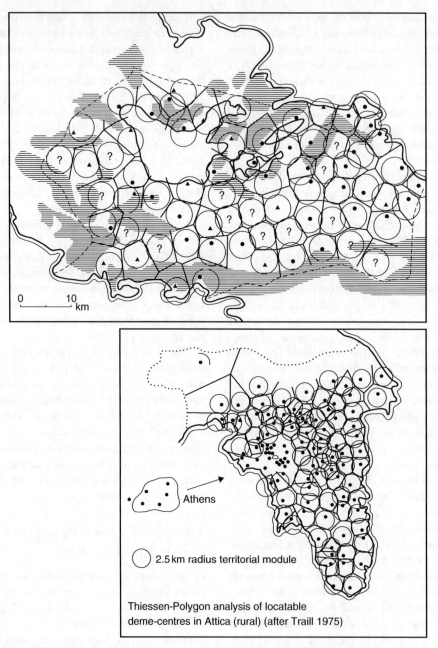

Figure 8.3   (Upper) The EIA to Archaic evolution of settlement foci in Boeotia. Known and hypothesized (question mark) nucleated settlements in later Geometric and Archaic times. By Classical times these multiple local foci have become separated into city-states (solid triangles) and their dependent villages (solid circles). Possible agricultural territories are marked by the polygons. (Lower) Territorial analysis of the historically and archaeologically located rural villages in the territory of Classical Athens, also showing urban (intramural) administrative units (rural and urban "demes"). Possible agricultural territories are marked by the polygons. J. L. Bintliff, "Territorial behaviour and the natural history of the Greek polis." In E. Olshausen and H. Sonnabend (eds.), *Stuttgarter Kolloquium zur historischen Geographie des Altertums*, vol. 4. Amsterdam 1994, 207–249. Published there as Figure 20 on Plate XXXIX, and Figure 36 on Plate LVI.

population centers "proto-poleis" (embryonic city-states) (Bintliff 1994), since many defend their independence and where possible expand territory by incorporating their neighbors. However, even in the EIA some foci were much larger than others, especially Thebes, and the dice are loaded against the more numerous smaller settlements. Through Late Geometric-Archaic times the many proto-poleis are absorbed peacefully or forcibly into a less numerous group of small and large poleis, which then conform to Ruschenbusch's (1985) statistical generalization, that an average Aegean Classical city-state was 5–6 km radius in territorial size and encompassed several thousand citizens. Clearly a typical successful polis will normally have absorbed one or more proto-poleis to achieve this scale.

In a path-breaking monograph the historical geographer Kirsten (1956) sought to solve a problem posed by his older mentor, Philippson, namely, "why were Greek towns so remarkably numerous, even in an ethnos [tribal] region such as Thessaly?" Kirsten's solution had hitherto not occurred to ancient historians, who focused on the legal nature of the polis and its political arrangements. As a geographer, Kirsten grasped from many case-studies what Ruschenbusch (1985) and recently Hansen (2004) later confirmed from large-scale databases for Greek city-states, that the *polis* was not usually a "city" at all, in the sense of a major urban agglomeration with an extensive dependent hinterland. Rather, the scale of the typical city-state (Ruschenbusch's *Normalpolis*), at, for the Aegean, around one hour's radius territory and with on average 2–4000 people (rural population included, with "cities" ca. 11–23 ha in extent) was that of the traditional larger Greek village of the Early Modern era, the *deme* (which also often included small dependent hamlets and villages). For Kirsten, the origin and general nature of the *polis* was a "village-state" or *Dorfstaat*.

However some *poleis* nourished ambitions to control entire regions as territorial states, and the most successful even transformed themselves in this fashion into "Megalopolis" (giant) cities (Kirsten) of one to several hundred hectares and with populations of 10–20,000. During the later Archaic era, the sixth century BC, the numerous Boeotian settlements in Figure 8.3 became either predators or victims as the

newly-created city-states competed to absorb lesser communities into their territories. This was largely successful when we count the smaller number of cities shown here for the late Classical period. Amongst these the city-state of Thebes grew into a "megalopolis"of over 300 ha, although there were only short periods when it actually dominated all the other 14 city-states.

Athens' region, Attica, may have followed the same route, but this happened earlier and hence went unrecorded in history, although possibly preserved in later legends. The final Archaic-early Classical village map (*demes*) (Figure 8.3, Lower) reveals a network of comparable community foci to those of contemporary Boeotia (*proto-poleis*), with 2–3 km radii in the areas beyond the immediate hinterland of Athens. We might suggest that a similar evolution to that in Boeotia occurred from a dense network of once independent, cell-like nucleated settlements into a much smaller group of competing early city-state centers. These were then absorbed successfully in this case into a single dominant "megalopolis," Athens. Consistent legends hint at an earlier stage in Geometric times when Athens competed with rival Attic centers, for example Marathon and Eleusis (Bintliff 1994).

The Southwest Argolid Survey (Jameson and Runnels 1994) also reconstructs from Late Geometric times a series of small *polis* foci in this area which later simplify into two larger territorial poleis. On Kea (Cherry *et al.* 1991), in Classical times the island possesses a series of roughly equal-sized territories, dominated by small poleis, with radii near the "Normalpolis" of 5–6 km. Whether earlier stages of the Iron Age saw more numerous nucleations is unclear, given the limited extent of intensive survey and the above-mentioned problems in clarifying the status of pre-Classical sites. In Thessaly, spatial analysis of Archaic-Classical urban centers (Auda *et al.* 1990) reveals a cellular network of "Normalpoleis" and larger poleis in most districts of this fertile region (territorial radii of 5–10 km), usually incorporating village satellites. Many of these foci are known to originate within PG and Geometric times, but whether this system crystallized out of more numerous proto-poleis is unknown. On Methana, regional survey (Mee and Forbes 1997) identifies three nucleated foci for Iron Age and Archaic settlement, with radii of some 3 km; by Classical times these are transformed into a single polis and two satellite villages.

Wilkinson's (1994) model for the rise of regional urban centers in dry-farming Northern Mesopotamia, though based on Early Bronze Age data, strikingly resembles the sequence just presented. Initial infill of the landscape creates numerous nucleated villages (comparable to 2–3 km radius "proto-polis" cells); subsequently, at a first stage of synoecism (political merger) groups of these come under the sway of local centers with resultant territorial radii of some 5 km (comparable to the Greek Normalpolis); finally, further competition results in incorporation of such groups into larger city-states (comparable to larger poleis in Archaic Boeotia), with territorial radii of some 15 km. Wilkinson rightly emphasizes as the driving force for these progressive absorptions of smaller centers the immense

advantage for the dominant towns of gaining access to increased food surpluses and human manpower, giving them a buffer against shortages and boosting military forces. Critically this allowed regional centers to outgrow the productive potential of their own immediate hinterlands. The overall picture also bears striking resemblances to geographical theories for the dispersal and relative size of Early Modern hamlets, villages, towns, and cities (Tidswell 1978, (his) Figure 11.1).

Landeskunde, Siedlungskammer, and community area theory

The next stage in our reconstruction is to highlight the importance of encapsulating the fragmentary data for EIA and early historic Greece within theories of how individual small landscapes are utilized in the long term, where the German *Landeskunde* approach should be central (following Text Box).

Landeskunde Theory

The German *Landeskunde* (landscape lore) tradition (represented for research in Greece by twentieth-century scholars such as Philippson, Kirsten, and Lehmann), takes as axiomatic the concept that settlement chambers (*Siedlungskammer*), or large areas of land with natural boundaries and with especially desirable resources to sustain lasting nucleated communities, will tend to be occupied in almost every period from the arrival of mixed farming in that area. Exceptions could be caused by endemic warfare or piracy, or recurrent plague epidemics, but arguably these constraints are likely to be short-lived compared to the episodes of continuous settlement believed typical of such landscapes. The size of the associated settlement

can fluctuate according to the particular social, political, and economic circumstances of each era. The theory does allow that settlement could be completely nucleated or partly or wholly dispersed through the settlement chamber. Yet the implication is that for most of the time we should expect such settlement chambers to contain settlement, even though, for historically-contextual reasons, settlement *locations* may shift around the chamber (making it more difficult to locate for each individual period). Lehmann (1939) was the first to apply the approach formally to Greece, identifying settlement chambers in Eastern Crete from the Bronze Age to the era of traditional villages, whilst similar analyses lie scattered throughout Philippson's multi-volume publication of the historical geography of Greece (1950–1959).

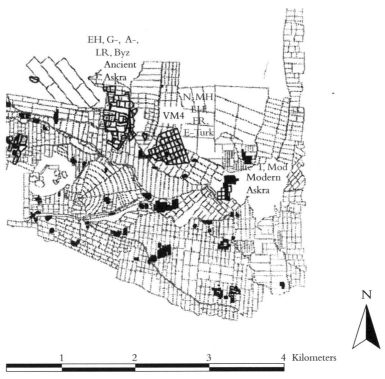

Figure 8.4   Settlement-chamber migration of nucleations in the Valley of the Muses. Askra is the sole nucleation in Early Bronze Age and Greco-Roman to Byzantine times, site VM4 is the sole village in Middle-Late Bronze Age, Frankish/Crusader, and Early Ottoman times, and the modern village is the only nucleation from Late Ottoman times to today. Author.

One very obvious internal relocation within settlement chambers might be expected in the EIA, when defensible positions may have been favored as a result of chronic insecurity. On Crete, for example, Nowicki (2000) has catalogued some 100 such refuge settlements between 1200 and 800 BC.

Two recent settlement-chamber case-studies are relevant to this chapter. Firstly, total-survey of all the cultivable area of the Valley of the Muses, Boeotia (Bintliff 1996), dealt with a fertile settlement chamber with mountains on three sides (Figure 8.4). This showed indeed that from Bronze Age to Turkish times there was always just one nucleated community in the Valley, although its location alternated between the valley bottom (Askra) and a nearby hillside (VM4), until the seventeenth century AD when the village shifted to today's location near the outer edge of the

Valley. There is one possible short desertion during the Early Roman Empire.

A second Boeotian example is a coastal basin comprising the territory of the ancient city-state of Khorsiai (Fossey 1986). Khorsiai is a proto-polis on an appropriately tiny territorial scale that retained a notional autonomy into Classical Greek times. Prehistoric activity is focused on the city hill (Kastron), but in the Dark Ages intensive survey revealed that the population moved to remoter Mali, on a rugged ridge east of the polis. By early historic times the main settlement returned to the city site, until relocation in the Middle Ages to modern Khostia village on the northeast rim of the basin.

From this discussion we discover that Southern Greece provides a laboratory to explore the concept of landscape "possibilism" favored by French regional geography (where a landscape offers *constraints* and *possibilities* rather than *determines* human settlement) (Vidal de la Blache 1926). Often natural geography has created settlement chambers encouraging repeated or continuous settlement by a farming community in many periods. But frequently the settlement-focus can migrate within these, so that only extremely intensive, source-critical landscape research can locate them. Equally common however are landscapes where larger bands of favorable land offer similar long-term opportunities for several communities, but without constraining their locations. Nonetheless, even here there are constraints on the *spacing* of settlements due to travel time to fields and the area needed to sustain a large settlement. In fact what we might conceive as "gravitational" attraction occurs: some very favorable niches for settlement may become fixed and hence cause a chain-effect on adjacent larger landscape blocs where settlement location is less restricted, through setting in motion a network of communities radiating outwards by natural patterns of settlement spacing. Thus can arise the "cellular" occupation revealed for Archaic Boeotia and Athens (Figure 8.3). The fusing of a mosaic of similar territorial units drawn into their locations by a few natural fixed foci is comparable to the concept in Chaos-Complexity theory of non-linear "attractors" (Bintliff 1997, Lewin 1993).

The trajectories of settlement: conclusions

In phases of full occupation of the countryside these possibilistic and gravitational factors will create networks of similarly-spaced communities; in times of reduced population we expect a more patchy settlement of the available community niches, rather than total abandonment of whole districts. Some settlement chambers might downscale to farmsteads, or even suffer brief abandonment, but when population recovers a full community should usually reappear in each chamber. During thin occupation episodes a community might even migrate to another settlement chamber if there was insufficient competition for each niche. Why could that happen? If in the Dark Age the local group was closely attached to a chiefly family,

rather than to a sense of land-rootedness, then with the dying out or loss of power of a particular family, that community might move to a different territory. Perhaps relocations symbolized a takeover by a new chieftain. Several well-known Dark Age settlements show discontinuous settlement histories (Lefkandi, Zagora). In contrast, as we shall see, major Mycenaean centers such as Athens and Thebes remained "town-like" throughout the "Dark Age" (Snodgrass Model 2), acting as fixed points to anchor expanding networks of smaller "proto-poleis" in the surrounding countryside, as well as posing a powerful threat to the ultimate independence of those networks.

Summarizing, most landscapes in Southern Greece probably retained elements of settled life throughout the EIA (if patchy and dispersed), providing seedcorn for the reinstatement of a complete, cellular network of settled communities by Archaic or Classical times. Through those latter periods, the gradual infill of the landscape by settlements of similar, modular size (proto-poleis and rare early towns), reduces the opportunity of settlement relocation within the Southern Aegean. Already by now, but increasing in pace comes competition between the dominant families resident in each community niche, for survival or for expansion to consolidate their own sustainability in food and manpower. The larger, older "town-like" communities probably have the edge in absorbing smaller or less well-established neighbors into satellite status. Thus are created those small networks typical for the "fat village": the *Dorfstaat* or *Normalpolis*. Always threatening these networks are even larger centers, whose success in absorbing clusters of Normalpoleis will allow Large Polis or even Megalopolis expansion in terms of settlement size and territorial radius. In parallel, the innumerable local chieftains postulated by archaeologists for dispersed proto-polis small settlements such as Lefkandi or Emborio, as well as in the rare "towns," but not necessarily permanently tied to one settlement chamber, eventually will become fixed in the landscape as all the available niches for settling a community are taken up. The Iron Age and early Archaic elite, the poet Hesiod's *basileis*, are initially resident in proto-poleis, but as these yield local power to higher-level centers, will probably move to the dominant polis to form an aristocratic class.

Developments in Northern Greece

In contrast to the tale of a decline in social complexity which still suits the EIA of Southern Greece, our limited knowledge of Northern Greece suggests a slow rise in complexity throughout the Bronze Age and, with no great disruption, on into the Iron Age (Andreou *et al.* 1996, Andreou 2001). As noted in earlier chapters, in the late LBA-EIA there is increasing evidence for the elaboration of district central-places, perhaps forming small regional states. In the earlier EIA outside influences remain small-scale, with Protogeometric ceramics imported and locally imitated in small proportions compared to traditional local hand-made wares (Snodgrass 1994, Papadopoulos 1996). But through the Geometric era southern styles become increasingly popular in pottery and other artifacts, showing growing exchanges, which culminate in southern colonies being planted along the coasts in Late Geometric and Archaic times. Although outside stimuli increase, assisting state-formation in Macedonia and Epirus, that process also appears to reflect indigenous responses to an EIA regional growth of population and economy. Northern polities would head in quite different and more hierarchical directions than those that give rise to the community-focused city-state in the Southern Aegean, culminating indeed in the formation of Northern Greek kingdoms by Archaic times.

Settlement and House Plans

The response of individual communities to the toppling of Mycenaean-Minoan civilization suggests that local political and military processes were decisive: initially many people fled to sizeable refuge sites in the final, post-palatial Bronze Age and earliest Iron Age, either new settlements or survivors of the thirteenth-century destructions (for example Tiryns, Perati, Asine, and Lefkandi). Some Mycenaean or Minoan centers were abandoned or shrank to hamlets, others revived as villages or even towns. Significantly, a number of remote, inaccessible "refuge sites" were already left for more practical agricultural locations by Geometric times, while others lasted through the EIA, only to be replaced in Archaic times by open-landscape sites at the time when the historical-

era city-states were becoming fixed centers. At that era, communities were relocating into more accessible new town-sites: urban locations include the "new towns" of Tanagra, Koroneia, and Thespiae in Boeotia.

Nichoria in the Southwestern Peloponnese is an excavated site that provides a glimpse of a small EIA settlement (McDonald *et al.* 1983). An earlier Mycenaean village at the site was a rural imitation of Bronze Age town life, with rectilinear houses in rows along the streets. After limited abandonment a new plan emerges: a less structured EIA settlement consists of individual houses dispersed over the site, at irregular angles to each other. Significantly, although material culture remains unimpressive, Nichoria sees its simple houses grow in size over the Geometric era, whilst a larger-scale chieftain's house is identified. Nonetheless, through the EIA until Late Geometric times, the typical Mainland family-home was a one-room curvilinear house. This plan was occasionally enlarged into a megaron form with a porch, main room, and storeroom in a simple access sequence, particularly in houses supposed to be of the elite (Dickinson 2006).

We have portrayed typical EIA landscapes as thinly settled by chieftain-focused hamlets or villages. A less numerous class of EIA settlements of a very different character usually retains its uniqueness into the subsequent early historic era. Many Mycenaean centers shrink to very small towns or villages (for example Mycenae), or remain unoccupied (Pylos), but a few (Athens, Argos, Thebes, Knossos) show continuity into Classical times, and moreover as extensive clusters of closely-spaced hamlets forming a "town in patches." Remarkably, the Classical historian Thucydides (*History of the Peloponnesian War* 1.10.2) and the philosopher Aristotle (*Politics* 1252b.28) describe this as the "traditional archaic" type of town, preserved to their time in the plan of Classical Sparta, a curious amalgamation of close villages. This multifocality might be giving us a map of several chiefs (*basileis*) with their retinues and serfs settled in each other's vicinity, keeping some social distance and with separate cemetery zones (Snodgrass urban origins Model 2, see earlier). At Eretria such a series of chief-centered house-clusters has been argued for from excavations of the Geometric predecessor of the later town (Crielaard 2007).

In contrast Old Smyrna on the west coast of Turkey has a fortification wall with signs of concentrated settlement within it (Snodgrass Model 1) already by the ninth century BC (Dickinson 2006). This might precociously anticipate its better-known plan by the end of the seventh century BC (Figure 9.3), when a dense Archaic township sits firmly enclosed within a circuit wall, a model for a typical Classical polis.

In landscapes mostly composed of small communities, the existence of an EIA town must at all times have exerted a gravitational attraction in its immediate region. It offered increased trade opportunities and social possibilities unobtainable elsewhere, and surely political influence over its neighbors (Lehmann 2004). Moreover a warlike elite society sees virtue in aggression and feuding to enhance its members' status and control over land and people, so that an imbalance of military capability in favor of such agglomerations could stimulate these larger communities into territorial expansion over lesser settlements in their vicinity. Multifocal Athens is remarkable in achieving dominance over the large region of Attica before recorded history begins (ca. 700 BC), and perhaps as early as 900 BC. By the end of the Geometric era Athens might already have possessed 10,000 inhabitants (Morris 2005), more than twice the size of a typical Classical city-state. Dark Age towns at Thebes, Argos, and Knossos also all rose to become the most powerful city-states in their regions, although at later dates.

Settlement and house-plan development over Geometric times

The Geometric settlement at Eretria on the island of Euboea may perhaps be typical. Under the Classical town lie many individual houses scattered without clear order, the only link between them being an orientation to the street plan. Lang (1996) terms this the *Einzelhaussiedlung* or Individual House Settlement model. Even the communal temple was initially comparable to surrounding houses (Figure 8.7). Eretria marks a new elite foundation at the end of the EIA, perhaps replacing nearby Lefkandi. Although the residence(s) of its chiefly rulers have yet to be clearly identified, their prestigious burials are placed inside the town, with associated cult (Crielaard 2007). At Geometric Emborio on the island of Chios (Figure 8.5, reconstruction), another *Einzelhaussiedlung* sprawls along a hillside

Figure 8.5   Settlement plan of Emborio on the island of Chios in the Early Iron Age.
A. Snodgrass, *An Archaeology of Greece. The Present State and Future Scope of a Discipline.* Stanford 1987, Figure 57. Reproduced by permission of University of California Press Books.

below a walled acropolis, within which lies a putative chieftain's house beside the eastern wall, indicating that the enceinte was plausibly a communal refuge in times of threat.

The development of the later major city of Corinth between Geometric and Archaic times is enlightening in documenting the transformation from such plans to a nucleated Archaic town-plan, the physical trace for the emergence of a city-state (Lang 1996). Like other "town-like" settlements such as Athens, initially village-hamlets lie dispersed around a large undefended area, whilst the lofty citadel of the Acrocorinth above the town provided refuge. In later Archaic times a city wall will enclose almost all the lower-town clusters. As at contemporary Eretria, an early stone temple from this transitional era seems to be symbolic of a communal identity, which the propinquity of the settlement clusters implies but cannot clearly demonstrate.

More exceptional and precocious is Old Smyrna, where as noted earlier the built-up and fortified small town of Archaic times may have been prefigured in a clustered house-plan of Late Geometric date (Dickinson 2006). Similarities appear at Zagora on the island of Andros, built on a coastal peninsula with a fortification wall protecting land access. It was created in the ninth century and abandoned ca. 700 BC (Snodgrass 1980, Lang 1996). Like other EIA sites, the Zagora community was focused around an architectural complex on the highest central point, which could have housed a leading family (although the distinctiveness and hence "status" assignation of this sector is disputed). However and significantly, instead of filling the enclosure with free-standing dispersed houses, the inhabitants were largely clustered in one-fifteenth of the defended area (around 1 ha), with many houses sharing a similar alignment on rectilinear plots (in terraced houses, also termed a *Reihensiedlung*). In its later stages Zagora's population is estimated as several hundred people. Are we seeing the early stages of an emergent city-state? At Old Smyrna certainly we are, where the nucleated settlement continues into the following period as a typical polis urban plan.

Vroulia on Rhodes provides a useful comparison (Lang 1996), a short-lived settlement occupied for a brief period soon after Zagora was abandoned. Around 700 BC, at the very end of the Geometric era,

a strictly-planned settlement was set out on a coastal promontory, with a land defense wall, behind which lay two regimented rows of terraced houses and a communal sanctuary. The population was also a few hundred, with the settlement being abandoned after a century. Between Zagora and Vroulia, we seem to observe a tightening of the architectural expression of a single community, anticipating the "Hippodamian" grid-plans of new towns in Classical times, with the "little boxes" marking seemingly equal citizen families. Nonetheless all these proto-urban (emergent town) settlements are within an aristocratic political system, where communal planning is elite-directed. And yet the concept of "community," expressed in integrated architectural blocks and defensive walling, equally reflects the emergence of a more homogenizing concept of a corporate society, "the citizens," and hence marks the rise of the "polis." Reinforcing this transformation is the displacement now of Vroulia town's burials outside of the defense walls – the separation of the society of the living from the "settlement of the dead" beyond a formal boundary.

Comparison with contemporary Late Geometric-early Archaic developments outside the Aegean are instructive. At this time there was a wave of Greek colony foundations abroad (see below). Typically the aristocratic founders of these new towns practiced a regular allotment of urban house-plots and an associated division of the surrounding agricultural land, providing attractive living and working conditions in order to encourage lesser-status families to depart from their homeland along with their aristocratic leaders. The Sicilian colony of Megara Hyblaea, founded in 728 by Megara for example, was a (rather irregular) grid-plan from its inception (Snodgrass 1980). However, the houses appear less regimented, and less like modern residential estates or the Classical "Hippodamian" plans. There is plentiful space for gardens and courtyards, and it is probable that class differences were marked by differences in the allotment of larger or smaller houses and rural estates.

If we turn to developments in the form of the domestic house, some at least of the Late Geometric sites so far discussed demonstrate that the private sphere of non-elite dwelling-houses is becoming more elaborately subdivided, which has been taken to be symptomatic of the evolution of a more complex

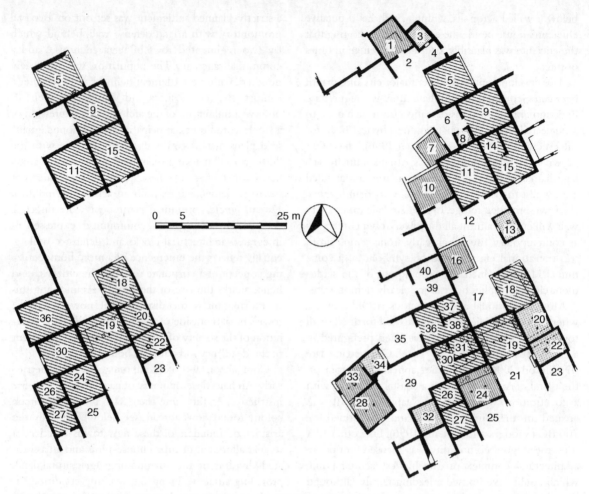

Figure 8.6 Elaboration of houses at Zagora during Late Geometric times.
F. Lang, *Archäische Siedlungen in Griechenland: Struktur und Entwicklung*. Berlin 1996, Figures 55–56. © Wiley-VCH Verlag GmbH & Co. KGaA, Weinheim.

society. Especially after ca. 750 BC the typical single-roomed curvilinear house, in mudbrick and wood, is replaced by rectangular houses, increasingly using stone foundations. At Zagora, the standard room plus porch, or megaron form, is replaced over the life of the settlement by multi-roomed houses often placed around a courtyard, inaugurating that more elaborate definition of social and economic space which is usually associated with the formation of the citizen family-based city-state (Figure 8.6, illustrating this transformation between LG1 and 2).

Technology and Trade

The shift to iron as the dominant metal for tools and weapons is generally a feature of the Protogeometric era, and may as Snodgrass claims be a combination of shortage of traded bronze or perhaps of the wealth to import its components, and the influence of precocious ironworking on Cyprus (Snodgrass 1983, 1989, Dickinson 2006). The surprising evidence for elaborate metallurgy at EIA Lefkandi suggests the survival of specialist craftsmen in the entourage of some chiefs:

alongside prestigious Eastern imports there is local metalworking producing bronze tripods and gold jewelry. Moreover, from Early Geometric times advanced craftwork with oriental parallels on Crete has led to the proposal that Levantine artisans may have settled there. Nonetheless, early imports are often antiques, and not very common, indicating limited supplies and their bringing prestige to new owners more from their exotic origin than their actual market value. Levels of import and export from the Aegean only recover Mycenaean standards by Archaic times (Dickinson 2006). However, much has been lost and recycled: unusually rich finds from a handful of excavated sites prompt caution in making wider generalizations. In the absence of strong regional authorities till the rise of the city-state and federal states of the Late Geometric-Archaic era, traders would have required guarantees of travel security and agreed terms of exchange, and this almost certainly occurred through personal agreements with local leaders sealed by gift exchange, hence the importance of exotic objects in EIA Greece. From the late Protogeometric onwards, Aegean pottery gradually spreads out of the Aegean, at first mainly amphorae and hence probably containing oil, but increasingly fine tableware as well. The latter may well have functioned as Eastern exotica had been doing in Greece, but now as Aegean "exotica" to please Levantine and Central Mediterranean clients (Dickinson 2006). Levels of trade and craft production take off in Late Geometric times, probably the result of internal growth in demand and security, linked to the expansion of town life, but also to greater intervention from oriental trading-partners.

The ceramic sequence

Human or animal representations from the PG to MG period are extremely rare (Lemos 2000), although the Lefkandi terracotta centaur-figurine shows that skill was available. Rather, the demand to create such communicative art was low. Crete is an exception, where the Minoan cultural inheritance remained strong through the EIA, stimulating more regular figural art. However, the intense geometric designs on Aegean ceramics, whose stylistic phases create the subdivisions of the EIA (PG, EG, MG, LG), probably possessed a symbolic charge hitherto beyond

our understanding (Figure 8.1; Color Plate 8.1). We are confronted with something totally "Other." To anyone familiar with the idealized reality of Classical Greek art, the repetitive rectilinear or circular patterns of PG and Geometric pottery seem "impoverished" (Spivey 1997).

One can say at least that, while some elements derive from the more varied repertoire of Mycenaean ceramics, much is reminiscent of textile patterns. Dress may well have been permeated with such striking designs, and judging by house and temple models from LG times, buildings were perhaps monumental "installations" of geometric painting.

Technically, PG-Geometric designs show a pleasing symmetry. Traditionally such pots were seen as benefiting from improved technology, a multiple brush attached to a compass, and a shift from a slow to a fast potter's wheel. But there seems no change in the potter's wheel and the compass already appears in final Mycenaean times. It is true that kiln improvements were responsible for the lustrous black gloss which appears from PG onwards, perhaps imitating luxury bronze vessels. Moreover, this predominantly abstract art is not static. The changeover from PG to Geometric around 900 BC is marked by the decline of circles and semicircles in favor of rectilinear images (meanders and running crenellations) (Spivey 1997), whilst other changes in shape and design allow subdivisions of Geometric (EG 900–850, MG 850–800, LG 800–700 BC).

If designs remain enigmatic, something can be done with shapes. In the later part of the era when cremations were common, men were generally buried in neck-handled amphorae, women in the belly-handled form, and this hint of a body association suits the observation that amphorae, and another major shape, the jug (oinochoe), seem to develop humanoid characteristics: shoulders, mouths, bellies, and feet. Seemingly the deceased are tied to their final resting place in "embodied" and gendered pots (Whitley 2001).

Finally we should note that Athens, where a large multifocal settlement existed throughout the EIA, formed a ceramic style-leader in PG and Geometric times for other areas of the Aegean. However, increasing knowledge of regional ceramic developments elsewhere shows that Athens was just one of several networks exporting ceramics or whose style was influential on a wider scale. Euboea and North-Central Greece form a rival sphere, perhaps linked to the metals trade (Crielaard 2006). Crete notably does not follow the classic Athenian ceramic sequence of PG-EG-MG. Its pottery retains more figured decoration in PG-Geometric and throughout Geometric times it shows a precocious Eastern or "Orientalist" influence in its pottery, which seems to reflect its early links in prestige exchange and metalwork with the Levant (Whitley 1998, 2001). On the Mainland, it is LG times when figural art returns regularly to ceramic decoration (cf. Colour Plate 8.1).

Social Archaeology

Our first historic sources around 700 BC in Southern Greece term the controlling elite the *basileis* (princes, lords). "Basileus" is a minor official in Mycenaean archives (*pa$_2$-si-re-eu*). Plausibly, during the collapse of palace civilizations, regional kingship disappeared, and power fragmented into a myriad of district chiefdoms. The Lefkandi-type residence fits this hypothesis well, as does the survival of the term.

Based on class distinctions and class sizes in Classical times, the EIA restriction of formal burial to an elite of some third to a half of the Southern Greek population (in Archaic times dubbed the "good" or *agathoi*), would encompass an upper *basileus* class but also a sizeable middle class of "yeoman farmer" rank (later dubbed the *hoplite* class). This middling group presumably controlled its own resources, whilst available as military support for the dominance of the basileis over the remaining half to two-thirds of the population: a subservient peasant class (in Archaic times designated the "*kakoi*" or the "bad"), whose land and labor appear to be controlled by the upper and middle classes. The existence of such distinctions within the "buried" elite in the PG-MG centuries is shown in grave gifts. One of the richest, presumably genuine aristocratic, graves is a cremation burial of EG period ca. 850 BC from Athens, accompanied by gold, faience, and glass jewelry. Being female, this burial underlines the centrality of kinship and wealth inheritance in the close-knit elite clans of this era. Crielaard (1998) notes that the EIA upper-class graves in Greece and Cyprus are marked by weapons, drinking, and dining equip-

ment including cauldrons and roasting-spits:"Eminent warriors and feasters" (p. 189).

For the EIA we have postulated a countryside with generally low populations and considerable uncultivated spaces, later to be filled and exploited (in some regions to crisis proportions), between Archaic and Early Hellenistic times (ca. 700–200 BC). In such landscapes land had low value and aspiring chieftains maintained power by controlling a more critical scarce resource: manpower. Arguably through a mutually beneficial alliance with the free middle class, basileis attached the lowest class of peasantry to their households. Chiefly power passed between families and this often encouraged continuity within settlement chambers, but perhaps equally commonly a change of elite might be signaled by a displacement of the seat of dynastic power, causing community migration around the thinly-settled countryside or even abroad.

How was the aristocratic grip on the working peasantry sustained? A popular model (Sherratt and Sherratt 1993) for such a comparatively undeveloped and fragmented society, not far from the expanding commercial power of the Levantine Phoenicians, would be a "core–periphery system." This model emphasizes the inflow of Eastern prestige goods for the Greek elite, in return for the latter supplying those raw materials and surplus foodstuffs that had been channeled into the local chieftain's trading capital as tribute from his dependents. However, the model fails to account for how peasant dependency arises in the first place and is then maintained. Intriguingly, changing clothing fashions in figured vases from LG to earliest Classical times (ca. 800–480 BC) indicate a stronger reason (van Wees 1998).

Although ceramics throughout the main part of the EIA avoid representing people (Lemos 2000), the situation changes dramatically in the eighth century BC "Renaissance" of the LG period (Hägg 1983), when in all aspects of life we see major positive changes toward a more populous, politically complex society in most parts of Greece, also artistically and architecturally experimental and ambitious. A striking series of large vases illustrate aristocratic life, with the addition of anachronistic details deriving from the popular legends of Troy and the Bronze Age heroic world (clearly to underline claims to heroic ancestry for the living elite) (Colour Plate 8.1). These large pots from Athens are also themselves power statements since they were placed above the graves of prominent individuals. Highly significant is the portrayal of the elite and their male retinue on these LG ceramics as armed at all times, with swords or spears.

The implication for the organization of EIA society is that force was law and a mere claim to preeminence was inadequate. Just as the chief, and the retinue he sustained (the middle class) through feasting and gift-giving, were always armed, ready to take on rival families or intruders from neighboring districts, so we could hypothesize that a similar threat of instant violence kept dependent peasantries in their place. The latter, through their labor and agricultural surpluses, were the essential foundation for the daily rations, banquets, gifts, and supply of metal which the elite superstructure required for its maintenance. The clashing clans of Romeo and Juliet's Verona come to mind, but closer to its time the episode of "The Return of Odysseus" in Homer's epic *The Odyssey* is a vivid illustration of the period's ethos. When Homer produced the definitive version, perhaps around 700 BC, of a series of overlapping epic poems, which seem to have been growing in scale and detail from the Middle Bronze Age into Homer's own time (the final Geometric-earliest Archaic era) (Sherratt 1990), much of the action is describing the poet's own society. So in this instance: in Odysseus' absence at Troy and then on his wanderings around the Mediterranean, a group of *basileis* insolently encamp in his palace on the island of Ithaka, hoping to marry the abandoned wife/widow, while squandering Odysseus' resources. Odysseus and his son secretly remove weaponry and armor hanging in the dining-hall, doubtless placed for his own followers, then massacre the defenseless suitors.

The Late Geometric "Renaissance"

The restriction in artistic representation of the era 1100–800 BC, as we have just noted, changes dramatically with the "LG Renaissance." An explosion of ornament occurs on decorated vessels in bronze and ceramic, whilst complex scenes in both media present the viewer with clear reminders of the correct social order. In the Kerameikos Cemetery, Athens (Color Plate 8.1), very large, highly-painted storage vessels (Dipylon vases) stood at elite graves over the crema-

tion burial-pit, kraters for men, amphorae for women. Some tombs were mounded and had stone constructions around and within them. Cemetery studies suggest that cremation burial may have begun in the EIA as an elite fashion, but across the Geometric era a more general shift away from inhumation reflects emulation of this practice amongst the "middle-class" elite. It was not a Mycenaean custom, but to suit contemporary aristocratic associations Homer's poems made it the custom of the "heroes" described in his tales of the Trojan War.

The funerary marker-vessels portray a "theater of power": in the example illustrated the aristocratic deceased lies on a high bier atop a horse-drawn cart, whilst a great crowd of mourners processes round the pot's profile (rows of war-chariots, lines of wailing men and women). It *is* likely that such public displays of prominent kin and large retinues occurred during elite funeral ceremonies, yet there are also conscious anachronisms. War-chariots and figure-of-eight shields are allusions to Homeric epics, half-remembered features of Late Bronze Age warfare, rather than contemporary realities. The eighth century is when the Homeric version of the epics finalized endless local versions of older tales. However, art until the later Archaic sixth century BC was still responding to wider, more varied heroic tales of the Iron Age and later Bronze Age (Snodgrass 1998).

The commissioners of these vases, by combining funeral scenes with pictorial references to the heroic life, expressed their belief in an afterlife where aristocratic death merged with the immortal community of legendary heroes, hence anachronism appears appropriate. This identification was reinforced by the probable development by the LG era, if not much earlier, of the elite feast or drinking party, later called the *symposium* (Murray in Hägg 1983, Morris 2000), where professional storytellers would perform the formulaic recitals of the epic tales, rehearsing the elite values to which references in art could be associated.

Indeed some believe that the erection of such power statements in contemporary cemeteries, commemorating prestigious public funerals, and the sudden burst of figurative scenes, are an elite response to a perceived threat to its dominance, due to the emergence of the city-state and the giving of new rights to non-elite males (such as the privilege of formal burial to the lower class) (Snodgrass 1980). Such art was then designed to remind onlookers that the city still belonged to its aristocratic families. Probably linked to display tomb-pots is the emergence in LG times of giant storage-vessels (pithoi) with elaborate decoration in relief (Ebbinghaus 2005), which would have been costly items. The conspicuous ornamentation combined with one's possession of numerous such storage-vats would have emphasized agricultural wealth in an increasingly competitive society. The supposed chief's house at Zagora had 16 pithos emplacements, mostly for vessels of this dimension.

The assertions of early historic elites that they were descended from royal families of the Mycenaean era are probably, with some exceptions, as unlikely as they were strongly emphasized by these local chiefly families. With much mobility around the landscape and the limited scope of district warrior-leaders, continuity of actual power and blood lines is rather implausible. But the aristocrats who were rather more reliant on a gang of armed followers and their own aggressiveness to claim power over a dependent peasantry, nonetheless were keen to bolster supposed ties to legendary Mycenaean heroes. Thus was born the later Classical Greek conception that there was no Dark Age, allowing the legendary Theseus to be both an early Mycenaean Athenian prince who destroyed the Cretan Minotaur (plausibly a memory of the Mycenaean takeover of the Minoan palace at Knossos ca. 1500 BC), and the founder of a unified Attic state focused on Athens in the middle era of the Early Iron Age some 700 years later.

These claims to ancestral power by LG-Archaic period elites have been associated with the widespread re-consecration of Bronze Age monumental tombs as foci of "hero cults" during this era (Snodgrass 1980, 1988, Antonaccio 1994). This late manifestation is also interpreted as a specific response to the changing conditions of the period 800–500 BC. Population rise, internal colonization of the landscape, and growing competition between elite families led to the need for traditional elites to reassert their authority over a burgeoning class of middling citizens and the lower classes in the emergent city-states and towns. One way to convince people that your family was descended from Bronze Age heroes is to identify an elite burial of that era and commence to make offerings to one's supposed ancestors in its precincts. It has

recently been suggested however, that such "created" links to "local heroes" may also have been instituted by the emergent city-state communities themselves, as they built up *their* sense of regional identity through claimed ties to the legendary past of their territories. This is also evidenced by cities erecting shrines over Bronze Age palaces (Hall 1997).

Feasting, so central to Homeric aristocratic gatherings, seems to have been equally important to the warrior-elite society of the Dark Age, and we can suppose that large buildings such as the EIA Lefkandi or Emborio houses were already the focus of elite-controlled banqueting, as well as a repository of prestigious items obtained by the upper class through trade, gift exchange or dowry, to emphasize their relative wealth and status to their middle-class retinue and the dependent peasants who were their clients. Mazarakis-Ainian (1997) has argued that communal cult activity was primarily based in the chief's house and under his supervision, a further source of power to reinforce armed might and stores of food and valuables, although we do have clear evidence of separate shrines and sacrificial places and the thesis is controversial (Dickinson 2006).

The Origins of the Greek Temple

Excavated Mycenaean shrines are generally small rooms or room clusters with ritual equipment. The palace reception rooms also probably witnessed political-ritual ceremonies. On Minoan Crete iconography and excavations suggest that alongside palatial ritual areas there existed true temple complexes as well as open-air sacrificial and ceremonial places, whilst Linear B archives and rare discoveries seem to indicate separate Mycenaean religious centers too. The Classical Greek temple however represents a complex fusing of several discrete EIA elements, although a striking central component appears to derive from the megaron-plan of the Lefkandi house and other larger residences believed to mark leading families. As noted above, this is considered to demonstrate that community leaders tied power to ritual, including ceremonies in their great houses. During the EIA, alongside the hypothesized ceremonial role

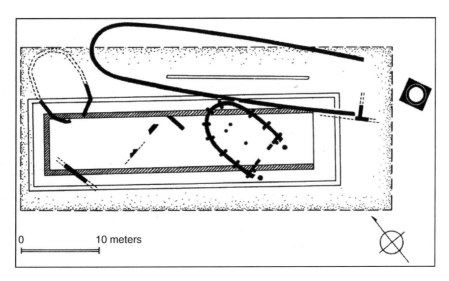

Figure 8.7 Eighth-century wooden temples of apsidal form underlying a later rectangular stone temple at Eretria. J. Whitley, *The Archaeology of Ancient Greece*. Cambridge 2001, Figure 7.6.

of the chieftain in his "great house" (Mazarakis-Ainian 1997), we also find open-air ritual foci. Votive deposits at Kalapodi (Central Greece) are associated with an altar and a claimed continuity of cult practices from the twelfth to seventh centuries BC. At several famous Classical sanctuary sites, ritual deposits including votives appear in limited quantities from the Protogeometric period onwards, whilst sacrificial altars are gradually monumentalized. Crete is exceptional, and it is suggested that Minoan traditions were stronger here throughout the EIA, with recognizable shrines within settlements and in the countryside, as well as continued use of cult figures and figurine dedications (Lebessi and Muhly 1990, Hayden 1991). Although the later, Classical complex of temple, external altar, and sacred enclosure encompassing them (*temenos*) is only identifiable on the Mainland and Cyclades as distinct from previous cult structures in Archaic times, it significantly marks the repackaging of earlier diffuse activities into a coherent ceremonial focus serving the communal interests of the emergent cities or federations of towns. Specialist studies of early cult-sites on the Mainland and Crete emphasize that both communal shrines and the rural sanctuaries (including later interstate centers of cult like Olympia), were places where ritual eating and drinking and animal sacrifice

typified communal ceremonies, under the leadership and to the prestige of leading local aristocratic families (Dickinson 2006).

The striking continuity of design elements needs detailing (Jameson 1990). One of the commonest forms of the earliest Greek temple plans of the eighth to seventh centuries BC is already in place at Lefkandi ca. 1000 BC: an elongated rectangle to which an apse (a semicircular wall) is added at one end, and with internal divisions denoting separate functions. When this particular hypothesized focus of community ritual separates from the elite dwelling, something seen in the critical LG eighth century BC (Figure 8.7), three key elements can be traced back into the elite house: an entry porch, a main room with a focus (originally a hearth, later the cult statue), and often an innermost chamber serving as private apartment-treasury (later temple treasury). Surely significantly, the word for the land domain reserved for the king in Mycenaean state archives (*te-me-no*), becomes from Homer's time onwards the term for the locality reserved for a god, enclosing his or her sanctuary.

The creation of a community temple complex, symbolizing the reorientation of society away from the residence of the elite and toward the symbolic residence of the city's patron divinity, is marked in another way (Snodgrass 1980).The oldest independent shrines receive a mere trickle of votive offerings until the era of state-formation in the eighth century BC, when the deposition of gifts develops into a flood. Moreover, many of these gifts are the result of a marked shift of deposition of dress-pins and weapons from individual burials to communal religious contexts, appearing to indicate a decline in the personalized social symbolism at funerals in favor of conceiving the public sanctuary as an arena of personal display for the evolving city-states.

The emergence of temples out of more multifunctional elite houses, means that non-residential cult houses only become generally distinct in the Archaic era, and can be ambiguous to interpret in their formative stages in the LG period (Snodgrass 1980, Morris 2000). In Figure 8.7, from the town of Eretria, there are two probable eighth-century temples underneath the Archaic Apollo temple. The earliest is an apsidal hut for a cult image, probably like the Perachora temple model with a high-pitched, thatched roof and a small portico with two columns. The second is larger and apsidal, reminiscent of Lefkandi; only the fact that its eastern end is open to face the altar makes it a temple. It still has a stone base with a timber frame and mudbrick wall supporting a thatched roof. The Samos Heraion illustrates the next stage in design development.This is a very early, still eighth-century, rectangular plan with a cult statue at the west and an entrance facing east to an altar; its dimensions already conform to the standard hundred-footer (*hekatompedon*) size for a Classical temple. Nonetheless, it still possesses a central row of columns suggesting a thatched roof. Ceramic roof-tiles are an innovation of earliest Archaic times, the seventh century, and first appear in the Corinth region, removing the need for a high thatched roof.

Bronze Tripods

One further element in domestic use which is more specific to the EIA and becomes less significant in Archaic to Classical times, when a more democratic society emerges, is the popularity of prestigious feasting vessels, cauldrons, especially of tripod-form. However these are rarely found before the time of spiraling prosperity in the eighth century BC. Is this because for much of the Dark Age, the general low level of bronze in circulation in society made large containers too expensive to use widely, or for the same reasons old vessels were recycled? We also have to bear in mind that most of our finds are votives from major sanctuary institutions and their deposits, which only take off in the Late Geometric era. In any case we can suspect that through the "Dark Age," and perhaps especially at its end, with growing access to trade and a rising population, there was elite investment in such great display pieces to show off at the traditional banquets in their households. Bronze cauldrons, often showpieces in museums today, were large cooking and warming vessels for communal eating. They were often highly ornamented, sometimes decorated with appropriate symbols of the warrior elite, for example a warrior with raised spear, a gesture which as Papalexandrou (2005) has shown, is the most frequent one associated with Homeric warriors in the epics. Tripods were suitable gifts between elites and later became a common reward for victors in competitions at the international festivals in Panhellenic (interstate) sanctuaries such as Olympia. But in the LG and early Archaic period tripods were, as Papalexandrou has stated:"the symbol of authority. Possession of tripods and their circulation through gift exchange, dedication and prize or dowry giving were key to the networks of aristocrats whose members vied for material and symbolic time [wealth, honor] and social prestige."

An Annaliste Perspective

In the long-term perspective, the "Dark" or "Early Iron" Age represents a prolonged phase of dislocation of complex society in the South Aegean and the Greek Islands, whilst it seems possible that North Greek societies were in a clearer but much slower trajectory of increasing social development. For the South, the *moyenne durée* is strikingly brought out in recent syntheses of the period: the twilight vestigial-Mycenaean world of the post-palatial centuries is replaced by the two to three centuries of EIA society with its reforged norms and socio-economic arrangements, then in the eighth century the "Renaissance" sees new developments in almost all areas of community life. The short term remains elusive, although an attempt to revive kingship at Tiryns offers potential in LH3C. Lefkandi is probably the best known of innumerable chieftain residences, although a special role for communities along the Gulf of Euboea in continuing long-distance exchanges may set the region's EIA settlements apart from others, implying that individuals such as the Lefkandi chief could have pioneered such activities. However Athens and Knossos are soon competing in social and economic networking so that a wider trend is visible beyond one historical individual.

A Personal View

One cannot but be awed by the spectacular collapse of Mycenaean civilization, and easily imagine the prolonged scenes of violence and forced migration which this entailed. The subsequent chieftain or Big Man-centered EIA society seems in many respects echoed in much of Homeric epic, if we focus less on kings and grand military coalitions and more on the competing "princes" on the island of Ithaka in the Odyssey. A matter still to be resolved is the catalyzing effect of Near Eastern trade and related diplomatic contacts with these small-scale Aegean societies: this was always accepted for the "Orientalizing" early Archaic seventh-century BC period, and more recently for the LG era in which the alphabet was adapted from Phoenician script and the basis for the first Greek written texts was laid, and trade rose exponentially (see following Chapters 9 and 10). But the latest discussions raise the question as to whether the gradual elaboration of Southern Aegean life from the PG through to MG was inextricably tied to stimuli brought by personal networks which linked Greek elites and craftsmen, both to the Levant but also to emerging native kingdoms (Phrygia and Lydia) in the hinterland of the Anatolian coasts (Morris 2000, and Chapters 9 and 10). I would nonetheless consider the most critical step – the creation of the polis and the victory of Morris' "middling" or community-focused political ideology – to be an internal development, as a far from inevitable outcome to the stresses brought on

traditional EIA societies through rising populations, growing wealth, and the military potential of a prosperous free farmer class.

References

Alcock, S. E. (1991). "Urban survey and the polis of Phlius." *Hesperia* 60, 421–463.

Alcock, S. E. *et al.* (2005). "Pylos Regional Archaeological Project, Part VII. Historical Messenia, Geometric through Late Roman." *Hesperia* 74, 147–209.

Andreou, S. (2001). "Exploring the patterns of power in the Bronze Age settlements of northern Greece." In K. Branigan (ed.), *Urbanism in the Aegean Bronze Age*. Sheffield: Sheffield Academic Press, 160–173.

Andreou, S., M. Fotiadis, and K. Kotsakis (1996). "Review of Aegean Prehistory V: The Neolithic and Bronze Age of northern Greece." *American Journal of Archaeology* 100, 537–597.

Antonaccio, C. (1994). "Contesting the past: Hero cult, tomb cult, and epic in Early Greece." *American Journal of Archaeology* 98, 389–410.

Auda, Y. *et al.* (1990). "Espace géographique et géographie historique en Thessalie." In *Archéologie et Espaces. Xe Rencontres Internationales d'Archéologie et d'Histoire, Antibes 1989*. Juan-les-Pins: Éditions APDCA, 87–126.

Bintliff, J. L. (1994). "Territorial behaviour and the natural history of the Greek polis." In E. Olshausen and H. Sonnabend (eds.), *Stuttgarter Kolloquium zur historischen Geographie des Altertums*. Vol. 4. Amsterdam: Hakkert Verlag, 207–249.

Bintliff, J. L. (1996). "The archaeological survey of the Valley of the Muses and its significance for Boeotian History." In A. Hurst and A. Schachter (eds.), *La Montagne des Muses*. Genève: Librairie Droz, 193–224.

Bintliff, J. L. (1997). "Catastrophe, chaos and complexity: The death, decay and rebirth of towns from Antiquity to today." *Journal of European Archaeology* 5, 67–90.

Bintliff, J. L. and A. M. Snodgrass (1988). "Mediterranean survey and the city." *Antiquity* 62, 57–71.

Bintliff, J. L., P. Howard, and A. M. Snodgrass (1999). "The hidden landscape of prehistoric Greece." *Journal of Mediterranean Archaeology* 12, 139–168.

Bintliff, J. L. *et al.* (2007). *Testing the Hinterland: The Work of the Boeotia Survey (1989–1991) in the Southern Approaches to the City of Thespiai*. Cambridge: McDonald Institute.

Cavanagh, W. *et al.* (eds.) (1996). *Continuity and Change in a Greek Rural Landscape: The Laconia Survey*. Vol. II. London: British School at Athens.

Cherry, J. F., J. C. Davis, and E. Mantzourani (1991). *Landscape Archaeology as Long-Term History*. Los Angeles: Institute of Archaeology, University of California.

Crielaard, J.-P. (1998). "Surfing on the Mediterranean web." In V. Karagheorghis and N. Stampolides (eds.), *Eastern Mediterranean: Cyprus–Dodecanese–Crete*. Athens: A. G. Leventis Foundation, 187–206.

Crielaard, J.-P. (2006). "Basileis at sea: Elites and external contacts in the Euboean Gulf region from the end of the Bronze Age to the beginning of the Iron Age." In S. Deger-Jakotzky and I. Lemos (eds.), *Ancient Greece: From the Mycenaean Palaces to the Age of Homer*. Edinburgh: Edinburgh University Press, 271–297.

Crielaard, J.-P. (2007). "Eretria's West Cemetery revisited." In A. Mazarakis Ainian (ed.), *Oropus and Euboea in the Early Iron Age*. Larisa: University of Thessaly Press, 169–194.

Dickinson, O. T. P. K. (2006). *The Aegean from Bronze Age to Iron Age*. London: Routledge.

Ebbinghaus, S. (2005). "Protector of the city, or the art of storage in Early Greece." *Journal of Hellenic Studies* 125, 51–72.

Fossey, J. M. (ed.) (1986). *Khostia. Results of Canadian Explorations and Excavations at Khostia, Boiotia, Central Greece*. Amsterdam: Gieben.

Hägg, R. (ed.) (1983). *The Greek Renaissance of the Eighth Century B.C.* Stockholm: Acta Instituti Atheniensis Regni Sueciae 30.

Hall, J. M. (1997). *Ethnic Identity in Greek Antiquity*. Cambridge: Cambridge University Press.

Halstead, P. (1996). "Pastoralism or household herding? Problems of scale and specialization in early Greek animal husbandry." *World Archaeology* 28, 20–42.

Hansen, M. H. (2004). "The concept of the consumption city applied to the Greek polis." In T. H. Nielsen (ed.), *Once Again: Studies in the Ancient Greek Polis*. Stuttgart: Franz Steiner Verlag, 9–47.

Hayden, B. J. (1991). "Terracotta figures, figurines, and vase attachments from Vrokastro, Crete." *Hesperia* 60, 103–144.

Jameson, M. H. (1990). "Domestic space in the Greek city-state." In S. Kent (ed.), *Domestic Architecture and the Use of Space*. Cambridge: Cambridge University Press, 92–113.

Jameson, M. H., C. N. Runnels, and T. H. Van Andel (1994). *A Greek Countryside. The Southern Argolid from Prehistory to the Present Day*. Stanford: Stanford University Press.

Kirsten, E. (1956). *Die griechische Polis als historisch-geographisches Problem des Mittelmeerraumes*. Bonn: Colloquium Geographicum 5.

Lang, F. (1996). *Archäische Siedlungen in Griechenland: Struktur und Entwicklung*. Berlin: Akademie-Verlag.

Lebessi, A. and P. Muhly (1990). "Aspects of Minoan cult: Sacred enclosures." *Archäologischer Anzeiger*, 315–336.

Lefkandi I–III = Popham, M. R. *et al.* (1979–1996). London: Thames & Hudson / British School at Athens.

Lehmann, G. (2004). "Reconstructing the social landscape of early Israel: Rural marriage alliances in the central hill country." *Tel Aviv* 31, 141–193.

Lehmann, H. (1939). "Die Siedlungsräume Ostkretas." *Geographische Zeitschrift* 45, 212–228.

Lemos, I. (2000). "Songs for heroes: The lack of images in early Greece." In N. K. Rutter and B. A. Sparkes (eds.), *Word and Image in Ancient Greece*. Edinburgh: Edinburgh University Press, 11–21.

Lewin, R. (1993). *Complexity. Life at the Edge of Chaos*. London: Dent.

Lohmann, H. (1993). *Atene. Forschungen zu Siedlungs- und Wirtschaftsstruktur des klassischen Attika*. Köln: Böhlau Verlag.

McDonald, W. A. and G. R. Rapp (eds.) (1972). *The Minnesota Messenia Expedition. Reconstructing a Bronze Age Regional Environment*. Minneapolis: University of Minnesota Press.

McDonald, W. A., W. D. E. Coulson, and J. Rosser (eds.) (1983). *Excavations at Nichoria in Southwest Greece*. Vol. III. *Dark Age and Byzantine Occupation*. Minneapolis: University of Minnesota Press.

Maran, J. and A. Papadimitriou (2006). "Forschungen im Stadtgebiet von Tiryns 1999–2002." *Archäologischer Anzeiger* 97–169.

Mazarakis-Ainian, A. (1997). *From Rulers' Dwellings to Temples*. Jonsered: Åström.

Mee, C. (ed.) (2011). *Greek Archaeology: A Thematic Approach*. Oxford: Wiley-Blackwell.

Mee, C. and H. Forbes (eds.) (1997). *A Rough and Rocky Place. The Landscape and Settlement History of the Methana Peninsula, Greece*. Liverpool: Liverpool University Press.

Morris, I. (1987) *Burial and Ancient Society*. Cambridge: Cambridge University Press.

Morris, I. (2000). *Archaeology as Cultural History*. Oxford: Blackwell.

Morris, I. (2005). "The growth of Greek cities in the first millennium BC." Stanford Working Papers in Classics 120509 (on-line).

Nowicki, K. (2000). *Defensible Sites in Crete c. 1200–800 BC*. Liège: Aegaeum 21.

Osborne, R. (1996). *Greece in the Making 1200–479*. London: Routledge.

Pakkanen, J. and P. Pakkanen (2000). "The Toumba building at Lefkandi: Some methodological reflections on its plan and function." *Annual of the British School at Athens* 95, 239–252.

Papadopoulos, J. K. (1996). "Euboians in Macedonia? A closer look." *Oxford Journal of Archaeology* 15, 151–181.

Papalexandrou, N. (2005). *The Visual Poetics of Power: Warriors, Youths, and Tripods in Early Greece.* New York: Lexington Books.

Philippson, A. (1950–1959). *Die griechischen Landschaften. Eine Landeskunde.* Frankfurt am Main: Vittorio Klostermann.

Popham, M., E. Touloupa, and L. H. Sackett (1982). "The hero of Lefkandi." *Antiquity* 56, 169–174.

Renfrew, C. and M. Wagstaff (eds.) (1982). *An Island Polity. The Archaeology of Exploitation in Melos.* Cambridge: Cambridge University Press.

Ruschenbusch, E. (1985). "Die Zahl der griechischen Staaten und Arealgrösse und Bürgerzahl der 'Normalpolis'." *Zeitschrift für Papyrologie und Epigraphik* 59, 253–263.

Shaw, J. W. (2006). *Kommos: A Minoan Harbor Town and Greek Sanctuary in Southern Crete.* Princeton: American School of Classical Studies at Athens.

Sherratt, S. (1990). " 'Reading the texts': archaeology and the Homeric question." *Antiquity* 64, 807–824.

Sherratt, S. and A. Sherratt (1993). "The growth of the Mediterranean economy in the early first millennium BC." *World Archaeology* 24, 361–378.

Snodgrass, A. M. (1977). *Archaeology and the Rise of the Greek State.* Cambridge: Cambridge University Press.

Snodgrass, A. M. (1980). *Archaic Greece: The Age of Experiment.* London: Dent.

Snodgrass, A. (1983). "Two demographic notes." In R. Hägg (ed.), *The Greek Renaissance of the Eighth Century BC.* Stockholm: Acta Instituti Atheniensis Regni Sueciae 30, 167–171.

Snodgrass, A. (1988). "The archaeology of the hero." *Annali Napoli* 10, 19–26.

Snodgrass, A. (1989). "The coming of the Iron Age in Greece: Europe's earliest bronze/iron transition." In M. L. S. Sorenson and R. Thomas (eds.), *The Bronze Age – Iron Age Transition in Europe.* Oxford: BAR Int. Series 483, 22–35.

Snodgrass, A. (1991). "Archaeology and the study of the Greek city." In J. Rich and A. Wallace-Hadrill (eds.), *City and Country in the Ancient World.* London: Routledge, 1–23.

Snodgrass, A. (1994). "The Euboeans in Macedonia: A new precedent for westward expansion." *Annali Napoli* 1, 87–93.

Snodgrass, A. (1998). *Homer and the Artists.* Cambridge: Cambridge University Press.

Spivey, N. (1997). *Greek Art.* London: Phaidon.

Tidswell, V. (1978). *Pattern and Process in Human Geography.* Slough: University Tutorial Press.

van Wees, H. (1998). "Greeks bearing arms. The state, the leisure class, and the display of weapons in archaic Greece." In N. Fisher and H. van Wees (eds.), *Archaic Greece: New Approaches and New Evidence.* London: Duckworth, 333–378.

Vidal de la Blache, P. (1926). *Principles of Human Geography.* Trans. M. T. Bingham from 1921 French edn. New York: H. Holt & Co.

Wallace, S. A. (2003). "The changing role of herding in the Early Iron Age of Crete: Some implications of settlement shift for economy." *American Journal of Archaeology* 107, 601–627.

Whitley, J. (1991). "Social diversity in Dark Age Greece." *Annual of the British School at Athens* 86, 341–365.

Whitley, J. (1998). "Knossos without Minos." *American Journal of Archaeology* 102, 611–613.

Whitley, J. (2001). *The Archaeology of Ancient Greece.* Cambridge: Cambridge University Press.

Wilkinson, T. J. (1994). "The structure and dynamics of dry-farming states in upper Mesopotamia." *Current Anthropology* 35, 483–520.

Further Reading

Bintliff, J. L. (1997). "Regional survey, demography, and the rise of complex societies in the Ancient Aegean: Core–periphery, Neo-Malthusian, and other interpretive models." *Journal of Field Archaeology* 24, 1–38.

Bintliff, J. (1999). "The origins and nature of the Greek city-state and its significance for world settlement history." In P. Ruby (ed.), *Les Princes de la protohistoire et l'émergence de l'état.* Rome: École Française de Rome, 43–56.

Boardman, J. (ed.) (1993). *The Oxford History of Classical Art.* Oxford: Oxford University Press.

Étienne, R., C. Müller, and F. Prost (2000). *Archéologie historique de la Grèce antique.* Paris: Ellipses.

Morris, I. (1991). "The early polis as city and state." In J. Rich and A. Wallace-Hadrill (eds.), *City and Country in the Ancient World.* London: Routledge, 24–57.

Pedley, J. G. (1993). *Greek Art and Archaeology.* New York: Harry N. Abrams.

Wells, B. and C. Runnels (eds.) (1996). *The Berbati-Limnes Archaeological Survey 1988–1990.* Jonsered: Åström.

9

The Archaeology of the Archaic Era
Demography, Settlement Patterns, and Everyday Life

Introduction

We have observed the likely continuity of a local elite political system in many parts of Southern Greece during the post-Mycenaean centuries, both in rural settlements and rare town-like, dispersed settlements later to play central roles in historic times (Athens, Argos, Corinth, and Knossos). The limited artwork and minor, largely reactive, participation in Mediterranean trade systems of the Protogeometric to Middle Geometric periods gave way to a "Renaissance" in the eighth century BC (Late Geometric era), with commercial expansion and significant ceramic and architectural works. Other major changes coincided, in a causal nexus: population rise, colonization both within the Aegean and into the wider Mediterranean, and the relaxation of lower-class burial restrictions. These transformations paved the way to the subsequent, earliest historic era, the Archaic, ca. 700–500 BC.

Political Developments

Apart from the vital improvement in our knowledge that the revival of literacy provides, a second great innovation is the spread of the city-state (*polis*) over large areas of Greece (Figure 9.1). This political structure was rapidly transported abroad through contemporary Greek colonial foundations around the Mediterranean and Black Sea. Essentially it signifies a form of state dependent on a single urban center, normally with villages and farms surrounding the latter as rural satellites. The agricultural basis of city-states in general (although there are rare exceptions, where commerce (Corinth) or empire (Athens) formed an equally important economic support), shapes the city-state as an inseparable duo of town and an agricultural territory (*chora*) belonging to it. Indeed most *polis*-citizens were required to own farmland to justify their political rights, whilst the typical territorial scale allowed all citizens, whether residing in the town or permanently in the country, to move in or out of the urban center in rarely more than an hour's journey-time on foot or donkey.

Politically, Classical Greece can be very broadly divided into two forms of state. In the first, mostly in the north, power remained with an elite or a king. These northern regions were dominated by a "tribal" or federal organization, the *ethnos*. The second form of state is found predominantly in the south and here state authority was vested in power-sharing between the middle (*hoplite*) class and an upper class, only rarely and discontinuously reaching down to the poorest free citizens. The Southern Mainland, and the Aegean and Ionian islands, thus adopted more egalitarian constitutions within a city-state organization. The transformation, so pregnant for European and later global history, from a common kind of elite politics

The Complete Archaeology of Greece: From Hunter-Gatherers to the 20th Century AD, First Edition. John Bintliff.
© 2012 John Bintliff. Published 2012 by Blackwell Publishing Ltd.

Figure 9.1 Map of the distribution of city-states or poleis in Classical Greece. The remaining areas were organized in "ethne" (tribal or confederate states) and/or kingdoms.

A. Snodgrass, *Archaic Greece. The Age of Experiment*. London 1980, Figure 43 (after Kirsten 1956). Courtesy of Professor A. Snodgrass.

found cross-culturally around the world, to a more unique experimentation with moderate democracy within Greece, took place essentially within the Archaic era (ca. 700–500 BC).

The *ethnos* and *polis*

The *ethnos* initially appears to be less a constructed civic community like the city-state, than a society resting on real or legendary kinship ties. Aristotle's negative distinction between the superior *polis* and the less advanced *ethnos* was followed till recently by historians and archaeologists researching how societies

like democratic Athens emerged out of the "Dark Age." Nineteenth and twentieth-century cultural evolutionary theory predicted that Greek society should pass from a "tribal" model, with or without "chiefdoms," toward "the state," with *ethnos* frequently translated as "tribe." Since *ethne* were often large regions (e.g., Thessaly or Boeotia), ethnographic evidence for tribal subdivisions of increasing geographical scale was successfully sought in ancient texts. Even Classical Athens possessed small-scale political and religious associations, the *phratry* and *genos*, whose names implied real or fictional kinship or neighborhood groupings. The idea arose that in the Early Iron Age all of Greece existed in kin-based and neighborhood-based political formations, sometimes linked into regional tribes. In the context of early migrations, such ethnic populations could probably cooperate on a larger scale, when people from a particular tribe spread widely around the Aegean, yet kept their original Greek dialect and specific aspects of cult (such as the Ionians or the Dorians). Arguably, as Greek society, especially in the precociously advanced Southeastern Mainland and the Cyclades, recovered population and a complex culture, these traditional forms of organization were replaced by the city-state and civic society, although remnants of the old kin system were retained for specific organizational purposes by the new states.

Over recent decades, this narrative has been widely deconstructed (cf. Snodgrass 1980). However this leaves archaeologists new problems. If we no longer accept the idea of large tribes acting in self-conscious coordinated polities in the EIA, we need to account for the historic existence in Archaic-Classical times of regions with named "peoples," some under kings, or forming confederacies. Even in the other world, of independent large and small city-states, we find occasional appeals to wider kinship affiliation (for political alliances), that are matched by the use of internal social divisions which are given an identical kinship terminology. Much light has been shed on these problems through the study of social anthropology and politics, notably by Hall (1997, 2004) who has applied such knowledge to questions of ethnicity and political organization in ancient Greece.

EIA Greece seems composed of a patchy dispersal of villages and rare small towns, organized around elite families, probably with much instability of power. Interactions within regions (due to intermarriage, migration, trade) probably account for the rise of large-scale patterns in ceramic styles during Geometric times (Snodgrass 1980), and, once literacy returns in early Archaic times, to regional variants in forms of the alphabet. In Early Modern Europe, farming villages and small agricultural town societies tend to practice exclusive identity politics ("campanilismo") (Tak 1990), so the dominant EIA social group may well have been the nucleated community one lived within. However, as groups of villages came under the sway of emergent city-states, or dominant towns in

ethnos regions, new identity requirements may have led to the naming of regions by a common identifier, probably taken from the dominant merger community, or some geographic or dialect label. Within these larger groupings older subdivisions may have persisted. Thus in the federal region of Boeotia (Central Greece) the "Boeotians" often act in war or religion together, but citizens preferred to be identified by their city of origin within the region. Hall (1997, 2004) and McInerney (1999: for the region of Phocis), argue that ethnic politics in Greece was creative and adaptive rather than reflecting an historical closed "race," and responded to changing social and political configurations. Luraghi (2002) believes that the Messenian "people" in the Southwestern Peloponnese, dominated by Sparta during the Archaic-Classical era, were largely "fabricated" into being at the time of their later revolt against Sparta. Their origin was forged at the rebellion's focus at the community of Messene. In conclusion, as local elites create larger political blocs from disparate local communities, appropriate new identities are formed, with suitable origin myths.

Current scholarship thus argues that the creation of regional federations and kingdoms, as well as the innumerable large, medium, and small city-states, found across Greece by early historic times (the seventh to sixth centuries BC or Archaic era), represents a political mosaic that is not due to inherent tendencies of character within "races" defined by Greek dialects, nor even by historical migration processes involving "peoples" (also marked by dialect distributions in historic times). The alternative scenario suggests that the final Bronze Age/earliest Iron Age disruptions initiated small and large population displacements as well as considerable population continuity at a reduced level of density. These were followed in the middle-late Geometric and early Archaic eras by the recrystallization of intercommunal political structures, ranging from "village-states" through territorial oligarchic states, to federations of towns or villages and finally to territorial kingdoms of towns and villages. Internal evolution is the central factor behind such emergent supra-family and supra-village communities, interacting however with external political and commercial contacts. It is further argued (Hall 2004, Tsetskhladze 2006) that the concept of a shared "Greek"

Solon's Reforms: An Archaeological Perspective

In mid-Archaic times, a severe crisis afflicted Athens, an impoverishment to the point of enslavement of many poorer citizens. The issue was rights over agricultural land, and although the exact nature of peasant indebtedness to rich citizens is unclear, the latter apparently possessed cripplingly exploitative control over peasant livelihoods. Solon found the land itself "enslaved," and his task was to "free" the land, rehabilitate peasant livelihoods, and release those sold into slavery from land-debt. However Solon clearly did not redistribute land in favor of the lower classes but probably gave them freehold rights to their existing plots. How did such indebtedness come about ca. 600 BC? Two major models are discussed by ancient historians:

1. Increasing population led to the poor being forced onto marginal land and a consequent dependency on the rich for economic help.
2. There had been a traditional dependency of the lower classes on the upper classes, dating back to the "Dark Age."

There is certainly an accelerating rate of settlement infill of the Southern Greek polis homeland landscapes from EIA through LG into Archaic and then Classical times (Bintliff 1997b). The issue here is the degree of pressure between population and available land by mid-Archaic times in the heartland of early demographic growth, which includes Athens and Attica.

Early Iron Age settlement in Southern Greece was low in density, nucleated, and typically consisted of small communities. Only in late Archaic times, the sixth century BC, but more especially in the Classical fifth to fourth centuries, will the Southern Greek landscape be filled in modular fashion by a complete network of villages and towns of comparable territorial scale. A further stage is very marked in intensive survey: the creation within the modular poleis and satellite village

(*kome*) territories of a dispersed settlement pattern of small farms and hamlets dependent on these nucleations. Yet Archaic farms and hamlets are rare and usually late in the period, compared to the explosion of Classical sites. Thus the database of landscape and urban surveys indicates an underpopulated Archaic countryside and cities yet to reach maximum size.

In contrast, Morris's reinterpretation (1987) of burial customs for Athens and Attica and by implication for other early polis societies, implies a rigidly enforced social gulf between an upper dominant and lower subordinate class throughout the EIA. Morris highlights the local peculiarity in Attica and Athens, that the opening up of burial to the lower class during the eighth century BC is subsequently rejected in the seventh century, where the old symbolism of exclusivity reappears, and only in the late sixth century will the "democratization" of burial return and persist. This seems to agree with the timing of the Solonic class crisis. The central problem for this elite of EIA chiefs and "middle-class" farmers was not land shortage or control over international commerce, but labor to work their fields *with* them (for the numerous second-rank elite) and *for* them (for the chiefly families). We can argue that Morris's upper class 33–50 percent of the population in Dark Age settlements used the labor of the lower class 67–50 percent to support them.

The Archaic crisis of Attic peasants, marked by their fluctuating burial rights, appears to have been solved by Classical times, but probably inaugurated an equally radical process of labor substitution for the other classes. The limits to production for ancient farmers were quite low (Foxhall 2003): cultivating a yeoman or hoplite farm of say 5–6 hectares (Burford 1993), as well as participating in political and military activity in the new polis center, normally required tied (tenant) or hired labor. Michael Jameson has argued that in Classical Attica agricultural slaves largely replaced tied labor for this essential role (Jameson 1977–1978, 1992). In Classical Boeotia, in contrast, calculations (Bintliff 1997a) suggest that the poorer half of the population could only have survived economically through working as paid labor on the estates of the middle and upper class (or as artisan and traders), leaving little scope for agricultural slavery, and not so surprising in a region where democracy was rarely in favor. In Classical city-states, whether fully democratic or run by the hoplite and noble class, the free lower class were a useful support force of lightly-armed troops (*peltasts*) or exceptionally (for Athens) this class manned the prime weapon of its Classical maritime empire, as warship rowers (the *thetes*). Unsurprisingly it is in Athens where this latter class achieves its greatest political freedoms. However in a considerable number of Archaic-Classical polis or ethnos regions, the support of the hoplite-elite class continued to rest on a large body of serfs; societies of this types could be found ranging geographically from Crete through the Peloponnese to Central Greece and Thessaly.

We might propose that in the EIA-Archaic era there were two forms of estate: the personal lands belonging to the middle and upper-class families, worked with the aid of the lower class and slaves, and the personal estates of lower-class peasants, which were subject to tenancy charges to the upper two classes. Crucially, this implies that the upper classes must have laid claim to all land taken into cultivation by the community, either by assuming direct, or indirect, rights to its surplus product. This model explains how peasant oppression remains in place, regardless of how intensely the countryside was being farmed. There was no land shortage at this point in Southern Greece, and colonization of the countryside was progressing at an increasing rate; but when peasants opened up

new land, the upper classes assumed rights to its surplus, as well as to the labor of the peasants on their own expanding acreage.

Why did this long-established system come into crisis in Athens ca. 600 BC? Historians suggest that the pressure for reform came from the middle class, and the gains for the lower class were modest. Plausibly, large-scale overexploitation of peasants by some groups of the elite classes appeared to threaten the effectiveness of their labor, making it preferable in the long term to give them freehold over their own land plots and eventually convert their tied labor on others' estates into free wage labor. In any case, political instability and limited rights for the lower class seem to continue through the sixth century in Attica, until Kleisthenes resolved their status more radically. Appropriately, as Morris shows, the changes in Attic burial norms closely reflect this.

We argued earlier that in the EIA the use of violence and armed men (van Wees 1998, 1999) enforced an unequal social structure, an alliance of the chiefs and the yeoman class keeping peasants in their place. Could peasants escape to live in free communities? Solon's claim that he brought back families who had fled abroad to avoid debt may reflect such refugees. Studies of peasant history however underline the risks of abandoning one's land to set up a new life far away, pressurizing peasants to choose security and past investment by remaining on tied farms. Just such risks however may have been taken, increasingly, by farmers in the Greek colonization movements of the eighth to sixth centuries BC, such as the poet Hesiod's father, who left Western Anatolia to create a new independent farm in Central Greece.

identity was weak until the Persian and Carthaginian Wars of the fifth century forged this in opposition to threatening civilizations.

In future city-state regions, the heartland for the rise of moderate democratic constitutions in some half of Classical Greece states, the tight control exercised over

peasant clients by warrior elites loosened in Late Geometric times, with the relaxation of the ban on lower-class formal burial. In the following early Archaic period a military reform occurred in which the cavalry and individualized combat on foot, centering on the rich, yielded on the battlefield to massed ranks of heavily-armed foot soldiers drawn mostly from the middle-class "yeoman" peasantry (the *hoplites*). Significantly, Morris (1987) estimates that one half to two-thirds of the population had suffered burial exclusion in the EIA. In Classical city-state armies, around half was aristocrat and middle (*hoplite*) class and the other half was composed of lightly-armed poorer citizens. This implies that the EIA elite was a very broad social group, later to form the upper *and* middle class of Classical times, whilst the EIA serf class usually remained a less privileged class of free citizens even in Classical city-states (Athens excepted). Thus the rise of moderate democratic institutions in Archaic-Classical times primarily reflects a shift in power from the dominant upper elite families to lesser, client-elite families, rather than the rise of a suppressed serf class.

The hoplite "reform"

Iron Age warfare in Homer's epics arguably portrays both contemporary (LG-early Archaic) fighting techniques and memories of Mycenaean practices. Nobles conduct personal combat with their peers in open skirmishes, utilizing chariots as "taxis" around the field of combat. There are bodies of support troops, but till recently these were dismissed as a second-quality mass whose success depended on the actions of their leaders. The contrast was drawn to the citizen armies of the mature Archaic polis, where the ranked formations of heavily-armed foot soldiers (*hoplites*) were decisive for any battle. This hoplite *phalanx* was predominantly composed of the middle-class citizenry rather than upper or lower class. Recent rethinking has nuanced this picture, arguing that IA-early Archaic aristocratic warriors were too small a group, so that successful warfare rested as much on the greater numbers of middling farmers, fit, healthy, and effectively armed from their own means or from equipment provided by their patrons (Raaflaub 1997). All this removes the lower-class peasantry, perhaps half the population, from a significant role in formal conflicts, apart from food support. This picture meshes well with Morris's pre-polis cemeteries, where the lowest class is absent, whilst the middle class is celebrated with the elite in formal burial rites.

Snodgrass forges a convincing compromise position (1980, 1993) by reanalyzing Homeric accounts

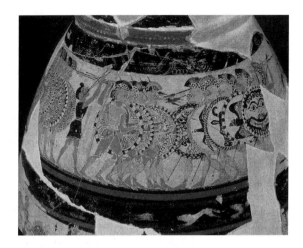

Figure 9.2 Early scene of a hoplite phalanx piped into battle ca. 675 BC.
Chigi jug, detail of warriors, c. 640 BC. Rome, Museo di Villa Giulia. © 2011. Photo Scala, Florence. Courtesy of the Ministero per i Beni e le Attività Culturali.

and scrutinizing the surviving bronze equipment of the Archaic period. Thus the open skirmishing in which elite individuals fronted their client soldiers, both groups in open formations, is reflected in limited heavy armor and helmets with easy vision to both sides as well as forwards. With the foundation of the polis it was the middle rather than the lower class which gained significant power-sharing with the traditional aristocracy, although legal rights were in theory open to all. The significance of this soon emerges in the appearance of a new military formation, a solid block of citizen-soldiers wedged together with spears to the fore like a hedgehog: the *phalanx*. The bulk of this army comes from the middle class, called the "hoplites" (from their heavy bronze and wood shields), with the aristocrats playing a minor role as support cavalry, or abandoning their horses and fighting on foot, anonymously, as hoplites. Often helmets reflect these new fighting conditions (Figure 9.2), with better side protection but a limited forward vision. A new heavier shield protected the left side of each warrior, the right being protected by the offensive weapons of spear and sword, but it also indicates limited mobility, as do metal greaves. The formation was key, not the individual, and once the phalanx was broken it was difficult to escape the subsequent rout. For Snodgrass the developing power of the middle-class citizens of the polis is still linked to a fundamental revolution in warfare, because it was precisely the military potential of the burgeoning hoplite class in LG-early Archaic times which challenged the traditional powerbase of the *basileis*. The threat of a coup from below, and/or the advantages of a hoplite phalanx in intercity warfare, were decisive considerations in persuading aristocrats to share power. The Archaic polis is defined less in terms of city walls (which are uncommon) but by its citizen-wall on the battlefield. As early as the end of the eighth century on Paros there has been claimed a possible communal military cemetery. Lower-class citizens could now act as light-armed support troops, but in Athens exceptionally, their decisive role as rowers in creating its maritime empire led to their achieving equal access to the other classes in holding all offices of the state during the Classical fifth century (Morris 2000).

The rise of tyrants in Archaic Greece

The emergence of the polis and the growing assertion of the middle classes not only leads to, or possibly is driven forward by, the hoplite reform in most city-states, but frequently to a further stage in which aristocratic domination of politics is confronted head-on. It seems that the pressure to broaden control of city-state decision-making, of the judicial process, and of rights to land, was being inadequately dealt with through partial concessions to the non-aristocratic classes. Two responses appear, sometimes both in the same city. Firstly, a dictator (*tyrannos*) may arise through manipulating the support of the competing factions, generally an opportunistic aristocrat. Alternatively the city may appoint an internal or external "lawgiver," to resolve the bitter and often bloody disputes between the classes, through creating a formal constitution enshrining an improved balance of citizen rights. The most famous tyranny is the Peisistratid dynasty in Athens, ruling for almost half the sixth century. Like tyrannies in other Greek states Athens experienced some beneficial effects, through sponsored economic growth as well as encouragement to the arts, especially if it served as propaganda for the ruler. Athens had already prevented revolution in the early sixth century through the reforms of the lawgiver Solon (see preceding Text Box), but after the ousting of

the last Peisistratid a second lawgiver was appointed, Kleisthenes. His remarkable constitutional reforms in 507 BC formed the basis for the inspirational Athenian democracy of Classical times.

The Archaic City

Cities emerged as expansions out of small EIA cores, or clusters of hamlets described by the Classical writer Thucydides as "the old form of cities," to create a characteristic typical built-up agglomeration of public and private sectors enclosed by a defensive wall, focused on a prominent urban sanctuary and public square (*agora*), and represented by the reconstructed seventh-century small polis of Smyrna (Figure 9.3). Walls were not only a sign of communal assertion, but in the world of Classical Greece, where warfare was endemic, a practical necessity against the aggression of neighboring states. However, Archaic fortifications develop unevenly. Many EIA villages have defensive walls protecting all of part of the settlement, but the larger, usually dispersed towns tend to develop circuit walls late and rely on a smaller defensible or defended *acropolis* (upper town) refuge (Corinth, Athens). When these more sizeable dispersed towns acquire lower city walls they will understandably enclose large areas of open ground as well as the original hamlet clusters.

Snodgrass (1980, 1986) has emphasized the role of the central urban sanctuary in defining the Greek Classical townscape. The form and central integrative communal role of the state temple probably originates in part from ceremonies within the great house of the EIA chieftains (*basileis*) (Mazarakis-Ainian 1997, Crielaard 2009), although it now seems likely that independent shrines within settlements also existed, if under the control of the elite (Dickinson 2006). As a sense of overriding citizenship arose, replacing orientations toward kin or a clientship centering around elite families, communal ritual and festivity were displaced to a community-focused imitation of the chieftain's great house. Nevertheless, temple construction and ornament did not escape from elite display, since a broad democracy, in which a large part of the free male citizens received significant political power, only emerges during the final Archaic and Classical periods.

Figure 9.3 Reconstruction of the city of Old Smyrna in the late Archaic period.
R. Cook, "Old Smyrna, 1948–1951." *Annual of the British School at Athens* 53 (1958–1959), 1–181.

Till then public shrines in town and country were generally sponsored by elites, who also were the main source of conspicuous dedications. Nonetheless, non-elite citizens were represented by smaller-scale offerings. Symptomatic of the rise of the polis is thus increasing investment in focal, monumental temples: perhaps already within the eighth century, pioneers are the "hundred-foot" (*hekatompedon*) temples on Samos and at Eretria (Hall 2007), and at least one Athena temple on the Athenian Acropolis. The carving of inscriptions with the laws of the state, valid for rich and poor, is highlighted as symptomatic of the Archaic-era trend toward democracy, but in this context it is

very significant that the majority of Archaic lawcode inscriptions are placed on temples or within their sacred enclosures (*temenoi*). This combination marks a deliberate link between the communal cult and equal justice for all citizens (Hölkeskamp 1994).

Since Archaic states were either run by kings, narrow oligarchies of a few families, or as compromises of middle-class "hoplite" males and aristocratic families, secular public buildings are of little significance till the end of the period, when novel democratic or semi-democratic constitutions call for prominent assembly-halls, chambers for state officials, and lawcourts. Less architecturally prominent but much more important in reality, however, was the main square of the city, the *agora*, which during this era was the space where public debate gave increasing scope to non-aristocratic political participation. Already present by the start of the Archaic era in the poetry of Homer and Hesiod, the agora housed an open-air assembly presided over by the *basileis* and other elders, where it is likely the rest of the citizens could merely register approval or disapproval (Hall 2007). It also formed an arena for the public dispensing of the law. Possibly at Late Geometric Zagora and Emborio open places by shrines mark an early agora, but archaeologically it is at late eighth-century Dreros on Crete and late seventh/early sixth-century Megara Hyblaea and Metapontum in Southern Italy where built structures seem more clearly to mark out such a central facility. Although at Athens the Classical agora was formally laid out with early public buildings in the late sixth century, textual and archaeological evidence suggest it replaced an earlier agora northeast of the Acropolis. But agoras also mark lively commerce, and their enhancement symbolizes the rise of a meritocratic (self-made) class in the polis as against the traditional dominance of aristocratic privilege.

In Morris's highly influential model (2000), the Archaic era is a political and intellectual battleground between polis factions: one supports an "elitist" international culture, the other advocates a "middling," internalized civic society. This conflict reflects the declining role of aristocrats and the rising power of the hoplite middle class. Mostly the latter wins out, marking Runciman's (1982) transition from a proto-state to a full-state community: segmentary, unstable control by competing *basileis* yields to the power of the assembly and lawcourts, in which greater consensus amongst all free citizens becomes possible, associated with written laws and edicts.

Systematic surveys of Aegean burial customs in Archaic times are lacking and scholars have relied heavily on the evidence from Athens and Argos. The Late Geometric revolution, when all classes gained entry to the city's cemeteries (Morris 1987), was followed slightly later by the disappearance of weapon burials and decreasing signs of wealth differentiation in grave goods. In the EIA-Geometric centuries, weapon graves (e.g., at Athens, Argos, Eretria) mark the elite amongst the privileged males receiving burial, but this probably reflects a distinction of class in burial rather than a limitation in access to weapons amongst the middle to lower classes (van Wees 1998). In these towns and more widely across South-Central Greece, the disappearance of weapons in graves at the turn of the Archaic era marks a watershed toward a civil society typical of the city-state, but in contrast the survival of the custom in more peripheral regions of the Aegean (such as at Knossos in Crete), demonstrates a conservatism in society manifested in other prominent ways. In parallel, from the seventh century most city-states banish burials, with rare exceptions, to outside the town, where they form communal, socially-mixed blocks, also seen as a sign of the victory of the "middling" mentality and civic solidarity (Morris 2000).

Unsurprisingly, since Archaic society remained controlled by an aristocracy, rising wealth and foreign inspiration encouraged the adoption of new status funerary display: tombs decorated with reliefs and inscriptions, or marked by the even more prestigious freestanding sculptures. However their scale declines by Classical times, reflecting the polis ethos, which condemned ostentation from the economically privileged (or maybe from the fear that the commercially active middle class could compete as *nouveaux riches*). In Archaic times, then, aristocrats and wealthier middle-class citizens could distinguish their graves, through tomb monuments of a "heroic" idealizing character, from surrounding lower-class burials, and through differential grave gifts, although significantly burial-wealth will progressively decline in city-states. A new city foundation, or the association of a particular clan with the emergence of a city-state, provided opportunities for underlining status, when a dominant family might receive a burial plot within the town. Here ancestor cults could be practiced communally to the "heroic" founders (as at Eretria). Nonetheless, the increasing disappearance of warrior burials signifies the city-state's role in the monopoly of force. Military equipment will now appear in civic contexts as spoils of communal war dedicated in the city's temples or in an international (Panhellenic) sanctuary. In a like manner, a reorientation from private to public conspicuous consumption is marked in the way that some bronze feasting-tripods are in Archaic and later times dedicated to temples by the citizen-body as well as by private members of the community. Nonetheless visitors would easily have distinguished the pottery dedications of ordinary folk from the valuable military equipment and prestigious bronze vessels presented by, and labeled as from, the rich (Hall 2007). Moreover in general, Archaic communities, now well represented in the symbolic sphere in their own right, still tolerated visible signs of the aristocrats when they represented "just" judges and politicians seeking the common good, as well as "heroic" warriors (Crielaard 1998).

Extramural and Panhellenic Sanctuaries

The centrality, literal and figurative, of the main sanctuary in each city-state or town for the self-definition of the new built-up community, is only part of religion's role in identifying city-state distinctiveness vis-à-vis other Greek states. We have seen that the "Normalpolis" and even more so, the Megalopolis, arose through assimilating surrounding villages and sometimes other proto-poleis into its territory. The identities of these formerly autonomous centers, forged through older cults, now required symbolic incorporation into the refocused sacred landscape radiating out from the new polis center. The city of Argos lay on the other side of the rich Argos Plain from the great sanctuary of Hera at the Argive Heraion, whilst a major cult of Demeter lay at Eleusis on the western border of Athens' territory. In both cases, sacred processions from the urban center to these satellite centers marked the possessive assertion of the chief regional city to spiritual (and potentially political) power which such older cult centers might lay claim to (Bintliff 1977, De Polignac 1995).

There were also "Panhellenic" (for all the Greeks) religious centers outside state boundaries which increasingly provided "international" theaters of display for city-state identities. The well-known, plus far more numerous little-known, interstate sanctuaries appear to have begun as centers of local communal

worship during the EIA, with occasional Mycenaean cult origins (for example at Epidauros). With population rise and landscape infill across large areas of the Southern Aegean and islands in the LG-Archaic eras, there was a proliferation of local and regional cult centers, and the more renowned progressively attracted worshippers from distant towns and villages. Legend accorded a remote origin for classic sanctuaries such as Olympia, with the first official games dated to 776 BC. Archaeological evidence for EIA ritual activity at such cult places reveals open-air sacrificial altars and deposits of votives left by worshippers. Temples and associated building complexes to service larger numbers of visitors are a later development, mostly a feature of the Archaic period, but the larger centers (Figure 9.4) are continuously extended throughout Classical Greek, Hellenistic, and Roman Imperial times to create sacred complexes both stupendous in their surviving major monuments, and at the same time for us today, bewildering ruin-fields of loose or stacked architectural fragments.

These sanctuaries seemingly began as religious and social foci for their immediate surrounding settlements. Arising within a stratified society, local elite families held control over ceremonial. Early dedications include imagery of horse- and chariot-riding, prototypically aristocratic sports.

Whether cult was always associated with games and other competitive performances, as claimed by ancient tradition, is unclear, but at Olympia significantly legend told how the Games originated with the funeral games for the mythical hero Pelops, whose tomb was believed to lie at the locality. Minor Bronze Age activity at the site has been documented, including an Early Bronze Age ritual tumulus which could have been the kind of monument encouraging later myths of heroes buried at the sanctuary. Significant cult activity begins here in the ninth century, whilst dedications only really take off in the eighth century.

Why did many such religious foci become centers for regional and interregional cult and games? A reputation for oracular divination (Delphi), or potent contact with the gods, could prompt more distant visitors to travel to them for worship. But during the

Figure 9.4 Reconstruction of the Panhellenic sanctuary at Delphi in about 160 AD.
Model by Hans Schleif, scale 1:200. General view showing Temple of Apollo and Theater from the south. Metropolitan Museum of Art, New York. Dodge Fund, 1930 (30.141.2). Photo © 2011 Metropolitan Museum of Art/Art Resource/Scala, Florence.

period 800–500 BC the elites of Geometric-Archaic society appear to have aspired self-consciously to "heroic" values, in which display rivalry was a central feature of elite reputation; this was not only served by warfare and colonial foundation, but also through temple construction and competitive appearances at interstate sanctuaries. Here prestigious dedications and monument building went hand-in-hand with striving for victory in those athletic or cultural competitions which were intimately associated with the worship of resident divinities. The rich elite not only competed against each other in acts of manly prowess, but were also able to gain international honor as sponsors of charioteers. On a more positive note, interstate oracles became a major force in polis decisions regarding internal and external affairs, and served to create a sense of shared values and norms

between the hundreds of emergent city-states (Snodgrass 1986).

Two further features of interest are worth mentioning. Firstly, in elite societies the role of women can be greater than in male-dominated "democratic" polities, as they form vital links in marriage and property networks. Thus it was possible for Archaic-era poetesses to perform at public competitive festivals. If tradition is correct, the Tanagra poet Corinna outperformed her male rival Pindar from Thebes in late Archaic or earliest Classical times. Secondly, although leisure for training was a natural privilege of the rich, giving them the advantage in athletic competitions, non-elites could with more success enter the musical and literary contests which were held at the same time. The poet Hesiod, a middle-class farmer, developed his literary gifts whilst shepherding on his native

Mount Helicon, but boasted of winning at regional competitions.

The rise of the middle class, intimately connected to the new dominance of the city-state over large parts of Greece, makes Hesiod an early harbinger of wider changes in the participants at Panhellenic games. As the communal focus shifted during Archaic times toward the city as a community, polis identity was affirmed through its finest young men bringing glory to their home-states through competing at the many interstate games. Intense rivalry in intercity competitions was another facet to the increasingly aggressive stance poleis took to their neighbors and rivals over the control of territory and trade opportunities, fostered by the introverted "corporate community" ethos of the Greek city-state. The view that interstate games were "war minus the shooting" (Spivey 2004) is underlined by the clear overlap between military training and competitive athletics in the Greek city-states. The centrality of the gymnasium for cultivation of male citizen fitness and male citizen bonding not only strengthened the "male club" which was the basis of polis life, but prepared the same male community for the regular interstate warfare which characterized Aegean life during the Archaic to Classical eras. There were even explicit links in events such as foot races in armor.

Expanding Horizons

So far we have described remarkable internal processes within the Aegean, in which the scattered, low-density settlements of the Iron Age were transformed through demographic and political change, between 800 and 500 BC, into a vibrant world of city-states, territorial states, and regional federations of towns and villages. Unsurprisingly these changes were increasingly associated with a revival of intensive cultural and commercial contacts both within the Aegean, but more significantly with peoples and landscapes elsewhere in the Mediterranean and additionally in the Black Sea coastlands.

We should first recall that Greece has never been a homogeneous country, geographically to be sure, but equally economically, demographically, culturally or ethnically. We have focused hitherto on the heartland

of Classical states in the Southern Mainland, and the Cycladic Islands adjacent to their east, based on historic sources, urban excavations, and regional field surveys. In this wide zone of Greece, urban and rural demographic takeoff and the associated proliferation of city-states and a rich artistic culture, are well developed during this key period of Late Geometric to Archaic times, but reach their greatest flourishing during the Classical fifth to fourth centuries BC (Bintliff 1997b). The key states in this early takeoff (Figure 9.5) include Athens, Corinth, Argos, Sparta, the Boeotian federation, and several Cycladic islands. The major players in Greek history throughout these centuries are exactly this group of named states. A review of developments in wider arcs beyond this heartland reveals a "wave-effect," with increasingly later takeoff chronologies for rural and urban population climax development in Crete and in Western and Northern Greece.

This pattern corresponds, intriguingly, to a power-shift over the same period. If the Southeastern "heartland" cities are the key players in Aegean politics from the eighth through early fourth centuries BC, they are then replaced by the emergent Northern Greek powers (Macedon, Aetolia, Epirus) in the final Classical and then the Hellenistic centuries (from the later fourth to second centuries BC). Crete, though not exercising wider military or political power within the Aegean, also emerges from political obscurity and an underdeveloped economy and demography toward the end of this latter period. If we focus on the many factors relevant to comprehending this regional diversity in growth, a combination of general (including geographical) circumstances, allied with unique historical processes, is the closest we can get to "explanation." I consider it unlikely, on present evidence, however, that external contacts were the central component in the precocious rise of the Southeastern states.

Nonetheless, external contacts played a significant role in the culture and economy of the rising states of Archaic Greece. After the limited external commerce of EIA Greece, it picks up dramatically from LG onwards, so that the early Archaic period is heavily enmeshed into the economic and cultural world of the more advanced states of the East Mediterranean, producing the "Orientalist" character of seventh-century cultural styles in Southern Greece.

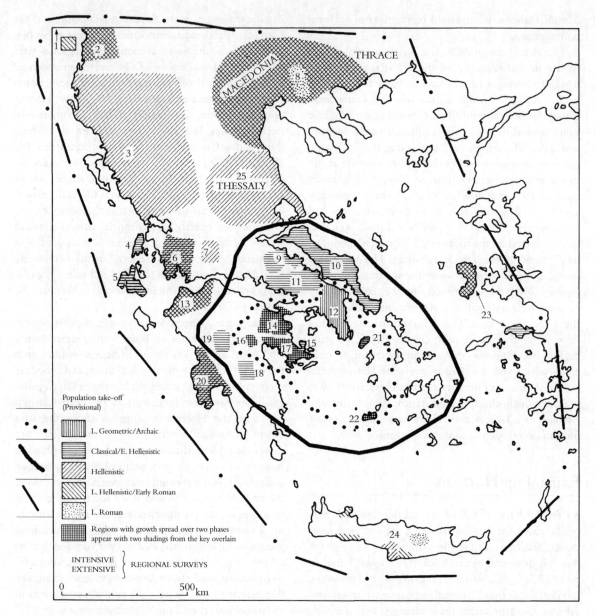

Figure 9.5 Waves of population and urbanization over time in the Aegean, from intensive and extensive survey data. J.L. Bintliff, "Regional survey, demography, and the rise of complex societies in the Ancient Aegean: Core–periphery, Neo-Malthusian, and other interpretive models." *Journal of Field Archaeology* 24 (1997), 1–38, Figure 10, revised.

Trade and Colonization

Thus the opening-up of the Aegean to the wider world was both an internal and external dynamic, a process in which the Greeks became far more active participants in Mediterranean life. The Aegean with its burgeoning population, growing surpluses in food and raw materials, and an expanding market potential for exotic luxury products, was ripe for exploitation by the enterprising merchant city-states of Phoenicia (modern coastal Syria and Lebanon), and to a far lesser extent the more introverted Egyptian state. Internally, the aristocratic society of the Aegean emulated the lifestyles of urban elites in these exotic regions and in the powerful native kingdom of Lydia in Western Anatolia, thereby enhancing Aegean-elite distinctiveness from local populations of lesser status, through acquiring and displaying in public their imported jewelry, clothes, tableware, and furniture. The close links between external trade and the upper class rests both on their control of wealth and also on the likelihood that most Aegean merchant ships venturing abroad were owned by the basileis class as a new form of wealth creation (Snodgrass 1980). This expanded on the elite's traditional reliance on landed estates and the patronage of regional craft populations. Importantly, Aegean commercial sailing not only responded to the rise of Levantine merchant arrivals by heading also toward Eastern markets, but was already from the LG era exploring the Central and West Mediterranean and the Black Sea, where less developed markets than the Aegean were to be found.

In a core–periphery model (Sherratt and Sherratt 1993), if Greece remained a subsidiary partner during this era to more advanced economies in the Near East, it could form a secondary core for the exploitation of economies to the North and West of the Aegean which were far less developed than itself. This relationship between the complex poleis of the Southern Aegean and indigenous tribal societies in Southern Italy and the Black Sea, was a mirror to the internal core–periphery relationships which the South Aegean states were establishing at the same period in the Mainland of Northern Greece (Bintliff 1997b). Generally, the core–periphery model sees core economies trading finished high-status goods, especially luxuries and military technology, for raw materials from the periphery (agricultural surpluses, metals, slaves).

At a certain point, successful commercial exchanges encouraged both Greek trading settlements at entrepôt points and genuine colonies. Generally, the nature of such communities reflects the level of political complexity of the exotic society into which Greeks inserted themselves. Thus the Etruscan city-states of North-Central Italy possessed a culture as elaborate as the states of the Archaic Southern Aegean, so that only formal entrepôts in delimited locations seem to have

been permitted, in order to encourage Etruscan trade with both Greek and Phoenician merchants and craftspeople. In Egypt a similar formal arrangement was achieved at the Nile-Delta port of Naucratis under the final native Egyptian dynasties before that country became incorporated into the Persian Empire during the course of the sixth century BC.

Till relatively recently, the much more widespread creation of autonomous Greek colonies outside of the Southern Aegean, a key feature of the LG-Archaic era (ca. 800–500 BC) (Figure 9.6), was considered to be a comparable phenomenon to global colonial expansion emanating from Western Europe in the sixteenth to nineteenth centuries AD. In this Early Modern period the home state encouraged merchants and potential commercial estate-developers to settle "undeveloped" countries, supporting such settlements militarily and through formal treaties with native societies, with the prime aim of increasing the supply of raw materials and manpower for European states, whilst creating vastly increased markets for European manufactured goods. At the same time, agricultural settlers from these European homelands, in part due to population pressure, took over fertile areas of undeveloped countries through violence, treaty or purchase, both to support a new life abroad under the protective arm of the homeland, and to develop commercial exports.

One of the first recorded Greek colonies abroad, at Pithecoussai near Naples, seems to fit this recent colonial model: a small rocky island (Ischia) was settled by a large population of Greeks from various homeland states (and other ethnic groups, including Phoenicians), argued to be offshore traders negotiating for the metal ores and other products of the indigenous early state societies of Central Italy. Shortly afterwards this entrepôt is replaced by a Greek colonial urban settlement at Cumae on the mainland, which, however, rapidly develops into a prosperous agricultural city on the model of Aegean poleis.

Actually the Early Modern parallels are problematic in both political and economic terms (Antonaccio 2007, Tsetskhladze 2006). Colonial Greek cities usually did not recognize their dependence on their mother-city. Indeed it was customary for colonies to be made up of settlers from various states; examples show that colonies could go to war with their founder-city. Secondly, Greek colonies were almost all intended to function like autonomous Aegean city-states, whose

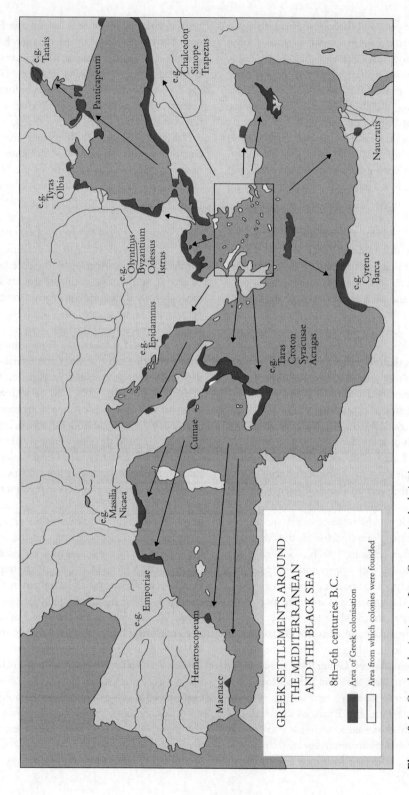

Figure 9.6 Greek colonization in Late Geometric–Archaic times.
A. A. M. van der Heyden, *Atlas van de antieke wereld*. Amsterdam 1958, Map 3.

populations farmed and herded, for the most part to feed themselves and supply regional rather than inter-regional markets, with a minor role for merchants, manufacturers, and export-oriented production. Moreover, both in the Black Sea and in Southern Italy it is increasingly suggested that local populations formed a significant component in the demography of "colonial" settlements. Thirdly, the evidence indicates that state-organized directional trade was highly uncommon, with various shippers from many states allowed to circulate goods from or to the same polis or ethnos.

This deconstruction of a commercial impetus might turn our attention to a rival scholarly opinion, that Greek colonies arose from overpopulation within the flourishing Aegean Archaic city-states. The difficulty here is timescale. The peak colonial era is Late Geometric to Archaic: even in the precocious zone of rising population and town size in the Southeast Aegean (Figure 9.5), the population climaxes, from surface survey and historic population statistics, occur in the Classical fifth to fourth centuries BC. That is not to say that certain cities did not become, for a time, population machines, supplying one colony after another with the core of its adventurous citizens. Eretria on the island of Euboea, or Miletos on the west coast of Anatolia, are striking examples. Yet historic and archaeological sources indicate that the lead city relied usually on volunteer colonists from many other states, as well as from indigenous groups in the newly settled regions, to make up the necessary numbers for a viable farming community capable of defending itself from potentially hostile "natives" and (frequently) aggressive neighboring Greek (and Phoenician) colonies. Colonial cities in the Aegean, with a few exceptions (such as the small arid island of Thera), seem to have possessed underused homeland countryside in the LG-Archaic era.

So why then were so many colonies set up over an intense phase of such activity? According to Crielaard (1992–1993) the dominant aristocratic class of this era dwelt in a mental world of "heroic" dynastic achievements and the tales of earlier (Bronze Age) elite warriors immortalized in Homer's epics. With food production ensured through a dependent peasantry, elite life was competitive and aggressive. Alongside clan and inter-state warfare, an ambitious aristocrat could also consider leading part of the community abroad, where city

foundation and the domination of much larger bodies of settlers was possible, all within a framework of a dangerous and heroic expedition into relatively unknown territory. Ancient sources also describe another frequent reason: factional conflicts stimulating particular *basileis* to leave for a new settlement abroad. Often the founder elite, once deceased, were literally worshipped as demigods in a "heroon" or burial and cult place at a prominent location in the new city. Increased power and prestige may then have been a central element in the aristocratically-inspired founding of foreign colonies. For Greek cities on the west coast of Anatolia a third major reason for colonial expansion in Archaic times was oppression by foreign powers.

What, though, was the advantage for the majority, lesser-status colonists who accompanied the founding family or families? Contemporary elites depended on supportive manpower: were the aristocrats' clients obliged to participate, or given encouragement through the promise of larger estates, or allowed the choice of remaining in the homeland? Clearly volunteers from other states were offered good conditions, perhaps without dues to the rich. In all cases, there should have been relatively free use of a town building-plot and a sizeable farm in the "chora" or hinterland of the new polis, for all willing to venture on a colonial project. We can suppose nonetheless that the elite would have required the labor or surplus of the peasantry, in some undetermined way, to ensure that their larger estates and more extravagant lifestyle were sustained in the "new world."

The arrival of Near Eastern merchants in the Aegean, and the knowledge of colonial foundations by Phoenicians in the West and Central Mediterranean, had clearly opened up the conceptual horizons of the Aegean Greeks, both in terms of stimulating a Greek colonial movement, but also in terms of increasing the production and consumption of trade items (whether raw materials or artifacts). This rise of a commercial sector in the Aegean was soon to be associated with the adoption of coinage.

Coinage

Significantly, like the return of literacy, this was an invention from the East, but this time from closer to the Aegean, from an early state in non-Greek

Southwest Anatolia, sixth-century Lydia. If at first denominations were large and of precious metal, more useful for paying mercenaries or other payments by the state authorities, before long smaller bronze denominations were created, allowing, and indeed signifying for us, the use of money in everyday transactions for ordinary citizens. It is clear that marketing of products, as well as wage payments, must have become a major aspect of Archaic Greek life in town and country. This had a considerable effect on the power-structure of Archaic states. The EIA system where the elite controlled ownership of precious metal and circulated it through gift and marriage exchange was now threatened by a coinage, mainly in silver, which the city-state allowed commoners to accumulate. Coinage was dangerously meritocratic. Citizens of any class might take advantage of a more open land market and rising possibilities for additional riches through investing in industry and commerce. Self-made men with such achieved wealth could claim greater access to the political and judicial system (Kurke 1999).

It can still be claimed that coinage was essentially a Greek phenomenon in its emergence as a vital form of exchange in the ancient Mediterranean world (Howgego 1995), because the rapid spread of its production and use out of its early sixth-century creation in Lydia was purely due to its adoption in the Greek world. By 500 BC a whole series of centers in the Aegean and the Greek Western colonies were minting (Color Plate 9.1). The Persian Empire adopted the practice late from their Greek dependencies, and Italy outside the Greek colonies was very tardy in producing coins. Although a major factor in city minting was a statement of autonomy and to enable the state to pay its citizens and other employees, as well as to receive financial support in return, the general opinion supports a more radical primary reason for the precocious use in the Greek world: the occurrence in Archaic times of an economic revolution in which market activity (primarily literally in the city agora) became a central feature of life for all citizens.

The Uses of Literacy

Amongst the innovations in Archaic Greece which arose from the growing intensity of trade with the Near East was the recovery of writing. Logically, this commercial context should have encouraged an initial use for marking goods, but in fact the first examples (eighth century, LG) relate rather to poetry, and the world of the elite (Snodgrass 1980, Morris 2000). Short texts inscribed on pots relate to Homeric allusions and erotic pursuits, suggesting prestige gained by the upper classes through their ability to communicate in ways impossible for their peasantry (Stoddart and Whitley 1988). Nonetheless before long and already during the Archaic seventh century BC, symptomatic of the changing politics of the South Aegean city-states, a very different use of literacy appears, inscribed lawcodes. The public display of laws was a fundamental feature of the rights of all citizens within the polis to equal treatment before the law, although our earliest autobiographical authority, the poet Hesiod, reminds us that the "bribe-eating basileis" strive to pervert that principle in his city-state around 700 BC. Yet codified and inscribed laws, usually in sacred but public spaces, mark a clear victory for civic values over the power of individual aristocrats, and set a precedent which in some states encouraged further moves toward democracy (Hölkeskamp 1992, 1994). Also as the Archaic era developed, writing spread into much wider use, weakening its value as a coded communication for elite distinctiveness, although most authorities argue that even Classical Greece remained essentially an oral culture, with literacy being confined to perhaps as little as 10 percent of the population (Whitley 1997).

References

Antonaccio, C. (2007). "Colonization: Greece on the move, 900–480." In H. A. Shapiro (ed.), *Archaic Greece*. Cambridge: Cambridge University Press, 201–224.

Bintliff, J. L. (1977). *Natural Environment and Human Settlement in Prehistoric Greece*. 2 vols. Oxford: BAR Supplementary Series 28.

Bintliff, J. L. (1997a). "Further considerations on the population of ancient Boeotia." In J. L. Bintliff (ed.), *Recent Developments in the History and Archaeology of Central Greece*. Oxford: BAR Int. Series 666, 231–252.

Bintliff, J. L. (1997b). "Regional survey, demography, and the rise of complex societies in the Ancient Aegean: Core–periphery, Neo-Malthusian, and other interpretive models." *Journal of Field Archaeology* 24, 1–38.

Burford, A. (1993). *Land and Labor in the Greek World*. Baltimore: Johns Hopkins University Press.

Crielaard, J.-P. (1992–1993). "How the West was won: Euboeans vs. Phoenicians." *Hamburger Beiträge zur Archäologie* 19/20, 235–260.

Crielaard, J.-P. (1998). "Cult and death in early 7th-century Euboea. The aristocracy and the polis." In S. Marchegay, M.-T. Le Dinahet, and J.-F. Salles (eds.), *Nécropoles et Pouvoir*. Paris: De Boccard, 43–58.

Crielaard, J.-P. (2009). "Cities." In K. Raaflaub and H. van Wees (eds.), *A Companion to Archaic Greece*. Oxford: Blackwell, 349–372.

De Polignac, F. (1995). *Cults, Territory, and the Origins of the Greek City-State*. Chicago: University of Chicago Press.

Dickinson, O. T. P. K. (2006). *The Aegean from Bronze Age to Iron Age*. London: Routledge.

Foxhall, L. (2003). "Cultures, landscapes and identities in the Mediterranean world." *Mediterranean Historical Review* 18(2), 75–92.

Hall, J. M. (1997). *Ethnic Identity in Greek Antiquity*. Cambridge: Cambridge University Press.

Hall, J. M. (2004). *Hellenicity. Between Ethnicity and Culture*. Chicago: University of Chicago Press.

Hall, J. M. (2007). "Polis, community, and ethnic identity." In H. A. Shapiro (ed.), *Archaic Greece*. Cambridge: Cambridge University Press, 40–60.

Hölkeskamp, K.-J. (1992). "Arbitrators, lawgivers and the 'codification of law' in Archaic Greece." *Metis* 7(1–2), 49–81.

Hölkeskamp, K.-J. (1994). "Tempel, Agora und Alphabet." In H.-J. Gehrke (ed.), *Rechtskodifizierung und soziale Normen im interkulturellen Vergleich*. Tübingen: Günter Narr Verlag, 135–164.

Howgego, C. (1995). *Ancient History from Coins*. London: Routledge.

Jameson, M. H. (1977–1978). "Agriculture and slavery in Classical Athens." *Classical Journal* 73(2), 122–145.

Jameson, M. H. (1992). "Agricultural labour in Ancient Greece." In B. Wells (ed.), *Agriculture in Ancient Greece*. Stockholm: Paul Åström, 135–146.

Kurke, L. (1999). *Coins, Bodies, Games and Gold*. Princeton: Princeton University Press.

Luraghi, N. (2002). "Becoming Messenian." *Journal of Hellenic Studies* 122, 45–69.

McInerney, J. (1999). *The Folds of Parnassos. Land and Ethnicity in Ancient Phokis*. Austin: University of Texas Press.

Mazarakis-Ainian, A. (1997). *From Rulers' Dwellings to Temples*. Jonsered: Paul Åström.

Morris, I. (1987). *Burial and Ancient Society. The Rise of the Greek City-State*. Cambridge: Cambridge University Press.

Morris, I. (2000). *Archaeology as Cultural History*. Oxford: Blackwell.

Osborne, R. (1996). *Greece in the Making 1200–479*. London: Routledge.

Raaflaub, K. A. (1997). "Soldiers, citizens and the evolution of the early Greek *polis*." In L. G. Mitchell and P. J. Rhodes (eds.), *The Development of the Polis in Archaic Greece*. London: Routledge, 49–59.

Runciman, W. G. (1982). "Origins of states: The case of Archaic Greece." *Comparative Studies in Society and History* 24, 351–377.

Sherratt, S. and A. Sherratt (1993). "The growth of the Mediterranean economy in the early first millennium BC." *World Archaeology* 24(3), 361–378.

Snodgrass, A. M. (1980). *Archaic Greece: The Age of Experiment*. London: Dent.

Snodgrass, A. (1986). "Interaction by design: The Greek city state." In C. Renfrew and J. F. Cherry (eds.), *Peer Polity Interaction and Socio-Political Change*. Cambridge: Cambridge University Press, 47–58.

Snodgrass, A. M. (1993). "The 'hoplite reform' revisited." *Dialogues d'Histoire Ancienne* 19, 47–61.

Spivey, N. (2004). *The Ancient Olympics: A History*. Oxford: Oxford University Press.

Stoddart, S. and J. Whitley (1988). "The social context of literacy in Archaic Greece and Etruria." *Antiquity* 62, 761–772.

Tak, H. (1990). "Longing for local identity: Intervillage relations in an Italian town." *Anthropological Quarterly* 63, 90–100.

Tsetskhladze, G. R. (2006). "Revisiting ancient Greek colonisation." In G. R. Tsetskhladze (ed.), *Greek Colonisation. An Account of Greek Colonies and Other Settlements Overseas*. Leiden: Brill, 23–83.

van Wees, H. (1998). "Greeks bearing arms. The state, the leisure class, and the display of weapons in Archaic Greece." In N. Fisher and H. van Wees (eds.), *Archaic Greece: New Approaches and New Evidence*. London: Duckworth, 333–378.

van Wees, H. (1999). "The mafia of early Greece." In K. Hopwood (ed.), *Organised Crime in Antiquity*. London: Duckworth, 1–51.

Whitley, J. (1997). "Cretan laws and Cretan literacy." *American Journal of Archaeology* 101, 635–661.

Further Reading

Kirsten, E. (1956). *Die griechische Polis als historisch-geographisches Problem des Mittelmeerraumes*. Bonn: Colloqium Geographicum 5.

Morgan, C. A. (2003). *Early Greek States Beyond the Polis*. London: Routledge.

10

The Built Environment, Symbolic Material Culture, and Society in Archaic Greece

The Revival of Monumental Figural Art

Beginning in the eighth and increasing in the seventh century BC, the previous rarity of human figured art yields to a proliferation of human and animal figures on a large scale, and in a range of media, from terracotta through wood and ivory to carved stone. The inspiration is clearly emulation of Levantine art, primarily from the Syro-Phoenician coastlands (especially for female statues, see Color Plate 12.1b), but Egyptian influence is equally recognizable (for male statues, see Figure 10.1 left) (See Text Box).

the stance

The Emulation of Levantine Art

During the Archaic era the stylized formality of these oriental sources (from our Western cultural bias, appearing rigid), was replaced by increasing naturalism and individualism (see Figure 10.1 right). There arises a new tradition of large-scale freestanding carved stone art which continues into the earliest Classical era. The idealized standing nude young males (*kouroi*), and richly-clothed young women (*korai*) are found at sanctuaries and cemeteries throughout the Mainland and South Aegean islands, although other poses are represented (seated figures, horsemen). Debate continues on what they represent: divinities, dedicatees, or memorialized dead. Few have inscriptions and context is ambiguous, since temple or cemetery locations do not pinpoint any one of these possible interpretations. Current views suggest that a fixed reading of these statues is erroneous: they represent an idealized young person, an appropriate image for a god or goddess, or of a praiseworthy deceased person, or of a devout dedicator of such an artwork (Fullerton 2000). Because the Greeks conceived of their divinities as beautiful humans, and perfect humans to be physically godlike, such ambivalence served its purpose. *like imago dei*

For the most part the commissioning of such prestigious sculptures (often life-size, some more than 3 meters tall), was the privilege of rich aristocrats, but sometimes a commoner might muster the considerable cost (one late sixth-century kore found on the Athenian Acropolis was dedicated by

the one in NY is a grave-marker of an Athenian Aristocrat

The Complete Archaeology of Greece: From Hunter-Gatherers to the 20th Century AD, First Edition. John Bintliff.
© 2012 John Bintliff. Published 2012 by Blackwell Publishing Ltd.

Figure 10.1   The development of male kouros statues from Early to Late Archaic times.
Colossal marble kouros from Cape Sounion (left). © De Agostini/SuperStock. Funerary kouros of Kroisos,
Paros marble, ca. 525 BC, from Anavyssos (right). © The Art Archive/National Archaeological Museum Athens/Gianni
Dagli Orti.

a potter). Generally, however, these imposing and once brightly-painted statues reminded local communities of the pronounced status differences characterizing the Archaic era.

The striking contrast between clothed maiden and naked youth is a gender distinction typical for Greek art until late Classical times. Significantly, the sculptural styles being emulated tend either to have clothed males and females or partially unclothed females (Egypt), or unclothed females and clothed males (the Levant). Bonnet and Pirenne-Delforge (2004) argue persuasively that the naked female in Near Eastern iconography does not indicate female emancipation in terms of political, economic or social status, but neither is she a mere sex object for male titillation. A more complex association is being affirmed, that of the fundamental life-giving power of female sexuality and reproduction, also directly related to the fertility of crops and animals: the life-force. As a distinct power, either as a mortal woman or as a goddess, the naked female can also appear as a suitable companion to warrior gods and heroes.

Interestingly, in some of the oldest, seventh-century examples of Greek appropriation of Levantine sculptural art, especially in the Cretan "Daedalic" style, female representations occur with this symbolism, including the attention being drawn by the figure to her breasts or womb. The association here with representations of heroized armed males is interpreted as channeling the life-force of woman into the making of citizen-soldiers. Yet as this Greek version of the style evolves, quite rapidly the naked female is accompanied, and then replaced, by clothed females. The male hero, at first clothed or naked, will become typically naked. These shifts in emphasis appear to demarcate the progressive marginalization of women in the polis-society of the Archaic to Classical South Aegean, neutralizing their potential power, whilst elevating masculine "heroic beauty." The polis as a "male club" is emerging symbolically.

Orientalizing and Orientalism

Greece's cultural and economic fascination with the more complex cultures of the Near East and Egypt, manifested in the widespread adoption of the alphabet, commercial links, a remarkable amount of mythology, and the revival of large-scale artworks, is so marked that the Archaic seventh century BC is termed "Orientalizing." Unsurprisingly the most active center is the commercial city of Corinth. It produced a colorful, richly-decorated ceramic style in this phase, "Proto-Corinthian" (Figure 10.2). Responding to the many Oriental trade and gift items which came to Greece during the "Late Geometric Renaissance" and the early Archaic, Corinth's pottery was traded back all over the Levant and also into the West Mediterranean, especially forms such as the *aryballos* for scented olive oil (Figure 10.2). Nonetheless Proto-Corinthian vases are covered with images largely derived from the Near East (especially an obsession with plant and animal motifs, notably monsters), even if the bands of design reflect local Geometric traditions.

Analyzing the iconography of Proto-Corinthian vases, Shanks (1993, 1999) found a selective concern for certain images and the neglect of others. Women are very rare, whilst scenes of aggression are remarkably common: predator animals hunt other animals, heroes fight dangerous animals or monsters, and men fight other men. The ethos represented reflects a male-centered polis society where citizen aggression is encouraged, brutalizing young men to form their bodies and minds as killing-machines, ready to take their place in the aristocratic raiding party and later the hoplite phalanx, whenever their clan, or later their polis, demands.

Till recently Oriental influences on the formation of Greek culture were downplayed as opportune interventions, serving merely to stimulate the far richer culture of Classical Greece. Martin Bernal, however, in his influential *Black Athena* volumes (1987, 1991), argued that Classical scholars had systematically suppressed the degree to which Archaic Greece arose from intellectual, cultural, technical, and even ethnic inputs from Egypt and the Near East. They did this to promote the Western ideal that modern civilization

Figure 10.2 Proto-Corinthian ceramic, fine ware from the final eighth to seventh centuries BC.
© Trustees of the British Museum.

developed in Europe out of Greek and then Roman culture, owing nothing significant to the stagnant backwaters of Middle Eastern traditions. Eighteenth- to early twentieth-century AD imperial and colonial agendas favored the view that Africa and the Middle East were from time immemorial the homes of peoples destined to be ruled by despots and lacking the spirit of technical and intellectual progress. Such concepts as democracy, independent thought, and innovation could only arise in the advanced city-state world of Athens. Bernal's ideas echo Edward Said's analysis of the West's negative views of the "eternal stagnation of the East" in his classic study *Orientalism* (1980), a widely accepted critique of Western scholarship regarding the Near and Far East since the eighteenth century AD.

Before *Black Athena*, Burkert's *The Orientalizing Revolution* (1992: first published in German in 1984) had anticipated this view. Subsequent to it, several major figures have reacted positively to the reorientation of Classical culture (Morris 2004), to show how many of Bernal's views are well-founded, and how many cannot be sustained, or are just downright wrong (such as his confusion between Sub-Saharan populations and the people of ancient Egypt, hence the "Black Athena," cf. Ray 1997). In particular, (Sarah) Morris (1992) and West (1997) have focused on the great debt that early historic Greece owed in religion, myth, and artistic production to the Near East. Archaic elites emulated more complex societies and lifestyles to the East, also including the neighboring non-Greek kingdom of Lydia, partly to dissociate themselves from the culture of their own clients and peasantry.

As for the context of Orientalizing influence, EIA settlements in the Aegean, as we have seen in Chapter 8, were in touch with commercial and probably diplomatic initiatives from the Levant and Cyprus by the tenth century BC. It is argued that Aegean trade partners were a peripheral market for Phoenician and other Near Eastern merchants and colonizers till the end of Geometric times, with Greeks in a relatively passive role. Eastern products were often obtained through diplomatic gift exchange, in which prestige objects from the East were often "antiques" valued for their exoticism in the Aegean. However, as these links grew and diversified, we have more evidence for proactive Greek colonial and merchant activities beyond the Aegean, especially in the LG phase. By the early Archaic, Greeks abroad were regularly encountering major architectural and sculptural complexes in the East Mediterranean and undergoing other forms of cultural absorption. Did the revival of stone monuments, large-scale art forms, and literature represent enthusiastic emulation of these inspiring contacts? Or did such encounters bring the desire to bring into more permanent form lost local Aegean Dark Age achievements in wood or ivory, in the same way as the ground plan of the Greek Classical stone temple is fundamentally a metamorphosis of its Lefkandi-class ancestor in purely organic materials? At the very least, awareness of Phoenician trading systems and colonies throughout the Mediterranean surely acted as a model for the adventurous expansion of Aegean ships and settlers in the final Geometric-Archaic centuries, inevitably bringing the potential for competition and conflict over trading

opportunities and colonial territory, although this was to become highly visible only in the sixth to fifth centuries.

Ceramic Art in Later Archaic Times

By the last third of the seventh century BC, Corinthian fine ware production has shifted toward the "Black-Figure" (BF) style (Figure 10.3), where the objects portrayed are silhouetted in glossy black paint against the bright yellow-orange of the natural color of the pot's clay. Details are picked out in white or with incisions. Similar BF wares were then produced in other city-states during the late Archaic era of the sixth century, notably in Athens, where the boom in urban and rural population, including many resident aliens specializing in trade and craft production, reflected the

Figure 10.3 Black-Figure Attic vase, typical fine ware from the late sixth to early fifth centuries BC.
Museum of Fine Arts, Boston/Henry Lillie Pierce Fund/ The Bridgeman Art Library.

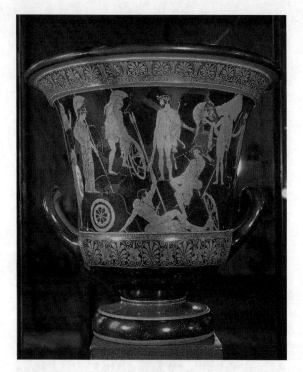

Figure 10.4 Red-Figure Attic calyx krater depicting Hercules wearing a laurel wreath with Athena and other Greek heroes, typical fine ware from the fifth to fourth centuries BC.
Niobid Painter (ca. 475–450 BC). Louvre, Paris/The Bridgeman Art Library.

connoisseurship by Beazley and later Boardman (Whitley 2001). Although RF wares are widely produced, Athens in the Classical centuries dominates the extra-Aegean market and also supplies a significant minority of RF wares to other Aegean states, to be used alongside their own versions.

On a lesser scale, white-background wares now appear with similar subtle scenes in varied color, especially for burial use and the female boudoir, such usage reflecting their more fragile surface decoration.

Dress Codes and the Rise of Civil Society

In the EIA "might was right" for the armed retinues of the *basileis*. With the rise of the integrated *polis*-state over large zones of the Archaic Aegean we expect evidence for Weber's definition of "the state," that it monopolizes the use of force. From figural representations on Archaic vases (van Wees 1998) disarmament develops slowly. In early Archaic, swords and spears remain typical dress for the elite household and its factious clans, but in the final Archaic period these and the open dress allowing rapid deployment of such weapons yield to a tight-fitting male dress copied from the Near East, linked to the disappearance of the sword. As the sixth century closes, the spear is replaced by a walking-stick, available to fend off vagrants, but no longer a serious weapon. Carrying the staff also makes plain that the owner is no artisan, needing hands free for labor, but a man about town, with wealth and leisure to conduct social and political affairs or attend the gymnasium. There is even a brief appearance of what later would be seen as "effeminate" Oriental fashion, the male parasol. At the same time, scenes of elite dining, which begin in Archaic times with a series of armor and weapons suspended above the diners, shift by early Classical times to a single set of military equipment, symbolizing the economic and political status of the head of family as a member of the middle or upper citizen class (the hoplite, having sufficient income to own the heavy equipment required of the citizen foot soldier in a typical Greek city-state). This symbolizes the transformation from private clan feuding to service for the community.

deliberate stimulus to the economy given by the Peisistratid dictatorship.

A further development in ceramic figure-painting attained an unparalleled sophistication in Athens in the final decades of the sixth century, lasting in popularity as a Mediterranean-wide export ware into the fourth century or earliest Hellenistic era: Red-Figure (RF) ceramics (Figure 10.4). Now the black gloss paint is confined to the non-figural areas as background for the representations, which are left in the natural red-brown clay color, but with details outlined with black and other fine paint lines. This transformation allows far greater refinement of portrayal, encouraging artists to develop personal styles of extraordinary beauty and expression. Individual examples of a particular artist's or workshop's output have been recognized through distinctive artistic traits in elaborate

Tripods

Whilst impressive three-legged bronze cauldrons ("tripods") formed a focus for elite feasts, gift exchange, and prestige dedications in LG–early Archaic times, a subsequent shift in their archaeological contexts and decoration marks the redirection of the city-state's population toward communal values. Ancient sources confirm that tripods could be won in athletic or artistic competitions by non-aristocratic citizens, whilst increasingly in Archaic times tripods were dedicated and displayed prominently by "the city" to honor its protective deities. Near the sanctuary of the local hero-god Ptoos, an alignment of tripods lined the road to the Boeotian city of Akraiphia, collectively dedicated by that city to express its religious identity. A number of Archaic tripods also seem to mark a civic identification when we see the former elite warrior ornament on their rims or handles replaced by unarmed youths "offering" the tripod, probably representing the collective of citizens (Papalexandrou 2005).

Nonetheless, tripods and other prestigious and expensive dedications remained a medium through which the rich and influential could remind people of their status, even in the more democratic ethos of the Classical city-state: rich sponsors of dramas or chariot-teams were entitled, even in extremely democratic Athens, to claim the tripod awarded to theater choruses or chariot-drivers, for themselves, in order to display these trophies in prominent urban locations. Just inside the pre-modern core of Athens, the Plaka, in the shadow of the Acropolis, just such a monument has survived, the fourth-century BC "choregic" victory column of Lysicrates (he subsidized the chorus of a successful drama).

Symposia and Their Aristocratic Origins

Although the chieftain's communal feast was being replaced by public feasts organized by city-state cult centers, Archaic elites retained private drinking-parties as a suitable venue for political and social networking between males of similar status. This custom, the *symposion*, probably evolved in early Archaic times as a merger of the older elite feast and emulation of Oriental dining habits. Murray has suggested (1990) that ninth-century kits of drinking equipment anticipate this culture of elite feasting, but the sharp rise in relevant ceramics and representations of symposia are a feature of the final seventh century. The distinctively Oriental contribution is for guests to recline on bed-like benches. A well-known illustration of this custom, on an early sixth-century BC Corinthian BF table-service jar (*krater*) for mixing water and wine (the central object in such drinking-parties), shows the hero Heracles dining with a king, whilst a frieze of horsemen underlines the aristocratic character of the scene. By the sixth century a whole range of drinking-cup shapes appears in Greek ceramics, to remain a very frequent find in archaeological domestic assemblages through Classical and Hellenistic times. Men-only was already becoming the norm for the guests at these formal meals, where politics, art, and literature mixed with social alliances and a form of extreme male-bonding which already produced a blatantly homosexual slant to the proceedings, enhanced by the sharing of couches by two males. Wives and daughters were becoming excluded, although the bisexual Greek male might, even if not that wealthy, pay for *demimonde* females to perform as musicians and/or sexual playthings at such gatherings. Indeed many of the first examples of the use of writing comprise love-messages or verses incised on symposium vases, generally male-to-male in character. By Classical times, however, a symposium space, the *andron*, was commonly created in the standard Greek middle-class home (Figure 12.8), in popular emulation of the elite lifestyle.

Monumental Architecture

Formal "architecture" reappeared in Greece when it was decided to invest major resources into buildings that went well beyond functionality (Tomlinson 1995). The Lefkandi structure (see Chapter 8) stood out from surrounding homes, either as the residence, or a copy of it, for persons of local distinction. In the transformation of this private monument into a communal temple, high status was being transferred to the god(dess) whose cult image was to be displayed inside

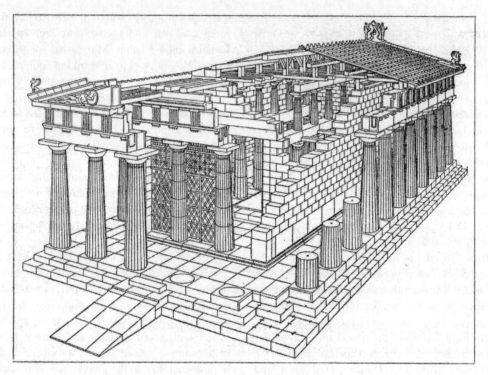

Figure 10.5   Late Archaic temple of Aphaea on the island of Aegina.
A. A. M. van der Heyden, *Atlas van de antieke wereld*. Amsterdam 1958, 30.

it, as an act of group devotion to the community's divine protector. Within the temple lay also a treasury of valuable or symbolic items dedicated to the divinity. However, the Greek climate encourages public activity to be outdoors, so that ancient Greek formal rituals took place at altars before the temple, watched and participated in by the community, who afterwards partook of the meat from the sacrificial animals in regular feasts. Once more a meaningful link is derivable back in time to communal feasting at the chief's great house, and to the prestige goods in his storeroom which evidenced his wealthy social connections, bridal gifts, and foreign exchange contacts.

During the early Archaic, temples achieve greater monumentality, through elaborate cut-stone foundations, stone superstructures for walls and roof-supporting columns, and terracotta-tiled roofs. The successful merging of the local great house with its organic architecture and the admired Egyptian and Levantine architecture, culminates in the characteristic Greek temple design (Figure 10.5). The significance of these structures, through investment in labor and materials, goes well beyond the desire of Greek cities to emulate the advanced cultures they were increasingly mixing with in the East Mediterranean and their own harbor-towns. They represent a reorientation of city-state society toward a new symbol of civic identity, the patron deity's sanctuary, for all citizens regardless of class. Furthermore, vigorous competition between poleis for land, trade opportunities, and prestige encouraged a rivalry in the size and ornamentation of temples (Snodgrass 1986). Outdoing neighboring or rival towns in the dimensions or cost of state temples spurred competitors to follow with a more impressive imitation. Tak (1990) describes similar rivalry between rural communities in Early Modern Italy, using the term "campanilismo," since rival villages try to outdo each other in the height and splendor of their prominent church bell-towers.

Panhellenic sanctuaries were equally arenas for interstate rivalry. Although their festival games were associated with a peaceable meeting of states (for the premier four-yearly Olympic festival heralds toured the Aegean announcing a cessation of interstate hostilities for its duration), less palatably those occasions were also "theaters" for chauvinistic competition and iconographic aggression. Many states dedicated small treasuries in temple form at the major interstate sanctuaries (Renfrew 1986, Snodgrass 1986), publicly displaying their sophistication and wealth, but also armor and weapons taken from campaigns against other Greek states. The treasury of Megara, ca. 510 BC, drew the viewer's attention to a recent military success over its larger neighbor Corinth (Spivey 1997): on its pediment the gods defeat a giant, whilst over this a looted shield was inscribed with the information that the victory spoils had paid for the monument.

Under the Tyrants, temple construction and its symbolic ornament introduced a more personal note to this competitiveness, as dictators embellished their towns with showpiece shrines and other public works (fountains or aqueducts), both to persuade citizens of their benevolent munificence and to impress neighboring states. In Athens Peisistratos, coming to power in 561 BC, had a long and probably benevolent rule, possibly residing on the Acropolis. Here fragments of a temple pediment may show Peisistratos uniting three regional power factions in Attica: the coastlands (waves), the plains (grain), and the hill-country (birds) (Fullerton 2000). Another pediment fragment ca. 545 BC shows Heracles, possibly adopted as propaganda for the tyrant as "strongman" (Spivey 1997). The Peisistratid Acropolis building program may represent several sacred buildings, but the central structure was one (or more) Athena temples. In the city below, this dynasty is linked to the formal layout of a new public square or Agora, with facilities for drainage, water supply, and road construction (Ammerman 1996). Traditionally, the formal presentation of plays in the Agora belongs to the same period, as does the first phase in the construction of a massive temple to Zeus to the southeast of the Acropolis, and the founding of the Dionysos temple on the Acropolis lower slope (Shapiro 2007). Finally, supporting the theory that increasing territorial control by city-states was

symbolized through their involvement in local cult foci in their dependent countryside (Bintliff 1977, De Polignac 1995), there was a major elaboration of Athens' distant cult center at Eleusis, on the western border of Attica, attributed to initiatives during the Peisistratids' reign.

We are witnessing the early stages in the characteristic physical appearance of the Classical city, a "city of images" (Bérard 1984): an urban environment where citizens are represented by, and visitors are confronted with, widespread art and architecture in the public and private sphere, which expresses the cultural aspirations and values of the city, as well as to a considerable extent those of Greek civilization in general.

Urban Plans

It is remarkable how little we actually know about ancient Greek cities, from texts or archaeology. Less than 10 percent of a recorded 1500 cities are carefully researched in the field, whilst just 50 or so have usable texts concerning aspects of their life (Whitley 2001). Athens, providing almost all the relevant ancient literary sources and archaeological attention, dominates what is written, despite it being highly abnormal as a rare giant agglomeration (Megalopolis), and imperial center.

Nonetheless the creation of the typical city plan, perhaps precociously seen in Archaic Old Smyrna (Figure 9.3), a walled community with densely-packed homes focused on an agora and a ritual complex (often on an acropolis), can be followed as we have already observed along two major trajectories (Snodgrass 1987–1989). A single Geometric-early Archaic settlement can explode into a much larger walled nucleation, or a community comprising several close hamlet-villages can coalesce through infill of the interstices. Athens and Corinth conform to the second model. At Athens (Figure 10.6) the separate burial places tied to discrete hamlets are banished to a new single urban periphery, whose border will later be marked by an early Classical city wall, whilst the associated rapid growth in population is estimated to rise from 10,000 to 20,000 (Morris 2005) across the Archaic centuries. In Corinth by the sixth century an

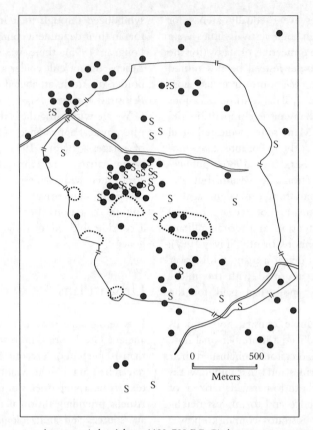

Area occupied at Athens, 1100–700 BC. Circles represent cemetery
remains; S represents settlement evidence. The continuous line marks the
course of the fifth-century wall. After Morris (1986) figures 17, 18 with
additions from *Arkhaiologikon Deltion* 34:2 (1979 [1987] 11–33).

Figure 10.6   The proto-historic dispersed plan of Athens with the later city wall.
I. Morris, "The early polis as city and state." In J. Rich and A. Wallace-Hadrill (eds.), *City and Country in the Ancient World*.
London 1991, 25–58, Figure 2. © 1991 Routledge. Reproduced by permission of Taylor & Francis Books UK.

extensive city enceinte was built around most of the
older hamlets, although infill of this vast space (4 km²)
was only gradual. Burial is also displaced, focusing on
the extramural North Cemetery.

The rise of larger, more integrated civil communities (*poleis*) caused the abandonment of previous
refuge-like clusters of houses around the residence
of chieftains (*basileis*), such as Emborio on Chios
(Figure 8.5), left around 600 BC for a more accessible
town site by the coast below.

Two forms are recognizable for Archaic town plans.
Older EIA towns grew organically. This tended to

create sprawling settlements lacking efficient communication networks, with limited open spaces. The latter were primarily reserved for an acropolis, a public
marketplace (*agora*), suburban sanctuaries, and those
important male gathering-places, gymnasia. Classical
Athens was described by contemporaries as such a
place. In contrast, when a new town was built it might
possess a regular plan from the beginning, encouraging a geometric grid for streets and house blocks. We
see this in the colonies as early as Late Geometric
times, at Megara Hyblaea in Sicily for example.
Nonetheless the Archaic period throughout the

Aegean witnessed the materialization of the polis concept in the form of defined and increasingly walled, built-up settlements of the living, formally isolated from the external *necropoleis* or "cities of the dead."

Houses remained rather randomly spaced in older-established settlements, and at the start of the Archaic era even city temples were little differentiated from the domestic structures which surrounded them. It was chiefly in the sixth century that we see the creation of small complexes of public buildings around agoras, and communal constructions such as spring-houses, water conduits, and even longer aqueducts. A rising "plantation" of inscriptions marking legal codes and polis decisions of a political, economic, and ritual character would be found at the major state sanctuaries and in the agora. Still, most Greek public events were open-air and the erection of stone buildings in Greek towns for communal affairs of various kinds did not mark the first practice of certain activities (Tomlinson 1995). More relevant is the symbolic statement being made by the polis in paying for costly monumental structures to house affairs of state.

The rights of citizens and their involvement in public affairs are materialized through the building of conspicuous lawcourts (*prytaneia*) and assembly-halls (*bouleuteria*), for example at Athens, the focus from the final Archaic period onwards of the most advanced experiments in democracy. However elsewhere a simpler solution was to hold public meetings in the courts of temples (in Crete at Dreros), or in theaters (Argos in the Peloponnese). Athens, with its final Archaic creation of a constituency-based parliamentary system, still seems in another league for democratic institutions, since assemblies were also held in its rural settlements (in the theater of Thorikos, whilst Sounion has several agoras) (Lohmann 1992). Yet these were probably provincial towns in their own right, thus functioning as mini-poleis.

Actually, after temples, the next city-center public building to appear was its most elegant, seen today in the Athenian Agora in the restored Hellenistic Stoa of Attalos. Archaic to Classical stoas were usually single-story, long, roofed structures with a deep colonnaded façade backed often by a parallel row of small rooms. The portico provided citizens with shelter or shade depending on the weather, but plenty of light and air, whilst the rooms to the rear could be deployed as shops, archives or other storerooms, galleries, or public dining-rooms. Generally stoas were placed along one side of city squares, or other public spaces where religious or secular communal gatherings took place. Eventually city agoras might be enclosed by bordering stoas on several sides. Stoas appear to originate in a sacred context, one of the earliest being the seventh-century example at the sanctuary of Hera on the island of Samos, erected for participants in religious ceremonies. Wood was normal in Archaic times, with stone constructions typical by the Classical era, probably following the earlier "lithicization" (conversion into stone) of temple colonnades (Tomlinson 1995). A less common form of public architecture was required in states with "Dorian" forms of communal male dining, where special buildings were erected in the city-center for these daily "rituals" (Haggis *et al.* 2007).

Greek stone theaters seem an even more typical urban monument, but surviving examples are generally late transformations of simpler constructions. Theatrical performances evolved from ritual dances and songs, usually originally presented in the agora. By Classical times regular excavated areas in natural hills became common, with wooden seating, and similar structures were in use for the Panhellenic Games. Stone seating and performance spaces become general only in late Classical and Hellenistic times (Tomlinson 1995). Although public celebrations of dance, music, poetry, and drama arose in Archaic times from religious festivals, the development of choruses and actors in the sixth century is associated with the city-state form of government and represented another aspect of civic debate on the nature of society which the polis stimulated (Rhodes 2003).

Over the Archaic period the "city as structure" crystallized into an integrated set of meaningful topographies: the religious, defensive, and secular civic built environment was complementary to that of private life (Hölkeskamp 2002, 2004). Monuments at prominent locations reminded the community of its past and present aspirations. The visual world of the "cityscape" acted in a dialectic with its occupants, both reflecting collective values but also educating citizens in those concepts. These concerns are to be associated with the expulsion of burials to extramural areas and the symbolic layout of cemeteries; the formal setting out and bounding of the agora; the construction of permanent highly-visible buildings for political and legal assemblies; the increasingly secluded nature of private homes; and finally the increasingly pretentious erection of major state sanctuary complexes at eye-catching points of the town. Civic religious proces-sions followed meaningful itineraries around this "city as structure" to reinforce awareness of the constituent parts of the polis as a collective life.

Houses and Archaic Society

The final Geometric-early Archaic era saw more elab-orate houses develop, multi-roomed rather than sin-gle-space, associated with defined courtyards, and rec-tilinear rather than oval-apsidal forms. The construction shows more investment with greater use of stone, whilst expensive terracotta roof-tiles become general. This house plan becomes the commonest form of Classical Greek home and appears to embody a pronounced conceptual contrast between the family, shielded from direct contact with others, busy with internalized social and economic activities (the prime domain of women), and the public (male) world of the city's public spaces.

Using the illuminating approach of "space syntax" (Hillier and Hanson 1984), a key part of which involves a systematic mapping of access routes through built structures, Lang (2005) shows how Iron Age homes are typically single linear sequences of one to a few rooms, and with rare multiple move-ment-paths. In Archaic times the number of rooms tends to rise at the same time as the access plan devel-ops into a more radial route system focused on an enclosed courtyard. If the Geometric house offers privacy with depth, its outside face (where most eve-ryday family life would have occurred) was public and unshielded from general view, whilst the spaces inside were a mere one to two rooms with minimal differentiation of function. In contrast, the Archaic house with its closed entrance leading into a private yard cuts the family off from public access and gaze. Once into the yard, a range of two to three and often several more roofed spaces are separately accessed, suggesting more differentiated activities, especially if

the closed yard is seen as a formal bounded space as well. A more elaborate and distinct life for the citizen family can be read as reflecting the rise of the city-state and its mentality. Jameson (1990) suggests that the creation of this typical "courtyard-house" for polis citizens arose from two sources: firstly from a conscious elaboration of more complex forms of liv-ing as the wealth and status of ordinary families improved, and secondly from copying the homes of the elite. In the "Dorian" type of serf-states (famously represented by Sparta), the emphasis on male citizen communal eating might be expected to reduce the focus on elaborating the citizen family house, and indeed excavated Cretan homes largely confirm this (see Chapter 12) (Westgate 2007).

The Archaic state is most commonly run by a class of aristocratic families. We therefore would expect to find wealthier mansions. Few are known, probably due to research limitations. We would need Archaic town quarters dug with extensive horizontal excava-tion to demonstrate a cross-section of social classes. Unfortunately most excavated Archaic homes are also from old projects where limited finds were kept (Lang 2005). Actually some putative Archaic town mansions exist, such as Building F in the periphery of the Athenian Agora, whilst the late phase at Zagora has distinct areas with larger and smaller homes perhaps denoting class differences (Hall 2007). City-states in the Eastern Aegean have also evidenced elite rural mansions from excavation (Crielaard 2009).

An Annaliste Perspective

The rise of literate state-societies in the Archaic Aegean is not an isolated phenomenon. The recovery of the Near East from similar political and military disruptions at the end of the Bronze Age was followed by the re-emergence of city-states and empires, whilst in Europe as a whole, the period paralleling Late Geometric-Archaic sees population boom and the crystallization of chiefdoms and states. Greater politi-cal stability and the impact of iron technology are amongst the key factors (Bintliff 1984), but as these societies expanded, their mutual interactions through trade, alliances, and cultural flows hastened the rise of more elaborate societies. In the *longue durée* then

LG–Archaic Greece is a part of this millennial trend to more populous and organized societies.

In the medium term, the heartlands of the Aegean see the rise of a cycle of flourishing, which will be followed by stagnation or decline after some 500 years. More peripheral regions however will take off later and their prosperity will last longer: ecological and socio-political factors can be invoked (Bintliff 1997).

As for the short term, Complexity Theory (Bintliff 2003) teaches us that local initial conditions can be critical for future developments. The contingent role of a lawgiver or tyrant in the social conflicts of Archaic Greece can direct a state's trajectory into divergent pathways, including the extreme democratic experiments of Athens. Yet similar variation can be seen in other, later city-state societies where the absence of a dominating outside political system allows small-scale states to experiment with their social organization, such as in late Medieval-Renaissance Italy (Waley 1988, Bintliff 2004).

A Personal View

Anthony Snodgrass's classic study (1980) dubbed the Archaic era the "Age of Experiment," and one remains amazed at the dynamism of this society, whether we look at the proliferation of hundreds of independent polities, the great wave of colonization around the Mediterranean and Black Sea, or the rapid developments in art and architecture. The above-noted absence of an overpowering empire, allowing so many "small worlds" to evolve, plus their internalized mentality and external aggressiveness to each other, seem to be elements stimulating unparalleled expressions of autonomy in the erection of monumental civic works, experiments in democracy, and remarkable explorations in the artistic and literary representation of everyday life and religious belief.

References

Ammerman, A. J. (1996). "The Eridanos valley and the Athenian Agora." *American Journal of Archaeology* 100, 699–715.

Bérard, C. (ed.) (1984). *La Cité des images. Religion et société en Grèce antique.* Lausanne: Fernand Nathan.

Bernal, M. (1987). *Black Athena: The Afroasiatic Roots of Classical Civilization.* Vol. 1. New Brunswick: Rutgers University Press.

Bernal, M. (1991). *Black Athena: The Afroasiatic Roots of Classical Civilization.* Vol. 2. New Brunswick: Rutgers University Press.

Bintliff, J. L. (1977). *Natural Environment and Human Settlement in Prehistoric Greece.* 2 vols. Oxford: BAR Supplementary Series 28.

Bintliff, J. L. (1984). "Iron Age Europe in the context of social evolution from the Bronze Age through to historic times." In J. Bintliff (ed.), *European Social Evolution.* Bradford: Bradford University Research Ltd, 157–225.

Bintliff, J. L. (1997). "Regional survey, demography, and the rise of complex societies in the Ancient Aegean: Core–periphery, Neo-Malthusian, and other interpretive models." *Journal of Field Archaeology* 24, 1–38.

Bintliff, J. L. (2003). "Searching for structure in the past – or was it 'one damn thing after another'?" In R.A. Bentley and H.D.G. Maschner (eds.), *Complex Systems and Archaeology.* Salt Lake City: University of Utah Press, 79–83.

Bintliff, J. (2004). "Time, structure and agency: The Annales, emergent complexity, and archaeology." In J. Bintliff (ed.), *A Companion to Archaeology.* London & New York: Blackwell, 174–194.

Bonnet, C. and V. Pirenne-Delforge (2004). " 'Cet obscur objet de désir.' La nudité féminine entre orient et Grèce." *Mélanges de l'École française de Rome. Antiquité* 116(2), 827–870.

Burkert, W. (1992). *The Orientalizing Revolution.* Cambridge, MA: Harvard University Press.

Crielaard, J.-P. (2009). "Cities." In K. Raaflaub and H. van Wees (eds.), *A Companion to Archaic Greece.* Oxford: Blackwell, 349–372.

De Polignac, F. (1995). *Cults, Territory, and the Origins of the Greek City-State.* Chicago: University of Chicago Press.

Fullerton, M. D. (2000). *Greek Art.* Cambridge: Cambridge University Press.

Haggis, D. C. *et al.* (2007). "Excavations at Azoria, 2003–2004, Part 1." *Hesperia* 76, 243–321.

Hall, J. M. (2007). "Polis, community, and ethnic identity." In H.A. Shapiro (ed.), *Archaic Greece.* Cambridge: Cambridge University Press, 40–60.

Hillier, B. and J. Hanson (1984). *The Social Logic of Space.* Cambridge: Cambridge University Press.

Hölkeskamp, K.-J. (2002). "Ptolis and agore. Homer and the archaeology of the city-state." *Storia e Letteratura* 210, 297–342.

Hölkeskamp, K.-J. (2004). "The polis and its spaces – the politics of spatiality. Tendencies in recent research." *Ordia Prima* 3, 25–40.

Jameson, M. H. (1990). "Domestic space in the Greek city-state." In S. Kent (ed.), *Domestic Architecture and the Use of Space*. Cambridge: Cambridge University Press, 92–113.

Lang, F. (2005). "Structural change in Archaic Greek housing." In B. A. Ault and L. Nevett (eds.), *Ancient Greek Houses and Households*. Philadelphia: University of Pennsylvania Press, 12–35.

Lohmann, H. (1992). "Agriculture and country life in Classical Attica." In B. Wells (ed.), *Agriculture in Ancient Greece*. Stockholm: Paul Åström, 29–60.

Morris, I. (2004). "Classical Archaeology." In J. L. Bintliff (ed.), *The Blackwell Companion to Archaeology*. Oxford: Blackwell, 253–271.

Morris, I. (2005). "The growth of Greek cities in the first millennium BC." Stanford: Stanford Working Papers in Classics 120509 (on-line).

Morris, S. (1992). *Daidalos and the Origins of Greek Art*. Princeton: Princeton University Press.

Murray, O. (ed.) (1990). *Sympotica: A Symposium on the Symposion*. Oxford: Clarendon Press.

Papalexandrou, N. (2005). *The Visual Poetics of Power: Warriors, Youths, and Tripods in Early Greece*. New York: Lexington Books.

Ray, J. (1997). "How black was Socrates?" *Times Literary Supplement* (14 February), 3–4.

Renfrew, C. (1986). "Introduction." In Renfrew and Cherry 1986, 1–17.

Renfrew, C. and J. F. Cherry (eds.) (1986). *Peer Polity Interaction and Socio-Political Change*. Cambridge: Cambridge University Press.

Rhodes, P. (2003). "Athenian drama and the polis." *Journal of Hellenic Studies* 123, 104–119.

Said, E. W. (1980). *Orientalism*. London: Routledge.

Shanks, M. (1993). "Style and the design of a perfume jar from an Archaic city state." *Journal of European Archaeology* 1, 77–106.

Shanks, M. (1999). *Art and the Early Greek State*. Cambridge: Cambridge University Press.

Shapiro, H. A. (2007). "Introduction." In H. A. Shapiro (ed.), *Archaic Greece*. Cambridge: Cambridge University Press, 1–9.

Snodgrass, A. M. (1980). *Archaic Greece: The Age of Experiment*. London: Dent.

Snodgrass, A. (1986). "Interaction by design: The Greek city state." In Renfrew and Cherry (1986), 47–58.

Snodgrass, A. M. (1987–1989). "The rural landscape and its political significance." *Opus. International Journal for the Social and Economic History of Antiquity* VI–VII, 53–70.

Spivey, N. (1997). *Greek Art*. London: Phaidon.

Tak, H. (1990). "Longing for local identity: Intervillage relations in an Italian town." *Anthropological Quarterly* 63, 90–100.

Tomlinson, R. A. (1995). *Greek and Roman Architecture*. London: British Museum Press.

van Wees, H. (1998). "Greeks bearing arms. The state, the leisure class, and the display of weapons in Archaic Greece." In N. Fisher and H. van Wees (eds.), *Archaic Greece: New Approaches and New Evidence*. London: Duckworth, 333–378.

Waley, D. (1988). *The Italian City-Republics*. London: Longman.

West, M. L. (1997). *The East Face of Helicon. West Asiatic Elements in Greek Poetry and Myth*. Oxford: Oxford University Press.

Westgate, R. C. (2007). "House and society in Classical and Hellenistic Crete." *American Journal of Archaeology* 111, 423–457.

Whitley, J. (2001). *The Archaeology of Ancient Greece*. Cambridge: Cambridge University Press.

Further Reading

Lang, F. (1996). *Archäische Siedlungen in Griechenland: Struktur und Entwicklung*. Berlin: Akademie-Verlag.

Morris, I. (1987). *Burial and Ancient Society. The Rise of the Greek City-State*. Cambridge: Cambridge University Press.

11

The Archaeology of Classical Greece

Demography, Settlement Patterns, and Everyday Life

Introduction

Around 500 BC Greece enters its Classical period, a civilization of lasting worldwide impact. The foundations of its reputation are: the development of democratic principles; major achievements in drama and poetry; the birth of the discipline of history; great advances in philosophy and speculative science (although significant work already began in later Archaic times); and magnificent monuments and high achievement in a range of fixed and mobile art forms.

We must first summarize historical events and trends of this period, which commences in the final decades of the sixth century in political terms, whilst for art historians a date around 480 BC is preferred. 500 BC is a reasonable compromise, and since these dates are based on events in Athens (the most significant single city in Classical Greece), precise dates are irrelevant for Greece as a whole.

Political Developments

In the late Archaic, the dominance of aristocracies in the city-states of Southern Greece (south of Thessaly) was frequently challenged through a combination of internal conflict between leading families, and pressure from the middle and lower classes in society (the hoplite and thetes/peltast groups respectively), who had varied grievances and ambitions. Disputes over political and legal rights, and over rights to land, were central, and historical sources indicate that radical changes occurred as a result, leading to a widespread creation of moderate democracies. However in Northern Greece city-states remained rare, and here confederacies of towns or even tribal non-urbanized peoples were dominant throughout the Classical era, led by aristocrats or kings, or a combination of both. Even within the city-state world of Southern Greece there were regions such as Laconia-Messenia (the territorial state of Sparta) and Crete, where power remained till the end of the Classical era in the hands of a dominant ruling class who controlled a numerous serf population.

Unsurprisingly, modern interest has focused on those poleis (city-states) where pressure induced a broadening of power to include significant political rights for the lower class. Symptomatic of late Archaic political turmoil were either coups by a "tyrant," generally an aristocrat who took sole control of the state, or invitations to outside "lawgivers" (rarely insiders) to legislate to resolve civil strife. In Athens the final expulsion of the Peisistratid dynasty at the end of the sixth century ushered in a wide-ranging democracy, which by the mid-fifth century experimented not only with voting and jury rights for all freeborn males, but allowed citizens of any wealth-status to stand for the highest offices. In Athens, the richest citizens were

The Complete Archaeology of Greece: From Hunter-Gatherers to the 20th Century AD, First Edition. John Bintliff.
© 2012 John Bintliff. Published 2012 by Blackwell Publishing Ltd.

exploited through "liturgies," requirements to subsidize warships (triremes) or dramatic choruses, yet allowed thereby to achieve public acclaim and influence. On the other hand, whereas the Aegean "Normalpolis," stretching, on average, over a radius of 5–6 km from city to state border, gave opportunities for every male citizen to be active in democratic processes, Athens' much larger hinterland (Attica) meant that it was city-dwellers and those living in the immediate rural suburbs (the "Asty" region) who effectively participated in the Assembly and lawcourts.

The democratic tide, which was happening in other city-states and was also stimulated by Athens wherever its power reached throughout the Aegean, survived and even extended its influence after Athens fell from imperial preeminence at the end of the fifth century BC. In the early fourth century, one of the successors to military hegemony on the Greek Mainland, the city of Thebes, spread such concepts through regions of Greece hitherto lacking such a constitution.

Significantly, in Sparta and Crete, and other "serf" societies, the class in power was wide enough to be comparable to the upper and middle class in more democratic city-states, so the real differences lie in the emancipation and empowerment of the other half of society, the lower class. Athens experimented with total suffrage of freeborn male citizens, an example inspiring all subsequent democratic movements throughout the world. Historians suggest that roughly half the 600–700 Classical city-states in the Aegean had at some stage a moderately democratic constitution. This means that political control over the state was shared between the upper-class and middle-class males, with usually lesser but significant legal and some political rights for the lower class.

Michael Jameson (1977–1978) has reminded us that a society like Athens was able to achieve a very broad participation in the political assembly and lawcourts from adult male citizens, regardless of income, through two compensatory mechanisms. Firstly the state gradually introduced payment for public service. It also could count on the fact that work on the family farm and in the home was assisted by household slaves, whilst much of the commercial economy was left to disenfranchised but free resident aliens (metics).

Slave plus metic numbers were large enough in Athens to almost represent the equivalent of the large serf populations in the "less advanced" societies of Sparta and the like. For Jameson, in a Marxist sense, both the "democratic" and the "serf" societies sustained plentiful free time for citizens' political activity, military training, and leisure, through similar substructures of unfree or disenfranchised classes. Exceptionally in Athens the creation of a tribute-paying empire, also without political representation, added yet another layer of undemocratic exploitation to sustain a special lifestyle for the small body of Athenian citizens.

Apart from the monumental constructions for lawcourts and the different political assembly-buildings which we saw being widely erected in city-states from the end of the Archaic era onwards, the broadening of citizen participation can be followed in greater detail in the placing of stone inscriptions to record the state's decisions, both in temple precincts and the agora/civic center. Not surprisingly, hyperdemocratic Athens' share of known inscriptions dwarfs those of other poleis.

Historical Outline

In the early fifth century BC, Athens and other democratic and oligarchic (aristocratic) cities were just exploring the potential of these wider freedoms when an overwhelming threat exploded into the fragmented Aegean political world: the encroachment of the enormous Persian Empire. The innumerable small and large states of Greece failed to unite against the imperial ambitions of this great Near and Middle Eastern power, leaving unstable coalitions of democratic and oligarchic states to pull off two remarkable feats: beating off an attack under the direction of King Darius in 490 BC on the coast of Athens' own homeland of Attica (the battle of Marathon, largely the victory of Athenian hoplites) and then a much more serious campaign led by King Xerxes in 480–479 BC in which a great sea battle (Salamis) followed by a great land battle (Plataea) gave alternate honors to the Aegean's leading maritime power (Athens) and its leading land power (the Spartans). This prolonged period of threat not only elevated to immense fame and importance those complementary states, but may well have encouraged their individual ambitions as well as their mutual rivalry within the resulting Persian-free Aegean. In any case, throughout the middle to late fifth century, an Athenian-led coalition was locked in intermittent warfare with a Peloponnesian coalition with Sparta and the city of Corinth at its head. On a more positive note, victory against the Persians gave Greeks a new sense of identity, which reinforced their traditional shared culture, language, and religion.

After the Persian wars, Athens excited envy and fear amongst its rivals by converting a religious confederacy, the Delian League, founded in 478/9 and devoted to preventing further Persian incursions, into a ruthless empire. Tribute was exacted as protection-money from a vast cluster of small states around the Aegean, under threat of siege, death, and enslavement for defaulters (Color Plate 11.1). Athens' vast fleet was the basis for "the Athenian maritime empire." If the large state of Sparta relied on its extensive serf-provinces to sustain its hoplite middle and upper class, Athens' population both in town and country grew to a scale well beyond its own rather infertile hinterland of Attica. Athens flourished through accumulating wealth from its tributary empire and the Attic silver mines, and perhaps through specializing in the export of Attic olive oil. Historians are increasingly linking Athens' foreign military adventures in Sicily, Egypt, and elsewhere to a desire to control imports of grain and timber at source.

The Persians had sacked Athens, demolishing its Archaic shrines on the temple hilltop (Acropolis) in the city-center. The Athenians buried the pillars and statues carefully on the Acropolis and in its perimeter wall, leaving the site open for decades, but then the climax of imperial power inspired the leading politician Pericles to restore the sacred hilltop on a massive scale (Figure 11.1). With a budget only possible from Athens' flourishing silver mines and the tribute of dependent cities throughout the Aegean, a series of remarkable ceremonial and cult buildings was erected from the 450s to the end of the century, turning the Acropolis of Athens into one of the great artistic achievements of European civilization. Athenian predominance in the Aegean also had longer-lasting effects well after the fall of its Empire, in the

Mediterranean-wide prestige of its art and literature and the ultimate adoption of its dialect as the standard international form of Greek.

The quarrelsome nature of Greek city-states and other forms of state within the Southern Aegean has resulted in historians recording hardly a single year in the fifth or fourth centuries BC without a war occurring somewhere. Large-scale conflicts involving the great powers of Athens, Sparta, and later Thebes, subsequently also the kingdom of Macedon in Northern Greece, drew in scores of lesser states on either side. Architectural skills deployed to make strong and beautiful temples to adorn cities and interstate sanctuaries, were used in equal measure to defend cities or erect border fortresses and signal towers across the countryside (and defend isolated farms). State budgets for military costs always far outstripped any other public expenditure (van Wees 2000).

In 404 BC Athens was finally defeated by the Peloponnesian coalition, after protracted conflicts ("the Peloponnesian Wars") since the 450s. Nonetheless, in the first half of the fourth century BC, Athens attempted to revive its maritime empire, countered again by its chief rival, Sparta, who likewise asserted its influence around the Aegean. Both yielded to a new power in the 370s and 360s, the city of Thebes, head of a federal state in Boeotia, Central Greece. Thebes' hegemony was short-lived, its forces and those of Athens being decisively defeated in 338 BC by a totally novel power in Southern Greek politics, the kingdom of Macedon in Northeast Greece, under the dynamic leadership of Philip II. After Philip's assassination in 336, the Greek states rose up, but his son Alexander swiftly suppressed the rebellion. With Greece securely under Macedonian dominion, Alexander "the Great" fulfilled his father's dream of invading the Persian Empire, beginning in Western Asia Minor where the Greek cities and native dynasties were still under Persian rule. By 323 when he died in Babylon, he had swept through the Middle East and Egypt to the frontiers of India and Afghanistan (Color Plate 13.1a). His generals carved "Successor Kingdoms" out of this vast realm (Color Plate 13.1b), significant parts of which survived till the spread of Roman power out of Italy in the late third to second century BC.

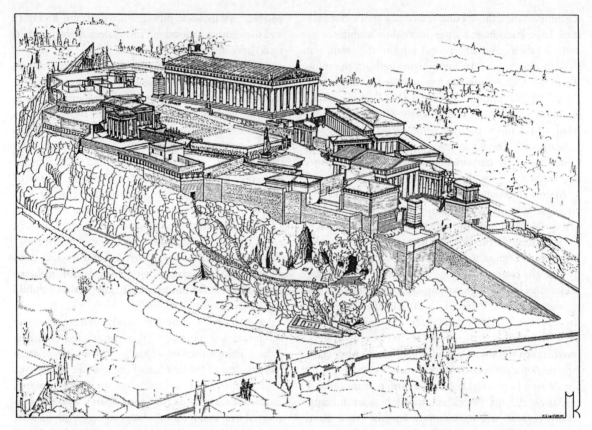

Figure 11.1 The Athenian Acropolis in Hellenistic times. Key Periclean monuments: immediately at the head of the entrance ramp is the Propylaea gate-complex, to its far right on a projecting wing the tiny temple of Athena Nike, then in the raised centre of the citadel is the temple of Athena Parthenos, and to its left adjacent to the perimeter wall the complex temple called the Erechtheion (dedicated to Athena and Poseidon Erechtheios).
Reconstruction drawing courtesy of Professor M. Korres.

Demography and Urbanism

Using intensive and extensive survey results to identify demographic climaxes and urban growth in diverse regions of Greece during antiquity (Bintliff 1997b), we find (Figure 9.5) that the florescence of town and country that had been largely focused in the Southeast Mainland during Late Geometric to Archaic times, has now in the fifth and fourth centuries spread more widely, encompassing much of the Southern Mainland from Central Greece down to the Central Peloponnese, together with the Aegean islands (Crete excepted) and the Western Ionian islands. The Great Power battles are between states in these regions,

but involvement of surrounding states spreads the conflict over the entire Aegean world and beyond. Add to this the demand of the major cities for timber, everyday and precious metals, mercenaries, and at times food supplies, then one can suggest that the maximally-dense regions of the South form a "core" having close and stimulating relations with a very large "periphery." Not surprisingly we find that as a result of interventions from the core in politics, military strategy, and interstate economics, parts of the periphery increasingly begin to enhance their militarism, their urbanism, and their investment in status monuments (such as temples) in order to promote their identity and significance.

Although in the core regions and adjacent Lowland zones of South-Central Greece, the basic network of nucleated local centers (proto-poleis and poleis: see Figure 8.3), was expanding through the Geometric era and probably reached its full numerical and spatial extent by the end of Archaic times, the Classical era in the core lands saw these centers grow in size and population. The increasing simplification of the nucleated settlement map into genuine political centers and lesser places subordinate to them (called "villages" (*komai*) or "demes") masks the fact that in the vital Southeast Mainland, population generally rose in major and minor towns, and also in villages, whilst the larger city-states such as Athens had incorporated into their swollen territory several town-like settlements, which continued their function despite downgrading to "village."

Estimating city size combines topographic survey, evidence from urban excavations, surface survey where towns lie today in cultivated or at least open ground, and (more rarely) textual sources. The area enclosed by defensive walls can be used, but critically, to suggest minimum areas for Classical towns, whilst the dating of circuit walls is a well-developed field within Aegean archaeology (Lawrence 1979). Nonetheless, since it is well attested in ancient and medieval urbanism that a town's population may outgrow its defense system, the existence of extramural domestic sectors should be tested. Legal requirements in general use throughout Greco-Roman civilization, from Classical Greek times onwards, prohibiting burial within a town's walls because of ritual pollution, make the mapping of cemeteries an additional helpful tool for confirming the likely edge of a nucleated settlement at any particular era.

Geometric-Archaic Greece was dominated by nucleated settlements, predominantly village or hamlet size to modern eyes, with occasional town-sized communities, often precursors of major Classical cities. The city-state emerged almost entirely from the smaller nucleations, hence the term "village-state" (Kirsten 1956, Bintliff 1994). Although most became incorporated as satellite settlements of slightly larger city-states of around 1 to 1,5 hours walking-radius territory by the fifth to fourth centuries BC (the "Normalpolis"), alongside the rarer, much larger "territorial states" ("Megalopoleis") such as Athens or

Sparta, their function usually continued throughout Greco-Roman antiquity as district centers of population, trade, industry, and farming. The reality of the Classical landscape is obscured by emphasizing formal state centers and forgetting the "urban" character of numerous large villages or small towns which existed within city-states and territorial states. In practice a 10 ha minimum size appears useful to consider a settlement as "geographically urban" (Bintliff 1997a), thus incorporating a large body of Classical villages, although there were exceptionally even smaller formal poleis which claimed independence despite limited demographic and economic resources.

Studying ancient urbanism from a geographical rather than legal and constitutional perspective is especially necessary when we enquire how the landscape was organized within the largest territorial states of Classical Greece. Attica, at around 2500 km², is the same size as neighboring Boeotia with its 14–15 city-states in a fragile confederacy, yet officially from its earliest accurate records possessed just one town, Athens, in a simple city-state structure. Yet we know that by the end of the Archaic era the population was divided into some 139 villages or "demes," within whose number Athens itself appears as an agglomeration of suburban quarters (also called demes). As we saw in Figure 8.3, the rural demes form a systematic grid of similar-sized territories, appropriate to villages or small towns, whilst the variable number of representative councillors each rural deme supplied to the state's executive council indicates indeed that demes must have run the entire range of sizes from hamlet to significant urban centers in their own right. Hans Lohmann has emphasized this variability in several studies of the still little-researched Attic countryside (Lohmann 1992, 1995).

At one extreme is the one deme we know almost everything about, Atene, due to Lohmann's remarkably fine survey of its territory (1993b). Here the community possessed no nucleated residential focus, consisting merely of rural estates, mostly large and well-established. However there must have been a central meeting-place where the necessary political, ritual, and social events required of demes took place. Perhaps several of the rural demes partially excavated to make way for the new (2004) Athens Airport in the central inland plain of Attica, the Mesogeia, may have had a similarly dispersed character (Tsouni 2001). Next, here and elsewhere in Attica, there are a few partially-excavated villages, both deme centers and subsidiary settlements to an official deme focus. Finally there are at least a handful of very large Attic demes, where the political quotas and/or the archaeological evidence indicate that the main settlement had a genuinely town-like character, such as Sounion, Acharnai, Rhamnous, and Thorikos. Not surprisingly, legends circulating in Classical Athens suggest that prior to the creation of the unitary territorial state of Athens, during the "Dark Age," there were several rival centers vying with Athens for regional power.

Similarly, within the large territorial state of Thespiae in Boeotia, focused on a very large polis of some 70 ha, minor district foci such as Askra, some 10–12 ha in size, appear to be officially villages but of an extent, according to our surface survey, to have accommodated around 1000 people; Askra possesses its own discrete fertile "settlement-chamber" and many farm satellites within that (see Figure 8.4). Both Kirsten's term "Dorfstaat" and an ancient Greek term *komopolis*, with a similar meaning, suit these villages with a town-like character.

The Classical Countryside

Ancient writers show little interest in everyday life in the countryside, if we except farming manuals, opening the thin textual evidence concerning rural life to contested interpretations. Alongside dense urban and village populations in the core regions of the Southeast Mainland, field survey identifies an almost ubiquitous settlement form: the isolated Classical farm or farm-cluster. From the 1980s onwards, a dispute arose as to whether these were farmhouses with a permanent occupation (family farms?), or seasonal huts occupied during peak agricultural work by farmers residing in towns or villages, or merely sheds and storehouses on rural estates (Osborne 1985, 1987, Snodgrass 1987, Jameson 1990, Lohmann 1992, 1993a).

Some small rural sites clearly lack finds-assemblages broad and rich enough for permanent residence, but most (given reasonable preservation and adequate pottery samples) indicate significant domestic use, if not permanent habitation. The evidence includes lamps for evening use, weaving equipment for cloth production, tableware and food preparation vessels for regular meals, and large and medium storage vessels for everyday needs and for storing agricultural surpluses. Such sites also have tiled buildings whose plan resembles townhouses. Nonetheless, sampling tens of Classical "farms" reveals a variable picture for the representation of these functional features, prompting Foxhall (2004) to range these sites along a continuum in permanence or regularity of use. However, there is always a sampling problem. The detection of artifact-types is primarily controlled by sample size as well as the chances of such finds appearing in deposits currently disturbed by plowing, grazing, or erosion. Thus surveyors often find one loomweight at supposed farm sites (and rarely more). Yet a working loom requires 12–50 weights. An additional form of evidence from survey projects that record "offsite" finds are "haloes" of dense domestic debris surrounding putative rural farms, indicating rubbish from prolonged and significant residence (Bintliff and Howard 1999). Summarizing such empirical evidence, it appears sensible to allow for a minority of sites to have been non- or periodically-residential rural sites, with the majority being permanent residences (see calculations in Bintliff 1997a). Also worthy of note is the fact that regular revisiting of rural landscapes suggests that perhaps as much as half of the small farmsites to be found in surface survey are not visible in any particular year of study, due to changing crops and natural vegetation as well as erosion and deposition of soils.

Hamlet, village, and urban sites also see parts of their visible surface manifestations come and go "like traffic lights" (Barker 1984), but such larger sites virtually never disappear from the surface record, if they are cultivated or at least not under dense woodland. Thus the main population centers are usually reliably represented, especially important since in the Aegean polis-world, two-thirds or more of the total Classical population probably dwelt in such nucleated communities, rather than in the infinitely more numerous small rural sites whose recognition and status are disputed by archaeologists and historians. For the Argolid and Boeotia Projects for example (Jameson *et al.* 1994, Bintliff 1997a), the size and population density of regional cities, compared to the potential inhabitants in hamlets and farms, place 70–80 percent of the population in towns. A wider analysis of Greek city sizes (Hansen 2004) has produced similar results. The simple reason is the close packing of cities and satellite village-towns in the Aegean, allowing most city residents to commute daily into their landscape to cultivate their estates and graze their stock over traveling distances generally of half an hour or rarely one hour (2–3, and 5–6 km radius respectively).

Why then did anyone bother to live in a rural farm, unless as a seasonal base? Although some misanthropes might avoid their fellow citizens for a quieter rustic life, more widely applicable factors are required. Living on the estate certainly allowed more time in its management. Secondly, we need not assume that farm occupants were the owners. Wealthier peasants, and even more likely, upper-class estate owners, may well have settled tenants, hired labor or slaves on their estates to carry out everyday work. In serf-states such as Sparta, although the citizen middle and upper classes had to maintain a successful farm to retain their political rights, the land was worked by the *helot*-serfs (Fisher 1998). Archaeologically such distinctions will be harder to detect than it might seem. Fine tableware in the Greco-Roman world has been known to be in the possession of slaves (from graffiti), whilst for comparison slaves in the pre-Abolition southern states of the USA have been found to own a surprising variety of consumer items (Orser 2004). Similar results have emerged from the excavation of peasant huts on eighteenth and nineteenth-century tenanted estates in Scotland (Symonds 1997).

Let us now examine some case studies in Classical rural life derived from regional field surveys.

The Atene Survey

The 20 km² territory of this Classical village of Attica was surveyed by Lohmann (1993b). This revealed large and small estate-centers, often intervisible, some beginning in late Archaic times, when this "deme" or village within the city-state of Athens already existed officially. The heyday of the dense farm system was the fifth to fourth centuries BC, followed by drastic abandonment of nearly all sites in Hellenistic times after ca. 300 BC.

For unclear reasons, whereas most other Southern Greek surveys uncovered innumerable small farms,

Atene possessed few such, the majority being extensive estate-centers indicating upper middle-class to elite landowners (Figure 12.11). Perhaps this can be linked to Lohmann's calculation that the deme's natural fertility was enhanced by some 40 percent through a massive investment in agricultural terracing, primarily for olive culture. Numerous olive presses were recorded from the farm complexes along with threshing floors and stock enclosures. Large-scale olive production is unsuitable for a family farm, where a balance of subsistence crops with a minor surplus for sale is typical. The local dominance of richer farmers and their high investment in a cash crop may demonstrate a major source of their wealth. The oil might have been sold in the vast market of Athens-Piraeus itself, or fed into the trade in which Attica's cereal shortages were met by regular grain shipments from the Black Sea. Some scholars believe Atene was unusual because its large-estate owners were directly involved in the Lavrion mines of eastern Attica, or were providing foodstuffs for their large workforce, but Lohmann argues that extensive survey elsewhere in the Athenian countryside documents similar large Classical farm complexes, whilst the landscape immediately around the mines has a settlement pattern no different from the rest of Attica (Lohmann 1995, 2005).

The Kea Project

The island of Kea/Keos lies near Attica, and one of its small Classical *poleis*, Koressia, has been field-surveyed in both town and country (Cherry *et al.* 1991). The city itself was a "Dorfstaat," technically 18 ha within its walls, but rocky slopes limited domestic settlement to 6–8 ha (perhaps 700–1000 residents). Textual sources suggest a total population around 1300 for town and country. The survey of the 15 km² *chora* (rural hinterland) of the city revealed a dense spread of Classical farm sites, but no villages, whilst individual "family farms" were probably occupied for only part of the overall Archaic-Classical-Early Hellenistic era they are datable within (ca. 600–250 BC).

However, how did Koressia sustain itself? In the nineteenth century AD farmers of the newly-independent Greek state were given rights to the land, and constructed a massive series of terraces across this hilly island to boost agriculture (Whitelaw 1998).

Without this investment farming would have been restricted to a mere 18 percent of the landscape, allowing only 200 people to be fed in the survey region. Although no clear traces survive to prove that Early Modern terracing replaced comparable ancient systems, the ancient texts and settlement-size calculations indicate that Classical production must have matched the nineteenth century: the population for all four city-state territories on the island was 4900, while ancient Kea was not a center of trade, industry or overseas empire and so had to support itself agriculturally. This means that a full landscape of Classical terraces has been hidden or destroyed. The evidence from Atene noted above makes clear that such human investment was being carried out elsewhere in the South Aegean at this time.

The Kea team have been able to compare the total number of Classical rural sites with those, the vast majority, which have yielded specific types of late Archaic-Classical drinking vessels. The importance of formal meals with appropriate tableware to Classical rural occupants of all free classes seems underlined, and supports the case that the farms are more than store-houses or siesta retreats for urban resident farmers. The survey team was nonetheless doubtful if most farms were permanently occupied, though this interpretation of rural farms is largely rejected by more recent surveys. If we were to suggest in contrast that the majority of their rural sites were residential, even if not all in contemporary use, this would bring the Project into harmony with the generalization that two-thirds or more of city-state populations dwelt in towns.

The Southwest Argolid Survey

This Southern Mainland survey (Jameson *et al.* 1994) also revealed a climax of settlement in town and country in Classical times. The range of surface ceramics confirmed the team's view that most rural sites were permanent farms and hamlets. The emphasis in settlement on soft rich soils suitable for olive and vine cultivation was seen as implying that the intensive land use and demographic florescence were driven by the regional economy becoming tied in to interregional commerce, the export of surplus oil and wine providing a growth stimulus. While this agrees with the Atene case study described above, the difference

here is the dominance of small estate-centers, as on Kea. It is debatable whether this commercial explanation works with small-scale farming. Most surveys in Southern Mainland Greece and the Islands (Crete excepted) have equally strong Classical rural climaxes but little signs of export orientation. A modest family farm required most of its production for its own needs, then part of its surplus for purchasing luxuries and hardware necessities from the nearest polis-center, leaving almost nothing for a major export industry.

Methana

This rocky, Southern Mainland peninsula (Mee and Forbes 1997) enjoys a Classical florescence, with one small city, two satellite villages, and a wide spread of small rural sites. The small farms were founded in the fifth century, with some decline already from the fourth century, presaging a steady reduction throughout the subsequent Hellenistic centuries. Comparison with Attica shows that the surface area of the pottery scatters is larger than the built areas of excavated farms. This is probably the "halo effect" first identified in Boeotia, where careful quantitative recording showed that farm buildings were ringed by a less dense zone of domestic rubbish, produced by: dispersal out by cultivation and weather; rubbish dumps on the farm edge; and manuring of gardens and infields (Bintliff and Snodgrass 1988b). One problem hangs over our understanding of the survey results: site gridding was confined to the nucleated sites and collections of sherds were small. The mapped Classical sites number 46, but only 22 had more than 5 Classical sherds brought back to be dated as such, and it is these "sites" which are shown on the histogram of site sizes. The significance of more than half of the localities with Classical finds is left unresolved (were they permanent residences, or just places with some farming or herding activity?), and they were excluded from further analysis.

The Berbati Survey

This fertile valley is located in the Peloponnese near Mycenae (Wells and Runnels 1996). Again rural settlement expanded in Classical times, but peaked during the Early Hellenistic era (ca. 350–250 BC). There is one village and the rest of the sites are farms or hamlets. Given the external location of the city-states to which the valley belonged (Mycenae and Argos probably alternated in control), the village formed the immediate focus for the resident farmers of the remaining smaller settlements. Study of the finds from the smaller sites recognized assemblage differences possibly distinguishing permanent residences from temporary storehouses/homes. The rarity of olive and wine presses plus the limited ceramic imports and fine wares led the team to conclude that the theory proposed by the Argolid Survey Project, linking a rise in Classical rural sites to their participation in cash-crop production for an international market, will not suit this region, where farmers were probably subsistence-focused.

The Pylos (PRAP) and Laconia Surveys

The serf-state of Sparta controlled not only Laconia but also Messenia, together a vast 8000 km² area spanning the southern half of the Peloponnese (Thomas 2000). Nearly all Spartan citizens and their families lived in the Sparta agglomeration itself, whilst the rest of the state was divided between the estates of the Spartans, worked by *helot*-serfs, and free communities with very limited rights, the *Perioeci*. The Laconia Survey close to Sparta found plentiful small rural sites and suggested that citizens intensified their estate-yields through placing their serfs directly on the estate, where they could also be personally supervised from the city (Cavanagh *et al.* 1996, 2003). In contrast, in distant Messenia, the PRAP survey has found few Classical rural sites, and suggests that helots lived in nucleated village settlements (Alcock *et al.* 2005). This may reflect more limited management of Messenian crop-production.

The Boeotia Project

The regional survey of this fertile agricultural province of Central Greece, directed by myself and Anthony Snodgrass since 1978, has been able to build up a complex understanding of Classical rural settlement (Bintliff and Snodgrass 1985, Snodgrass 1990, Bintliff 2000, Bintliff *et al.* 2007). In the hinterland of the several cities surveyed we found the usual abundance of small sites at this period in the countryside,

with a lesser number of larger estates and hamlets. Field surveyors have answered Robin Osborne's (1985) challenge to demonstrate that small rural sites were actually residential, by analyzing the dwelling-structures and farm assemblages recovered at such sites. If we apply Whitelaw's approach (1998) on the Kea Survey, where surface finds are grouped into different use-categories, to the Boeotia rural sites (Bintliff *et al.* 2007), it is clear that the Classical farms are rich in tableware, with a secondary interest in food processing and a low interest in storage/transport vessels. This suits better with domestic occupation. The fragment of an olive or wine press is a rare find, but these are to be associated with specialized crop-processing with a more commercial emphasis, and for preparing family supplies of such crops such stone presses are not necessary (Mattingly 1994). The invaluable aid of subsurface electrical, magnetic, and radar geoprospection to reveal ground plans of farmsteads, as well as the use of soil chemistry to indicate large-scale accumulations of household rubbish at these sites, have strengthened the case that most Classical rural surface sites represent permanent residence. Classical sources provide reasonably reliable regional population figures, although only for citizens, leaving uncertainties about the level of slave-owning and of resident aliens from other states. Nonetheless, the approximate size of the 14–15 cities of Boeotia, and the frequency of satellite villages, plus the more precise data gathered on small farm density within "windows" of intensive surface prospection, encourage the exercise of relating the archaeological settlement hierarchy to population levels that can be reconstructed from ancient sources. Since Boeotia was essentially a mixed-farming landscape with only minor evidence for trade and industry, we can also compare the demographic level with the potential "carrying capacity" of the landscape to support it through food production:

1. 11 regions, each contributing to a federal army 1000 hoplites (heavy-armed troops), 1000 light-armed troops, 100 cavalry. The confederacy possessed a fleet of 50 triremes = 10,000 men. Total forces = 33,100 men × 5 for family and one slave = 165,500 minimum total population derivable from sources ca. 400 BC.

2. Ancient Boeotia=2580 km². In 1961 one-third was considered officially as cultivable land, anciently perhaps one half? A hoplite (middle-class citizen) family landholding is some 5,4 ha (from various ancient sources). Cultivated land was probably rotated, so either 50 percent or 33 percent in any one year would be left fallow. Cereal yields were probably on average about 9–12 bushels per acre. Food needs: 1000 kg "wheat-equivalent" (cereal or an equivalent food crop) per family (+250 kg per slave) per year.

3. If we give all the Boeotian hoplites and the cavalry (usually aristocrats) the minimum hoplite farm, then 12,100 hoplites/cavalry×5,4 ha = 653 km² needed for food production for these two classes.

4. If we assumed in Classical times that one third (860 km²) or one half (1290 km²) of the land was cultivated, then either 207 or 637 km² was left for lower-class families. This would create less than 1 ha, or 3 ha, for each lower-class family to live off.

Classical farmers were clearly maximizing regional land potential, to sustain estimated populations in town and country remaining unmatched till the twentieth century AD. Even if we allowed a larger area of land in use than recently, under ancient cropping conditions over half was required merely to provide a modest estate of 5,4 ha for the middle and upper classes. The latter certainly owned more than this, customarily the minimum landholding expected of the official status of a (hoplite) middle-class landowner. In contrast a farm of 1 ha would normally have been inadequate for self-sufficiency and even one of 3 ha would have been a difficult basis for long-term risk-free subsistence. An estimated half of the population of lower-class status was thus left with much less than the desirable comfort and economic security of a 5,4 ha estate per family. The upper figure of 3 ha allows for Classical farmers extending land use into present day marginal land by a factor of 1,5. Survey has located such farms in modern scrub, but not to such a degree, so an alternative solution would have been to combine significant use of poorer land with a degree of constant cropping, predicting unparalleled intensification of crop production but a very risky strategy in the longer term due to declining yields.

However, the maximum area of farmland easily cultivated by an ancient nuclear family was 2–3 ha (Foxhall 2003). Here we can see the likely solution in Classical Boeotia for feeding the lower half of society, that poorer peasants supplemented their own smallholdings with labor on the larger estates of the middle and upper classes. In other Greek states it has been argued that agricultural slaves, or serfs, supplied the necessary extra labor to work such larger estates.

The Boeotia survey results seem to correspond remarkably well to the population density implied by our regional documentary sources, and both point to an astonishing demographic pressure which remained unmatched till the end of the twentieth century AD.

Offsite archaeology and the Aegean landscape

Regional survey has increasingly adopted the American approach to landscape archaeology, of treating the single "artifact" (ancient find) on the surface, rather than the archaeological site, as the basis for recording human activity in the Greek landscape. But the application of this concept and even more the interpretation of its results remain surprisingly controversial. Our recent fieldwork in the city and countryside of ancient Tanagra in Boeotia has shed much light on the so-called "site halo" and "offsite carpet" phenomena which appear when we study the distribution of all the individual ancient artifacts across the countryside (Bintliff et al. 2004–2005, 2007). It turns out that "non-site" archaeology can reveal remarkable information about ancient population and land use.

Whilst fieldwalking in the outer countryside of Tanagra's rural territory, our counting of surface pottery densities has provided a very clear image of human activity debris (Color Plate 11.2a). In this computer-generated map by Emeri Farinetti the densities of surface pottery are given in color grades, whilst "sites," here farms and hamlets of Classical, Roman, and Medieval age, are indicated with blue dots and numbers. Very few to no finds are noted in the areas with the lowest, first two density levels (marked with grey and pale blue color). These are dominant, large areas, as each marked fieldwalker strip is usually 20×200 meters in size. Here human activity debris is very slight. In contrast, significant pottery spreads occur around those very high concentrations we have defined as habitation sites, where the density rises from outermost green through dark blue to pink. After fieldwalking, putative sites are gridded and more refined density maps are made in groups of 10×10 or 20×20 meter squares. In this district when we did this it became clear that the settled area of these sites is confined to the dark blue zone for small sites, or even just part of that zone, or the pink zone for larger sites. This creates two further divisions after the genuinely largely empty landscape: the habitation zone and an immediately surrounding zone of human debris, the "site halo."

This "halo" around "site cores" is a feature we have confirmed for domestic sites in Boeotia without exception since 1978, and it accounts here for almost all the dark green sectors. A part of this scatter of material at lesser density than the occupied site core is due to ploughing or the weather moving surface finds out of the core into a limited area around it, but we have shown and this is clear here too, that such haloes can often lie uphill from sites and occur at distances and in quantities too great to be accountable solely to these forces. Additional elements need to be introduced. The simplest can be seen in any modern farm, that is piles of debris, in or out of use, lying on the edges of the occupation area. Nowadays this is plastic or metal, but in pre-modern times far more use was made of ceramics. Furthermore, whilst today we have centralized large-scale rubbish disposal, till recently the world dumped its discarded organic and inorganic debris near its place of production and consumption. Moreover, in most mixed-farming cultures waste material had a value, even a high value, for immediate recycling. Broken roof tiles could be used to patch up roofs, from their first widespread use in Archaic times onwards, and from Roman times onwards, tile old and new is a very common construction material in walls and foundations. Food debris, human and animal urine and feces, and processing debris from farming and herding, were seen as very useful compost material for spreading on kitchen gardens and also open fields. It is well evidenced that the storage and recycling of domestic

rubbish for manuring did not involve as today a careful filtering of distinct forms of rubbish. In one fortunate excavation context, that of the Classical city of Halieis, houses were found to have pits filled with all manner of unsorted domestic rubbish including discarded tile, interpreted as collections for rural manuring on their owners' estates (Ault 2005). Thus accumulations of broken pots and tiles found their way into the more useful organic rubbish, although ethnographic evidence shows that adding sherds to manure has an additional value in aerating and moisturizing soil which has long been appreciated. A generation ago Anthony Snodgrass and I (1988b) proposed that the wider spreads of sherds of ancient and post-Roman age in the immediate surroundings of sites ("haloes") and sometimes much further afield ("sherd carpets"), could reflect intentional spreading of such fertile compost onto farm gardens and the "infield" areas (those closest to occupation sites) of agricultural land.

As we can see, the dark green areas regularly extend 200 meters or more out from the site core. Since in many cases the topography here is very level, it is inconceivable that this can be explained through plough or rain dispersal out from the settlement. It is worth noting that the biggest site with the widest human impact into its surroundings (TS30) is a Byzantine-Frankish village, with the remainder mostly composed of Classical rural farms and Roman farms and villas. Haloes are thus a cross-cultural and cross-period aspect of rural estate life. Incidentally the existence of so much rubbish, even from a "family farm" such as TS33, is as powerful an argument as any for sustained domestic life. Finally let us note that the densest haloes (where dark blue replaces the more typical dark green code for density) come from the largest sites (the medieval village and Roman villa TS28), which is appropriate to the greater scale of their human activity.

From Tanagra city's remoter hinterland let us move (Color Plate 11.2b) to the countryside immediately outside the city walls (marked red) of ancient Tanagra. Here we see the density of surface pottery running in four directions up to 1 km away. The same color codes as in the previous map allow a direct comparison between the outer and inner *chora* (city rural territory). Strikingly, there are virtually no low-sherd or sherd–empty fieldwalked strips (note these are usually 100×20 meters here). The rest of the landscape is one continuous giant human artifact, a vast carpet of broken pottery. The densities are almost entirely in the dark green, darker blue, and pink grades, which we saw were confined in the deep countryside to site cores and their surrounding haloes. There are indeed sites here: many small Classical cemeteries, one or two Classical farms, and several Roman villas. When these sites were gridded in small units, we can still record even higher densities for their habitation areas and haloes than their wider surroundings. So the novelty we have to explain are the high-density carpets of pottery that fill almost all the landscape between sites. One important clue is that these sherd-carpets all rise in density the closer we get to the city. Another is that sometimes, as in the west and south, blocks of land have contrasted levels of density: where the land is flat, the carpets are denser than when they lie on hilly slopes. Even on steep terrain however, densities remain at the level of site haloes in the outer countryside.

How can we account for the difference between the landscape nearest the city and that much further away? We can rule out influence from rural sites: their density and size are broadly comparable from inner to outer *chora*. Since most of Tanagra was enclosed in its ancient walls and the land here mapped outside is mostly uphill from the city, there is no question of these immense sherd scatters being washed out of the town itself. So how can it be that the typical densities up to 1 km from the city wall, in *every* part of every field, would be at site halo or site level in the outer countryside?

There is surely only one explanation possible: the presence of a 55 ha-plus ancient city of some 7000 or so inhabitants. It can only be their accumulated rubbish, artificially transported into the entire adjacent landscape, which could have provided what will amount to several million pieces of broken sherds and tile spread evenly into its immediate hinterland. Urban manuring into the landscape is the mechanism, whilst almost certainly the vast majority of the city-dwellers were farmers whose estates were concentrated into the first 5 km or one hour travel radius out from the urban center

(the outer landscape used for comparison lies some 7 km distant).

The particular relevance of this phenomenon to Classical Greek times can be illustrated from another Boeotian city landscape, that of ancient Thespiae, where we already have available a reliable sample of dated sherds from the offsite carpets surrounding the town. The totally-dominant period is Classical Greek. Such labor-intensive manuring to boost crop production is thus exactly in that era when population levels were at their pre-modern highest in the region. Controversy over Classical manuring (Alcock *et al.* 1994, reply by Snodgrass 1994; Pettegrew 2001, Barker *et al.* 2000, Osborne and Foxhall 2001, Bintliff *et al.* 2002), stems in part from doubts as to whether these carpets could be due essentially to plowing scatter and erosion out of ancient sites. For Boeotia I hope we have demonstrated from our comparison of the inner and outer countryside of Tanagra, that only small parts of the site haloes are significantly affected by such phenomena; the wider carpets are almost certainly urban manuring, confined to accessible haulage distances from the town itself.

The pioneer survey work on manuring was achieved by Wilkinson in a series of Near Eastern landscapes (1989, 1990), and he made it clear firstly that such exhaustive practices occurred rarely in any particular landscape, and secondly that their chronology might differ from region to region. The common factor was typically that the landscape in question seemed to have been maximizing its agricultural productivity to sustain an exceptionally high population. Comparison of regional growth curves for the ancient Aegean (Bintliff 1997b; Figure 9.5) show that population climaxes have systematically been out of phase across Greece as a whole, during a 1000-year period (Greco-Roman times), with the Classical climax being essentially focused on the Southeastern Mainland and the Aegean islands. We have also seen other mechanisms for boosting farm production, such as the intensive terracing in Attica. In Boeotia for certain, the Thespiae evidence for an essentially Classical era for urban manuring matches perfectly with regional population reconstructions and the fact that the city itself is larger by almost a factor of two in this period than at any other time in its history.

The Cultural Biography of Rural Surface Sites

The development of smaller Classical rural settlements opens a window into the vicissitudes of the social and economic role of the countryside. In the Classical Southeastern Aegean heartlands there is a high frequency of "family farms" compared to other eras. Beginning in late Archaic times, most actually commence in the high Classical or Early Hellenistic period, whilst almost all appear abandoned by Late Hellenistic or Early Roman times. The scale and social group size is reasonably assured through analysis of the site data. A minority stay in use through Roman to Late Roman times, and perhaps a majority are reused after abandonment, in Late Roman times. Field surveyors can usually recognize a site's existence from the localized high density of finds, but the problem lies in how to disentangle the history of occupation over several phases of use, merely from collecting a sample of sherds. In Roman Britain for example, there are numerous well-excavated villa sites where sufficient areas have been opened to allow a series of reconstruction images of the estate-center from century to century, nearly always showing radical changes in the size and complexity of the villa (Millett 1990). Rescue excavations in Northern Greece have revealed similar complex building sequences (Adam-Veleni *et al.* 2003).

Greek survey specialists from the 1970s onwards, when focusing on Greek and Roman landscapes, prioritized detecting as many sites as possible, estimating their approximate size and dating their period of use through a small surface collection. This has allowed us to see widespread phenomena of vital historical value, such as the rise and fall of the Classical "family farm" and the revival of many landscapes in the Late Roman period. It is a more recent concern that leads us to ask how particular rural sites developed over time. Moreover, the broad-brush results from the 1970s and 1980s surveys may conceal finer details which we need to evaluate, not merely to deepen knowledge but also to correct possible errors from the assumptions made in interpretation.

A practical example. Most Aegean surveys need to cover large areas in a few seasons to get economical results from limited research funds. A quick, almost standard, method estimates the size of a surface site by placing two lines at right-angles across the site and counts finds at regular intervals along them. Where the dense sherd scatter stops is the site edge, and by interpolation the remaining borders can be inferred. The sherd sample is often focused on these thin strips too, together with a quick grab collection from the rest of the site (the "quadrants"). Also to save time, the number of sherds taken from each site tends to be quite small, of which often only a minority are datable to a particular period. Now this need not be too problematic for a one-period site, as the maximum size of the site coincides with the site date, and only the small samples may prevent a clear study of the full range of activities carried on there. But sadly, on almost all intensive Aegean surveys, the majority of sites have turned out to be multi-period.

Excavated rural sites in other parts of Europe which span two or more periods of use, many hundreds or even a thousand years of activity, almost invariably evidence dramatic changes in the size, and type of use, of the site. In Chapter 8 on the Archaic period we introduced the case-study site LSE1 (Thespiae Hinterland Survey), where a rural estate-center exhibited a striking change in extent and function between Geometric-Archaic and Classical times. This was only detected because the entire site had been divided into a regular grid of samples, and then a large collection of sherds had been gathered from the surface. After the Classical period, there are some further mysterious contrasts here in period presence evidenced from datable sherds collected: Classical Greek 305, Roman 83, Late Roman 22.

To make the analysis more complicated, our site (the white grid in Figure 11.2) lies close to the city of Thespiae, and in the district surface sherd-density map has visibly massive interference from the urban discard halo spreading over it from the west (left). So first of all we need to clarify how much pottery could be being introduced by local offsite activities *onto* the site, rather than signifying occupational site-use. Our

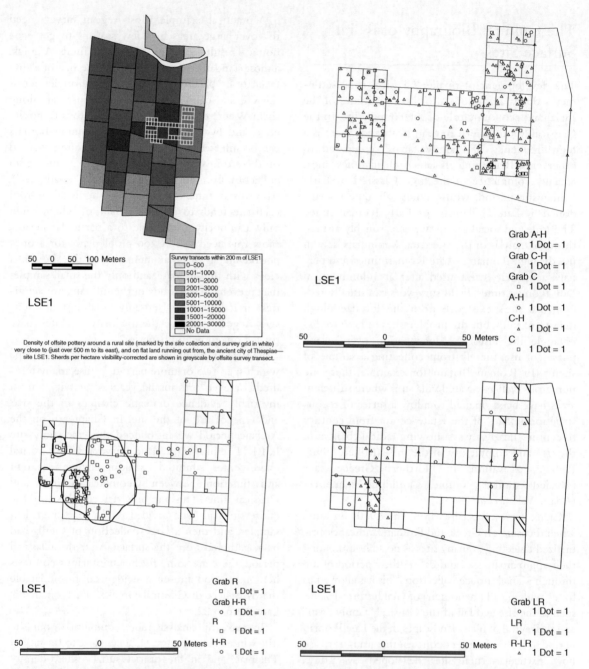

Figure 11.2   The site of LSE1. (Top left) Local surface pottery density around the site (gridded in white). (Right and lower) Sherd foci for Classical, Roman, and Late Roman times.

Elements taken from J. L. Bintliff and P. Howard, "A radical rethink on approaches to surface survey and the rural landscape of Central Greece in Roman times." In F. Kolb and E. Müller-Luckner (eds.), *Chora und Polis*. München 2004, 43–78, Figures 11, 22, 23, and 24.

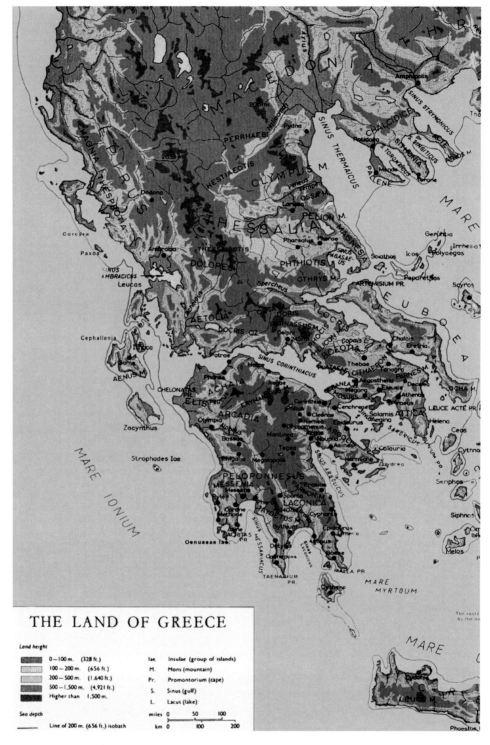

THE LAND OF GREECE

Land height

	0 – 100 m. (328 ft.)
	100 – 200 m. (656 ft.)
	200 – 500 m. (1,640 ft.)
	500 – 1,500 m. (4,921 ft.)
	Higher than 1,500 m.

Iae.	Insulae (group of islands)
M.	Mons (mountain)
Pr.	Promontorium (cape)
S.	Sinus (gulf)
L.	Lacus (lake)

Sea depth

——— Line of 200 m. (656 ft.) isobath

miles 0 ⸺ 50 ⸺ 100
km 0 ⸺ 100 ⸺ 200

Plate 0.1 Map of Greece and the Aegean Sea with ancient regions and major ancient sites indicated. A. A. M. van der Heyden, *Atlas van de antieke wereld.* Amsterdam 1958, Map 1.

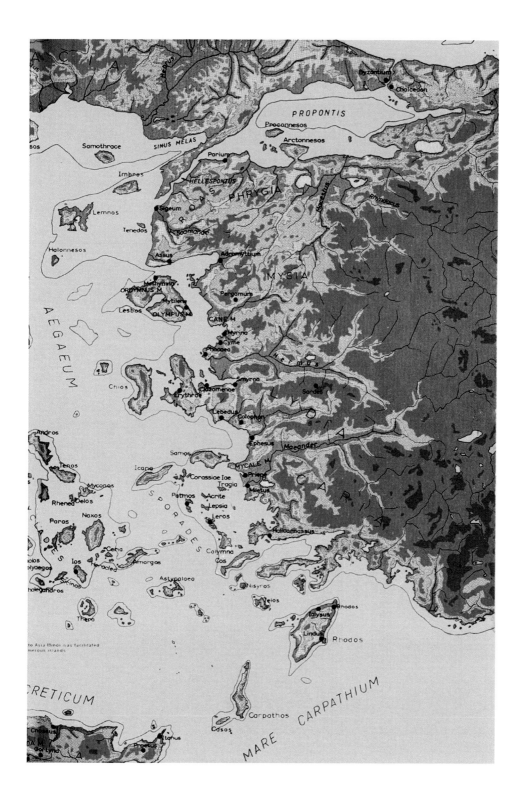

PROPONTIS

Byzantium
Chalcedon

Proconnesos

SINUS MELAS
Arctonnesos

Samothrace

Parium

Imbros

HELLESPONTUS

Sigeum

PHRYGIA

Lemnos

Rhyndacus

Tenedos

Scamander

Assus

Adramyttium

Halonnesos

MYSIA

Methymna
ORDYMNUS M.
Mytilene
OLYMPUS M.

Pergamum

Lesbos

CANE M.

Myrina

AEGAEUM

Cyme
Phocaea

Chios

Hermus

Smyrna

Clazomenae
Erythrae

Sardes

Lebedus
Colophon

Andros

Ephesus

Maeander

Tenos

Samos

MYCALE M.

Myconos

Icaria

Corassiae Iae
Priene

Rhenea
Delos

Patmos

Tragia
Miletus

Paros

Naxos

SPORADES

Acrite

Lepsia

Leros

Ceba

Ios
Heraclea

Amorgos

Calymna

Halicarnassus

Polyaegos

Sikinos
Pholegandros

Astypalaea

Cos

Nisyros

Telos

Thera

Ialysus
Camirus
Rhodos

Lindus
Rhodos

to Asia Minor was facilitated
numerous islands

CRETICUM

Carpathos
MARE CARPATHIUM

Casos

Chersus
Gortyna
Praesus

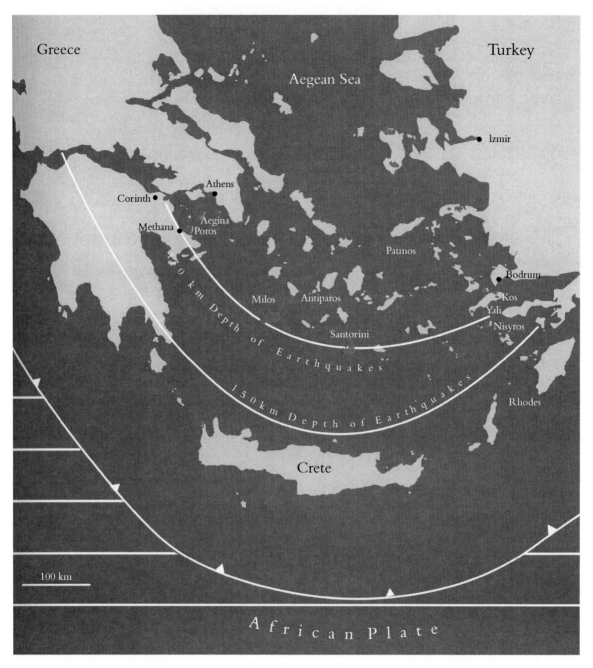

Plate 1.1 Earthquake and volcanic arcs in the Southern Aegean. Active volcanic areas in recent geological time shown in red. W. L. Friedrich, *Fire in the Sea. The Santorini Volcano: Natural History and the Legend of Atlantis.* Cambridge 2000, Figure 2.3.

(a)

(b)

Plate 1.2 Greek landscape types 1. (a) Rocky islands and sea, Aegina. (b) Large fertile alluvial plains of Northern Greece.
(a) Author. (b) © Ekdotiki Athenon, Athens.

(a)

(b)

Plate 1.3 Greek landscape types 2. (a) Dry Pleistocene plains of Southern Greece with soft limestone hills leading to hard limestone mountains, Plain of Argos. (b) Deep soft limestone hill land, Plain of Sparta.
Author.

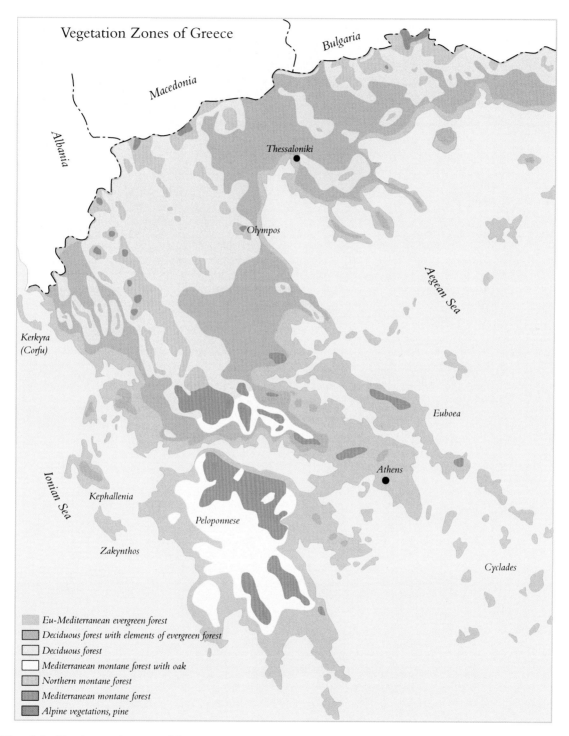

Plate 1.4   Zonal vegetation map of Greece.

Modified from J. Kautzky, *Natuurreisgids Griekenland. Vasteland en Kuststreken*. De Bilt 1995, map on p. 21.

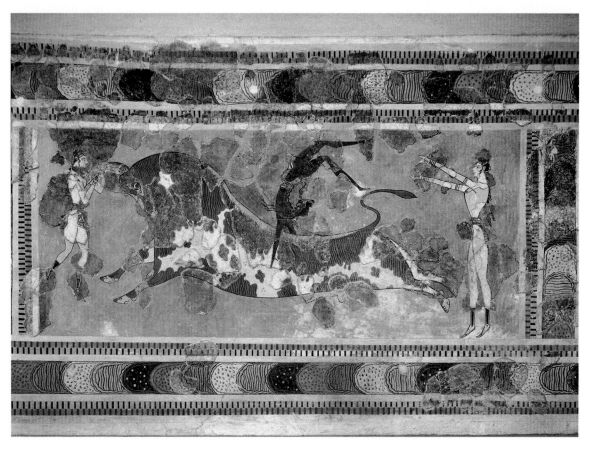

Plate 5.1 Jumping bull fresco from Knossos, restored, h. 86 cm, Minoan, sixteenth century BC. © akg-images/Erich Lessing.

Plate 6.1 Scene from the Miniature Fresco including a sea battle, and a town with emerging soldiers and residents. Akrotiri, Thera, Late Cycladic period.
National Archaeological Museum, Athens. © akg-images/John Hios.

Plate 8.1 Late Geometric elite burial marker vase with funeral scene. The abundant figures mark a clear break to preceding Protogeometric and Early-Middle Geometric ceramic decoration. Dipylon series, Kerameikos cemetery, Athens. The Art Archive/National Archaeological Museum, Athens/Gianni Dagli Orti.

(a)

(b)

Plate 9.1 (a) Silver stater from Aegina, late 6th century BC; obverse: turtle; reverse: abstract design. (b) Athenian silver five-drachma coin, "owl," ca. 480 BC; obverse: head of Athena; reverse: owl.
Silver stater, with a turtle and Goddess Athena tetradrachm of Athens. Both images © The Trustees of the British Museum.

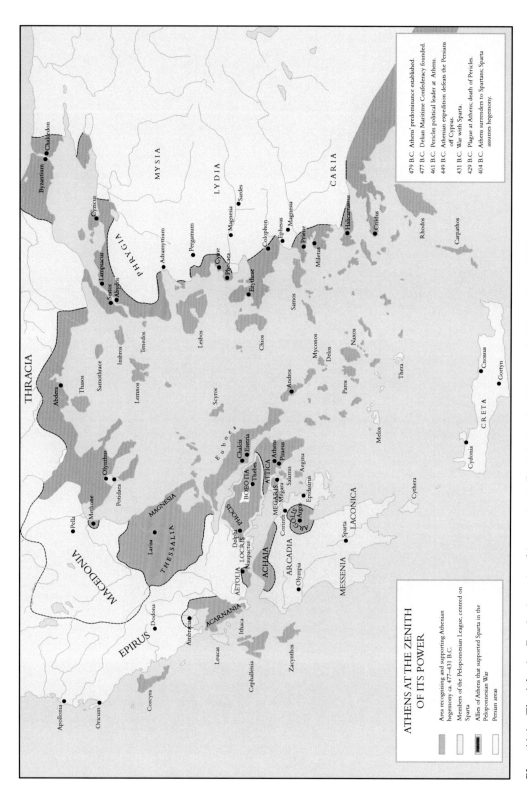

Plate 11.1 The Athenian Empire (green) and its enemies (yellow) during the Peloponnesian Wars, 457–404 BC.
A. A. M. van der Heyden, *Atlas van de antieke wereld*. Amsterdam 1958, Map 6.

ATHENS AT THE ZENITH
OF ITS POWER

Area recognising and supporting Athenian
hegemony ca. 477–431 B.C.

Members of the Peloponnesian League, centred on
Sparta

Allies of Athens that supported Sparta in the
Peloponnesian War

Persian areas

479 B.C. Athens' predominance established.
477 B.C. Delian Maritime Confederacy founded.
461 B.C. Pericles political leader at Athens.
449 B.C. Athenian expedition defeats the Persians
          off Cyprus.
431 B.C. War with Sparta.
429 B.C. Plague at Athens; death of Pericles.
404 B.C. Athens surrenders to Spartans; Sparta
          assumes hegemony.

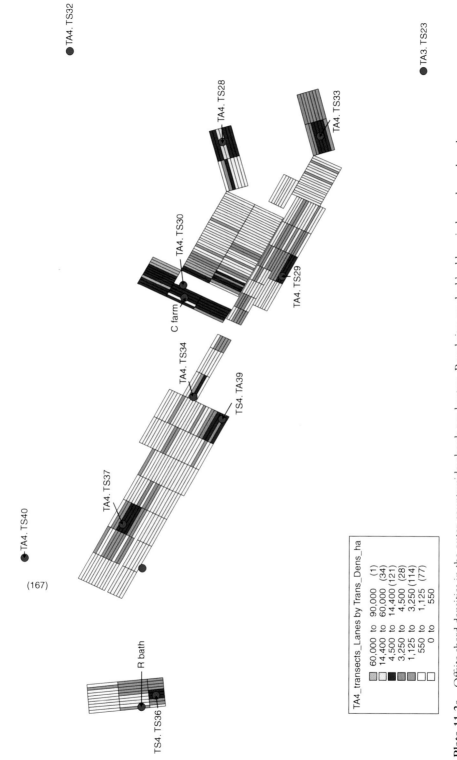

(167)

Plate 11.2a Offsite sherd densities in the outer countryside; sherds per hectare. Rural sites marked by blue circles and numbered.
J. L. Bintliff, "The Leiden University Ancient Cities of Boeotia Project: 2005 season at Tanagra." *Pharos. Journal of the Netherlands Institute in Athens* 13 (2006), 29–38, Figures 2–4.

TA4_transects_Lanes by Trans_Dens_ha

60,000	to	90,000	(1)
14,400	to	60,000	(34)
4,500	to	14,400	(121)
3,250	to	4,500	(28)
1,125	to	3,250	(114)
550	to	1,125	(77)
0	to	550	

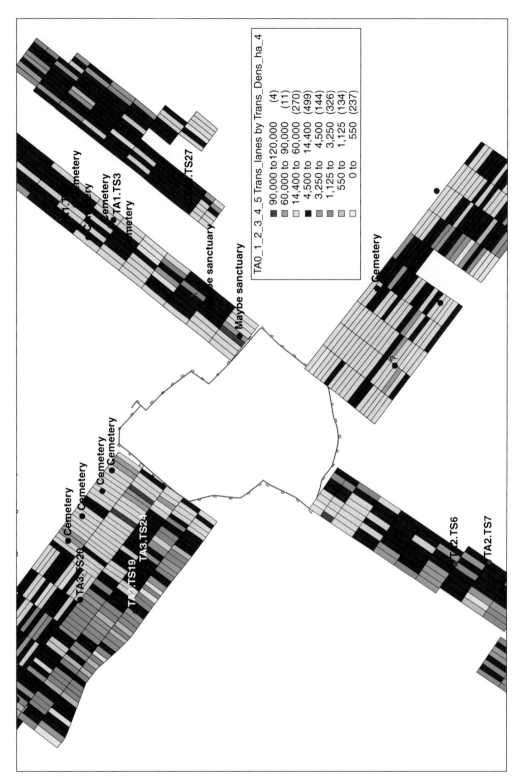

Plate 11.2b Offsite sherd densities in the innermost countryside of the ancient city of Tanagra, Boeotia; sherds per hectare. Rural sites marked by blue circles, numbers or function. Tanagra city marked by its city wall in red. Author.

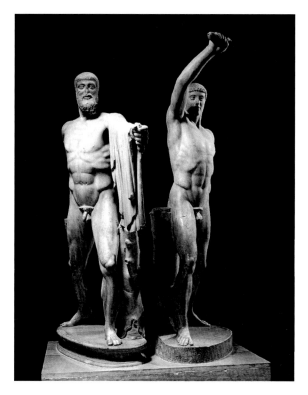

Plate 12.1a Classical sculpture group, Harmodius and Aristogeiton, the "Tyrant Slayers," Roman marble copy, after a Greek bronze original of the fifth century BC.
Naples, Museo Archeologico Nazionale. © akg-images/De Agostini Picture Library.

Plate 12.1b Restored and coloured cast of the Peplos Kore.
© Museum of Classical Archaeology, Cambridge.

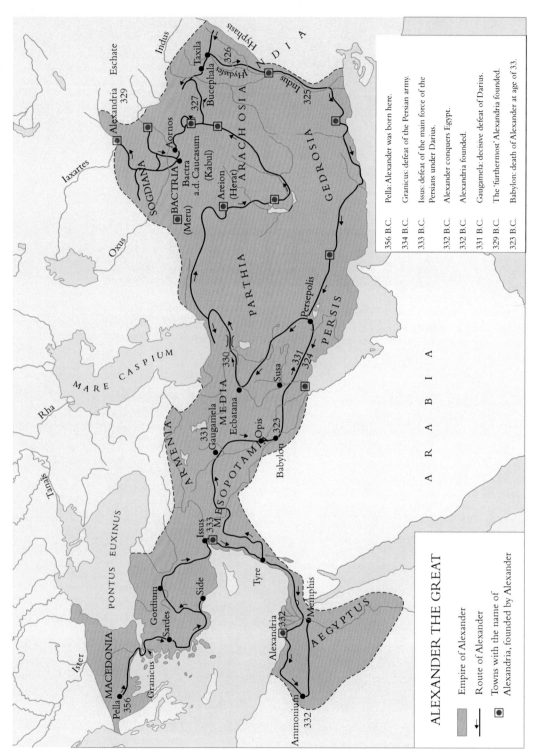

ALEXANDER THE GREAT

Empire of Alexander

Route of Alexander

Towns with the name of
Alexandria, founded by Alexander

356 B.C. Pella: Alexander was born here.

334 B.C. Granicus: defeat of the Persian army.

333 B.C. Issus: defeat of the main force of the
Persians under Darius.

332 B.C. Alexander conquers Egypt.

332 B.C. Alexandria founded.

331 B.C. Gaugamela: decisive defeat of Darius.

329 B.C. The 'furthermost' Alexandria founded.

323 B.C. Babylon: death of Alexander at age of 33.

Plate 13.1a The Empire of Alexander the Great, 336–323 BC.
A. A. M. van der Heyden, *Atlas van de antieke wereld*. Amsterdam 1958, Map 7.

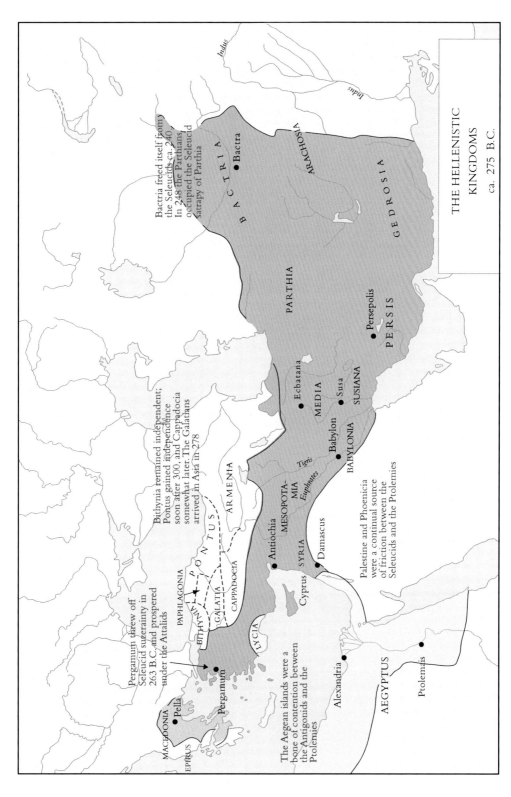

The following labels appear on the map:

Indus

Bactria freed itself from
the Seleucids ca. 240.
In 248 the Parthians
occupied the Seleucid
Satrapy of Parthia

Bithynia remained independent;
Pontus gained independence
soon after 300, and Cappadocia
somewhat later. The Galatians
arrived in Asia in 278

Pergamum threw off
Seleucid suzerainty in
263 B.C. and prospered
under the Attalids

THE HELLENISTIC
KINGDOMS
ca. 275 B.C.

B A C T R I A

• Bactra

ARACHOSIA

G E D R O S I A

P A R T H I A

• Persepolis
P E R S I S

• Ecbatana
MEDIA
• Susa
SUSIANA

• Babylon
BABYLONIA

MESOPOTA-
MIA
Euphrates
Tigris

A R M E N I A

P O N T U S

PAPHLAGONIA

BITHYNIA
GALATIA
CAPPADOCIA

LYCIA

• Antiochia
SYRIA
• Damascus
Cyprus

Palestine and Phoenicia
were a continual source
of friction between the
Seleucids and the Ptolemies

The Aegean islands were a
bone of contention between
the Antigonids and the
Ptolemies

• Alexandria

AEGYPTUS

• Ptolemais

MACEDONIA
• Pella
EPIRUS

• Pergamum

Plate 13.1b The Hellenistic Successor Kingdoms: the Ptolemies in Egypt, Seleucids in the central Near East, the Antigonids in Macedonia and the Attalids in Pergamum.

A. A. M. van der Heyden, *Atlas van de antieke wereld*. Amsterdam 1958, Map 8.

Plate 14.1a "The Deer Hunt": mosaic floor from the andron of the House of the Abduction of Helen, Pella, fourth century BC.
© World History Archive/Alamy.

Plate 14.1b "Tomb of Philip" at Vergina, Greece (ancient Aigai, principal city of the Macedonian kings), discovered in 1978, if not for Philip II then possibly the grave of Alexander IV, murdered in 311 BC. View from the outside.
© akg-images/Hervé Champollion.

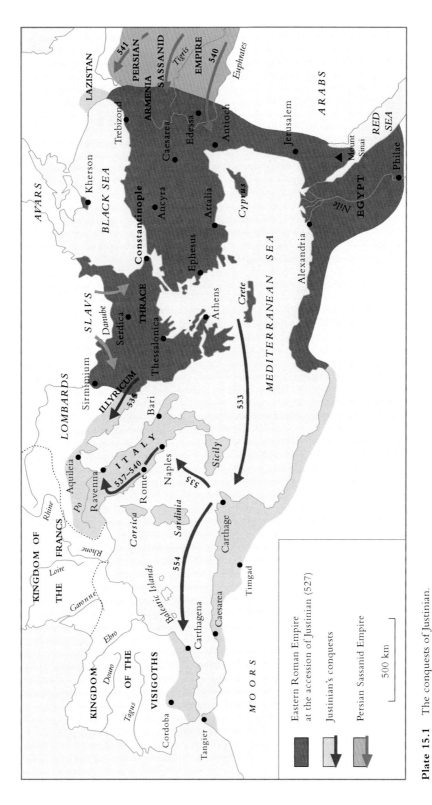

Plate 15.1 The conquests of Justinian.

F. Delouche (ed.), *Illustrated History of Europe*. London 1993, Figure 2, p. 96.

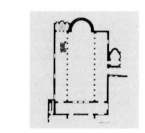

Plate 16.1a   The later fifth-century AD basilica church of Acheiropiitos, Thessaloniki, view and plan.
E. Kourkoutidou-Nicolaidou and A. Tourta, *Wandering in Byzantine Thessaloniki*. Athens 1997, Figures 219 and 220. © Kapon
Editions.

Plate 16.1b   The Acheiropiitos church, interior photo: it retains its original marble floors, pillars, and mosaics.
E. Kourkoutidou-Nicolaidou and A. Tourta, *Wandering in Byzantine Thessaloniki*. Athens 1997, Figure 223. © Kapon Editions.

Plate 16.2 A military saint from the fifth-century AD mosaics of the Rotunda, Thessaloniki.
E. Kourkoutidou-Nicolaidou and A. Tourta, *Wandering in Byzantine Thessaloniki*. Athens 1997, Figure 59. © Kapon Editions.

(a) (b)

Plate 17.1 Early to Middle Byzantine ceramic forms. From left to right: Slav ware from the Olympia cemetery; Cretan painted ware; Green-and-Brown Painted Ware; Fine Sgraffito Painted Ware; Slip-Painted Ware.
Courtesy of A. Vionis.

10 m

Plate 18.1 Plan of the Middle Byzantine double-churches at the monastery of Osios Loukas, Central Greece. Upper: the Panaghia. Lower: the Katholikon. The Katholikon has two entrance halls, the outer numbered 135–137. The crossing of the cross plan with the main dome is marked in the two churches by numbers 139 and 134. The most exclusive sacred areas are the two apse groups to the east (right of the image) shielded by screens.

J. Lowden, *Early Christian & Byzantine Art*. London 1997, Figure 133. Courtesy of Professor J. Lowden.

Plate 18.2   The domed centre of the Katholikon of Osios Loukas, ca. 1011–1030 AD, interior view looking east toward the screened apse.
© akg-images/Paul Ancenay.

Plate 18.3a   Middle Byzantine mosaic of Holy Luke in the Katholikon church at Osios Loukas.
© akg-images/Paul Ancenay.

Plate 18.3b Late Byzantine Resurrection fresco, Chora monastic church, Constantinople (Istanbul), fourteenth century AD.
© Godong/Robert Harding.

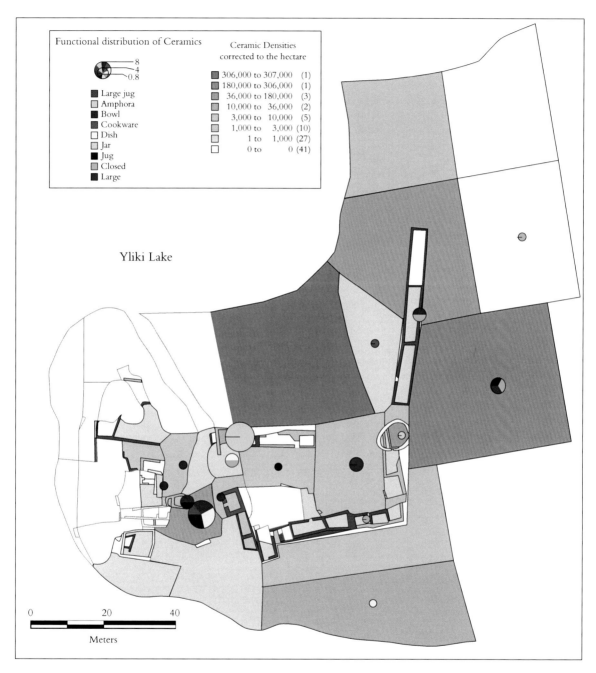

Plate 19.1 The Crusader feudal estate centre at Klimmataria. Plan with ceramics of all periods at the site plotted by type. The central tower is in purple, the internal courtyard to its right.

E. Sigalos, *Housing in Medieval and Post-Medieval Greece*. Oxford 2004, 202.

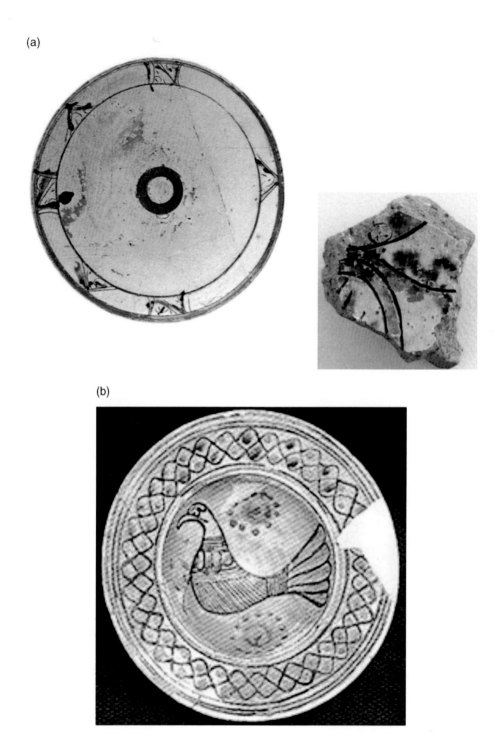

Plate 19.2 Late Byzantine-Frankish ceramics. (a) Zeuxippos ware bowl and fragment of Green and Brown Sgraffito. (b) Proto-Majolica dish.
Courtesy of A. Vionis.

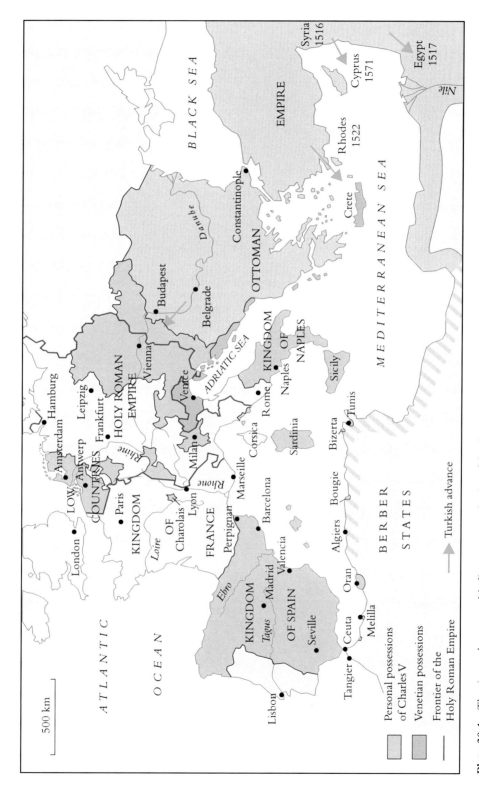

Plate 20.1 The sixteenth-century Mediterranean territories of the Ottoman Empire.
F. Delouche (ed.), *Illustrated History of Europe*. London 1993, Figure 4.

Plate 20.2a   Sixteenth-century Iznik ware tulip mug.
© Chris Hellier/CORBIS.

Plate 20.2b   Eighteenth-century Kütahya plate.
Courtesy of A. Vionis.

(a)

(b)

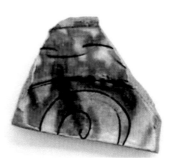

Plate 20.3 Ottoman-Venetian era ceramics. (a) Polychrome painted Majolica jug from Pesaro, Italy, mid-eighteenth to early nineteenth century. (b) Aegean imitation of Italian Majolica jug and Late Green and Brown Sgraffito pottery fragment. Courtesy of A. Vionis.

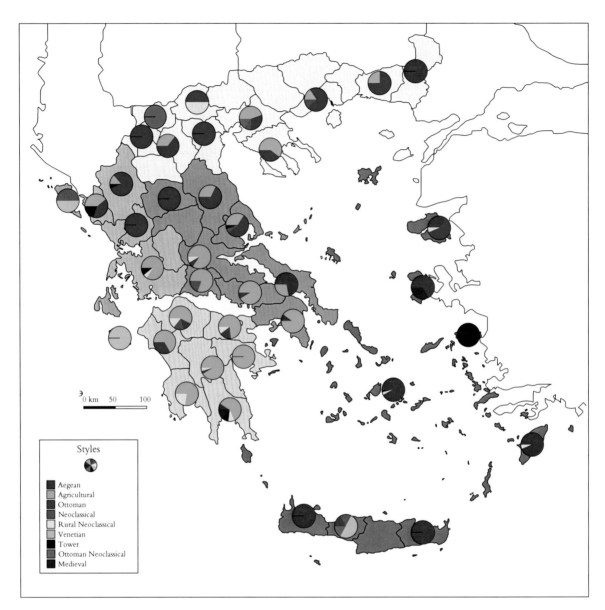

Plate 21.1a Distribution of vernacular house types in Greece based on a survey of published surviving historic buildings. Note the dominance of the longhouse-style (Agricultural) for the southern Mainland, Frankish-Venetian styles (Aegean-Venetian) on the islands and Ottoman for the northern Mainland.

E. Sigalos, *Housing in Medieval and Post-Medieval Greece.* Oxford 2004, Figure 82.

Plate 21.1b   The traditional single-story or one-and-a-half-story longhouse is the commonest form within the category Agricultural of the distribution map. A seventeenth-century example is illustrated here from Boeotia.

N. Stedman, "Land-use and settlement in post-medieval central Greece: An interim discussion," in P. Lock and G.D.R. Sanders (eds.), *The Archaeology of Medieval Greece*. Oxford: Oxbrow, 1996, p. 189, Figure 2. Courtesy of the author.

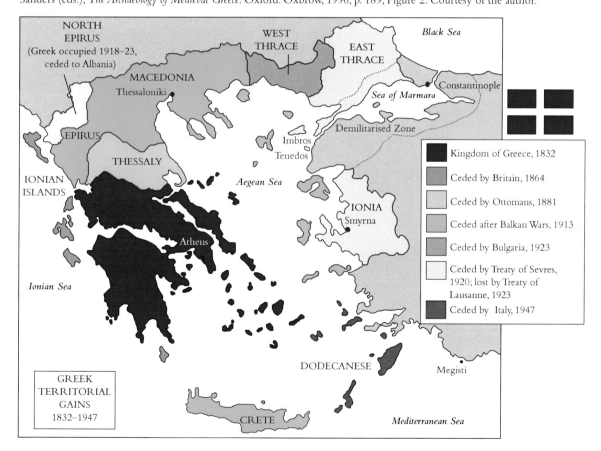

Plate 22.1   The growth of the Modern Greek State.
Wikipedia image.

Plate 22.2a   Early Modern Aegean decorated wares. Left to Right: Polychrome Sgraffito jug (from West and Northern Greece), late eighteenth to late nineteenth century; Çanakkale Ware dish (Northwest Turkey), eighteenth to mid-nineteenth century.
Courtesy of A. Vionis.

Plate 22.2b   Early Modern Aegean decorated wares. Left to Right: Transfer-printed dish (from Syros/Europe), late eighteenth to early twentieth century; Grottaglie Ware bowl (Southern Italy), late eighteenth to early twentieth century, Benson Collection, Zurich and Montefioralle.

Plate 22.3a Traditional meets modern rural housing. Outside of abandoned longhouse on the main street of Aghios Thomas village, Boeotia.
Author.

Plate 22.3b Traditional meets modern rural housing. A modern villa and behind it the original family longhouse of the plot still in secondary use along the same street, Aghios Thomas village, Boeotia.
Author.

Plate 22.4   Traditional female costume of Tanagra village, Boeotia. Dora Stratou Dance Theatre, Athens www.grdance.org.

Plate 22.5a   An Achilles statue in the garden of the Achilleion, Corfu.
Author.

Plate 22.5b Village cemetery at Asi Gonia, Crete.
www.imagesofgreece.co.uk.

Residual Analysis technique (Table 11.1) compares site surface pottery totals with the level of finds for each period throughout the surrounding district. The "predicted" finds are the amount of pottery we would expect to find at the location even if no settlement was present, based on the levels of density for the whole district around the site. Only if site levels are

well above expectation can we begin to argue that in each period there was a real occupation there.

Here, despite the massive Classical Greek offsite carpet in this area, our location remains even for this period an abnormally high density focus. Also the Roman finds are well above local expectations, since Roman is rare in the offsite. As for Late Roman, also rare in offsite, the site finds are not very elevated but "something" is happening here. Having shown that all three periods show a real focus of activity at site LSE1, we now have to account for the gross differences in these period frequencies. Here the necessity for full gridding becomes clear: the sherds collected for the three phases of activity reflect a large farm in Classical times, then a much smaller Roman farm, followed by at most a shed or temporary field base in Late Roman times.

This approach aims to write a "cultural biography" for surface sites. Just to underline that these sequences of striking transformations may be the norm for multi-period sites, Table 11.2 provides the trajectory

Table 11.1   Residual Analysis for site LSE1.

Period	Archaic to Hellenistic	Roman	Late Roman
Actual	305	83	22
Predicted	153	16	7
Residual	+152	+67	+15

Actual = recorded density.
Predicted = expected density from surrounding fields for this district of the *chora*.
500-sherd sample.

Table 11.2   Changing site sizes (ha) and functions in the south *chora* of Thespiae city, Boeotia, together with the size of the contemporary city of Thespiae.

Site	Classical-Hellenistic	Hellenistic	Hellenistic-E Roman	Early Roman
LSE1	1,2 hamlet	1,2 hamlet	0,2 small farm	0,2 small farm
LSE2				
LSE3	1,8 hamlet	0,15 Farm	Low activity	Low activity
LSE4	<1,5 cemetery			
LSE5	0,45 medium farm	0,45 medium farm	Low activity	Low activity
LSE6	0,8 hamlet	0,8 hamlet	0,4 medium farm	0,4 medium farm
LSE7	0,7 hamlet	Abandoned?		0,6 large farm/ villa
THS1	<0,03 cemetery			
THS2			Low activity	0,34 Small–medium farm/villa
THS3	0,26 cemetery	0,26 cemetery		
THS4			0,4 medium farm	0,4 medium farm
THS11	0,03 cemetery			
THS12	0,5 medium farm	0,5 medium farm?	0,2 farm?	0,5 medium farm/villa
THS13				0,2 small farm
THS14				
THS15	<0,06 cemetery			
THS16	1,06 hamlet	1,06 hamlet	0,4 farm cluster/medium farm	0,4 farm cluster/ medium farm
THS17	0,27 small farm	Abandoned? Late?		Low activity
PK-Apot	2,5 hamlet + cemeteries?	2,5 hamlet?	Abandoned?	2,5 hamlet + cemetery?
Th City	95,02 major city	95,02 major city	42 medium-large city	42 medium-large city
Totals	9,28 + 95,02	6,66 + 95,02	1,4–1,6 + 42	5,54 + 42

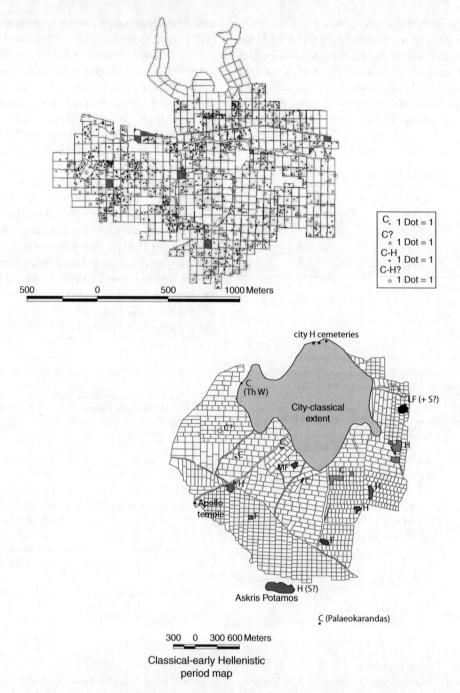

Figure 11.3   (Upper) Surface survey of Thespiae city shows its maximum extent of 70–100 ha during the Classical to Early Hellenistic era. (Lower) Total rural survey south of the city revealed an inner ring of small rural cemeteries (C), then a ring of large to medium-sized farms (MF, LF) and hamlets (H), followed by small farms (F), and finally a large hamlet (Askris Potamos). Upper: author. Lower: J. L. Bintliff *et al.*, *Testing the Hinterland: The Work of the Boeotia Survey (1989–1991) in the Southern Approaches to the City of Thespiai*. Cambridge 2007, Figure 9.4.

of size and function changes for the whole series of sites surveyed in the southern hinterland of Thespiae (Bintliff *et al.* 2007), from Classical to Early Roman.

The changes to many of these sites in Middle and Late Roman times are often equally dramatic. Putting all the individual "cultural biographies" together makes it possible to offer a far more nuanced view of the types of activity in the Classical countryside. Figure 11.3 shows the city size, and then our reconstructed rural landscape for the first 3 km out from ancient Thespiae city, during Classical to Early Hellenistic times. The city itself is of imposing size, never matched before or after, and its rural hinterland has a wide scatter of farm centers and hamlets of different sizes. Between these country residences lay an immense carpet of offsite Classical ceramics, marking the presence of intensive farming carried out largely by commuting city-dwellers.

In this elaborate methodology I have tried to demonstrate that analyzing an ancient landscape must go well beyond putting "dots on a map," where some pottery of a particular period found in a field is read as an occupation focus. Only through intensive grid-based recording and collection of large pottery samples, set into the context of intensive analysis of the "offsite" finds around the site, can we offer a reliable interpretation of the scale and nature of human activity in the countryside.

The Ceramic Assemblage

Classical pottery assemblages are rich in forms, although many of the dominant shapes are also found in Archaic and Hellenistic times. This means that many of the finds from surveys or excavations cannot be securely pinned down to particular centuries, and there is a tendency to squeeze sherds which *could* be Classical into the fifth to fourth centuries, making the periods either side appear problematically impoverished. We touched on the main types of figured tableware in Chapter 10. Although it is now clear that red-figure tablewares were not expensive, we lack reliable statistics to clarify how far down the social scale they were in use, although Lohmann (1993b) suggests they are confined to a minority of rural farm sites in comparison to wider use in the city. The importance

of formal drinking at all levels of society is emphasized by the major proportion of cups and *kraters* (jars for mixing wine and water) in typical assemblages. There is an explosion of their production in Greece from the mid-sixth century BC, although their use included ritual, festivals, symposia, and more private home-use. In comparison to Hellenistic and Roman times, amphorae appear less frequently, which implies that long-distance export of bulky food products was at a lower scale, and local consumption dominant. Nonetheless recorded prices place wine-amphorae and honey at modern semi-luxury levels, compared to oil and cereals and figure-painted pottery. The high occurrence of ceramic beehives on town and rural sites is thus not surprising. We noted in Chapter 8 that giant storage-vessels (*pithoi*) were expensive although useful for decades. Our assemblage illustrated in Figure 11.4 presents the everyday household wares, minus the fine tablewares and large pithoi.

The Economy Beyond Agriculture

Agriculture may have provided the mainstay of Classical Aegean state economies but other products could be a major source of income at a secondary level. Mines for example brought relatively short-lived wealth to Athens (silver and lead), and Siphnos (gold and silver), and timber and gold helped to boost the rise of the kingdom of Macedon. Intensive research at the Athenian Lavrion mines has shown a massive and elaborate production area over many square kilometers, although the figure of 20,000 slaves employed there seems a fantasy (Lohmann 2005). Other aspects of the economy are not easily analyzed from ancient sources due to their limited interest in detail and quantification, as well as their imbalance toward Athens, not a typical polis in any respect. Craft workshops were usually home and family based, as were shops, and are well evidenced archaeologically, but seem very rarely to have employed significant groups of artisans. Although banking could be profitable, especially for commercial maritime financing, most citizens preferred to borrow from relatives and friends. However, a few cities where Aegean trade was focused, such as Athens-Piraeus and Corinth, made substantial profits from import-export taxes.

Figure 11.4   Domestic ceramics of the Classical era.
B. A. Sparkes, "The Greek kitchen." *Journal of Hellenic Studies* 82 (1962), 121–137, composite from Plate IV pots 1, 2, 3, 5; Plate V pots 2, 6, 7; Plate VI pots 2, 5.

Nonetheless, there is clear evidence that through the later fifth century in Athens a class of assertive *nouveaux riches* emerged whose income came largely from craft and trade rather than primarily from land. This development may have been resisted by large sectors of the citizen body, but ultimately presaged a general reorientation of Aegean society in Hellenistic and Roman times away from the "hoplite-farmer" lifestyle and mentality so central to the rise of the polis-state (Burke 2002, Rosenbloom 2002).

In contrast, state finances were small-scale, hence the need to call on wealthy citizens to subsidize cultural and military investments. Persian subsidies to favored Greek states, from its vast empire, were able to tip the balance of power in the Aegean in the late fifth and early fourth century (van Wees 2000).

References

Adam-Veleni, P., E. Poulaki, and K. Tzanavari (2003). *Ancient Country Houses on Modern Roads. Central Macedonia.* Athens: Archaeological Receipts Fund.

Alcock, S. E., J. F. Cherry, and J. L. Davis (1994). "Intensive survey, agricultural practice and the classical landscape of Greece." In I. Morris (ed.), *Classical Greece. Ancient Histories and Modern Archaeologies.* Cambridge: Cambridge University Press, 137–170.

Alcock, S. E. *et al.* (2005). "Pylos Regional Archaeological Project, Part VII. Historical Messenia, Geometric through Late Roman." *Hesperia* 74, 147–209.

Ault, B. A. (2005). *The Excavations at Ancient Halieis 2: The Houses. The Organization and Use of Domestic Space.* Bloomington: Indiana University Press.

Barker, G. (1984). "The Montarrenti Survey, 1982–83." *Archeologia Medievale* 11, 278–289.

Barker, G. *et al.* (2000). "Responses to 'The hidden landscape of Prehistoric Greece'." *Journal of Mediterranean Archaeology* 13, 100–123.

Bintliff, J. L. (1994). "Territorial behaviour and the natural history of the Greek polis." In E. Olshausen and H. Sonnabend (eds.), *Stuttgarter Kolloquium zur historischen Geographie des Altertums, 4.* Amsterdam: Hakkert Verlag, 207–249.

Bintliff, J. L. (1997a). "Further considerations on the population of ancient Boeotia." In J. L. Bintliff (ed.), *Recent Developments in the History and Archaeology of Central Greece.* Oxford: BAR Int. Series 666, 231–252.

Bintliff, J. L. (1997b). "Regional survey, demography, and the rise of complex societies in the Ancient Aegean: Core–periphery, Neo-Malthusian, and other interpretive models." *Journal of Field Archaeology* 24, 1–38.

Bintliff, J. (2000). "Deconstructing 'the sense of place'? Settlement systems, field survey, and the historic record: A case-study from Central Greece." *Proceedings of the Prehistoric Society* 66, 123–149.

Bintliff, J. L. and P. Howard (1999). "Studying needles in haystacks. Surface survey and the rural landscape of Central Greece in Roman times." *Pharos* 7, 51–91.

Bintliff, J. L. and A. M. Snodgrass (1985). "The Cambridge/Bradford Boeotian Expedition: The first four years." *Journal of Field Archaeology* 12, 123–161.

Bintliff, J. L. and A. M. Snodgrass (1988a). "Mediterranean survey and the city." *Antiquity* 62, 57–71.

Bintliff, J. L. and A. M. Snodgrass (1988). "Off-site pottery distributions: A regional and interregional perspective." *Current Anthropology* 29, 506–513.

Bintliff, J. L. *et al.* (2002). "Classical farms, hidden prehistoric landscapes and Greek rural survey: A response and an update." *Journal of Mediterranean Archaeology* 15, 259–265.

Bintliff, J. L. *et al.* (2007). *Testing the Hinterland: The Work of the Boeotia Survey (1989–1991) in the Southern Approaches to the City of Thespiai.* Cambridge: McDonald Institute.

Bintliff, J. L. *et al.* (2004–2005). "The Tanagra project: Investigations at an ancient city and its countryside (2000–2002)." *Bulletin de Correspondance Hellénique* 128–129, 541–606.

Burke, E. M. (2002). "The early political speeches of Demosthenes: Elite bias in the response to economic crisis." *Classical Antiquity* 21, 165–194.

Cavanagh, W. *et al.* (1996). *Continuity and Change in a Greek Rural Landscape: The Laconia Survey.* Vol. II. London: British School at Athens.

Cavanagh, W. *et al.* (2003). *Continuity and Change in a Greek Rural Landscape: Laconia Survey.* Vol. I. London: British School at Athens.

Cherry, J. F., J. C. Davis, and E. Mantzourani (1991). *Landscape Archaeology as Long-Term History: Northern Keos in the Cycladic Islands.* Los Angeles: Institute of Archaeology, University of California.

Fisher, N. (1998). "Rich and poor." In P. Cartledge (ed.), *Cambridge Illustrated History of Ancient Greece.* Cambridge: Cambridge University Press, 76–99.

Foxhall, L. (2003). "Cultures, landscapes and identities in the Mediterranean world." *Mediterranean Historical Review* 18(2), 75–92.

Foxhall, L. (2004). "Small, rural farmstead sites in ancient Greece: A material cultural analysis." In F. Kolb (ed.), *Chora und Polis.* München: R. Oldenbourg Verlag, 249–279.

Hansen, M. H. (2004). "The concept of the consumption city applied to the Greek polis." In T. H. Nielsen (ed.),

Once Again: Studies in the Ancient Greek Polis. Stuttgart: Franz Steiner Verlag, 9–47.

Jameson, M. H. (1977–1978). "Agriculture and slavery in Classical Athens." *Classical Journal* 73(2), 122–145.

Jameson, M. H. (1990). "Domestic space in the Greek city-state." In S. Kent (ed.), *Domestic Architecture and the Use of Space.* Cambridge, Cambridge University Press, 92–113.

Jameson, M. H., C. N. Runnels, and T. H. Van Andel (1994). *A Greek Countryside. The Southern Argolid from Prehistory to the Present Day.* Stanford: Stanford University Press.

Kirsten, E. (1956). *Die griechische Polis als historisch-geographisches Problem des Mittelmeerraumes.* Bonn: Colloquium Geographicum 5.

Lawrence, A. W. (1979). *Greek Aims in Fortification.* Oxford: Clarendon Press.

Lohmann, H. (1992). "Agriculture and country life in Classical Attica." In B. Wells (ed.), *Agriculture in Ancient Greece.* Stockholm: Paul Åström, 29–60.

Lohmann, H. (1993a). "Ein Turmgehöft klassischer Zeit in Thimari (Attika)." *Mitteilungen des Deutschen Archäologischen Instituts Athenische Abteilung* 108, 101–149.

Lohmann, H. (1993b). *Atene. Forschungen zu Siedlungs- und Wirtschaftsstruktur des klassischen Attika.* Köln: Böhlau Verlag.

Lohmann, H. (1995). "Die Chora Athens im 4. Jahrhundert v. Chr.: Festungswesen, Bergbau und Siedlungen." In W. Eder (ed.), *Die athenische Demokratie im 4. Jahrhundert v. Chr.* Stuttgart: Franz Steiner, 515–548.

Lohmann, H. (2005). "Prähistorischer und antiker Blei-Silberbergbau im Laurion." In Ü. Yalçin (ed.), *Anatolian Metal III.* Bochum: Deutsches Bergbau-Museum (*Der Anschnitt* Beiheft 18), 105–136.

Mattingly, D. J. (1994). "Regional variation in Roman ole-oculture: Some problems of comparability." In J. Carlsen, P. Ørsted, and J. R. Skydsgaard (eds.), *Land Use in the Roman Empire.* Rome: 'L'Erma' di Bretschneider (Analecta Romana Instituti Danici, Supplementum XXII), 91–106.

Mee, C. and H. Forbes (eds.) (1997). *A Rough and Rocky Place. The Landscape and Settlement History of the Methana Peninsula, Greece.* Liverpool: Liverpool University Press.

Millett, M. (1990). *The Romanization of Britain.* Cambridge: Cambridge University Press.

Orser, C. E. J. (2004). "The archaeologies of recent history." In J. Bintliff (ed.), *A Companion to Archaeology.* London & New York: Blackwell, 272–290.

Osborne, R. (1985). "Buildings and residence on the land in Classical and Hellenistic Greece." *Annual of the British School at Athens* 80, 119–128.

Osborne, R. (1987). *Classical Landscape with Figures.* London: George Philip.

Osborne, R. and L. Foxhall (2001). "Response to David K. Pettegrew, 'Chasing the Classical farmstead'." *Journal of Mediterranean Archaeology* 14, 212–222.

Pettegrew, D. K. (2001). "Chasing the Classical farmstead: Assessing the formation and signature of rural settlement in Greek landscape archaeology." *Journal of Mediterranean Archaeology* 14, 189–209.

Rosenbloom, D. (2002). "From *ponêros* to *pharmakos*: Theater, social drama, and revolution in Athens, 428–404 BCE." *Classical Antiquity* 21, 283–346.

Snodgrass, A. (1987). *An Archaeology of Greece.* Stanford: Stanford University Press.

Snodgrass, A. M. (1990). "Survey archaeology and the rural landscape of the Greek city." In O. Murray and S. Price (eds.), *The Greek City from Homer to Alexandria.* Oxford: Oxford University Press, 113–136.

Snodgrass, A. (1994). "Response: The archaeological aspect." In I. Morris (ed.), *Classical Greece. Ancient Histories and Modern Archaeologies.* Cambridge: Cambridge University Press, 197–200.

Symonds, J. (1997). "The Flora MacDonald Project." *Current Archaeology* 152, 304–307.

Thomas, R. (2000). "The classical city." In R. Osborne (ed.), *Classical Greece.* Oxford: Oxford University Press, 52–80.

Tsouni, K. (ed.) (2001). *Mesogaia.* Athens: Athens International Airport.

van Wees, H. (2000). "The city at war." In R. Osborne (ed.), *Classical Greece.* Oxford: Oxford University Press, 80–110.

Wells, B. and C. Runnels (eds.) (1996). *The Berbati-Limnes Archaeological Survey 1988–1990.* Jonsered: Paul Åström.

Whitelaw, T. (1998). "Colonisation and competition in the polis of Koressos." In L. Mendoni and A. Mazarakis Ainian (eds.), *Keos-Kythnos: History and Archaeology.* Athens: National Hellenic Research Foundation, 227–257.

Wilkinson, T. J. (1989). "Extensive sherd scatters and land-use intensity: Some recent results." *Journal of Field Archaeology* 16, 31–46.

Wilkinson, T. J. (1990). "Soil development and early land use in the Jazira region, Upper Mesopotamia." *World Archaeology* 2, 87–103.

Further Reading

Étienne, R., C. Müller, and F. Prost (2000). *Archéologie historique de la Grèce antique.* Paris: Ellipses.

Whitley, J. (2001). *The Archaeology of Ancient Greece.* Cambridge: Cambridge University Press.

12

Symbolic Material Culture, the Built Environment, and Society in Classical Greece

Classical Art: General Considerations

The art of the Classical Greek era is remarkable for its high quality, although original surviving works are rare. Wooden statues, and paintings on organic surfaces, appear to have been common, but almost never survive the Greek climate. Even marble or bronze statues representing known Classical artists or schools are usually Roman copies, and may not always be precise reproductions; some now appear to be pastiche imitations of Classical style (Beard and Henderson 2001).

Here we shall focus on how symbolic representations illuminate society. Classical Greek art, just as much of its formal literature, has been characterized as primarily a public representation of self-definition or identity by an individual or a city (Fullerton 2000). An early Classical sculptural example is the Tyrant-Slayers (Color Plate 12.1a), a dramatic figure-pair adorning the community center (*agora*) in Athens, portraying a moment in the rise of democracy. Indeed, since only a minority was literate, public art was a more accessible form of communication, so reading it as a coded text offers a plausible approach (Ridgway 1994). It is unsurprising then that human figures dominate late Archaic-Classical ceramic tableware, hence their labels Black-Figure and Red-Figure (Beard 1991). Hallmarks of the post-Archaic style are

greater naturalness and a sensitivity to mood. But historical context is important, as the men represented (Harmodius and Aristogeiton) are being publicly commemorated for assassinating a member of the Peisistratid tyranny shortly before the latter's expulsion and the founding of Athenian democracy at the end of the sixth century BC. But why are both men shown as physically perfect, and naked? Is there significance to the bearded and beardless contrast? We shall see later that these features illustrate Athenian concepts of gender, politics, and personal relations.

Ancient texts and surviving sculptures make clear that every Greek polis, and towns in other political formations such as ethnic federations or kingdoms, were adorned with expensive, finely-made statues. Mostly these were dedications by individuals or the state to communal sanctuaries, both those belonging to states and also interstate sanctuaries. Such standing figures might also mark burials of wealthier members of society, although some states such as Athens prohibited such status markers, to promote its democratic ethos. Stone grave-markers (*stelae*) were also decorated with relief sculptures, which were expensive and thus represented the upper half of society. Rarely, the state erected or allowed the public placing of sculptures to mark exceptional events or individuals, but this was unusual, especially as the latter also contravened the communal ethos of the polis.

A popular misconception, based on their present appearance, assumes that ancient sculptures, as well

The Complete Archaeology of Greece: From Hunter-Gatherers to the 20th Century AD, First Edition. John Bintliff.
© 2012 John Bintliff. Published 2012 by Blackwell Publishing Ltd.

as temples and their sculpted ornament, were austere white or shades of yellow and grey, the color of their stone. But it has long been known that added color was ubiquitous, elaborate, and to our modern eyes, garish. Color was added through both painting and varied types of stone or metal inlays (Color Plate 12.1b). The British Museum's claim that the "Elgin Marbles," priceless sculptures from the Parthenon marble pediments, frieze, and metopes, were safer in London than had they been left in Greece, were seriously undermined when it was admitted that at one point they were scrubbed with metal brushes and chiseled to restore their supposed pristine whiteness! On this issue, this author strongly believes "the Marbles" must be returned to the nation which created them, especially now a state-of-the-art museum has been built specifically to house them. Incidentally, another aspect of the Greek love of polychrome was its Oriental associations, reminding us how Early Modern Eurocentric views of Ancient Greece preferred white austerity to the original rich palette.

Although freestanding or monument-based marble sculptures are given central attention by Classical art specialists, their high color reminds us that the underlying material was chosen primarily for durability, with (mostly lost) bronzes being infinitely more expensive. Nonetheless, recent research has argued that multiple reproduction of similar bronze statues was carried out even by the most famous artists.

Another class of Classical art which does survive in impressive numbers is figure-decorated fine ware pottery, primarily tableware and hence for social display. So attractive is this class of artifact that the products of the leading producers, especially from Athens, found their way not only throughout the Greek homeland and colonial world, but also in smaller quantities into every settled landscape of the Mediterranean and even into "barbarian" tribal societies and chiefdoms in temperate Europe. The commonest form, Red-Figure, used the natural reddish color of the ceramic for the objects portrayed, set in contrast against a background of glossy black paint, but with details painted onto the paler areas with black and white paint. This allows finer detailing than was possible with Black-Figure wares. Although most Greek city-states produced non-figured black gloss pottery, and some Red-Figure

ware too, Athens monopolized the trade in finer versions of the style.

The naturalism and sophisticated designs strike modern eyes as exceptional, if not masterly, a reaction which has helped these vases being treated in Art History as surpassing the products of most other world cultures. Unsurprisingly, Classical figured-wares reach high, occasionally astronomical, prices on the art market. Greek Classical art has always been presented, since Roman times, as symbolic of the unsurpassable quality of Greek civilization, which in turn has featured in an origin myth for the global importance of Europe in the development of world civilization. When Greek vases were first marketed on a significant scale from the late eighteenth century, by entrepreneurs such as Sir William Hamilton (although at first they were assumed from their find-spots to have been made in Etruria under Greek inspiration), their value was promoted by the suggestion that such fine works were originally prestigious possessions.

Connoisseurship went hand in hand with commerce, and Art History went further, appropriating an anachronistic model of art production which derived from the Renaissance era and afterwards in Europe: the artist as a creative genius, whose unique luxury products were recognizable by distinct stylistic features within a generic tradition for each age. It was the lifetime achievement of John Beazley (1895–1970) to have claimed, by meticulous study of a large corpus of Athenian Classical vases, to have identified a series of such master painters (Spivey 1997b, Whitley 2001). In the absence of associated names for all but a few (and the significance of many of the latter is disputed in terms of their role in the production process), he assigned these anonymous craftsmen a title based upon their favorite subject or a stylistic attribute (e.g., the Midas Painter), and their products have been further studied by his successors, gifted analysts such as Boardman (2006).

It is difficult to place figured vases back into their original context, especially when traditional museum presentation, in serried ranks of glass cases, proclaims them "works of art," obscuring their everyday role in ancient Greek life (Shanks 1997). Yet in ancient sources, potters were people of low status, along with most craftsmen. In contrast, sculptors and fresco-painters were widely known by name and work, and the most sought-after were appreciated more like modern artists. Vickers (1990, 2004), Gill (1988), and Vickers and Gill (1995) consistently criticize the concept of figured vases as articles of high value, produced by master craftsmen.

The prices on vase-sets (Johnston 1991) seem clear evidence that black gloss tableware was not vastly more expensive if it possessed painted scenes (figureless was 25–50 percent cheaper), and both were of moderate cost, within the reach of all but the poor. More controversial is Vickers and Gill's claim that many features of figured ware are imitations of tableware in bronze, silver, and gold: cheap copies of vessels of genuine value. Even experts in the Beazley-style attribution of pots to a particular workshop have offered unintentional support. Studies of Athenian Black-and-Red-Figure workshops have estimated that their typical production by potter-painters of low social status in small-scale workshops might have run at 5–6 painted vessels per working day (Stissi 2002; H. Brijder, *pers. comm.*). It is probable that wealthy citizens accumulated quality metalware in bronze, silver, and gold as capital and for home display to their peers, almost all of which has vanished through ancient recycling. When Philip II sacked the town of Olynthus in 348 BC his soldiers took the metalware, but left plenty of ceramic tableware (Cahill 2002). Vickers provocatively calculates the following Classical Greek vase value ratio: painted pottery 1, bronze 10, silver 1000, and gold 10,000.

If wealthy people deployed expensive metalware for the table, and most others used figured or plain black-gloss wares, there was also a pottery class designed primarily for funerary deposition, White-Ground ware, especially in the *lekythos* form, containing an offering of oil for the deceased. This is a tall, narrow fine ware vase with a flaring rim and attached handle for easy pouring, used for anointing the body and the tomb before being deposited with the burial. The fine white surface would not survive regular handling in a household context, but such wares were certainly used for unguents in the home (Nevett 1999).

The high frequency of human figures on Classical tablewares indicates a system of signs, where selective aspects of contemporary society are repeatedly on display (Beard 1991). We should therefore focus on the viewer rather than the artist. Yet "reading" Classical art is beset by a weighty scholarly heritage. The historian Plutarch, part of an Early Roman cultural revival of all things Classical Greek (the "Second Sophistic"), gave us the concept of a High Classical flowering, climaxing in the later fifth century BC, notably in the buildings on the Athenian Acropolis. This marked a standard against which all subsequent art was to be compared. We are today struck by the development from a rather formal Archaic art, growing more naturalistic in the early Classical "Severe Syle" at the start of the fifth century, and then reaching a remarkable harmony of ideal beauty with close attention to naturalistic detail in mid-century. Some, however, see later fifth-century Athenian art as a partial retreat into a formalistic, programmatic, arid beauty. The explanation for these revolutionary explorations of representation is nowadays sought less in the inherent genius of European peoples, and Greeks in particular, but rather in historical context. The dramatic experience of the Persian Wars and the highly personal involvement of citizens in the Greek polis in all its public manifestations stimulated a sharpened sense of human freedom and personal responsibility, as well as an almost arrogant self-comparison to the Gods (Fullerton 2000). At the same time, both Fullerton and Spivey (1997) emphasize the competitive ethos within the polis. These forces built a favored iconography of ideal figures, modeled on perfect versions of living people, capable of anything and masters of their own destiny.

Temple Art in the Classical Period

Classical cityscapes remained dominated by the major temples of the city's patron divinities, especially when their location was elevated above the politico-legal, domestic, and business quarters of the town, as most famously in the city of Athens. Because Athens has always stood in the Western mind as the greatest of Greek cultural centers, so too its symbolic heart, the Acropolis, has been given intensive scholarly and touristic attention from the early pioneers of Classical Archaeology in the late eighteenth century AD (Stuart and Revett 1762–1816) onwards (see following Text Box).

The Athenian Acropolis

Many questions remain concerning the great building program here of the later fifth century BC, in which the Athenians constructed a new set of religious buildings to match their rich and powerful empire (Hurwit 1999, Beard 2002). The new design replaced monuments of the Archaic era, but on a grander scale (see Figure 11.1). A great entrance-portal, the Propylaea, brought the visitor onto the flat summit of the limestone hill which dominates the center of Athens. To the right of this monumental gate-complex is set the beautiful, small temple of Athena Nike (Athena Victorious), whilst directly ahead lay the great rectangular Parthenon temple (Athena the Maiden), containing a giant ivory and gold (chryselephantine) statue of the goddess. Left of the Parthenon a complex, split-level double sanctuary, the Erechtheion, celebrated Poseidon, Athena, Hephaestos, and a legendary hero Erechtheus. The rest of the hilltop gradually filled up with dedicatory statues and inscriptions throughout the era and into Roman times, since the entire Acropolis was now reserved for public cult and the display of the records cut in stone of individuals and the state.

The decorative scheme which ornaments the classic architectural design of the Parthenon (Figure 12.1) is in the most general terms well understood, but in critical details also poorly understood and subject to increasingly divergent theories. Let us start with the areas of general agreement.

The most visible artistic zone is at both ends of the building, where a large triangular area (*pediment*) tops the pillared façades. One end depicts the birth of Athena, the other the contest of Athena and Poseidon for the honor of being Athens' patron; thus both celebrate the eponymous deity of the city and infer that even the Gods would fight for that privilege. Also, on the outside of the temple and above the outer ringing (*peripteral*) portico on the long and short sides, a regular series of square panels (*metopes*), show scenes familiar from other polis temples, portraying warfare of distinct types. An *Ilioupersis* commemorates the legendary Greek war at Anatolian Troy, whilst an *Amazonomachy* shows Greek warrior males defeating the female warriors of mythical barbarians in the region of the Black Sea. A *Centauromachy* displays a fight between drunken, lascivious Centaurs (half man, half horse) and Lapiths, a civilized mythical people defending their womenfolk. Finally the *Gigantomachy* shows

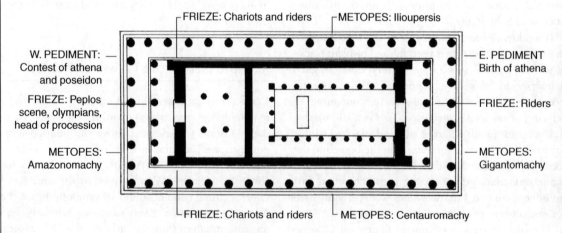

Figure 12.1   The decorative scheme of the Parthenon.
M. D. Fullerton, *Greek Art*. Cambridge 2000, Figure 35. © Cambridge University Press.

the epic battle of the Olympian Gods against the Giants. All these scenes have in common the contest of Classical Greek polis values against "The Other," ways of life in various respects which are non-Greek and represent a threat to the Classical Greek world (Fullerton 2000). This opposition was both symbolic and real in contemporary power-politics. Thus for the Greeks, non-Greek invading armies were a permanent danger in the sixth and fifth centuries BC (Persians for the Aegean homeland, Phoenicians for the Greek colonial West, "barbarian" tribes and kingdoms for the Greek colonies around the Black Sea).

Invoking the Trojan War aligned Greek victories over such enemies with the heroic achievements of their ancestors, of particular resonance in Athens which had played a central role in the defeat of the Persians and still maintained vigilance through its maritime empire against further threats. The monstrous, primitive giants likewise were a symbol of the enormous armies of the Greeks' enemies, whilst the Olympian gods were made in the form and character of the Greeks' own concept of themselves as a people. Centaurs and Amazons challenged the mentality of Greek polis life. Civil disorder, abuse of hospitality and of individual rights were defended by the civilized Lapiths. The Amazon race of warrior women represented the overturning of the male domination of the polis, both by claiming equality in physical accomplishment and heroism with men, and in spurning the correct female values of domesticated marriage, child-rearing, and breast-feeding, central to the inferior place allotted to respectable women in the Classical city-state.

Interpretive disagreement concerns the frieze above the interior wall on the long sides and above the interior portico on the short sides of the Parthenon. This location, together with the frieze's height, makes visibility from the ground very difficult, although the craftsmen tilted the frieze downwards so that its features were somewhat clearer. As with much Greco-Roman monumental art, however, this rather challenges modern expectations that art is primarily there for anonymous viewers, whereas an equal role could be as a

statement by the work's commissioners, or for the Gods to appreciate.

The frieze has one theme, a procession winding around three sides of the temple, culminating with the head of the procession meeting a group of seated Gods and forming the "Peplos Scene" at the west end of the Parthenon. The traditional reading sees the people of contemporary Athens processing to the Acropolis, where they will sacrifice to Athena, and in the presence of the Gods dedicate a new garment (*peplos*) to the ancient statue of the goddess in the Erechtheion. An appropriate occasion was the four-yearly state procession and games of the Great Panathenaia. But there are unresolved difficulties. For example the "Peplos Scene" does not clearly show the presentation of the goddess's new garment but perhaps something else. Alternative theories have been proposed, some obscure and perhaps incomprehensible to non-Athenian admirers visiting this monument of imperial propaganda. I still feel that the traditional reading is the most economical, and if we accept it then an interesting conclusion has been drawn by Foxhall (1995). A feature of the Classical polis was its careful prohibition against enhancing individual status, mindful of the not-long-distant threat of tyranny and elite families to the democratic citizen ethos dominant in at least half of Classical city-states. It is exceptional rather than common to find living people portrayed, and these are victorious generals or Olympic victors representing the community. But here the people of Athens represent themselves on their most elaborate state monument, at the highpoint of their city, and of course as a nation of perfectly-formed human beings. Moreover, as a sign of arrogance, even the Gods sit and admire this citizenry in a scene where both occupy the same stage. The Parthenon frieze represents overreaching self-admiration and a claim to superiority, matching the speech in praise of Athens by its first citizen Pericles as reported (or imagined?) by the contemporary historian Thucydides (*History of the Peloponnesian War* 2.38.2.), both basking in the great success of the Athenian imperial venture.

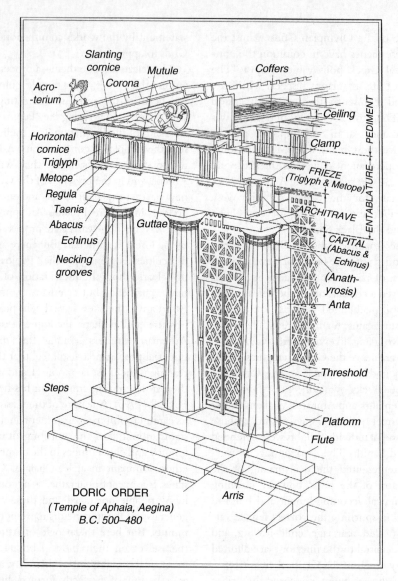

Figure 12.2   The Doric architectural order.
A. W. Lawrence and R. A. Tomlinson, *Greek Architecture*. New Haven 1996, xiv, unnumbered figures.

Finally and on a more general note, we should mention that the two main Classical architectural "orders" (Figures 12.2 and 12.3) were used widely and even in the same Greek sanctuary complexes, so that style and context are more important than any link to dialect or ethnicity which the labels "Doric/Ionian" might imply (Lawrence and Tomlinson 1996).

Theaters

We have seen the agoras of polis-centers becoming filled with civic buildings for political, legal, commercial, and cultural-social purposes from late Archaic times onwards, but one building sees considerable monumentalization in the Classical era: the theater. Although this institution was widespread amongst Greek states, its

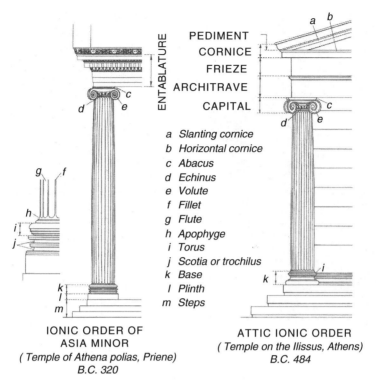

Figure 12.3   The Ionic architectural order.
A. W. Lawrence and R. A. Tomlinson, *Greek Architecture*. New Haven 1996, xv, unnumbered figures.

role in Athens was truly exceptional, since the vast majority of Classical dramas were composed and first performed there. Both here and in other states, drama began as part of religious festivals in which choruses performed dances alongside spoken and sung texts. The special emphasis on the exploration of individual and community beliefs and actions which the Greek polis engendered, not only led to the high significance attached to citizen participation in political assembly debates and legal cases, but also to a form of public presentation of contemporary issues through increasingly sophisticated tragedies and comedies (Rhodes 2003). As noted earlier, appropriately theatrical events once staged in the agora or on hill slopes were seen in the fifth to fourth centuries as worth embedding into large and expensive stone complexes. These incorporated tiered seating adequate for a large proportion of male citizens, a near-circular dance-chorus floor at its base (*orchestra*), and behind this a raised stage with rear rooms for changing and arranging appearances.

Gender Relations, Family, and Class: The Iconography of Figured Vases and Tombstones

For an archaeologist, Black- and Red-Figure fine tableware is less interesting for its disputed status as evidence for master craftsmen, than for the insights it offers into how Greek society worked, or was supposed to work, as represented on such vases. Figure 12.4 offers an excellent introduction to the study of Classical gender relations (Beard 1991).

This image, used repeatedly, follows clear conventions, allowing us to recognize a house interior, with the wife intently spinning on a chair, whilst her husband watches carefully. He stands over her, close enough to be almost threatening, but his walking-stick informs us he is either on his way out of the home or just arrived back, and that he is a man-about-town of sufficient income not to need to use his hands

Figure 12.4   Red-Figure Attic vase showing a household scene.
© Trustees of the British Museum.

for manual work. A female servant appears from behind the housewife with a box, perhaps the wife's jewelry. The latter activity is generally shown separately, where the wife examines her adornments alone with her servant. In Greek art it was permissible to show sequent activities on the same panel ("synoptic" scenes). Very similar scenes appear on the gravestones of women (Stears 1995, Leader 1997).

The relative body positions of the man and woman indicate the dominance of the husband, and the importance he attaches to her wifely duties. Another common task portrayed is the wife looking after the children (usually male). If the woman's place is in the home, the man appears to be "not at home" but calling in, between his activities in the outside world of the city. Some representations however show an old man, seated, but with a walking-stick. This seems to illustrate the fate of this male age-group, unable to spend the day out in the town due to age and infirmity, but perhaps wishing to be there. The opposition between *oikos* (the home) and *polis* (the public side of city life), is a central theme of such scenes, symbolizing gender roles. As we shall see later, recent research identifies the entire house (the formal dining-room excepted) as the women's area. Appropriately, male grave reliefs show a different role "persona" (Leader 1997): hoplite, athlete, or man-about-town.

However, purely chauvinistic readings of such scenes require some "deconstruction." The presentation of the wife's jewelry casket is a good place to start, especially if we link this with women depicted on vases and gravestones looking into mirrors. A modern reading might identify a male stereotype of women as obsessed with outward appearances, but there are strong reasons to reject this. The wife's dowry was fundamental to most marriages, whilst she was also responsible for the household economy; if divorce occurred, her own family was entitled to reclaim her bride-wealth. Thus the jewelry box symbolizes her contribution to the couple's assets (money, land, stock, textiles). The mirror scenes contain another message. On one tombstone with such a portrayal, a text informs the passer-by of the inner beauty of the deceased. The deceased woman looking at herself in the mirror symbolizes her relatives looking admirably into her remembered character.

Other vase images show a very different world, orgiastic parties in the *andron* or formal dining-room of the house. Textual sources indicate that the participants are the male household-head and his male relatives and acquaintances, the only females being party entertainers or prostitutes. Appropriately the scene is found on drinking-cups (*kylix* or *skyphos*) used on such occasions. Also of note, females paid to entertain men are allowed to drink reclining like men, whereas wives and daughters in domestic scenes are seated in upright chairs. Wild symposia of this kind were probably restricted to the wealthy sector of the polis, whilst more typical gatherings were perhaps better seen as the ancient equivalent of the Early Modern Greek male-only coffee-house (*kapheneion*) where men bonded and arranged marriages, land-deals and exchanged reflections on the contemporary world (Jameson 1990b). Returning to the issue of gender portrayals, it is striking that female nudity in Classical Greek art is extremely rare outside such "lowlife" contexts. Introducing the female nude into public art, including religious art, even of the love-goddess Aphrodite, was highly unusual. When the late Classical sculptor Praxiteles carved a titillating nude Aphrodite (Figure 12.5), the citizens of Cnidus set it into a

Figure 12.5 The Cnidos Aphrodite. Marble. Roman, ca. 180 AD. Slightly altered copy of the Aphrodite of Cnidos by Praxiteles, ca. 350 BC.
Vatican Museums, Rome, inv. no. 474. akg-images/ Nimatallah.

portico peep-show; it became a focus of sensational pilgrimage (Spivey 1997b).

In contrast to "respectable women," male nudity was ubiquitous and appears gratuitous and celebratory, in vase-painting, freestanding sculpture, and friezes. A well-known tombstone of two youths has one entirely nude; they are seemingly citizens of Athens who perished in battle, from the hoplite equipment they bear. But this cannot be so, since Athens had a special funeral place for its heroic war dead, and this monument is part of the general cemetery memorials. Rather the deceased appear with appropriate symbolism for their stage in life. A young free male at 18 became a citizen, and in the following years he accrued rights and duties: firstly to fight for his city, training initially in border-patrols. Ideally he would exercise frequently in the gymnasium in preparation for war. Only later was he allowed to vote in the assembly and the lawcourts. The men are shown in youthful prime, physically ideal. The nakedness of the front figure is clearly designed to display his beautiful physique to the admiring onlooker. In the same way aristocratic members of the Parthenon procession frieze include naked riders.

The contrasted representation of female and male bodies in Classical Greek art proves extremely enlightening for our understanding of the social reproduction of polis society (Stewart 1997, Spivey 1997). Although the home in art and texts formed the domain of women, whilst male citizens were expected to be outside, busy with the wider life of the city, this has to be significantly nuanced. Firstly, as in Western society until recently, this gender division was desired by the middle and upper classes, based on achieved income by the husband, or inherited wealth from both partners. But perhaps one half of the free population belonged to the poorer citizenry, where family labor sustained the household. Most Greeks were full- or part-time farmers, and although only the poorest citizens were without slaves (Jameson 1977–1978), the assistance of wife and children in farming or artisanal work would probably have been normal for the lower and lower-middle income groups. This would have meant daytime absence from the house, and communal work, for women and daughters, something rarely visible in Classical art, where the lifestyle of the upper half of society dominates. Nonetheless, modesty remained important to a patriarchal society, and arranging female work in public within a wider circle of relatives and friends would have been the first protection of female virtue, followed by modesty in clothing. But for the upper-middle and upper-class families, the desirability of female seclusion in the enclosed house is suggested by ancient sources and house designs. As for permitted travel into public areas by such women, accompanied by suitable male escorts, there is considerable evidence for their use of veiling in the presence of strangers (Llewellyn-Jones 2004).

Women were a guarded resource. Firstly because they brought wealth to the household, but secondly because the polis monitored the parenthood of offspring to ensure their legal and political rights. Moreover, in a severely chauvinistic society, the respect of male citizens was at risk from the sexual attentions of other men toward their womenfolk. The naked female body was usually displayed in art, as in public, to represent non-respectable females, their immodesty marking their role in society as marginalized taboo-breakers exciting the lust of men.

But why the constant exposure of the male body? The traditional answer connects ideal forms of human to the ideal gender: male. Contemporary texts classify women as weaker physically and intellectually than men, their role being to support the male citizen through a well-run home and by producing male children. The higher aim of the human species was (male) participation in the introverted society of the polis, through its communal political and legal institutions, and equally important, being able to defend the polis against its enemies (often close neighbors).

The Olympian gods were, with few exceptions given perfect human bodies with supernatural powers, and chief among them were the males. Legendary heroes possessed similar attributes. The ideal form for a citizen was therefore a well-proportioned, athletic male, and we can see this aspect in sculpture and gravestones, or figured vase scenes, where the male is often gratuitously naked. Experts such as Richter (1971) focus therefore on the anatomical exactness of the male body-beautiful (Figure 12.6) as the explanatory key to repetitive male nudes in Classical art. Furthermore ancient writers report that leading sculptors (such as here Polycleitos) consciously designed figures with mathematically balanced proportions (Spivey 1997a).

And yet, there is much more being expressed here. Stewart (1997) and Beaumont (1994, 1998) emphasize the divergent trajectories of male and female citizens at puberty. In Athens, where our sources are richest, girls were married as young as possible, often from age 13, passing from their mothers' tutelage to the control of a husband, who was typically twice their age. They moved from learning to practicing wifely skills. Teenage boys were expected to mix with male relatives, male peers, and also older unrelated males. Sports and military training provided indoctrination into the outdoor world of masculine citizens, whilst here and through the participation of youths at the symposium, came intimate relations with older men. If men generally married in their late 20s, then male sexual desires from puberty might be directed to prostitutes, but especially through homosexuality. Indeed the partnership of young males and older men was considered a respectable

Figure 12.6 The Garlanded Youth (Diadumenos) by Polycleitos. Marble, h. 186 cm. Fifth century BC. Ancient copy from Delos.
akg-images/De Agostini Picture Library.

and desirable form of male citizen bonding, achieving a broader intimacy and education into the society of male citizens than relatives might provide. Revisiting the public statues to Harmodius and Aristogeiton, which opened this chapter, the bearded and beardless pair shows the age difference between two male lovers, whose quarrel with the ruling family of tyrants in late sixth-century Athens was as much about sexual rivalry as violent politics. On Athenian figured vases (Bérard 1984), a recurrent theme is the pursuit of youths by older men, portrayed metaphorically through the hunt, a dog chasing a hare, and more direct scenes of gifts of wild game (dead, or playfully alive) to such boys, symbolizing the same romantic metaphor.

For Stewart (1997), the obsession with nude masculinity in Classical Greece reflected a highly successful strategy, where adolescent male sexual desire was diverted from largely unavailable female sexuality in order to strengthen a male-bonded public life.

Sometimes this culminated in an extreme public self-sacrifice, when an elite core of the polis army comprised pairs of male lovers, who would perish rather than flee even in defeat, to avoid shame in their partner's eyes.

Nonetheless, we cannot underestimate the significant, if secondary, place assigned to women citizens in the Classical polis. In fifth-century Athenian cemeteries there are as many female as male figured gravestones, and as many as both combined where males and females are portrayed together (Stears 1995). In contrast to the Archaic period, where rich males dominate figured-stelae graves or graves with sculptures above, the Classical repertoire represents a broadening to middle-class use and a new balance in the genders, whilst the scenes highlight how men and women equally maintain society. In democratic states anti-elite legislation led to the decline of the more prestigious grave sculptures, but in those that remain from Athens the equal emphasis on men and women served the state's purposes by advertising the legitimacy of offspring as born of two citizen parents. On a more positive note, much of the art expresses a broader set of approved norms for women as household manager, dowry-bringer, manufacturer of home textiles, and carrier of admired virtue, rather than *merely* as childrearer.

The complexity of funerary art symbolism reminds us that communal cemeteries were visual highpoints in the cityscape. Graves were not just in use at the time of bereavement, but witnessed regular ceremonies of memorial by relatives. Urban necropoleis were often located by roadsides leading out of the town so that passers-by were drawn to "view" them; they were thus theaters of representation of desired social relations, at least for the middle to upper classes who could afford such monuments and aspire to the lifestyle portrayed.

In contrast, at least in Boeotia, where surface survey has located numerous dispersed *rural* cemeteries marking the estates of Classical farmers, computer-aided spatial analysis indicates that most family grave groups were rarely visible from roads or other farms, and were largely placed for the benefit of the landowning families themselves as they worked their farms, and their guests, and to remind others who strayed onto an estate whose land it was (Bintliff *et al.* 2004–2005, 2007).

Women on figured pots and grave sculptures are rarely shown in professions. Apart from entertainers, servants assist their housewife-mistresses, their lower status emphasized through lighter, more revealing clothing, shorter hair, and often in reduced scale. This underlines these scenes' class bias, working-class farmers' wives and street vendors also being unsuitable models for representation. A potter's workshop shown on a figured-vase, where one painter is clearly female is a rare glimpse of underrepresented realities.

Closer analysis of women on figured vases (Bérard 1984) encourages the view that although middle- and upper-class wives were constrained by male-focused conventions, they could create a parallel world in which perhaps men were intruders. Women reading to each other, performing music or dancing, were private, small-scale forms of "resistance" to their exclusion from public artistic expression, yet some would link such rarely-portrayed scenes to a broader world of female companionship, in which women are shown swimming in the countryside, and even using the gymnasium (speculatively on special women's days?). Additionally women were the central figures in rites concerned with death and commemoration of family dead. Finally, women had public and private cults of their own in which they could find organizational and spiritual fulfillment and a shared female perspective. One was a house-cult of Adonis, when women decorated the roofs.

Beaumont (1998) points out that in Greek Classical art, female goddesses are adult and powerful, and should not be shown as children. Aphrodite and Athena were indeed born as adults. A childlike weakness, assumed by Greek culture to be typical of mortal women throughout their lives, cannot be permitted with the gods. The need to draw the line between allowing immortal women to hold sway over a man's world, and the tight subordination of mortal women, is clearly expressed in iconography and myth.

In late Classical times, the power of most poleis declined, and specialists have seen a corresponding rise in a more sympathetic portrayal of women, children, and the family in art, as society turned more inwards to the individual and private life (Leader 1997, Beaumont 1994, 1998). Sojc (2005) has sensitively charted this trend toward a broader and subtler humanity in grave reliefs. At the same time, as family begins to take precedence over community, art and house design show more obvious class distinctions. Yet even in Athens during the highpoint of its democracy, there was always scope for elite families to emphasize their distinctiveness, whether in deploying advantages in education and leisure to lead the city in political or military matters, or being allowed to continue taking traditionally privileged roles in religious cults, or being blatantly milked by the city through compulsory contributions to the construction of warships and the sponsoring of dramatic choruses (*leitourgia*).

Slaves were depicted in smaller scale than citizens, like children, and indeed the same word *paidia* was used for both. Conditions varied from family to family as to how household slaves were treated, although in formal respects they were treated as family members and were often honored thus in death. Yet literature and iconography includes examples suggesting that abuse of slaves, including physical and sexual maltreatment, need not arouse communal disapproval. Nonetheless inscriptions show that building projects, craft workshops, and farming were widely carried out by mixed teams of citizens, free aliens (*metics*), and slaves. Only in projects such as the Athenian silvermines at Lavrion were many thousands of slaves employed in generally brutal conditions, but even here it is argued that skilled technicians amongst them lived like prosperous citizens (Lohmann 2005).

Houses and Town Planning

Typically, Classical towns with long histories of urban development, commencing in Geometric-Archaic times, grew "organically": clusters of houses aggregated around public foci such as an acropolis, agora or major temple. Larger settlements had several nuclei of dispersed hamlets which gradually merged over time into irregular blocks separated by narrow, winding streets. This contrasts with rarer examples of more regular settlement plans from later Geometric-early Archaic times (such as Vroulia on Rhodes, and early colonies such as Megara Hyblaea in Sicily). Here it seems that aristocratic elites set out a formal land division, made possible by colonization of a new site, whilst conceiving of regular alignments of small house-plots as appropriate spaces for peasant families.

Earlier, we observed the tendency over Geometric-Archaic times for individual houses to grow in size and in the number of formal spaces. In parallel more privacy

was achieved through the layout of the multi-roomed home and its more limited access and visibility to neighbors. These developments relate closely to the contemporary emergence and proliferation of the city-state. Even in regions formally "*ethne*" or federal-tribal states with multiple nucleated settlements, such as Thessaly (Auda *et al.* 1990), we find comparable towns. For all these polis and polis-like cities, the rise of citizen rights and the enhanced importance of birth legitimacy (so as to be entitled to citizenship) stimulated investment in house architecture which enclosed the family as a private unit for citizen reproduction, biologically and socially. At the same time rising wealth and aspiration encouraged all but the poorest families to create or commission homes with separate built spaces for human residents, animals, and the reception of visitors.

Thus despite the overall contrast between Athens, notorious for its unplanned domestic districts, and the rigid house-block grids of the replanned "New Town" of Olynthus in the later fifth century BC, most recorded Classical townhouses have comparable plot sizes and internal designs. Moreover, from late Archaic times the rise of grid-pattern town planning appears to reflect a conscious concept of dividing both town and country space into modular units appropriate to a citizen-farmer family of middling wealth. Although fifth-century regular grid-plan towns are associated with the city planner Hippodamus, he merely elaborated and advertised the concept through high-profile commissions such as the new Athenian port-town of Piraeus, and at Rhodes. Significantly, such grid-plans are organized around units of house blocks (*insulae*) rather than the custom of Roman towns, which were articulated through city gates, the central square (*forum*), and other major public buildings (Jameson 1990b).

The Mediterranean climate and the economics of everyday life make a courtyard a natural focus for the home, so that all the main design variants recognized by specialists differ in the way surrounding rooms relate to this open space. Only in the largest cities of the wider Greek world (Alexandria, Antioch), and significantly in Hellenistic times, did modern-style housing pressure lead to tower-like apartment plots with at best only internal lightwells for air and sunlight added to rare external windows. Typical houses from the Northern Greek city of Olynthus can thus illustrate the general nature of the Greek home for average families. (Following Text Box.)

Housing at Olynthus

Olynthus (Figure 12.7) was occupied on its South Hill from ca. 1000 BC, but during the fifth century BC it expanded considerably, mainly due to immigration from other settlements in its region, the Chalkidike peninsula. This "*synoecism*" or merger of communities was probably in reaction to the rising threat from the hinterland kingdom of Macedon. Indeed Philip II of Macedon besieged and destroyed the town in 348 BC, after which only insignificant reuse is attested. The preceding urban expansion focused on a grid-planned "New Town" on the North Hill and part of the adjacent plateau to its east. During the 1920s, a Greek-American excavation undertook large-scale research on the North Hill, producing what is still today the most extensive sample of Classical housing in the Aegean (more than 100 houses excavated, 50 of which are completely planned). Although by modern standards the recording and recovery of structures and finds was limited, the excavation was exceptionally good for its period, allowing Cahill (2002) to reanalyze the impressive series of site monographs and the plentiful unpublished dig-records, and find remarkable insights into everyday life in the town during the period immediately prior to its sack.

As might be expected, limited trials on the older-settled South Hill found an irregular layout, whilst the "New Town" on the North Hill was largely composed in the now popular Classical style of regular blocks of homes, each two rows of five separated by an alley and surrounded by grid-plan streets. House plots were broadly equal, on which homes of closely similar design were erected on stone foundations with mudbrick superstructures. Many showed signs of an upper story, but it remains unclear if this was normal. The repeated plan (Figure 12.8) has a single entrance to the street, from which the focal, often paved yard is accessed (i on the plan). The latter links together all the other built spaces, emphasizing its importance in daily household life, a fact underlined by its abundant artifact finds and the fact that adjacent rooms were largely lit from its daylight.

A portico faces the court (f), offering shelter from sun, wind, and rain, whilst allowing sunlight and air to circulate, and acts therefore as an extension to the fully open yard. At a deeper access-level, a series of small rooms behind the portico form the household living-quarters (a–e), incorporating units for washing and cooking with special drainage and draught facilities (c–d respectively), the others serving storage and daily family life. They are usually unpaved. Separately accessed rooms (h) may be stables or additional general storage and family space. The formal dining room (*andron*, "male room") (k) and an antechamber for food preparation or serving in that space (j) (bottom right) are distinctly furnished rooms, also separately accessed from the yard. The andron has settings for dining-benches, mosaic or plaster floor, and decorated walls. Some houses had a room on the street without internal access, seen as a shop or workshop. Although contemporary texts suggest separate areas for women and men, only the dining-room appears gender-linked. Visitors emerge directly into the courtyard, where normally family members of both sexes doubtless spent much of the day. However, the lost upper floor, and uncertainty over its frequency, makes it plausible that distinct female quarters were here, in the most remote place from stranger-access.

Since ground floor windows were high and small, whilst the entrance door was a substantial barrier, the overall design emphasizes family seclusion rather than gender or class division, for no obvious areas for slaves or servants can be identified (Jameson 1990a–b). As for fixed features, immobile storage vessels are rare, suggesting many rooms were multifunctional. Fixed hearths are uncommon, suggesting that portable braziers were used for heating and cooking, and this suits activities moving around rooms and also into the portico and yard as the weather and company dictated.

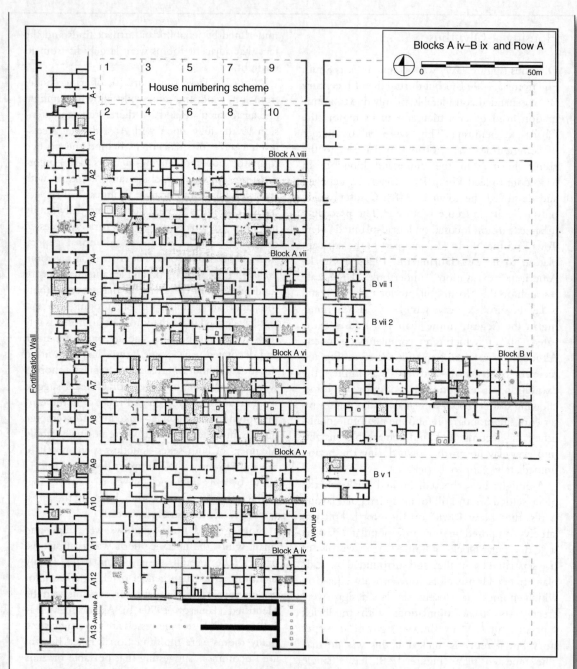

Figure 12.7   A series of house blocks on the North Hill, Olynthus.
N. Cahill, *Household and City Organization at Olynthus*. New Haven: Yale University Press 2002, Figure 7.

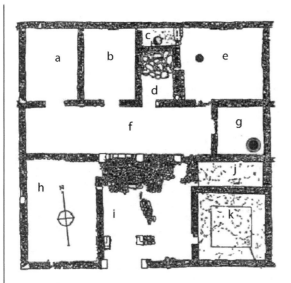

Figure 12.8   A typical Olynthus house plan.
M. H. Jameson, "Domestic space in the Greek city-state."
In S. Kent (ed.), *Domestic Architecture and the Use of Space.*
© Cambridge University Press 1990, Figure 7.6.

Why did citizens prefer to live side-by-side in these small habitations, where work, leisure, storage, some animals, family, slaves/servants, and guests were accommodated at varying times, rather than in the countryside, closer to the primary income source for most Classical Greeks, their estates, and where land was cheaper and hence habitation space could be wider? Following Höpfner and Schwandner (1994), the primacy of the city-state or urban-citizen mentality overrode convenience, with the majority of families choosing life in a town-like nucleation to that in villages or farms. Moreover the uniformity of the necessarily small plots and almost identical house plans reflected a shared ethos of citizen equality before the law, and in at least half of Greek city-states, of major political rights for free male household-heads. Almost all Olynthus house plots are 200–300 m², comparable to those in fifth-century BC grid-planned Piraeus.

More irregular houses have been excavated around the Athenian Agora, where individual homes are identified through separate courtyards, but even here the larger houses are only of the normal Olynthus size, making the smaller appear rather impoverished. Athenian sources state that some poorer folk did not possess storage space. Overall, an immense gulf appears between the size and grandeur of public (religious and secular) architecture and that applied to private life in the Classical Aegean city, reinforcing the primacy of the *polis* over the *oikos* (home).

The majority of Greeks were farmers but additionally urban dwellers: agricultural processing and the storage of estate produce took place in the house plot. Animals were probably few per family, larger flocks of sheep/goats or cattle being managed on the large estates of the rich, or group-managed for several families by rural shepherds. Urban families probably had traction or pack animals such as donkeys, and small stock such as milk-goats and chickens in their household enclosures. A typical family possessed large storage jars for water, oil, and wine. But surprisingly little clearly differentiated space exists to reflect these activities. Hints such as rare wheel-ruts in thresholds point to transport to estates. At the town of Halieis the unusual scale of olive production, where four of the 24 excavated homes possessed large oil presses, leave the remaining known townhouses without obvious working fixtures. It should be recalled that such presses suggest commercial specialization above household needs. Perhaps they processed the olives of other families, but since a family could also make oil for itself without them, alternatively they might indicate owners of larger olive-groves. Shops and workshops are more recognizable as small rooms only accessible from the street, though still part of a typical house complex. One fifth of Olynthus houses had such a dedicated space. The home-based, small-scale nature of most Greek craft and industry is clear.

The limited range of townhouse sizes is matched by the rarity of elaborate decoration. A friend of the fifth-century BC Athenian politician Alcibiades was criticized for luxurious living through using marble in his home, as was the politician himself when he employed a famous artist to do wall-paintings for him. The Athenian orator Demosthenes bemoaned the decline of unostentatious living between that century and his own time of the mid-fourth century, claiming that if you know houses of the famous personalities of *that* era you cannot see them differ from the common man, whilst today every politician has a house so remarkable that it is more magnificent than public buildings.

Archaic house plans, not surprisingly for an era of aristocratic control, show the existence of "immodest homes," before the Classical inauguration of the ethos of citizen equality encouraged at least a superficial similarity of homes in the *polis* world. We may assume that outside that world, where elites continued in power through Classical times around the Aegean, peasant huts lay alongside the mansions of the rich into Hellenistic times. As the fourth century progressed, leading into the autocracies of the Hellenistic kingdoms, we might also expect a relaxation of the citizen-equality of uniform houses. Indeed during the fourth century some houses do appear of well above average proportions, and exhibit a new architectural ostentation, such as the House of the Mosaics from Eretria. Interestingly, here the traditional family home has now been pushed to the fringes of the complex, with its own now private court, kitchen, washroom, and family spaces. The visitor enters an impressive reception court, with a portico on all sides (*peristyle*), opening onto no less than four mosaic-floored rooms for entertaining guests. This 625 m² home is more than twice the size of the normal Classical module, although it lacks an upper story. At Olynthus the late fifth to early fourth-century New Town also has a minority of extra large, well decorated suburban "*villae*," especially in the Eastern Plateau extension.

Moreover, the relative modesty of the typical Classical house hides variable cost. At Olynthus and Athens (Cahill 2002) standard house prices range from 1000 to 5000 drachmas, with 10,000 for a fine house. A reasonable annual family income might be 200 drachmas, thus buying a new home was a major investment. Customary fittings like giant storage pithoi or replacement rooftiles were also costly.

A major variable was house location, and Olynthus inscriptions record (unsurprisingly) that house prices rose in more desirable quarters, such as near the town center.

Concerning gender relations within the Greek house, iconography and texts announce that the woman's place is the home, the man's place is outside in the city. Some ancient sources separate a female area of the home (*gynaikonitis*), perhaps lockable but also possibly more decorated than that for men, from a male area (*andronitis*). Protecting women from encountering non-family males appears a primary goal. The *andron*-room for formal drinking-parties is associated by modern house analysts with the males of the family and their male guests. Yet the commonly recognizable andron might also have seen wider use. Texts mention special family celebrations, which might have taken place in the andron; indeed in sanctuaries, women celebrated festival dinners in similar symposium rooms. The courtyard would have been a major activity focus for both genders through the year, easily accessible to all the ground floor roofed spaces. Managing female seclusion became therefore a time-scheduling affair, clearing areas of women and girls on the approach of visitors.

One favored solution to the apparent conflict between texts and plans proposes that the upper floor was a zone of female seclusion. This would be the place for sleeping and a refuge when male guests penetrated the courtyard and ground-floor rooms, as well as housing a female boudoir as identifiable on vase-paintings. Stone footings for stairs rarely survive, suggesting that access staircases were normally of wood and mudbrick. Moreover, since house foundations are not massive, upper floors cannot have possessed heavy mobile or fixed contents, so that fallen traces onto excavated ground floors would be rather uninformative, as is indeed the case. In genuine single-floor houses, time-scheduling for the temporary seclusion of women would involve their retreating into slightly less accessible inner rooms, and the latter's nightly conversion to bedrooms from more everyday living-rooms. But throughout this discussion, we need to separate the lifestyle of the middle and upper classes from those of the equally sizeable lower class. Peasants and artisans frequently required wives and daughters to help with agricultural and craft work, outside as well as inside the home, so that restrictions on female movement and mixing with non-family males may have been relaxed for practical reasons.

Both house plans and images in art indicate that the house was primarily a female and family space, with a male presence highlighted only by the andron. Women controlled everyday household activities, not only the children and the work of servants, but its budget. Greek states encouraged the presence of its middle- and upper-class males in public spaces: the lawcourts, the assembly or gymnasium in the more democratic poleis, or the barracks and dining-clubs as well as gymnasia for the serf societies such as Dorian Crete and Laconia. The home as a complementary space for female power and sociability, however confining, suits its relative openness and the multifunctionality of its spaces.

The economy of Classical Greek society rested on slaves, serfs or tenants; texts characterize a completely impoverished citizen as one lacking such tied labor. Female slaves assisted citizen-wives in housework (Figure 12.4), while agricultural slaves/serfs or tenants were probably fundamental to the middle-upper class of citizen farmers of the democratic polis, and their class counterparts (the normal citizen) in serf-states (Jameson 1977–1978). But hardly any built spaces seem designed as living space for slaves or servants, apart from occasional tiny rooms by the entrance-door which possibly housed a porter, and are usually post-Classical, when class divisions became more visible. Texts portray house-slaves as household members, whilst maidservants probably slept in the same area as the free women of the house. As just noted, the view of many, that the lost upstairs rooms were the prime bedroom space, would leave few excavated traces.

In contrast to Early Modern Greek homes, a small fixed household shrine is not characteristic for Classical houses. A minority of excavated homes possess a stone altar in the courtyard but portable altars were perhaps moved round the house according to need. Texts suggest that rituals were common and conducted ubiquitously within the home, often being a simple scattering of offerings of food or liquid over a fire or into the ground, to bless the varied house localities. Miniature cups recovered from homes at Halieis could represent such practices. The cult of Zeus Ktesios, for protecting and enriching family property, was focused on a jar of seeds and fruits; this was kept in a storeroom and deployed on special occasions, such as if a new slave or married couple joined the household, when they were showered with the contents.

Texts such as fifth-century Athenian confiscation-inscriptions or the Hellenistic temple-estate inventories from Delos caution us that much may not survive for house archaeology (Whitley 2001). We noted that the rich in Athens could employ renowned painters for interior décor. As for movable contents, sums of 1000–1500 drachmas are given for portable items confiscated from homes by the Athenian state, to set against a reasonable annual income of 200 drachmas. More unexpectedly, Delian houses were let without doors or windows, wooden fittings being so valuable on smaller Aegean islands that people took them when moving.

Nevett (1999) explored house interior scenes on vases. If room furnishings consistently matched activities, they might indicate functional spaces. A computer analysis indicates sets of regularly co-occurring pot types on vase scenes, which are correlatable to their likely purposes in the home. One clear grouping seems to be set in the female boudoir. Other contexts are religious libation-pouring for both sexes, washing, and male symposia; the first two associate pots with activities rather than distinct spaces, but the symposium can be located in the andron with its dining-benches and male-only clientele (flute-players etc. excepted!). This analysis can nonetheless identify the probable multipurpose use of rooms when combined with archaeological house inventories.

Olynthus remains our largest excavated house sample. However, excavated generations ago, only small samples of finds were recorded, from which a further selection occurred before publication. On average three finds per room were recorded: in the best conditions, the maximum finds per house were 268. This is very low compared with the recent high-quality excavation at Halieis (Ault and Nevett 1999, Ault 2005), where House E produced 4100 ceramic finds, excluding roof tile, plus additional non-pottery objects. Nonetheless, the best large-scale data on house contents come from intelligent reworking of the excavation records of Olynthus town (Cahill 2002).

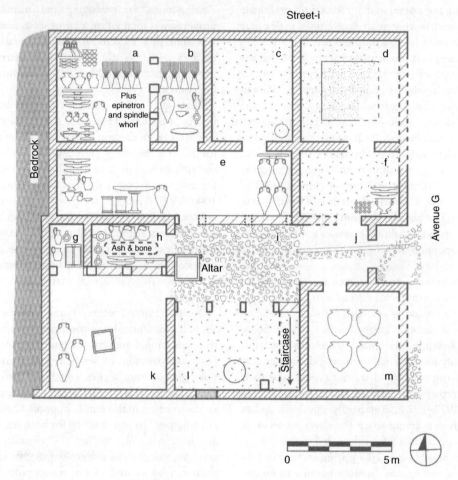

Figure 12.9   An example of Cahill's Olynthus house analysis.
N. Cahill, *Household and City Organization at Olynthus*. New Haven: Yale University Press 2002, Figure 16.

Figure 12.9 shows Cahill's artifact-coding and its deployment to illustrate space-use for one Olynthus home. Spatial patterns do become apparent, some artifact types being localized, others ubiquitous. A series of house-contents analyses reveals interesting trends. The *andron* (d) is generally kept clean, but its function emerges from the benches and fixed décor. The associated anteroom (*f*) has a mixing-bowl and plates in store. Weaving equipment can occur in almost any room in Olynthus houses, underlining the likely absence of permanent gender seclusion (in Figure 12.9, loomweights occur in "a" and "b"). Women probably prepared cloth in the court or in various internal ground- and upper-floor rooms,

dependent on time of day, season or personal preference. Storage rooms or spaces, and shops, often show up well from their limited range of vessels (e.g., in Figure 12.9, rooms "k" and "m").

Cahill's detailed house analyses led him to argue that rows of houses were in part or whole purchased by social groups with related space needs: either people with similar economic profiles, or relatives. In particular, the North Hill had much commerce and industry, in comparison to the often larger and more agriculturally-focused houses on the Eastern Plateau extension. Such social and economic zoning belied the generally similar appearance and size of homes, and although the North Hill includes many slightly wealthier homes, their higher frequency on the Eastern Extension agrees with storage provision being generally much higher there. Maybe North Hill residents combined small-scale farming with a trade, whilst the Extension farmers had larger estates, which were perhaps more commercially oriented.

From his analyses Cahill concludes that Höpfner and Schwandner's (1994) thesis that regular "estate-towns" such as Olynthus offer concrete expression for an overriding egalitarian ideal needs significant modification. Actually, contemporaries such as Demosthenes inform us that fourth-century norms (the main period of Olynthus' occupation) had relaxed from those of the fifth century, permitting status families to occupy more visibly spacious homes.

Classical texts, essentially elite-focused, denigrate artisans, so one might have expected to find them on the urban periphery as a marginal social group. The Olynthus house-finds allow easy recognition of sculptors, potters, figurine- and weapon-makers, also cloth- and food-processing on a scale beyond household needs (Cahill 2002). Surprisingly however, trade was not banished to urban fringes or special quarters: at least one quarter of 100 excavated houses, widely distributed, revealed such domestic industries, including presses and press-floors, and large grain-grinder collections, all of which suggest the provision of services for other households (as possible at Halieis, see above).

Till recently the variety of Classical housing was illustrated mainly through contrasting irregular Athens, where limited domestic areas were known, and the large database from the planned town of Olynthus. Now excavations well away from such famous towns are revealing what may have been the "norms" for most Classical Greeks, who lived in smaller cities (the "Normalpolis") which were sometimes grid-planned from late Classical or Hellenistic times, and perhaps as often not. A Greek team led by Adam-Veleni (2000) has been excavating such a small town in inland Northern Greece, whose ancient name is even unclear. Although its remains belong to Hellenistic times, just a few aspects may reflect that late date, and the rest could represent a small town in a hilly region typical for much of the Classical Aegean. The reconstructed town plan shows houses in irregular groups following the contours of the hill and with winding small streets for foot and donkey passage. Perhaps just one wider street existed to allow wheeled traffic to cross the city. Houses, usually on two floors, average 180–200 m². Upper storys are of light materials to reduce the load on the floor and lower foundations. The excavator argues that the common one-and-a-half story house-type was adapted to steep slopes. Its andron was on the upper level of the house-front, facing the street. The rear of the house, at a lower level, possessed a backyard with a stair to a veranda (comparable to the *hagiati* of Early Modern Greek houses) from which one accessed a large upper-floor backroom for women. Finds show that ground floors were used for storage, shops or workshops, and also for cooking and stables. Upper rooms from their fittings did for once allow spatial separation of males (andron with symposia equipment) and females (looms and a shrine).

Fascinating new studies have investigated housing arrangements in the very conservative serf-states of the Classical Aegean. Much of Crete followed a "Dorian" mode of society comparable to ancient Sparta. A broad upper-middle class dominated an equally numerous dependent lower class who worked the land for the former as tied labor. Trade and industry were largely left to resident aliens. The political solidarity of the free ruling-class was emphasized by male citizens eating in communal dining halls (*syssitia*), to which each free household contributed 10 percent of its agricultural production. Westgate's (2007) examination of domestic house plans of several Cretan towns reveals greater resemblance to Iron Age homes than those of Mainland Classical cities (Figure 12.10). The access diagrams reveal a simple linear progression which we saw typical for pre-Classical homes. Only the uppermost house on the plan shows Mainland polis influence in its more complex radiating plan. There is thus a lack of development regarding the space for the citizen family. In contrast, work at the small East Cretan city of Azouria (Haggis *et al.* 2007) shows the monumental construction of public dining and storage complexes in the center of the town. In these cities then the focus of the town is shared male citizen activity, preventing the emergence of elaborate homes marking household autonomy, which is all consistent with our historical evidence.

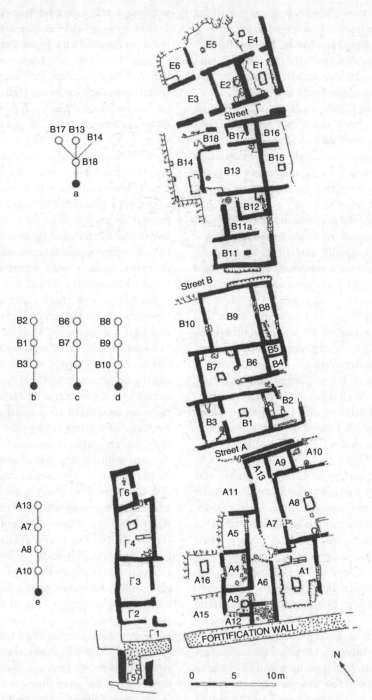

Trypetos, plan and access maps of selected houses (drawing by H. Mason; after Vogeikoff-Brogan and Papadakis 2003, fig. 22).

Figure 12.10   Access analysis for the settlement at Trypetos, Crete.

R. C. Westgate, "House and society in Classical and Hellenistic Crete." *American Journal of Archaeology* 111 (2007), 423–457, Figure 12. Reproduced by permission of Archaeological Institute of America (Boston).

Country Houses

Increasingly numerous plans exist of country houses, allowing comparison between townhouses and the rural built environment. A simple home may consist of a two-roomed structure with a small yard. Most recorded townhouses are larger, although Athens evidences some of this small size. Presumably their occupants were poor peasants, agricultural tenants or slaves, but alternatively some might be seasonal field-houses for urban-dwelling farmers of higher status. In contrast the excavated farms on Delos and at Vari in Attica are similar, or larger, than typical townhouses, and the latter estate-center clearly possesses a farmyard larger than urban norms. Nonetheless rural residences repeat the standard plan of the townhouse: a family structure with at least two rooms, and usually additional rooms ranged around a walled farmyard. The larger country residences exhibit more spacious and numerous room-clusters around a veranda-courtyard, not infrequently set off by expensive, prominent towers. An increase in area for rural homes may reflect the lower cost of rural land whilst the obvious dominance of agricultural activities benefited from larger farmyards. Rural courtyards can equal the rest of the farm enclosure in size, whereas the yard commonly occupies just one quarter to one fifth of a standard Olynthus townhouse. Nonetheless regional surveys in Greece have identified a predominance of relatively small "family farms," with surface areas commonly less than half a hectare plotted by pottery scatters, although ensembles of sites in contiguous blocks of countryside reveal a hierarchy of rural residences which include rarer larger estate-centers and rural hamlets (Bintliff *et al.* 2007).

These rural farms, known from standing, aboveground foundations, or (still rare) excavations, can be accompanied by threshing floors, small rough enclosures (probably for stock), terracing to conserve soil on hilly terrain, and stream dams to limit erosion. Occasionally, as in the remarkable network of larger farms mapped by the Atene survey in Attica (Lohmann 1993) wall-lines survive indicating estate-boundaries for specific identified farm sites, further allowing the estimation of landholding sizes (Figure 12.11). Most plans come from stony land where house foundations are visible on the present surface, but where soils are deeper, such as in Boeotia (Central Greece), much can still be achieved through combining non-destructive subsurface probes such as the geophysical tools of resistivity, magnetometry or georadar with exhaustive plotting of the differential spreads of domestic rubbish and collapsed roof tile which mark Classical farms on the surface. A typical small "family" farm has a pottery scatter of some 25 meters radius, which compares well with a basic farmhouse-complex plus a yard of some 200–300 m^2 at its heart (some 9–10 meters radius), surrounded by working areas or gardens, together with rubbish heaps and pits (Bintliff 1997b). Surveyors have additionally noted enhanced quantities of domestic debris surrounding these pottery scatters or "site cores" of Classical age. On our Boeotia Survey, mapping these "site haloes" suggests concentrated rubbish disposal for fertilizing infields of more intensive cultivation (see Chapter 11).

The range of pot types from such sites offers a full spectrum of functions suitable for a permanent residence, but caution is needed. On the Methana Survey farm-site sample collections were small, so that, unsurprisingly, any individual site has a low number of shapes which can be tied to particular activities. Foxhall (2004), as noted previously, compared this composite assemblage of all the pot types from the rural sites with the selection found at individual farms. She interpreted divergence to suggest that some sites were not the location of full domestic activities. However, a more limited range of pot types collected by surveyors can be expected as a result of their differential survival and limited presence on the surface, as well as stemming from the tiny sample of finds brought back and datable, bringing her conclusions into question.

Although farmers of similar income could probably purchase larger rural properties for the same cost rather than buy a smaller townhouse, many estate-centers are so much larger and better-equipped that they seem to reflect wealthier owners. The pseudo-egalitarian ethos which permeates many planned Classical towns may have been relaxed in the countryside where pretentious houses were far from jealous eyes (Jameson 1990a–b). The late Classical author Isocrates remarks for Athens that the better houses and furnishings are rural.

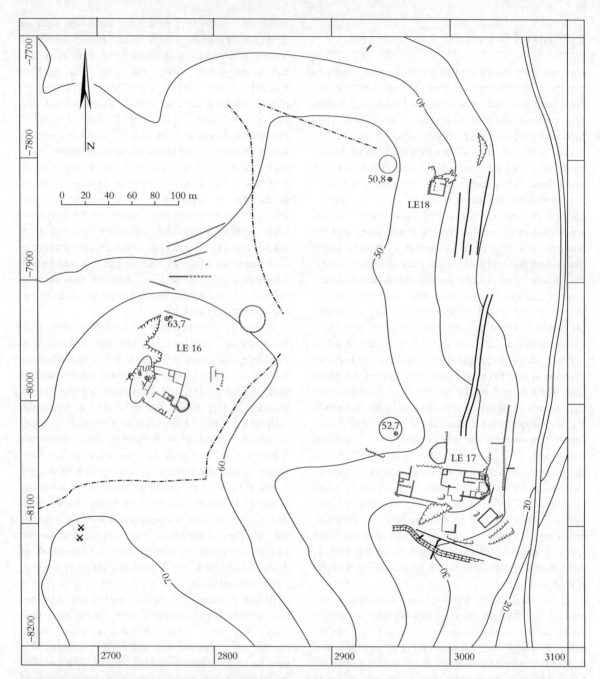

Figure 12.11 Atene deme's thin eroded soil allows Classical farm foundations to stand on the modern surface. Three farms, numbered, are shown with circular threshing-floors and estate boundaries.

H. Lohmann, *Atene. Forschungen zu Siedlungs- und Wirtschaftsstruktur des klassischen Attika*. Köln 1993, Figure 36.

At regular intervals across the countryside there were villages, arguably acting as secondary or tertiary foci for surrounding rural farmsteads when distance from the city reached several kilometers. We have many such sites from surface survey but few are excavated. A village in Attica at Ano Voula has been partially exposed (Lohmann 1992, 1993). Wide streets articulate a loose settlement structure comprising large walled or fenced enclosures. Within these are houses but also associated gardens (the latter match surface survey "site haloes" which rural sites show extending well outside the likely house positions). Several towers are integrated into homes, also recorded from a minority of rural estates in Attica and elsewhere. In towns and villages these are largely for prestigious display, whereas in dispersed farms they also (as texts confirm) have a defensive role against robbers. Finally village social life is revealed by dining-rooms for communal male clubs, and several small shrines dot the street-plan rather like modern Greek versions (*iconostaseis*).

Lohmann's (1993) Atene deme survey provides our best window into Classical rural life within one ancient city-state. In comparison to richer farming landscapes such as Boeotia, where perhaps 50 percent of the surface was cultivated in Classical times, Atene is a rocky $20 \mathrm{km}^2$ district. To compensate, farmers invested in a massive terracing program, largely for olive groves, enlarging the cultivable surface by an extra 38 percent. Even so, the ca. 445 ha then in use represented only 22 percent of the total deme area. Nonetheless survey located 36 sites (farms and other rural activity-foci), and Lohmann suggests that a further 15–20 farms have been lost to erosion, cultivation, and other disruptions. Numerous rural cemeteries were mapped, all but one associated with a farm site.

Figure 12.11 (upper left) shows a typical larger farm complex, that of LE17, and its close distance to similarly-sized neighbor LE16. Traces of intervening estate boundary-walls survive (dashed lines). The status of the small site LE18 to the north of site LE17 is unclear. Since there is no village center for Atene and we are far too remote from Athens, such a site cannot be a seasonal residence for a farmer living in a nucleation, so the question is whether this was an independent small farm or a satellite to its larger neighbor

LE17. Possessing its own threshing-floor might indicate its independence, although it could still be a tenancy to LE17.

An Annaliste Perspective

In the long term, the European Iron Age sees interactions between the positive impact of iron technology and other advances in agriculture and craft, boosting population levels to new highs, and growing political, commercial, and cultural exchanges between its high cultures and civilizations (Bintliff 1984, 1997a). Complex societies develop in parallel in Greece, Anatolia, Italy, Spain, and Temperate Europe. For the medium term, cycles of several hundred years mark the rise and fall of such societies or their transformation into radically different forms: ecological failings, military expansion, and the unsustainability of particular political systems all play a role. Much of the South Aegean sees such a cycle between 600 and 200 BC. The typical fragile small polis can flourish in a large space free from overpowering empires for a limited time, before it either succumbs to such systems intruding from *outside* (surviving the Persian attempt, but not the Roman), or from empires arising out of megalopoleis or non-polis territorial states *within* the Aegean (Athens, Sparta, Thebes, and then Macedon in chronological order). The fate of Italian city-states between 1100 and 1600 AD follows a very similar path (Waley 1988). In the short term, the decisive intervention of a person or event can open up surprising opportunities: the defeat of the Persians, Themistocles' ability to divert Athens' silver from short-lived handouts to its citizens into a great fleet, and the supernova ability of Alexander to conquer enormous foreign lands and change the place of the Aegean in the Greek world for ever. How often events and their wider consequences might have turned out otherwise.

A Personal View

Classical Greece, especially Athens, was an inspiration that made me, from age 10, want to be an ancient historian or archaeologist. It still overpowers me with the extraordinary cultural achievement and political experiments of relatively small and often very small communities. I have learnt to be less wholeheartedly enthusiastic, of course, about *every* aspect of the era: the subordination of women, the vital role of slaves, the murderous competitiveness of the city-states are always at the back of one's mind. Even the Acropolis brings admiration with a taste of doubt at the brutal treatment of the "subjects" who helped pay for it, and of the many thousands of slaves in the silver-mines who also were necessary to fund its construction. Yet the freedom all this gave to Athenians to create a functioning egalitarian democracy lifts their society onto a new level, still a model for global politics to try to match. And in any case, the widespread achievement of legal rights and some form of political engagement for all free male citizens was something many hundreds of other city-states put in place, symbolized materially by the standard "citizen house." Culturally, again, individual competitiveness and that between cities spurred on artistic production to heights the equal of any world civilization. For Athenians to see themselves like gods was indeed an illusion and high arrogance, although defeating the vast Persian Empire certainly fostered that illusion and helped to stimulate an almost godlike beauty in all the visual arts.

References

Adam-Veleni, P. (2000). *Petres of Florina.* Thessaloniki: Greco-Roman Museum.

Auda, Y. *et al.* (1990). "Espace géographique et géographie historique en Thessalie." In *Archéologie et Espaces. Xe Rencontres Internationales d'Archeologie et d'Histoire, Antibes 1989.* Juan-Les-Pins: Éditions APDCA, 87–126.

Ault, B. A. (2005). *The Excavations at Ancient Halieis 2: The Houses.* Bloomington: Indiana University Press.

Ault, B. A. and L. C. Nevett (1999). "Digging houses: Archaeologies of Classical and Hellenistic Greek domestic assemblages." In P. Allison (ed.), *The Archaeology of Household Activities.* London: Routledge, 43–56.

Beard, M. (1991). "Adopting an approach II." In T. Rasmussen and N. Spivey (eds.), *Looking at Greek Vases.* Cambridge: Cambridge University Press, 12–35.

Beard, M. (2002). *The Parthenon.* London: Profile.

Beard, M. and J. Henderson (2001). *Classical Art: From Greece to Rome.* Oxford: Oxford University Press.

Beaumont, L. (1994). "Constructing a methodology for the interpretation of childhood age in Classical Athenian iconography." *Archaeological Review from Cambridge* 13(2), 81–96.

Beaumont, L. (1998). "Born old or never young? Femininity, childhood and the goddesses of ancient Greece." In S. Blundell and M. Williamson (ed.), *The Sacred and the Feminine in Ancient Greece.* London: Routledge, 71–95.

Bérard, C. (ed.) (1984). *La Cité des images. Religion et société en Grèce antique.* Lausanne: Fernand Nathan.

Bintliff, J. L. (1984). "Iron Age Europe in the context of social evolution from the Bronze Age through to historic times." In J. Bintliff (ed.), *European Social Evolution.* Bradford: Bradford University Research Ltd, 157–225.

Bintliff, J. L. (1997a). "Regional survey, demography, and the rise of complex societies in the Ancient Aegean: Core–periphery, Neo-Malthusian, and other interpretive models." *Journal of Field Archaeology* 24, 1–38.

Bintliff, J. L. (1997b). "Further considerations on the population of ancient Boeotia." In J. L. Bintliff (ed.), *Recent Developments in the History and Archaeology of Central Greece.* Oxford: BAR Int. Series 666, 231–252.

Bintliff, J. L. *et al.* (2004–2005). "The Tanagra project: Investigations at an ancient city and its countryside (2000–2002)." *Bulletin de Correspondance Hellénique* 128–129, 541–606.

Bintliff, J. L. *et al.* (2007). *Testing the Hinterland: The Work of the Boeotia Survey (1989–1991) in the Southern Approaches to the City of Thespiai.* Cambridge: McDonald Institute.

Boardman, J. (2006). *The History of Greek Vases.* London: Thames & Hudson.

Cahill, N. (2002). *Household and City Organization at Olynthus.* New Haven and London, Yale University Press.

Foxhall, L. (1995). "Monumental ambitions. The significance of posterity in Greece." In N. Spencer (ed.), *Time, Tradition and Society in Greek Archaeology. Bridging the 'Great Divide'.* London: Routledge, 132–149.

Foxhall, L. (2004). "Small, rural farmstead sites in ancient Greece: A material cultural analysis." In F. Kolb (ed.), *Chora und Polis.* München: R. Oldenbourg Verlag, 249–279.

Fullerton, M. D. (2000). *Greek Art.* Cambridge: Cambridge University Press.

Gill, D. W. (1988). "Expressions of wealth: Greek art and society." *Antiquity* 62, 735–743.

Haggis, D. C. *et al.* (2007). "Excavations at Azoria, 2003–2004, Part 1." *Hesperia* 76, 243–341.

Höpfner, W. and E.-L. Schwandner (1994). *Haus und Stadt im klassischen Griechenland.* München: Deutscher Kunstverlag.

Hurwit, J. M. (1999). *The Athenian Acropolis.* Cambridge: Cambridge University Press.

Jameson, M. H. (1977–1978). "Agriculture and slavery in Classical Athens." *Classical Journal* 73(2), 122–145.

Jameson, M. H. (1990a). "Private space and the Greek city." In O. Murray and S. Price (eds.), *The Greek City from Homer to Alexander*. Oxford: Oxford University Press, 171–195.

Jameson, M. H. (1990b). "Domestic space in the Greek city-state." In S. Kent (ed.), *Domestic Architecture and the Use of Space*. Cambridge: Cambridge University Press, 92–113.

Johnston, A. (1991). "Greek vases in the marketplace." In T. Rasmussen and N. Spivey (eds.), *Looking at Greek Vases*. Cambridge: Cambridge University Press, 203–232.

Lawrence, A. W. and R. A. Tomlinson (1996). *Greek Architecture*. New Haven: Yale University Press.

Leader, R. E. (1997). "In death not divided: Gender, family, and the state on Classical Athenian grave stelae." *American Journal of Archaeology* 101, 683–699.

Lehmann, S. (2007). "Zeus und seine Heiligtum in Olympia." *Antike Welt* 38(6), 8–16.

Llewellyn-Jones, L. (2004). *Aphrodite's Tortoise: The Veiled Women of Ancient Greece*. Swansea: The Classical Press of Wales.

Lohmann, H. (1992). "Agriculture and country life in Classical Attica." In B. Wells (ed.), *Agriculture in Ancient Greece*. Stockholm: Paul Åström, 29–60.

Lohmann, H. (1993). *Atene. Forschungen zu Siedlungs- und Wirtschaftsstruktur des klassischen Attika*. Köln: Boehlau Verlag.

Lohmann, H. (2005). "Prähistorischer und antiker Blei-Silberbergbau im Laurion." In Ü. Yalçin (ed.), *Anatolian Metal III*. Bochum: Deutsches Bergbau-Museum (*Der Anschnitt* Beiheft 18), 105–136.

Nevett, L. (1999). *House and Society in the Ancient Greek World*. Cambridge: Cambridge University Press.

Rhodes, P. (2003). "Athenian drama and the polis." *Journal of Hellenic Studies* 123, 104–119.

Richter, G. (1971). *Sculpture and Sculptors of the Greeks*. New Haven: Yale University Press.

Ridgway, B. S. (1994). "The study of Classical sculpture at the end of the 20th century." *American Journal of Archaeology* 98, 759–772.

Shanks, M. (1997). *The Classical Archaeology of Greece*. London: Routledge.

Sojc, N. (2005). *Trauer auf attischen Grabreliefs*. Berlin: Reimer Verlag.

Spivey, N. (1997a). "Meditations on a Greek Torso." *Cambridge Archaeological Journal* 7, 309–317.

Spivey, N. (1997b). *Greek Art*. London: Phaidon.

Stears, K. (1995). "Dead women's society. Constructing female gender in Classical Athenian funerary sculpture." In N. Spencer (ed.), *Time, Tradition and Society in Greek Archaeology. Bridging the 'Great Divide'*. London: Routledge, 109–131.

Stewart, A. (1997). *Art, Desire and the Body in Ancient Greece*. Cambridge: Cambridge University Press.

Stissi, V. (2002). "Pottery to the people." PhD thesis, University of Amsterdam.

Stuart, J. and N. Revett (1762–1816). *The Antiquities of Athens*. 4 vols. London: John Haberkorn, John Nichols, T. Bensley.

Vickers, M. (1990). "The impoverishment of the past: The case of classical Greece." *Antiquity* 64, 455–463.

Vickers, M. (2004). "Was ist Material wert? Eine kleine Geschichte über den Stellenwert griechischer Keramik." *Antike Welt* 35(2), 63–69.

Vickers, M. and D. W. Gill (1995). *Artful Crafts: Ancient Greek Silverware and Pottery*. Oxford: Oxford University Press.

Waley, D. (1988). *The Italian City-Republics*. London: Longman.

Westgate, R. C. (2007). "House and society in Classical and Hellenistic Crete." *American Journal of Archaeology* 111, 423–457.

Whitley, J. (2001). *The Archaeology of Ancient Greece*. Cambridge: Cambridge University Press.

Further Reading

Carter, J. C., S. M. Thompson, and J. Trelogan (2004). "Dividing the chora." In F. Kolb (ed.), *Chora und Polis*. München: R. Oldenbourg Verlag, 127–145.

Goldberg, M. Y. (1999). "Spatial and behavioral negotiation in Classical Athenian city houses." In P. Allison (ed.), *The Archaeology of Household Activities*. London: Routledge, 142–161.

Hurwit, J. M. (1988). *The Art and Culture of Early Greece*. Ithaca: Cornell University Press.

Renfrew, C. (1986). "Introduction." In Renfrew and Cherry 1986, 1–17.

Renfrew, C. and J. F. Cherry (eds.) (1986). *Peer Polity Interaction and Socio-Political Change*. Cambridge: Cambridge University Press.

13

The Archaeology of Greece in Hellenistic to Early Roman Imperial Times

Demography, Settlement Patterns, and Everyday Life

Introduction

Within 500 years, from 323 BC (when Alexander's death inaugurates the Hellenistic era), to the transition from Early to Middle Roman times ca. 200 AD, the changes the Aegean world underwent were out of all proportion to those of the preceding 500 years. At the start of this era, the Aegean was still a world of hundreds of city-states, of varying size and importance, plus larger confederacies and kingdoms focused in the more mountainous, less Mediterranean Northeast and Northwest of Greece. The premature disappearance of the invincible young King of Macedon in a distant part of his overstretched Asiatic empire (Color Plate 13.1a) could have precipitated its collapse, during which several powers in Greece might have reasserted their independence and prolonged the life of the autonomous polis (city-state).

This was not to be: historical parallels teach us that the flourishing of a host of tiny statelets is not unusual but generally occurs in the temporary absence of adjacent great powers, since the resources and cohesion of the former are generally doomed against the might of the latter. Within Greece this scenario had already been played out in Classical times, with sequent attempts at Aegean hegemony by Athens, Sparta, and Thebes. Alexander's successor generals or "Diadochi" lost no time carving out more manageable dynastic kingdoms for themselves (Color Plate 13.1b), keeping as firm a grip as possible on the aspirations of the numerous Greek and non-Greek states, kingdoms, and tribes which had been conquered in the whirlwind Macedonian campaigns of the 330s and 320s. Despite losing the furthest eastern realms to resurgent native states and especially the Parthians, the Seleucid dynasty regrouped around the Levant from a base in Syria, the Ptolemies founded their dynasty in Egypt, and the Antigonids tried to control Greece from the traditional Macedonian homeland. True however to Greek tradition these Successor Kingdoms wasted resources fighting each other to extend their individual sway. A small but for the Aegean influential kingdom escaped from these power-blocs during the third century, that of the Attalid dynasty in Pergamon (Western Anatolia).

Nonetheless, the Aegean outside the state of Macedon was now a marginal region in a vaster Greek-dominated world in which innumerable local cultures were infused by "Hellenization" or central aspects of Greek lifestyle. Apart from a shared form of Greek language, the *koine*, this "New World" was tied by common ceramic styles, coins, domestic practices, and building types. In return, increased mobility led to a growing popularity, even in the Aegean, across the Hellenistic period (and enhanced further under Roman rule), for Eastern gods such as Isis, Sarapis, and Levantine forms of Aphrodite (Mikalson 2006).

The Complete Archaeology of Greece: From Hunter-Gatherers to the 20th Century AD, First Edition. John Bintliff.
© 2012 John Bintliff. Published 2012 by Blackwell Publishing Ltd.

Alexander's unexpected death encouraged a large-scale revolt in Greece against Macedonian rule, but after Athens and other major southern cities were defeated and democratic constitutions annulled, the Macedonian successor kings sponsored the general installation of, or support for, rule by oligarchy or monarchy in the Aegean and the wider Greek world (Cartledge 1998). The city-state survived to manage its local affairs, but in foreign affairs poleis could at most maneuver beneath the favor or disfavor of the rival Hellenistic kingdoms, all of whom were active in the Aegean. Nonetheless for lengthy periods leagues of Greek states were established to try and counter the dominance of the dynastic kingdoms through equivalent merged resources, the most significant being the Achaean and Aetolian Leagues centered in their regions (van Wees 2000).

The organization of the Macedonian kingdom shows the contrasted nature of Hellenistic states from preceding city-states. An autocratic dynasty bonded its large territorial state through incorporating regional elites into the Royal Court and as elite cavalry. A large professional army led by full-time officers, who were rewarded with estates in conquered lands, mixed novel units (cavalry and light-armed troops) with a vastly more deadly version of the phalanx. All this was supported by economic resources in food surpluses and minerals far beyond the scale of Classical city-states (Osborne 2000). The immense wealth garnered during Alexander's foreign conquests and the tributary demands made on dependent small states by the Hellenistic kingdoms, ensured the powerlessness of all but a few Aegean states; their financial and military capacity was no match for the Hellenistic superpowers. The progressive decline of the citizen hoplite-army occurred from the fourth century, with mercenaries widely employed both within and against the standing armies of the Hellenistic dynastic states. With city-states no longer reliant on the middle, hoplite citizen-class, inequalities in landholding caused decreasing concern and the era sees widespread evidence in historic sources and rural survey for the decline of the free peasant class and a displacement of control over the landscape toward wealthy landowners. This can also be tied to the visible differences now permitted between the urban houses of the rich and those of other citizens, and a relaxation on displaying wealth in tombs.

In the second century BC wars within and between these Hellenistic kingdoms provided an excuse for a new aggressive, expansive power, Republican Rome, to intervene in the politics of the Eastern Mediterranean. Over the following two centuries what now seems a relentless absorption of the Hellenistic world by Rome took place. Both ancient and modern historians see the sack of Corinth in 146 BC, with the abolition of the Macedonian state and the creation of the first Roman province in Greece covering the Northern Mainland, as the effective arrival of Rome as the lord of the Aegean. Like the Diadochoi before them, the Late Republican Roman conquerors benefited from gaining control over the stored-up wealth of the rest of the Mediterranean (Howgego 1992). This fed their irresistible colonial expansion, both in military terms, but also to the economic advantage of Italian settlers in new provinces such as the Aegean, where upper- and middle-class immigrants invested in estates, commerce, and industry, internationalizing the leading sectors of Greek life. Finally with the defeat of the last Ptolemy, Cleopatra at Actium (31 BC), and the complete dominance of the first Roman emperor, Octavian-Augustus, over the Eastern Mediterranean world, from Greece via Anatolia and Syro-Palestine to Egypt, the total suppression of Aegean autonomy both in internal and external affairs was enforced under Roman rule. Administrative authority at the city level was delegated by Rome to local elites under the watchful eye both of provincial governors and of the emperor and senate in Rome itself.

The second century BC had witnessed prolonged, diffuse warfare between Rome and various East Mediterranean powers of Hellenistic origin, in which vast territories and innumerable cities were laid waste. In the first century BC civil wars between Roman warlords exacerbated this: Marius and Sulla, Caesar and Pompey, the Triumvirate and Caesar's assassins, finally Octavian and Mark Antony. Much of this took place in the East. Whilst therefore Roman expansion into Western Europe stimulated rapid prosperity in town and country, frequently the opposite was the case in the previously flourishing world of the Aegean city-states and ethnos states, and the Hellenized Eastern Mediterranean kingdoms. The historical and archaeological record for the Late

Hellenistic era (ca. 150–31 BC), is unsurprisingly disruptive at province and city level.

For the Late Hellenistic-Early Roman Imperial era (LH–ER), a developmental scenario for Rome's Eastern Provinces is also appropriate to many (but not all) regions of Greece. It sees an early phase of often brutal disjunction resulting from the local impact of Rome (at varied moments regionally between the second century BC to first century AD), when destruction or limited growth, if not stagnation, are apparent in town and country. This is followed by stabilization and greater prosperity in Middle Roman Imperial times (second to fourth centuries AD).

By the first century AD all the Roman provinces benefited from internal imperial peace, the *Pax Romana*, whilst commercial networks prospered from growing income and demand in the recently acquired Western and North African provinces. Till the late second century AD we might expect Greece in this Early Roman era to still be recovering from the internal decline of Late Hellenistic times in many regions, and the violent disruptions of the same period associated with Roman impact.

As the Aegean settled into Roman Imperial rule, a reorientation of urban foci was soon evident. Instead of the many hundreds of city-states which had formed significant centripetal (local focus) tendencies for regional populations, a small number of key administrative centers dominated territories of a much larger scale (Alcock 1993). The creation of numerous Roman colonies, such as refounded Corinth and Patras, and a major new city in Northwest Greece at Nicopolis (designated a Roman colony although largely made up of displaced Greeks from a wider region around), were amongst this select set of towns. Other favored cities were Thessaloniki in Northeast Greece and Knossos and Gortyn on Crete (see Figure 13.2).

"Romanization" is a significant concept in assessing the character of Early Roman (ER) Greece. It brought major political change and the penetration of Roman tax-raising, economic systems, and cultural influences. There were also more direct local interventions: the founding of colonies of retired Roman soldiers or other Italians. In return, as the Roman poet Horace remarked, "Captured Greece subdued her fierce conqueror, and introduced the arts to rustic Latium" (*Epistles* 2.1.156). Greece "captured" Rome

in cultural terms, since the Roman elite, including several emperors, cultivated a cultural persona based on idealized Classical-Hellenistic Greek art, architecture, and literature, and forms of social interaction such as luxurious social dining and palatial private homes. However, as far as the Aegean is concerned, what not long ago was seen as a positive advance when Greece joined the Roman Empire, is today viewed more critically in the light of the violent breakdown of society in very many cities in the early phase, and then the dramatic contrasts in wealth within and between the various Aegean regions during later centuries of Roman sway. Significantly, Roman admiration for Greece, "Philhellenism," was insufficient to foster sympathetic treatment of the bulk of its people, Athens excepted: "general attitudes to Greeks and matters Greek had little impact on actual policy" (Briscoe 1986, 94). That Roman domination, although eventually bringing welcome peace to Mediterranean peoples, was also driven by the economic self-interest of the conquerors, underlies Pliny the Elder's writing (*Natural History* 14.2): "Everyone is aware that as a result of the world being united under the majesty of the Roman empire life has improved thanks to trade and the sharings of peace." A similar materialism, though likewise tinged with accurate realism of the advantages to the provinces of Roman technological improvements, appears from another first-century AD author Julius Frontinus, who comments that the Egyptians made useless pyramids, the Greeks much-admired but also useless monuments, whilst the Romans made innumerable and necessary aqueducts (Doukellis *et al.* 1995).

It seems likely that outside of the numerous Roman colonies in Greece, Roman power and culture in the period 200 BC to 100 AD were often unpopular amongst the general population, although the local elite cultivated influential Romans whether politicians, generals, traders or bankers. This phase however gave way by the second century AD to an acceptance of Rome as a master under whom many cities could flourish, helped by intermarriage having created a new international ruling-class in the Aegean. Not only Augustus in the first century BC, but later philhellene (Greece-loving) emperors of the second century AD such as Hadrian and Marcus Aurelius, promoted Greek culture as a formative inheritance adopted by Roman civilization. Marcus Aurelius' contemporary Pausanias wrote a travel-guide to Greece, where the Aegean becomes a past unity akin to a museum landscape (Elsner 1992). In response, Greek elites copied Roman custom in stressing an illustrious family-tree, through genuine or spurious connections to famous names from the Greek Classical era (Luraghi 2008). Significantly in the Early Empire it was only ambitious Greeks of status who adopted Latin names, in order to further their careers *outside* their immediate Aegean environment.

Settlement and Population

The Early Hellenistic period in town and country offers for most regions of Greece a continuation of the picture in town and country of late Classical times. In contrast in LH-ER times, for many of the best-known regions of Classical Greece, there is a marked contrast between on the one hand, the image from the cities presented by art and architecture, and on the other, the evidence from texts and archaeology. A notable reorganization of the Greek provinces also becomes clear at the macroscale of urbanization and population levels.

Historical sources offer a drastically disturbed scenario for large areas of the Aegean from the third century BC on till the early second century AD (Bintliff and Snodgrass 1985, Alcock 1993), almost the entire LH-ER era. Contemporary Greek commentators (Polybius, Strabo, Pausanias) depict severe decline, abandoned or run-down cities, emptied countrysides, social disintegration, and moral decline. Roman, or Romanized Greek, writers used these factors to account for Rome's rise and the concomitant decline of Greek states. For these reasons modern historians were often skeptical of the reality behind these comments. Was this not a comfortable, simplistic literary device (*topos*) to delight Roman audiences and conveniently explain to Greek readers how they fell from greatness?

Hellenistic and Roman buildings have been excavated in long-studied and high-profile centers such as Athens, Corinth, Olympia, Delphi, and Delos, where the wealth and display needs of Hellenistic dynasties, Roman generals and emperors, as well as foreign and indigenous elites, ensured a steady flow of new prestige monuments throughout the period, giving an impression of relative prosperity. Kahrstedt's pioneering (1954) volume on the archaeology of Roman Greece, based on excavation reports, however, showed symptoms of widespread urban decline (towns shrinking to rural estates for example), and a shift in the open countryside toward villa estates, representing a non-peasant class. Yet the data were thin and often ambiguous, preventing general acceptance of his narrative of large-scale decline. A generation later, our intensive field-survey in the rural landscape of Boeotia, Central Greece (Bintliff and Snodgrass 1985) demonstrated that ancient accounts of widespread depopulation and decline in land use, characterizing LH-ER, actually matched the archaeological realities (Figure 13.1, top). During the mid-1980s our attention turned to Boeotian cities: thanks to a continuing emphasis on regional agriculture most remain in open cultivation suitable for surface survey. This confirmed (Bintliff and Snodgrass 1988, Bintliff 2000) that the decline was equally valid for Boeotian city life. Haliartos town, destroyed by the Roman army in 171 BC, clearly never recovered throughout the Early and Middle Roman Imperial era. The small town of Askra (Figure 13.1, below), and a larger city at Hyettos, saw severe contraction.

The survey of the small city-state of Koressia on Kea island (Cherry *et al.* 1991) reinforced the evidence from Boeotia. By Late Hellenistic times the polis shrank to a village and no recovery occurred even in Late Roman times. The Kea countryside also saw severe rural depopulation, lasting through ER, but reviving in LR times. ER rural sites remained small and could still be family farms, although poor assemblages suggest instead that they were bases for hired or tenant labor within larger estates, whose owners dwelt in urban centers elsewhere. In the Northeastern Peloponnese the Berbati Survey (Wells and Runnels 1996) follows the Southeastern Mainland norm: dramatic emptying of the landscape in LH-ER, with only one significant site for the entire valley. Although this was arguably a large estate-center occupying land previously farmed by many small farms, its modest size implies that most of the district was out of intensive use. In the deme of Atene in rural Attica farms are almost all abandoned in mid-Hellenistic times, with limited reuse of the landscape by Late

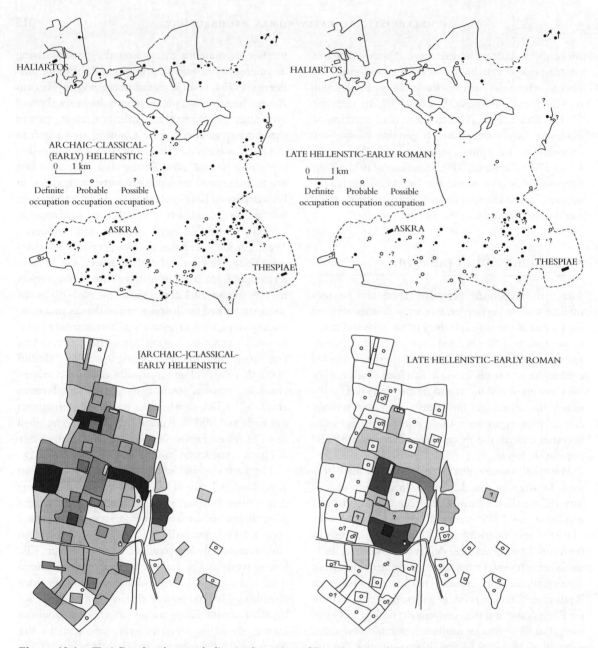

Figure 13.1 (Top) Rural settlement decline in the region of Boeotia, Central Greece belonging to the ancient cities of Thespiae and Haliartos (located in the Southeast and Northwest of the maps). Many rural farms and hamlets disappear between Classical-Hellenistic and LH–ER times, many more cease to be flourishing settlements (low ceramic finds indicate site shrinkage or temporary rather than permanent use = "probable/possible" occupation).

J. L. Bintliff, "The Roman countryside in Central Greece: Observations and theories from the Boeotia Survey (1978–1987)." In G. Barker and J. Lloyd (eds.), *Roman Landscapes. Archaeological Survey in the Mediterranean Region*. London 1991, 122–132, Figures 2 and 4.

(Below) Surface collections from the small town of Askra show severe contraction between Classical Greek and Early Roman times. Open circles denote sample areas lacking finds of the mapped period, grayscale shading increases in darkness with higher density of dated finds for the mapped phase.

J. L. Bintliff and A. M. Snodgrass, "Mediterranean survey and the city." *Antiquity* 62 (1988), 57–71, Figures 2b and 2c.

Roman pastoral enclosures, probably belonging to large estates (Lohmann 1993). In Laconia the LH-R era sees a marked decline in site numbers from survey evidence (Mee and Cavanagh 1998) paralleled by the evidence from the Megalopolis project.

The early results of several survey projects were summarized in their historical context by Alcock (1993). She emphasized the disjunction of the Greek landscape caused by Roman incorporation. Firstly, the Romans created new colonial towns with planned influxes of foreigners. Secondly they administered Greece within much larger political units (provinces) than the old city-states and ethnic-territorial states. Most of Southern Greece formed the province of Achaea, administered from Corinth. Northwest Greece eventually formed the province of Epirus, focused on Nicopolis, whilst Northeast Greece, the province of Macedonia, was centered on Thessaloniki. Crete was exceptionally dislocated from the Aegean, and together with the region of Cyrenaica in coastal Libya formed the province of Crete and Cyrene, whose Cretan capital was Gortyn (dominating the fertile Mesara Plain). The refocusing of Aegean political life led to parallel centralization of social and economic activities into this smaller number of favored provincial capitals, and other older towns who had wisely supported Roman expansion. Indigenous populations, especially those who had been hostile to Rome, were relocated to boost new colonial foundations.

According to Alcock, local elites who prospered with the Roman assumption of power were drawn to these flourishing agglomerations, weakening their traditional support to smaller towns. Such absentee landowners were less likely to oversee intensive farming on distant estates, contributing to an overall decline in crop production, now centered on managers, slaves, and tenants. For the Nemea Survey project in the Northeastern Peloponnese, in contrast, she argued that rural peasants fled deteriorating conditions in the countryside, moving to town to take advantage of other economic opportunities opened up by the Roman Empire. Her urban survey of the associated small town of Phlius used surface ceramic distributions to evidence urban growth in ER times, seemingly going against the downward trend of cities elsewhere in the Southern Mainland (Alcock 1991). The rise of

a few "supercities" such as Corinth, Nicopolis, and Thessaloniki (Figure 13.2), and Roman stimulus for the flourishing of its colony at Patras and favored traditional centers like Athens, Argos, Messene, and Sparta, compensated, Alcock said, for the decline of smaller centers (Phlius curiously excepted), and perhaps therefore the rural depopulation merely reflected a move of dispossessed small farmers to favorable towns. In fact her study has been widely interpreted as indicating a displacement of population rather than decline, both to towns as a whole when peasants abandoned the countryside for alternative craft, trade, and service jobs in cities, and from shrinking towns to those growing through Roman favor. The *topos* of an impoverished Aegean is therefore an illusion (cf. Woolf 1994a, Étienne et al. 2000, Grandjean 2008).

Revaluation of such work, and a wider perspective over the Aegean, are both necessary and possible now, resulting in more nuanced interpretations of the transformation between Hellenistic and Early Roman Imperial times. "Source Criticism" of survey interpretations, for example, raises doubts about the Roman expansion of Phlius. The well-dated sherds suggest that the city grew in size from Archaic through Classical to reach a peak in Hellenistic times, then declined somewhat in ER and even further in LR times. The apparent ER growth is due to including an arbitrary share of sherds assignable to more than one period, which are far more likely to be dominated by the phases shown in the certainly-dated categories. Furthermore, as we shall see below, claims for supercities absorbing displaced persons from declining towns elsewhere are not supported by the archaeological data, which in total suggest a decline in urban populations for the Aegean as a whole.

By chance, most intensive survey projects in the 1980s and early 1990s (Boeotia, Kea, the Argolid, Methana, Atene) lay in relative proximity, in the South-Central Mainland. The long-term picture they revealed was remarkably similar, supporting ancient sources for these regions: a climax Classical-Early Hellenistic flourishing of town and country, decline in Late Hellenistic to Early Roman times, and (unanticipated in the sources) dramatic recovery (at least in the countryside) in Late Roman times. However, subsequent synthesis of accumulating extensive and intensive surveys (Figure 9.5; Bintliff

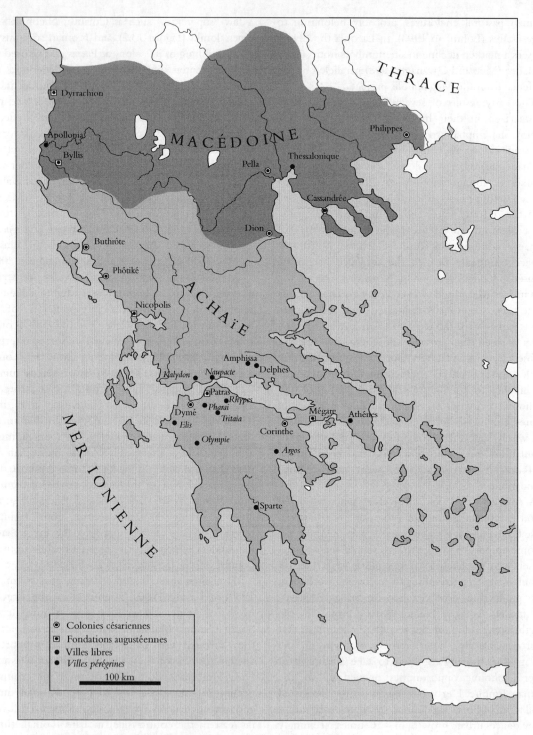

Figure 13.2 Early Roman Greece, its provinces, colonial foundations by Caesar (colonies césariennes) and Augustus (fondations augustéennes), and privileged indigenous cities (libres, pérégrines).
R. Étienne *et al.*, *Archéologie historique de la Grèce antique*. Paris 2000, Figure 137.

1997), covering the whole of Greece, confirms other indications from historical sources that regional growth and decline patterns were more varied. Many regions are strikingly out of phase with each other in their development, contrasted with the more internally-consistent set of regions where the major early surveys were carried out: they represented a "core" of precocious takeoff and, perhaps not coincidentally, early decline.

Regional divergence is notably pronounced for the ER period, but continues at a lesser scale in LR. The early takeoff in demography and urbanization in Geometric-Archaic times of the Southeast Mainland in Attica, Argos, and Corinth, followed during Classical times by neighboring regions Laconia, Boeotia, and Thessaly in Southern, Central, and North-Central Greece, corresponds with powerful states during the Archaic-Classical eras. The Late Classical-Hellenistic era sees the decline of most of these "heartland" landscapes, complemented by the emergence of important North and Northwest Greek ethnic states or confederacies: Macedonia, Aetolia, and Acarnania. In Late Hellenistic and Roman times the island of Crete emerges out of obscurity into a major growth phase in town and country, paralleled in the northern Peloponnesian region of Achaea (see Patras Survey, Petropoulos and Rizakis 1994).

These displacements of prosperity reflect historical contingency and geography. The Archaic-Classical highpoint regions possessed reasonably fertile soils for Mediterranean polyculture (cereals, olives, and vines), high communication potentials by land and sea (including early exposure to Oriental culture and commerce), and a stressful climate favoring state expansion to secure resources. They were also at risk from overgrowth, especially when export markets or food imports were threatened by a decline in the military power of these core states, but also from internal overpopulation confronted by unstable climates and poorly regenerating soils with a high erosion potential. These factors combined to weaken those states, whilst other regions, which for various reasons had witnessed slower demographic growth and political elaboration over the same era, now expanded their urban and rural populations, to usurp Aegean military dominance. The Macedonian kingdom was the greatest Aegean power throughout Hellenistic times, but in second place came the kingdom of Epirus and the ethnic confederacies of the Aetolians and Acarnanians, as well as the city-state federation of the Achaean League, all of whom wrote history against a backdrop of decline in the famous states of the Southeastern Classical core lands.

If Macedonia with its vast territory of upland and lowland plains, mountains, and hill country was a late developer in Aegean demography during the Iron Age up till Philip II, its potential was very considerable, and once having taken off economically it was not to decline in antiquity. In contrast, the Northwest provinces of Acarnania, Aetolia, and Epirus had very low agricultural potential, were benefiting more from large territories whose scattered populations were slowly urbanizing, and as agglomerates were more than a match militarily for the depopulating states of the Southeast core lands. The medium-term (scale of centuries) prospects of such powers were limited, since their ascendance depended on tapping the superior agricultural resources of more naturally fertile regions. Aetolian and Acarnanian populations who survived their war with Rome were deported, mostly as slaves to Italy, but a minority were sent to boost new foundations of Roman veterans or freedmen, such as Nicopolis on the coast of Epirus, Patras on the coast of Achaea, and the city of Corinth (burnt by the Romans in 146 BC, refounded by Caesar in 44 BC). Thus we find these poorly-favored regions sinking by the Roman occupation into their more natural adaptive mode of low and scattered population with modest relations to the outside world, excepting a few prosperous coastal ports. Another late developer, Crete, however, once it had expanded to its full demographic potential, remained flourishing throughout the Roman era, including Late Antiquity, but here in proportion to its high fertility. The region of Achaea (Petropoulos and Rizakis 1994), took off in ER times, then declined during LR, possibly due to limited agricultural potential and regional political factors. Each city in Greece tried to survive through alliances and crisis measures in the last two centuries BC, but based on the latest textual and archaeological information, just a few regions seem to have escaped a calamitous downturn in population and economy (Rizakis and Touratsoglou 2008).

Nonetheless, why did the formerly densely occupied and flourishing landscapes of the early core homelands not recover their populations and prosperity under the Pax Romana? At least for Boeotia and Attica, environmental problems and the loss of dominance of outside markets for import and export of agricultural products, respectively, played a major role in the persistence of depopulated landscapes in major parts of both regions. These problems were in addition to the impact of the short-term destructiveness of Roman and other powers that afflicted both regions from the second century BC till the reign of Augustus. Textual evidence makes clear that wide swathes of established Greek cities had become severely impoverished through losses and exactions caused by these recurrent wars, often turning to Italian moneylenders to keep themselves solvent. Some resorted to asking wealthy volunteers to sponsor public inscriptions. But still we might expect that the beneficial effects of incorporation into the Roman Empire would nourish recovery in demography and general prosperity. We need to introduce further explanatory factors.

Rural Transformation

There are clearly vital landownership changes throughout the Aegean. In formerly flourishing Classical-Hellenistic landscapes, sparser Roman-era villas of wealthier individuals replace the denser networks of independent family farms typical for the Classical-Early Hellenistic centuries. Did this lower the intensity of land use, and the size of working populations on the land, whilst at the same time removing the stimulus for productivity for a new class of tenants and sharecroppers, hired estate labor and agricultural slaves or freedmen? The destruction of cities and crops, at times the enslavement of populations, when followed by opportunistic expansion of larger estates by wealthy locals and foreigners, may provide a key background.

In those parts of the Aegean where growth in town and country had been slow in Archaic-Classical times, and really took off in Hellenistic or Early Roman times, a picture of expansion in rural settlement and in town plans under the impact of Rome can certainly be clearly registered, one more typical from the new provinces of the Western Empire, though once

again it is larger estates which predominate. Such villas probably mark opportunistic land-grabbing by foreign elites and their local clients. Rome from as early as the second century BC and on into the second century AD was reorganizing significant parts of the Greek landscape, often using new land divisions (*cadasters*), not just to allot land to Italian colonists, but to punish Aegean cities for disloyalty and reward its own elites and favored Greek communities (Doukellis 1988). This is a major background to the collapse of small indigenous farms in many landscapes and the rise of villa-estates, and an increasing polarization of wealth. A second observable aspect of domestic life may explain the increasing numbers of larger rural estate-centers, and that is the common elaboration of the middle- and upper-class urban house toward semi-public display and reception, increasingly limiting or even excluding the processing and storage of farm products (Westgate 2000). Many wealthier townhouses, unless they were residences for specialist merchants and manufacturers, would now require a country base for such purposes, where a slave or free manager supervised the supporting estate.

It is noteworthy that the Macedonian kingdom had always been unashamedly hierarchical, so that its own agricultural intensification might be expected to encourage sizeable rural estates. We know that the state's expansion saw elite families gifted with lands in areas absorbed in the fourth century onwards, and now excellent recent rescue excavations by Greek archaeologists have revealed substantial farms suggested to include such "colonial" elite "villas" (Adam-Veleni *et al.* 2003). Likewise in the countryside of Miletos in coastal Anatolia, a city of oligarchic (aristocratic) constitution, rural survey shows site expansion in late Classical-early Hellenistic times, but with finds of large monumental graves hinting at land concentrated into larger estates (Lohmann 2001). Just as the Hellenistic conquests abroad could spread rural growth in which the rich were notably benefiting, so in the Aegean, Macedonian rule favored the upper class and we may expect here too that the decline of family farms and the rise of villas may be a trend that rises steadily through Hellenistic into Roman times. Indeed recent survey in Messenia (Alcock *et al.* 2005) has found that once Spartan control of this province was broken by the mid-fourth century BC and the region became independent, rural settlement expanded dramatically, as local cultivators were now able to keep the profits of their labor; but significantly new estates include villas and wealthy graves. Similar evidence comes from adjacent Elis. Overview studies of Roman villa-landscapes in the Mediterranean (Leveau *et al.* 2000) argue that their particular focus was generally commercial agriculture, or large-scale stockraising, thus representing the estates of the upper half of society. They are often linked with nearby villages (*vici*) where their dependent labor resided.

A less obvious but perhaps major change could have occurred in the support system for the lower classes in the Aegean. When community-focused city-states were common, state-funded provision of grain in times of scarcity (even if often subsidized by rich citizens) could protect those vulnerable to food shortages. With the LH-ER rise of a commercial economy in foodstuffs and the general impoverishment of city finances, the rich who controlled the majority of surplus production could exploit scarcity for profit, exacerbating the gulf between income classes. On the plus side, the obligation for most Aegean residents to pay cash taxes to Rome brought far greater interaction with marketing, with the result that provincial farmers of all classes gained easier access to international trade goods.

We are still collecting the vital quantitative data on the numbers of rural sites in LH-ER times and the likely populations involved, but provisionally it remains the case that for most Southern Mainland landscapes a real decline in both rural population and land-use intensity can be registered, whilst in previously less developed countrysides in a wider arc of the Aegean, this period can witness a major expansion in rural life. Nonetheless in both kinds of landscape-use, larger estates are the most prominent feature. It is highly unlikely that small-town inhabitants and occupants of attested villages were essentially craft and trade specialists, and we can assume that peasants now concentrated their own subsistence plots around these nucleations where they mostly now dwelt, and provided a major if not the main workforce as hired labor or share-cropper tenants on the estates of the rich which dominated the open countryside. While major movements of Greek population to the Hellenistic conquered lands in the East and large-scale enslavement by Roman armies can help account for temporary reductions in Aegean populations (Davies 2006), that cannot explain why subsequently so many Greek poleis did not compensate through increased births to infill abandoned lands. The texts we have and the archaeological evidence all seem to indicate that the land, in later Hellenistic and ER times, was progressively absorbed into the control of wealthy families, whose preferred exploitation was commercial but localized. Peasant farmers appear to lack the finances or perhaps access to use the remaining landscape in the intensive manner we have postulated for Southern Greece in Classical-Early Hellenistic times. By the mature Roman Empire, both field survey and excavations indicate Aegean landscapes dominated by villa-estates, alongside a lesser number of smaller farms which may well be largely tenanted rather than independent smallholdings.

Urban Life in Hellenistic Times

In the vast territories Alexander conquered, subsequently carved out into kingdoms by his royal Macedonian successors, old cities were reorganized to varying degrees along Greek lines, and entirely new cities were built. In Greece, the majority of cities continued in use with minor alterations, notably in personalized monumentality for ruler propaganda, and also to take account of major advances in siege warfare, but there were also new cities to reflect the grand schemes of Hellenistic dynasts (such as Demetrias and Halos in Thessaly, and Thessaloniki in Macedonia). The traditional royal residence at Aegai was replanned on a vast scale (Figure 14.1) to suit the rapid rise to Aegean dominance of the Macedonian state, whilst an entirely new capital was constructed by Archelaos ca. 400 BC in a more accessible position near the sea at Pella in the plain of Western Macedonia (Figure 13.3). The formal geometric grid-planning of these new towns was not new however, as we have seen from earlier periods.

In a small settlement-chamber on the Gulf of Volos in Thessaly there had arisen in the Archaic era a typical network of small towns. These were abruptly closed down at the end of the fourth century when the Antigonid dynasty decided to create a strategic

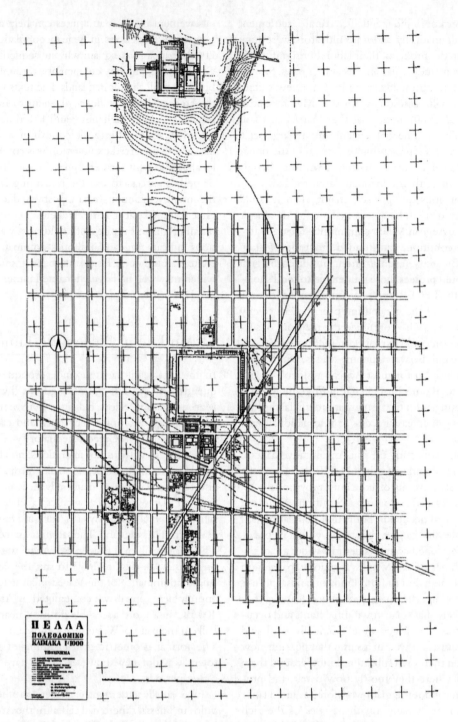

Figure 13.3 Pella: palace/acropolis to north, agora center, and wealthy mansions to its south.
M. Lilimpaki-Akamati and I. M. Akamatis (eds.), *Pella and Its Environs*. Athens 2004, Figure 8.

fortified city in North-Central Greece, Demetrias, as a base for the Macedonian fleet and as a second residence after northern Pella (Marzolff 1999). The giant proportions of the "megalopolis," some 440 ha, were filled by forced migration into it from surrounding urban centers, hence by later Hellenistic times almost no surrounding settlements are recorded.

The fate of existing towns or new towns arising in late Classical to Hellenistic times was dependent both on earlier regional development trajectories (Bintliff 1997) and the favor or disfavor of the new powers of the Aegean, the monarchies and city leagues. Messene, for example, was founded as a giant new town with the freeing by Thebes of Messenia from Spartan domination in the early fourth century. Both town and country took off after centuries of repression, the city becoming highly ornamented with monuments gifted by local Hellenistic elites and later Roman patrons.

Alexander founded a series of cities to memorialize his reputation and consolidate a core Greek colonial presence throughout his vast empire, a custom continued by his successor rulers based in the Aegean and Asia. Additionally, in Hellenistic times cities everywhere became the focus of pronounced advertising for the great princes of the East Mediterranean and their leading wealthy supporters in each provincial city, who now held the key power, since the Successor Kings favored oligarchic rule. This contrasts with the major Classical building programs, which had been paid for by the city, the rich being allowed to gain public approbation by part-funding festivals, public monuments or warships. Those theaters and stadia which were still of earth and wood, could be recast in expensive cut-stone with architectural and sculptural embellishments at the cost of kings and dominant urban elites. The small, ambitious breakaway Pergamon kingdom in Western Anatolia fancied itself as a second Athens: to underline the comparison its kings embellished their own city with remarkable buildings but also decorated Athens with flashy monuments in eye-catching places. Eumenes II constructed a giant stoa along the southern slopes of the Acropolis in the early second century BC, whilst later in the same century Attalus II built the great stoa on the east side of the Agora (now reconstructed).

Older, Classical monuments of the Aegean cities were not immune from the new power politics and its local interventions emanating from the great Hellenistic rulers. Thus when in 306 BC Demetrios Poliorcetes drove out of Athens his rival Cassander's puppet-ruler Demetrios of Phaleron, the Athenians showed no self-respect in their gratitude (Hurwit 1999). Poliorcetes and his father Antigonus were deified and awarded royal status while gold portraits were voted for public display. According to the ancient sources, as if Poliorcetes wished to degrade Athens yet further, he gained approval to occupy the west room of the Parthenon where he held orgies with his mistresses, deploying the temple plate for his dinner parties.

Despite the real subordination of almost all Aegean states to the great dynastic powers, cities continued to busy themselves with their internal affairs and tried to ensure their future by seeking the most promising patrons amongst the rival kings. Stone inscriptions thus remain very common amongst Hellenistic cities. With the help of external patrons and rich citizens these towns were often more splendid than in Classical times, adding in the second to first centuries BC innovative features such as arched gateways and colonnaded avenues to the uniform grid-plan favored in new or replanned infrastructures. But local investment in religious architecture, more vital to self-identity than the display-pavilions of foreign potentates, shows a widespread decline across the Hellenistic era (Shipley 2005). A vigorous growth area however was in the building of gymnasia, now usually in town centers than as previously on urban peripheries: with political activity marginal, wealthier citizens cultivated traditional civic identity in athletic and general body-culture, associated with higher education and anachronistic military exercises (Rizakis and Touratsoglou 2008). Their design with grand entrances, a large open space, and inspiring statues seems to replace the older community agora as the focus of elite culture (Kousser 2005).

A definite redirection of citizen activity from politics and cult toward commerce is marked by the new prominence of business premises in urban spaces. The immense agora at Pella (Figure 13.3) has a limited area devoted to public buildings, being dominated by shops and workshops dealing in pottery, terracottas, metal objects, and foodstuffs (Siganidou and Lilimpaki-Akamati 2003). Urban club-houses proliferated in Hellenistic and then Roman times, especially for particular professions, and increasingly as venues for foreign merchants and businessmen exploiting the wider economic horizons opened up by their empires. The Cycladic island of Delos offers several examples such as a large complex built for traders and shippers from Berytus (Beirut in Lebanon), combining warehouse, offices, assembly-rooms, accommodation, and a shrine (Stewart 2006). A decrease in city autonomy is also marked by a general opening up to allow foreigners to gain citizenship, marry into, and own land in previously closed polis communities, clearly a strategy to bring more wealth and counter demographic decline (Thompson 2006). Cities reoriented themselves around the power of their leading families and to an ethos where wealth creation was primary in a world of expanding commercial markets. The resulting more cosmopolitan connections opened up the Hellenistic city to other communities, new cults from the East, and allowed elite women a new and active role in communal affairs (Shipley and Hansen 2006).

The rise of female influence in the urban world seems to follow from the emergence to dominance during Hellenistic times of a class of wealthy landowners, who monopolize public office and deploy their wealth to subsidize public events and urban infrastructure. This power of leading families elevates the scope for their female members to share in distributing what was joint wealth, and hence encouraged towns to allow them a wider set of civic positions as well as the resultant rewards of honorary inscriptions and statues. However van Bremen (1983) considers that greater female power was not a result of a changed perception of gender equality, but the inevitable effect of changes in class structure and sheer wealth. Nonetheless one must consider that greater visibility and respect for at least elite females may have eventually shifted public opinion away from the official disrespect for women's public potential characteristic of our Classical sources.

We are still some way off achieving an Aegean-wide overview of the state of cities across the Hellenistic era. Balancing the regions which appear to see an expansion in the size and number of towns,

such as the kingdoms of Northern Greece, there is the combined testimony of epigraphic and historical texts and archaeology to a serious decline in urban life over large parts of Southern Greece and the Islands during the Late Hellenistic era (Bintliff 1997, Rizakis and Touratsoglou 2008). Overpopulation and land exhaustion, economic, military, and social crises all seem to be involved at different times and places in contributing to this phenomenon.

Urban Life in Early Roman Times

Alcock's admirable analysis of Roman Greece (1993) showed how drastically Rome transformed the Aegean, but suggested that instead of an overall decline in town and country, displaced and depressed populations and elites migrated to a few, especially the larger, urban centers. We have seen that most surveyed Aegean landscapes register rural decline, whilst a minority see rural colonization stimulated by Roman favor or previous underdevelopment (Bintliff 1997). On balance I see lower *total* rural populations, frequently focused on larger estates. But in Classical-Hellenistic times Aegean populations were predominantly urban (perhaps commonly 70–80 percent), so the real issue is the fate of Aegean towns. Here again, most landscapes see shrinkage or even disappearance of the typical small-to-medium Classical town, with more positive exceptions being isolated or in selected regions. A central issue then is whether new "super-cities" formed poles of attraction, draining lesser Aegean towns for their own growth, and hence sustaining similar *total* levels of Aegean urban populations to pre-Roman times.

The two outstanding case studies must be Nicopolis and Corinth, the former created by Augustus by moving surviving Greek inhabitants from many surrounding towns and villages, the latter being a genuine colony of Italians introduced by Caesar. In Acarnania, in the wider region south of Nicopolis, Lang (1994) records urban centers for Classical-Hellenistic times with a total walled area of 630–700 ha. By ER times no towns survive apart from Nicopolis and the other city given a share in that landscape, the Roman colony at Patras across the Gulf of Corinth: villages and villas are the replacement. To the north of Nicopolis, in Epirus, in a region where 70 towns were destroyed and their inhabitants enslaved by Rome in the second century BC and mostly deported to Italy, the ER settlement system is likewise one of villa-estates and small nucleated settlements, with only two towns likely to survive, the earlier cities being either abandoned or shrunk to villages (Doukellis *et al.* 1995, Murray 2003). Roman Patras is not an extensive city, whilst even the much larger Nicopolis is estimated at 130 ha. The evidence appears to indicate a catastrophic decline in urban populations for Northwest Greece, which Nicopolis and Patras fail to balance.

Corinth, capital of Roman Southern Greece, is given the enormous size of 725 ha by Alcock, based on the Archaic-Classical walls, in which the town itself makes up some 500 ha, with an additional 200+ ha taken up with an area enclosed by Long Walls which ran to and included the port of Lechaion. Even for Classical-Hellenistic times these figures do not represent occupied area. Lechaion possessed no major domestic settlement, neither then nor in Roman times (Rothaus 1995), whilst the Long Walls were to safeguard Corinth's strategic access to its port during an enemy siege. Classical and Roman sources indicate that the Long Walls enclosed open fields. These were formally set out as a cadastral (estate allotment) grid for agricultural use in the early era of the Roman colony (Romano 2003), although a small part nearest the city on archaeological evidence appears to have been for extramural cemeteries (D. Romano, *pers. comm.*). Even the Classical 500 ha city wall included the largely barren mountain of Acrocorinth, while the current excavation team considers the remainder was never fully built up. In any case, using the Archaic-Classical city wall as a guide to Roman Corinth is inappropriate, since we now know from Romano's urban and rural survey (2003, and *pers. comm.*) that the new colony had an entirely different plan (Figure 13.4). The Roman colony was laid out at ca. 240 ha, but seems to have been replanned on a diminished scale (ca. 140 ha) within a few generations to match real population needs. In Late Roman times less than half of even this seems still to be in urban use. In conclusion, Roman Corinth was probably one-third the size of its Classical predecessor.

These reanalyses of settlement patterns in Roman Greece do reinforce the point (Alcock 1993, Bintliff 1997) that the different regions and cities of the Aegean pursued radically divergent pathways throughout the historical era. But they also emphatically indicate that Greece *taken as a whole* in the Early Roman Empire was less populated, less intensively cultivated, and less urbanized than in preceding centuries. This can be counterbalanced by the evidence from sources and archaeology that at least where towns survived, and more rarely expanded (especially during the second century AD), there were major public works (monumental civic buildings, odeia (theaters), amphitheaters and stadia, aqueducts and fountain-houses), lavish townhouses, and, in the countryside, innumerable well-furnished villas. As noted earlier, a polarization of wealth and the occasional intervention by emperors and governors essentially explain this contrast. An even more interesting observation can be brought to bear: current research at Leiden University on the urbanization rate of Roman Italy (De Ligt, de Graaf, *pers. comm.*) has found a dominant pattern of around 20 percent urban, 80 percent rural population, the exact inverse of Classical-Early Hellenistic Greece. Many towns seem to be occupied by the upper class, officials, and residents servicing rural populations and elites (market central-places), whilst in Classical Greece the majority of townsfolk were commuter-farmers. It may be that the "decline of the Aegean town" under Rome was less a failure to recover a desired pattern than a restructuring of Greece into a more Italian settlement-system. But let us make no mistake: the net effect appears currently, if we take the Aegean as a whole, to have been a smaller population, less intense land use, an enlarged wealthy class, a severely diminished middle class, and a smaller and marginalized lower class.

The Character of Roman Cities

Roman impact in Greece was an arbitrary mix of pillage and embellishment. Athens (Walker and Cameron 1989, Hoff and Rotroff 1997) provides a good example for the latter (following Text Box).

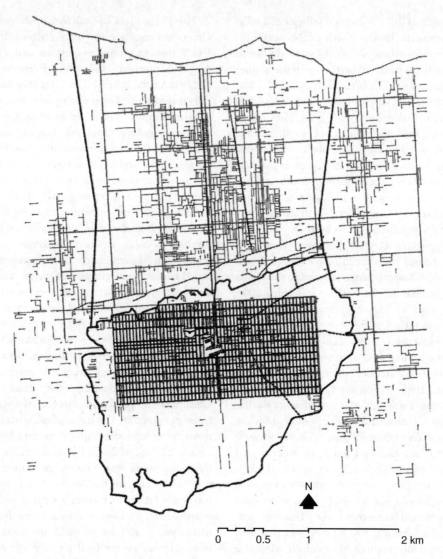

Figure 13.4   The gridplan of the Roman colony of Corinth was set within the pre-Roman city-walls. Also marked is the acropolis (far southwest) and the former Long Walls (to the north running to the coast), together with the Roman agricultural land-division for the colonists around the city.

R. Étienne *et al.*, *Archéologie historique de la Grèce antique*. Paris 2000, Planche XIV.3.

A manifestation that Athens and other famed cities whose glory lay in the pre-Roman past could now count on income from admiring cultured benefactors, students, and tourists emanating from Italy, is the travel-guide prepared by the Romanized Greek Pausanias in the late second century AD (Elsner 1992, Arafat 1996, Alcock *et al.* 2001). For some 30 years he toured the Aegean to "present all things Greek" to the

educated Roman, with an emphasis on artistic and architectural sights. This agenda became the main strength (and ultimately limitation) of the sub-discipline of Classical Archaeology during its development in the period 1750–1960.

Between 167 and 88 BC the Cycladic island of Delos, gifted to Athens by the Romans but as a free port to assist its own merchants, became one of the

The Roman Embellishment of Athens

In the second century AD, Roman elite culture particularly enthused over its debt to Greek civilization (the "Second Sophistic" movement; Spawforth and Walker 1985, 1986). Emperors Hadrian and Marcus Aurelius cultivated a Greek appearance and sponsorship of the arts. Hadrian instituted a league of Greek Cities, the Panhellenion, with claims to ancient prestige, and being an ardent fan of Athens made that city its base, perhaps in a large basilica near the Roman Agora (Hurwit 1999). He also improved Athenian grain and water supplies, and further reoriented the old, disorganized Classical town toward the growing number of Roman public monuments surrounding the new Roman Agora, where he constructed a library and "university" complex.

East of the Roman Agora Hadrian built a "New Town," marking the transition with a still-surviving arch: on the "Old Town" side was inscribed "Here begins the City of Theseus" (legendary King of Athens) and on the "New Town" side "Here begins the City of Hadrian." The most spectacular monument in Hadrian's New Town was the Temple of Olympian Zeus (Olympeion), a gigantic structure which had been begun in Archaic times and fitfully worked on in the intervening centuries.

A more controversial figure later in the same century was the Greek millionaire Herodes Atticus (Tobin 1997, Welch 1998). Originating from Marathon in the Attic countryside he grew up in Rome, rising to senator then consul, eventually becoming an intimate of the philhellene Marcus Aurelius. Accused of embezzling a bequest of his father to the people of Athens, he replied with vast and expensive public monuments. Their success is measurable through their reuse today for similar events by Athens' citizens and visitors: on the south slope of the Acropolis a great odeion or concert hall (venue for the modern Athens Festival, west of the Theater of Dionysos), and in the east of the "New Town" a stadium rebuilt in marble for the Panathenaic Games (restored for the first modern Olympic Games in 1896). Herodes Atticus was also busy self-promoting in other high-profile venues: he refurbished the Delphi stadium in stone, whilst a large architectural setting (*exedra*) at Olympia displayed sculpture representing members of his and the Imperial family.

Clearly Roman gifts to Athens' townscape reflect its new status as progenitor of Rome's own cultural sophistication: lecture-halls, odeia, gymnasia, and libraries (Camp 2001). For intellectuals outside the circle of the Roman dynasts, Greece could also offer a prestigious platform to display claims to cultural achievement. The great Roman orator Cicero wrote that he was planning some monument near the Academy: "I am very fond of the city of Athens. I should like it to have some memorial of myself" (Camp 2001).

Athens was understandably slavish to powerful Romans (Hurwit 1999). Flattery for Nero led to a long inscription on the Parthenon exterior. A staggering 94 altars are known from Athens dedicated to the "god" Hadrian. Athens' enthusiasm for cultivating Roman favor was however poorly matched to her impoverished resources, prompting widespread recycling of older statue-dedications and inscriptions, described by one commentator as "all expense spared." A monument to her Hellenistic Attalid patron Eumenes of Pergamon, standing at the Acropolis entrance-gates, was briefly rededicated to Antony and Cleopatra, then again to their naval vanquisher Agrippa. More remarkably, the Erechtheion was rededicated to Julia Domna, the emperor Septimius Severus' wife, whilst statues of the "god" Hadrian and Julia Domna were added to Athena's statue in the Parthenon.

The "wandering temple" reflects another aspect of Roman impact in Greece. In Attica and other Southern Greek regions, survey and excavation indicate widespread rural depopulation of lesser nucleations and smaller estate-centers in LH–ER times (Lohmann 1993, 2005). This probably led to the running-down or even abandonment of their associated temples. During the Early Roman era a fifth-century BC Ares temple from the rural Pallene deme was dismantled and re-erected in

Athens' ancient Agora, whilst temple architecture from elsewhere in Attica was removed to the capital. Walker (1997) however, challenges the standard view that the deliberate infill of the Athenian Agora was a political statement, replacing democratic opportunities by: "otium [leisure] in the Odeion, nostalgia in the reconstructed fifth-century temple, and flattery in the shrines and statues to an alien ruling elite." She suggests rather that Roman novelties to the ancient urban fabric are products of the "classical revival" encouraged by Augustus, a reaffirmation of Rome's cultural roots in the city most associated with its inspiration in Classical Greece.

most prosperous commercial centers in the Mediterranean. It represents an early intimation of the way Roman power would remove old boundaries to human migration and the circulation of goods, as well as the key role played in the future Empire by entrepreneurial bankers and traders (van Berchem 1991, Étienne et al. 2000). Italians were perhaps dominant in Delian business, followed by Athenians and then various Eastern communities, whilst freedmen and even slaves were very active in finance and commerce for wealthy patrons. So cosmopolitan is this society that neither Hellenization nor Romanization adequately encompass it. Symbolic for all these developments is the Agora of the Italians: the largest complex on the island, more than 5000 m², it possessed statues of Roman magistrates, a public bathhouse, and vast open and porticoed spaces for social and economic interaction. It has little room for traditional religious structures but appears to be devoted to the new god of international business.

Another example of outstanding Early Roman urban development is the city of Thessaloniki (Grammenos 2003) (Figure 13.5). Major rebuilding in modern Greece's second city has allowed large-scale excavations to reveal a monumental Early Imperial city center. As so often, unpredictable politics in the late Roman Republic played their part: Thessaloniki backed the right side in the first-century BC Civil Wars and became the favored regional center for Roman rule at the expense of the older Macedonian capital of nearby Pella, which consequently declined rapidly. Wealthy Roman businessmen and landowners moved in and the town was already highly prosperous by the time of Augustus. Then followed a major building boom in the second century AD in which the vast new Forum was constructed (Velenis 1990–1995). By

this time inscriptions indicate that local and Roman elites were well integrated into a dominant urban class. A general trend for Greek cities to allow their fortification walls to fall down or their stones to be recycled is recorded already in the first century BC for Thessaloniki by Cicero. Fortunately the city authorities rebuilt them in the less secure conditions of the Middle Empire, in time to withstand devastating barbarian raids into Greece by the Heruli tribe during the late third century AD. Athens was less successful, parts of the city including the Stoa of Attalus being sacked in 267 AD; sources however claim there was a spirited defense of the city by a local militia led by the philosopher Dexippos which finally drove off the invaders (Gregory 1992).

Argos in the Peloponnese exhibits typical ER developments (Piérart and Touchais 1996). Although becoming a minor regional center in the shadow of more prosperous and favored cities such as Sparta and Corinth, its small oligarchy of rich families is largely responsible for new buildings in the agora, an odeion (theater/concert hall) and new temples. Statues of the elite naturally deck the town, whilst one local worthy even acquired hero status and was buried with gold finery in a mausoleum in the agora. At Sparta, the local dynast Julius Eurycles, a favorite of Augustus, was probably responsible for the marble theater constructed ca. 30–20 BC: a grandiose design recalling Classical predecessors and the Dorian heritage of the city, it nonetheless introduced state-of-the-art Italian-style mobile stage machinery (Waywell et al. 1998). On Crete the Romans, probably to spite hostile Knossos which was made into a colony, elevated the minor town of Gortyn to become the island's capital (Francis and Harrison 2003). In Early Roman times the Hellenistic town continued but a Roman-style

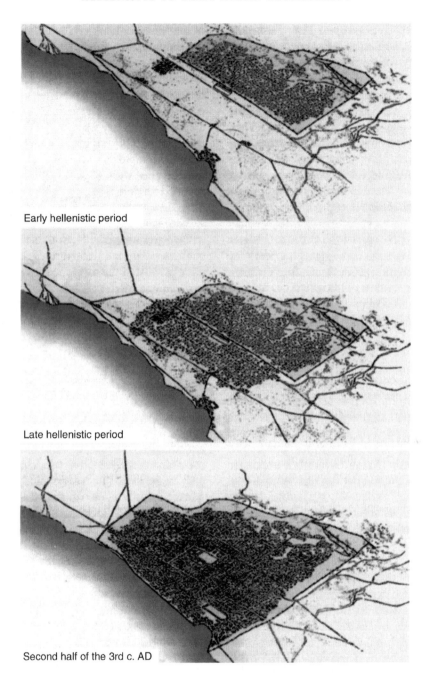

Early hellenistic period

Late hellenistic period

Second half of the 3rd c. AD

Figure 13.5 Development of Thessaloniki from a secondary center within the Macedonian Hellenistic state, to the capital of the Roman province of Macedonia.
D. V. Grammenos (ed.), "Roman Thessaloniki." Thessaloniki, Archaeological Museum Publications, 2003, 124.

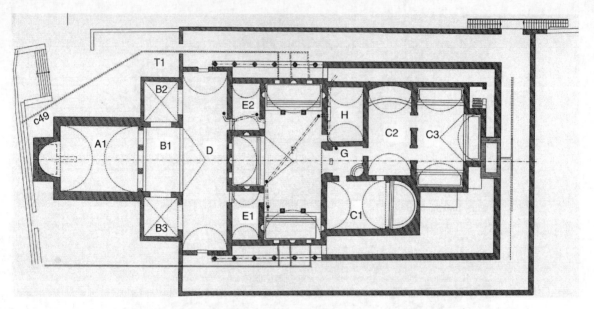

Figure 13.6   Argos: Roman bath complex.
M. Piérart and G. Touchais, *Argos. Une ville grecque de 6000 ans.* Paris 1996, 79.

extension grew up outside it, fitted with an amphi-theater, circus, and *praetorium* (governor's residence).

Beneath the glitter and apparent prosperity of the major Romanized towns we can glimpse a major shift in wealth and influence toward Italian entrepreneurs of both aristocratic (senatorial) and wealthy commoner origin (*equites*), as well as to their clients amongst their peers in the Aegean cities. On Crete for example, sluggish in development during the Archaic to Hellenistic centuries, prosopographical study (using names to create collective biographies from inscrip-tions), evidences a flood of Italian and other immi-grants to the island, who develop the economy to an international scale and promote key centers such as Gortyn (Baldwin Bowsky 1999). Such changes are associated with a widening gulf between richer and poorer citizens, evidenced by contrasted living stand-ards and house sizes in towns, as well as the already-noted dominance in the countryside of larger estate-centers and villages (where perhaps tenants and wage-laborers rather than independent smallholders resided). For the wealthy, the "globalization" of com-merce was aided by the Pax Romana: this brought security, a vast maritime traffic subsidized by the Empire, and at least from the second century AD a

major system of long-distance roads (Rizakis 1996). Also positively, elite women appear in many cities to have gained even further influence on civic life than during Hellenistic times, doubtless tied to Roman customs impacting on the provinces. In Roman soci-ety women were given greater respect and allowed more freedoms than in traditional Greek society (see further Chapter 14). We find from inscriptions at many cities of the Roman East that females of wealthy families are allowed to hold varied public offices well beyond their older association with female cult-centers. These included becoming gymnasiarchs (gymnasium-managers), or the officials responsible for public revenues. As a result honorific statues and ded-icatory inscriptions to elite women begin to form a significant part of the Roman "city of images"(van Bremen 1983, Lefkowitz 1983).

Because of the traumas of the Late Republic there is often little urban construction then in the Aegean except in new foundations, but recovery spreads in the following two centuries of the Early Empire. A pride in Greek traditions may explain why many cities con-tinued to employ cut stone for public buildings and made little use of Roman concrete and brick (Tomlinson 1995), while traditional Greek athletic and cultural festivals remained extremely popular into the third century AD, with Romans eager to participate (Spawforth 1989). The Roman elite and emperors also left prominent constructions in famous sanctuaries. It is rather from the second century and especially during the Middle Imperial era of the third to fourth centuries that Italian innovative materials come into general use and Greek cities introduce more Roman building types, marking as seen earlier a wider process of Greco-Roman integration (Woolf 1994b). Roman games featuring gladiators and beast fights now became widely popular, causing modifications to existing stadia and theaters or calling for purpose-made constructions (Welch 1998). Theaters were built or rebuilt in lavish stone in the Roman style from the second century AD, with semicircular orchestras, a podium stage, and increasingly elaborate stone back-scenery ornamented with statues (where donors, gods, and emperors were promoted) (Tomlinson 1995). Aqueducts are a clear improvement to urban life which the Romans introduced on a scale without previous parallel (Étienne et al. 2000). The grandest is Corinth's, running 100 km from the Central Peloponnese, but Nicopolis' was more than 70 km and Athens' 20 km. Crossing many former independent states most aqueducts remind us of the dissolution of borders, whilst the flourishing of public baths in Athens and elsewhere (Figure 13.6) both stimulated the (usually imperial) gift of aqueducts and shows the partial Romanization of Greek society.

Hellenistic and Early Roman Trade, Economics, and Craft Production

In the Classical era it is generally argued that the vast majority of city-states consumed most of their own food and raw material products, with external commerce being of minor economic importance. Exceptions such as Athens, where total population well outgrew the food-production of Attica, could compensate for this through tribute from its imperial dependencies and the settling of its own citizens on their land, but it also relied on its own silver mines to boost its economy. Yet a sign of longer-term trends is the evidence that Athens promoted the export of olive oil to balance its import of grain. Although then agricultural wealth still remained the foundation of Athenian citizen income, there were important profits from industry and trade, even if these were largely gained by resident aliens (metics). A significant role for such external economic factors does create a difference from typical states where citizen wealth grew from a largely internal market.

In Hellenistic times there are increasing signs of a growth in such contributions from intercity commerce toward wealth creation. Rhodes developed a powerful combination of a dominant aristocracy whose incomes linked major agricultural production to shipping and a strong democracy (Gabrielsen 1997). The Rhodian battle fleet was part-public, part-private and defended the independence of the island as well as protected the private merchant fleet.

The collapse of independence for most other Aegean states, even if they could attempt to play one dynastic patron against the others, had two potential effects on citizen motivation. Firstly it may well have redirected citizens' energy away from the affairs of the polis into the promotion of personal wealth, going well beyond traditional needs, which had been an adequate surplus to fund dowries, necessary equipment, and minor luxuries. This was rapidly becoming a society where the display of wealth in house sizes and furnishings was encouraged, breaking earlier restraint. Secondly the vast scale of the new dynastic kingdoms, all of whom were active in the Aegean, opened up cultural, social, and economic exchanges on an unparalleled level. In line with the rising status of women, we find them engaged in effectively independent financial deals on a large scale.

Coinage can be used to shed light on the intensity of market behavior. The immense bullion from the Persian Empire, released into circulation through the minting by Alexander and his successor dynasts to pay armies, seems to have been a major element in stimulating increased monetarization of the Hellenistic world (Davies 2006). Grandjean (2006) argues that the degree of monetarization of a society and thus its commercial complexity can be measured on a spectrum: from a minor level, where coins, especially low-value pieces, are rare and concentrated in the largest urban centers, near major land and sea routes, to a high level where coins of all values are plentiful and reach remoter rural sites. Although the database remains small, her analysis suggests that Classical monetarization was mainly at the lower end, whilst over the Hellenistic era and even more into the Early Roman Empire most societies in the Aegean were moving progressively toward the higher end of this spectrum. She links the increasing dominance of leading families in cities in the LH-ER era, from the second century BC onwards, and their close involvement in commerce, with the rapid growth in Aegean monetarization.

These developments are increasingly seen as moving into yet another dimension with the rise of Roman influence in the Aegean. Older views in which Hellenistic and Roman economies were set far apart from capitalism and modern economics (Finley 1973) have yielded to a proto-capitalist, "globalist" perspective, where significant changes in the former era lead on to even more dramatic transformations in economic behavior under Rome (Davies 2006). Nothing marks the intensification of interregional movement of goods better than the chart of Central and West Mediterranean shipwrecks (see Davies 2006 updating earlier work by Parker) where a logarithmic rise and fall can be dated from the second century BC to the end of the second century AD.

Although the Aegean largely lay outside the main ER trade routes (Abadie-Reynal 1989) and lacked the economic stimulus of military bases (as it remained a demilitarized zone far from the imperial frontiers), individual cities could benefit from through-trade, imperial favor, and patronage by rich international entrepreneurs. The colony at Corinth was a key port and transit center. Not surprisingly some 85 percent of its amphorae are imported compared to 50 percent elsewhere, whilst these come from a wide range of destinations (Slane 2003, Gregory 2006b). Likewise Late Republican importation of Italian red-gloss (*sigillata*) tableware shows Corinth's Roman settlers looking west, whilst such wares are rare in indigenous Southern Mainland cities till the Early Empire (Étienne *et al.* 2000). Crete, critically aligned on the northern maritime route linking the East and West Mediterranean, also took advantage from commerce which otherwise avoided the inner Aegean (Haggis 1996). At Gortyn (Francis and Harrison 2003) a

precocious link-up with trade from the Western Mediterranean is clear from ceramic studies.

The overall impression is that the Aegean became drawn into the more commercialized Roman economic sphere from the second century BC onwards, both through imports and business practices, although there is extreme regional variety based on the particular historical trajectory of each Greek city (Hoff and Rotroff 1997). It is surely in this context that we should understand the widespread disappearance of small farms and their replacement by a lesser number of larger estate-centers or villas. Significantly: "There was nothing like a middle class in the Roman Empire" (Gregory 2006a). It is arguable that this fact encapsulates the decline of city economies dominated by lower-middle- and lower-class farmers largely consuming their own products, with minor marketing to local towns. Instead, larger commercially-focused estates supply the same towns but also, to a much greater extent than previously, exports to a wider region. This is quite different from seeing the Aegean as a major exporter to the *whole* Hellenistic or Roman world. Current data suggest it was a relative backwater economically in this larger framework, with the exception of cities astride through-traffic which crossed the South Aegean Sea between the two halves of the Mediterranean, or cities acting as economic "gateways" to Greece such as Corinth (Abadie-Reynal 1989). Nonetheless, Roman businessmen, especially the upper-income group called *negotiatores*, formed a major predatory class in the last two centuries BC in the Aegean, lending money to weakened cities and buying up estates on a large scale, as well as setting up craft workshops and commercial networks. Ultimately, through intermarriage with Greek magnates, they would create a single ruling class controlling Aegean towns during the Early Empire (Rizakis 2001).

Paterson (1998) notes that the expansion of commerce and finance that marks the rise of Rome in the Mediterranean reaches a peak in the Augustan era, when markets are still rising due to new provinces, increased urbanization, and the stimulation created by the Italian entrepreneurial community abroad. From that point each region of the Empire establishes its own systems of production and exchange, regional economies largely designed to meet regional needs (although the scale is as large as the Aegean as a

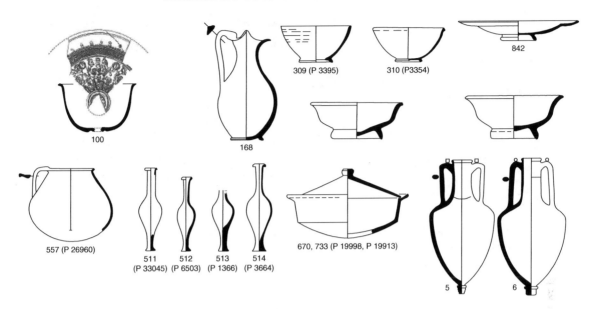

Figure 13.7(a) Drawings. A typical assemblage of Hellenistic date. Top: (left to right) table cups, jug, and serving bowls. Lower: (left to right) cookpot, unguentaria (oil-flasks), casserole, and amphorae. Courtesy of Mark van der Enden.

whole). In a series of sequent phases, individual regions appear to capture a wider market for particular products and expand their circulation over many or all of the Empire's regions. In an "economy of substitution" such goods can now only achieve interregional success by displacing others. Paterson attributes these "hotspots" of production, especially clear from the changes in the sources of tablewares and transport amphorae, to competition between different business communities around the Empire, and changes in taste. However, major shifts in the location of the dominant exporters of olive oil, wine, and fish-sauce are also known to be linked to the dynamics of the state-sponsored provisioning of Rome and the frontier armies in these and other products (chiefly grain) (Fulford 1987, 1992).

As regards Hellenistic household ceramic containers (Figure 13.7a), alongside the shift in oil-flasks from figure-decorated *lekythoi* to minimally-decorated *unguentaria*, Red-Figured tableware also declines swiftly in Hellenistic times (Hayes 1991). After experimentation with polychrome painting, plain black- or grey-gloss wares take over with impressed and incised ornament, blatantly imitating the silver and gold

tableware of the urban and dynastic elites of the age. Is this competitive emulation of the rich, with an escalation of values? Hayes suggests further that the massive decline in sanctuary dedications of miniature pots from the third century BC implies that "such minor offerings were deemed insufficient" in an atmosphere of competitive wealth-display.

The use of ceramic molds points to more uniform, larger-scale production of pottery, which agrees with recent tendencies to see the Hellenistic era as well on the way to more commercial and capitalist forms of economics, parting increasingly with the household dominance of Classical craft-production. The shift to red-gloss molded wares (Eastern Sigillata) occurs in the Late Hellenistic period in the Near Eastern Greek world, rather than in Greece, which has very variable imports of such products, perhaps linked to the highs and lows of each region's prosperity in the troubled era 200–1 BC (Bes 2006). It is with transport amphorae where the rise of commercial trade is most clearly demonstrable (Rotroff 2006), with a "staggering variety" of forms widely traded around the Aegean (although wine and oil will have been their dominant contents). The increasing use of

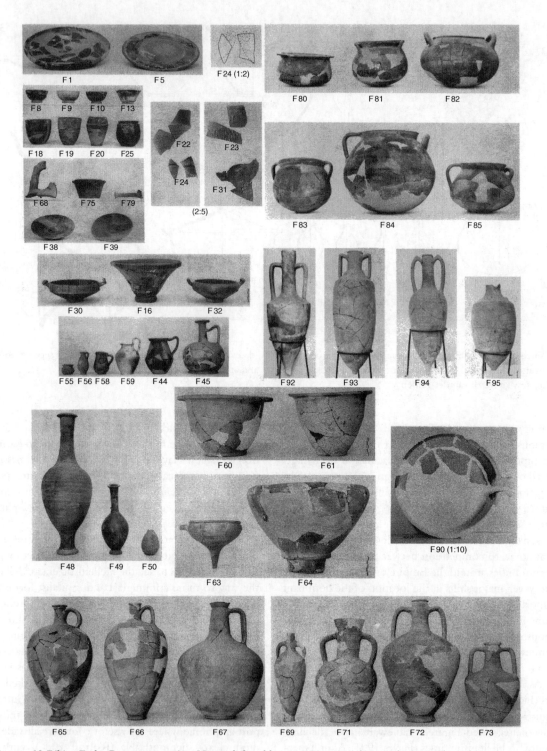

Figure 13.7(b) Early Roman ceramics. Upper left: tablewares. Upper right: amphorae and cooking ware. Below, unguentaria, kitchen, and other plain wares.

Philip Bes after H. S. Robinson, *Pottery of the Roman Period. Chronology* (= *The Athenian Agora*, Vol. 5). Princeton 1959, with permission of Professor J. Camp.

stamps marks both the commercial character of this trade and state monitoring.

Specialists in Roman pottery (Figure 13.7b) agree that the expansion of Roman economic and political influence was associated with a further heightened level of industrial production in most spheres, not least ceramics. The scale of manufacture and the reach of major pottery-production centers is one of the striking features of the Early Empire. Although in the Aegean regional and even city-based production of everyday wares usually remained predominant, we find in both excavation and survey collections that the role of non-Aegean medium- and long-distance imports and exports rises dramatically. The most obvious areas of the assemblage concerned are the red-gloss (sigillata) tablewares and transport amphorae (containing oil, wine, and fish-sauce especially). It has long been noted that the penetration of such highly commercialized wares into every corner of the Empire is remarkable and generally not repeated till the Early Modern era marketing of factory products (Blake 1980). The period 100 BC to 100 AD sees an influx of Italian sigillatas to the Aegean, followed in the subsequent second-century recovery era of the Aegean world by a colonization of the tableware market by Eastern variants. But significantly Eastern tablewares have now adopted Italian shapes, angular over curved (Bes 2006). Moreover Italian eating styles are also adopted in the Greek world: its cups and plates for example. But suiting the marginal and sluggish nature of Aegean economy in the LH-ER era, pots and lamps of Hellenistic style continue to be made into the first century AD before converting to Roman designs (Rotroff 2006). By the second century AD, Corinth was producing lamps following Roman tastes for distribution throughout Greece, such as those found at Messene with gladiators and erotic scenes (Themelis 2003). The virtual cessation of small dedications (miniature vases and figurines) at Roman-era sanctuaries in Greece, appears to mark a collapse of investment in such activities by the average citizen, possibly linked to the greater materialism which had begun in later Hellenistic times. This is also seen in the decline in specific products made for funerary dedications.

In other aspects of technology (Keyser and Irby-Massie 2006), there are progressive advances during Hellenistic times in the milling of flour and olive oil, symptomatic of greater commercialization of agriculture and heightened industrialization of production. More to the advantage of ordinary citizens was the invention of blown glass, probably in the Levant ca. 50 BC, making glass tableware and body-care wares common in Roman Greece.

References

Abadie-Reynal, C. (1989). "Céramique et commerce dans le bassin égéen du IVe au VIIe siècle." In C. Morrisson and J. Lefort (eds.), *Hommes et richesses dans l'empire byzantin, IVe–VIIe siècle*. Paris: Éditions P. Lethielleux, 143–159.

Adam-Veleni, P., E. Poulaki, and K. Tzanavari (2003). *Ancient Country Houses on Modern Roads. Central Macedonia*. Athens: Archaeological Receipts Fund.

Alcock, S. E. (1991). "Urban survey and the polis of Phlius." *Hesperia* 60, 421–463.

Alcock, S. (1993). *Graecia Capta. The Landscapes of Roman Greece*. Cambridge: Cambridge University Press.

Alcock, S.E., J.F. Cherry, and J. Elsner (eds.) (2001). *Pausanias. Travel and Memory in Roman Greece*. Oxford: Oxford University Press.

Alcock, S. E. et al. (2005). "Pylos Regional Archaeological Project, Part VII. Historical Messenia, Geometric through Late Roman." *Hesperia* 74, 147–209.

Arafat, K. W. (1996). *Pausanias' Greece. Ancient Artists and Roman Rulers*. Cambridge: Cambridge University Press.

Baldwin Bowsky, M. W. (1999). "The business of being Roman: The prosopographical evidence." In A. Chaniotis (ed.), *From Minoan Farmers to Roman Traders*. Stuttgart: Franz Steiner Verlag, 305–347.

Bes, P. (2006). "The ICRATES Platform: Tablewares in the Roman east. A case study: Late Hellenistic and Early Imperial Greece (60 BC–AD 150)." In M. Kerkhof et al. (eds.), *SOJA-bundel 2005*. Leiden: Stichting voor Onderzoek door Jonge Archeologen, 25–34.

Bintliff, J. L. (1997). "Regional survey, demography, and the rise of complex societies in the Ancient Aegean: Core–periphery, Neo-Malthusian, and other interpretive models." *Journal of Field Archaeology* 24, 1–38.

Bintliff, J. (2000). "Deconstructing 'the sense of place'? Settlement systems, field survey, and the historic record: A case-study from Central Greece." *Proceedings of the Prehistoric Society* 66, 123–149.

Bintliff, J. L. and A. M. Snodgrass (1985). "The Cambridge/Bradford Boeotian Expedition: The first four years." *Journal of Field Archaeology* 12, 123–161.

Bintliff, J. L. and A. M. Snodgrass (1988). "Mediterranean survey and the city." *Antiquity* 62, 57–71.

Blake, H. (1980). "Technology, supply or demand?" *Medieval Ceramics* 4, 3–12.

Briscoe, J. (1986). "Review of E. S. Gruen *The Hellenistic World and the Coming of Rome* 1984." *Classical Review* 36, 91–96.

Camp, J. M. (2001). *The Archaeology of Athens*. New Haven: Yale University Press.

Cartledge, P. (1998). "Historical outline c.1500–146 BCE." In P. Cartledge (ed.), *The Cambridge Illustrated History of Ancient Greece*. Cambridge: Cambridge University Press, 54–73.

Cherry, J. F., J. C. Davis, and E. Mantzourani (1991). *Landscape Archaeology as Long-Term History. Northern Keos in the Cycladic Islands*. Los Angeles: Institute of Archaeology, University of California.

Davies, J. K. (2006). "Hellenistic economies." In G. R. Bugh (ed.), *The Cambridge Companion to the Hellenistic World*. Cambridge: Cambridge University Press, 73–92.

Doukellis, P. (1988). "Cadastres romains en Grèce. Traces d'un reseau rural à Actia Nicopolis." *Dialogues d'Histoire Ancienne* 14, 159–166.

Doukellis, P., J.-J. Dufaure, and É. Fouache (1995). "Le contexte géomorphologique et historique de l'aqueduc de Nicopolis." *Bulletin de Correspondance Hellénique* 119, 209–233.

Elsner, J. (1992). "A Greek pilgrim in the Roman world." *Past and Present* 135, 3–29.

Étienne, R., C. Müller, and F. Prost (2000). *Archéologie historique de la Grèce antique*. Paris: Ellipses.

Finley, M. I. (1973). *The Ancient Economy*. London: Chatto & Windus.

Francis, J. and G. M. W. Harrison (2003). "Review article: Gortyn: First City of Roman Crete." *American Journal of Archaeology* 107, 487–492.

Fulford, M. (1987). "Economic interdependence among urban communities of the Roman Mediterranean." *World Archaeology* 19, 58–75.

Fulford, M. (1992). "Territorial expansion and the Roman Empire." *World Archaeology* 23, 294–305.

Gabrielsen, V. (1997). *The Naval Aristocracy of Hellenistic Rhodes*. Aarhus: Aarhus University Press.

Grammenos, D. V. (ed.) (2003). *Roman Thessalonike*. Thessalonike: Archaeological Museum Publications.

Grandjean, C. (2006). "Histoire économique et monétarisation de la Grèce à l'époque hellénistique." In R. Descat (ed.), *Approches de l'économie hellénistique*. Saint-Bertrand-de-Comminges: Entretiens d'archéologie et d'histoire 7, 195–214.

Grandjean, C. (2008). "Introduction." In C. Grandjean (ed.), *Le Péloponnèse d'Épaminondas à Hadrien*. Paris: De Boccard, 11–17.

Gregory, T. E. (1992). "Kastro and diateichisma as responses to Early Byzantine frontier collapse." *Byzantion* 62, 235–253.

Gregory, T. E. (2006a). *A History of Byzantium*. Oxford: Blackwell.

Gregory, T. (2006b). "The Corinth centennial: 100 (+10) years of work in the Roman city." *Journal of Roman Archaeology* 19, 632–636.

Haggis, D. C. (1996). "The port of Tholos in Eastern Crete and the role of a Roman horreum along the Egyptian 'corn route'." *Oxford Journal of Archaeology* 15, 183–209.

Hayes, J. W. (1991). "Fine wares in the Hellenistic world." In T. Rasmussen and N. Spivey (eds.), *Looking at Greek Vases*. Cambridge: Cambridge University Press, 183–202.

Hoff, M. C. and S. I. Rotroff (eds.) (1997). *The Romanization of Athens*. Oxford: Oxbow Books.

Howgego, C. (1992). "The supply and use of money in the Roman world 200 B.C. to A.D. 300." *Journal of Roman Studies* 82, 1–31.

Hurwit, J. M. (1999). *The Athenian Acropolis*. Cambridge: Cambridge University Press.

Kahrstedt, U. (1954). *Das wirtschaftliche Gesicht Griechenlands in der Kaiserzeit*. Bern: Francke.

Keyser, P. T. and G. Irby-Massie (2006). "Science, medicine, and technology." In G. R. Bugh (ed.), *The Cambridge Companion to the Hellenistic World*. Cambridge: Cambridge University Press.

Kousser, R. (2005). "Creating the past: The Venus de Milo and the Hellenistic reception of Classical Greece." *American Journal of Archaeology* 109, 227–250.

Lang, F. (1994). "Veränderungen des Siedlungsbildes in Akarnanien von der klassisch-hellenistischen zur römischen Zeit." *Klio* 76, 239–254.

Lefkowitz, M. (1983). "Influential women." In A. Cameron and A. Kuhrt (eds.), *Images of Women in Antiquity*. London: Croom Helm, 49–64.

Leveau, P., P. Gros, and F. Trément (2000). "La recherche sur les élites gallo-romaines et le problème de la villa." *Bulletin Ager*, 2–10.

Lohmann, H. (1993). *Atene. Forschungen zu Siedlungs- und Wirtschaftsstruktur des klassischen Attika*. Köln: Böhlau Verlag.

Lohmann, H. (2001). "Survey in der Chora von Milet 1999 Abschlussbericht." In *18. Arastirma Sonuclari Toplantisis 2. Cilt*. Ankara: Ayribasim, 11–22.

Lohmann, H. (2005). "Prähistorischer und antiker Blei-Silberbergbau im Laurion." In Ü. Yalçin (ed.), *Anatolian Metal III*. Bochum: Deutsches Bergbau-Museum (*Der Anschnitt* Beiheft 18), 105–136.

Luraghi, N. (2008). "Meeting Messenians in Pausanias' Greece." In C. Grandjean (ed.), *Le Péloponnèse d'Épaminondas à Hadrien*. Paris: De Boccard, 191–202.

Marzolff, P. (1999). "Zentrum und Peripherie im Wandel der Besiedlungsstruktur an der Bucht van Iolkos." In E.-L. Schwandner and K. Rheidt (eds.), *Stadt und Umland*. Mainz: Philipp von Zabern, 168–185.

Mee, C. B. and W. G. Cavanagh (1998). "Diversity in a Greek landscape: The Laconia Survey and Rural Sites Project." In W. G. Cavanagh and S.E.C. Walker (eds.), *Sparta in Laconia*. London: British School at Athens Studies 4, 141–148.

Mikalson, J. D. (2006). "Greek religion. Continuity and change in the Hellenistic period." In G. R. Bugh (ed.), *The Cambridge Companion to the Hellenistic World*. Cambridge: Cambridge University Press, 208–222.

Murray, W. M. (2003). "Foundation and destruction: Nicopolis and northwestern Greece." *Journal of Roman Archaeology* 16, 475–478.

Osborne, R. (2000). "The fourth century: Political and military narrative." In R. Osborne (ed.), *Classical Greece*. Oxford: Oxford University Press, 197–222.

Paterson, J. (1998). "Trade and traders in the Roman world: Scale, structure, and organisation." In H. Parkins and C. Smith (eds.), *Trade, Traders and the Ancient City*. London: Routledge, 149–167.

Petropoulos, M. and A. D. Rizakis (1994). "Settlement patterns and landscape in the coastal area of Patras." *Journal of Roman Archaeology* 7, 183–207.

Piérart, M. and G. Touchais (1996). *Argos. Une ville grecque de 6000 ans*. Paris: CNRS.

Rizakis, A. D. (1996). "Les colonies romaines des côtes occidentales grecques. Populations et territoires." *Dialogues d'Histoire Ancienne* 22, 255–324.

Rizakis, A. D. (2001). "Les Cités péloponnésiens entre l'époque hellénistique et l'Empire: le paysage économique et social." In R. Frei-Stolba and K. Gex (eds.), *Recherches récentes sur le monde hellénistique*. Bern: Peter Lang, 75–96.

Rizakis, A. D. and Y. Touratsoglou (2008). "L'Économie du Péloponnèse hellénistique: un cas régional." In C. Grandjean (ed.), *Le Péloponnèse d'Épaminondas à Hadrien*. Paris: De Boccard, 69–82.

Romano, D. (2003). "City planning, centuriation, and land division in Roman Corinth." In C.K. Williams and N. Bookidis (eds.), *Corinth, the Centenary 1896–1996*. Athens: American School of Classical Studies, 279–301.

Rothaus, R. (1995). "Lechaion, western port of Corinth: A preliminary archaeology and history." *Oxford Journal of Archaeology* 14, 293–306.

Rotroff, S. I. (2006). "Material culture." In G. R. Bugh (ed.), *The Cambridge Companion to the Hellenistic World*. Cambridge: Cambridge University Press, 136–157.

Shipley, G. (2005). "Between Macedonia and Rome: Political landscapes and social change in Southern Greece in the Early Hellenistic period." *Annual of the British School at Athens* 100, 315–330.

Shipley, D. G. J. and M. H. Hansen (2006). "The polis and federalism." In G. R. Bugh (ed.), *The Cambridge Companion to the Hellenistic World*. Cambridge: Cambridge University Press, 52–72.

Siganidou, M. and M. Lilimpaki-Akamati (2003). *Pella. Capital of Macedonia*. Athens: Archaeological Receipts Fund.

Slane, K. W. (2003). "Corinth's Roman pottery. Quantification and meaning." In C. K. Williams and N. Bookidis (eds.), *Corinth, the Centenary 1896–1996*. Athens: American School of Classical Studies, 323–335.

Spawforth, A. (1989). "Agonistic festivals in Roman Greece." In S. Walker and A. Cameron (eds.), *The Greek Renaissance in the Roman Empire*. London: British Institute of Classical Studies Supplement 55, 193–197.

Spawforth, A. and S. Walker (1985). "The world of the Panhellenion I." *Journal of Hellenic Studies* 75, 78–104.

Spawforth, A. and S. Walker (1986). "The world of the Panhellenion II." *Journal of Hellenic Studies* 76, 88–105.

Stewart, A. (2006). "Hellenistic art. Two dozen innovations." In G. R. Bugh (ed.), *The Cambridge Companion to the Hellenistic World*. Cambridge: Cambridge University Press, 158–185.

Themelis, P. G. (2003). *Ancient Messene*. Athens: Ministry of Culture, Archaeological Receipts Fund.

Thompson, D. J. (2006). "The Hellenistic family." In G. R. Bugh (ed.), *The Cambridge Companion to the Hellenistic World*. Cambridge: Cambridge University Press, 93–112.

Tobin, J. (1997). *Herodes Attikos and the City of Athens: Patronage and Conflict under the Antonines*. Amsterdam: J. C. Gieben.

Tomlinson, R. A. (1995). *Greek and Roman Architecture*. London: British Museum Press.

van Berchem, D. (1991). "Commerce et écriture. L'Exemple de Délos à l'époque hellénistique." *Museum Helveticum* 48, 129–145.

van Bremen, R. (1983). "Women and wealth." In A. Cameron and A. Kuhrt (eds.), *Images of Women in Antiquity*. London: Croom Helm, 223–242.

van Wees, H. (2000). "The city at war." In R. Osborne (ed.), *Classical Greece*. Oxford: Oxford University Press, 80–110.

Velenis, G. (1990–1995). "The Ancient Agora of Thessalonike." *Athens Annals of Archaeology* 23–28, 129–142.

Walker, S. (1997). "Athens under Augustus." In M. C. Hoff and S.I. Rotroff (eds.), *The Romanization of Athens*. Oxford: Oxbow, 67–80.

Walker, S. and A. Cameron (eds.) (1989). *The Greek Renaissance in the Roman Empire: Papers from the Tenth*

British Museum Classical Colloquium. London: Institute of Classical Studies.

Waywell, G. B., J. J. Wilkes, and S. E. C. Walker (1998). "The ancient theatre at Sparta." In W. G. Cavanagh and S. E. C. Walker (eds.), *Sparta in Laconia*. London: British School at Athens Studies 4, 97–111.

Welch, K. (1998). "Greek stadia and Roman spectacles: Asia, Athens, and the tomb of Herodes Atticus." *Journal of Roman Archaeology* 11, 117–145.

Wells, B. and C. Runnels (eds.) (1996). *The Berbati-Limnes Archaeological Survey 1988–1990*. Jonsered: Paul Åström.

Westgate, R. C. (2000). "Space and decoration in Hellenistic houses." *Annual of the British School at Athens* 95, 391–426.

Woolf, G. (1994a). "Town, country and imperialism in Roman Greece." *Journal of Roman Archaeology* 7, 417–420.

Woolf, G. (1994b). "Becoming Roman, staying Greek: Culture, identity and the civilizing process in the Roman East." *Proceedings of the Cambridge Philological Society* 40, 116–143.

Further Reading

Arafat, K. W. and C. A. Morgan (1998). "Architecture and the other visual arts." In P. Cartledge (ed.), *The Cambridge Illustrated History of Ancient Greece*. Cambridge: Cambridge University Press, 250–287.

Bintliff, J. and P. Howard (1999). "Studying needles in haystacks. Surface survey and the rural landscape of Central Greece in Roman times." *Pharos* 7, 51–91.

14

Symbolic Material Culture, the Built Environment, and Society in Hellenistic and Early Roman Greece

Urban Residential Life

Hellenistic Era

As noted in the preceding chapter, quite a number of significant "Hellenistic" trends derive from the Late Classical fourth century BC world, not least in the kingdom of Macedon, so I will take the liberty at times in this chapter to include slightly earlier aspects that predate the death of Alexander. Notable already during the late Classical fourth century, and increasingly pronounced for the Hellenistic era, is a relaxation of the outwardly egalitarian "polis" ethos of domestic housing (Westgate 2000). Differentiation increases both in house size and decoration. Private as well as public life openly reflect the display of personal status within a blatantly stratified society, modeled upon the traditional dynastic-oligarchic combination found in Greece's conquerors, the Macedonian Kingdom. Macedonian towns and houses form influential models throughout the Greek world for status dwellings.

For Hellenistic dynasts the palace (*basileion*) replaced the agora of Archaic-Classical Greece as the setting for the reproduction of public life (Étienne *et al.* 2000). An early example is the Vergina-Aigai royal palace, the traditional Macedonian capital and site of the royal tombs (Figure 14.1). The plan of the palace is seen in its late fourth-century form. The approach was dominated by a monumental east façade, leading via a tunnel into a vast 2000 m² court. Around this opened a series of medium to large meeting-rooms, including several banqueting chambers supplied with mosaic floors and couches (rooms E and F, and M1–3, of which the latter are each 300 m² or larger than a typical Classical house). West of the Great Court was a smaller version, perhaps the private apartments for the ruling elite. At the succeeding capital of Pella two major palaces have been uncovered, also on a massive scale (Palace 1 is 7500 m²), with a similar emphasis on large courts and assembly/dining rooms, linked by formal porticoes. Although the plans of Macedonian palaces are not fully understood, especially the location of administration (the grand east portico at Aigai was maybe for the civil service), it is clear that a central feature of the power structure was provision for large-scale formal banqueting where relations between the dynasts and their upper-class retinue were regularly affirmed and negotiated.

In the excavated town of Pella late fourth-century private house-blocks (*insulae*) incorporate spacious mansions for the wealthy and powerful. Sources indicate that major officials and junior members of the royal house occupied such urban villas, appropriate to their scale: often 1000–2000 m², whilst the Villa of Dionysos is over 3000 m². The latter has an entrance-door with Ionic capitals and both its courts are *peristyle* (pillar-surrounded) display spaces,

The Complete Archaeology of Greece: From Hunter-Gatherers to the 20th Century AD, First Edition. John Bintliff.
© 2012 John Bintliff. Published 2012 by Blackwell Publishing Ltd.

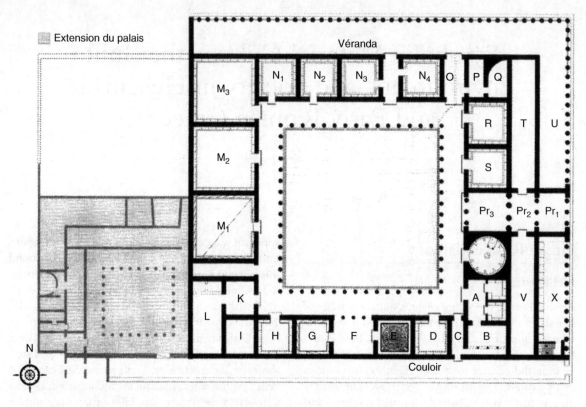

Figure 14.1   Plan of the Aegai palace.
R. Étienne *et al., Archéologie historique de la Grèce antique*. Paris 2000, Figure 113.

although the northern with its series of smaller rooms and an upper story doubtless included more private and service functions. Macedonian elite homes represent small-scale imitations of palaces: porticoed courts, often more than one, are surrounded by rooms with decorated mosaics or murals (Color Plate 14.1a) for the reception or dining of guests, the whole ornamented in terracotta and sculpture. These changes were both copied throughout the Greek world but were independently occurring in other states with the widespread decline of the city-state ethos. Already by late Classical times, for example, the great houses at Eretria (on the island of Euboea) had become bi-focused with a double court.

Architectural splendors formerly reserved for public secular and sacred buildings of the Classical polis are now imported into private homes, where just a single *andron* suite with modest décor had formed an exception. The enhanced display function shows that the homes of wealthier individuals are no longer secluded private residences where the front door led directly into family space. Judging by the multiplication of ornamental courts and entertainment rooms in late Classical-Hellenistic houses of middle to large scale, the house has become a semi-public zone (see Figure 14.2 for Delian homes). From the late Classical era through the Hellenistic, mosaics primarily for house ornament become increasingly popular and technically sophisticated, a sure sign of growing conspicuous consumption at the family level. Nonetheless, Hellenistic palaces still stood out through scale and prestigious façades, advertising a new hierarchy of power.

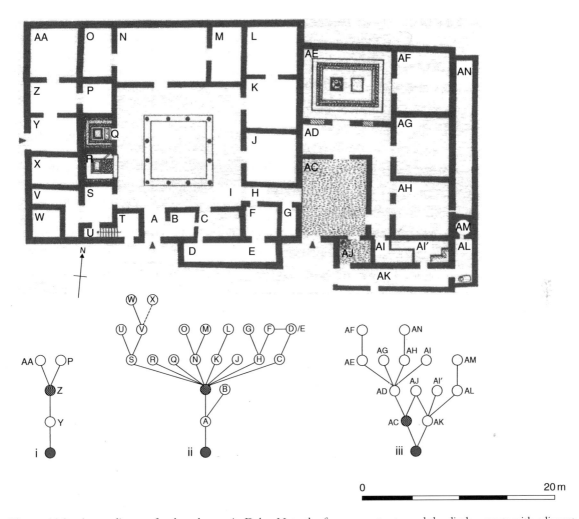

Figure 14.2 Access diagram for three houses in Delos. Note the focus on entry toward the display courts with adjacent mosaic-floored entertainment rooms and the marginalization of family and service suites.
R. C. Westgate, "House and society in Classical and Hellenistic Crete." *American Journal of Archaeology* 111 (2007), 423–457, Figure 1. Reproduced by permission of Archaeological Institute of America (Boston).

In many houses the architectural embellishment of the main, sometimes only court, indicates a reduction in its functional household activity role in favor of leisure and guest reception. There is evidence that upper rooms were becoming more decorated, possibly hinting at a more relaxed attitude to female seclusion in Hellenistic times. The often multiple dining-rooms may indicate sensitivity to different statuses of guests, whilst contrasts in the art of small versus large reception rooms are interpreted as designed to impress visitors of greater or lesser sophistication. Additionally the number of couches may rise from the Classical norm. Contemporary texts inform us that dinner-parties were important for integrative networking ("social reproduction"). As for citizen homes below the rich, they also seem to exhibit minor differences reflecting their means. On the other hand, time-scheduling probably removed the inconvenience of losing traditional family space to display areas, allowing domestic activities to spread into reception areas when guests were absent.

Town life and the rise of Rome in the Aegean

During the transitional era from Hellenistic to Early Roman times, the second to first century BC, when most excavated Delos houses are dated, the display courts of its larger residences possess fountains, ponds, and ornamental sculpture. For the island's flourishing merchant community of Greek, Italian, and others of foreign origin, social display through opening up the home for acquaintances, clients, and business colleagues was a priority. In the group of three houses from Delos (Westgate 2000) shown in Figure 14.2, the *left* example (if truly an independent residence) seems a very simple home for someone of modest means. Its access diagram recalls Iron Age homes with a basic linear progression from public to private (or storage). In contrast the homes in the *center* and *right* offer very elaborate access routes. Entry to the home is conceived as a display opportunity, as the visitor arrives in a colonnaded court from which one or several decorated reception rooms are accessible (here Q and R in the central house, AE for the right). The service rooms are marginalized within the complex (via rooms S, H, and C in the central house and AJ or AK for the right example).

In terms of urban fabric, the Delian townscape in this era resembles that of Early Modern European towns (Trümper 2005). There are many social gradations from the hyper-rich multi-courted villas, through middle-class traditional-sized homes, then to the lower classes in small to very small apartments or tiny homes, or even above shops. Yet all classes and occupations live side by side, whether in privately owned plots of very small to very large extent, or in sublet sectors of elaborate house-blocks owned by wealthier residents.

By the Early Roman imperial era the dominance in every aspect of city-life of an integrated ruling class of indigenous and Italian origin was also clear to all citizens through the proliferation of honorific statues at every point of the town plan, as well as through the numerous public buildings and facilities gifted by this elite. With the decline of city finances such wealthy families were the default source of income for new or renovated civic monuments, apart from the occasional gift from the Imperial family or a provincial governor.

The first-century BC Roman authors Cornelius Nepos and Vitruvius observed that Romans allowed women to share in social life, including dinner-parties, whilst Greeks confined women's society to their relatives, denying them access to social dining. However such references probably referred to the pre-Roman era rather than contemporary Greek customs, and at least by the time of the late first and early second century AD the Greek author Plutarch tells us his wife was well esteemed by his friends, implying easy familiarity between the genders. This may fit with a notable alteration in house access (Nevett 2002). Whereas the Hellenistic double-court, one for display, brought a semi-public area within the home, the retention of a separate domestic court at a further level of accessibility or on a divergent route, still indicates a restriction on the movements of non-family members. Nevett highlights a significant change with many Roman-era Aegean homes. Characteristic is the house-access shift between a fourth-century and first-century BC house at Kassope. Here the original single house-access to a court and andron, shielding easy access to inner private open and roofed spaces, is replaced by two different house-entrances, removing movement barriers. The easier circulation created into and around the house may well indicate that everyone was socialized with little restriction. Delian houses sometimes likewise show an opening up of their façades through eye-level windows, or bays for creating attractive views (Étienne et al. 2000).

One wonders if the impact of Roman entrepreneurial culture, a major form of Italian influence on Greece, did not undermine traditional class and gender distinctions to promote the maximum freedom of movement and interaction to assist unimpeded wealth-creation. A large proportion of resident Italians in Greece were actually freedmen or even slaves employed by elite patrons to conduct their business, and indeed the important Roman colony at Corinth had a core of freedmen at its foundation. In time some Roman Corinthians became sufficiently wealthy to marry into established Greek elite families.

In Roman-era houses, on occasion, the display court becomes so elaborate that its use for household work becomes less likely. If there is no second, more domestic court, this raises the question where everyday work (weaving, food preparation, agricultural-processing, and house-based artisanship), can have taken place. An example is the Areopagus House in Athens, with a walled garden, pond, and well. In Delos especially such courts had wall-paintings, architectural features, reliefs, statues, and barriers. Often the narrow entrance-doors rule out farm vehicles entering such houses. Two solutions are likely. Firstly, plans can oversimplify actual use. Everyday work might, as we saw for Hellenistic courtyards, have continued in the peristyle verandas surrounding these leisure-courts. Secondly, the wealthier households may have dedicated their townhouses to social life and removed associated craftwork and agricultural processing to rural estate-centers; in turn, this could be linked to the proliferation of villa-type establishments in the Greek countryside in Roman times.

In the increasingly elaborate town mansions of the Roman Imperial period particular attention was paid to the dining-rooms, or *triclinia*, where complex mosaic designs were so placed to suit the viewpoint of guests reclining on three sides of the room. At Knossos the second-century AD Villa Dionysos has a peristyle garden with four highly-decorated reception rooms opening off it, including very fine mosaic floors, marble veneer, wall-painting, and stucco moldings; a fountain and a grand pillared entrance for the house complete the image of a wealthy mansion in or near the town (Paton 1998). By Middle Imperial times (ca. 200–400 AD), Roman entrance-hallways or *atria* appear, and these can also have a shallow pool and mosaics: probably clients of lower status were received here as opposed to one's social equals who were invited further into the house, where the more elaborate reception and dining-rooms were situated around an inner court or garden (as at Sparta, Raftopoulou 1998).

Hellenistic Art

The royal tombs at Vergina

Although the Classical polis-world knew visible displays of wealth in burials, expressed in elaborately carved monumental tombstones, such minor infringements of citizen egalitarianism pale into insignificance when we enter the Hellenistic era. The kingdom of Macedon, always a highly stratified society, had never experienced a democratic ethos, so as its Aegean power grew it combined lavish burial for leading families with Classical art forms adopted from the South Aegean states. Most spectacular are the monumental burials associated with the royal family at the original capital of Aegai (modern Vergina). Andronikos' excavations (1989) revealed, within a series of traditional tumuli, complex stone-built tombs with fabulously rich gifts and elaborate painted decoration (see following Text Box).

Repackaging the Macedonian kingdom, often considered "barbarian" by the Aegean city-states, into a heroized state with mythical Greek roots, began in the early fifth century BC with King Alexander I: an imaginary history of the royal house traced it back to Hercules via the Peloponnesian city of Argos. The next step was to claim divine status for the dynasty. Already during Philip II's reign, he erected a circular shrine to himself and his family at the Panhellenic sanctuary of Olympia, and here and also in a surviving sculpted head from Athens the portrayal of his son Alexander is already that of the propaganda ideal that the latter would promote around the Mediterranean and Near East. The autocrat as a god (on death, and even when alive), was easily accepted in most regions of the Near East where a comparable concept had been common for millennia (particularly in Egypt), but in Greece it represented a stronger break with Classical tradition. However, since Olympian gods and mythical heroes were conceived as ideal mortals, the emergence of supernatural associations for rulers of unparalleled and awesome power in the Hellenistic world would ultimately not have seemed unimaginable to the Greek mind. Yet one did not offer prayers or dedications to Hellenistic dynasts or expect supernatural miracles from them, and it appears rather that their cults reflected gratitude, fear, and respect toward new powers who wielded an influence on ordinary people previously associated with divinities (Mikalson 2006).

The Alexander cult

If Philip II was nonetheless considered by contemporaries in the city-states as an upstart dictator, fighting his way to controlling Classical Aegean civilization

Macedonian Royal Tombs

Many scholars accept one tomb (Color Plate 14.1b) as that of the founder of Macedon's hegemony, Philip II, based on the finds-chronology and physical details uncovered by facial reconstruction of the skull, although just as many prefer another member of the dynasty and dispute the same evidence. In any case, this tomb has armor and crowns emphasizing political and military power and contains 20 miniature ivory images which are probably portraits of family members. The objects selected for Macedonian burials and accompanying murals were carefully chosen to symbolize central aspects of elite society (Étienne et al. 2000): purple cloth and crowns for royalty, military paraphernalia to represent an ethos of conquest, hunting scenes representing aristocratic manliness and companionship, banquet couches and luxury tableware recalling the central role of large-scale social dining, and bath implements to symbolize Greekness through gymnasium culture.

This elaborate funerary presentation of Macedonian royalty builds on the older Southern Greek tradition of hero cults, where mythical associations were created to suggest semi-divine status for the elite. Moreover, the merging of imported architectural elements derived from South Aegean public buildings, with the regional tumulus-burial tradition, created a novel monument of enhanced prestige: the "Macedonian Tomb." Its façade resembles a Greek temple, behind which a barrel vault roofs one or more chambers containing the burials and gifts of the elite, all enclosed by a traditional Macedonian earth tumulus. Such tombs, the palace-towns at Aegai and Pella, and an iconography of dynastic power, sustain what anthropologists have called the "Theatre State" (Geertz 1980, Spivey 1997), where pomp and pageantry are deployed to reinforce the power of ruling elites. The two-story monumental façade of the Aegai palace, later adopted for Hellenistic stoas in agoras and temple complexes, likewise offered "grandstanding" as well as theatrical backdrops for public events in an age where spectacle might replace substance (Stewart 2006).

from a peripheral "barbarian" kingdom, his son rapidly shifted everyone's perceptions through his remarkable success in carrying Greek arms to the ultimate borders of the vast empire of that traditional enemy, the Persians. During his lifetime he encouraged the act of prostration before himself for formal reception, an Oriental custom, and consciously cultivated divine status through stage-managed visits to foci of mythical and religious associations. Although not demanded of Aegean cities, he ordered his colonial foundations in Asia to establish cults for his worship (Spivey 1997). As befitted a self-created god, Alexander carefully controlled the propagation of his ideal image in sculpture, painting, gems, and coins, selecting the artists who would bring his desired appearance and qualities to the great world he had conquered. The battle-scene where Alexander charges toward a terrified King Darius, copied in a mosaic from Pompeii two centuries later, is probably based on a lost contemporary painting, and if so, already gives the audience a reworked propaganda image of the great hero rather than a taste of realism.

Hellenistic sculptural traditions

Attalos I, king of the small state of Pergamon in Northwest Asia Minor (Color Plate 13.1b), achieved spectacular military victory in 237 BC over invading tribes of Gauls ("Galatians"). His propaganda machine portrayed this as a new episode in the Greeks' defeat of threatening Barbarians, a topos (literary cliché) traceable back to the Sack of Troy by way of the two successful defeats of the invading Persians in the early Classical era. His son and successor Eumenes II achieved further victories over the Gauls, and these dynasts were also able to defeat the Macedonian and Seleucid states. In part to celebrate this ostentatiously, Eumenes commissioned the "Baroque" giant sculptural frieze at the Great Altar in Pergamon, full of symbolism of the mythical roots of the Pergamene state and its superhuman victories. This style, favored by dynasts and other members of the Hellenistic elite, was named from its similarity to a post-Renaissance artistic tradition of exaggerated expressionism. Contorted bodies and gestures, grandiose poses, offer a populist "comic strip" iconography, suitable for emphasizing "the Other," whether Barbarians or the extraordinarily powerful Hellenistic dynasts themselves. "Barbarians" could also however be identified in a contemporary Greek form. In 200 BC, when Philip V of Macedon threatened Athens, Attalos I seized his chance to protect this now minor state on which he was modeling his own. Although his reaction was more diplomacy than armed protection, so that Athens suffered considerable death and destruction before Philip withdrew, the city was duly grateful, with Attalos receiving public honors and a hero cult.

To permanently commemorate this intervention, making its symbolism timeless, Attalos presented a series of sculptures, mounted on a discontinuous plinth over 100 meters long, to be displayed on the Athenian Acropolis (Stewart 2004). The themes were: (1) a battle of Gods and Giants; (2) a battle of Athenians and Amazons; (3) Athenians fighting the Persians; and (4) the Pergamon warriors fighting the Galatians. All four themes represent the forces of (Greek) civilization defeating the (Barbaric) "Other," while the ensemble cleverly evokes the Attalids' claim to be the modern defenders of Greek life and values. Even the tortuous twists of the various enemies' bodies and their manic glances show their "abnormal" non-Greek emotions (Figure 14.3). Their manufacture in bronze with details picked out in metal, glass, and stone inlay increased their high visibility, but their placing, near the Parthenon with closely-related themes on its external sculpted metope-panels, was an unmistaken cross-reference to Athenian Classical propaganda.

Alongside such power-statements of the all-controlling elite at the royal and city level, with exaggeratedly ideal sculptural representations of the Great and the Good borrowed from the Classical tradition of merging gods with men, a quite contrasting style of human representation developed. This is a very different reaction to the violent discontinuity that was

occurring in the way of life of all Greeks, being a turn to realism and the individual. The Hellenistic era brought an end almost everywhere to the democratic world of the Classical polis, relegating the ordinary citizen from any major role in the vital political decisions concerning the state he belonged to, unless he happened to be rich and powerful. This resulted in a refocusing on "the basics": making the most of one's profession, high or low, and taking a closer look at the remaining arenas of social life, the neighbors, the craftsmen or entertainers. A world formerly centered on participation in popular politics and the citizen-to-citizen bonding of army service, has become reoriented toward individualism and the search for wealth and status, where attention turns to smaller-scale networking. Artistic concerns reflect these trends, portraying the unique features of the people, or of a common "type," one encountered within more confined social networks.

Parallel to the godlike transformation style for elites, then, another genre arose, the "warts and all" confrontation with a real person, or a generic character that was set apart from other human types or lifestyles. The democratic orator Demosthenes, portrayed ca. 280 BC, could represent a "people's politician." A boxer was no longer the "Adonis" athlete of the Classical sculptor Praxiteles, but a punch-drunk, broken-nosed bruiser, although inspiring empathy. In another genre, the theater, the same shift is striking: Classical Old Comedy with its political references and Athenian master-playwrights, was replaced by the New Comedy, often composed by writers from diverse cities, in which stock characters of the town played out domestic comedies (Walton and Arnott 2001). Even rulers sometimes deploy this style to suggest to their enemies that they are tough and pragmatic opponents. In a more negative sense, Athens in the final century BC and first century AD experienced considerable popularity for this "verismo" style, since its unflattering and cynical reflection of the world symbolized a city which had been taken over by a new class of *nouveaux riches* businessmen (Stewart 1979). The turn to the individual can also be linked with the rise in popularity of the cults of Dionysus, Asklepios, and Isis, offering their devotees personal health, security, and the good life now and after death (Mikalson 2006).

Figure 14.3   The Baroque: defeated Barbarians from the Attalid dedication on the Parthenon.
Left: National Archaeological Museum of Venice. Right: © 2011. DeAgostini Picture Library/Scala, Florence.

Within the more personal, realist tradition such as the subgenre of "worthy citizen, orator or philosopher" seen in the serious, Classical derivative Demosthenes statue, Stewart (1979), focusing on Hellenistic and Republican Roman-era sculpture in Athens and Delos, observes a sociological sea-change which portraits have undergone since Classical times. Athens till the fourth century honored its rich and powerful office-holders and benefactors with citizenship, tax-breaks or votes of thanks. Now a portrait commission became common. The weakened Aegean poleis had grown increasingly dependent on leading individuals within or outside their citizen-communities. Fifth-century portraits were usually created posthumously, now they represented living heroes, the more elevated of whom received divine honors and formal worship.

As well as flattering patrons who might continue to act for a city, portraits could offer compensation for a feeling of impotence on the "world stage," substituting a "local hero" statement to elevate activities on a lesser scale. As Stewart remarks, this shows how a minor notable, a provincial but prominent person, was "asserting his own individual worth and significance by literally carving himself a niche in history." The individual and polis reconstituted their relations through the central medium of the portrait, where private virtue and public need and advantage coincided.

Traditionally Greek art studies have adopted an evolutionary sequence based on formal styles, essentially focusing from Archaic times onwards on Athens. But already in the Hellenistic era (and regionally earlier), both public and private patrons could select a sculptural style or genre from a wide range to suit varied contexts (Fullerton 2000). Thus earlier scholars could be misled into taking LH-ER sculpture as copies of Classical-early Hellenistic originals. The famous Venus de Milo, for example, now appears to be a pseudo-Classical statue of Aphrodite ca. 150–50 BC, once standing in the gymnasium of Melos, but modified with some baroque stylistic features and betraying its lateness by clearly representing a sensuous female nude (Kousser 2005).

Hellenistic figured vases, funerary art, and society

Radical changes in Hellenistic private life are also reflected in vase scenes and family portrayals on tombstones. From the fourth century onwards, baby goddesses appear more frequently on vase-painting, tied to the increased role of the home, wives, and children (Beaumont 1998). On tombstones, late Classical scenes increasingly show family groups (Leader 1997), whilst some evidence a further symbolic novelty when portraying a husband and wife bidding a forced farewell imposed by death (Stears 1995). Whilst Classical husbands were shown taking physical "possession" over a new bride, through grasping her wrist, now at times an equal handshake appears, or even the roles in reverse with the wife's grip dominant. Family life as an enhanced focus of attention in an era of declining public commitment seems to explain the development of "hero" cults even for non-elite families, centered on small shrines with statues of family ancestors (for example on Thera) (Thompson 2006).

An enhanced female profile of women in the more home-centered Hellenistic world could expand outwards into the polis. If powerful families now held control in Greek cities, in alliance with elite clans ruling the dynastic states above them, then women, being central to such groups, could find new scope for involvement in both affairs of state and urban affairs. As noted earlier, it thus became acceptable for wealthy, powerful women to contribute to polis monuments or infrastructure, thereby receiving civic honors and statue dedications (van Bremen 1996).

Athens, which till now has formed the main focus of study for grave monuments (the corpus of fourth-century decorated graves alone registers 1800), provides an impoverished record for Hellenistic times. However, the puppet-ruler Demetrios of Phaleron (installed in Athens by Cassander) had authorized a decree in 317 BC banning all but simple monuments and brief inscriptions (Stears 2000). This reacted

against a growing trend for ever larger funerary monuments with a theatrical relief style, part of wider tendencies seen in houses and sculpture toward the relaxation of democratic ideals in favor of a greater display of individuality and wealth. Presumably this law would squash any opportunity for local elites to assert undue power in cities within the sphere of Hellenistic kings and generals. Tombstones became limited to a small column or table. Unsurprisingly these restrictions remained under successive external powers till the second century BC. Intriguingly a more hidden aspect of burial ritual alters likewise to a simpler form in Hellenistic times, since finely-painted *lekythoi* were replaced as standard grave goods in Athens by cruder oil-flasks (*unguentaria*). Nonetheless, even where expensive burials were banned, those elites favored by the great kings were still able to exhibit their status publicly through dedicating civic monuments and being awarded statues in public places. This kind of greater visibility was easier to control by the dominant powers.

However the Athenian bias in Greek archaeology has been rectified for the Hellenistic era by well-published excavations in Macedonia. Here a society which throughout Greco-Roman times was very hierarchical gives evidence for rich elite burials from Archaic times onwards, and in particular the Hellenistic era provides an equivalent range of burial wealth and elaboration of tombs to parallel the varied statuses amongst the living (Ginouvès 1994). Beyond the spectacular royal tombs of Aegai, other centers such as Pella (Siganidou and Lilimpaki-Akamati 2003) possess cemeteries which range from simple cist and earth tombs for ordinary citizens, through larger, vaulted chamber tombs for middle-class family use, up to "Macedonian Tombs" for the elite, imitating on a smaller scale the mounded chambers of royalty. The middle- and upper-class burials possess plentiful gifts, including precious metal, as well as wall-paintings and architectural settings.

Insights into personal representation and gender roles can also be gained from changes in grave goods. Till the end of the fifth century BC strigils (metal scrapers for cleansing the body with oil, traditionally linked with males) and mirrors are rare, but in Hellenistic times they increase ten-fold, and now both appear in women's burials. Heightened body-care may reflect the rise of individualism and the participation of women can be linked to new perceptions of women as primarily attractive, desirable persons beyond their earlier chief role as wives or mothers (Naerebout 2001–2002, Rotroff 2006).

Terracottas

Terracotta figures become an important minor art form in late Classical and Early Hellenistic times in Greece, especially known from cemeteries at the Boeotian city of Tanagra (Higgins 1986). Flourishing from the later Classical era till around 200 BC, they contrast with the traditional grand art of Greece in temples and grave-monuments through focusing on everyday life, and recognizable individuals, in highly detailed miniature human or animal figurines. Usurping the dominance of gods and goddesses in Archaic to Classical figurines, the genre includes numerous representations of contemporary ordinary folk. This more personalized and sensitive art once more spotlights the particularities of real persons at a local, neighborhood scale, as the affairs of the polis retreat into the hands of the rich and powerful few. Figurines of divinities do of course continue to be made, and here it is noteworthy that statues of a nude Aphrodite become common, illustrating a more blatant interest in female sexuality in Hellenistic times, if not female power. This suggestion agrees with other figurines of clothed contemporary women who are attractive, but lacking obvious signs of motherhood or housewifery (Rotroff 2006).

Art and Architecture in the Aegean in the Early Roman Period

The presence of Romans and other Italians in Greece became noticeable from the late third century BC onwards, as diplomats, soldiers, and businessmen. Their influence increased inexorably, so that actual annexation was the formalization of a process begun long before. But let us recall Horace's quip cited in Chapter 13, that "captured Greece took its wild conqueror captive," in at least the cultural sense. Like many upwardly-mobile societies rising to prominence through hard-nosed commerce and aggressive militarism, the Romans soon sought some cultural

credentials. Their natural model was Greece, already influential on proto-historic Italian states from the eighth century BC. Taking on the mantle of cultural eminence could be obtained in two ways: the easiest, widely adopted, was carrying off by force or purchase as many Greek works of art as possible, to adorn the townhouses and rural villas of the Italian elite, as well as Italian public buildings and open spaces. The sack of rich ancient towns such as Corinth and Athens provided rich booty, whilst large-scale tomb-robbing increased the haul. A more creative response by culture-hungry Italians was to commission new works of art by Greek artists or in a Greek style. This process revolutionized art and architecture in Italy itself, but there are also many products of this initiative within the Roman Aegean.

The demand for varied decoration in rich houses and prestige buildings belonging to Italians or their Greek protégés in the Aegean further enhanced Hellenistic eclecticism. "Off-the-shelf" styles reflecting different periods or contexts of earlier Greek art could be selected for a particular room or temple façade for aesthetic purposes, style becoming a timeless commodity. On the other hand Italians had new needs for art, retaining sufficient sense of a separate identity to inspire a merger of the fine art traditions of Classical Greece with a self-perceived rugged individuality, proper to traditional Roman elites and *nouveaux riches* alike. Statues of implausibly ideal bodies topped with heads of a no-nonsense soldier or businessman (Figure 14.4) look rather absurd to us, but represented consumer choice by a new society aware of its position in history (Fullerton 2000). Nonetheless these are not quite realistic portrayals of pragmatic merchants, bankers, and generals: their serious, unflattering appearances express generic values which these patrons projected as personalities, just as their ideal bodies are hardly those of the person represented.

The Cycladic island of Delos was a major market for such works, but their Athenian sculptors were also active in Athens itself (Stewart 1979). Athens, with Roman encouragement, made the island its colony in 168 BC. As a free port, it became a magnet for a rising international trade, especially in slaves, attracting a large population of resident Italians. Their taste and purchasing power stimulated a boom in sculpture and other arts, in both eclectic and Classicizing-realist

Figure 14.4 A Roman entrepreneur from Delos, first century BC, in Classicizing physique, a "pseudo-athlete." © Erin Babnik/Alamy.

styles, and they commissioned sculpture and a range of other artworks for their homes and to adorn public monuments gifted to Greek cities and sanctuaries. On Delos private houses of Italians and Athenians could possess portrait-busts or statues of their owners or patrons (Étienne *et al.* 2000).

The new semi-realist style was not confined to Italian patrons but spread wider into Athenian society (Stewart 1979). As noted earlier, from the second century BC, a social revolution occurred in Athens: a *nouveau riche* class, enriched by commerce on Delos, took over Athens' government. Foreigners were

incorporated into the citizen-body, women allowed greater freedoms, and an assertive middle- and even lower-class majority set the lifestyle and attitudes of the city. Replacing a pale imitation of the Classical style, a more open society favored sculptures projecting strong, self-made personalities.

Flourishing workshops produced cultural goods in marble, ivory, bronze, silver, and gold, symbolizing a highly materialistic consumer culture where styles had become disembedded from a particular era (Fullerton 2000). One class of luxury objects worth mentioning here is that of large marble vases and altars, for conspicuous consumption in house interiors, deliberately referencing Greek Classical and Hellenistic art, hence termed "Neo-Attic." The success of this industry may, it now appears, have led to chronological confusions amongst previous generations of Classical art historians (Beard and Henderson 2001).

In the Roman Aegean leading families aimed to dominate the "city of images" through multiple statues and public monuments advertising their achievements and generosity. A spectacular example of dynastic propaganda comes from the city of Messene, where in the second century AD the Saithidai family restore the theater in Roman style with elevated scenery and a great number of statues to their dynasty, so that the audience must have felt it was in a monument to this clan (Luraghi 2008). These honorific statues are often influenced by propaganda images of the emperor and his family, although more private images make free use of stylistic eclecticism to express varied attributes of the sitter. The first Roman emperor, Augustus (reigned 27 BC–14 AD), had favored public images in a rather severe form of Athenian Classical imagery, alongside that of military virtue. In the second century AD several emperors cultivated a more Hellenistic, intellectual appearance, with the styled hair and beards of the "philosopher" persona (Smith 1998). Exceptionally they might also create art in Greece where they inserted their personal mythology into Greek traditions, as with Hadrian's sculptural program in his restoration of the Theater of Dionysos in Athens.

In the Hellenistic era the showplaces for the great kings were primarily the Panhellenic sanctuaries and then certain cities significant for their diplomacy, but with the total domination of Rome every city competed to show enthusiasm for the imperial family and provincial officials. Pride of place was the essential construction of a temple with associated art for the cult of the emperor, in whose honor games and other festivals were organized by local notables wishing to affirm their loyalty to Rome. An inflation of value occurred, where civic power was so closely linked to a town's notables and their contacts in the provincial administration of Rome, that even a modest contribution to a town's finances was rewarded with a public statue (Hojte 2002). However in the early phase of Greece's relations with Rome many cities had weak finances and we find older honorific statues to Hellenistic kings rededicated to influential Roman patrons.

Funerary art

A notable feature of the Hellenistic era is the widespread revival of the display of wealth and status in burials (Athens excepted, as noted earlier). Macedonian tombs were copied elsewhere in Greece, but other forms of grave monumentalization appear, while grave goods vary significantly in value. Whereas in hierarchical societies such as Macedonia these class distinctions had existed since the Iron Age, they became general with the rapid emergence in Hellenistic times of dominant elite families in Aegean towns. Messene favored its leading citizens exceptionally through a series of family tombs inside the town, including within the gymnasium, beginning in the third century BC, as if to provide role models for other citizens to admire and emulate (Fröhlich 2008). In the Early Empire this reached its peak with the Heroon or monumental family tomb to the important local family the Saithidai, placed at one end of the intramural stadium and on the city wall (Luraghi 2008). In Roman times, cemeteries outside settlements usually had clearly defined statuses exhibited in their burials, reflecting the formal hierarchy of Roman society in general. Thus outside the town of Messene stone family mausolea with marble sarcophagi adjoin cist-graves and simple tile-graves for the non-elite classes (Themelis 2003).

Where genuine Roman settlers were brought into Greece, cultural importations are apparent. Burial monuments at Corinth and Patras show Italian styles such as street tombs, and altar or temple graves with urn niches (*columbaria*) (Flämig 2003). Nicopolis mixes alien and Greek burial traditions, as its hybrid population would suggest. In contrast, in remoter, more provincial Greece, local conservative "Classicizing" or Hellenistic traditions persist into the Early Roman era, although concessions are made to Roman dress and hair codes. For example at Palatiano (Macedonia), a leading family erected a "heroon" (ancestor cult shrine) in this hybrid style (Flämig 2003). At Knossos Hellenistic burials respect the location of older graves whilst the layout makes a spatial connection to earlier interments as a sign of continuity. When the city was refounded as a Roman colony, a punishment for resisting Rome, no such reverence was observed. The Italian colonists, emanating from Capua, are buried in a new part of the extramural landscape and show a great interest in robbing earlier burials for simple wealth but also for antiquities, much desired by Roman collectors (Grigoropoulos 2004).

Stylistic references to past days of Greek glory appear in funerary monuments of the flourishing "museum" city of Athens. The enforced disappearance of expensive grave reliefs due to overbearing Hellenistic monarchs and their lackeys, could be relaxed under a Roman rule which positively encouraged wealth creation and display, and significant social mobility. The most spectacular example occupies an eye-catching location on a hilltop opposite the Athenian Acropolis, the tomb of Philopappos, a Greek descendant of Hellenistic rulers, a Roman consul (109 AD) and honorary citizen of Athens. A new production of male and female grave reliefs arises, often reflecting a nostalgia for Athenian Classicism. Although it is tempting to read this as "cultural resistance" to Roman rule, Bergemann (2003) argues that it merely responds to the wider mood of the Early Empire, where Augustus had set the lead of reviving that Classical Athenian art style as appropriate to the peace and stability of the ordered, authoritarian state he inaugurated (Zanker 1988).

Indeed an important form of multiple identity formation occurred in Athens, but was known throughout the Eastern Provinces, still permeated (though much less so for Egypt) by Hellenistic Greek culture (Smith 1998). On the one hand, retrospective artistic references to the great centuries of Classical-Hellenistic Greece reveal a current awareness of Greek-speakers' pride in tradition. On the other, Greeks are perfectly willing to seize the benefits available, by "buying in" to the administrative, economic, and social opportunities which have arisen through incorporation into the Roman world, and other forms of art show this clearly too. Thus in Athens some citizens advertise their "Roman-ness" by commissioning gravestones imitating current styles of honorary portraits of "the great and the good," whilst at the same time occasional graves reject such urban modernity, preferring symbols of Attic rustic life (farmer's dress, vine-trimming tools, ploughs) (Gray 2006). The latter are not actually based on Classical precursors, but form a material complement to contemporary texts which praise "the old ways of life," the survival of a pure Attic dialect in the countryside, and a number of rural hero cults associated with a nostalgia for tradition. But for the bulk of the population, this mix of identities was unproblematic, as the popularity of gladiatorial games in cities such as Thessaloniki attests.

An Annales Perspective

In the long-term perspective (*longue durée*), the absorption of small political units by ever larger ones seems to be a global trend, bringing us today to a world with some 200 states in total. In the context of the ancient world the acquiring of economic and manpower resources through conquest or peaceful absorption increases the power of a state. The Hellenistic kingdoms and Roman empire follow this path. The medium-term dimension of our era allows more differentiation: the cyclical rise and fall of regions does not coincide with the trajectories of the great states just noted, reflecting their own earlier trajectories and contingent interactions with wider events and trends. Finally the short term shows us human lives and lifestyles which were altered for centuries by the victory of the Macedonian kingdom over its opponents within Greece and throughout the Near East. Art and architecture also speak volumes about the shifting mentalities of the age.

A Personal View

The decline of citizen democracy over this era causes sadness, whilst at the same time the relentless rise of "capital" brings recognition that over the LH-ER period many aspects of modern economic activity become visible, together with a vast range of wealth and statuses that also reminds me of the inequalities created by contemporary processes of globalization. Yet out of this transforming period we see ordinary people emerge to express themselves in the plays of the Athenian New Comedy, the Tanagra figurines, and the individualized statues of the great and minor figures of the age.

References

Andronikos, M. (1989). *Vergina. The Royal Tombs*. Athens: Ekdotike Athenon.

Beard, M. and J. Henderson (2001). *Classical Art: From Greece to Rome*. Oxford: Oxford University Press.

Beaumont, L. (1998). "Born old or never young? Femininity, childhood and the goddesses of ancient Greece." In S. Blundell and M. Williamson (eds.), *The Sacred and the Feminine in Ancient Greece*. London: Routledge, 71–95.

Bergemann, J. (2003). "Klassizismus im kaiserzeitlichen Griechenland: Klassische Kunst zwischen Romanisierung, Resistenz und vorbildhaftem Geschmack." In P. Nölke (ed.), *Romanisation und Resistenz*. Mainz: Philipp von Zabern, 560–562.

Étienne, R., C. Müller, and F. Prost (2000). *Archéologie historique de la Grèce antique*. Paris: Ellipses.

Flämig, C. (2003). "Grabarchitektur als Spiegel der historischen Prozesse und der Bevölkerungsstruktur im kaiserzeitlichen Griechenland." In P. Nölke (ed.), *Romanisation und Resistenz*. Mainz: Philipp von Zabern, 563–575.

Fröhlich, P. (2008). "Les tombeaux de la ville de Messène et les grandes familles de la cité à l'époque hellénistique." In C. Grandjean (ed.), *Le Péloponnèse d'Épaminondas à Hadrien*. Paris: De Boccard, 203–227.

Fullerton, M. D. (2000). *Greek Art*. Cambridge: Cambridge University Press.

Geertz, C. (1980). *Negara: The Theatre State in Nineteenth Century Bali*. Princeton: Princeton University Press.

Ginouvès, R. (ed.) (1994). *Macedonia. From Philip II to the Roman Conquest*. Princeton: Princeton University Press.

Gray, C. L. (2006). "The bearded rustic of Roman Attica." In R. M. Rosen and I. Sluiter (eds.), *City, Countryside, and the Spatial Organization of Value in Classical Antiquity*. Leiden: Brill, 349–368.

Grigoropoulos, D. (2004). "Tomb robbing and the transformation of social memory in Roman Knossos." In B. Croxford *et al.* (eds.), *TRAC 2003. Proceedings of the Thirteenth Theoretical Roman Archaeology Conference Leicester 2003*. Oxford: Oxbow Press, 62–77.

Higgins, R. (1986). *Tanagra and the Figurines*. Princeton: Princeton University Press.

Hojte, J. M. (2002). "Cultural interchange? The case of honorary statues in Greece." In E. N. Ostenfeld (ed.), *Greek Romans and Roman Greeks*. Aarhus: Aarhus University Press, 55–63.

Kousser, R. (2005). "Creating the past: The Venus de Milo and the Hellenistic reception of Classical Greece." *American Journal of Archaeology* 109, 227–250.

Leader, R. E. (1997). "In death not divided: Gender, family, and the state on Classical Athenian grave stelae." *American Journal of Archaeology* 101, 683–699.

Luraghi, N. (2008). "Meeting Messenians in Pausanias' Greece." In C. Grandjean (ed.), *Le Péloponnèse d'Épaminondas à Hadrien*. Paris: De Boccard, 191–202.

Mikalson, J. D. (2006). "Greek religion. Continuity and change in the Hellenistic period." In G.R. Bugh (ed.), *The Cambridge Companion to the Hellenistic World*. Cambridge: Cambridge University Press, 208–222.

Naerebout, F. G. (2001–2002). "The Baker dancer and other Hellenistic statuettes of dancers." *Imago Musicae* 18–19, 59–83.

Nevett, L. (2002). "Continuity and change in Greek households under Roman rule." In E. N. Ostenfeld (ed.), *Greek Romans and Roman Greeks*. Aarhus: Aarhus University Press, 81–97.

Raftopoulou, S. (1998). "New finds from Sparta." In W. G. Cavanagh and S.E.C. Walker (eds.), *Sparta in Laconia*. London: British School at Athens Studies 4, 125–140.

Paton, S. (1998). "The Villa Dionysos at Knossos and its predecessors." In W. G. Cavanagh and M. Curtis (eds.), *Post-Minoan Crete*. London: British School at Athens Studies 2, 122–128.

Rotroff, S. I. (2006). "Material culture." In G. R. Bugh (ed.), *The Cambridge Companion to the Hellenistic World*. Cambridge: Cambridge University Press, 136–157.

Siganidou, M. and M. Lilimpaki-Akamati (2003). *Pella. Capital of Macedonia*. Athens: Archaeological Receipts Fund.

Smith, R. R. R. (1998). "Cultural choice and political identity in honorific portrait statues in the Greek East in the second century A.D." *Journal of Roman Studies* 88, 56–93.

Spivey, N. (1997). *Greek Art*. London: Phaidon.

Stears, K. (1995). "Dead women's society. Constructing female gender in Classical Athenian funerary sculpture." In N. Spencer (ed.), *Time, Tradition and Society in Greek Archaeology. Bridging the 'Great Divide'*. London: Routledge, 109–131.

Stears, K. (2000). "Losing the picture: Change and continuity in Athenian grave monuments in the fourth and third centuries BC." In N.K. Rutter and B. A. Sparkes (eds.), *Word and Image in Ancient Greece*. Edinburgh: Edinburgh University Press, 206–227.

Stewart, A. (1979). *Attika. Studies in Athenian Sculpture of the Hellenistic Age*. London: Society for the Promotion of Hellenic Studies.

Stewart, A. (2004). *Attalos, Athens and the Akropolis*. Cambridge: Cambridge University Press.

Stewart, A. (2006). "Hellenistic art. Two dozen innovations." In G. R. Bugh (ed.), *The Cambridge Companion to the Hellenistic World*. Cambridge: Cambridge University Press, 158–185.

Themelis, P. G. (2003). *Ancient Messene*. Athens: Archaeological Receipts Fund.

Thompson, D. J. (2006). "The Hellenistic family." In G. R. Bugh (ed.), *The Cambridge Companion to the Hellenistic World*. Cambridge: Cambridge University Press, 93–112.

Trümper, M. (2005). "Modest housing in Late Hellenistic Delos." In B. A. Ault and L.C. Nevett (eds.), *Ancient Greek Houses and Households*. Philadelphia: University of Pennsylvania Press, 119–139.

van Bremen, H. C. (1996). *The Limits of Participation. Women and Civic Life in the Greek East in the Hellenistic and Roman Periods*. Amsterdam: J. C. Gieben.

Walton, J. M. and P. D. Arnott (2001). *Menander and the Making of Comedy*. Westport: Greenwood Press.

Westgate, R. C. (2000). "Space and decoration in Hellenistic houses." *Annual of the British School at Athens* 95, 391–426.

Zanker, P. (1988). *The Power of Images in the Age of Augustus*. Ann Arbor: University of Michigan Press.

Further Reading

Hurwit, J. M. (1999). *The Athenian Acropolis*. Cambridge: Cambridge University Press.

Tobin, J. (1997). *Herodes Attikos and the City of Athens*. Amsterdam: J. C. Gieben.

15

The Archaeology of Greece from Middle Roman Imperial Times to Late Antiquity

Demography, Settlement Patterns, and Everyday Life

Introduction

As we saw in Chapter 13, the Roman impact in Late Republican and Early Roman imperial Greece was all too often in the form of destruction and stagnation in the cities and countryside. But this generally led into an era of greater prosperity in Middle Roman (MR) imperial times (second to fourth centuries AD), although this period was punctuated by occasional phases of stress (the plague of the second century AD, widespread financial problems and Barbarian raids in the third century).

The final, Late Roman (LR) phase from ca. 400 to the mid-seventh century AD in the Eastern Mediterranean forms a strange conjunction of continuity and discontinuity, demolition and vigorous new building, a vigorous international economy but social decline, and increasing military insecurity. On the other hand, compared to the collapsing Western provinces, the Eastern provinces are entering a boom time (Bintliff and Snodgrass 1988a). The Eastern provinces witness an extraordinary flourishing during this period, with almost unparalleled levels of activity in the countryside and in villages and towns, matched by a staggering outburst of construction in monuments to the new official state religion of Christianity – churches and monasteries, as well as in secular urban and rural villas. As a result of the late third-century

reforms of Diocletian and subsequent emperors, the courts of the emperor, co-emperors, and junior Caesars were displaced away from Rome and, in both Eastern and Western provinces, moved closer either to the threatened frontiers (Milan, Trier, Thessaloniki) or to safer locations (Ravenna, Constantinople). When Constantine the Great elevated the last-named regional center of Byzantium to a "New Rome" (dedicated in 330 AD), as a rival to the "old," he recognized the unequal resources now favoring the Roman East, unintentionally setting in motion a progressive transference of the Empire's heart toward his foundation. Constantine's other remarkable innovation, to tolerate (312 AD) and then encourage Christianity, changed the physical and mental world of the Empire as well as offering a new framework for holding its communities together against the overwhelming military threats stacked against its survival. His instinct was correct: Rome and the Western provinces fell into Barbarian hands in the fifth century and were converted into their kingdoms, but the Eastern provinces survived intact till the mid-seventh century and in parts even till the fifteenth century.

For archaeologists who focus on material culture, Late Antiquity is usually characterized as "Late Roman" because of the major continuities in ceramics and architecture, whereas art historians prefer to begin "Byzantine" civilization and history with this era of ca. 330–ca. 650 AD. We shall adhere to the former tradition in this volume and advise the reader that our "Early Byzantine" is the next, very different period from ca. 650–850 AD, when a new society arises which is the basis for the Greek Middle Ages.

In various regional projects within the Aegean the case is strongly made for an MR–LR landscape of great estates or villas, with dependent workers living within the villa complex or in separate nucleated or dispersed rural sites. The pottery is heavily dominated by so-called transport and storage amphorae, often distinctively combed on the outside, suggestive of commercial production for wide markets. Abadie-Reynal (1989) argues that the collapse of Rome and Italy to waves of Barbarians in the final fourth through late fifth century, the florescence of the Eastern Roman provinces, and the new focus of Constantinople at the head of the Aegean Sea, converted Greece, hitherto a sleepy backwater with low external imports and exports, into the heart of empire. Moreover, the evidence of amphorae and tableware shows that exports from the East, including the Aegean, now flowed to the Western Mediterranean and even to Southwestern Britain (Fulford 1989).

Great Eastern cities such as Constantinople, Antioch, and Alexandria, and the frontier armies, needed vast amounts of food and other material. The explosion of rural sites in Greece and other parts of the Eastern Empire from the 4th century on arose, to a significant extent, as commercial estates to service these needs. The local market town however lost importance and rarely increased in size. Many became village-like and rural, with agoras taken over by industrial workshops, burials, and market stalls, and show little sign of secular investment. Only the Christian church forms a focus of new construction: even shrunken village-towns usually boast new basilica-form churches with recycled architecture built into their walls or altars from abandoned pagan monuments. In fact the central role of Christianity in everyday practical and spiritual life cannot be underestimated. Cormack (1985) emphasizes the key changes by the mid-sixth century as the rise of the "holy man," the development of monastic life, the growth in the power of bishops with their significant role in the management and sustenance of communities, and the rise of religious icons as foci of worship and presumed supernatural power.

Already from the third century and with increasing frequency and ferocity Barbarian tribes were raiding into the Empire from its northern frontiers, while the rising Persian (Sassanid) Empire attacked its eastern provinces. In response most cities construct a small internal fortification-wall during the third to sixth centuries AD well inside older, more extensive urban defenses, hastily made with ancient *spolia* (reused blocks and inscriptions of earlier centuries) (Gregory 1982, 1992). Though towns indeed usually shrink in total area, surface survey and excavation show that many cities included extramural settlements with churches outside these Late Roman fortresses. The walled *kastra* (castles) were often designed primarily to house garrisons of local militia and imperial troops, alongside the imperial administrators, the bishop, and ecclesiastical staff who now ran the towns. Large numbers of the class of rich landowners who used to control the city (*curiales*) had retreated to their rural estates, the great cities of the Empire, or imperial administration to avoid increasingly burdensome civic duties (Haldon 1990). Some have argued that many lesser Greco-Roman cities became villages associated with a fort (Foss 1977, 1996).

The Empire from the third century AD onwards, when the first Barbarian incursions successfully penetrated its borders, also began to redeploy its armies from concentrations along the borders to defense in depth. This encouraged the refortifying of neglected ancient city walls, but also the reconstruction of older landscape defenses within the provinces (Gregory 1992). Examples of the latter include one at the Thermopylae Pass, a key route between Northern and Southern Greece, and the *Hexamilion* wall which blocked access to the Peloponnese at the Corinth Isthmus (Gregory 1993). The mobile professional, full-time army (*comitatenses*), was placed in strategic hinterland points where Barbarian threats were expected, but its increasing weakness in stopping deeply-penetrating enemy incursions into the heart of the Empire led to greater reliance over time on local soldier-farmer militias (*limitanei*), who had a vested vital interest in defending their families and possessions from their bases in the continuous network of *kastra* (Liebeschuetz 2007).

The highpoint of the Late Roman Eastern Empire is marked by the meteoric career of the emperor

Justinian I (reigned 527–565 AD). The sustained economic and demographic expansion of the Roman East lay behind his ambition to reconquer the Western provinces (Color Plate 15.1). His general Belisarius arrived in North Africa in 533, conquered the Vandal kingdom and advanced into Italy in 535. The ruling Ostrogoths were a tougher challenge, and although their capital at Ravenna was taken in 540, imperial forces waged a further 15 years of warfare before mastering the rest of Italy. Meanwhile parts of Spain were regained from the Visigoth kingdom. Success in Italy was however reversed with the arrival of a stronger invader, the Longobards, whose stubborn resistance eventually led to the loss of Italy apart from footholds in the north and center such as Ravenna, and large parts of the south with Sicily, all of which remained largely in imperial control for several centuries to follow.

After ca. 540 AD the Eastern Roman Empire experienced continuing crises which almost exterminated it, although the worst time is the mid-seventh century AD which ushers in the Early Byzantine period (or "Dark Ages"). Exhaustive warfare against the Persian Sassanid Empire permanently weakened both the Eastern Romans and Sassanids, laying them open to an unexpected and devastatingly successful military empire expanding out of Arabia in the early seventh century, that of Islam. It was the Arab conquests that definitively removed North Africa and the Near East, Anatolia excepted, from Eastern Roman control. In the Aegean disasters include bubonic plague, major earthquakes, and invasions: from the late sixth century Slavic tribes penetrated the Balkans and gradually took over the countryside from imperial power, leaving coastlands and major towns as islands of Roman authority. The general prosperity of the early sixth century is thus all but destroyed by its end, when we begin to see a progressive deconstruction of the Greco-Roman way of life in both town and country (Bintliff 1997a, Liebeschuetz 2001). This prepares the way for new forms of society in a transformed, shrunken Eastern Empire, after the seventh century, in the guise of Byzantine civilization.

A final notable general feature of Late Antique society was the high profile of women (Gregory 2006). The weakness of the Empire encouraged attempts to secure succession to the throne through kinship, allowing mothers and sisters as well as wives to intervene, sometimes decisively, in politics. Even more in religion, the still formative Christian Church was an environment favorable to indirect forms of female power. Elite women were prominent in the foundation of churches and monasteries, with an early example being Constantine the Great's mother Helena. More pervasively the rise of the personal worship of *icons* (religious images) in the home is associated particularly with women, whose public role in organizing worship was already denied (Cormack 1985).

The Middle to Late Roman Countryside

Although the Late Hellenistic and Early Roman periods are poorly represented in many intensive Aegean surveys, probably resulting from political and economic instability during those centuries in those regions, Middle Roman times are far more visible; the transformed countryside which now emerges will be expanded in Late Roman times. If we revisit the Aegean-wide picture of the first florescence of town and country in historic times (see Figure 9.5), there are occasional landscapes where this first occurs as late as this era, for example in Eastern Macedonia (Kotsakis 1989, 1990). Even where the first apparent population and urbanism highpoint is pre-Roman, the Late Roman period commonly witnesses revival after stagnation (notably on the Southern Mainland), or a deepening of previous growth (such as on Crete).

For most studied regions however the innumerable small Classical-Early Hellenistic peasant farmsteads have long ago drastically declined, replaced in MR–LR if not earlier (LH–ER), by fewer but larger estate-centers, as well as a continuing number of village foci. Most of the new larger sites classified as "villas" suggest extensive estates. Even if only a minority have certain evidence for wealthy owners (attached bath-houses, architectural ornaments, complex room plans, mosaic and other decoration), this probably implies that managers ran the remaining such establishments for wealthy owners. It is generally agreed that exploitation of the countryside has shifted toward a wealthier class of landowners than in Classical-Hellenistic times. Indeed tax data from the LR Aegean (Jameson *et al.* 1994) indicate that estates are typically three to four times larger than normal for Classical-Hellenistic farms.

Such a reading nonetheless fails to address conditions of labor and tenure, a telling criticism by Garnsey (1979) of early interpretations of the survey evidence for the landscapes of Roman Italy. Where does the workforce for these larger rural sites reside? If on the estate, then we can stay with our initial model: the generally larger estate-centers *are* the signs of a landscape controlled by villa elites. But to judge by ethnographic and historical parallels in the Mediterranean, it is equally likely that a waged labor-force, or a share-cropping tenantry (farmers working others' land for a share of the harvest), cultivated rich people's estates from villages or the nearest town, instead of or alongside villas with resident labor. If we still find smaller rural sites appropriate for cultivation by "lesser folk," and significantly this tends to be in parts of the countryside more remote from the urban centers (such as upland Methana), are these dispersed tenant-farmers, or survivors of the free peasantry of Classical times? For Methana in fact, the investment in commercial processing-equipment suggests tenants.

However, if poorer people worked *their own* land from villages and towns, as was the norm for Archaic to Hellenistic times, it is not always easy to separate their settlement pattern from the tied-labor model. Commuter-farming is mostly physically "invisible" in the countryside (unless it is unusually intensive, producing evidence of manure "carpets" discussed earlier), since the visible farmsteads represent a minority of people active in the landscape, most families not maintaining a rural house as well as their main home. This should caution us from equating the visible MR-LR "villa" landscape with a single form of land use and landownership without additional evidence.

Nonetheless the balance of probability agrees with Alcock (1993), that the decline of small rural sites in favor of rising villa-type sites indicates a shift in relations of landownership toward the wealthy. Although the share of land use remaining in the hands of a lower and lower-middle class of farmers is problematic, as is the status of farmers living in the LR villages and

towns, textual sources indicate increasing levels of dependency (as tenants, laborers) without excluding small-scale peasant subsistence farming (Haldon 2000).

Let us consider case-study archaeological surface surveys on these important issues. On the Kea Survey (Cherry *et al.* 1991) in LR times there is a clear revival in site numbers, and although most sites remain small, a minority in the 1,5–2 ha size are likely to be larger estate-centers. However these latter lack trademark signs of villa life (wall-painting fragments, mosaics, etc.) suggesting that their wealthier landowners are not in residence. It is argued that managers, tenants or wage-laborers were responsible for cultivation at both site-types, on behalf of absentee landowners. The lack of urban revival at the former urban center of Koressia underlines the distinctly limited nature of the LR recovery. For comparison the Argolid Survey (Jameson *et al.* 1994) and the Methana Survey (Mee and Forbes 1997) show vigorous rural recolonization after ER-MR limited activity.

Site numbers for the Argolid Survey:

Date	Definite occupation	Possible occupation
Early Roman	6	20
Middle Roman	4	21
Late Roman	66	33

Site numbers for the Methana Survey:

Date	Definite occupation	Possible occupation
Early Roman	2	18
Middle Roman	3	25
Late Roman	36	22

However, these statistics need critiquing. Most surface pottery of the ER-MR periods cannot be closer dated than "Roman," which covers both their time spans. On Methana 10 sites had enough finds of this broader period to be seen as occupation sites. As just one had only such finds, the others having some ER or MR sherds, the real number of ER or MR definite settlements should be two to three times higher than the 2 or 3 sites listed above. Furthermore on many surveys everyday rather than fine ware ceramics show little change between ER, MR, and LR, and are therefore classified as ER–LR. They are usually left out of calculations, or may be shared out equally across the ER, MR, and LR; the first procedure reduces generic Roman activity levels, the second blurs contrasts across the 600–700 years of such activity.

Moreover recognition of LR ceramics is easier than ER–MR (Pettegrew 2007). Most LR sites have high numbers of distinctive ribbed-amphora sherds, whereas ER–MR presence is usually distinguished by much rarer imported red-gloss tableware or its local imitations. A typical Roman Mediterranean urban pottery assemblage produces 50–85 percent amphorae (Hayes 1997), a generalization referring chiefly to the LR era. LR tableware, notably distinctive imports like African Red Slip Ware or East Mediterranean variants, adds to the visibility of sites from this phase. All these factors may bias against recognizing site use during ER–MR as opposed to LR times, unless the site was large and a sizeable collection was made. Unfortunately most surveys gather small collections of sherds.

Furthermore we often lack detailed spatial distribution at rural sites, in order to query *what kind of activity* is being evidenced by the less abundant finds of ER–MR date. Most surveys estimate the maximum site extent, then use this for *all periods* in which the site sees activity. Usually only a handful of urban or village sites are more carefully gridded, allowing the team to collect dated sherds from different sectors of the occupied surface and thence suggest how the settlement expanded or contracted from period to period. Both the Argolid and Methana surveys suffer from these spatial resolution problems. Individual periods on multi-period sites are almost certainly occupying different surface areas, and unless this is mapped by subsampling the site surface, population estimates based on maximum site area will be seriously unreliable.

Finally, study of assemblages from Classical-Hellenistic sites shows a higher proportion of drinking and eating vessels than for ER–LR sites, regardless of site size. Overall consumption of ceramics may have been higher and hence leaves disproportionately greater sherd numbers on Classical-Hellenistic sites, making ER–MR rural sites appear impoverished. Equally, LR sites appear abundant in surface finds. This is partly attributable to their abundance in storage and transport amphorae, which seem comparatively underrepresented in Classical-Hellenistic and ER–MR rural sites, and being generally large containers tend to break into far more fragments than other pots.

We can now ask ourselves what "possible occupation" finds of ER–MR could mean, why they seem different from Classical-Hellenistic rural sites and why LR rural sites are often distinct in character from both earlier periods. In fact the difficulties just itemized have a positive side, as they seem to be telling us something about changing social and economic conditions in the countryside.

Let us begin with sherd quantities. In regions with an early population takeoff, abundant finds at Classical-Hellenistic rural sites (especially for food consumption), dominated numerically by putative "family farms" of less than a dozen people, and the low presence of transport amphorae, indicate prosperous small farmers without a major orientation to commercial food production, but with a cultural commitment to social dining. Larger sites include wealthier estates and villages, and for the former it is widely accepted that commercial market production was important. In ER–MR times two common scenarios appear: old-occupied regions see decline or stagnation, whilst underdeveloped regions expand rural settlement. Leaving aside the often dominant "villa-type" sites in both, the remaining sites with ER–MR finds fall into two groups: a minority continue to show heavy domestic use and suggest that some small farms survived, whilst a majority have impoverished assemblages (although partly due to recognition problems), suggesting the shrinkage of larger Classical-Hellenistic sites and impermanent use of small sites as sheds or temporary field-houses. The rarity of pots concerned with social dining may indicate a decline in the economic status of those rural workers using ER–MR sites on a permanent or temporary basis.

In LR times the great rise in "definite" sites in both newly colonized and previously depressed regions of the Aegean indicates a surge of activity levels in the

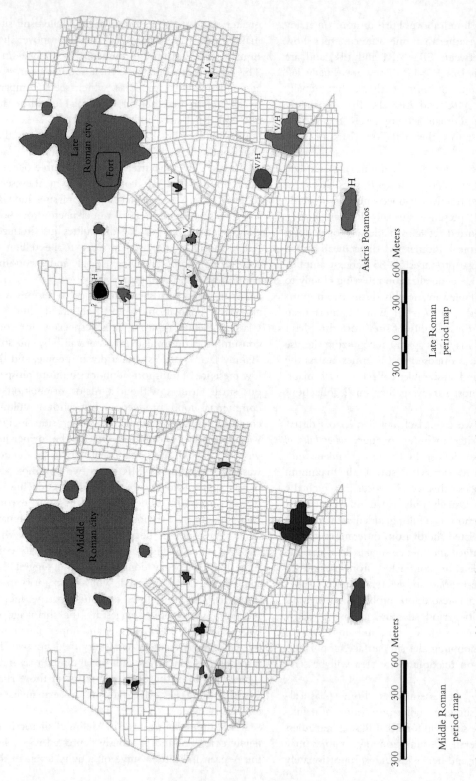

Figure 15.1 Sequence of landscape change in the countryside of Thespiae, Boeotia in MR–LR times. Villas (V) and putative villa-estate hamlets (H) concentrate in the southwest and west districts, with an increase in site area over time. Redrawn from J. L. Bintliff et al., *Testing the Hinterland: The Work of the Boeotia Survey (1989–1991) in the Southern Approaches to the City of Thespiai*. Cambridge 2007, Figures 9.10 and 9.15.

countryside: seemingly permanent occupation rose dramatically, perhaps returning to Classical-Hellenistic levels. The recovery of activity is undeniable but exaggerated because of the high recognizability of LR ceramics, underlined by the observation (cf. Pettegrew 2007) that the ratio of certain to possible sites in surveys rises dramatically from the ER-MR phase. Moreover we have also challenged the view that more and often larger rural sites document a return to a fully-populated countryside (Bintliff *et al.* 2007), at least in Central Greece.

In Boeotia (Figure 15.1), we have argued that these sites are estate-centers for commercial crop production, destined primarily for wider markets, with a limited permanent staff of slaves and farm-managers, whilst their labor force were wage-laborers or tied tenants residing in nearby towns and villages. Wickham (1984) and Haldon (2000) have argued that the larger estates of the wealthy relied especially on slave workforces in the Early Empire, only to replace them with tied tenants in Late Antiquity. The low level of LR villa domestic debris contrasted with high tile and amphora finds, reflects the small resident labor force and the investment in farm storage structures and vessels for collecting and transporting commercial products such as wine, oil, and cereals to regional and interregional markets. Comparable to the "agro-towns" of post-Medieval Southern Italy and Sicily (Blok 1969, Ikeguchi 1999–2000), peasants were grouped into nearby nucleations whose regular spacing facilitated seasonal commuting onto the estates of wealthier landlords, whilst probably those laborers or tenants also possessed small subsistence plots or gardens in the vicinity of their communities. Similar amphora and tile sites appear common in many areas of LR Greece. The clinching and quite independent evidence in Boeotia for this interpretation is the lack of widespread offsite sherd carpets around towns and rural villas, suggesting lower populations and a reduction in the extent and intensity of farming overall.

Nonetheless there are certainly sites on all surveys which produce exceptions to these features, and some whole landscapes differ from these generalizations: on Methana for example as noted earlier, LR activity is focused on a rash of small sites with more balanced domestic assemblages. The Methana team however believe on local and general textual evidence that the LR rural workers were tied labor, but the rugged topography of Methana peninsula made it less efficient to locate estate workers in the single nucleation, Methana city. Instead it is suggested that they were sent out to live in the uplands on small tenant farms, through which large estates were cultivated. The seeming contrast between Boeotia and Methana may be a response to the logistics of farming in very different topographies. The fact that most small to medium Methana farms have presses for oil or wine suggests that it was more efficient for tenants to process their cash crops on the spot than convey them as raw crop to central facilities for the estate as a whole (as well as indicating an economy beyond peasant needs). There are also textual references indicating that Methana lands were passing into the control of external elite groups, an observation also confirmed for the ER-LR Argolid region (Jameson *et al.* 1994). Significantly, the Methana sites already in ER and MR yielded international traded ceramics, revealing that their lowly workers were tied to a more interregional economy. The Atene survey in Southeast Attica (Lohmann 1993) shows a more extreme form of large-estate specialization: after a very full mixed agricultural use in Classical-Hellenistic times, the only evidence for ER-LR land use is a series of pastoral enclosures, interpreted as reflecting the development of commercial sheep and goat herding.

The commercialization of estates is evidenced in a different fashion in the LR era, when over very large areas of Greek coastline on the Mainland and the Islands we find a rash of sites on small and large bays, suitable for coastal loading and unloading of merchandise. In some cases there is associated archaeological material pointing to mineral mining and export (such as on Melos: Bintliff 1977, Renfrew and Wagstaff 1982), but most examples must be staging points for the primary exportable produce of Greece in this era, commercial crops for the new imperial capital at Constantinople and the armies on the Danube frontier. For the latter products we see the development of widespread ceramic production centers for the manufacture of appropriate transport amphorae for oil, wine, and grain, often also by the coast as natural foci for assembling such cargoes. Abadie-Reynal (1989) has used the presence and quantity of traded ceramics to model the possible variation in the strength and direction of ER-LR trade affecting the Aegean. In ER-MR times Greece is a relative backwater in the imperial Mediterranean but in LR times a massive surge in trade washes throughout the region. Greece is not gifted with vast food or mineral surpluses compared to other provinces and was in ER times in many regions suffering demographic and economic crisis. Yet a few regions of the Aegean could already benefit then, such as Crete, firstly because it lay *en route* for strong merchant flows running from the Eastern provinces toward Italy and Rome, and secondly because it had not succumbed to the Hellenistic-ER decline and was in fact entering a florescence unparalleled since Minoan palatial times (Bintliff 1997b).

What changed in Late Antiquity was that the reorientation of the entire Empire to Constantinople, lying just northeast of the head of the Aegean, funneled immense flows of merchant traffic through the Aegean Sea, stimulating subsidiary feeding of regional surpluses into the wider supplying of "The City" as it came to be known, with the progressive loss of the other giant Roman cities between the fifth and seventh centuries AD. To this we can add the archaeological evidence for massive revival of land use in almost every corner of Greece, arguably driven by commercial rather than subsistence production. The needs of the frontier and interior armies must also be met on an increasing scale, with escalating warfare throughout the LR era and the abandonment of productive land along the imperial borders due to insecurity. The LR fort at the Isthmus of Corinth, for example, was probably sustained both by resident soldier-farmers but also from a constellation of contemporary villa-estates in its surroundings (Gregory 1990).

The evidence from the Argolid and Methana surveys can still be read as indicating a severe rural decline during ER-MR times, with dramatic revival of activity in LR times, yet our reanalysis suggests that ER-MR site *use* may be more significant than claimed, and LR site *occupation* less significant. This helps to explain a very frequent observation in Greek surveys: a large number of rural sites are in use in the Classical-Hellenistic era, then see reoccupation in LR. For the intervening periods of LH-ER and MR, either no activity is found or very sparse ceramic finds. Although some locations are obviously favorable for siting an

estate-center, most of these resettlements are not of especially distinctive localities, and we must accept that the landholding and its associated former residence survived in some recognizable form during the intervening centuries. I suspect that many sites with scant recognized ER-MR finds were impoverished farms, temporary land-use bases for large estates, or at least their land plots were perhaps cultivated as units by labor based in villages and towns. When the LR revival of land use arose, these landholdings see higher activity levels for various reasons: some had tenants resettled on them, others were utilized more intensively from residences elsewhere, and all have more recognizable broken pots as the high commercial bias favored tiled storage structures and amphorae. Finally, let us not forget the bias to more datable sherds which elevates the visibility of LR activity. Nonetheless, there surely was a population rise in LR Greece, if considerably less impressive than usually conceived, and in no way comparable to earlier Classical Greek levels.

One Mainland project however directly highlights the role of large landownership. The Berbati Survey area (Wells and Runnels 1996) recovers from virtual abandonment in LH-ER times and shows a characteristic recolonization during MR-LR times. The relevant distribution map combines both MR and LR but essentially almost all sites shown are the product of a revival in MR and a peak of activity in LR. These sites concentrate in the lowest and most fertile lands but the team argue that there may have been just one great estate exploiting the valley by Late Antiquity. At its heart is a villa with mosaics, architectural decoration, and a bath complex. Nearby lie a water cistern and water-mill perhaps for milling grain, whilst numerous finds of olive presses add to a picture of a large-scale commercial estate, whose wealthy owners are probably to be identified with an elaborate hypogeum (underground cut chamber) grave some distance from the villa. A cluster of sites around the villa itself are suggested to constitute worker accommodation, industrial areas, and a cemetery for the labor force (this valley lacks a contemporary town or village as a source of labor).

Much evidence thus comes from rural sites, but is this usually where the countryside is largely being exploited from? Much depends on the level of population in contemporary villages and towns.

We should recall that in Classical-Hellenistic times the real weight of population lay not in the innumerable farms but primarily in the close-spaced cities and their dependent villages. I suspect that this may often have remained the case even in ER-LR times, as we shall shortly investigate.

A question under lively discussion at the present is the effect on rural life of the rising inability of the Empire to protect the Greek provinces from Barbarian raids, whose tempo, range, and depth of devastation in the Balkans as a whole increase from the third through sthe seventh centuries AD (Poulter 2007). Abandonment or destruction dates for open settlements such as villas suggest a parallel rate of emptying of the landscape to match the scale of raids and warfare, especially from the mid-sixth century AD. Textual sources record large-scale enslavement of captured populations who did not make it to the nearest fortified town or village (Liebeschuetz 2007). From the fifth century, invaders such as the Huns could storm cities as well, and with the Slav raids and then invasions of the late sixth through seventh centuries only the largest towns and strips of coast protected by the imperial fleet could be held permanently by the Roman army (Whitby 2007). The North Balkans suffered far more initially through propinquity to the frontiers in the early phase of LR, whilst in Greece villa landscapes usually survive into the time of the more serious and permanent invasions by the Slavs. But throughout the Balkans populations increasingly sought refuge in the fortified towns or clustered inside a new class of fortified village or castle (kastron), sometimes reoccupying hilltop locations last used in pre-Classical times. Whilst hundreds of such sites are recorded in the lands north of Greece, their study is just beginning in the Greek Aegean. Our own survey in Boeotia, Central Greece, has located a fortified LR hilltop-village 2 km east of the ancient and contemporaneously refortified city of Tanagra, at Aghios Constantinos (Figure 15.2a). It is possible that this focus for rural populations eventually became the home for the inhabitants of Tanagra during the "Dark Age" of the seventh century onwards, as the latter had a weak defensive position.

Heather (2007) emphasizes the critical significance of the loss of villa-estates in the final LR landscape: the landed elite had been the mainstay of civic organization and cultural investment and in turn it was the town which held together the Greco-Roman world, so that the necessary disappearance from any

Figure 15.2a The fortified hilltop of Aghios Constantinos represents a class of walled villages typical for the Balkans in the fifth to seventh centuries AD.

district of its landed magnates ultimately caused a vacuum into which a different kind of society would emerge in subsequent centuries.

Towns in the Middle to Late Roman Eras

Textual references to Roman towns in Greece are twofold. Inscriptions inform us of public affairs or family and personal history, whilst official histories by near-contemporaries offer details of general conditions. But such documents become much rarer in MR-LR times. The "epigraphic habit" of erecting inscriptions declines dramatically following Emperor Caracalla's gift of citizenship in 212 AD to all free inhabitants of the Empire, removing the stimulus to advertise one's citizen status (Meyer 1990). Although archival history becomes thinner and the geographies and tourist manuals fade away after the second century AD, the letters, saints' lives, and formal records of the Christian Church form a new, compensatory source for general and local conditions.

For local civilian elites heightened taxes and crises made public service as councilors and other official urban positions increasingly unpopular. To compensate, authority over cities gradually shifted to a pairing of state representatives and (from the fourth century AD) the local bishop and clergy. This caused a widespread decline in the traditional ostentatious erection of urban inscriptions and inscribed secular public monuments by local grandees, together with statues honoring them. There *are* rare examples of honorific statues in LR towns, but these now focus on powerful representatives of the state (Poulter 2007).

The outstanding exception to all this is an extraordinary burst of church-building, consuming most of the funds and motivation for prestigious urban construction. Nonetheless, we should not overestimate the speed of Christianization within the Empire: edicts continue till the end of the seventh century to ban pagan practices (Chrysos 1997) and it seems that a significant degree of tolerance in the fourth and early fifth centuries accounts for the fact that most of the typical basilican churches of the Aegean were built from the mid-fifth century onwards (Oikonomou-Laniado 2003).

Our textual sources allow historians to paint a general picture of MR-LR urban life. During the MR era, most Aegean cities remain dominated by an elite, often one or two powerful families. Increasingly, especially in the LR era, rising taxation and currency instability, taken with escalating costs of urban maintenance (such as the need to rebuild and maintain city walls during the Barbarian incursions), cause many such families to emigrate to the great cities (after the early fourth century, especially Constantinople), or to great estate-centers. However, it is frequently from the ranks of regional wealthy landowning families that the Church recruits its bishops, who often assume the neglected role of the urban managerial elite (*curiales*). It is also argued (Heather 2007) that the former urban elites have turned to serving in the imperial service as officials in the same regions, remaining an important force despite withdrawal from central roles in urban management.

These historical trends do not allow us to estimate the overall state of city life in Greece in the mature to late Empire, but do provide a helpful background to the decline in public secular building (defenses excepted) and a corresponding flourishing of urban church construction. For a more realistic take on the scale of town life we need to turn to surface survey and major urban excavations.

When field survey revealed the dramatic changes in many parts of the Southern Aegean countryside between Classical-Hellenistic and Roman times, indicating a severe decline in rural population and land use, some scholars suggested a flight of peasants into expanding Roman towns, with little change in total demography. As we saw in Chapter 13, this argument was challenged in Central Greece when the Boeotia Project followed up rural survey with the complete survey of three town sites, Thespiae, Haliartos, and Askra (Bintliff and Snodgrass 1988b). Contemporaneous with rural depopulation came abandonment or dramatic shrinkage of all three nucleated sites. Subsequently the same result was demonstrated at the city of Hyettos. Notably, although surrounding rural sites pick up in number and size through MR and chiefly in LR times, these urban sites do not recover their Classical-Hellenistic size (except for the village-town of Askra).

On the Argolid Survey (Jameson *et al.* 1994), the city of Halieis was abandoned during Hellenistic times, and on its ruins, significantly, by LR times a villa with a bath-house was erected, with 26 poor graves probably marking its labor force. Another city, Hermione, survives but in a shrunken size from its Classical Greek peak. On the Methana Survey (Mee and Forbes 1997), two of the three nucleated sites of Classical-Hellenistic times lose that status, whilst the remaining example, the town of Methana, loses two-thirds of its former extent by Roman times. In the Patras region of Achaea, extensive survey and excavation (Petropoulos and Rizakis 1994) evidence population and economic growth in ER times, in both town and country, far beyond Classical-Hellenistic levels when the region was not highly developed. However in LR times not only does the town follow the Greek norm in shrinking in size but rural sites buck the wider trend and decline in number by a half. The island of Kea (Cherry *et al.* 1991) seems to have lost three out of four of its Classical towns by LR times, with only Ioulis retaining its urban character.

Yet an intriguing contrast emerges if we focus on the traditional subject-matter of Classical archaeology: art and architecture. All investigated Late Antique towns in Greece look flourishing if we ignore the widespread evidence for their contraction and focus on monumental buildings. With the arrival of Christianity as the state religion, whilst pagan sanctuaries are converted to churches or more commonly demolished for building material (recycled as *spolia* into city-wall renewals, private houses, and church construction), a great spate of new churches, monasteries, and baptisteries sweeps over every surviving urban center and every village. At Patras, where we just noted urban shrinkage and declining rural site numbers, the LR city has nonetheless well-built baths and Christian basilicas. Corinth boasts in its port at Lechaion one of the largest basilican churches in the Roman world (Rothaus 1995). Yet Corinth shows a decline in its urban fabric progressively over the fifth and sixth centuries, reflected in a shrinkage in its public bath facilities, piecemeal disuse of its agora buildings, and then displacement of the town center, leaving the former agora outside the final fortified settlement, whose size indicates a community perhaps a third of its ER predecessor. The Lechaion basilica was probably paid for by the emperor and major

improvements to its harbor are recorded as the gift of the provincial governor. Decaying civic centers may be left to encroachment by housing and industry, while a church complex can form a new urban focus elsewhere, such as at Cretan Gortyn (Francis and Harrison 2003). In Athens (Figure 15.2b) a new city wall of reduced circuit leaves the Classical Greek Agora outside it, no longer in active civic use, whilst pagan temples and secular public buildings in the remainder of the town are converted into churches (Camp 2001). At Argos around 400 AD (Oikonomou-Laniado 2003), the city center (including the agora, baths, theater, and odeion) loses its role and is taken over by houses and workshops, whilst the focus of life shifts to the east around new church buildings; the mid-sixth to seventh centuries see urban shrinkage and further decline in town life. For Thessaloniki, the agora and its public buildings appear to go out of use from the fourth century onwards, allowing pottery kilns to colonize the civic center in the fifth century: again the contemporary creation of churches in new areas and wealthy mansions indicate drastic urban reorganization (Velenis 1990–1995, Poulter 2007).

For most Aegean towns a combination of surface prospection, planning of surface architecture, and small-scale excavation now offers the best insights for the MR-LR era. Till the 1980s all that was known of the large Greco-Roman city of Thespiae in Boeotia was a largely demolished LR stone and tile fortress of an irregular shape (*kastron*), 12 ha in extent. Total urban survey showed that it lay central to a much greater Classical Greek city, almost 70 ha (see Figure 11.3). Shrinking drastically in LH-ER times, the city saw a modest re-expansion in the LR era (Figure 15.1). In the center of the artificial surface collection grid an irregular circle marks the fort built in the late fourth to early fifth century out of recycled architectural pieces from the earlier city. The surface finds indicate that although activity was most intense within the fort, a large extramural settlement existed to the east of it, whilst to the far east, and to north, south, and west, scatters of LR sherds denote the extensive cemeteries of the town, with dispersed foci of activity (including probably cemeteries) in the intervening formerly built-up areas. Within the eastern extramural settlement three small basilican churches survive as surface ruins, whilst a fourth lies within the Kastro. It may be

Figure 15.2b   The Late Roman wall of Athens.
Author.

suggested that the restricted Kastro served as the residence of a militia, the bishop and his entourage, and the imperial officials now responsible, together with the Church, for urban management. To judge by the remarkable concentration of ceramic wasters (production debris) in the Kastro and hardly anywhere else, and their mostly LR date, we can suppose that this locality, the former civic center of the Classical town was also a significant area for industrial production. The town of Sparta appears to have had a similar *kastro* plus extramural domestic zone (Zavvou 2006).

As well as encouraging urban refortification and village fortification, the state was compelled from the third century onwards to set up military bases within provinces well behind the frontiers, as Barbarians succeeded in penetrating the borders (Gregory 1982, 1992). A well-studied example is the fifth-century AD Hexamilion wall that ran across the Isthmus of Corinth, guarding northern approaches to the Peloponnese and the provincial capital of Corinth (Gregory 1993). A major military

base attached to it has also been subjected to intensive analysis (Kardulias 1992, 2005, Gregory 1993). The land wall and fortress utilized pillaged blocks from the nearby major Classical Greek sanctuary at Isthmia. Surface architectural debris and geophysical tests allowed the American research team to make an internal plan of the major buildings within the fort, which also showed a considerable amount of industrial activity. In the LR period military bases made and repaired much of their own equipment, but it is common, especially in the sixth and early seventh centuries, to see a blurring of the use of urban space in general, where "dirty" productive activities colonize formerly "clean" public spaces such as the major streets and agoras of Roman towns (Potter 1995, Liebeschuetz 2001). Perhaps similar trends are active in Thespiae and the Hexamilion fort, mixing military and domestic life. For the latter, the finds indeed support the idea that the military unit included resident families, and was involved in artifact production, whilst international ceramic imports and mosaic floors all add up to a small town-like community, probably representing a local militia and their households combined perhaps with imperial troops. Kardulias (2005) suggests that the fort is a microcosm for a late antique society where the traditional Greco-Roman cities and their associated cult-complexes, with their civic or ritual architecture and infrastructure, are widely replaced by such *kastra*: small defended communities oriented around defensive militarism and the Christian Church.

The detailed stages of such urban decline or abandonment due to Barbarian invasions and Slavic colonization are still archaeologically unclear, whilst the historic sources are suspected of exaggeration and are often contradictory. There is also evidence for a major blow to urban prosperity already with the Gothic invasions of the late fourth century, such as at Corinth and Argos (Oikonomou-Laniado 2003). Slavic colonization into the imperial Balkans seems to have begun by the later sixth century, and Slavic raids into Greece likewise, but despite earlier claims for urban destructions at this time, scholars today appear to favor a permanent and large-scale loss of imperial control over much of the Mainland countryside to Slav settlers as occurring later, in the seventh century. The so-called "Slav Ware" (see Color Plate 17.1) in its sporadic sixth-century appearances in the Aegean is perhaps a local, hand-made supplement to traditional Roman-style wheel-made wares, although later variants genuinely seem to represent the typical wares of the Slav settlers in Central and Eastern Europe and the Balkans, most notably in the Slavic village which was erected on the ruins of the sanctuary of Olympia. In any case, there seems a general agreement that between the mid-sixth and late seventh centuries nearly all of the numerous towns of the Aegean suffered shrinkage, infrastructural decay, and demographic collapse. Most would not survive as cities: only a minority, with powerful defenses, a sizeable population, and/or on the coast and protected by the imperial fleet, remained in any sense urban into the next, Early Byzantine era.

Death and Burial

Late Roman cemeteries continue class-based traditions of earlier pagan times in the Aegean. The upper elite are buried in marble sarcophagi, lower elite and middle-class groups can possess vaulted chamber tombs, whilst the majority of the population appear in dense clusters of cist-graves or tile-graves, rarer in amphorae or other everyday vessels, or even simple earth graves. In the second to third centuries at Thessaloniki (Kourkoutidou-Nicolaidou 1997), Christian graves, although in pagan extramural cemeteries, are sometimes recognizable through gifts or paintings using Christian symbolism. Conversely, many pagan themes continue to the end of the LR era in the now largely Christian cemeteries, since they could be reinterpreted in new ways, or could represent a pagan desire for a form of earthly paradise in Heaven. However in most parts of Greece the LR era sees a decrease in funerary gifts, in part reflecting the Christian emphasis on a spiritual rather than materialistic after-life, but also probably due to the increasingly impoverished status of the rural and urban lower classes. A polarization in wealth is indicated by the continuance of extravagantly-carved marble sarcophagi for the secular and ecclesiastical elite (a third-century example from Thessaloniki is shown in Figure 15.3). However the disintegration (or perhaps radical restructuring) of the traditional Classical townscape is marked from the sixth century onwards by the colonization of the intramural area by graveyards, as at Argos (Oikonomou-Laniado 2003).

Ceramics, Economics, and Trade

We have seen that commerce picks up to an unprecedented level in MR-LR times, marked by the high proportion of interregional tablewares and the increasing dominance of transport-amphorae in assemblages (Figure 15.4).

The typical red-gloss sigillata tableware of the Early Empire, not very common in the Aegean and often showing an Italian origin, are gradually replaced in the MR period by Eastern Sigillata from Anatolia and other Near Eastern provinces. But in the LR era, North African red-slip variants often dominate (Slane 2003), competing with Western Anatolian Phocaean red-slip (François 1994), both being frequently encountered in Aegean rural and urban assemblages. These trends seem to follow the rise and fall of wider exports from these ceramic-producing regions.

Figure 15.3   Marble sarcophagus from Thessaloniki, third century AD.
Archaeological Museum of Thessaloniki, inv. no. MΘ 1247. © Hellenic Ministry of Culture and Tourism/Archaeological
Receipts Fund.

LR amphora manufactories are widespread in the
Aegean, especially the LR2 form, mainly used for
olive oil, but the region also receives amphorae and
their contents from Western Anatolia (LR3),
Southeastern Anatolia/Syria (LR1), and Palestine
(LR4–6), all primarily containing wine and oil
(Abadie-Reynal 1989). Fulford (1987) has argued
cogently that the long-range flows of tablewares are
largely riding on the back of bulk exports of such
staple (amphora-borne) foods, whilst the latter are
heavily driven by the shifting routes to the great cities
of the Empire and the frontier armies (the "command
economy") (Fulford 1992). The great expansion of
Aegean amphorae in LR fits with the proliferation of
harbor-sites and the dominance of villas in the countryside, all arguing for a central focus of the Aegean
economy on commercial crops, their target markets
being both regional and interregional, especially
north to Constantinople and the Balkan provinces.

We have cast doubt on the benefits of this expansive, commercial LR economy for both population

levels and personal prosperity for all social classes.
In Central Greece at least the hypothesized rich
villa-owning elite and their dependent labor probably
had increasingly divergent incomes and only a modest
growth in demography can be supported since ER
times (Bintliff *et al.* 2007). But more positive evidence
for rising populations and overall wealth-creation
comes from elsewhere in the Roman East, such as
upland Syria (Tate 1997), and this could also apply to
other regions of Greece when wider research is carried out. Perhaps significantly in the Syrian example,
"cooperatives" of peasants rather than landed magnates are the driving force. The immense activity in
the "busy countrysides" (Pettegrew 2007) of the LR
Aegean certainly cannot be imagined without many
hands at work.

The central significance of commercial farming in
Late Antiquity is borne out not merely by the proliferation of villa-estates, commonly on sites out of
occupation since Classical times, but in manuals such
as that of Palladius Rutilius (fourth century) on land

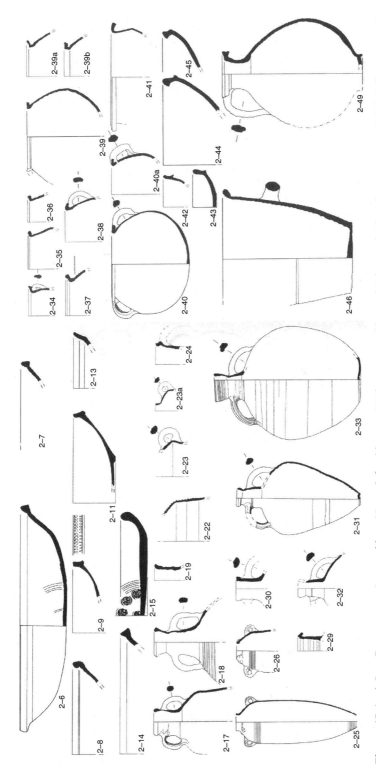

Figure 15.4 A Late Roman ceramic assemblage. Upper left: tablewares. Right upper and lower: kitchen and other domestic wares. Below left: storage and transport amphorae.

Philip Bes after K. W. Slane and G. D. R. Sanders, "Corinth: Late Roman horizons." *Hesperia* 74/2 (2005), 243–297. Reproduced with permission of American School of Classical Studies at Athens.

use and villa construction (Arce 1997). It is debated if the villa focus implies "de-urbanization," but certainly the largest estates show almost town-like, self-sufficient economies with craft production, cemeteries, and elaborate reception rooms for clients and peers, whilst the presence of activity at virtually every small bay in the Aegean may represent significant amounts of the estate-surpluses bypassing towns for wider regional and interregional markets. Yet as we have argued, most Aegean towns may have been homes to agricultural tenants and others servicing the landowning class, so their integration into the villa economy was intense, and indeed their populations must have been sustained largely by the villa-estate economy. The scale of Eastern Empire LR trade can be measured by its products reaching through the Barbarian states of Western Europe and into the chieftain-societies of Dark Age Britain (Lebecq 1997).

The catastrophic loss of provinces which the Empire suffered due to the early seventh-century Islamic conquests, following on the failure to reincorporate the lost Western Roman provinces into permanent parts of the state, needs to be given an economic value. Haldon (2000) estimates that in the mid-seventh century the Empire had merely one-quarter of its income of the mid-sixth century AD, and this enforced a total reorganization of civil and military life. In parallel, we must consider the catastrophic intra-Aegean effects, for the maintenance of cities and standing armies, of the abandonment of its commercial villa economies due to Germanic raids and subsequent conquest of the Mainland interior by Slavic subsistence-farmers (Heather 2007). The subsequent "Dark Ages" till the ninth century, with the temporary loss of most of Mainland Greece from imperial control and the disappearance of most towns, are easier to comprehend in this light. Naturally the large-scale production and distribution of transport ceramics and fine tablewares rapidly drops away, to be replaced by a thinner but continuing circulation of such wares and by more regional or even local products of lower sophistication, including handmade wares, from the second half of the LR era onwards (see the following chapter, and Oikonomou-Laniado 2003, Sodini 2008, Vionis et al. 2009).

References

Abadie-Reynal, C. (1989). "Céramique et commerce dans le bassin égéen du IVe au VIIe siècle." In C. Morrisson and J. Lefort (eds.), *Hommes et richesses dans l'empire byzantin, IVe–VIIe siècle*. Paris: Éditions P. Lethielleux, 143–159.

Alcock, S. E. (1993). *Graecia Capta. The Landscapes of Roman Greece*. Cambridge: Cambridge University Press.

Arce, J. (1997). "Otium and negotium: The great estates, 4th–7th century." In L. Webster and M. Brown (eds.), *The Transformation of the Roman World AD 400–900*. London: British Museum Press, 19–32.

Bintliff, J. L. (1977). *Natural Environment and Human Settlement in Prehistoric Greece*. 2 vols. Oxford: BAR Supplementary Series 28.

Bintliff, J. L. (1997a). "Catastrophe, chaos and complexity: The death, decay and rebirth of towns from antiquity to today." *Journal of European Archaeology* 5, 67–90.

Bintliff, J. L. (1997b). "Regional survey, demography, and the rise of complex societies in the Ancient Aegean: Core–periphery, Neo-Malthusian, and other interpretive models." *Journal of Field Archaeology* 24, 1–38.

Bintliff, J. L. and A. M. Snodgrass (1988a). "The end of the Roman countryside: A view from the east." In R. F. J. Jones et al. (eds.), *First Millennium Papers: Western Europe in the First Millennium AD*. Oxford: BAR Int. Series 401, 175–217.

Bintliff, J. L. and A. M. Snodgrass (1988b). "Mediterranean survey and the city." *Antiquity* 62, 57–71.

Bintliff, J. L. et al. (2007). *Testing the Hinterland: The Work of the Boeotia Survey (1989–1991) in the Southern Approaches to the City of Thespiai*. Cambridge: McDonald Institute.

Blok, A. (1969). "South Italian agro-towns." *Comparative Studies in Society and History* 11, 121–135.

Camp, J. M. (2001). *The Archaeology of Athens*. New Haven: Yale University Press.

Cherry, J. F., J. C. Davis, and E. Mantzourani (1991). *Landscape Archaeology as Long-Term History: Northern Keos in the Cycladic Islands*. Los Angeles: Institute of Archaeology, University of California.

Chrysos, E. (1997). "The empire in east and west." In L. Webster and M. Brown (eds.), *The Transformation of the Roman World AD 400–900*. London: British Museum Press, 9–18.

Cormack, R. (1985). *Writing in Gold: Byzantine Society and its Icons*. London: George Philip.

Foss, C. (1977). "Archaeology and the 'twenty cities of Asia'." *American Journal of Archaeology* 81, 469–486.

Foss, C. (1996). *Cities, Fortresses and Villages in Byzantine Asia Minor*. Aldershot: Variorum Reprints.

Francis, J. and G. M. W. Harrison (2003). "Review article: Gortyn: First City of Roman Crete." *American Journal of Archaeology* 107, 487–492.

François, V. (1994). "De la céramique en contexte à Istanbul." *Journal of Roman Archaeology* 7, 512–519.

Fulford, M. (1987). "Economic interdependence among urban communities of the Roman Mediterranean." *World Archaeology* 19, 58–75.

Fulford, M. G. (1989). "Byzantium and Britain: A Mediterranean perspective on post-Roman Mediterranean imports in western Britain and Ireland." *Medieval Archaeology* 33, 1–6.

Fulford, M. (1992). "Territorial expansion and the Roman Empire." *World Archaeology* 23, 294–305.

Garnsey, P. (1979). "Where did Italian peasants live?" *Proceedings of the Cambridge Philological Society* 205, 1–25.

Gregory, T. (1982). "The fortified cities of Byzantine Greece." *Archaeology* 39, 14–21.

Gregory, T. E. (1990). "Geophysical and surface surveys in the Byzantine fortress at Isthmia." *Hesperia* 59, 467–511.

Gregory, T. E. (1992). "Kastro and diateichisma as responses to Early Byzantine frontier collapse." *Byzantion* 62, 235–253.

Gregory, T. E. (1993). *Isthmia IV: The Hexamilion and the Fortress*. Princeton: American School of Classical Studies.

Gregory, T. E. (2006). *A History of Byzantium*. Oxford: Blackwell.

Haldon, J. F. (1990). *Byzantium in the Seventh Century. The Transformation of a Culture*. Cambridge: Cambridge University Press.

Haldon, J. F. (2000). *Byzantium. A History*. Stroud: Tempus.

Hayes, J. W. (1997). *Handbook of Mediterranean Roman Pottery*. London: British Museum Press.

Heather, P. (2007). "Goths in the Roman Balkans c.350–500." In A. Poulter (ed.), *The Transition to Late Antiquity on the Danube and Beyond*. Oxford: Oxford University Press, 163–190.

Ikeguchi, M. (1999–2000). "A comparative study of settlement patterns and agricultural structures in ancient Italy: A methodology for interpreting field survey evidence." *Kodai. Journal of Ancient History* 10, 1–59.

Jameson, M. H., C. N. Runnels, and T. H. Van Andel (1994). *A Greek Countryside. The Southern Argolid from Prehistory to the Present Day*. Stanford: Stanford University Press.

Kardulias, P. N. (1992). "Estimating population at ancient military sites: The use of historical and contemporary analogy." *American Antiquity* 57, 276–287.

Kardulias, P. N. (2005). *From Classical to Byzantine: Social Evolution in Late Antiquity and the Fortress at Isthmia, Greece*. Oxford: BAR Int. Series 1412.

Kourkoutidou-Nicolaidou, E. (1997). "From the Elysian fields to the Christian paradise." In L. Webster and M. Brown (eds.), *The Transformation of the Roman World AD 400–900*. London: British Museum Press, 128–142.

Lebecq, S. (1997). "Routes of change: Production and distribution in the West (5th–8th century)." In L. Webster and M. Brown (eds.), *The Transformation of the Roman World AD 400–900*. London: British Museum Press, 67–78.

Liebeschuetz, J. H. W. G. (2001). *The Decline and Fall of the Roman City*. Oxford: Oxford University Press.

Liebeschuetz, J. H. W. G. (2007). "The Lower Danube region under pressure: From Valens to Heraclius." In A. Poulter (ed.), *The Transition to Late Antiquity on the Danube and Beyond*. Oxford: Oxford University Press, 101–134.

Lohmann, H. (1993). *Atene. Forschungen zu Siedlungs- und Wirtschaftsstruktur des klassischen Attika*. Köln: Böhlau Verlag.

Mee, C. and H. Forbes (eds.) (1997). *A Rough and Rocky Place. The Landscape and Settlement History of the Methana Peninsula, Greece*. Liverpool: Liverpool University Press.

Meyer, E. A. (1990). "Explaining the epigraphic habit in the Roman Empire: The evidence of epitaphs." *Journal of Roman Studies* 80, 74–96.

Oikonomou-Laniado, A. (2003). *Argos Paléochrétienne. Contribution à l'étude du Péloponnèse byzantin*. Oxford: BAR Int. Series 1173.

Petropoulos, M. and A. D. Rizakis (1994). "Settlement patterns and landscape in the coastal area of Patras." *Journal of Roman Archaeology* 7, 183–207.

Pettegrew, D. K. (2007). "The busy countryside of Late Roman Corinth: Interpreting ceramic data produced by regional archaeological surveys." *Hesperia* 76, 743–784.

Potter, T. W. (1995). *Towns in Late Antiquity: Iol Caesarea and its Context*. Oxford: University of Sheffield/Oxbow.

Poulter, A. (2007). "The transition to Late Antiquity." In A. Poulter (ed.), *The Transition to Late Antiquity on the Danube and Beyond*. Oxford: Oxford University Press, 1–50.

Renfrew, C. and M. Wagstaff (eds.) (1982). *An Island Polity. The Archaeology of Exploitation in Melos*. Cambridge: Cambridge University Press.

Rothaus, R. (1995). "Lechaion, western port of Corinth: A preliminary archaeology and history." *Oxford Journal of Archaeology* 14, 293–306.

Slane, K. W. (2003). "Corinth's Roman pottery. Quantification and meaning." In C. K. Williams and N. Bookidis (eds.), *Corinth, the Centenary 1896–1996*. Athens: American School of Classical Studies, 323–335.

Sodini, J.-P. (2008). "Conclusions." *Mélanges de l'École française de Rome. Médiévale* 120(2), 419–425.

Tate, G. (1997). "Expansion d'une société riche et égalitaire: les paysans de Syrie du Nord du IIe au VIIe siècle."

Comptes-rendus des séances de l'année. Académie des inscriptions et belles-lettres 141(3), 913–941.

Vionis, A. K., J. Poblome, and M. Waelkens (2009). "The hidden material culture of the Dark Ages. Early medieval ceramics at Sagalassos (Turkey): new evidence (ca. AD 650–800)." *Anatolian Studies* 59, 147–165.

Wells, B. and C. Runnels (eds.) (1996). *The Berbati-Limnes Archaeological Survey 1988–1990.* Jonsered: Paul Åström.

Whitby, M. (2007). "The Late Roman army and the defence of the Balkans." In A. Poulter (ed.), *The Transition to Late Antiquity on the Danube and Beyond.* Oxford: Oxford University Press, 135–161.

Wickham, C. (1984). "The other transition: From the ancient world to feudalism." *Past and Present* 103, 3–36.

Zavvou, E. *et al.* (2006). *Sparta. An Archaeological and General Guide.* Sparta: Municipality of Sparta.

16

Symbolic Material Culture, the Built Environment, and Society in Middle to Late Roman Greece

Houses and Society in the Later Roman Aegean

In the Middle to Late Roman Empire (ca. 200–650 AD) there is a clear trend for even greater differences in private-house size and sophistication than we observed for LH-ER times (Scott 1997). Palatial mansions have been excavated in all the major cities of the Aegean, whilst we observe the largest number of extensive estate-centers known at any time for the Greek countryside (except Late Ottoman times, see Chapter 21). However although rural villas with impressive architecture are known in survey and excavation, many, perhaps most, lacking such luxurious facilities, may have been foci for estates whose owners lived in distant centers.

The town houses of the wealthy and powerful often have facilities for receiving their peers, clients or tenants on a large scale, prominent sizeable rooms often with an elevated apse where the elite family could entertain and address dependents. In Thessaloniki, 10 excavated, substantial Late Roman (LR) villas have been linked to the rise of a class of imperial administrators and military officials, who were largely replacing the traditional wealthy local councilor elite (*curiales*) (Grammenos 2003). Constructed in the north and east of the town where building density was light, they provided seclusion from the bustle of the downtown and harbor zones

and a more favorable climate. All were based around a large reception room (*triclinium*) possessing the usual elevated niche at one side. The pragmatic attitudes of suburban villa-owners are clear from the juxtaposition in the same complexes of luxury fittings (wall-paintings, stucco, mosaics, marble revetments), with cottage industry and storerooms.

In Athens, several large villas have been identified around the Acropolis and neighboring Areopagus hill. Some may reflect a special source of wealth in the Roman-era city, in modern terminology "private colleges" (Camp 2001). Athens' educational reputation was already attracting young members of the Roman elite in late Republican times, and this was only enhanced by the greater catchment which opened up through incorporation into the expanding Roman Empire. One mansion could as well belong to a successful philosophy professor as to a wealthy landowner or imperial official, and, like others in this quarter of fourth- to sixth-century AD Athens, it had private baths, marble peristyle courtyards, sculpture collections, and rich wall décor. At Sparta mansions outside the restricted LR "kastro" walls have gardens, private baths, and elaborate decoration for the *triclinium*, where mosaics with figure patterns were set to delight the reclining diners around them (Raftopoulou 1998). At Argos luxurious homes are notable from the fourth century onwards, some with their own bath complexes (Oikonomou-Laniado 2003): as elsewhere

The Complete Archaeology of Greece: From Hunter-Gatherers to the 20th Century AD, First Edition. John Bintliff.
© 2012 John Bintliff. Published 2012 by Blackwell Publishing Ltd.

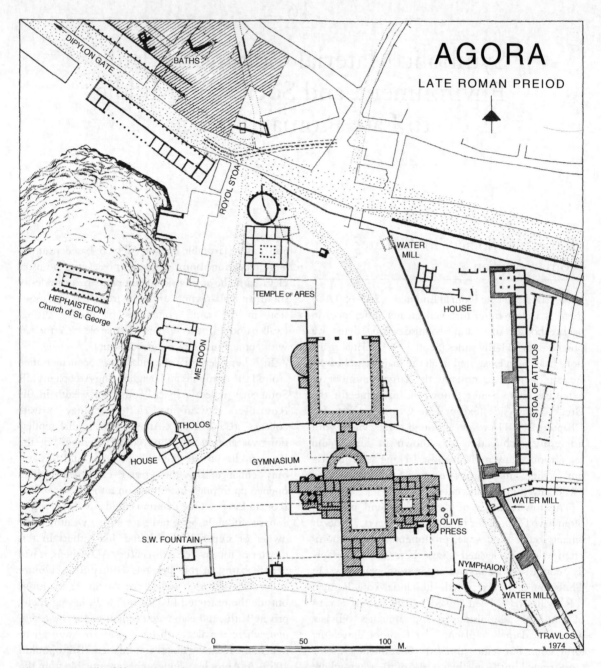

Figure 16.1   The fifth-century palace in the Old Agora, Athens, lying outside the new city wall on its right. J. M. Camp, *The Archaeology of Athens*. New Haven 2001, Figure 224.

in Greece, mosaic scenes emphasize elite pastimes such as hunting, the seasons, and appropriately Dionysos and his entourage with their associations of feasting and leisure. Since wealthy individuals were commonly donors of churches, their taste could intrude into Christian basilica floors, and similar scenes are often found there.

It has been suggested that the weakening of civic culture led to even greater dependence on patron–client relationships in Late Antiquity, stimulating larger spaces in elite mansions for the entertaining of followers (Scott 1997). With parallels in the private Triconch palace at Butrint (Albania) and Diocletian's retirement palace at Split (Croatia), a massive palace was constructed in the fifth century amidst the ruins of the Athenian Old Agora, now left outside the fortifications (Figure 16.1), although it is unclear if it was for a very wealthy private individual or an imperial official (Camp 2001).

Symbolic Culture

The decline of civic culture outside the contrastingly booming life centered on urban churches is marked by the rarity of new secular public buildings, public inscriptions, and honorific statues to local councilors. Those statues which *are* erected are often to the new power-foci, the governors and other imperial officials, who with the bishop were largely responsible for regional management in the Late Empire. Statues in Athens to the prefect Herculius can be matched by crude statues of generals from Corinth, one being identified interestingly as of Germanic origin. Vanderpool (2003) notes that LR statues from both towns use recycled marble from older works.

In palaces, town houses, suburban villas, and the larger rural villas, Roman naturalistic art flourished amongst the prosperous upper-class communities of the Middle to Later Roman Empire in Greece. This same style was adopted by the first Christian communities in their necessarily private religious art in house-churches and foci of worship in communal underground cemeteries (*catacombs*). But with the edict of tolerance in 312 AD and the subsequent adoption of Christianity as the state religion, followed gradually by the banning of pagan worship and the closure of temples, radical changes affected the architecture and art of the LR Aegean.

Temple complexes dedicated to the Olympian gods and Oriental cults were systematically demolished or converted to Christian use, hence the survival of Classical temples such as the "Theseion" in the Athens Agora (Figures 16.1-2) and the Parthenon itself. All LR cities exhibit "spolia," recycled architectural material from redundant shrines or pagan burial-monuments, placed in the new Christian churches, private houses, and notably in the great rebuilding of town defenses spurred on by the Barbarian invasions from the third century onwards. Nonetheless the late foundation dates of most Aegean churches and repeated imperial legislation indicate that paganism was mostly tolerated until the age of Justinian, so that temple destruction or conversion often occurs in practice in the fifth or even sixth and seventh centuries.

At the same time there was a dramatic need to create new, capacious places of worship now Christianity could be practiced in public and was attracting growing congregations. Its establishment as the state religion brought an unparalleled demand for large churches, as attendance was now associated with the institutional structure of the city (Color Plates 16.1a–b).

Greco-Roman temples housed cult statues and a treasury for dedications; formal worship was focused outside around altars and on temple steps. Christian worship however developed from Jewish traditions of communal worship inside a roofed space, requiring architects from Constantine the Great's time onwards to elaborate an appropriate large-scale hall. Actually there already existed an ideal form in the public urban *basilica*, a rectangular building which could have galleries and naves, developed in the Roman world as a space for judicial proceedings and other public assemblies. Basilicas often possessed an apse for the presiding magistrate or official of the state to be seated in a dominating location. In the canonical new Christian temple, however, the axis of attention in the basilica moved from the entrance and apse facing each other in the center of each long side, to their placement at the opposing short ends. The altar and seats for the clergy and bishop (replacing the pagan judge and administrators), were located in the apse, often on a raised platform, with the congregation facing them in a clearly subordinate position (Runciman 1975).

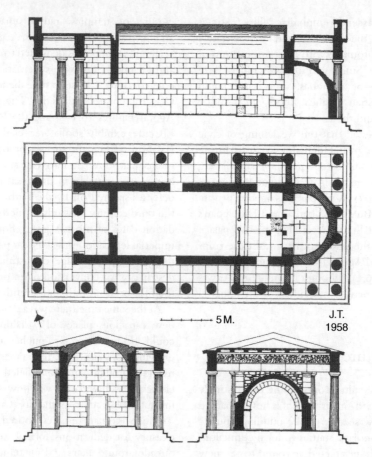

Figure 16.2   The "Theseion" (Hephaisteion) converted to a church, Athens.
J. M. Camp, *The Archaeology of Athens*. New Haven 2001, Figure 231.

The basilican hall would remain the characteristic church design for some 500 years (for a map of significant LR Greek examples see Sodini 1975).

The longitudinal organization of the basilica reflected the importance of movement in the physical performance of worship (Mathews 1998), with four processions: when the clergy made their entry, when Bible readings were given, when bread and wine were presented, and finally when communion was shared. Wall decorations accompanied these movements with dynamic narratives lining the nave, focusing attention on a stillness at the apse where the ceremonies culminated and whose art symbolized the communion act.

In Late Antique towns the clergy were given increasingly wider functions in the running of public affairs, so that ecclesiastical complexes formed one of the main foci for urban life. Since LR towns often witnessed radical shifts in zones of occupation, this new religious focus often lay in a different sector than the traditional Greco-Roman forum (Bintliff 1997). The importance of local martyrs also encouraged major churches at the edge of town, where their executions had occurred.

In the sixth century the emperor Justinian recovered large swathes of the former Western Empire, whilst encouraging monumental church-building as a symbol of Eastern Roman power. The most famous survivors of his program of new buildings or renovated structures are great churches at the port-town of Ravenna in Northeastern Italy and in Constantinople, but in Greece there are innumerable contemporary examples. Although these large churches were ubiquitous, only a minority survive as standing monuments, since many rural examples and those in smaller towns were not to outlast the abandonment or shrinkage of their settlements in the "Dark Ages" of the seventh to eighth centuries AD. Yet it is possible to rediscover even major churches which are invisible on the surface, as an example from the abandoned city of Tanagra (Boeotia) demonstrates. Here geophysical survey has revealed monuments such as two large Early Christian basilican churches, while subsequent targeted surface architecture collection ("ground-truthing") has documented innumerable decorative elements from distinct parts of their plans (Bintliff and Slapsak 2007; for a parallel from Philippi see Provost and Boyd 2002).

A rarer MR-LR building type was a round, domed construction (*rotunda*), also of pagan origin. This had earlier served as a monumental tomb design or an imperial showpiece temple. The gigantic palatial complex of the emperor Galerius at Thessaloniki included a colossal circular domed temple-mausoleum, ca. 300 AD. The Rotunda was converted into a Christian monument, probably by the late fourth-century emperor Theodosius the Great, after which it was decorated with one of the earliest surviving large-scale Christian mosaic programs (Color Plate 16.2) (Nasrallah 2005). This domed and centralized plan, usually adopted in LR times for Christian mausolea (especially martyria) or baptisteries, was the seed of a far greater development within Byzantine church architecture. This is also anticipated in the greatest achievement of LR ecclesiastical construction at the "New Rome" of Constantinople, Justinian's stupendous Aghia Sophia church (532–537 AD), the cathedral of the Eastern Empire (Mainstone 1988). Looking both backwards and into the future, it combines a giant basilica adorned with naves and galleries with a vast 30 meter-wide dome soaring 55 meters over its heart.

Late Antique churches were decorated primarily with striking, abstract surface ornament: intricate hollow-carved pillar-capitals, columns and screens of marble and other bright stones, veneers of colored stone on the walls (cleverly covering the underlying rubble, spolia, brick, and concrete construction). Often the upper walls and ceiling glittered with polychrome mosaics. Frescoes had been overtaken in popularity by mosaics, an art of display which suited the more dramatic forms of symbolic culture characteristic of Late Antiquity. Here Eastern Roman and later Byzantine artists became specialists in atmospheric light effects. Firstly, windows were few and often filled with alabaster sheets which diffused the light, then additional illumination from candles and lamps formed glowing pools which chained from one wall or icon to another. Mosaicists were also skilled in varying the angle of each cube to enhance the indistinct flickering of the flames illuminating them. The impression aimed for was to get the church and its decoration to shimmer with movement and the eye to be taken round the building and its images (Runciman 1975; cf. also Mathews 1998). The rising demand for church art stimulated regional mosaic and marble sculpture workshops to develop throughout the Aegean, although high-profile commissions such as the giant basilica at Corinth's port of Lechaion (perhaps an imperial donation), used imported marble, ready-prepared pieces, and skilled workers alongside local artisans (Sodini 1970, 1977). Already in Constantine the Great's first churches in the early fourth century, figurative Christian art could appear, raising even in this early period a debate on the risk of "idolatry" which would resurface more dramatically in the Byzantine era (Gregory 2006).

Public Non-ecclesiastical Architecture

During Middle Roman times the provinces became increasingly significant as "players" in the Empire, with emperors often rising from them and their fates gradually diverging from that of Rome and Italy (Elsner 1998). The East had always been apart with its alternative Hellenic identity, together with lesser regional identities such as Egyptian and Aramaic. The dominance of the Roman East begins in Middle Roman times and peaks in Late Roman, indeed after Rome has fallen to "the Barbarians," and after its replacement capital of Constantinople had begun its extraordinary development. Intimations of this future centrality of the Eastern, "Greek" provinces, anticipating Byzantine civilization, are visible in the special place of Aegean Thessaloniki in the late third to early fourth centuries AD (Kourkoutidou-Nicolaidou and Tourta 1997, Grammenos 2003, Nasrallah 2005).

When the emperor Diocletian (284–305 AD) reorganized the sprawling, struggling Empire into more manageable quarters (the Tetrarchy), appointing a second emperor (*Augustus*) to himself and under both a junior (*Caesar*), a successful general Galerius, born near Sofia (Bulgaria) as an uneducated peasant, became first a Caesar and later Augustus (293–311 AD). He chose as his seat the city of Thessaloniki, constructing a 15 ha palace-complex near the eastern fortification walls close to the harbor. His giant palace, a sequence of courts, included a sealed passage to the imperial box in a new hippodrome. A large basilica was constructed for state embassies and council meetings, whilst a giant arch commemorated Galerius' victories over Rome's chief enemy in the East, the Parthians. Finally he erected the great domed temple (*Rotunda*), probably in honor of the gods of the four rulers of the Roman world, the Tetrarchs, and planned to become his own mausoleum (though he was actually buried elsewhere). The palace-complex and associated art represent a mini-Rome in the East, a precedent followed by Constantine the Great, a mere decade or so later, when he took the momentous step of founding a "New Rome" in an Eastern city. Indeed Thessaloniki was considered a possibility for this ultimate accolade, before Byzantium-Constantinople received final approval.

"Style" in Late Antiquity

In the MR era, public art had continued its careful manipulation of the Hellenistic "reality" forms, as well as the serious, remote idealism inherited from Classical Greece, producing alternatively naturalistic or idealized images of the ruling class. Subsequently, during the Late Roman fifth and sixth centuries, "official" art underwent a style transformation (*Stilwende*) (Elsner 1998). Late Roman public representations often take the appearance of modern "comic books." The elite are portrayed on a larger scale than lesser citizens, striking exaggerated poses of power. Moreover after Constantine the Great's reign, the dominance of Christianity in the Empire necessarily elevated the emperor to a pivotal position in the Christian model of the universe. As early as Eusebius' (ca. 264–340)

Figure 16.3 Image of the victorious Christian emperor Justinian. Byzantine, early sixth century AD ivory diptych relief, made in Constantinople.
The Art Archive/Musée du Louvre, Paris/Gianni Dagli Orti.

Ecclesiastical History, world history ends with the ideal Christian ruler Constantine. Although in practice successor emperors were intended to be selected by their predecessor in advance, with the agreement of the influential army and the Senate, by the age of Justinian (emperor 527–565 AD), he was considered to have a "special relationship" with God and be His appointee. This is fundamental to his formal portraits and was reinforced by the custom of formal prostration and silence practiced by those entering his presence. The image of Justinian in Figure 16.3 combines Christian imagery (the blessing offered above the warrior emperor by Jesus, not shown on this close-up view) with the pagan winged goddess of victory (Nike) on his right side.

The third-century crisis of the Empire and the sustained pressures that did not disappear in the entire LR period are considered to be a potent force in the creation of these new, expressionist tendencies in the art of that era (Gregory 2006). For similar reasons, after Diocletian, emperors became more secluded from the public and cultivated a mystique of remote, awe-inspiring power through elaborate court ceremonial and dress codes.

Icons

Images of Christian saints and divinities are central to Greek Orthodox symbolic culture, and were well established in the Byzantine world (the direct descendant of the LR Eastern Empire) by the ninth century AD. They form a material "portal" where supernatural power communicates with the world of mortals, and still today attract fervent belief in their healing and protective powers. Technically, experts restrict the term "icon" to sacred representations painted on wood, and these have the particular potential to be opened and shut with door-panels, conveyed from church to church or around a town and also borne into battle (Cormack 1985). But from Late Antiquity onwards such images were closely related to similar pictures in mosaic or paint affixed to church walls and ceilings (Color Plate 16.2). As these icons played a key role in the identity of what became Byzantine society in Greece, and indeed provide spiritual continuity with Modern Greek culture and the far wider Eastern Orthodox religious communities, we shall discuss the origins of this phenomenon.

There are pagan examples within the Roman Empire of the private ownership of small images of divinities painted on wood. They already diverge from the remote Classicizing statues found in public temples through their frontal stare at the worshipper, commanding attention and signifying a personal eye-contact with the supernatural protector. Painted haloes or fires may enhance the imagined power of the sacred beings (Elsner 1998), whilst lids protect the images and shield their fearful gaze from casual view. Possibly these little-known household icons were set within a framework of candles, incense-burners, and cushions for the worshipper. Christians appear to have borrowed these customs for early representations of saints, and indeed the world of the home remained the special sanctuary for icons whereas their popularity

in churches fluctuated. This created an opportunity, seized by women, to reset the balance of public worship, where they were marginalized physically and as participants.

In creating images of their new divinities Christian artists had little or nothing to rely on for authenticity and increasingly adopted appropriate iconography from pagan sacred art to create powerful effects. Thus in our earliest images Jesus is a young beardless man with short curly hair, but gradually another type grew in popularity to become today's standard representation, a bearded man with long, parted hair. The fifth-century bishop Gennadius was in no doubt about the source of the second form when he healed the withered hand of "a painter who dared to paint the Savior in the likeness of Zeus" (as recorded by the sixth-century Church historian Theodore the Reader).

Icons increasingly invaded the space of the community church. In the sixth century, figurative images were especially common in the focal apse and on the low screen or *templon* which, placed between apse and nave, separated clergy from congregation. Moreover as this display area grew in symbolic prominence, more prestigious materials were employed there, marble and mosaic. In so doing, the Church emphasized its power over the people through spatial barriers marked by potent images. By the seventh century prominent icons were borne in public to counter Barbarian attacks on Eastern Roman towns, and were attributed miraculous healing-powers.

One little-preserved locale for Christian art was the decorated tombstone or family vault. Thessaloniki possesses one of the finest collection of such wall-paintings in the Aegean region (Kourkoutidou-Nicolaidou 1997) from the third to sixth centuries. They develop from traditional pagan themes, imitations of luxury homes with marble veneer walls and scenes of the "good life" expected hereafter, to Christian spiritual symbols such as the lamb, deer, and lion, or biblical characters taken from the Old and New Testament.

Even rarer are the splendid luxury silver and gold chalices and plates used in church liturgy, similar to those present at the dining-tables of the non-ecclesiastical elite. Greek representatives were mostly lost in the wars and destructions which the Aegean suffered in Medieval and post-Medieval times, but similar objects from the Late Roman world appear in rare buried hoards of treasure, in cathedral treasuries in Western Europe, or as gifts, trade items or simple plunder in the graves of Barbarian chiefs (such as the royal grave at early seventh-century Sutton Hoo in England, Lebecq 1997).

An Annales Perspective

Both historical and archaeological eras seem often to enclose cycles of growth and decline of cultures and institutions over the middle term of several hundred years. The LR era is no exception and it is clear that scholars have found the third-century crisis and the subsequent reshaping of the Empire by Diocletian and Constantine to have inaugurated new structures of empire, a distinctive phase which then loses its coherence during the sixth to early seventh centuries, calling forth yet another remaking of empire during the following "Dark Ages." The challenge and response met by the Roman polity allowed the emergence of a major cultural achievement in Late Antiquity. Out of the *subsequent* crisis the Eastern Empire would be reborn as Byzantine civilization. Over the short term the endless saga of good/bad emperors, or victories and defeats over foreign enemies, is reminiscent of the Early Empire, although the Late Empire increasingly runs out of resources to sustain the former's geographical and political scale. Unique circumstances, notably the elevation of Constantinople to rival Rome, and Constantine's promotion of Christianity, are probably unpredictable "events" with the kind of long-term impact not far off the legendary butterfly-wings in Tokyo causing a tornado in Florida familiar from Chaos Theory (Lewin 1993, Bintliff 1997).

A Personal View

Late Antiquity, especially the often forgotten "after-life" of the Eastern Empire following the Fall of Rome, has till recently been neglected by archaeologists and many historians, more interested in the supposedly linear evolution of modern European states from the Barbarian kingdoms that replaced the Western Empire. Now, if anything, more publications appear for Late Roman than for Early, but welcome all the same, because it is an extraordinary age of dramatic contrasts: between devastating wars and the slow death of cities, and the giant Christian basilicas with their emotive mosaics and the sprawling town-like estates of the powerful landowners. No wonder that a major style of this period's art is an almost "comic strip" of "superheroes," emperors, generals, saints, or Christ himself. The worse things got, the more loudly the secular and religious leaders needed to shout to prevent their world collapsing completely under both internal and external threats to its very survival.

References

Bintliff, J. L. (1997). "Catastrophe, chaos and complexity: The death, decay and rebirth of towns from antiquity to today." *Journal of European Archaeology* 5, 67–90.

Bintliff, J. L. and B. Slapsak (2007). "Tanagra: la ville et la campagne environnante à la lumière des nouvelles méthodes de prospection, par les universités de Leyde et de Ljubljana." In V. Jeammet (ed.), *Tanagras. De l'objet de collection à l'objet archéologique*. Paris: Musée du Louvre Éditions, 101–115.

Camp, J. M. (2001). *The Archaeology of Athens*. New Haven: Yale University Press.

Cormack, R. (1985). *Writing in Gold: Byzantine Society and Its Icons*. London: George Philip.

Elsner, J. (1998). *Imperial Rome and Christian Triumph*. Oxford: Oxford University Press.

Grammenos, D. V. (ed.) (2003). *Roman Thessaloniki*. Thessaloniki: Archaeological Museum Publications.

Gregory, T. E. (2006). *A History of Byzantium*. Oxford: Blackwell.

Kourkoutidou-Nicolaidou, E. (1997). "From the Elysian fields to the Christian paradise." In L. Webster and M. Brown (eds.), *The Transformation of the Roman World AD 400–900*. London: British Museum Press, 128–142.

Kourkoutidou-Nicolaidou, E. and A. Tourta (1997). *Wandering in Byzantine Thessaloniki*. Athens: Kapon Editions.

Lebecq, S. (1997). "Routes of change: Production and distribution in the West (5th–8th century)." In L. Webster and M. Brown (eds.), *The Transformation of the Roman World AD 400–900*. London: British Museum Press, 67–78.

Lewin, R. (1993). *Complexity. Life at the Edge of Chaos*. London: J. M. Dent.

Mainstone, R. (1988). *Haghia Sophia: Architecture, Structure and Liturgy of Justinian's Great Church*. London: Thames & Hudson.

Mathews, T. F. (1998). *The Art of Byzantium*. London: Weidenfeld & Nicolson.

Nasrallah, L. S. (2005). "Empire and apocalypse in Thessaloniki: Interpreting the Early Christian Rotunda." *Journal of Early Christian Studies* 13, 465–508.

Oikonomou-Laniado, A. (2003). *Argos Paléochrétienne. Contribution à l'étude du Péloponnèse byzantin*. Oxford: BAR Int. Series 1173.

Provost, S. and M. Boyd (2002). "Application de la prospection géophysique à la topographie urbaine. II. Philippes, les quartiers Ouest." *Bulletin de Correspondance Hellénique* 126, 431–488.

Raftopoulou, S. (1998). "New finds from Sparta." In W. G. Cavanagh and S. E. C. Walker (eds.), *Sparta in Laconia*. London: British School at Athens Studies 4, 125–140.

Runciman, S. (1975). *Byzantine Style and Civilization*. London: Penguin Books.

Scott, S. (1997). "The power of images in the late Roman house." In A. Wallace-Hadrill and R. Laurence (eds.), *Domestic Space in the Roman World: Pompeii and Beyond*. Portsmouth, RI: Journal of Roman Archaeology Supplementary Series 22, 53–67.

Sodini, J.-P. (1970). "Mosaiques paléochrétiennes de Grèce." *Bulletin de Correspondance Hellénique* 94, 699–753.

Sodini, J.-P. (1975). "Notes sur deux variantes régionales dans les basiliques de Grèce et des Balkans." *Bulletin de Correspondance Hellénique* 99, 581–588.

Sodini, J.-P. (1977). "Remarques sur la sculpture architecturale d'Attique, de Béotie et du Péloponnèse à l'époque paléochrétienne." *Bulletin de Correspondance Hellénique* 101, 423–450.

Vanderpool, C. de G. (2003). "Roman portraiture. The many faces of Corinth." In C. K. Williams and N. Bookidis (eds.), *Corinth, the Centenary: 1896–1996*. Princeton: American School of Classical Studies at Athens, 369–384.

Part III

The Archaeology of Medieval and post-Medieval Greece in its Historical Context

17

The Archaeology of Byzantine Greece
Demography, Settlement Patterns, and Everyday Life

Introduction

Timothy Gregory's entry on Byzantine Archaeology in *The Oxford Dictionary of Byzantium* (Kazhdan 1991) began by commenting that this field hardly existed, reinforcing similar comments by Rautman (1990). Crow's latest review (2010) continues the criticism of the slow development of an independent archaeological approach to Byzantine civilization, although in contrast Athanassopoulos's review (2008) suggests that Greek Medieval Archaeology has finally "come of age." The splendid Thessaloniki exhibition of Byzantine everyday life certainly succeeds in embedding museum objects into the wider society that produced and used them (Papanikola-Bakirtzi 2002). Nevertheless whilst the churches and art of the independent Byzantine empire from the later seventh to early thirteenth centuries, and of the divided empire of the subsequent era to 1453 AD (when much of the Aegean had been conquered by Crusaders or "Franks"), have been thoroughly studied for many generations, archaeology as the total integrated examination of society has barely begun, by the standards of West European Medieval Archaeology. We refer to the survey and excavation of farms, villages, cemeteries, town quarters, isolated defenses and castles, industrial zones, harbors, monasteries, etc.

Yet a more holistic approach to Byzantine material culture began already a century ago, when large-scale American excavations uncovering major Classical monuments in the ancient Agora at Athens and in ancient Corinth revealed significant overlying Medieval levels. Very creditably the excavation directors commissioned pioneering studies of the finds (e.g., Frantz 1938, 1942), the most substantial of which, Morgan (1942), remains a major source-book for Byzantine and Frankish ceramics in the Aegean. Even earlier, a group of British archaeologists with remarkably wide period-interests were publishing papers on Byzantine and Frankish churches and castles at the beginning of the twentieth century (Wace, Traquair, and others). Over the last two decades an explosion of new data has emerged from two parallel developments. Firstly, interest has been renewed in post-Roman excavated deposits from urban excavations, especially at Corinth (Sanders 2000). Secondly, widespread evidence for Medieval rural life has emerged from regional surface surveys.

As a result, a better understanding of the ceramic sequence has been called for, not just the fine tablewares which had already been published as art objects, but of the domestic and coarse wares which dominate archaeological assemblages. Notable advances have been made by combining ceramic studies from production sites, excavated town sites, and the often large collections of surface finds from regional survey. Key works for Medieval-Postmedieval Aegean ceramics include the

Saraçane excavation in Constantinople (Hayes 1992); Hayes' contributions to regional rural surveys (Kea: Cherry *et al.* 1991; Boeotia: Bintliff *et al.* 2007); Bakirtzis on medieval cooking, storage, and transport wares (1989); Papanikola-Bakirtzi on medieval glazed wares (1992, 1999); Sanders' studies of urban deposits from Corinth (2000); and overviews by Vroom (2003, 2005) and Vionis (2001). Coarse wares and fabric studies now extend the diagnosticity of assemblages beyond traditional reliance on decorated pottery (Lang 2009).

Additionally the Austrian *Tabula Byzantina* project has since 1976 issued atlases of the Byzantine empire, province (*theme*) by province (Koder 1996). Alongside excellent maps showing the location of monuments, excavations, and literary topographic references, the texts of these volumes offer historical-geographical reviews, upon which intensive regional surface survey can build up local detail.

Reflecting this broadening of approaches, several significant volumes dealing with Medieval Greece have appeared (Lock and Sanders 1996, Caraher *et al.* 2008, Bintliff and Stöger 2009). Alongside these are excellent recent studies of Byzantine history, including archaeological information (Foss and Magdalino 1977, Ducellier 1986, Haldon 2000, Gregory 2006).

Chronology

It is first necessary to clarify our terminology when dealing with Byzantium. Once Constantine the Great had created his "New Rome" at the strategic position of Byzantium (modern Istanbul) in 330 AD, the Roman Empire reoriented itself to a new focus, not only administratively but also in economic and military organization. The association of this change with official tolerance and soon state support for Christianity represents another vital rupture in the Roman way of life as it had developed over the preceding 1000 years. For these reasons many scholars commence the Byzantine era in the early fourth century AD. This "Byzantine" civilization would only last some 300 years in all the Roman provinces which the Empire lost to the advance of Islam from the seventh century AD (North Africa and the Levant), so scholars of the Levant call the last part of this period Late Byzantine. This is confusing, since in the core

regions of the new Roman world which from the fifth century were ruled from Byzantium-Constantinople (the South Balkans and Anatolia), Eastern Roman imperial power is in force till 1204 AD, and, after an interruption between then till 1261 when Crusader Franks occupy the capital, "Roman" power is restored till 1453 when the capture of the city by the Ottoman Turks definitively ends the Eastern Roman Empire. For Greek scholars then, Early Byzantine can begin with Constantine, Middle Byzantine with an important change in the nature of the Empire in the ninth century AD, and Late Byzantine with the Frankish occupation, ending with the Ottomans.

Actually, many archaeologists (including myself) prefer a different scheme to suit the material realities of Eastern Roman life. Till the seventh century AD the Roman Empire remained dominant in its Eastern provinces and its material culture and organization rest on forms and models which had developed in the third and fourth centuries AD. From the mid-sixth to the eighth century, by which time the Western Roman provinces had been lost to Barbarian kingdoms (with brief episodes of recapture and with minor footholds surviving in Southern Italy), a series of crises afflicted the surviving Eastern Empire, almost destroying it on many occasions. However, by the ninth century it re-emerged as a great power in the Mediterranean world. This imperial renewal also coincides with major changes in material culture (especially the emergence of a distinctively "medieval" ceramic assemblage), novel urban forms, church architecture, and art, and is associated with a series of effective emperors (the Macedonian dynasty). Hence we shall define the era ca. 400–650 AD as Late Roman; the transitional era ("Dark Age") 650 to mid-ninth century as Early Byzantine; and the era of greatest flourishing, from then to 1204 AD, as Middle Byzantine; finally 1204–1453 AD forms the Late Byzantine period. The latter includes Frankish-Crusader times when Greece was divided between Byzantines and these hostile colonizers.

"Byzantine" civilization was coined by Early Modern Enlightenment scholars. The inhabitants of that society called themselves "Romans" (*Rhomaioi*), expressing their sense of continuity as the surviving Eastern Roman Empire. Even modern Greeks, aware of their rich Medieval heritage, call the essence of Greek identity "*Rhomaiosyne*" (literally Roman-ness) (Leigh Fermor 1966). Nonetheless this "Eastern Roman Empire" from ca. 650–1453 underwent transformations, so although there was much inherited from the wider Empire before the collapse of the Roman West in the fifth century AD, there was far more change within the following 800 years. Latin, for example, did not survive for long as an official language once Constantinople formed the focus of the Eastern Empire, unsurprising when even in Rome's heyday the Eastern Provinces had remained dominated by Greek and local languages such as Aramaic.

As yet Byzantium is little known outside the Southern Balkans, and is seen as a strange culture with wonderful art but disreputable politics, in any case out of the path linking the great achievements of the Ancient Greeks and Romans to Modern Western Civilization. Hence the prolonged neglect of its archaeology and history by students and the general public outside of Greece (Gregory 1984, 2006). Historical sources are also surprisingly limited for such a powerful and long-lived civilization, but this is mostly due to their destruction through war. A popular image is of a static, backward society run by corrupt priests and tyrannical emperors or their scheming courts ("byzantine" is a term used today to denote a tortuous and possibly devious administrative organization). The seeming lack of development in its best-known remains, churches and their icons, appears to confirm its stagnant nature. Yet of course no civilization could really survive so long without adaptation. But there is a core of truth in the stereotype of continuity within Byzantine history: the basic notion of the Empire remained the same. It was the Kingdom of God on Earth, a pale reflection of the Kingdom of Heaven, and the emperor was God's earthly ruler. Since the emperor was expected to maintain order on Earth in imitation of that in Heaven, ritual and ceremonial were a central feature of court life (Haldon 2000).

The Early Byzantine (EB) Period (ca. 650–842 AD)

If the period 400–550 AD had seen Greece in a phase of revival and heightened activity in town and country, not least because it had become one of the

near-hinterland regions of a Roman Empire focused on Constantinople at the head of the Aegean, the succeeding centuries saw rising crisis and a constant threat of the complete disappearance of Eastern Roman power. Following immense depopulation occasioned by the first outbreak of the (probably bubonic) Plague in the mid-sixth century (Durliat 1989), continual recurrences till the eighth century ensured that Greece was underpopulated and its economic productivity shrunken. The migration of Slav peoples from the Baltic regions of North Europe had been underway throughout Central-Eastern Europe for some centuries, so that their arrival in the South Balkans in the late sixth century found insufficient resistance from a weakened Byzantine army or local militias to prevent their rapid colonization of the countryside, from Macedonia in the north to the Peloponnese in the south (Malingoudis 1991). The Empire was preoccupied with prolonged wars in the East against the Persian Sassanian Empire and then, from the seventh century, against the seemingly irresistible Arab armies. The available forces to meet this Slav challenge were only capable (with the help of the imperial fleet), to retain Byzantine control over the capital, major towns, and many coastal strips and islands. Essentially the Mainland Greek countryside left imperial control for much of the period 600–800 AD and came under the dominance of Slav tribes. But evidence on the Aegean islands during the EB era for churches and walled military posts confirms a tenuous grip by the Byzantine fleet on many coastal localities.

The permanent loss of Byzantine control over its Levantine and North African provinces in the seventh century to a new Islamic empire arising in Arabia, although confining the Empire to the South Balkans, Anatolia, and restricted parts of Italy (Figure 17.2), at least allowed it to direct all its energies to reorganizing its rump state and recapturing its core hinterland in Greece. During this phase of crisis a new system of provincial management emerged, where the surviving Empire was divided into a series of small provinces or *themes* (Haldon 1990), each with an integrated government combining military and socio-economic control. Soldier-farmers ensured the regional productivity needed to make each theme both economically viable and defensible. Steadily between the seventh and early ninth centuries imperial forces defeated the

Slavs and reincorporated the Aegean countryside into the Empire, as well as stabilizing the frontiers to North and East, respectively against new Slav states and the dynasties of the Islamic Empire (the Umayyads and their Abbasid successors).

Settlement in Early Byzantine town and country

Late Roman ceramics up to the early seventh century can be understood reasonably well, evolving out of forms arising in the earlier Empire (Hayes 1972, 1997). Fine wares, especially from North Africa and in lesser quantities from the East Mediterranean, and transport amphorae from numerous centers in the East Mediterranean and the Aegean, allow collections to be dated with considerable accuracy (Pettegrew 2007). Increasingly, the domestic and coarse wares (generally locally made in each region) are also being classified for many provinces, including the Aegean variants. Field survey, our most significant tool for the history of rural sites between Late Antiquity and the Middle Byzantine period, demonstrates that despite the accumulating crises, people continued to dwell or exploit rural estates till the end of the LR era. On the Methana Survey for example (Mee and Forbes 1997), 11 LR sites survive into the seventh century AD. The large villa at the abandoned city of Halieis in the Argolid, partly excavated, was deserted after fire destruction in the seventh century (Jameson *et al.* 1994). Late Antique towns were hit by a succession of catastrophes, not only natural ones such as earthquakes and the Plague, but increasing Barbarian raids from the third through sixth centuries, culminating in the permanent settlement of the Slav tribes in the sixth and seventh century. Nonetheless many small and large Greek urban sites continued to be occupied throughout the sixth even into the early seventh century AD (the last imports of African red-slip tablewares being a primary dating tool), including excavated sites such as Corinth as well as town sites explored by intensive surface survey, such as the several Boeotian cities.

Archaeological research in Greek cities and rural sites focusing on the post-Roman periods remains very rudimentary, further compounded by a severe problem in recognizing assemblages typical for this period, whether in provincial towns or in the countryside. The archaeological evidence in the Aegean is, however, extremely scanty for this period. If we accept that population was brought to a very low level from the sixth century onwards as a result of warfare and recurrent Plague outbreaks, then the amount and dispersal of material culture should be limited for this phase of two hundred years, with the exception of the larger towns. Even there, however, our recovered evidence remains slight, despite historical sources confirming their widespread continued existence through Early Byzantine times.

When the Byzantine Empire recovers its demographic, military, and economic power from the ninth century onwards, there are also radical developments in material culture, one of which is a new ceramic assemblage of "medieval" character, paralleled around this period in both other Christian lands of Southern Europe and in the Islamic Near East and North Africa. The easily-recognizable feature is glazing on table and other wares, initially perhaps to make them watertight and cleanable, soon however for visual attractiveness (probably imitating expensive metal containers). Such wares spread slowly out of precocious seventh-century production foci such as Egypt, Syria, and the city of Constantinople. It is generally in the tenth to eleventh centuries that they become common in the Byzantine provinces, by which time they had already stimulated imitative local production. Outside major cities and maritime-oriented smaller settlements, a serious gap in recognized ceramics for the crisis phase, the later seventh to later ninth centuries, hinders understanding of everyday Aegean life.

As in Italy (Potter 1987), pushing back regional glazed ware production to meet the last early seventh-century Late Roman forms is unsupported, leaving rare occurrences of glazed white wares exported from Constantinople to the provinces as occasional dating evidence (Sanders 1996). What is beginning to be confirmed is that the "Dark Age" saw derivatives of Late Roman wares, chiefly local domestic and coarse ceramics, but also in lesser amounts red-slip and amphora types, survive until the appearance of the "medieval" assemblages (Armstrong 2009, Vionis *et al.* 2009). Since we still lack a clear assemblage for EB sites after the mid-seventh and until the tenth century AD in the Greek provinces, only future research will create regional settlement maps for Greece during these centuries, or a plan of occupation zones in a surviving town site. Instead we can at least present case studies from rural settlements and excavated urban sites.

The failure of a distinctive Slav culture in Greece to fill the gap surprises scholars. Slav-occupied areas in East-Central Europe do possess distinctive assemblages, although in the early period of migration it is usually in cemeteries that such wares are most clearly recognized. But in Greece comparable pottery is very rare and often their forms and decoration merely assign them to either an earlier or later time-period within the seventh to tenth century AD. Our historical sources (Malingoudis 1991) leave no doubt that the Slav colonization of Greece was a large-scale population movement. Thessaloniki, second city of the Byzantine Aegean, was besieged by a sea of Slav settlers from the surrounding countryside, and Slavs exercised genuine control over the Greek rural landscape rather than existing as harmless infillers of land left empty by earlier depopulation. Indeed for this reason we could not accept the apparent emptiness of the EB landscape, since such colonizers undoubtedly revived land use and settlement activity. We can also dismiss the theory that early Slavs lacked tangible houses, pottery or mixed farming: all these features are well-evidenced throughout the remaining Slav world (Malingoudis 1991).

The Greek peasant population which survived the raids and plagues of the LR era we might suspect largely stayed in their landscapes and intermarried with Slav incomers, hence the occurrence of sub-Roman ceramics in the EB period. Our working hypothesis to account for the rarity of "Slav" ceramics is that Roman-derivative wares were preferred by both population groups. This merger was aided by the creation of a minor but widespread local production of hand-made coarse wares in final LR times, perhaps to substitute for declining professional supplies, which look similar to genuine Slav ceramics (Gregory and Kardulias 1990, Rautman 1998, Oikonomou-Laniado 2003). On present knowledge, the colonizers arrived with their own Slav ceramic traditions but rapidly converted to utilizing regional pottery in a sub-Roman tradition, making their presence almost invisible in the archaeological record. Up till 2005, our Boeotia

project in Central Greece, despite having surveyed many Late Roman villas, villages, and urban sites, and numerous Medieval villages and farms, producing a database of 100,000 sherds, included just one piece of "Slav ware," from ancient Hyettos city. We favor the view that a mixed Slav-Hellenic peasant population occupied many of our sites during EB times but their ceramic culture lies largely unrecognized in the innumerable "LR" sherds which lack a distinctive fine-dating. The latest research (Vionis *et al.* 2009) shows that careful examination of such assemblages and those of "medieval" settlements can reveal new variants of older Roman wares, or distinctive new unglazed wares, as probable type-fossils (recognizable types) for the EB era.

Finding EB settlements may be hindered by a new preference for surviving local populations to occupy isolated hilltop refuges, little researched in Greece. Such locations, analogous to post-Bronze Age refuge sites, are widely documented historically and archaeologically throughout the rest of the LR Balkans (Dunn 1997, Poulter 2007), and we discovered one such (Aghios Constantinos) near Tanagra, Central Greece (see Chapter 15). In Italy similar resettlements occur (Francovich and Hodges 2003). But the incoming Slav colonizers were confident militarily, and skillful farmers seeking the best land (Malingoudis 1991); this would surely encourage them rather to reoccupy ancient village and city locations. Surface survey and place-name evidence support this second scenario for the EB era, and if some open locations retained existing peasant occupants there may well have developed a peaceful coexistence with dominant Slav settlers. We do however have one very clear Slav community discovered archaeologically. The ancient sanctuary at Olympia lost its ritual role probably in the fifth century, but was occupied by a domestic Late Roman settlement till perhaps the early seventh century, sheltering behind a fortification (recalling Aghios Constantinos village). It is argued that this community left and was soon replaced by a Slav village, only recorded from a cremation cemetery of at least 35 burials (Vida and Völling 2000). The typology of these burial urns, beginning with early hand-made, undecorated forms and continuing into increasingly more complex wavy-line ornaments and the use of the potter's wheel, suggests a period of use

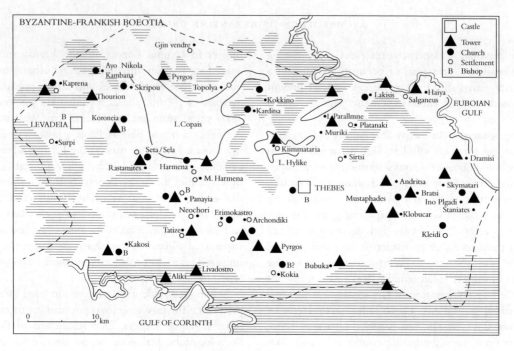

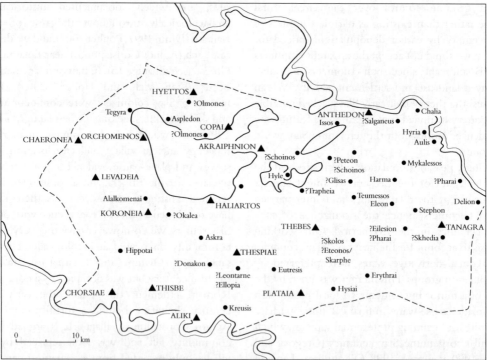

Figure 17.1 (Upper) Generalized distribution of major foci of settlement in Byzantine and Frankish Boeotia, from extensive and localized intensive survey, compared with (Lower) the distribution of Greco-Roman cities (triangles) and villages (circles) in Boeotia. A high proportion of settlements are in use in both eras, but their names changed in the intervening period.

J. Bintliff, "Reconstructing the Byzantine countryside: New approaches from landscape archaeology." In K. Blelke *et al.* (eds.), *Byzanz als Raum*. Wien 2000, 37–63, Figures 11 and 12.

of some 200 years over the seventh and eighth centuries, paralleling sequences in the Lower Danube and Dniepr Valleys in the North Balkans. Other evidence suggests that we are on the right track.

Thus a map of known Byzantine-Frankish settlements in Boeotia (but excluding small farms and hamlets) is strikingly similar to that of Greco-Roman towns and villages (Figure 17.1). We might argue that in EB times some elements of a reduced Greco-Roman population remained on or near former LR foci of settlement from Late Roman times, merging through intermarrying with incoming communities of Slav farmers. A subsequent major rise of population and regional prosperity during mature to final Middle Byzantine (MB) times (tenth to twelfth centuries AD), predicted from traditional study of church-building and the historical sources, is certainly matched by a dramatic increase in rural sites from our intensive survey in Boeotia, generally without LR or possible EB occupation. Yet I would suggest that this later phase of revival builds upon the "survival capsules" of "Sub-Roman" times, which in their turn are a simplified network of the Greco-Roman settlement system. We also suggest that these EB sites are in two forms: defensible locations used by indigenous communities on or near antique settlements, as widely evidenced in the north Balkans (Liebeschuetz 2007), at least in the most insecure early part of the EB period, and open sites also on or near ancient sites, where Slav farmers settled down with or without local surviving peasant families.

In the *Siedlungskammer* (settlement-chamber) model of the German *Landeskunde* (landscape-knowledge) school (see Chapter 8; Lehmann 1939, Bintliff 2000a–b) diversified landscapes create "constraints and possibilities" for settlement, often in or around certain recurrent places in the landscape (the product of physical topography, soil types, technological and land use regimes, and natural paths of communication). Apparent continuities in the placing of settlements over time can thus result from natural conditions, or recurrent ways of using the landscape, and need not imply genuine continuities of local peoples.

To clarify these contrasted processes we need more precise information. Intensive survey of small districts at the *Siedlungskammer* scale, combined with historical and archival evidence, can provide major insights in Boeotia (following Text Box).

The Transition from Antiquity to the Middle Ages in Boeotia

The Valley of the Muses is a small, largely enclosed upland valley landscape, which has in the long term normally only seen one nucleated settlement (see Figure 8.4). Intensive survey (Bintliff 1996) found some 50 archaeological sites dating from Neolithic to Turkish times. In Greco-Roman antiquity the central nucleation was a large village at Askra, which was particularly flourishing in Late Roman times. Byzantine ceramics from Askra securely dated to the ninth to twelfth centuries AD suggest a smaller village, but are associated with a large church in the south center of the site (Bintliff and Snodgrass 1988). Lock (1995) has argued that this community is "Zaratova," which gained an Orthodox bishop by the twelfth century, one of several new bishoprics established by the bishop of Thebes to serve a rapidly growing rural population in later MB Boeotia, very much supporting other evidence we have for general revival in the Aegean from the ninth and tenth centuries onwards.

Only hints of possible EB wares at Askra suggest continued use of the site after its LR florescence, but restudy is in progress. Provisionally more help comes from archival sources. The replacement of ancient Askra with Byzantine Zaratova indicates a dominant linguistic presence of Slav-speakers, the place-name "of the mountain" suiting this upland basin enclosed on three sides by imposing Mount Helicon. The toponym points to the settlement of Slavs in an open, non-defensive site surrounded by highly fertile land, exactly at the period where our ceramic evidence is still ambiguous for continuity of site use at Askra. Boeotia was recovered by the Byzantine army by the ninth century. The subsequent Hellenization and Christianization of the Slavs in Greece explains why by the end of the Middle Ages the village had acquired a Greek

Orthodox name, Panaghia (signifying the Virgin Mary). The precise overlying of the Medieval over the Greco-Roman village might hint at a merger of surviving local peasants and a dominant incoming Slav community, which we hope to test through re-examination of the survey ceramics.

Haliartos, a Greco-Roman city also in Boeotia, offers similar evidence (Bintliff 2000a–b). Destroyed by the Roman army in the second century BC, it never revived as a nucleated settlement during Antiquity. Our total urban survey found scanty Medieval activity, but when we surveyed around and between the houses of the adjacent, modern Haliartos town, we collected plentiful finds of Middle Byzantine, Frankish, and Early Ottoman times. The MB extramural village blossomed into a populous community in the thirteenth to sixteenth centuries AD, with the name Harmena or Charmaina. The reasons for postulating an EB settlement rest again on that community's name: it appears to be a Slav name

for a church (P. Soustal *pers. comm.*), associated with earlier rather than later Slav settlements. Indeed toponyms may offer complementary evidence to archaeology elsewhere in Greece: the Slav languages underwent major changes from the tenth century, but most of the Greek villages with original Slav names belong before this transformation (M. Kiel *pers. comm.*).

Thespiae offers a further parallel. The Late Roman town is replaced by two villages with the Greek name Erimokastro, in place by MB times on the far eastern periphery of their urban predecessor, according to texts and abundant surface finds. There is now strong reason to support continuity of occupation at the city, if only at village level, during the intervening EB period, both by A. Vionis' recognition of sporadic EB ware amongst the sherd finds from our 1980s city survey, but also by M. Karambinis' discovery that fragments of church architecture from the LR Kastro also belong to the "Dark Age."

The Boeotian evidence resonates with the wider picture: "most of the cities of the Balkan area ceased to exist in the late sixth and/or the seventh century, and social life changed dramatically" (Gregory 2006, 158), but their village replacements are very common. A relatively small number of larger or more strategically vital towns did survive in Greece through the EB era, and we shall present their evidence later in this chapter in the context of their subsequent MB revival.

The Middle Byzantine Peak: Ninth Century to 1204 AD

Under the vigorous and powerful Macedonian imperial dynasty, lasting 200 years from the late ninth century, the Byzantine Empire strengthened and at times extended its borders (Figure 17.2), which however remained overall in the same lands as previously: the South Balkans with Greece, Anatolia, and a foothold

in southern Italy and the Crimea. Alongside strong rulers and military power, the final victory of the "iconophiles" in 843 (the supporters of religious representative art and its mystical authority, see Chapter 18) encouraged greater internal coherence around the symbolic power of the Empire as God's kingdom on Earth, and brought a spiritual dimension to the defenses of the Empire against its Slav and Islamic neighbor states. The grandson of the first Macedonian emperor Basil I (acceded in 867) was Constantine VII Porphyrogenitos (acceded 913), from whose reign colorful texts and images survive to illuminate the elaborate ceremonies and politics of the Empire.

Slavs within the revived Empire had been incorporated into the Byzantine state during the eighth and ninth centuries, whilst their Christian conversion followed a policy pursued by the Byzantine church and state, which led ultimately to the "Hellenization" of the probably large share of the population of Greece which derived from the Slav colonization. One means through which successful Hellenization was achieved

Figure 17.2 The Byzantine Empire in 1025.
C. Mango (ed.), *Oxford History of Byzantium*. Oxford 2002, 178 (unnumbered figure). © Oxford University Press.

was through imperial initiative in appointing tribal leaders as "archons" or regional representatives, tied to recognition of Byzantine authority and the payment of tax or tribute (Megaw 1966). Although we know the names of certain leading families of Slav origin in later times, most not only Christianized but adopted Greek names and kept no roots in their culture of origin. This is of course a sensitive topic even today for a nation like Greece with appropriate pride in its national heritage from Classical Greek times. As a result, the Slav presence in Medieval to Modern Greece has been subject to both academic and popular controversy. The provocative thesis of Fallmerayer in the nineteenth century, that Modern Greeks were almost entirely a Slav replacement of the vanished Hellenic stock, no longer stands academic scrutiny, but neither does the nationalistic opposite, sometimes voiced even by Greek academics, that the Slavs made no significant contribution to the population, perhaps even going "home" after a time in Greece. Malingoudis' (1991) measured small volume on this topic is an excellent antidote to nationalists on either side of the debate. Equally important to the integration and sur-

vival of Byzantine civilization was the Christianization of the Slav states surrounding the Empire to its North and West, spearheaded by the monks Saint Cyril and Saint Methodius in the ninth century, which gave the Byzantines a powerful spiritual influence on their often dangerous neighbors.

On the other hand, there were also signs of internal changes of a less positive character in later MB times, particularly when the Comnenoi dynasty assume imperial power in the late eleventh century. In the Aegean Mainland countryside the reduced populations suggested from textual and archaeological evidence up until the tenth and eleventh centuries, following a period under Slav control when imperial authority was largely absent, is associated by Byzantine historians with a strong peasantry and a village-based organization of the landscape. A text called *The Farmer's Law* (early eighth century AD?) is seen as illustrating this phase of MB peasant life (Gregory 2006). This is contrasted with the dominant model of the Late Roman period, when peasants are considered to have been largely tied (*coloni*) to the estates of large landowners. By the late MB however the sources evidence an increasing conflict between the independent villager and a new class of landowners (secular but also clerical, with the expansion of monastic holdings), intent on absorbing them into their expanding estates, a battle where the emperors regularly intervened on the peasants' side but ultimately without great success. At the time of the Crusader conquest of Greece and Constantinople from 1204 AD, many historians argue that the Greek peasantry was widely tied to a form of magnate lordship, as tenants, sharecroppers or even serfs, so that the introduction of Western feudalism by the Franks meant no radical change for many rural communities.

The Macedonian dynasty had achieved a long period of growth and prosperity but from the late eleventh century, when the Comnenoi dynasty (1081–1185) assumed power, the Empire began to suffer increasing problems from within and without which were inexorably going to cause its decline and demise, even if the last blow was the definitive capture of the capital, Constantinople in 1453 by the Ottoman Turks. The Empire became constantly on the defensive from external aggression, at the same time as increasing indications of internal breakdown became manifest, including the loss of income and authority to a "semi-feudal" provincial landlordism. Normans based from the later eleventh century in their new state in Sicily and South Italy attacked the Byzantine Balkans from the West, whilst the Seljuk dynasty led colonizing Turks at the same time into Anatolia. Although the Normans were rebuffed from the Balkans (not before sacking the second city of Thessaloniki and other major towns such as Thebes), the Turks gradually took over Anatolia except the coastlands.

John Haldon (1992) has suggested a cyclicity in the development of the Byzantine state, paralleled by similar processes in its ultimate replacement, the Ottoman state. The Byzantine Empire initially deployed the "Ancient Mode of Production" whereby free peasants were taxed at low levels to sustain its central state bureaucracy and its regional urban administration, and were also expected to provide recruits for the army. Over time however, a "service" military-bureaucratic class diverted control over the peasantry and tax income into its own hands, aspiring to a hereditary society of wealthy landowners dominating a tied peasantry. This weakened the emperor's grip on his people and territories. Armies became increasingly dominated by foreign mercenaries, whose cash demands raised taxes, already reduced by a siphoning-off of state revenue into the pockets of the landowners. An early tight control on trade within the Byzantine world was replaced by concessions to the commercial fleets of the entrepreneurial Italian trading cities such as Venice and Genoa, blocking the rise of a middle class of wealth-creating manufacturers and traders within the state and subverting its entire economy. The early Byzantine Empire had been sustained by tax and peasant army recruits from independent rural communities, largely producing their own food and supplying sufficient small surpluses for the minor demands of the state. In contrast, the mature to late Byzantine state was being cut apart by the scissors of a declining income from its peasantry and an economic peripheralization as its wealth was being drained by the expanding proto-capitalist Italian commercial world. Unsurprisingly, the coinage, hitherto a "gold standard" for Mediterranean trade that had maintained its value for some seven centuries, now became devalued (Gregory 2006).

Whereas in feudal Western Europe a defined hierarchy of power existed, Byzantium allowed greater mobility, with two avenues to power: the civil elite with administrative roles in Constantinople and the military leadership provided by provincial landed magnates. However intermarriage and success in building up dynastic privilege led by the twelfth century to a concentration of wealth and status in a limited stratum of families, largely responsible for the commissioning of monastic and church foundations and their famous art (Cormack 1985). This meant that a powerful landowner elite dominated social life at all levels and especially in provincial towns, limiting the development of a middle class (trade and manufacture were considered unsuitable career paths for the elite) and causing a widening gulf between relatively poor peasants and the wealthy magnate class (Gregory 2006). The result was a predictable inability of the Byzantine economy to compete with that of the Italian mercantile families who, massively supported by their commercial republics, represented a foreign capitalist elite in the Byzantine homeland.

Developments in the Middle Byzantine Greek countryside

The development of rural life in the Byzantine provinces has traditionally been reconstructed from literary sources: agrarian laws, saints' lives, contemporary chronicles, and monastic archives. In second place has come the study of monuments surviving in the landscape, especially churches and monastic foundations, with much less attention being given to defensive structures such as castles and towers (which generally remain poorly dated and recorded), and the rather sparse record of modern excavation. The atlas for each Byzantine province (*Tabula Imperii Byzantini*) now helpfully synthesizes this information. However the richest database for writing the history of the Byzantine countryside lies invisible to all but surface artifact survey teams, ceramic scatters found across provincial landscapes. Although the first intensive surveys were only able to date pottery to very broad periods ("Medieval" or even "Medieval to Turkish"), it is now possible, with the help of a handful of experts, to assign surface finds of tableware to periods of one to two hundred years, whilst advances in establishing fabric and style typologies for domestic and coarse wares often allows their assignation to broader but still useful periods such as Middle Byzantine, Frankish, Early- or Late Ottoman, and Early Modern.

The results of regional surface surveys confirm fundamental changes in Byzantine society during the MB era: a major population growth and the rising productivity of the countryside, which sustained a parallel growth in the number and size of towns (Armstrong 2003) (Figure 17.3). This economic expansion continues into the Frankish thirteenth and fourteenth centuries, forming a steady trend not anticipated by historical sources. It may be objected, as noted earlier, that we have no accurate idea of the settlement patterns for the preceding Early Byzantine era, and indeed we have suggested that most settlements remain invisible archaeologically owing to our inadequate knowledge of the pottery assemblage and the scarcity of coin finds. But several arguments can be deployed to argue that there was a real MB takeoff in rural and urban population.

Firstly, historical sources give clear signs of land intake, deforestation, village foundation, multiplication of bishoprics, and urban revival (Harvey 1983, 1990). A first peak of such prosperity around the late MB period fits the independent evidence of archaeological survey, where a dramatic rise of nucleated hamlet and village sites can be seen across Greece in the eleventh to twelfth centuries, often without prior occupation in Late Roman times or with any ceramics of the ninth to tenth centuries. There is also growing evidence from rescue excavations in Greece for the flourishing of small Middle Byzantine rural settlements (such as in Attica, Gini-Tsofopoulou 2001). Whereas an absence of datable seventh- to eighth-century finds is unreliable when we are just beginning to characterize contemporary wares, the widespread lack of the typical "medieval assemblage" forms including glazed wares from the ninth and tenth centuries is strikingly consistent. The delayed explosion of rural settlements is partly due to the fact that even though from the ninth century the Empire was growing strong and flourishing again, there were regional difficulties and setbacks. The decline of Aegean piracy was held back till Crete was recaptured in 961 whilst Bulgarian invasions hit Greece severely in the tenth century (Bouras 2006).

At the same time the chronology of church architecture gives a suitable rise in dated monuments: there are just a handful erected outside the major towns in the EB period, a few churches for the early MB, and then a proliferation during the eleventh and twelfth centuries and also during the first century of Frankish power over much of Greece, the thirteenth century. The example of Messenia is shown in Figure 17.4. Boeotia provides another example (Megaw 1966). After the definitive reconquest of the province from the Slavs by the end of the eighth century AD, several major church foundations from the mid-ninth century in the regional capital Thebes coincide with similar examples from Athens, as well as with the building of the famous Boeotian rural monastic church at Skripou (modern Orchomenos). Historic sources indicate that the ancient city of Orchomenos, reduced to a village by Roman times, saw this new monastic church constructed in 872 AD in the open countryside, with much *spolia* from its ruins, on the estate of a magnate and regional government official from the provincial center at Thebes. The location was very exposed to attack, so the important new

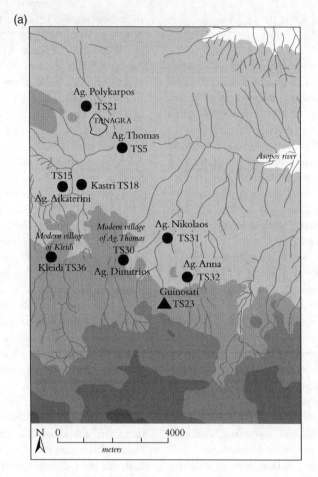

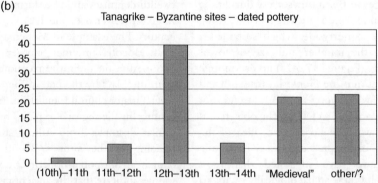

Figure 17.3 (a) Deserted medieval villages (black circles) in the region of ancient Tanagra city, Boeotia. (b) The chronology of their surface finds.

A. Vionis, "Current archaeological research on settlement and provincial life in the Byzantine and Ottoman Aegean." *Medieval Settlement Research* 23 (2008), 28–41, Figures 5 and 13.

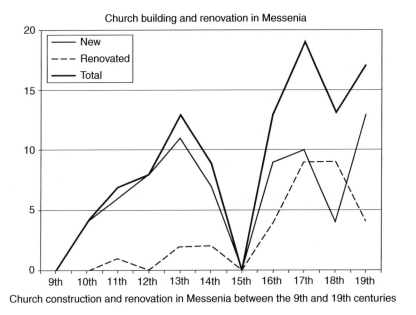

Church construction and renovation in Messenia between the 9th and 19th centuries

Figure 17.4 Chronology of church construction in Messenia.
E. Sigalos, *Housing in Medieval and Post-Medieval Greece.* Oxford 2004, Figure 187.

monastery reflects the establishment of firm imperial control in the region. The revival of the nearby settlement of Orchomenos and other parts of the adjacent countryside seems to occur later in the MB era, further symptom of that sustained wider demographic and economic growth over the period, to judge by the two small churches of eleventh-century date in the modern town and the nearby twelfth- to thirteenth-century rural church of Aghios Nikolaos sta Kampia. This is in keeping with our own intensive survey results from several other districts in Boeotia which indicate that the proliferation of villages associated with parish churches marks the late phase of the MB period, from the tenth and more usually eleventh or twelfth centuries AD, confirming the historic sources for agrarian expansion in contemporary texts such as the cadasters (landholding records) from Thebes (Svoronos 1959, Harvey 1983).

Finally we can cite the evidence of coinage. Experts in numismatics suggest that the Early Byzantine era was one which virtually lost the everyday use of money, relying on exchange in kind or services. From the ninth century however, for example at the town of Corinth, coin finds indicate a recovery of coin circulation, pointing to the revival of marketing and commerce, whilst increased production of small change, the opening of provincial mints, and tax changes confirm a rise in monetarization at the everyday level (Harvey 1990, Sanders 2003, Gregory 2006). Dunn (2007) has contributed an important study on MB peasant productivity (seen as very favorable) and rural markets, whilst an insightful analysis of Byzantine urban market areas can be found in Koder (2006). Dunn (2009) also discusses the existence of entrepôts on the Strymon Delta in Macedonia, which serviced the export of surpluses from estates in its fertile hinterland as well as the channeling of imports inland.

The archaeology of Byzantine villages poses one of the greatest areas of research potential in the period. There are clearly many hundreds if not more deserted sites from the EB through LB era awaiting survey and excavation, whilst at least from the tenth century, when, or soon after, the majority were founded, the ceramics are both datable and rich. Moreover since the typical Byzantine town was small, with the revival of imperial control the village became a fiscal unit, rather than as in Classical and Roman times being merely a rural suburb of a city district. This indicates that the backbone of Byzantium was its rural population (Haldon 2000). In keeping with this observation, larger villages are known to have stimulated considerable cottage industry to supply their own inhabitants: monastic records for the village of Radolibos in Macedonia for example evidence a population of around 1000 people, with more than 20 shoemakers and two potter's workshops (Laiou-Thomadakis 1977). Fairs occurred not only in towns but in villages and the open country, to further expand the reach of products to rural populations in the absence of a dense network of urban centers and the lack of large-scale manufacture and marketing within them. Even the industrial establishments excavated at Corinth are described by the excavators as "cottage industry" (Sanders 2003).

The revival of town life

Although historical sources are thin for events outside the two greatest cities of the Byzantine world, Constantinople and Thessaloniki, it is likely that (as with Anatolia and Byzantine Southern Italy), most Aegean towns lost their urban status in the EB era if not already in the final centuries of LR, whilst many suffered destruction and despoiling of their ruins. Just a few cities lasted as real centers in EB, notably when bases for the army and as *theme* (province) capitals (for example Thessaloniki in Greece and Amorium in Anatolia). But from the ninth century onwards there is clear revival of provincial small towns, with a wave of construction of churches and defense-works and the expansion of domestic quarters. By the tenth century there were some 40 towns above village status in the Peloponnese, although even the largest such as Corinth at its twelfth-century peak may have contained just 10,000 people (Sanders 2003). Some are officially "refounded" as they come back into full imperial control. Argos may be typical of the fate of larger centers: it shows continuity of activity on a very limited scale in the EB, seen as a village by French excavators (Piérart and Touchais 1996), then with the reconquest of the Peloponnese it is reborn as a major provincial center and archbishopric with numerous churches and a kastro (fortified refuge and

military base) above it. At Sparta, whereas the EB population appears to have withdrawn to the acropolis for security, where behind the walls of the LR kastro houses were built inside the abandoned theater, during the tenth to twelfth centuries the town spread out into the former lower town, where rescue excavations have uncovered new public and private buildings, churches, baths, and workshops (Zavvou et al. 2006). At Athens (Camp 2001) the town survives through the EB era but in severe decline, with minimal evidence for occupation until a clear revival in the eleventh to twelfth centuries, when a thriving town re-emerges with numerous small churches marking its parishes. At some former cities however the fortified EB kastro may have been accompanied by small hamlets nearby in parts of the abandoned ancient settlement (Haldon 2000).

The Byzantine town differed, however, in several significant ways from the Greco-Roman cities it replaced as "central-places" in each region (Haldon 2000). Firstly, apart from Constantinople and Thessaloniki, other Aegean towns were very small. Even the great cities lacked a gridded street plan of wide avenues, although they still possessed substantial public squares, but in typical provincial towns the extensive central Greco-Roman fora were replaced by small squares or street widenings. Roads were narrow and winding, and house-blocks irregular. Towns could be fortified, or possess a separate kastro, but the key to their internal organization was a network of parish churches or monasteries, creating local neighborhoods where much welfare and education provision as well as communal activities were focused around the Orthodox Church. In fact in contrast to the ancient city, where aristocrats and wealthy businessmen had frequently invested in public secular amenities and games to attract approval, these groups now primarily displayed their wealth through the construction and decoration of religious institutions (Cormack 1985). The great communal baths of the Roman era, as much social as exercise centers, went out of use in Late Antiquity, to be replaced by much smaller establishments open to the public but run as private ventures or attached to religious complexes, as much victims of economic decline as the underlying disapproval of the Church (Magdalino 1990).

The functional role of Byzantine towns is controversial. A major debate has been running for over two decades on the fate of towns in former Roman provinces between Late Antiquity and the Middle Ages (Barnish 1989). One view emphasizes the decline of their industrial and commercial activities during the "Dark Ages" in response to the collapse of markets and trade-routes. An alternative thesis stresses the continuing significance of the social and political role of surviving or re-emergent towns in the Early Medieval era. For the Byzantine Aegean provincial towns, it seems likely that they functioned essentially as regional market centers providing services and craft products, with a solid local agricultural base, as well as acting as foci of provincial military, political, and ecclesiastical administration. Long-distance trade and manufacturing for an interregional market appear to be of lesser importance, although we know of clear exceptions where towns had industries producing for a wider consumer zone than just their region. If the various workshops at Corinth, for example, show typical service industries for the townsfolk and surrounding villages (pottery, metalworking, and metalwork), sources tell us of major silk manufactories there and also in Thebes of international importance (Jacoby 1991–1992). However, at Sparta as at these other towns, it was especially a Jewish colony that was prominent in the processing and commerce of textiles and local agricultural surpluses. Moreover the presence of Venetian merchants at provincial towns in our sources also suggests that local entrepreneurs were slow to take advantage of such flourishing populations and regional production (Zavvou *et al.* 2006), although at the same time it does evidence a surplus of wider marketability. A few centers also benefited from holding international fairs, such as Thessaloniki, where merchants from the Christian West, the Islamic Near East, and Southern Russia were active (Gregory 2006).

Schreiner (2001) observes that in Byzantium a broad urban culture, so well known from contemporary Western Europe, is poorly represented, and then chiefly in its final LB two centuries. This reflects the high centralization of the court and the state's policy of limiting the powers of provincial towns. All who could, went to Constantinople to make careers and wealth. With the later decay of the capital and imperial power, however, rival centers emerged, Trebizond

as a second imperial city from the thirteenth century in Northern Anatolia, and Mistra likewise dominating the Peloponnese; but both remained focused on the residence of imperial court personnel. Only Thessaloniki shows signs of the development of a politically-assertive urban bourgeoisie, linked to the importance of its commercial community in Late Byzantine times.

In the later phase of MB it appears that Italian entrepreneurs took advantage of flourishing urban centers in the Byzantine world to dominate their financial and commercial affairs, which restricted their own citizens' ability to participate in wider Mediterranean economic opportunities. Advantages given by the Byzantine state to such Italian businessmen in terms of trading privileges were partly to blame, a combination of a lack of awareness of the negative effects on its own trading communities, and pressure (including military) on Byzantium to perpetuate these inequalities. However the restrictive practices of the Byzantine guild system were also a major factor in limiting the ability of local producers and merchants to compete with the flexible, state-sponsored commercial families of Northern Italy. The truncated potential of Byzantine commerce can be indicated from an exception, its flourishing entrepôts in the Black Sea during the eleventh and twelfth centuries, walled emporia run by magnates paid by the state (Stephenson 1999). Nonetheless, to confound the expectations of historians, who have derived from political history the image of a declining state and economic crisis, the twelfth century sees a flourishing urban network in the Aegean. Although much was being both siphoned off and run by Italian and Jewish businessmen, there was sufficient wealth for rich Byzantines to fill these towns with their endowments to monasteries and churches, paralleling a countryside dense with populous villages.

The Late Byzantine Period (1204–1453 AD)

The decisive shift in the fortunes of Byzantium was unsurprisingly to come from the West, through an unholy alliance between the ruthless maritime, commercial empire of the Republic of Venice and a mot-

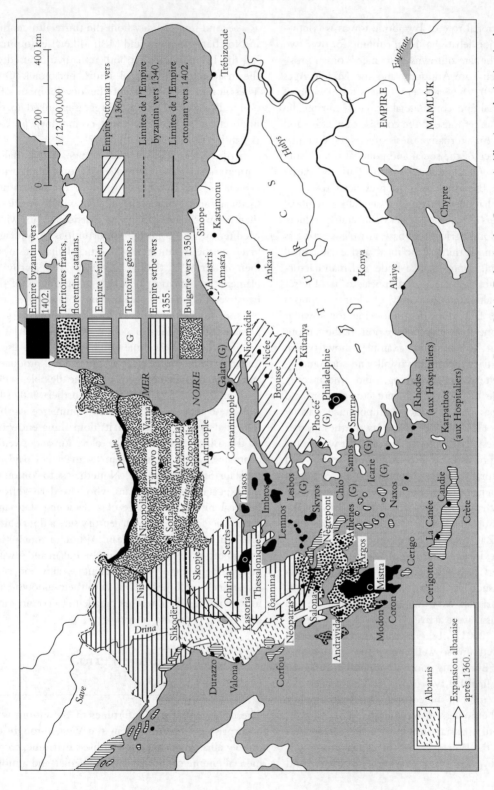

Figure 17.5 The fragmented territorial powers of the Aegean in 1402 (Venice, Genoa, Serbia, Bulgaria, the Ottomans). Albanian colonization is also indicated. Residual pockets under Byzantine rule are in black.

A. Ducellier, *Byzance et le monde orthodoxe*. Paris 1986, 8, bottom figure. By permission of Éditions Armand Colin.

Map labels:

Empire byzantin vers 1402.

Territoires francs, florentins, catalans.

Empire vénitien.

Territoires génois.

Empire serbe vers 1355.

Bulgarie vers 1350.

Empire ottoman vers 1360.

Limites de l'Empire byzantin vers 1340.

Limites de l'Empire ottoman vers 1402.

1/12,000,000

0   200   400 km

Albanais

Expansion albanaise après 1360.

MER NOIRE

Danube

Save

Drina

Euphrate

EMPIRE MAMLŪK

Trébizonde

Kastamonu

Amastris (Amasra)

Sinope

Ankara

Konya

Alaiye

Chypre

Rhodes (aux Hospitaliers)

Karpathos (aux Hospitaliers)

Nicomédie

Nicée

Brousse

Kütahya

Philadelphie

Phocée (G)

Smyrne

Galata (G)

Constantinople

Andrinople

Mésembria

Sozopolis

Varna

Târnovo

Nicopolis

Sofia

Niš

Skopje

Serrès

Ochrida

Kastoria

Iōannina

Néopatras

Salona

Andravida

Thessalonique

Thasos

Imbros

Lemnos

Lesbos (G)

Skyros

Chio (G)

Samos (G)

Icarie (G)

Naxos

Athènes (G)

Négrepont

Argos

Mistra

Coron

Modon

Cerigo

Cerigotto

La Canée

Candie

Crète

Corfou

Valona

Durazzo

Shkodër

Maritsa

Ioannina

TAUROS

ley collection of Frankish (mainly French and Italian) barons. The Fourth Crusade diverted its forces from the increasingly difficult war in the Holy Land, where the Crusader states were losing their territories to Islamic armies, to sack a softer target, the capital of another Christian state, Constantinople, in 1204. The conquest of much of Byzantine Greece followed, which was partitioned between major and minor Western feudal lords. Important pockets of Byzantine power under aristocratic families survived: in Epirus the Despotate of Arta under the Angeloi, an imperial statelet at Nicaea in Northwestern Anatolia under the Lascarids, and another on the Black Sea at Trebizond under the Comnenoi. Although the Byzantines recaptured the capital in 1261, expelling the Frankish emperor and establishing their own, final dynasty, the Palaeologi, and although the Peloponnese saw the creation and steady expansion of a Palaeologan satellite province at Mistra, the disintegration of the Byzantine heartland was now irreversible.

The Western Crusaders and their allies the Venetians occupied large areas of Greece, but Serbia and Bulgaria also extended their realms into Byzantine Greece during the fourteenth century. By this time the Turks had occupied most of Anatolia, providing a launching-pad for one of their constituent statelets, the Ottomans (founded by Osman) in the Northwest of the region, to steadily expand Islamic conquest into Greece and the Balkans. By the beginning of the fifteenth century, Byzantine power was confined to the capital and its hinterland, Thessaloniki its second city, some island pockets, and a portion of the Peloponnese centered on Mistra (Figure 17.5).

The capital itself in this "Late Byzantine" era (contemporary to the "Frankish period" in Crusader-occupied Greece, see Chapter 18), degenerated into a series of villages amid ruins and gardens, with perhaps 50,000 occupants remaining from tenth-century estimates of 500,000, and its trade largely in the hands of resident Italians. If anything the provincial city of Mistra near ancient Sparta was more prosperous. Despite or perhaps even because of all this (see Chapter 18), a Late Byzantine florescence in art and architecture is attested, with a distinctive style, strongly influential on the emergent Italian Renaissance. In return, Palaeologan architecture incorporates Western features.

Developments in the Late Byzantine town and country

Our knowledge of rural archaeology from historic sources and regional surface survey shows that, despite disruption caused by the Frankish conquest, the progressive infill of the Greek countryside by a dense network of farming villages from the eleventh century onwards does not cease until the fourteenth century. Moreover, although the official sources for political and social history have suggested worsening conditions for Byzantine society in town and country from a highpoint in the eleventh century, the archaeological picture contradicts this, whilst the latter matches local archives such as monastic records, from which trends concerning village numbers and their populations can be inferred. If the central state became terminally weak and its income minimal, the dense villages and numerous towns of the Aegean indicate a parallel, more flourishing image. Clearly rural productivity was high, allowing provincial magnates to live in some style in towns, import fine ceramics and luxuries, and invest in monastic and church endowments. The balance between those towns which were primarily residences to their rentier class and provided local markets and services, and those which were significantly producing industrial products and agricultural surpluses for interregional trade, remains, as we have seen, disputed, but will emerge from increasing archaeological investigations. The failure of a widespread entrepreneurial middle class or assertive artisan class to emerge in the towns, for example stimulating the rise of a more autonomous "communal" politics, seems at present to argue for the former view of urban society. Only Thessaloniki, with an exceptional international role in trade, produces a short-lived emergence of popular power.

Nonetheless, all our sources confirm a general collapse of settlement in both Byzantine and Frankish areas during the fourteenth century. The impact of the Black Death from the mid-fourteenth century is considered to have reduced European populations by a third to a half, whilst Greece's woes were augmented by constant aggression from Byzantium's enemies over its remaining territories, as well as their own mutual wars (Bulgarians, Serbs, Turks, Venetians, Catalans, Navarrese, Florentines, etc.). A similar demographic collapse occurred not only in the two great cities of the Empire but throughout its few other remaining regional towns. This chaos was resolved by the conquest of Constantinople by Ottoman armies under Mehmet the Conqueror in 1453, linked to the absorption of the Greek Mainland and almost all the Aegean islands, as well as virtually all of the Slav states of the Balkans, into the rapidly-expanding Ottoman Empire. The subsequent "Ottoman Peace" (*Pax Ottomanica*), offered the opportunity for native Greek populations to recover from the military and economic disasters of the preceding 150 years. Despite being now within an Islamic state, this is remarkably what occurred in the following period up till 1600 AD.

Byzantine Everyday Material Culture

The ceramics of the EB era are still being slowly understood and remain largely unrecognized. Amongst forms now assignable are the handmade "Slavic Wares," locally produced and found in many sites in Greece, seemingly both an indigenous replacement for the general disappearance of local industrial products and also produced by genuine Slav settlers from outside the Balkans (Color Plate 17.1). They date from the sixth to seventh centuries for undecorated hand-made varieties, then comes a decorated (incised linear and wavy-lines designs), wheel-made series in the eighth and ninth centuries. These were used both for cooking and as tablewares. Other wares reflect a clearer development as sub-Roman ceramics (Armstrong 2009, Vionis *et al.* 2009), such as Red-Painted Ware manufactured on Crete during the seventh and eighth centuries, originating out of the LR tradition of Red-Slip Ware of the sixth to seventh centuries in the Aegean (Color Plate 17.1). Recent research indicates that Red-Slip wares are also still being made locally into the 8th century. Constantinople White Ware (named from its fabric), is a yellow-green pioneer glazed ware found rarely in the EB provinces. Pamela Armstrong has argued that although White Wares are already common in the capital from the seventh century, they spread widely in the ninth and tenth centuries, reflecting both the recovery of Byzantine power over the Aegean and also the desire of provincial populations to acquire exotic tableware from the cultural center of their civilization (Armstrong 2001).

Transitional amphorae types of globular form from the seventh to ninth centuries have been identified across the Aegean and the Eastern Mediterranean in recent years, especially the Sarachane 35 amphora. Shapes show continuity from Late Roman forms into the Early Byzantine period in the Eastern Mediterranean, and the wide spread of such transport wares indicates that maritime commerce did not cease during the "Dark Ages."

With the Middle Byzantine era the ceramic assemblage becomes much clearer. In tablewares the commonest types (shown in Color Plate 17.1) are (1) Green and Brown Painted Ware (maybe Persian-influenced), eleventh to early thirteenth centuries; (2) Early Sgraffito (incised) Ware (Islamic-influenced), eleventh and twelfth centuries; and (3) Slip-Painted Ware, eleventh century to Modern era. These wares are normally covered with a clear or colored lead-glaze to protect their surfaces and assist cleaning and impermeability. But even in provincial trading towns such as Corinth, such glazed wares are less than 1 percent of the weight of excavated pottery in the tenth and eleventh centuries, then rise gradually to 20 percent in the thirteenth century (Sanders 2003). Nonetheless, although the vast bulk of glazed tableware was made regionally, the burgeoning commerce of the late MB and LB Aegean, even if increasingly in Italian hands, was moving tableware as well as the more predictable oil and wine amphorae around the coastlands, as the twelfth-century Alonissos shipwreck underlines (Papanikola-Bakirtzi *et al.* 1999). Byzantine plain wares, for food preparation and serving, and for cooking, have been published by Bakirtzis (1989).

We shall cover LB ceramics in Chapter 19. One other artifact can at times shed important light on Byzantine society, lead seals (Polychronaki 2005). They were used to guarantee the confidentiality of correspondence, authenticating the author and also used to seal merchandise. As official archives are almost all lost, lead seals can shed light on state mechanisms, as its administration required a constant exchange of letters.

Byzantine Burial Traditions

Many traditional forms of interment continue from Antiquity (Rautman 2006). The commonest recorded is a brick-lined tomb sealed with roof tiles or stone slabs, the inhumation being accompanied by small gifts such as coins, jewelry, and pottery and the deceased dressed in clothes indicating their status in life. Pots and lamps used in funeral meals by family members may leave surface debris for archaeologists, to add to that from the grave-gifts when a tomb is disturbed by cultivation or later constructions. From the Late Roman era onwards, burials were made not only in older cemeteries extramural to towns and villages, but clustered around the graves and shrines of Christian martyrs both outside and inside settlements (Kourkoutidou-Nicolaidou 1997). By the eighth or ninth century the Church specified that the burials of ordinary citizens should be confined to the precincts of churches and monasteries, by now commonly intramural in both towns and villages. Elite figures from public and ecclesiastical life were permitted to be interred inside churches to emphasize their status. Wealthy families generally invested their wealth in such foundations to increase their chances of divine grace on decease.

References

Armstrong, P. (2001). "From Constantinople to Lakedaimon: Impressed white wares." In J. Herrin et al. (eds.), Mosaic. Festschrift for A.H.S. Megaw. London: British School at Athens Studies 8, 57–67.

Armstrong, P. (2003). "The survey area in the Byzantine and Ottoman periods." In W. Cavanagh et al. (eds.), Continuity and Change in a Greek Rural Landscape. The Laconia Survey. Vol. I. London: British School at Athens, 330–402.

Armstrong, P. (2009). "Trade in the east Mediterranean in the 8th century." In M. M. Mango (ed.), Byzantine Trade, 4th–12th Centuries. Farnham: Ashgate, 157–178.

Athanassopoulos, E. F. (2008). "Medieval archaeology in Greece: An historical overview." In W.R. Caraher, L. J. Hall, and R. S. Moore (eds.), Archaeology and History in Roman, Medieval and Post-Medieval Greece. Aldershot: Ashgate, 15–35.

Bakirtzis, C. (1989). Byzantine Tsoukalolagena. Athens: Publications of the Archaiologikon Deltion 39.

Barnish, S. J. B. (1989). "The transformation of Classical cities and the Pirenne debate." Journal of Roman Archaeology 2, 385–400.

Bintliff, J. L. (1996). "The archaeological survey of the Valley of the Muses and its significance for Boeotian history." In A. Hurst and A. Schachter (eds.), La Montagne des Muses. Geneva: Librairie Droz, 193–224.

Bintliff, J. L. (2000a). "Reconstructing the Byzantine countryside: New approaches from landscape archaeology." In F. Hild et al. (eds.), Byzanz als Raum. Wien: Österreichisches Akademie der Wissenschaften.

Bintliff, J. L. (2000b). "Deconstructing 'the sense of place'? Settlement systems, field survey and the historic record: A case-study from Central Greece." Proceedings of the Prehistoric Society 66, 123–149.

Bintliff, J. L. and A. M. Snodgrass (1988). "Mediterranean survey and the city." Antiquity 62, 57–71.

Bintliff, J. L. and H. Stöger (eds.) (2009). Medieval and Post-Medieval Greece. The Corfu Papers. Oxford: BAR Int. Series 2023.

Bintliff, J. L. et al. (2007). Testing the Hinterland: The Work of the Boeotia Survey (1989–1991) in the Southern Approaches to the City of Thespiai. Cambridge: McDonald Institute.

Bouras, C. (2006). Byzantine and Post-Byzantine Architecture in Greece. Athens: Melissa.

Camp, J. M. (2001). The Archaeology of Athens. New Haven: Yale University Press.

Caraher, W. R., L. J. Hall, and R. S. Moore (eds.) (2008). Archaeology and History in Roman, Medieval and Post-Medieval Greece. Aldershot: Ashgate.

Cherry, J. F., J. C. Davis, and E. Mantzourani (1991). Landscape Archaeology as Long-Term History. Los Angeles: Institute of Archaeology, University of California.

Cormack, R. (1985). Writing in Gold: Byzantine Society and Its Icons. London: George Philip.

Crow, J. (2010). "Archaeology." In L. James (ed.), A Companion to Byzantium. Oxford: Blackwell, 291–300.

Ducellier, A. (ed.) (1986). Byzance et le monde orthodoxe. Paris: Armand Colin.

Dunn, A. (1997). "Stages in the transition from the Late Antique to the Middle Byzantine urban centre in S. Macedonia and S. Thrace." In Aphieroma ston N.G.L. Hammond. Thessaloniki: Etaireia Makedonikon Spoudon, 137–151.

Dunn, A. (2007). "Rural producers and markets: Aspects of the archaeological and historiographic problem." In M. Grünbart, E. Kislinger, and A. Muthesius (eds.), Material Culture and Well-Being in Byzantium (400–1453). Vienna: Austrian Academy of Sciences, 101–109.

Dunn, A. (2009). "Byzantine and Ottoman maritime traffic in the estuary of the Strymon." In J. Bintliff and H. Stöger (eds.), Medieval and Post-Medieval Greece. The Corfu Papers. Oxford: BAR Int. Series 2023, 15–31.

Durliat, J. (1989). "La Peste du VIe siècle." In C. Morrisson and J. Lefort (eds.), Hommes et richesses dans l'empire byzantin, IVe–VIIe siècle. Paris: Éditions P. Lethielleux, 106–119.

Foss, C. and P. Magdalino (1977). Rome and Byzantium. Oxford: Elsevier-Phaidon.

Francovich, R. and R. Hodges (2003). *Villa to Village: The Transformation of the Roman Countryside*. London: Duckworth.

Frantz, M. A. (1938). "Middle Byzantine pottery in Athens." *Hesperia* 7, 429–467.

Frantz, M. A. (1942). "Turkish pottery from the Agora." *Hesperia* 11, 1–28.

Gini-Tsofopoulou, E. (2001). "The Mesogaia from Early Christian times to the Ottoman conquest." In K. Tsouni (ed.), *Mesogaia*. Athens: Athens International Airport, 148–197.

Gregory, T. (1984). "Cities and social evolution in Roman and Byzantine South-East Europe." In J. L. Bintliff (ed.), *European Social Evolution: Archaeological Perspectives*. Bradford: University of Bradford Research Ltd, 267–276.

Gregory, T. E. (2006). *A History of Byzantium*. Oxford: Blackwell.

Gregory, T. E. and P. N. Kardulias (1990). "Geophysical and surface surveys in the Byzantine fortress at Isthmia." *Hesperia* 59, 467–511.

Haldon, J. F. (1990). *Byzantium in the Seventh Century. The Transformation of a Culture*. Cambridge: Cambridge University Press.

Haldon, J. F. (1992). "The Ottoman state and the question of state autonomy: Comparative perspectives." *Journal of Peasant Studies* 18, 18–108.

Haldon, J. F. (2000). *Byzantium. A History*. Stroud: Tempus.

Harvey, A. (1983). "Economic expansion in Central Greece in the eleventh century." *Byzantine and Modern Greek Studies* 8, 21–28.

Harvey, A. (1990). *Economic Expansion in the Byzantine Empire, 900–1200*. Cambridge: Cambridge University Press.

Hayes, J. W. (1972). *Late Roman Pottery*. London: British School at Rome.

Hayes, J. W. (1992). *Excavations at Sarachane in Istanbul: The Pottery*. Princeton: Princeton University Press.

Hayes, J. W. (1997). *Handbook of Mediterranean Roman Pottery*. London: British Museum Press.

Jacoby, D. (1991–1992). "Silk in Western Byzantium before the Fourth Crusade." *Byzantinische Zeitschrift* 84–85, 452–500.

Jameson, M. H., C. N. Runnels, and T. H. Van Andel (1994). *A Greek Countryside. The Southern Argolid from Prehistory to the Present Day*. Stanford: Stanford University Press.

Kazhdan, A. P. (ed.) (1991). *The Oxford Dictionary of Byzantium*. Oxford: Clarendon Press.

Koder, J. (1996). "Perspektiven der Tabula Imperii Byzantini." *Geographia Antiqua* 5, 75–86.

Koder, J. (2006). "Land use and settlement: Theoretical approaches." In J. F. Haldon (ed.), *General Issues in the Study of Medieval Logistics*. Boston: Brill, 159–183.

Kourkoutidou-Nicolaidou, E. (1997). "From the Elysian fields to the Christian paradise." In L. Webster and M. Brown (eds.), *The Transformation of the Roman World AD 400–900*. London: British Museum Press, 128–142.

Laiou-Thomadakis, A. E. (1977). *Peasant Society in the Late Byzantine Empire: A Social and Demographic Study*. Princeton, NJ: Princeton University Press.

Lang, F. (2009). "A method for the activity analysis of Medieval sites." In J. L. Bintiff and H. Stöger (eds.), *Medieval and Post-Medieval Greece. The Corfu Papers*. Oxford: BAR Int. Series 2023, 157–165.

Lehmann, H. (1939). "Die Siedlungsräume Ostkretas." *Geographische Zeitschrift* 45, 212–228.

Leigh Fermor, P. (1966). *Roumeli: Travels in Northern Greece*. London: John Murray.

Liebeschuetz, J. H. W. G. (2007). "The Lower Danube region under pressure: From Valens to Heraclius." In A. Poulter (ed.), *The Transition to Late Antiquity on the Danube and Beyond*. Oxford: Oxford University Press, 101–134.

Lock, P. (1995). *The Franks in the Aegean 1204–1500*. London: Longman.

Lock, P. and G. D. R. Sanders (eds.) (1996). *The Archaeology of Medieval Greece*. Oxford: Oxbow.

Magdalino, P. (1990). "Church, bath and diaconia in Medieval Constantinople." In R. Morris (ed.), *Church and People in Byzantium*. Birmingham: Centre for Byzantine, Ottoman and Modern Greek Studies, Birmingham University, 165–188.

Malingoudis, P. (1991). *Slavi sti Mesaioniki Ellada*. Thessaloniki: Ekdoseis Banias.

Mee, C. and H. Forbes (eds.) (1997). *A Rough and Rocky Place. The Landscape and Settlement History of the Methana Peninsula, Greece*. Liverpool: Liverpool University Press.

Megaw, A. H. S. (1966). "The Skripou Screen." *Annual of the British School at Athens* 61, 1–32.

Morgan, C. H. (1942). *Corinth, XI: The Byzantine Pottery*. Cambridge: Harvard University Press.

Oikonomou-Laniado, A. (2003). *Argos Paléochrétienne. Contribution à l'étude du Péloponnèse byzantin*. Oxford: BAR Int. Series 1173.

Papanikola-Bakirtzi, D. (ed.) (2002). *Everyday Life in Byzantium*. Athens: Ministry of Culture.

Papanikola-Bakirtzis, D., E. D. Maguire, and H. Maguire (1992). *Ceramic Art from Byzantine Serres*. Urbana and Chicago: University of Illinois Press.

Papanikola-Bakirtzi, D., F. N. Mavrikiou, and C. Bakirtzis (1999). *Byzantine Glazed Pottery in the Benaki Museum*. Athens: Benaki Museum.

Pettegrew, D. K. (2007). "The busy countryside of Late Roman Corinth: Interpreting ceramic data produced by regional archaeological surveys." *Hesperia* 76, 743–784.

Piérart, M. and G. Touchais (1996). *Argos. Une ville grecque de 6000 ans*. Paris: CNRS.

Polychronaki, M. (2005). "Late Byzantine lead seals from the Demetrios Economopoulos Collection." *Museum of Byzantine Culture* 12, 67–80.

Potter, T. W. (1987). *Roman Italy*. London: British Museum Press.

Poulter, A. (ed.) (2007). *The Transition to Late Antiquity on the Danube and Beyond*. Oxford: Oxford University Press.

Rautman, M. L. (1990). "Archaeology and Byzantine Studies." *Byzantinische Forschungen* 15, 137–165.

Rautman, M. L. (1998). "Handmade pottery and social change: The view from Late Roman Cyprus." *Journal of Mediterranean Archaeology* 11(1), 81–104.

Rautman, M. L. (2006). *Daily Life in the Byzantine Empire*. Westport: Greenwood Press.

Sanders, G. D. R. (1996). "Two kastra on Melos and their relations in the Archipelago." In P. Lock and G. D. R. Sanders (eds.), *The Archaeology of Medieval Greece*. Oxford: Oxbow, 147–177.

Sanders, G. D. R. (2000). "New relative and absolute chronologies for 9th to 13th century glazed wares at Corinth: Methodology and social conclusions." In F. Hild and J. Koder (eds.), *Byzanz als Raum*. Wien: Österreichisches Akademie der Wissenschaften, 153–173.

Sanders, G. D. R. (2003). "Recent developments in the chronology of Byzantine Corinth." In C. K. Williams and N. Bookidis (eds.), *Corinth, the Centenary 1896–1996*. Athens: American School of Classical Studies, 385–399.

Schreiner, P. (2001). "Drei Kulturen in Byzanz." In C. Stiegemann (ed.), *Byzanz. Das Licht aus dem Osten*. Mainz: Philipp von Zabern, 2–18.

Stephenson, P. (1999). "Byzantine policy towards Paristrion in the mid-eleventh century: Another interpretation." *Byzantine and Modern Greek Studies* 23, 43–66.

Svoronos, N. (1959). "Recherches sur le cadastre byzantin et la fiscalité aux XIe et XIIe siècles: le cadastre de Thèbes." *Bulletin de Correspondance Hellénique* 83, 1–145.

Vida, T. and T. Völling (2000). *Das slawische Brandgräberfeld von Olympia*. Rahden: Verlag Marie Leidorf, Archäologie in Eurasia 9.

Vionis, A. K. (2001). "Post-Roman pottery unearthed: Medieval ceramics and pottery research in Greece." *Medieval Ceramics* 25, 84–98.

Vionis, A. K., J. Poblome, and M. Waelkens (2009). "The hidden material culture of the Dark Ages. Early medieval ceramics at Sagalassos (Turkey): new evidence (ca. AD 650–800)." *Anatolian Studies* 59, 147–165.

Vroom, J. (2003). *After Antiquity: Ceramics and Society in the Aegean from the 7th to the 20th Century A.C.* Leiden: Leiden University Archaeological Studies 10.

Vroom, J. (2005). *Byzantine to Modern Pottery in the Aegean. An Introduction and Field Guide*. Utrecht: Parnassus Press.

Zavvou, E. *et al.* (2006). *Sparta. An Archaeological and General Guide*. Sparta: Municipality of Sparta.

Further Reading

Dunn, A. (1999). "From polis to kastron in southern Macedonia: Amphipolis, Khrysoupolis, and the Strymon Delta." In A. Bazzana (ed.), *Castrum 5. Archéologie des espaces agraires méditerranéens au Moyen Âge*. Madrid: Casa de Velázquez, 399–413.

Vionis, A. (2008). "Current archaeological research on settlement and provincial life in the Byzantine and Ottoman Aegean." *Medieval Settlement Research* 23, 28–41.

18

Symbolic Material Culture, the Built Environment, and Society in the Byzantine Aegean

The Early Byzantine Period (ca. 650–843 AD)

Cormack (1985) has argued that Byzantine civilization was dominated by the Church. It deployed art, for whom it was the chief patron, as a means to reproduce a particular mentality which aimed to discipline everyday public and private life. The Byzantine world was portrayed as aspiring as closely as possible to Heaven on Earth, with the emperor and priesthood God's representatives in this grand design. Art could thus complement military action, strengthening the Byzantines' sense of destiny when the Eastern Roman Empire was threatened with total destruction during the Dark Age centuries.

Cormack uses the example of Saint Demetrius in his great pilgrim church at the city of Thessaloniki. Martyred in the fourth century AD, his symbolic role as divine patron of the town was soon a focal point of resistance to enemy attacks. In the late sixth century large Avar and Slav forces besieged the town but the threat was beaten off, not least by the saint himself, whose supernatural embodiment took to the walls to repel the invaders. A celebratory depiction of ca. 620 (Figure 18.1) shows the saint with one arm round the city's religious head, the bishop, the other around the regional military and civil governor, the *eparch*. Although the saint's body had not been preserved, a special shrine (*ciborium*) had been erected. This was a highly-decorated locale with dedications and artworks donated by the poorer faithful and local elites, and it became a focus for bringing the sick for miraculous healing, for prayers of personal intervention, and even for timely manifestations of the saint to assist the city in times of need. These might include, alongside sieges, food shortages and civil unrest. The Church encouraged this local "hero cult" to control and inspire the town's population.

We can also observe that wealthy aristocrats had by now diverted the wealth they had in pagan times spent for public entertainments and civic monuments, into the construction and decoration of churches and monasteries. Here they were often portrayed as pious donors, alongside the saints and even more powerful Christian figures such as Mary or Jesus.

The intimate relationship between Byzantine life and Orthodoxy meant however that crisis in society could be refracted into religion. Since Christian symbolic culture and its associated rituals were the central medium for reproducing Orthodoxy, it becomes less surprising to find that the "Dark Ages" of the seventh to mid-ninth centuries also provoked an Empire-wide assault on icons known as *Iconoclasm* ("the smashing of images"). From the early seventh century onwards, Islamic armies had swept out of Arabia and in astonishingly rapid conquests had driven Byzantine

The Complete Archaeology of Greece: From Hunter-Gatherers to the 20th Century AD, First Edition. John Bintliff.
© 2012 John Bintliff. Published 2012 by Blackwell Publishing Ltd.

Figure 18.1 Saint Demetrius mosaic, Thessaloniki (ca. 620 AD).
E. Kourkoutidou-Nicolaidou and A. Tourta, *Wandering in Byzantine Thessaloniki*. Athens 1997, Figure 191. Photo © Kapon Editions.

power from the Levant and North Africa. They then raided and threatened the surviving rump Eastern Roman territory for the succeeding two centuries. At the same time the Church grew immensely rich and politically influential, encouraging the populace to orient their mentalities to the magical power of icons and the mystical power of the clergy, rather than to the army and the emperor. An influential sector of the Byzantine secular elite, as well as more fundamentalist Eastern church leaders, began to believe that the defeat of the Empire and its threatened imminent demise was due to God's displeasure at the perversion of his commands. Was it not forbidden by Moses' Commandments to create graven images to worship? The cult of icons encouraged embracing and kissing of images, the belief that many were of

supernatural rather than human manufacture, and widely-accepted tales that they could weep or bleed, and that their subjects could step out of the icon to work wonders. Was it not Islam which was more in God's favor, with its stricter adherence to the non-portrayal of human or divine forms in its religious art, and hence the bringer of justified chastisement on Byzantine idolatry?

Between 726 and 780 and again from 813 to 843 AD, the imperial power and a body of favorable church leaders pursued a policy of Iconoclasm throughout the Empire: figurative church images were destroyed or painted over, and replaced by simple crosses and similar aniconic symbols. Contemporary historical sources may exaggerate the scale of destruction (Haldon 2000) and in Greece it may have been weakly implemented (Bouras 2006), but nonetheless this was an attempt to reorient deeply-rooted ways of thought in Byzantium public life. Icons had become a significant personal focus in the home, where women played a role in private worship denied them in public religious affairs, and it seems that iconoclasm was resisted in many domestic circles, not least because icon-worship offered women personal fulfillment, nor was this sphere a focus of official persecution. Significantly, it was indeed females of the imperial family who were responsible for the revival of icons which ended both periods of Iconoclasm.

We must always recall, however, that alongside the well-preserved religious art surviving today in churches, museums, libraries, and private collections, there was also a secular art, of hunting, battle, circus, and erotic scenes, almost all destroyed, just occasionally intruding into Christian contexts (Effenberger 2001, Maguire 2005).

Symbolic Culture of the Middle Byzantine Era (843–1204 AD)

The ninth century marks a turning-point in Byzantine fortunes. Over the preceding century the Greek countryside had been reconquered from Slav tribes, and now the Arab threat was increasingly distanced through successes by the army and fleet. A strong dynasty, the Macedonian, seized power in 867 AD under Basil I and this inaugurated an era of sustained prosperity for the Byzantine Aegean until the late eleventh century.

This new confidence encouraged the public revival of the icon, as the powerful focus of an empire representing itself as the closest mankind could get to God's Kingdom on Earth, with its saints physically approachable and conceived as regularly active within everyday public and private life. A more confident secular power could allow the Church and its powerful symbolic propaganda machine back into partnership in controlling the Byzantine people and their mentality. This was also made clear in Byzantine coinage (Gregory 2006), the essential way in which the emperor became known to his subjects. From the end of Iconoclasm one face had the emperor with his symbols of power, accompanied by Christ, the real ruler; on the reverse came the imperial family crowned by Christ or Mary. In the representational arts and literature, imperial revival stimulated imitation of Classical forms (Greek and Roman) to remind citizens and Barbarians that what we term the Byzantine world was the unconquered Eastern Roman Empire.

Even more significant was a major transformation in the way that a new form of church corresponded to a novel iconographic program, which together almost universally separates the monuments of the Late Roman and Early Byzantine epochs from those of Middle to Late Byzantine times. Actually the change in design appears to have occurred during the political and iconoclastic crisis of the seventh to eighth centuries AD but the all-important new world of images awaits the end of iconoclasm and the recovery of the Empire's confidence in the ninth century (Mathews 1998). Whereas the earlier church design, dominated by longitudinal basilicas, created open, public areas, decorated with flexible narrative scenes, the majority of later monuments are compressed, multiple-enclosure areas, usually variations on a domed cross-in-square plan (Color Plates 18.1 and 18.2), and with a more controlled program of symbolic forms, that are also formally blocked into specific interior spaces. The new church concept, the commonest (but far from exclusive) design till the present day, envisaged it as a container for a particular religious experience in which the separate elements of its iconography are actively participating. At the

same time, the shift from early to later church design reflects a redirection of ceremonial from longitudinal processions in which the congregation had participated, suited to the basilica, to rituals centering on the frontal appearance and special acts of the clergy, with the congregation boxed into a focal central space and as largely passive observers (see following Text Box).

It has been observed that typical public Middle Byzantine (MB) churches are normally smaller than their predecessors, attributed to smaller populations (hence smaller congregations), and less surplus wealth, as the Empire slowly recovered from its Dark Ages. The comparison is certainly overdrawn since MB rural parish and monastic churches are ubiquitous. Moreover many large urban EB basilican churches were still in use and thus covered the needs of considerable congregations. In addition, smaller size is somewhat illusory, as traditionally Orthodox services have spilled out into the areas around the church, with doors open so that large bodies of worshippers can swell the numbers present inside and still participate in the service. Worship also emerges into the open air for processions and outdoor ceremonies.

In rural districts the simpler basilica construction continued to be built as a minority (and cheaper) alternative to the new centralized domed form (Bouras 2006). Indeed in many, perhaps most Greek provincial landscapes, there exist innumerable small churches of a different and so simple a plan that they are so far very hard, or even impossible, to date (Bouras 2006, Nixon *et al.* 2009). Still what is clear about the new, dominant church design is the marshaling of the inner congregation into an almost spotlighted central space beneath the main dome, where participants receive spiritual power from the religious activities directly before them at the apse screen, and from the all-surrounding sacred beings who line the walls up to and including the roof itself.

Outside of the great cities such as Constantinople or Thessaloniki, where multi-story apartment blocks competed with religious domes for the townscape skyline, the larger class of the new churches dominated the typically low-elevation ordinary houses and the occasional larger town house or palace of the upper classes. This accentuated the "monumental time" which they represented, in contrast to the more perishable secular buildings (Cormack 1985). The individual quarters of

The Cross-in-square Church Design

The key to the new church design that emerged from the EB era was a cross shape, whose arms were enclosed into corners to make a square, then roofed correspondingly by four barrel vaults or subsidiary domes over the arms, and a central dome over the crossing. The dome's thrust was transferred to its corner piers and the secondary vaults, as well as the enclosing corners between the arms. The design created a large, high auditorium, the center of the cross, where the congregation stood to receive spiritual power from all sides. Before them lay the apse(s), where the clergy conducted the key Orthodox rituals. The apse initially was set apart by a low screen with marble panels, but increasingly this rose higher to become a total barrier to vision onto which more and more icons accumulated, and behind which the priests gathered invisibly and prepared for dramatic appearances before the worshippers. With larger churches, the cross-in-square was preceded by one or two entrance-chambers (*narthex, exonarthex*).

The likeliest origins of the new plan are firstly, a small number of Justinian-era and subsequent EB churches, including Aghia Sophia in Constantinople, of basilica plan but enhanced by a dome above the space before the apse, and secondly, the Holy Apostles imperial mausoleum in the capital, a cross-form basilica with domes over sanctuary and arms (begun by Constantine the Great and rebuilt by Justinian). The MB design would thus combine the two main Early Christian monument forms (Bouras 2006, Papacostas 2010). So far the earliest examples of the full cross-in-square church are eighth- to early ninth-century monuments at Arta in Epirus, on the Cycladic island of Naxos, in the Propontis near the capital, and in Constantinople itself (Bouras 2006).

Outside, the new churches were ornamented with brickwork, mosaics, and inset glazed ceramics. The exterior tile and brick patterns can reflect cultural borrowing from the aniconic (non-representational) Islamic mosque, and include stylized Koranic script, such as the pseudo-Kufic designs at Osios Loukas in Central Greece. The interior of the MB church was a single vast icon with a relatively fixed program, relating particular themes to specific locations within the building. The inner frescoes and mosaics surrounded the congregation on all sides and also from above at increasing heights. According to the new programmatic placing of images (Mathews 1998), the ground level directly confronting the worshipper comprised "everyday" saints, including clergy (nearest the altar), the military, women, and healers. It became traditional to visit these individually, offering the *proskynesis* (a triple bow), the *apasmos* (kissing the image), then a personal address which might include a request. Intimacy with the lesser saints made worshippers aware of their real presence in the sacred space and inspired hopes to share in their eternal world, enhanced by their usual representation as standing figures, seemingly populating the same space as the worshipper.

The theme of physical and spiritual merging with the divine is continued at the next height level, the vaults beneath the dome, where the Body of Christ dominated narrative compositions. In contrast to Western Christianity, Christ was portrayed as muscular and sensuous, his body symbolizing transformation into eternal life in scenes of his baptism, crucifixion, burial, and transfiguration. In the apse there was often a Virgin and Child, a prominent but notably inferior placing; this recalls again the "embodiment" of God in Jesus, but also celebrates the remarkable religiosity and silent witness of women in Orthodox Christianity. Before the apse lay the screen, a decorated barrier to vision, with doorways sealed from sight by curtains. Behind the screen only clergy were active, and the steps of the screen, the doorways and the hidden rear space were used to create ritual dramas. The Bible readings, the sermons, the preparation and display of the elements of the mass, all became choreographed to the unaccompanied chanting of the priests and congregation, so as to create a striking effect on the worshippers. Once again the theme of God's body is central, with the mass being the climax, when the faithful consume the body and blood of Christ, and are thus physically and spiritually assimilated in turn into him.

At the next level up in the church iconography, in the various domes, we see Heaven, whilst the Evangelists, the Prophets, and Mary are shown as mediators between humans and God. But the central dome, high and directly above the congregation, is totally dominated by the image of Christ offering a blessing with his right hand. He embraces the worshippers below in his benediction and in his remote elevation symbolizes transforming strength, hence the naming of this image the *Pantocrator* (all-powerful).

The church's entrance gallery, the *narthex*, being naturally well-lit, could be used for daily prayers but also commonly served for burial rites, and hence is frequently painted with scenes of the Day of Judgment and Resurrection, focusing the worshippers' attention, on entering and leaving, on their eternal hopes as well as mortality.

As a visual unity, the Middle Byzantine church, the model for the commonest large Orthodox church plan up to the present day in Greece, not only portrayed in "surround-image" the community of the saints, apostles, and great divinities, but materialized the belief that during the sacred rituals this other world becomes alive and joins with the congregation in the ceremonies taking place. Middle Byzantine representational art of this period is thus austere and powerfully confrontational, well illustrated by the mosaic of Holy Luke in the Katholikon church of his monastery (Color Plate 18.3a).

Holy Luke is a monastic church complex, and indeed although most other new MB church buildings are small, many of the larger, such as this double church, are the result of the endowment of churches and monasteries by the rich and powerful, not only the royal family and top administrators, but also provincial elites. Such foundations allowed the ostentatious display of status and piety before the community, but could also include the mausolea of donor families and ensure continual prayers for their departed members. The imperial family regularly deployed church iconography to boost its secular image. Conquering emperors would be surrounded by military saints, whilst imperial families and other church donors appear, unselfconsciously, carrying bags of money for a church donation. "[I]n the 9th and 10th century [church] building activity was becoming one of the political activities of the Byzantine empire, the objective being to strengthen its authority in remote regions, where it had been weak or ignored for many years" (Bouras 2006, 70).

Byzantine towns were focused on churches and especially monasteries, not merely due to the rituals drawing in local inhabitants (services in and around them, processions emanating from or coming to them), but also because they were community welfare centers, their complexes including schools, hospitals, old people's homes, and soup-kitchens.

Whereas the official Church was close to the imperial court, monastic institutions were not and were in fact commonly hostile to the secular authorities and hence closer and more influential to the people (Schreiner 2001). Monks traveled and spoke demotic (everyday) Greek, as opposed to the almost incomprehensible classicizing use of language in court life. The popular influence of monks was also enhanced by the ubiquitous dispersion of small monasteries and the power and pilgrimage attraction of major monastic centers such as Mount Athos.

By the end of the MB era monasteries owned vast swathes of the landscape, forming small semi-urban foci of agricultural production, craftwork, and art. Their usual plan (Gregory 2006) was a walled rectangle, around whose periphery lay the abbot's or abbess's residence and the monks' or nuns' cells and a formal reception-room. Central to the complex was a church or even two, one for visitors and the other for the monastic community. There were also service buildings and rooms for study and art production. Apart from market- and kitchen-gardens within and around the monastery, its extensive agricultural estates might be so distant that satellite estate-centers (*metochia*) were set up to manage them. The greatest center of monastic life in Greece, and the richest landowner collectively, was the multiple monastery peninsula of Mount Athos in coastal Macedonia, where the earliest communities settled in the ninth century and the first major monastic complexes date from the late tenth century (Cormack 1985).

The artists

We can truly marvel at the power and beauty of Byzantine art and architecture. Its craftsmen were not surprisingly in demand in neighboring societies, either sent from within the Empire or working from surviving schools of Christian art within the Islamic world. The Early Islamic Dome of the Rock Mosque in Jerusalem and the Great Mosque in Damascus employed Christian mosaicists for their decoration, whilst the spectacular Great Mosque in Cordoba culminates in a prayer-niche (*mihrab*) which glows with mosaics made by craftsmen sent on request from the Byzantine emperor. Likewise in Italy, the revival of mosaic art in Rome from the ninth century, in the mosaic decoration of Saint Mark's Cathedral in Venice between the eleventh and thirteenth centuries, and in the great churches in the Norman kingdom of Sicily in the twelfth century, all betray the inspiration of MB church art and at times the hands of Greek craftsmen (Runciman 1975).

Nonetheless Middle Byzantine artists were not the high-profile, named individuals we are familiar with from Renaissance Italy. Instead their status was as skilled craftsmen, who at their highest level were an imperial "civil service team." Their goal in Church art was the reproduction of the essential concepts of belief on which Byzantine mentalities were rooted. Inevitably, the representation of eternal truths, and the close links between artist and ecclesiastical patron, encouraged the enforcement of conventions in religious art: how particular saints or secular figures

should be shown, appropriate gestures and colors, tended toward a formal pattern, limiting experimentation. We may find this constricting, and indeed it has resulted in lesser works, to be found in most Orthodox churches today, unadventurous copies of standard images, still made in styles developed 1000 years ago. Yet Orthodox believers rightly challenge "Western" expectations of artistic individuality. Byzantine art is deliberately "traditional," ultimately connected with Neoplatonic ideas emphasizing the unchanging qualities of the sacred world and its divinities, which lie "beyond time." In the essential element, the icon, a saintly face is characteristically frontal to the viewer, with little background to distract attention, its large staring eyes opening a direct avenue of communication to the divine (Cormack 1985). It is deliberately two-dimensional, formalized, and symbolic rather than realistic (Gregory 2006). Moreover, the higher-quality products of Byzantine art *did* witness changing styles, even within the confines imposed by a commitment to numerous traditional conventions.

The material culture of status and ceremonial

Byzantine secular and religious life were manifestly integrated through ritual processions: through communities, and into, out of, and between churches and monasteries. Elites were prominent in such events, which could occur on a weekly basis. In Modern Greece, important Orthodox ceremonies retain this character.

Secular power was also supported by a gradual elaboration of court and provincial ceremonial, culminating in instructions within the *Book of Ceremonies* compiled by the tenth-century emperor Constantine Porphyrogenitus. The imperial bureaucracy was extremely hierarchical and this was expressed in rules of precedence, complex dress codes (forms and color), and set modes of address. On the most formal occasions the place and movements of officials or representatives of the people could be choreographed and even set to music.

Embassies from the medieval West were surprised by the lavish ornamentation of the body for both sexes in elite Byzantium, including precious metal jewelry, gemstones, and enamel. Silk production was an imperial monopoly. If we add to this the fact that particular colors and a special cut to clothes were used to define official status, we can see that control over prestige dress formed a source of power (Jacoby 1991–1992). Gifts of Byzantine silk were diplomatic items in external relations, hence their survival in royal and cathedral treasuries in Western Europe and not in the plundered Empire itself (Fulghum 2001–2002).

Dress codes allows us a brief comment on attitudes to gender in Byzantine society. As with Classical Greece, our sources suggest that wealthy women were expected to cultivate modesty and seclusion in the presence of male strangers in the home, deploying veils or retiring to a women's quarter. Some Orientalists have even suggested that Islamic veiling may have arisen under Byzantine influence. But as with the ancient parallels, working women moved freely and without veiling whether in urban trades or assisting with agricultural tasks in the country. Ibn Battuta noted for fourteenth-century Constantinople that women were omnipresent in retail occupations and craftwork (Sigalos 2004b). In fact Byzantine women appear to have enjoyed greater freedom to work in a range of jobs, and engage in business management and legal affairs, than their antique predecessors (Herrin 1983). At the highest level, several empresses ran the Empire for under-age male heirs or arranged their own marriages to retain power.

Symbolic culture during the Comnenoi dynasty, 1081–1185

It is widely accepted that the shift in public mentality from confidence in the eternal order of the Byzantine world, symbolized in the Macedonian era (867–1081) by a strong, if not severe, art style, to the contrasted experience of political turmoil and imperial decline under the Comnenoi dynasty and in the subsequent Late Byzantine eras, stimulated new and remarkable artistic achievements. These can be characterized as experiments in surrealism and emotional expressionism, with more depth and dynamism to the images. The embattled state, under regular attack from the medieval West and the Seljuk East, as well as undermined by the growth of rapacious landlordism in its own countryside, nourished a change in mentality

which finds expression in a more sensitive, humanistic religious art (Cormack 2000).

The imperial family and powerful state officials still commanded sufficient wealth to endow churches and monasteries with buildings and artworks, where this new more personal view of the world can be seen. Especially popular was the image of Mary as the compassionate Mother, loving of her Son but also grieving in anticipation of His fate (the *Eleousa*). The most famous example is an icon (the "Virgin of Vladimir") gifted to the Duke of Kiev by the Patriarch of Constantinople. This art style was highly influential in Italy, for example in the twelfth-century churches of the Norman kingdom of Sicily and the mosaics of the Byzantine-style cathedral in Venice. Mosaics were increasingly replaced by frescoes, cheaper in a declining state economy, but also, with their stronger outlines, more suited to the new intimate humanistic style, compared to the remoter glow of ideal forms in earlier glittering mosaics.

Symbolic Culture of the Late Byzantine Era

The Peloponnesian town of Mistra, center of a flourishing but isolated Byzantine province, by this period surrounded by Frankish territory, provides another "gallery" of church art in the new late style of Byzantium (closely paralleled in the wonderful Late Byzantine churches of Constantinople such as the Chora monastery, Color Plate 18.3b). Fantastic colors and expressionist composition join with emotional humanity to create a last flowering of independent Byzantine art in the final centuries of the fragmented and besieged Empire, especially in the fourteenth-century churches of the Aphentiko and Peribleptos. Also exceptional is the art in a series of churches in the empire's second city Thessaloniki, founded by the city's ecclesiastical hierarchy rather than the imperial family and regional aristocracy, reflecting the town's more socially diverse commercial culture (Rautman 1989).

This Late Byzantine humanist style was clearly the basis for the earliest art of the Italian Renaissance, where Duccio and Giotto elaborated their masterpieces from a thorough grounding in the "Greek

Style" (*maniera greca*). Yet here is a difference: whereas the Byzantine anonymous masters still strove to present realistic images of eternal figures, the Italian pioneers transformed designs copied from imported icons by rooting their subjects in a precise time and place and person (Mathews 1998), commencing a very different concern with the world here-and-now, and with the individual. However, Byzantine art itself reflects the mutual entanglement between its society and that of the West, created through commerce, warfare, and the Frankish colonization of the Aegean. It can be seen to develop new aspects from this era onwards which reflect artistic trends in Italy: for example in the twelfth century some Byzantine artists sign their name (Cormack 1985), something that becomes common in post-Medieval Orthodox churches.

The Urban Built Environment

Byzantine power recovered from the ninth century onwards, encouraging prosperity and expansion in both the capital and regional towns. Although the higher Byzantine elite considered life outside Constantinople as a form of banishment, and provincial towns (Thessaloniki excepted) were far less grandiose and cosmopolitan, literary sources make clear that in Middle Byzantine times regional towns accumulated wealth from commerce and manufacturing, as well as from their mainstay of income from surrounding agricultural estates. Nonetheless sources report that even Constantinople had very few streets wide enough for carriages, and off these one entered a rabbit-warren of winding alleys navigable on foot or with pack-animals. Unsurprisingly, limited excavations reveal that provincial towns were unplanned mosaics of meandering streets around irregular house-plots (Gregory 2006), which developed organically rather than to a set geometric plan. Nonetheless, in Corinth (Figure 18.2) within the old forum, by at least the eleventh century, the town center was flourishing, eventually comprising a wide street flanked by shops, including temporary affairs marked by post-holes, and with multiple workshops for bronzesmiths and for ceramic and glass production (Sigalos 2004a). Mistra also had a great open square before the Palace

for public gatherings. However major exchanges between town and country and at the interregional level often took place in extramural markets and fairs. Apart from the capital and Thessaloniki, with their large quarters for foreign merchants, another exception to the typical urban design of the town-plus-castle (essentially a market and service center for an agricultural region), was the coastal port-town of Monemvasia in the Peloponnese, which specialized in trade and piracy: the Upper Town was reserved for the governor, the elite, and major churches, the Lower for sailors and merchants (Avramea 2001).

The commonest Byzantine town plan (Avramea 2001) was a fortified settlement with separate citadel and lower town, the latter organized round parish churches and monasteries (see Mistra Text Box). Much of the population owned farmland and many commuted out to work in their fields, whilst usually a household owned a vegetable plot by the house or within the walls for kitchen-produce. The town was run by the governor, the bishop, and the local elite of officials and landowners ("the powerful" or *dynatoi*), the latter two possessing multi-story mansions contrasted with the simpler, single- or two-story rectangular homes for ordinary citizens. The elite founded monasteries and small churches within the urban fabric, further embellished by founders' inscriptions and paintings, as well as burial chapels reserved for them.

The archaeology of the Byzantine house is still in its infancy and just hints emerge from published plans and textual comments (Sigalos 2004a–b). For the first stage, the Early Byzantine centuries of crisis, we might expect limited new construction and patching-up of those buildings still in use from Late Roman times, amidst much abandoned space due to depopulation in towns. Certainly written sources agree, offering a semi-rural picture even for Thessaloniki in this phase. Excavations in Athens, Corinth, Thebes, and Thessaloniki show continued use of Late Roman houses with some internal modifications. This practice continues into MB times, where we have excavated house areas from Corinth and Athens for example. These courtyard houses continue ancient forms, mostly reusing existing Roman structures of this design, but in Corinth it seems that this type clusters near the center of the town, has

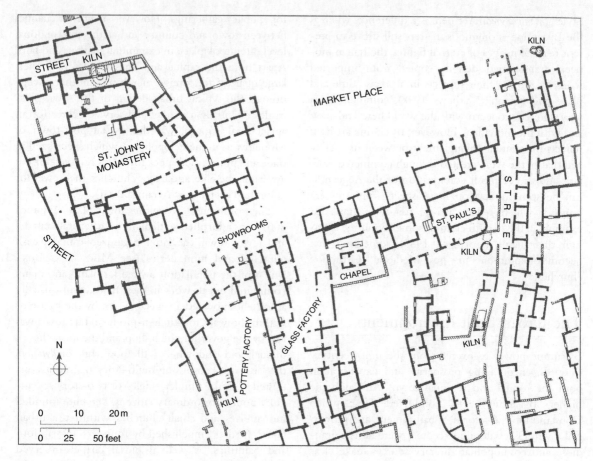

Figure 18.2   The center of the town of Corinth in the eleventh to twelfth centuries.
C. Mango (ed.), *Oxford History of Byzantium*. Oxford 2002, 200 (unnumbered figure). © Oxford University Press.

much storage space, and is associated with signs of urban commerce and artisan production. Probably it belongs to a wealthier class of resident, prosperous from the economic revival of this period. Although dating from the subsequent Frankish period, one good example is a domestic-cum-manufacturing complex located in a large courtyard house. Within this, the small, one-roomed ground floor units were probably workshops and shops, with bronze-working the chief activity. It is likely that domestic accommodation existed above on the first floor. The entire house might have been the property of a wealthy citizen, for which parallels exist in texts. Such elaborate houses have some half dozen rooms and areas 200–300 m² or more.

A more typical middle-class two-story courtyard house seems to have located animals and stores on the ground floor and domestic accommodation above (Gregory 2006). One central aspect of the Greek traditional two-story house is the elevated open balcony (*hagiati*), offering an intermediate working and living space between indoor and outdoor space. An enclosed projecting upper story (*ondas*) can also increase living space and the circulation of light and air into living-rooms. Although the precise form and functions of the *hagiati* and *ondas* in traditional Greek houses are closely associated with Oriental house influences, there is evidence that the basic habit of allowing the upper story of a house to encroach over the street below, projecting out from the ground floor, whether fully walled-in or open in parts as a balcony, also existed in Byzantine urban settlements. Some larger houses at Mistra for instance show enlarged balconies, although there are Italian architectural influences in this late town which may also be a design source for this feature.

A second excavated house type is usually single-story, has two or more rooms, and lines the street and/or borders a yard. At Chalcis for example, larger numbers of such simpler homes have been found further out near the edges of the town, interpreted as working-class or urban-farmer accommodation, and when they occur in direct association with workshops might be homes for a lower artisan class (Sigalos 2004a–b). Such simpler linear houses often have just one or two, occasionally three to four rooms and may have no yard areas, and average 50–100 m². A busy neighborhood in Chalcis gives a picture of this poorer end of the urban environment.

Contemporary sources have led to suggestions that Byzantine women were secluded within the home, in a *gynaikonitis* (female apartment). We lack house details to confirm this image, but might be suspicious of the applicability of the custom outside the mansions of the rich.

At Athens, Corinth and elsewhere, the growth of the city is marked by MB expansion from Late Antique and Dark Age limits. In general the evidence from texts and archaeology reinforces the view of Alan Harvey (1990) that links demographic upturn in country and town with the rise of towns, both servicing, and supported by, increasing rural populations. The market for the expanding commerce and manufacturing seen in excavated town quarters would rest on a flourishing agrarian surplus and rising rural demand, and a modest interregional trade.

Rural Settlement Design and House Culture

If Byzantine towns created opportunities for a range of social classes to occupy houses from small dwellings, comparable to rural homes, to palatial multi-story mansions, it seems likely that villages and hamlets remained simple in their layout and the variety of their housing. It is suggested that Greek peasants in general occupied houses of limited size and internal complexity till the late nineteenth century, often on the Mainland just single-story (except in steep terrain where a basement was both necessary and easier to construct). The Mainland Agricultural Style (Sigalos 2004b) of rural settlement, consisting of a loose dispersal of longhouses with a broad façade, allowing much space between homes for open-air activities, appears already in MB times, and seems typical for a mixed-farming economy right up to living memory in many regions. One to two rooms, and animals under the same roof as the extended family, can reasonably be inferred from more recent use of such houses (see Color Plate 21.1b).

As for rural estate-centers of the rich, we are very poorly informed both from texts and archaeology. Some sources suggest that rural towers are not merely a Crusader introduction but were in use in Byzantine areas both to mark status and as protection for estate staff. A rare excavated example of an isolated complex estate-center from Pylos (in the province of Elis) dates from the twelfth century and has a square, two-story plan a little reminiscent of a tower house from later centuries, but is on a much smaller scale (Coleman 1969, 1986). Perhaps we can use the description provided by the fourteenth-century statesman Michael Choniates of his semi-rural palace in the outermost suburb of Constantinople as a guide to rural villas of the elite (Magdalino 2002): set within farmland the estate-center was vast, including domestic structures with upper galleries surrounding a paved courtyard, a church, gardens, cisterns, and aqueducts.

An Annales Perspective

The *long-term* perspective for Byzantium clearly challenges us to set this civilization as it saw itself, as a thousand-year empire which was "Part II" of the preceding thousand-year Roman Empire. In many respects there were important continuities. The emperor aspired to absolute power over remodeled provinces in the Eastern Mediterranean; the economy was of "ancient economy" type, resting at least initially on the tax of free town and village populations, which in turn relied essentially on agricultural surpluses primarily consumed regionally; at least initially, the

The Town of Mistra (Figure 18.3)

After 1204, Greece was divided into Frankish feudal realms, with just three major pockets of Byzantine resistance in Epirus and Anatolia. But by 1261 the Byzantines had driven the Crusaders out of the capital, and over the following two centuries they nibbled away at the Frankish dukedoms and baronies with considerable success. Mistra (Runciman 1980, Avramea *et al.* 2001, Chatzidakis 2003, Sigalos 2004a, Gregory 2006) had been founded in 1248 as a castle dominating the Vale of Sparta in the Southeastern Peloponnese, by the Frankish Prince of Achaia William II Villehardouin, but had to be surrendered to the revived Byzantine state in 1262. The citizens of the nearby regional town of Sparta migrated to this safer walled town, which became the seat of a semi-independent statelet or Despotate ruled by junior members of the imperial family, whose wealth and importance grew continually to the fifteenth century, as Mistra expanded its power over most of the Peloponnese. The enlightened patronage of the city's secular and ecclesiastical elite encouraged a circle of philosophers, writers, and artists to reside there, making it a vibrant center for a late flourishing of Byzantine culture.

The town has four parts (Figure 18.3). Initially the Frankish settlement focused on the uppermost, walled citadel (16), and below it the Upper Town (Kastro) with the first stages of the Palace (17) and some of the oldest houses. After the Byzantine takeover important monasteries developed below the walled Upper Town and these were subsequently incorporated inside a Lower Town (Mesokhorion) wall, within which gradually many additional houses were built, especially mansions of the leading families, as well as the Cathedral. Finally an extramural settlement developed beyond the Lower Town (Katochorion).

A series of impressive churches and monasteries scattered amongst the often expansive private mansions of the wealthy and powerful document a town that seems more prosperous than the capital itself, despite its far smaller scale. Nonetheless the impact of Frankish and especially Italian architecture is visible, in the foreign introduction of bell-towers, and design aspects in the homes of the elite and the Palace of the Despots (17). Second-story balconies supported with arcades, Gothic windows, towers, and large reception-halls seem to reflect Western influences in the town's mansions.

The houses, smaller and larger, follow however typical provincial town plans elsewhere on the Mainland, with a basic rectangle aligned across the slope, which is here steep enough usually to allow an extra story downslope (usually for stores), onto which additional units can be added longwise or at a right-angle, and in grander mansions also upwards. The austere stonework is relieved by large windows and doors, and the decorative use of brick and tile. Houses are often separated by open space and do not form coherent planned geometric blocks. Grander mansions have towers and many houses have a first-floor veranda with a view over the Sparta Valley (Figure 18.4). A large room on the first or second floor was the main domestic space, used for eating, socializing, and sleeping (*triklinion*), and can have spacious windows; wooden partitions may have offered privacy. The Palace of the Despots possesses a giant throne room on its second floor with Gothic features.

The streets were steep and narrow and not suited for carriages, thus used for foot, horse, and mule transport. Before the Palace was a large square for administrative and economic activities, although much marketing took place outside the Upper Town gate. Exceptionally a new aqueduct was built for import of clean water into the city, probably linked to cisterns and terracotta distribution-pipes.

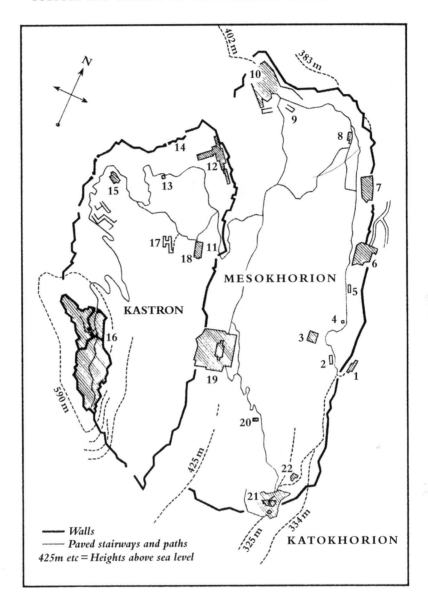

Mistra   1 Marmara, 2 Church of St Christopher, 3 Lascaris mansion, 4 well, 5 passage,
6 fortification, 7 Metropolitan Church, 8 Church of the Evanghelistria, 9 Church of
the Sts Theodore, 10 Hodeghetria Church, 11 Monemvasia Gate, 12 Palace of the
Despots, 13 Chapel, 14 Nauplia Gate, 15 Church of St Sophia, 16 Castle, 17 Palataki,
18 Church of St Nicholas, 19 Pantanassa, 20 Phrangopoulos mansion, 21 Church
of the Peribleptos, 22 Church of St George

Figure 18.3   Mistra: general town plan. Citadel = 16, Upper Town = Kastro, Lower Town = Mesokhorion, Extramural
Settlement = Katochorion.
S. Runciman, *Mistra: Byzantine Capital of the Peloponnese*. London: Thames and Hudson Ltd 1980, 94. Drawn by
Hanni Bailey.

Figure 18.4 The "Laskaris House," an aristocratic mansion at Mistra.
N. V. Georgiades, *Mistra*, 2nd edn. Athens 1973, Figure 6. Drawn by A. K. Orlandos. The Archaeological Society at Athens.

army rested on peasant conscripts; art and ceremonial show strong continuities with the Roman world, especially the former in periods of conscious "Classical revival." But the differences are as great: the total dominance of Christian belief being the chief novelty, not only in the balance between Church and State, but at times in open rivalry with the State. If we note the changes over time toward a dependent peasantry and mercenary armies, these were also features of the Late Roman Empire, but the lack of a strong regional urban identity with powerful, largely self-governing elites to whom provincial rule could be delegated strikes one as a fundamental contrast to the city-based world of Greek and Roman antiquity. Indeed apart from Thessaloniki, Byzantine towns were small and irregular.

In the *medium term* the rise and fall of Byzantium appears to follow many other cultural examples, and as so often internal decay and external aggressors can be invoked, although the novelty here in a World History perspective is the aggressive intrusion of the North Italian capitalist economy into that of the Byzantine world. For the *short term* both the success and failure of individual emperors or dynasties are relevant, as are certain events: such as the defeat of the imperial army by the Seljuk Turks at Manzikert in 1071 (leading to the loss of most of Anatolia), and the temporary destruction of the latter's successor, the rising Ottoman state, by the Mongol Khan, Tamerlane the Great, in 1402 (giving the Byzantine Empire another half century of life).

The overall mentality of the Byzantine world shows powerful strands of a central continuity, giving its citizens and elites a confidence in their superiority over other cultures and the will to survive. The focal belief in the state and the emperor as God's representatives on Earth further assisted in the reproduction of a significant military and cultural power in the Old World.

A Personal View

Byzantium has had a "bad press" since scholars of the European Enlightenment consigned it to a deviant, non-progressive path on their models for the gradual improvement of civilization. It remains a neglected area in the study of European and World History, and archaeologically we are, if one excepts the rich tradition of studies in ecclesiastical art and architecture, in the formative stage of a genuine discipline for Byzantine Archaeology where everyday life and settlement analysis are concerned. Closer examination of this impressive culture however makes clear that for many centuries the ruling classes in the rest of Medieval Europe and Russia saw Byzantium as a splendid civilization which they sought to emulate. Furthermore, the abundant remains of Byzantine life to be found in abandoned villages and small fortified towns throughout Greece, and indeed in other parts of the former Empire (Southern Italy, the Black Sea, Anatolia, and the wider Southern Balkans), would be an ideal focus for attracting the interest of young archaeologists looking for new research areas to colonize, away from the overpopulated discipline of Classical Archaeology.

References

Avramea, A. (2001). "Byzantine towns." In A. Avramea, D. Eugenidou, and J. Albani (eds.), *The City of Mystras*. Athens: Ministry of Culture, 23–31.

Avramea, A., D. Eugenidou, and J. Albani (eds.) (2001). *The City of Mystras*. Athens: Ministry of Culture.

Bouras, C. (2006). *Byzantine and Post-Byzantine Architecture in Greece*. Athens: Melissa.

Chatzidakis, M. (2003). *Mystras*. Athens: Ekdotike Athenon.

Coleman, J. E. (1969). "Ileia: Excavation of a site (Elean Pylos) near Agraphidochori." *Archaiologikon Deltion* 24B1, 155–161.

Coleman, J. E. (1986). *Excavations at Pylos in Elis*. Athens: American School of Classical Studies, Hesperia Supplement 21.

Cormack, R. (1985). *Writing in Gold: Byzantine Society and Its Icons*. London: George Philip.

Cormack, R. (2000). *Byzantine Art*. Oxford: Oxford University Press.

Dark, K. (ed.) (2004). *Secular Buildings and the Archaeology of Everyday Life in the Byzantine Empire*. Oxford: Oxbow Books.

Effenberger, A. (2001). "Kunst und Alltag in Byzanz." In C. Stiegemann (ed.), *Byzanz. Das Licht aus dem Osten*. Mainz: Philipp von Zabern, 65–75.

Fulghum, M. M. (2001–2002). "Under wraps: Byzantine textiles as major and minor arts." *Studies in the Decorative Arts* 9(1), 13–33.

Gregory, T. E. (2006). *A History of Byzantium*. Oxford: Blackwell.

Haldon, J. F. (2000). *Byzantium. A History*. Stroud: Tempus.

Harvey, A. (1990). *Economic Expansion in the Byzantine Empire, 900–1200*. Cambridge: Cambridge University Press.

Herrin, J. (1983). "In search of Byzantine women: Three avenues of approach." In A. Cameron and A. Kuhrt (eds.), *Images of Women in Antiquity*. London: Croom Helm, 167–189.

Jacoby, D. (1991–1992). "Silk in Western Byzantium before the Fourth Crusade." *Byzantinische Zeitschrift* 84–85, 452–500.

Magdalino, P. (2002). "Review of J.F. Featherstone 'Theodore Metochites's Poems'." *Byzantine and Modern Greek Studies* 26, 339–345.

Maguire, H. (2005). "'A fruit store and an aviary': Images of food in house, palace, and church." In D. Papanikola-Bakirtzi (ed.), *Food and Cooking in Byzantium*. Athens: Ministry of Culture, 133–146.

Mathews, T. F. (1998). *The Art of Byzantium*. London: Weidenfeld & Nicolson.

Nixon, L., S. Price, and J. Moody (2009). "Settlement patterns in Medieval and post-Medieval Sphakia." In J. Bintliff and H. Stöger (eds.), *Medieval and Post-Medieval Greece. The Corfu Papers*. Oxford: BAR Int. Series 2023, 43–54.

Papacostas, T. C. (2010). "The medieval progeny of the Holy Apostles: Trails of architectural imitation across the Mediterranean." In P. Stephenson (ed.), *The Byzantine World*. Abingdon: Routledge, 386–405.

Rautman, M. L. (1989). "Patrons and buildings in Late Byzantine Thessalonika." *Jahrbuch der Österreichischen Byzantinistik* 39, 295–315.

Runciman, S. (1975). *Byzantine Style and Civilization*. London: Penguin Books.

Runciman, S. (1980). *Mistra: Byzantine Capital of the Peloponnese*. London: Thames & Hudson.

Schreiner, P. (2001). "Drei Kulturen in Byzanz." In C. Stiegemann (ed.), *Byzanz. Das Licht aus dem Osten*. Mainz: Philipp von Zabern, 2–18.

Sigalos, E. (2004a). "Middle and Late Byzantine houses in Greece (tenth to fifteenth centuries)." In K. Dark (ed.), *Secular Buildings and the Archaeology of Everyday Life in the Byzantine Empire*. Oxford: Oxbow Books, 53–81.

Sigalos, E. (2004b). *Housing in Medieval and Post-Medieval Greece*. Oxford: BAR Int. Series 1291.

19

The Archaeology of Frankish-Crusader Society in Greece

Introduction

The main era of Frankish-Crusader rule in Greece lasted from 1204 AD till the early fifteenth century. In a wider context, its image is rather unfavorable. Compared with Byzantine civilization, which it helped to destroy, Frankish Greece appears as an episode with restricted geographic scope and even less cultural significance, and no lasting heritage. This phase of Western intrusion into the Aegean is moreover unknown to all but a few educated visitors to Greece and plays no significant role in the traditional "History of Greece." As for archaeology, it will be no surprise that a research focus on Frankish Greece hardly existed, apart from an obscure corner within the specialist field of "Castle Studies," until it was formally created in 1996, with the publication by Lock and Sanders of *The Archaeology of Medieval Greece*.

I was myself long mystified by the curious title "Duke of Athens" given to Theseus in Shakespeare's play *A Midsummer Night's Dream*. The Dukes of Athens and Thebes were in fact major players in the remarkable history of the Frankish adventurers who, in the wake of the Crusader conquest of Constantinople, carved out small states from the Mainland and Aegean islands (see Figure 17.5). Their story is available through contemporary chronicles in various Frankish languages, reflecting not only the diverse source of the conquerors of 1204, but also several waves of subsequent West European adventurers. After the initial dominance of French, Genoese, and Venetian colonizers, came the Catalans, Navarrese, and Florentines. The Venetians were always present and their possessions grew over time as the other Frankish states weakened; their avarice was indeed the prime force behind the diversion of the Fourth Crusade from recovery of the Holy Land to the easier prey of the terminally-weakened Byzantine Empire. These contemporary chronicles, and obscurer archives of secular and papal authorities, have long attracted medieval historians, producing most notably Miller's highly entertaining yet scholarly *Latins in the Levant* (1908), and a series of studies by Bon (e.g., 1969) and Setton (e.g., 1975). As noted previously, windows into rural life during these Frankish-Late Byzantine centuries appear in great detail from monastic records (Laiou-Thomadakis 1977, Lefort 1986). From the latter part of the Frankish era onwards there are also maritime charts and early maps of the Aegean to illustrate contemporary texts (Avramea 1985, Tolias 1999).

Historical sources, from political chronicles to monastic records and the earliest Ottoman imperial tax archives after their takeover of the Aegean, suggest a flourishing society in the Frankish sphere during the thirteenth and early fourteenth centuries, followed by a catastrophic decline in the late fourteenth to mid-fifteenth centuries, as the Crusader possessions

The Complete Archaeology of Greece: From Hunter-Gatherers to the 20th Century AD, First Edition. John Bintliff.
© 2012 John Bintliff. Published 2012 by Blackwell Publishing Ltd.

are afflicted by large-scale depopulation resulting from the great plague know as the Black Death, and constant warfare between the Franks, the Byzantines, and the Ottomans. In an effort to repopulate largely deserted agricultural lands, the last generation of Frankish lords and subsequently the earliest Ottoman administration encouraged a major rural resettlement by farmers and herders from Albania. Only a minority of Greek villages now survived, refuge communities lying in upland or otherwise remote locations where they had escaped pillage and enslavement; the Albanian colonizers spread like a tidal wave around them to dominate the Southern Mainland rural landscape (Bintliff 2000b, Kiel 1987).

Those striking landmarks of Western feudal power in Greece, the castles, had also inspired pioneer papers (e.g., Traquair 1905–1906), then classic publications by Bon (1937, 1969) and Andrews (2006 [1953]). Other aspects had attracted the interest of early archaeologists who had not yet learnt to confine themselves to particular periods of the Greek past, such as Wace's (1904–1905) study of Frankish sculpture in the Peloponnese. Additionally, major excavations on Classical sites such as the Athenian Agora and the center of ancient Corinth by American teams throughout the twentieth century revealed, and took appropriately seriously, significant overlying layers of Frankish occupation (when both towns were major feudal centers). Indeed today it is continuing work on Frankish Corinth (Sanders 2000, 2003, MacKay 2003, Williams 2003), which is providing the key sequence for Frankish-era ceramics and trade, as well as knowledge of Mainland urban planning. Corinth's Frankish town, with the adjacent massively-fortified acropolis mountain of Acrocorinth, was a significant possession of the Princes of Achaia, one of the most powerful baronies of Crusader Greece, whose residence was however closer to Western shipping at the still-imposing castle of Chlemoutsi and its nearby towns of Glarenza and Andravida, in Elis (Northwest Peloponnese).

For the wider landscape, the Austrian *Tabula Imperii Byzantini* (Koder 1996) provides for all relevant Byzantine provinces a gazetteer and map for all published Frankish-era monuments and excavations, together with places mentioned in historical sources. But it has been the rapid rise of regional surface

survey from the late 1970s which has provided a third pillar in the revival of Frankish Greece as a major focus of academic research. Intensive, multi-period surface survey, with its impartial interest in all periods of occupation of the Greek landscape, has found ample evidence of the Frankish era, and here our own experience on the Boeotia Project in Central Greece is indicative.

When Anthony Snodgrass and I commenced this regional surface survey in 1978, our interest was in reconstructing the prehistoric and Greco-Roman history of the landscape. We did not consider that the survey might reveal significant evidence for Medieval or post-Medieval Greece, and there was no serious published work to suggest this was feasible, given the sparse literature on monuments and ceramics for those eras. This rapidly changed when our ceramic assemblages from a series of farms and villages were dated by John Hayes, utilizing his immense experience in processing excavated post-Roman pottery from many countries of the Mediterranean. What previous survey projects had largely been confined to, assigning sites merely as "post-Roman" or "Medieval," shifted to dating them far more precisely. The possibility of a detailed phase by phase reconstruction of landscape developments within the lengthy interval 700–1900 AD immediately became apparent, and we seized this opportunity (Bintliff and Snodgrass 1985, Bintliff 1996b, 2000a).

Our expectations of the potential of surviving Frankish monuments also changed rapidly. In the early 1980s, as our survey teams walked large areas, we became ever more aware of a striking series of isolated towers which punctuated the Boeotian landscape, clearly of post-Roman age and adapted to pre-cannon warfare from their rudimentary defenses and arrow-slits (Figure 19.1). We invited a medieval historian and architectural expert, Peter Lock, to research the Boeotian towers. He later studied comparable structures in adjacent Attica and Euboea, including a giant medieval tower on the Acropolis in Athens which had been demolished in 1875. The implications of Lock's researches (1986, 1996, 1997) were considerable for the future development of Frankish Archaeology, since he concluded that most towers were probably built as rural control points for their village *fiefs* (land assigned to them) by the incoming thirteenth-century

Crusaders. With our new confidence in the datability of Medieval village surface ceramics, the opportunity opened of linking peasant villages to Frankish feudal towers, which proved itself almost immediately with the ideal example in site VM4 in the Valley of the Muses (see below). Meanwhile Lock updated older histories of the period with a new synthesis, *The Franks in the Aegean 1204–1500* (1995). The Frankish era was also well integrated into contemporary Late Byzantine history in the historical overview of Byzantium edited by Ducellier (1986). But archaeological survey teams still need to be more sensitive to the potential and pitfalls of using historical sources without experts on their project staff (Tsougarakis and Angelomatis-Tsougarakis 2009).

In the later 1980s and 1990s further survey projects followed our example in mapping the Frankish era in other regions of Greece: in the Peloponnese at Nemea (Athanassopoulos 1997), Asea (Forsen and Forsen 2003), the Corinthia (Kardulias 1997), and on the Pylos Project (Davis and Bennet 2009); on Crete the Mesara Survey (Watrous *et al.* 2004) and the Sfakia Survey (website http://sphakia.classics.ox.ac.uk/); and in the Cyclades on Kea (Cherry *et al.* 1990) and other island groups (Sanders 1996, Vionis 2001b, 2005).

In contrast to Boeotia and the Peloponnese, where barons and knights from France were initially in control, the dominant Frankish power in Crete and the Aegean Islands was the Venetian maritime empire. Significantly, whereas the first group of Frankish principalities was based locally and we lost almost all their records with their fall, except for narrative chronicles preserved in Western Europe, the "Serenissima" or "sublime" power of Venice kept a very close eye on its colonial empire from the city itself, where far richer archival sources still survive.

Frankish control in the Aegean did not completely disappear with the Ottoman conquests of the fourteenth and fifteenth centuries. Whilst the other Frankish powers were wiped out by the Ottoman conquest, the Venetians hung on to fragments of their Aegean Empire (Crete and some smaller Aegean islands and Mainland coastal dependencies), and made a serious attempt at reconquest of large sectors of Southern Greece as late as the end of the seventeenth century. For Venetian dependencies from the thirteenth to seventeenth centuries in Greece, plentiful archives exist (cf. McKee 1995), and a plethora of largely unpublished monuments (to modern standards that is). Although the Frankish principalities in the Peloponnese were largely non-Venetian until the Ottoman conquest, in the seventeenth century Venice briefly seized the peninsula from the Ottomans, leaving highly detailed landscape records now being exploited by regional survey teams (Davies and Davis 2007, Davis and Bennet 2009). The first results of combining regional survey and individual site survey with the Venetian archives are now appearing. This later Venetian archaeology will be covered with the archaeology of its contemporary Ottoman era in the Aegean in the following chapters.

Frankish Society

Western medieval society was relatively open for the free, non-serf population, in terms of marriage and landholding rights across the whole of Christendom, provided that the individuals concerned paid their allegiance, taxes, and if necessary military obligations, to higher authorities, whether kings, barons, or city councils. Given the small scale of the Frankish emigration to Greece during and after the Fourth Crusade, many local Greek notables could thus be conveniently and usefully incorporated into the Frankish power and landholding structure, although they retained their Orthodox faith. In fact the Catholic Church made little headway in converting Greeks to the Latin rite, except for the heavily Italianized Cyclades where a more significant immigrant population existed. As we have observed in previous chapters, later Byzantine society had been moving inexorably toward a semi-feudal structure, making intercultural cooperation that much easier. The elite families from both local and colonizing groups intermarried and we can see mutual influences in dress, ceremony, art and architecture, and ceramics.

The serious undermanning of Frankish fiefs in Greece was a more general problem with Crusader states in the Eastern Mediterranean, since large numbers of Westerners participated through allegiance to their overlords for the duration of specific campaigns of conquest, and having obtained, they hoped, some wealth from gifts of land and a share of booty, would leave for home (Phillips 1997). However a distinction needs to be made between this picture, typical for the Mainland landed Frankish elite, and that in the capitalist-minded regions dominated by Venice, such as the Cyclades, Crete, the Ionian Islands, and key fortified ports on the Mainland, where larger colonial populations resided and a more intense link between commercial estates, industry, and trade were encouraged by the highly interventionist Republic of Venice.

In terms of economy, Italian merchants were already a dominant force in the Aegean before the conquest of Constantinople, and were even more significant in the mature Frankish era and beyond. There is widespread evidence that the concurrent expansion of Italian commercial networks and Frankish colonization stimulated new levels of international trade and cultural exchange throughout the Mediterranean. Craftsmen may also have settled in the major centers, such as the Italian glassworkers suggested by Whitehouse (1991) to have set up production in Corinth.

Stone Centers of Power

Appropriately for a colonial expansion into an alien environment, increasingly detailed studies have appeared of the fortified centers of Frankish power, even if we still await modern archaeological and architectural study of the castles to match meticulous holistic monographs such as that for the contemporary Crusader castle of Belmont in the Kingdom of Jerusalem (Harper and Pringle 2000; cf. also Kennedy 1994). But there is a growing body of castle studies, building on older summaries by Bon (1937, 1969) and Andrews (2006 [1953]). This includes a Minnesota University team (Brenningmeyer *et al.* 1998, Cooper 2002, Coulton 2009), case studies by Burridge (1996), Gregory (1996), Vionis (2006), and the *Archi-Med* Venetian fortification project (Triposkoufi and Tsitouri 2002). The elaboration of Byzantine strongholds which were contemporary to Frankish states can best be seen in the remarkable ruins of the town and castle of Mistra (the latter originally constructed by the Franks) studied by several Greek scholars since Orlandos in the 1950s (Avramea *et al.* 2001).

Pringle's (1989) remarks for the Crusader Kingdom of Jerusalem serve equally well for Frankish Greece: the fortified centers of power were alien features in the landscape, representing both physically and symbolically the imposition of a foreign military elite upon a largely peasant native population. Frankish strongholds either mark the residences of the major barons (such as Chlemoutsi, the Athenian Acropolis, the Kadmeia at Thebes), or key strategic strongholds for movement by land or sea (such as Acrocorinth or Monemvasia). Contemporary texts allow distinctions between landscapes controlled directly by aristocrats from castles or fortified towns, and those where a few castles of the great lords were surrounded by innumerable towers where their dependent knights or soldiers dominated Greek villages. Attica, centered on Athens, and Boeotia, with its twin towns of Thebes and Livadheia, seem to be typical for the latter, whilst much of the Peloponnese seems organized in the first fashion with many striking castles.

It was formerly assumed that the Attic-Boeotian towers were built to police routes, but careful analysis (Lock 1986, 1996, Langdon 1995) shows otherwise (Figure 19.1). Firstly they are, in contrast to the isolated military watchtowers of Classical-Hellenistic Greece, rarely in very high locations permitting intervisibility with each other, or even commanding wide views in varied directions. Secondly, they are usually associated with an indigenous contemporary village. Their typical design is a two- to three-story rectangular structure with access via a door only at the first or even second floor, reached by a wooden stairway. The ground floor, accessible purely from within through an opening from the first floor, for defensive reasons, is a barrel-vaulted storeroom, whilst the upper floors form the public rooms and private living quarters of the permanent inhabitants. A fighting platform appears at roof level, and in well-preserved cases this is crenellated.

Sources and parallels from Western Europe whence the occupants and the design originated, indicate that these towers housed knights and even men-at-arms (*milites*), who administered Byzantine villages as fiefs within the lordship of regional barons. The ground-floor stores housed provisions against attack, but more normally contained the tax-dues in various agricultural products from dependent Greek villages. The

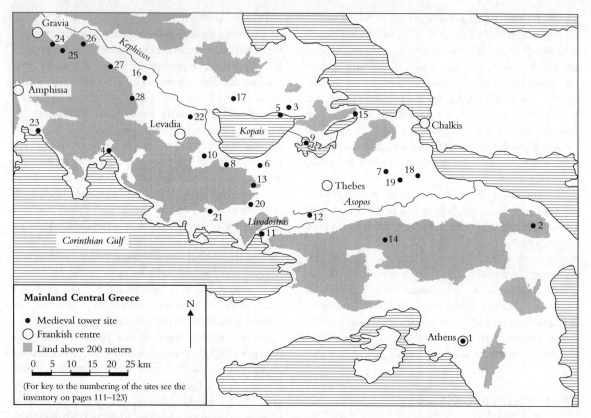

Figure 19.1 Distribution of Frankish-era feudal towers and urban centers in Boeotia. The now destroyed tower on the Athens' Acropolis is also marked.

P. Lock, "The Frankish towers of Central Greece." *Annual of the British School at Athens* 81 (1986), 101–123, Figure 1.

public rooms were necessary for administration, including judicial procedures, since the feudal elite had wide-ranging legal powers over their peasantry. Much grander versions, but with similar plans, appear as strongpoint-keeps and symbols of power built into the castles of the regional barons (such as that formerly at the entrance to the Athens Acropolis, demolished in 1875, and a survivor lying within the Museum at Thebes).

The intimate ties to local villages can be illustrated by the tower on the approaches to the modern town of Haliartos, in Boeotia. Although lying on the former main road linking the Peloponnese to Northern Greece, its location on a small rise is poorly suited to spot enemy movements, and is invisible to other local towers. Our surface survey around the houses of modern Haliartos revealed a Byzantine, Frankish, and

Early Ottoman village underlying the present town, which the feudal tower looked down onto.

The number of surviving towers in Attica-Boeotia is impressive, despite the destruction of many noted in Early Modern Travelers' accounts. Our fieldwork argues that Frankish towers control existing Byzantine villages which either survived as settlements from Late Antiquity, or reflect the ninth- to eleventh-century recolonization of the countryside. The major Frankish centers were usually ancient towns, such as Thebes and Livadheia for Boeotia, and elsewhere Corinth and Athens.

The immigrant colonizing power was insecure, not only through the antagonism of the surviving Byzantine forces, but from other potential conquerors in Greece, who proved successful in the case of the Catalan mercenary Grand Company of the early

The Village of VM4 Zaratova-Panaya

In the micro-landscape of the Valley of the Muses (see Figure 8.4), the Frankish impact is dramatic (Bintliff 1996a, Vroom 1999). Early in the thirteenth century, a feudal tower is erected 500 meters from the low-lying Byzantine village of Askra-Zaratova, on a high crag, and concurrently the majority of the villagers were displaced to a hillside immediately below the tower. Papal letters show that the new Catholic bishop, imported by the Franks, remained at Askra, and became the object of predation by the minor feudal occupier of the tower, a mere "soldier" (*miles*) rather than a proper knight (Lock 1995). Symptomatic of a class of unscrupulous adventurers who headed East to make their fortunes by exploiting local populations and other colonizers, this tower-holder beat the bishop up and burnt his crops, then calmly proceeded to Thebes to receive mass from the superior bishop! The new village (site VM4) shows a more extensive area than Middle Byzantine Askra, reflecting that continuous expansion of population seen elsewhere, despite increased feudal pressure on villagers.

fourteenth century, and the Ottoman Turks of the fifteenth century. The towers from which dependent villages were controlled were thus necessarily constructed against raids rather than for comfort. Finding the best location for a tower could mean moving the dependent village a kilometer or more, as happened in the case of Askra-Zaratova, relocated to our site VM4 but still within its definable settlement-chamber (see Box), or at Mount Tsalika in the Peloponnese (Gregory 1996). Where an ancient city site shrank to a Byzantine village, an interval tower of the Classical fortifications could be remodeled into a Frankish tower, seen in Boeotia at Thisbe and Chaeroneia. Near ancient Tanagra in Boeotia, a series of Middle Byzantine villages remain flourishing, from our surface ceramic study, in their Frankish phase. At two at least, a tower was constructed, one through remodeling its existing church.

A more spectacular example of Frankish rural settlement appeared during a severe drought in 1989, which lowered the surface of Boeotian Lake Ylike to levels rarely seen since the nineteenth century. Old reports of a submerged Frankish tower led us to visit the Klimmataria location, where we discovered not only the tower but a contemporary surrounding farm-complex (rather than an indigenous older village), its walls washed clean by the lake and the similarly washed ceramics lying in each room and open space. We were able to make a detailed plan of the site and collect the ceramics in each architectural context (Color Plate 19.1). Parallels can be found for such rural estates from the contemporary Crusader Kingdom of Jerusalem (Ellenblum *et al.* 1996, Ellenblum 1998) and with an excavated example from the Mesogaia rescue excavations in Attica (Gini-Tsofopoulou 2001). The medieval phase architecture of the site is highlighted in the colors red, light brown, and purple (the last-named is the feudal tower). It consists of a rectangular courtyard, with the small (at least two-story) feudal tower in its western edge. Rectangular rooms, probably only single-story, range the four sides of the court, with an exit to the northeast leading to an outer sector in which a range of three very long rooms, also single-story, project away from the court (stables?). West of the tower there are additional structures, in part built onto Greco-Roman buildings. Following Western feudal custom, the lord's own share of the land (*demesne*), separate from the villagers under his control whose surpluses came to him by right, was farmed separately, and perhaps the Klimmataria estate center, far from any known village, represents such a rural focus.

In contrast to the Latin Kingdom of Jerusalem, where large numbers of Frankish peasant villages were established, on the Greek Mainland Byzantine villages provided the base level of the feudal pyramid. Most appear to have stayed in their location, with the parasitical Westerners locating their controlling towers nearby.

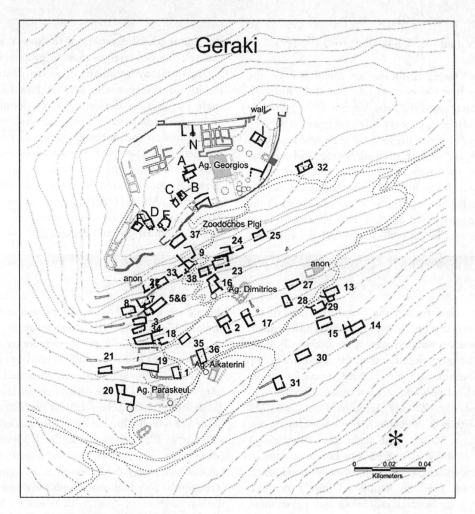

Figure 19.2   Castle settlement at Geraki, Peloponnese.
E. Sigalos, *Housing in Medieval and Post-Medieval Greece*. Oxford 2004, 202.

We already observed in the preceding, Byzantine chapters that indigenous Greek Medieval rural settlements are currently hypothesized for the Mainland to be weakly-structured nucleated villages or hamlets, with dispersed longhouses the norm, rarely more than one story, emphasizing the agricultural activities associated with the house, or sometimes craft production for the community. We are better informed for Frankish-controlled settlement plans, although published examples are mostly settlements associated with feudal fortifications of the small castle or tower variety. In these sites, there may also be a

defensive enclosure around the whole settlement, reminiscent of the Italian practice of *incastellamento*, where the lord walled in the dependent villagers, both to protect and to control them. The Frankish tower settlement at Panakton in Boeotia, perhaps only occupied for a few generations in the fourteenth and fifteenth centuries (Gerstel *et al.* 2003) possesses an inner enceinte around the feudal lord's tower, then a larger outer defense enclosing a dispersed collection of irregularly-aligned longhouses and small rectangular buildings. In the center of the outer settlement is an East-West single-aisle church.

The rugged Frankish-Late Byzantine castle-village of Geraki (Figure 19.2) (Simatou and Christo-doulopoulou 1989–1990, Sigalos 2004) in Laconia in the Peloponnese possesses a more elaborate plan. The lord's castle dominates with its elevated enceinte, centering on the Aghios Georgios church, with the complex building to its north probably the lord's residence. Other houses are more typically scattered irregularly around the upper enclosure. In the lower settlement houses are of longhouse or smaller rectangular type, the majority being aligned along the contours of this steep slope. Some longhouses lie across the contours, and on sloping sites this usually indicates that they took advantage of the elevation difference to construct a cellar-floor on the downslope end of the building, creating a "one-and-a-half-story" house. It would be normally suggested that the feudal elite, their retainers, and craft specialists dwelt in the upper settlement, the dependent peasantry in the lower. However it has been suggested that in the outer settlement those houses with extra floors may mark status or wealth divisions within the non-lordly class.

Additional studies of Peloponnesian fortified castle-villages have been published by Burridge (1996: Vardounia), Gregory (1996: Mount Tsalika), and Ince and Ballantyne (2007: Paliochora), the former two constructed by the early Franks, the last-named largely under the control of Venetian feudal lords. In these examples a feudal keep and/or mansions for the elite contrast with simple homes for the dependent peasantry, and site locations are highly defensible. Multiple churches of simple plan seem to be chiefly donated by the elite members of such settlements. An inner, foreign elite enclosure, and external Greek peasant enclosure, recall sites already mentioned and also the castle-village of Kephalos on the Cycladic island of Paros (Vionis 2006).

Although we lack rural open settlement plans for this period, we can probably see their character from those of the lower, indigenous peasant classes attached to feudal strongpoints, since as we have seen, almost all Frankish towers or small castles exploited nearby or immediately adjacent peasant communities. Similar peasant settlement- and house-plans continue to be the norm throughout the Ottoman and Early Modern period. In general, Aegean rural settlement is typically nucleated from Early Byzantine to the end of Ottoman times, with isolated farms becoming common only in the later nineteenth century AD. Independent rural estate-centers of feudal lords and the wealthy Ottoman landowners were the major exception to this tendency, and perhaps Klimmataria (above) represents an example. The Frankish conquest generally appears to have stimulated even denser rural settlement than previously and also growth in earlier villages. On Crete, survey also indicates that the Venetian impact is associated with a notable increase in population density over Middle Byzantine levels (Nixon et al. 2009).

Frankish Towns

On the Cyclades, Crete, and the Ionian Islands, Venetian maritime power came to dominate, although the Genoese and other Italian states colonized Greek islands on a lesser scale. The Cycladic islands were taken over by aristocrat families and their followers, creating genuine colonial urban enclaves within a wider and denser rural landscape of Greek villages. The favored locations for these foundations were visible and defensible locations, and here a highly nucleated town plan was introduced from Italian urban experience (Sanders 1996, Vionis 2001b, 2005, Sigalos 2004). The edges of the colonial settlement were either provided with a wall, or an outer ring of multi-story houses created a defense barrier. The residence of the dominant lord of the island was a central tower or small castle within this nucleation. Regular planning was preferred, for example on Antiparos (Figure 19.3b), but where the terrain was very hilly the rows of domestic houses and the narrow streets run along the contours, as on Siphnos or Astypalaia (Figure 19.3a). Some of these Italian planned towns were new foundations, others redeveloped sites used in earlier eras, but they begin in their planned form from the thirteenth-century Latin conquest of Greece, and most still preserve the main lines of their urban plan and individual house design.

The design scheme seems to echo not surprisingly the built environment of Medieval towns in Italy, with prominent residences for the ruling elite (fortified palaces for dukes and bishops, towers for leading landed

Figure 19.3a Astypalaia town with its focal Venetian castle.
E. Sigalos, *Housing in Medieval and Post-Medieval Greece.*
Oxford 2004, Figure 7.

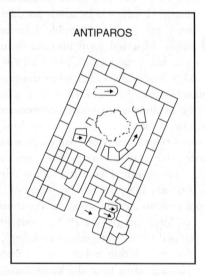

Figure 19.3b Plan of the old town on Antiparos centering
on the lord's castle or tower.
E. Sigalos, *Housing in Medieval and Post-Medieval Greece.*
Oxford 2004, Figure 12.

families), and street-lining rows of terraced multi-story
houses for the rest of the population (comparable to
"Borgo" habitations in Renaissance Italy, Sabelberg

1985). There is a significant difference however. In
Italy both wealthy and poor citizens of the town lived
in the same streets, regardless of class, except for the
uppermost stratum of aristocracy. In the colonial towns
established on the Aegean islands, the colonial settlers,
traders, manufacturers, and landowners occupied the
new planned settlements, whilst the Greek peasantry,
working for the incomers, occupied rural villages or
the irregularly-developing fringes of the colonial
town. The colony was centered on the local lord's keep
and an adjacent public square, which represented a
spatial and social focus for the community. This echoes
on a far larger scale the same concept as the courtyard
which accompanied many private family residences.

Within these towns the ordinary colonist house
(Vionis 2001b, 2005) was of two storys, terraced with
similar neighbors along the street front. The adoption
of flat roofs was a reflection of the dry Aegean climate,
and it is interesting that also in the Crusader states of
the Levant, colonial settlements made the same adaptation (Boas 1999). Often the ground floor was used
for animals, storage of agricultural produce, craft production or shops, but sometimes different families
occupied the lower and upper floors. Generally however the house was for one household with domestic
accommodation in one or more rooms on the upper
floor. A simple division in these homes in their Early
Modern occupation of less public, more private space
toward the interior, could well be applicable to their
Medieval use. In recent times the public outer half of
the domestic space was ornamented with textiles and
ceramics. There could also be a courtyard for work
and leisure, although the flat roofs and the streets
would also have been in use for various purposes as
house extension spaces. It is usually argued that
increasing elaboration in the number of built spaces,
with associated separation of room functions, including conceptual divisions between animals and humans,
is a mark of increasing social complexity (Kent 1990).
However the vertical layering of domestic housing in
the island colonial towns was just as much a consequence of the compression of large numbers of citizens in Italian towns with high prices for land plots
and the constraints of an urban defense wall, as symptomatic of a bourgeois mentality of domestic life.

What is unique in the Aegean is the remarkable
conservation till today of what are largely thirteenth-

century AD settlement and house designs. The Aegean islands certainly suffered from regular pirate raids, but were little transformed by Ottoman rule, or the devastations of the War of Independence and later industrial developments. Only Syros saw major rebuilding in the nineteenth century, when it briefly formed a national center of commercial shipping wealth and became a focus of Neo-Classical architecture (Kartas 1982). At the beginning of the twentieth century, with the rise of Modernism in Western European architecture, the replicated Medieval whitewashed box-agglomerations of the Aegean island towns had survived to stimulate architects such as Le Corbusier (Michaelides 1972).

On Crete and the Ionian Islands, direct rule from Venice as opposed to the indirect rule on the Cyclades through dominant Venetian families, led to a series of port-towns where characteristic features of North Italian and Venetian Adriatic urban planning and architecture are found: urban defense works which grow increasingly massive over time (Triposkoufi and Tsitouri 2002), major squares associated with state offices, warehouses and fleet facilities, stylish mansions renewed at intervals in fashionable styles for the wealthy elite, and Italianate churches. In the countryside villas accompanied extensive commercial estates, also in imported styles. The physical presence of Venice, in particular in Cretan Rethymnon, has both inspired a pride in the historic role of the town but also modern resentment at restrictions its citizens now endure when wishing to modernize it (Herzfeld 1991).

Mainland towns under both Frankish and Byzantine control benefited from the rise, beginning in later Middle Byzantine times, of a wealthy residential class, combining extensive landowning with investment in regional trade and manufacture. This class of *archontes* was very significant to the flourishing of provincial towns, some of which received formal privileges in the Late Byzantine-Frankish era as "communes." With the political fragmentation of power due to the multiple competing states and duchies, towns could gain more autonomy and economic initiative, which was also stimulated by the general penetration throughout the Aegean of the boats and merchants of the highly commercial Italian states such as Genoa and Venice. The Latin Conquest, in enhancing the inroads of Western commerce, had

at least one positive effect in increasing urban exchanges and a greater commercialization of rural markets. In the major commercial towns there were quarters for merchant families of different statehoods, including warehouses, offices, and residences for traveling traders. However, we should not overestimate the urban scale of Frankish towns. MacKay comments: "Corinth was no city, and in the Frankish period probably never much of anything but a fortress town and ecclesiastic center, but it did harbor foreign merchant enclaves" (2003, 419).

At Athens the successive dukes dwelt on the Acropolis, where massive fortifications were erected (Figure 19.4). They converted the ancient entrance-complex or Propylaea into a palace dominated by an immense tower. The Parthenon of the goddess Athena was appropriately rededicated as a church to the Virgin Mary (Camp 2001).

The rather grander Mainland houses in larger villages, castle-settlements, and towns, which could represent ruling elites, are two or more storys high, with separate access to a domestic first floor from the ground floor. The latter was often barrel-vaulted and in use for storage, stabling, and workshops and could enclose a cistern fed by rainwater. An open yard spread before the house, which in some cases could be fortified, with loopholes for archery, although the yards are not normally walled. At the first-floor domestic access point, open balconies can be found of a *hagiati* type, which thus allowed house occupants to vary their activities flexibly between indoors, outdoors or in an intermediate climate. Rarely a tower is incorporated into such larger houses, of two or three storys in height. The main reception room on the first floor (*triklinos* in the Byzantine sources) was a long chamber combining, as in the smaller colonial houses on the Cyclades, public social as well as private living space. The display side of wealthier homes and also feudal towers can be seen in architectural refinements on the main reception floor (first or second), such as Gothic tracery windows and vaulting. The lack of genuine private space remains the case for all but three-story mansions, where the extra floor was free of public access. In the case of feudal towers, as noted earlier, the main reception floor could be used for public affairs of the district such as judicial proceedings and the reception of serfs and tenants.

Figure 19.4 The Frankish Athenian Acropolis. Lower right, the Propylaea converted into an impressive palace for the Dukes of Athens. The Parthenon, already a Byzantine church, was rededicated as a Catholic cathedral to the Virgin Mary. The entire hill was massively refortified. On the left are the ruins of the older temple of Athena and next to them the Erechtheum. © Dimitris Tsalkanis, www.ancientathens3d.com.

In summary, if we except the built colonial towns of foreign aspect implanted in the Aegean and Ionian islands and on some colonial outposts on the Mainland, we might characterize the remaining Medieval Greek settlements as articulated by a small number of narrow and winding streets flanked by freestanding houses with attached open yards in a generally dispersed pattern. Numerous churches would mark distinct neighborhoods and might reflect building and furnishing dedications by the wealthier families.

Frankish Churches and Monasteries

The Pope and Frankish lords encouraged the settlement of Western clergy, but Catholicism never gained a major foothold in the Aegean area outside of some Cycladic islands (Lock 1995). Despite gifts of land and other support, the Latin Church was a small, dispersed community with limited wealth compared to its Western counterparts. The monastic orders invited to settle in the countryside were also typically those with an austere lifestyle, so that the few surviving ecclesiastical complexes are simple rectangular basilicas with Gothic ornament applied sparingly, notably in the sanctuary (Panagopoulos 1979). Pitched wooden roofs accompany a vaulted sanctuary apse. In the few major towns there were also parish churches and monasteries, such as the excavated Saint John's monastery in Corinth. The focus of Frankish power in the Peloponnese was in Elis, close to contacts westwards by sea. Here the Villehardouin dynasty used the town of Andravida as their capital, and nearby built the giant stronghold of Claremont (Chlemoutsi), and three Gothic churches for various Latin monastic orders. That of Saint Sophia has been studied (Cooper 1996, Coulson 1996, Bouras 2006) and originally had a large central nave suitable for convening the court, and a smaller aisle for ceremonies of the monks (Figure 19.5a–b). Like most of the few surviving, and

Figure 19.5a The Frankish dynastic church of Saint Sophia, Andravida, Elis, Western Peloponnese. Photo Tasos D. Zachariou.

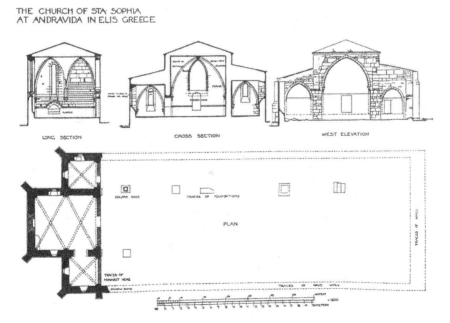

Figure 19.5b Plan from R. Traquair, "Frankish Architecture in Greece." *Journal of the RIBA* 31 (1923), 34–48 and 73–83 (also monograph, London 1923).

in any case originally rare, Latin churches on the Crusader Mainland, the plan is an apsed basilica with limited Gothic ornament. Such churches also preserve a fortified appearance, reflecting the insecurity of their founders in a hostile landscape.

In keeping with both Byzantine and Frankish practice, the Frankish elite were buried within churches, for which sadly only fragmentary inscriptions and architectural embellishments survive (Ivison 1996). Near Andravida the now-destroyed mortuary church of the Villehardouins of Saint James has yielded the thirteenth-century tombstone of Princess Agnes in a mixed Frankish-Byzantine style. The Byzantine church at Daphni in Attica became a Cistercian monastery and the burial-place of the Frankish Dukes of Athens: representing this elite are several recycled ancient sarcophagi found in the floor and the crypt, again combining elements of both Frankish and Byzantine art. The Athens Parthenon was also used for the burial of higher clergy and the Florentine Dukes of Athens; fragments of Gothic tomb architecture mixed with Byzantine styles survive as well as epitaphs on the columns. Ivison argues that Mainland Franks were more integrated into indigenous society and hence funerary art was hybrid, whereas on the islands of Chios and Cyprus a more exclusively Western society produced purely Gothic and Italian styles.

Ceramics and Frankish–Late Byzantine Society

Already from the MB era onwards, cultural interactions between Italy, the Aegean, and the Islamic Near East had given rise to shared technologies and styles in fine-ware production, although the initiative until the Italian Renaissance remained with Islamic manufacturers, who in turn were often inspired by Persian and Chinese ceramics. The lively trade around the East Mediterranean encouraged by the establishment of the Frankish principalities, and especially stimulated by Italian merchants, was enhanced by the close political links forged between them, which included the new Frankish-Crusader polities throughout the Aegean. Nonetheless because this stylistic network-

Table 19.1 Better-quality tableware on typical Italian rural sites (after Blake), for comparison with the Greek evidence.

1050–1350	Exotica and tin-glazed types absent
1350–1500	Tin-glazed (majolica) present
1500–1700	Slip-coated types replace majolicas
1750–1900	Peak in cheap (increasingly factory-made) glazed wares

ing around the Eastern Mediterranean had already been shared from preceding centuries, in many respects the early Frankish levels at the town of Corinth show much similarity in pottery to the underlying MB ones (Williams and Zervos 1993). Although functional analysis of Frankish period rural sites is still in its infancy, most studied so far show access to wider interregional trade in ceramics, although the bulk of pots were locally made. Suiting Hugo Blake's (1980) generalizations for Italian rural life (Table 19.1) during the same High Medieval period, so also the Greek rural world possessed good but not highest-quality table wares. The latter are found in numbers in major towns with significant international trade connections, such as Thebes, Corinth, and the Venetian colonies.

However a different aspect of social history relates to the story of dining habits in Europe. Our medieval assemblages are comparable to those not only of the preceding Middle Byzantine era, but also to other South European countries such as Italy and Spain during the period 1000–1400 AD. People of all classes ate seated on chairs or benches, and consumed their various dishes from wide, open serving dishes shared by several adjacent diners. Only at the very end of the Middle Ages, during the fifteenth century, did it become common in Italy to introduce individual bowls and plates for each diner. Whilst however this tendency in Western Europe was to develop further in association with the rise of Capitalism and individualism, resulting in a full suite of personal ceramics, glasses, and table cutlery (Gaimster 1994), Greece shifted during Ottoman times into Oriental eating (both in culinary terms and in table manners), as we shall see, and still focused on central shared dishes. Nonetheless some changes are visible in the ceramics of the Frankish period in the Aegean (Vionis 2001a,

2009). Dishes become deeper, which in Western Europe has been linked with a growing tendency to stew main meals in their juices, rather than rely on roasted meat. More dishes seem to appear on some scenes of dining in this period, which might be the first signs of catering to some extent to the individual diner, but could equally mark a wider range of side-dishes to supplement the main item on the menu, placed centrally in the largest dish on the table. Contemporary sources tell us that the Byzantines disapproved of Frankish cuisine, where greasy spitted or stewed meat dishes were the most desired, themselves favoring a more varied diet including salads and vegetables. Could the occasional scenes of mixed dishes mark a merger of Western and Eastern tastes?

In the LB-Frankish period glazed wares rise in their share of assemblages (Sanders 2000) and spread wider from tableware and into domestic shapes (see Color Plate 19.2a–b for tableware variants). The thirteenth-century innovation of tripod-stilts (to allow easier stacking in the kiln) and other improvements to production seem to have increased the supply to markets. But social dining seems to have been very important even in rural hamlets, to judge by the remarkably high levels of decorated tableware on Boeotian deserted villages (Vionis 2008). Sgraffito (incision-decorated) wares continue to be very popular (Vionis 2001a), some of them traded around the Eastern Mediterranean, such as the finely-made Zeuxippos Ware (Color Plate 19.2a) and a thicker version called Aegean Ware (both primarily thirteenth-century). A common difference to MB Sgraffito is a rise in deeply grooved designs (gouged), including wares where large areas of the surface have been cut away to leave designs in relief (*champlevé*). But most pots were locally made, especially in the style called Brown and Green, or Late, Sgraffito, which continues from the late thirteenth to the seventeenth centuries (Color Plate 19.2a). This tends to be rather carelessly decorated with incised squiggles, wavy lines, and rarer flowers or animals, with added random splashes of green and brown paint. For details and fine illustrations of Frankish-era Sgraffito products see Ministry of Culture (1995), Papanikola-Bakirtzi (1999), and Papanikola-Bakirtzi *et al.* (1999).

Especially in the towns with good commercial links to the West, such as Corinth, more exotic imports are common (Vionis 2001a, MacKay 2003,

Sanders 2003, Ince and Ballantyne 2007). These include the polychrome RMR ware from Southern Italy (thirteenth to fifteenth centuries), the early tin-glazed wares such as South Italian Proto-Majolica (late twelfth to fifteenth centuries) (Color Plate 19.2b), and North Italian Archaic Majolica (thirteenth to seventeenth centuries). The taste of the Frankish colonizers will often have been met by their Western merchants in this way, although some of these wares are met occasionally on indigenous settlements too. Nonetheless case studies suggest that the Italian imports are generally found on colonial sites, and inside these are associated with the foreign elite quarters, while local wares typify the Greek domestic zones (Vionis 2006, Ince and Ballantyne 2007). Athens seems to have little of such Western wares and is more provincial (MacKay 2003).

The Fourteenth-Century Collapse

As we have noted earlier, despite the recorded shrinkage of the Byzantine capital during the Late Byzantine era, and the catastrophic contraction of the Empire due to the settlement of the Franks and the Ottoman Turks, those villages which we have studied in Boeotia and which came under Frankish rule from the early thirteenth century, show no clear decline from the archaeological evidence. If we consider their size and external trade contacts as evidenced in pottery finds, if anything there may be continued growth in rural settlements during the Frankish thirteenth century. As noted by Gregory (2006) here archaeological realities appear to contradict the historical sources, which emphasize warfare and disruption to life in the Aegean of this era. But all this changes drastically during the fourteenth and fifteenth centuries AD.

Although most surface ceramic finds can only be generally dated to a transitional period termed "Late Frankish-Early Turkish," which covers the fourteenth to sixteenth centuries, it is notable that on Greek village sites studied from surface survey in Boeotia, distinctive fourteenth- to fifteenth-century pieces are usually absent, in contrast to those of the thirteenth or sixteenth centuries. This archaeological evidence now goes well with official history of this era, with incessant warfare between the Franks and the Byzantines, both

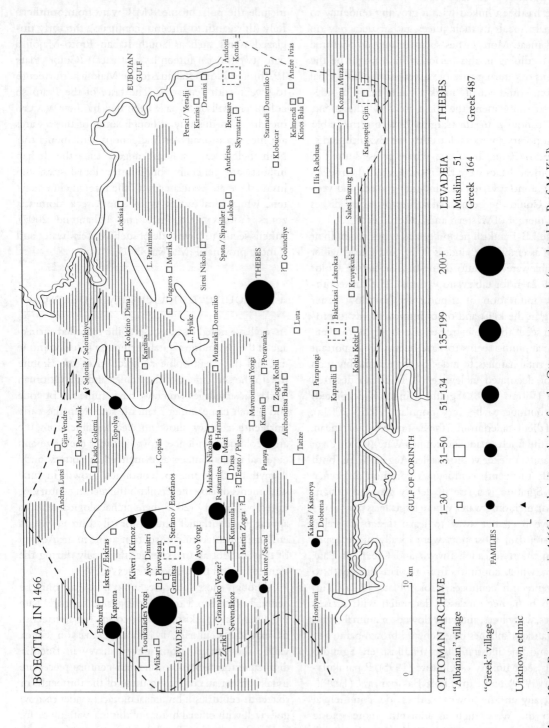

Figure 19.6 Boeotian settlements in 1466 by ethnicity and size after the Ottoman tax records (translated by Prof. M. Kiel). J. L. Bintliff, "The two transitions: Current research on the origins of the traditional village in Central Greece." In J. L. Bintliff and H. Hamerow (eds.), *Europe Between Late Antiquity and the Middle Ages*. Oxford 1995, 111–130, Figure 11.

against the marauding Turks, and fighting too between different Frankish armies. In 1311 for example, a mercenary army of Catalans wiped out the majority of the established French nobility of Central Greece and assumed their fiefs. Even more destructive was the European-wide eruption of the Great Plague from the 1340s onwards, which may have killed up to one half of urban and rural population in its recurrent outbreaks. Meanwhile, Ottoman Turkish raids on the coastlands were enslaving rural populations and driving others into more remote upland refuge sites. The famous cliff-top monasteries at Meteora in Thessaly begin in the fourteenth century in a remote environment (Gregory 2006). Excavations at Frankish Corinth also show a total decline in the town during the fourteenth century (MacKay 2003).

Late Byzantine monastery estate-records support fourteenth-century decline (see Chapter 17). Uniquely detailed records of the demographic devastation of this era also come from an unexpected source, the Ottoman Imperial Tax archives (Kiel 1997). One of the earliest of these "defters" comes from 1466, not long after the Ottoman conquest of Greece, and the full effects of the cumulative catastrophic events can be seen in this first preserved Ottoman tax register for the province of Boeotia (Figure 19.6), a kind of "Domesday Book" of Final Medieval Boeotia. The population described as "Orthodox Greek" is confined to the two towns of the province, Thebes and Livadheia, and to a handful of large villages around the Mount Helicon massif (including the tower-site VM4 ["Panaya"] discussed earlier). Elsewhere it is apparent that the landscape has been largely deserted by its Byzantine inhabitants. The nominal authority in Boeotia in the final century before the Ottomans, the Dukes of Athens and Thebes, fully aware of the disastrous consequences of depopulation both on agricultural production and the ability of the Duchy to withstand the threat of Ottoman conquest, invited large-scale immigration into the region by semi-nomadic Albanian clans, who were in any case migrating by force into Southern Greece (Jochalas 1971).

In the 1466 defter the "newly-settled" Albanian (*Arnavaudan*) clans (as they are usually described, since the process continued under Ottoman encouragement), can be seen as a wide scatter of small semi-

mobile hamlets (*katuns*). Careful work on the location of these Albanian villages shows that there must have been a deliberate policy to direct the newcomers to locations close to deserted Byzantine-Frankish village sites. Thus in the region in the north-center of the map above Lake Copais, just one tiny Greek village survives in 1466 (Topolya), but we see four small new Albanian hamlets. In the preceding Byzantine-Frankish era our field survey located several Byzantine villages and hamlets near these new colonies. One of the new Albanian foundations, Gjin Vendre, replaces a now-abandoned large Byzantine and Frankish village we termed site CN3, which in turn is a possible replacement for the adjacent ancient city of Hyettos (all three settlements are just a few hundred meters apart). We can assume that the inhabitants of CN3 and nearby Frankish-period hamlets, who may have been descendants of the ancient Hyettos city population, were either enslaved or killed by the natural or human threats of the fourteenth century, or had fled to one of the 1466 refuge "Greek" villages (shown in black). This required almost complete repopulation of the district by immigrants.

At another ancient Boeotian city, Thisbe, the case for a continuity of population on the ancient site, through Byzantine and Frankish times, together with a possible Slav admixture, is also strong (located in the southwest of the map, at the 1466 settlements Kakosi and Dobrena). Here depopulation during final Frankish times was severe but not complete, creating a fascinating settlement scenario. In 1466, next to the now inadequately small "Orthodox Greek" hamlet of Kakosi-Kastorya, which had formerly been a large, long-established and important Byzantine settlement, we find a new Albanian village, Dobrena (a name which may point to an abandoned Slav settlement selected for Albanian colonization). Here it seems the regional authorities, final Franks or the first Ottoman administration, deemed it advisable to boost the shrunken Greek community with new population.

In contrast, at the site of the ancient city of Thespiae, which continued as a village throughout the Byzantine and Frankish era, and where the Frankish lords were an Italian monastic order housed in a prominent tower, neither of the Frankish-period villages located by our survey survived the fourteenth-century crisis. This led to a sponsored recolonization, but onto a hill above the ancient and medieval settlements, by Albanian colonizers, founding the modern village till recently called Zogra Kobili (west of Thebes in the center of the map).

In the available series of villages studied by surface survey in Boeotia, despite the close spacing of Middle Byzantine and Frankish (Late Byzantine) villages, they are mostly small during the eleventh to thirteenth centuries. Nearly all are then abandoned during the crisis fourteenth century (cf. Figure 17.3b). But if the later fourteenth and early fifteenth centuries are a period of generalized indigenous depopulation, they are clearly also one of a concentration of Greek survivors into large refuge villages, all within the context of disruptive warfare and piracy.

Moreover, if the policy of Albanian repopulation failed to prevent Ottoman conquest of the Southern Mainland during the fifteenth century, both events succeeded in providing a strong basis for the agricultural and demographic recovery once the privations of the Conquest had passed, in which the small number of large Greek refuge villages would prosper exceptionally well, as we shall see.

An Annales Perspective

The expansion of military and commercial populations from Western Europe is the product of a medium-term cycle of recovery and growth there from the ninth to thirteenth centuries AD, after the traumas associated with the collapse of the Western Roman Empire. The eruption into Greece was anticipated by Norman colonization of Southern Italy, whilst Germanic and Scandinavian warriors and traders were active in settling and trading into Slavic Central and Eastern Europe. A particular extra element for the Aegean was the early capitalist commercial impact on the region from neighboring Italy. Climatic improvements in the same period ("The Early Medieval Warm Era") are also linked to demographic growth in Western Europe. The fourteenth-century population decline is a general European phenomenon too, combining a phase of climatic deterioration, ecological problems due to over-exploitation of land, and increasing civil and foreign warfare. In the long term, the Byzantine-Frankish rise and

decline is part of an agrarian demographic and economic cycle seen as characteristic for pre-industrial European mixed-farming populations (Ladurie and Goy 1982). Only one clear element sets this cycle apart, and that is the first development of Italian commercial states, which begin to create new mentalities and conditions of life in the Aegean during this period, and lastingly in the regions where Venice maintains control into the post-Medieval era. For the short term, the temporary capture of Constantinople by the Franks and their conquest of large areas of Greece appear less significant in the framework of the already advanced domination of the Byzantine economy by Italian commercial interests. Cultural mergers make a similar point, as does the convergence of Byzantine semi-feudalism with the full Frankish form for Greek peasantries. A clearer historical disruption is formed by the relentless rise of Turkish states in Anatolia. The weakness of the hinge region of Greece and the Balkans between powerful Islamic states and similarly strong Christian states further west meant that the fate of this area was unpredictable. In fact the decisive division of power was to be set in the Adriatic, so that only the Ionian Islands remained beyond Islamic control.

A Personal View

The Crusaders remain in Western (but certainly *not* Eastern) eyes a romantic community of fearless adventurers in picturesque costumes, notably restored to attention by the recent film *The Kingdom of Heaven*. Modern scholarship more soberly, and with an eye to "post-colonial" critiques, has reminded us of a ruthless, avaricious streak that ran through all the Crusades. The sacking of Christian Constantinople and the conquest of the Byzantine Aegean become unsurprising in this more negative perspective. Yet to be honest, one's sense of adventure can still be stirred by the description of Frankish life in Greece, as accessibly told by Miller (1908), and all of us involved with Frankish Archaeology in Greece are rather enthralled by detecting the material culture associated with the Villehardouin, the de la Roche, the de Brienne, and other great houses. More positively, the cultural exchanges and indeed intermarriages between Franks and Byzantines have long-term impacts, such as the stimulus given to early Renaissance art in Italy by exposure to Late Byzantine painting, and the never-broken commercial links between Western capitalist commerce and some Greek communities (especially on the Aegean islands), which will increasingly encourage the development during the Ottoman period of a wealthy, internationalizing Balkan merchant class.

References

Andrews, K. (2006 [1953]). *Castles of the Morea*. Princeton: American School of Classical Studies at Athens.

Athanassopoulos, E. F. (1997). "Landscape archaeology of Medieval and pre-Modern Greece: The case of Nemea." In P. N. Kardulias and M. T. Shutes (eds.), *Aegean Strategies*. Lanham: Rowman & Littlefield, 79–105.

Avramea, A. (1985). *Chartes ke chartographoi tou Aigaiou pelagos*. Athens: Olkos.

Avramea, A., D. Eugenidou, and J. Albani (eds.) (2001). *The City of Mystras*. Athens: Ministry of Culture.

Bintliff, J. L. (1996a). "The archaeological survey of the Valley of the Muses and its significance for Boeotian history." In A. Hurst and A. Schachter (eds.), *La Montagne des Muses*. Geneva: Librairie Droz, 193–224.

Bintliff, J. L. (1996b). "The Frankish countryside in central Greece: The evidence from archaeological field survey." In P. Lock and G. D. R. Sanders (eds.), *The Archaeology of Medieval Greece*. Oxford: Oxbow, 1–18.

Bintliff, J. L. (2000a). "Reconstructing the Byzantine countryside: New approaches from landscape archaeology." In K. Blelke *et al.* (eds.), *Byzanz als Raum*. Wien: Österreichische Akademie der Wissenschaften, 37–63.

Bintliff, J. L. (2000b). "Deconstructing 'the sense of place'? Settlement systems, field survey and the historic record: A case-study from Central Greece." *Proceedings of the Prehistoric Society* 66, 123–149.

Bintliff, J. L. and A. M. Snodgrass (1985). "The Cambridge/ Bradford Boeotian Expedition: The first four years." *Journal of Field Archaeology* 12, 123–161.

Blake, H. (1980). "Technology, supply or demand?" *Medieval Ceramics* 4, 3–12.

Boas, A. J. (1999). *Crusader Archaeology. The Material Culture of the Latin East*. London: Routledge.

Bon, A. (1937). "Forteresses médiévales de la Grèce centrale." *Bulletin de Correspondance Hellénique* 61, 136–208.

Bon, A. (1969). *La Morée franque*. Paris: De Boccard.

Bouras, C. (2006). *Byzantine and Post-Byzantine Architecture in Greece*. Athens: Melissa.

Brenningmeyer, T., F. Cooper, and C. Downey (1998). "Satellites, silicon and stone: Spatial information and Greek archaeology." *Geo Info Systems* 8(1), 20–28.

Burridge, P. (1996). "The castle of Vardounia and defence in the Southern Taygetos." In G. Lock and G. D. R. Sanders (eds.), *The Archaeology of Medieval Greece*. Oxford: Oxbow, 19–28.

Camp, J. M. (2001). *The Archaeology of Athens*. New Haven: Yale University Press.

Cherry, J. F., J. C. Davis, and E. Mantzourani (1991). *Landscape Archaeology as Long-Term History*. Los Angeles: Institute of Archaeology, University of California.

Cooper, F. (2002). *Houses of the Morea: Vernacular Architecture of the Northwest Peloponnesos (1205–1955)*. Athens: Melissa.

Cooper, N. K. (1996). "The Frankish church of Hagia Sophia at Andravida, Greece." In P. Lock and G. D. R. Sanders (eds.), *The Archaeology of Medieval Greece*. Oxford: Oxbow, 29–47.

Coulson, M. E. (1996). "The Dominican church of Saint Sophia at Andravida." In P. Lock and G. D. R. Sanders (eds.), *The Archaeology of Medieval Greece*. Oxford: Oxbow, 49–59.

Coulton, M. B. (2009). "The Morea Vernacular Architecture Project." In J. Bintliff and H. Stöger (eds.), *Medieval and Post-Medieval Greece*. Oxford: BAR Int. Series 2023, 153–156.

Davies, S. and J. L. Davis (eds.) (2007). *Between Venice and Istanbul. Colonial Landscapes in Early Modern Greece*. Athens: American School of Classical Studies, Hesperia Supplement 40.

Davis, J. L. and J. Bennet (2009). "The Pylos Regional Archaeological Project." In J. Bintliff and H. Stöger (eds.), *Medieval and Post-Medieval Greece*. Oxford: BAR Int. Series 2023, 89–91.

Ducellier, A. (ed.) (1986). *Byzance et le monde orthodoxe*. Paris: Armand Colin.

Ellenblum, R. (1998). *Frankish Rural Settlement in the Latin Kingdom of Jerusalem*. Cambridge: Cambridge University Press.

Ellenblum, R., R. Rubin, and G. Solar (1996). "Khirbat al-Lawza, a Frankish farm house in the Judaean Hills in Central Palestine." *Levant* 28, 189–198.

Forsen, J. and B. Forsen (eds.) (2003). *The Asea Valley Survey. An Arcadian Mountain Valley from the Paleolithic Period until Modern Times*. Stockholm: Swedish Institute in Athens.

Gaimster, D. (1994). "The archaeology of post-Medieval society, c.1450–1750: Material culture studies in Britain since the war." In B. Vyner (ed.), *Building on the Past. Papers Celebrating 150 Years of the Royal Archaeological Institute*. London: Royal Archaeological Institute, 283–312.

Gerstel, S. E. J. et al. (2003). "A late medieval settlement at Panakton." *Hesperia* 72, 147–234.

Gini-Tsofopoulou, E. (2001). "The Mesogaia from Early Christian times to the Ottoman conquest." In K. Tsouni (ed.), *Mesogaia*. Athens: Athens International Airport, 148–197.

Gregory, T. E. (1996). "The medieval site on Mt Tsalika near Sophiko." In P. Lock and G. D. R. Sanders (eds.), *The Archaeology of Medieval Greece*. Oxford: Oxbow, 61–76.

Gregory, T. E. (2006). *A History of Byzantium*. Oxford: Blackwell.

Harper, R. P. and D. Pringle (eds.) 2000. *Belmont Castle. The Excavation of a Crusader Stronghold in the Kingdom of Jerusalem*. Oxford: Oxford University Press.

Herzfeld, M. (1991). *A Place in History: Social and Monumental Time in a Cretan Town*. Princeton: Princeton University Press.

Ince, G. E. and A. Ballantyne (2007). *Paliochora on Kythera: Survey and Interpretation*. Oxford: BAR Int. Series 1704.

Ivison, E. A. (1996). "Latin tomb monuments in the Levant 1204–ca.1450." In P. Lock and G. D. R. Sanders (eds.), *The Archaeology of Medieval Greece*. Oxford: Oxbow, 91–106.

Jochalas, T. (1971). "Über die Einwanderung der Albaner in Griechenland." *Beiträge zur Kenntnis Südosteuropas und des Nahen Orients* 13, 89–106.

Kardulias, P. N. (1997). "Reconstructing Medieval site locations in the Corinthia, Greece." In P. N. Kardulias and M. T. Shutes (eds.), *Aegean Strategies*. Lanham: Rowman & Littlefield, 107–122.

Kartas, A. (1982). *Syros. Elliniki paradosiaki architektoniki*, Vol. 2. Athens: Melissa.

Kennedy, H. (1994). *Crusader Castles*. Cambridge: Cambridge University Press.

Kent, S. (1990). "Activity areas and architecture: An interdisciplinary view of the relationship between the use of space and domestic built environments." In S. Kent (ed.), *Domestic Architecture and the Use of Space*. Cambridge: Cambridge University Press, 1–8.

Kiel, M. (1987). "Population growth and food production in 16th century Athens and Attica according to the Ottoman Tahrir Defters." In J.-L. Bacque-Grammont and E. van Donzel (eds.), *Proceedings of the VIth Cambridge CIEPO Symposium*. Istanbul-Paris-Leiden: Divit Press, 115–133.

Kiel, M. (1997). "The rise and decline of Turkish Boeotia, 15th–19th century." In J. L. Bintliff (ed.), *Recent Developments in the History and Archaeology of Central Greece*. Oxford: BAR Int. Series 666, 315–358.

Koder, J. (1996). "Perspektiven der Tabula Imperii Byzantini. Zu Planung, Inhalt und Methode." *Geographia Antiqua* 5, 75–86.

Ladurie, E. L. R. and J. Goy (1982). *Tithe and Agrarian History from the Fourteenth to the Nineteenth Century*. Cambridge and Paris: Cambridge University Press/Éditions de la Maison des Sciences de l'Homme.

Laiou-Thomadakis, A. E. (1977). *Peasant Society in the Late Byzantine Empire: A Social and Demographic Study*. Princeton: Princeton University Press.

Langdon, M. K. (1995). "The mortared towers of central Greece: An Attic supplement." *Annual of the British School at Athens* 90, 475–503.

Lefort, J. (ed.) (1986). *Paysages de Macédoine*. Paris: De Boccard.

Lock, P. (1986). "The Frankish towers of Central Greece." *Annual of the British School at Athens* 81, 101–123.

Lock, P. (1995). *The Franks in the Aegean 1204–1500*. London: Longman.

Lock, P. (1996). "The towers of Euboea." In P. Lock and G. D. R. Sanders (eds.), *The Archaeology of Medieval Greece*. Oxford: Oxbow, 107–126.

Lock, P. (1997). "The Frankish period in Boeotia: Problems and perspectives." In J. L. Bintliff (ed.), *Recent Developments in the History and Archaeology of Central Greece*. Oxford: BAR Int. Series 666, 305–313.

Lock, P. and G. D. R. Sanders (eds.) (1996). *The Archaeology of Medieval Greece*. Oxford: Oxbow.

MacKay, T. S. (2003). "Pottery of the Frankish period." In C. K. Williams and N. Bookidis (eds.), *Corinth, the Centenary 1896–1996*. Athens: American School of Classical Studies, 401–422.

McKee, S. (1995). "Households in fourteenth-century Crete." *Speculum* 70, 27–67.

Michaelides, C. E. (1972). "Aegean island towns: A current view." In O. B. Doumanis and P. Oliver (eds.), *Shelter in Greece*. Athens: Architecture in Greece Press, 53–63.

Miller, W. (1908). *Latins in the Levant. A History of Frankish Greece (1204–1566)*. London: John Murray.

Ministry of Culture, Greece (1995). *Syllogi Dimitriou Oikonomopoulou*. Athens: Archaeological Receipts Fund.

Nixon, L., S. Price, and J. Moody (2009). "Settlement patterns in Medieval and post-Medieval Sphakia." In J. Bintliff and H. Stöger (eds.), *Medieval and Post-Medieval Greece. The Corfu Papers*. Oxford: BAR Int. Series 2023, 43–54.

Panagopoulos, B. K. (1979). *Cistercian and Mendicant Monasteries in Medieval Greece*. Chicago: University of Chicago Press.

Papanikola-Bakirtzi, D. (1999). *Byzantine Glazed Ceramics. The Art of Sgraffito*. Athens: Archaeological Receipts Fund.

Papanikola-Bakirtzi, D., F. N. Mavrikiou, and C. Bakirtzis (1999). *Byzantine Glazed Pottery in the Benaki Museum*. Athens: Benaki Museum.

Phillips, J. (1997). "Who were the first crusaders?" *History Today* (March), 16–22.

Pringle, D. (1989). "Crusader castles: The first generation." *Fortress* 1, 14–25.

Sabelberg, E. (1985). "Die 'Süditalienische Stadt'." *Erdkunde* 39, 19–31.

Sanders, G. (1996). "Two kastra on Melos and their relations in the archipelago." In P. Lock and G. Sanders (eds.) *The Archaeology of Medieval Greece*. Oxford: Oxbow Books, 148–177.

Sanders, G. (2000). "New relative and absolute chronologies for 9th to 13th century glazed wares at Corinth: Methodology and social conclusions." In K. Blelke *et al.* (eds.), *Byzanz als Raum*. Wien: Österreichische Akademie der Wissenschaften, 153–173.

Sanders, G. (2003). "Recent developments in the chronology of Byzantine Corinth." In C. K. Williams and N. Bookidis (eds.), *Corinth, the Centenary 1896–1996*. Athens: American School of Classical Studies, 385–399.

Setton, K. M. (1975). *Athens in the Middle Ages*. London: Variorum Reprints.

Sigalos, E. (2004). *Housing in Medieval and Post-Medieval Greece*. Oxford: BAR Int. Series 1291.

Simatou, A. M. and R. Christodoulopoulou (1989–1990). "Observations on the Medieval settlement of Geraki." *Deltion tis Christianikis Archaiologikis Etaireias* 15, 67–88.

Tolias, G. (1999). *The Greek Portolan Charts*. Athens: Olkos.

Traquair, R. (1905–1906). "Laconia. I. The Mediaeval fortresses." *Annual of the British School at Athens* 12, 258–276.

Triposkoufi, A. and A. Tsitouri (eds.) (2002). *Venetians and Knights Hospitallers. Military Architecture Networks*. Athens: Ministry of Culture.

Tsougarakis, D. and H. Angelomatis-Tsougarakis (2009). "The archaeologist and the historian." In J. Bintliff and H. Stöger (eds.), *Medieval and Post-Medieval Greece. The Corfu Papers*. Oxford: BAR Int. Series 2023, 67–72.

Vionis, A. K. (2001a). "Post-Roman pottery unearthed: Medieval ceramics and pottery research in Greece." *Medieval Ceramics* 25, 84–98.

Vionis, A. K. (2001b). "The meaning of domestic cubic forms: Interpreting Cycladic housing and settlements of the period of foreign domination (ca. 1207–1821 AD)." *Pharos* 9, 111–131.

Vionis, A. K. (2005). "'Crusader' and 'Ottoman' material life: Built environment and domestic material culture in the Medieval and post-Medieval Cyclades Islands, Greece (c.13th–20th [centuries] AD)." University of Leiden, PhD thesis, Faculty of Archaeology.

Vionis, A. (2006). "The thirteenth–sixteenth-century *kastro* of Kephalos: A contribution to the archaeological study of Medieval Paros and the Cyclades." *Annual of the British School at Athens* 101, 459–492.

Vionis, A. (2008). "Current archaeological research on settlement and provincial life in the Byzantine and Ottoman Aegean." *Medieval Settlement Research* 23, 28–41.

Vionis, A. (2009). "Material culture studies: The case of the Medieval and post-Medieval Cyclades, Greece (c.AD 1200–1800)." In J. Bintliff and H. Stöger (eds.), *Medieval and Post-Medieval Greece. The Corfu Papers*. Oxford: BAR Int. Series 2023, 177–197.

Vroom, J. (1999). "Medieval and post-Medieval pottery from a site in Boeotia: A case study example of post-Classical archaeology in Greece." *Annual of the British School at Athens* 92, 513–546.

Wace, A. J. B. (1904–1905). "Laconia. V. Frankish sculptures at Parori and Geraki." *Annual of the British School at Athens* 11, 139–145.

Watrous, L. V., D. Hadzi-Vallianou, and H. Blitzer (2004). *The Plain of Phaistos. Cycles of Social Complexity in the Mesara Region of Crete*. Los Angeles: Cotsen Institute of Archaeology, University of California.

Whitehouse, D. (1991). "Glassmaking at Corinth." In D. Foy and G. Sennequier (eds.), *Ateliers de verriers de l'antiquité à la période pré-industrielle*. Rouen: Association française pour l'archéologie du verre, 73–82.

Williams, C. K. (2003). "Frankish Corinth. An overview." In C. K. Williams and N. Bookidis (eds.), *Corinth, the Centenary: 1896–1996*. Princeton: American School of Classical Studies at Athens, 423–434.

Williams, C. K. and O. H. Zervos (1993). "Frankish Corinth: 1992." *Hesperia* 62(1), 1–52.

20

The Archaeology of Ottoman and Venetian Greece

Population, Settlement Dynamics, and Socio-economic Developments

Introduction

The Ottoman state was one of several Islamic Turkic polities which arose in thirteenth-century Anatolia. Its location in the Northwest as the closest to unconquered Byzantine and Frankish lands encouraged a remarkably successful imperial expansion in that direction through conquest of the Balkans, only subsequently advancing back through Anatolia to incorporate almost all the Middle East during the fourteenth and fifteenth centuries (Lawless 1977).

It remains a commonplace of popular histories of Greece, that after the Ottoman Turkish conquest of Constantinople in 1453 AD, the Aegean succumbed to an unrelieved era of wicked Turkish oppression lasting till 1830 or longer. This view is also surprisingly common even in some academic publications. The stereotypical features of this disastrous four centuries generally include: a population nadir which stays low throughout the period, associated with the flight of the ethnic Greek population to the hills to plan their eighteenth- and nineteenth-century commercial rise and then the Revolution which led to Greek Independence. Then we learn that the Ottomans were a barbarous people with little cultural achievement in Greece, and worse still, they were prone to exercise a negative effect on the gifted Greeks by banning the construction of churches and converting most existing examples to mosques. Finally, we read that no notable changes occurred within the Ottoman period of rule, except due to the initiatives of their subjects.

What should strike us immediately as strange, is that the Ottomans' own perception of themselves was one of a cultivated society. Any modern visitor to the Old City in Istanbul needs no convincing of the undoubted artistic and architectural achievements of Ottoman civilization. Just a brief visit to the remarkable religious, educational, and welfare complex (*kulliye*) called the Suleymaniye will do (see Goodwin (1971) for an authoritative overview of the splendors of Ottoman architecture).

We can begin our deconstruction of the above stereotype history by noting that both the traditional Greek, and customary West European, view of the Ottoman Empire stem from the final era of its decline. Then there was indeed widespread arbitrary violence and corruption, and a lack of economic, technological, and political progress compared to the West. However, in the sixteenth and early seventeenth centuries Westerners had a very different, and frequently admiring view of the Ottoman world, which was plainly undergoing a great flourishing of population and productivity. The popularity of products of that world, such as its prestigious carpets and tapestries, like those shown on paintings such as Holbein's

The Complete Archaeology of Greece: From Hunter-Gatherers to the 20th Century AD, First Edition. John Bintliff.
© 2012 John Bintliff. Published 2012 by Blackwell Publishing Ltd.

The Ambassadors (Jardine 1996), matches the healthy respect shown to Ottoman military prowess abroad.

By its sixteenth-century climax, the Ottoman empire (Color Plate 20.1) covered all the Balkans apart from Slovenia and coastal Croatia, the Middle East excluding Persia, and North Africa from Egypt through to tributary states in Tunisia and Algeria. As a matter of policy the empire was multinational and consciously drew its high officials and much of its elite army officers from non-Muslims (*reaya*).

In its early phase, to the late sixteenth century, taxes were low and the countryside was dominated by independent villages, with the state intervening to restrict rural lands being dominated by a particular family (Keydar 1983), but over the middle (late sixteenth to early eighteenth century) to late (late eighteenth to early twentieth century) phases internal breakdown and external military and commercial pressures led to rising taxation, insecurity, and the increasing conversion of rural peasants into estate-serfs of rich landowners. The empire became dependent on West European merchants and bankers, but this also had the positive effect of stimulating the growth of a class of Balkan entrepreneurs, traders, and shipowners, who were fundamental to the creation of national identity in Greece and other Balkan countries, and thus prepared the path for national independence as the empire fell apart piecemeal over the nineteenth and twentieth centuries (Lawless 1977, Inalcik 1972, Inalcik *et al.* 1997). However there are some Aegean regions where later Ottoman times saw continuing prosperity, such as the Cyclades (Vionis 2005a), and upland communities exploiting new opportunities in textile manufacture or long-distance commerce (Thessaly and other areas in Central-Northern Greece for example).

In the early empire manufacturing was widespread but not generally large-scale or primarily designed for long-distance trade, but significant textile production is already noted in Thessaloniki and the towns of Thessaly. Significant exports from a region of a wide range of products, even to other Ottoman provinces as well as internationally, were subject to special authorization and generally discouraged, in order to ensure local needs and prevent their shortfall through private profiteering. The quality of craft products and access to membership of craft communities was managed by the state through a guild system, which whilst protecting skilled workers, would gradually prevent innovation and entrepreneurial competition, necessary to combat a steady rise in the proportion of goods and their shipping within the empire controlled by Western Europeans. With a weak urban hierarchy, fairs often met the need for rural populations to get goods to cover a year or more (shoes, ceramics, cloth) (Sigalos 2004). The immense needs of the capital Istanbul-Constantinople naturally affected production in a wide radius, so that a large part of the surplus grain from Thessaly, Macedonia, and Thrace was demanded as tax-in-kind from the state.

Our available resources for Ottoman and Venetian Greece are rich if little-known and only gradually being used for archaeological research programs (Bintliff 1995, Kiel 1997, Zarinebaf *et al.* 2005, Davies and Davis 2007 (Introduction), Stallsmith 2007). They include: the imperial tax records and local Ottoman and Greek archives (Davis 1991, Kasdagli 2007); travelers' reports (Tsigakou 1981, Angelomatis-Tsougarakis 1990); maps and naval charts (Sphiroeras *et al.* 1985, Tolias 1999); then material remains such as public religious and secular buildings, urban and rural domestic-houses, water-management systems, furniture, dress and other textiles, and finally ceramics and additional everyday portable artifacts (Kiel 1990, Vionis 2005a–b, 2009, Bintliff 2007). A model study of texts, buildings, and settlement geography is already available for the island of Lesbos (Karidis and Kiel 2002).

The Venetians kept control of Crete till 1669, and lost their Cycladic dependencies in a gradual progression of Ottoman power between the mid-sixteenth century and the early eighteenth, whilst the Ionian Islands were effectively under Venice from the thirteenth century till 1797. A Venetian archaeology of the Aegean has not fared any better than the Ottoman (Davies and Davis 2007, Introduction), but is likewise now taking off through a major initiative by the PRAP project in the province of Messenia (cf. Davies 2004). As with the Ottoman case, however, there were already well-studied aspects, such as the remarkably detailed Venetian land registers (in contrast to the Ottoman, provided with detailed maps of landholdings) (cf. Dokos and Panagopoulos 1993), personal archives (McKee 2000), and early studies of elite architecture and Venetian fortifications (for example by the Italian scholar Gerola in a series of papers in the 1920s and 1930s). Renewed interest in Venetian fortifications is signaled in Triposkoufi and Tsitouri (2002). Ceramic studies are so rare that their authors make a point of mentioning this (MacKay 1996).

In contrast to early Ottoman policy, Venetian land-holding, as befitted a capitalist and commercial state, was very much focused on the accumulation of estates by wealthy individuals, either Italian colonial settlers or local elites, who were utilized by Venice as managers of peasant populations (for detailed study of land use on Venetian Crete see Stallsmith 2007). In the Cyclades, their gradual absorption into the Ottoman empire and low interference or settlement by Turks subsequently, left local Venetian-Greek magnates in control of the bulk of the land into late Ottoman times (Vionis 2005a). Comparison of rural life under successive Venetian and Ottoman control in the same districts is a fascinating insight into historical processes at spatial levels appropriate to regional archaeological survey investigation (Zarinebaf *et al.* 2005, Malliaris 2007, Stallsmith 2007). A similar comparison between Late Byzantine and Ottoman life can be explored in Bryer and Lowry (1986).

Ottoman-era ceramics (ColorPlate 20.3a–b)

One major tool assisting a deconstruction of past biases is advances in our knowledge of the material culture of the Ottoman era. In the Aegean our ability to recognize Ottoman-era ceramics has leapt forward over the last two decades. Whilst still in the 1980s most field projects did not systematically collect post-Medieval finds, and if they did had to be content to classify them as Turkish/Venetian to Modern (or even just Medieval to Modern), we are now in a situation where most pottery sherds found even in the damaged condition of surface finds on regional surveys, whether coarse, domestic or fine ware, can be phased not merely into broad chronological divisions such as Byzantine, Frankish, Ottoman, and Early Modern, but through assemblage reconstruction into subdivisions such as Early, Middle or Late Ottoman (as for example with the recent analyses of deserted village assemblages on the Tanagra Project: Vionis 2004–2005,

2006b). This means that we can approach an Ottoman farm or village with the aim of using its surface ceramic finds to inform us of that community's relative wealth, economic behavior, and mentalities.

Rural Villages in the Early Ottoman Period

The Ottomans found a generally depopulated Greek countryside and shrunken towns, whilst even the capital Constantinople was more a collection of villages than a great city. The earliest Ottoman census and tax records from several regions of Greece, studied by several Greek and foreign experts, fit well with the gradually emerging archaeological evidence for settlement decline in the final Frankish-Byzantine era of the fourteenth to early fifteenth century. Thus for example the great plains of Thessaly (Kiel 1996), were virtually empty in 1388 when the Ottomans took over, requiring planned resettlement by population displacement from Western Anatolia, and the encouragement of Greek communities who had retreated to the hilly fringes to descend to the lowlands. By the mid-sixteenth century this policy had proved highly successful. An identical story is given by the archives for Attica (Kiel 1987) and Boeotia (Kiel 1997) (where Albanian colonists were encouraged), for the Peloponnese (Zarinebaf *et al.* 2005), and indeed for the Balkans in general. Turkish populations were predominantly urban in the Balkans, with only local pockets of planned Turkish rural colonization (for example in Thrace), so that farmers were Christians of various indigenous backgrounds (Braude 1985).

Some of the factors responsible for the fourteenth-century nadir were common to Europe as a whole, such as the recurrent devastations of the Black Death and high levels of warfare. Likewise the great demographic and economic recovery of the sixteenth century is not confined to the regions sharing in the benefits of the Pax Ottomanica (the two centuries of relative peace and prosperity of Early Ottoman rule), since the period is widely prosperous in many regions of Europe. In the Peloponnese in the Southern Mainland the reconstruction by Barkan of sixteenth-century population levels indicates some quarter of a million inhabitants, an observation fitting well with a peak of church construction (Sigalos 2004, see Figure 17.4).

The regime of landholding under which most Greek farmers were to operate in the first period of Ottoman rule, conceived of the land as belonging to the state. The non-Islamic population, or *reaya*, always the vast majority in the Aegean, paid tax for their freehold right to cultivate, whilst land plots were treated as contributory tax units for the sum needed (*timar*) to support the permanent army, in particular a *sipahi* or cavalryman. The other main use of such taxes was to pay the limited imperial bureaucracy, the elite foot regiments or *Janissaries*, and to contribute to the financial support of the main cities. The arriving Ottoman population was freed from most taxes, and conversion to Islam brought similar privileges, which accounts for a not-inconsiderable level of conversion from Christianity in many Balkan countries. Greece in general was not one of them, the Orthodox Church having already easily weathered the attempted imposition of Catholicism under the Franks. In any case, Ottoman policy followed the general norm amongst Islamic empires, allowing a high degree of freedom to indigenous faiths, especially those of the other "People of the Book" – the Jews and Christians. Its constituent populations were allowed a considerable degree of management of local affairs under their own secular and religious leaders, and this, combined with freedom of worship, led to a major influx of Jewish communities fleeing from persecution in Christian states.

If local populations paid their taxes regularly, they were given a remarkable amount of freedom, including selling their produce for profit. These favorable conditions, not least a great increase in security (the "Pax Ottomanica"), help to explain the general flourishing of societies throughout the Ottoman Empire in its first and greatest phase, from the later fourteenth to late sixteenth century. Although the vast lands of the Orthodox churches were reduced to smaller proportions, their estates and incomes were treated as those of mosques (*vakf*) and subject to minimal tax, which together with the overall favorable demographic and economic conditions of the early Empire, helps to explain why so many monasteries and churches were built, repaired, and lavishly decorated in this era.

On our own project in Boeotia, Central Greece, we have been exceptionally fortunate to have had already since the 1980s the involvement of John Hayes for fine-dating our post-Roman surface survey finds, followed by younger scholars such as Joanita Vroom and Athanassios Vionis. In addition, the services of a renowned expert in Ottoman archives, as well as Ottoman-era architecture, the Dutch scholar Machiel Kiel, has provided us with detailed breakdowns of the Ottoman imperial tax archives for the fifteenth to eighteenth centuries AD. In particular the collaboration between Kiel and my own work on locating and surveying deserted villages has provided a very detailed illustration of the historical processes at work on a regional landscape in the long period from early Frankish rule to the post-Ottoman period (Bintliff 1995, Kiel 1997).

If the first preserved defter of 1466 (Figure 19.6) reflects, in its restricted spread of Greek villages, the devastating collapse of Greek populations, it already points to planned recovery with invited Albanian communities. If we take away these new colonists we see that over two-thirds of the Byzantine-Frankish settlements must have been abandoned. On many deserted Frankish-era villages in Boeotia, we have now been able to demonstrate this chronology from surface finds (see Figure 17.3b). The large size of the few survivor indigenous villages, such as Panaya, must reflect their status as refuge communities for wider areas.

The subsequent tax records show that the small Albanian hamlets (initially some 30 families or less), multiplied and grew larger, and the larger Greek villages also grew even further. The seasonal Albanian "katuns" became permanent villages with tree crops and other products comparable to the Greek settlements. The effects of the new stability in increasing population levels and promoting economic prosperity are seen in the successive tax defters of 1506, 1522, 1540, and finally 1570, generally the defter with the highest figures for population, crop, and stock (Figure 20.1). Intensive archaeological survey at villages such as Panaya in the Valley of the Muses (see Text Box below) gives closer detailed confirmation of the tax records.

Blake's (1980) use of survey ceramics in Italy to highlight the degree of access to expensive fine wares for rural farming communities, indicated a relatively poor peasant society in High Medieval times, wealthier rural proto-capitalist communities

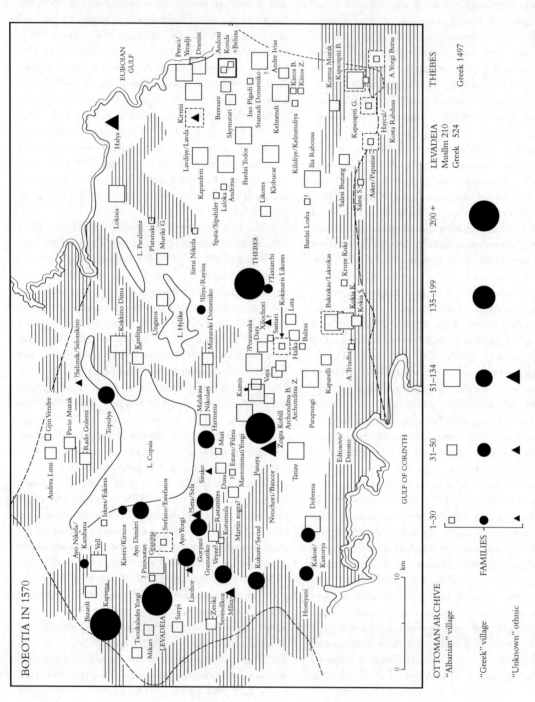

Figure 20.1 Settlement size and ethnicity from the Ottoman tax defter for Boeotia in 1570, locatable and approximately-locatable villages only shown (Ottoman texts translated by Prof. M. Kiel).

J. L. Bintliff, "The two transitions: Current research on the origins of the traditional village in Central Greece." In J. L. Bintliff and H. Hamerow (eds.), *Europe Between Late Antiquity and the Middle Ages.* Oxford 1995, 111–130, Figure 12.

in the Renaissance era of the later fourteenth and fifteenth centuries (wide access to Majolica products), then rural impoverishment for the sixteenth to early eighteenth centuries (cheaper slip-coated earthenwares being the best quality obtained), followed by rural improvement in the later eighteenth and nineteenth centuries (renewed penetration in quantity of exotic glazed wares, increasingly factory-produced).

If we set this alongside the Greek evidence, the High Medieval period (Frankish-Late Byzantine), may be comparable, not too surprising considering the incorporation of Mainland Greece into Western feudal politics and economics in this era. Blake's second, "Majolica" phase is a century later for Greece. Its framework in Greece, however, is pre-capitalist, communal village farming, along the Medieval model. Despite this, it is apparent that economic conditions for the villagers became very favorable. Imported tin-glazed wares from Italy, white-paste wares of comparable appearance with a high-quality body including clay, quartz, and glass (fritware) from Anatolia (Iznik) (Color Plate 20.2a), and locally produced tin glaze or pseudo-tin-glaze wares, are common on our village sites for this period, indicative of rural prosperity.

Although the Greek Ottoman rural highpoint is later than that in rural Italy, both are marked amongst other indicators by widespread access to relatively more expensive tin-glaze dishes and jugs (Majolica), and it is notable that Greece produced its local versions of these Italian wares. Likewise in Italy the remarkable Anatolian Ottoman glazed pottery made chiefly at Iznik (Atasoy *et al.* 1994) was both a status imported tableware and locally imitated, as well as being found in surface collections at contemporary village sites in Greece. We do have some evidence for tableware production of less costly, standard lead-glaze types at the large village of Panaya in Boeotia, but more exotic wares such as the Italian and Anatolian imports and Aegean tin-glazed products would probably have been bought at provincial market towns, in this case Thebes or Livadheia, and also at a well-recorded feature of the Ottoman Balkans – district fairs. As already in Medieval Europe, it was convenient for traders to circulate around country districts utilizing periodic rural

fairs, where goods for a whole year and not locally produced could be purchased. The Ottoman tax records note for example, halfway between the two market towns noted above, a fair at the large village of Rastamites. Traditionally in Early Modern Greece, and this must also have been the case in Ottoman times, peddlers toured villages selling small-scale products, and it may be that some ceramic pieces reached rural settlements this way too. Their place today is taken by the truly exotic sight of sub-Saharan Africans, whom one finds in the remotest villages, passing from café table to table, offering small African art objects as well as the normal fare of cheap watches and pirated CDs.

In the Attic region immediately southeast of Boeotia centered on the city of Athens, exactly as in Boeotia, after serious depopulation in final Frankish times the number and size of settlements in the countryside grows in the early Ottoman period to 1570 AD, as study of the early Ottoman tax records makes clear (Kiel 1987). Here again, the countryside is largely made up of recently-arrived invited Albanian settlers, who kept their language, as in Boeotia, into the opening decades of the twentieth century. A similar picture of rural growth appears in the settlement analysis for the mountainous province of Aetolia in North-Central Greece for the fifteenth and sixteenth centuries (Doorn 1989), also based on the archival research of Machiel Kiel.

Intriguingly, the match of tax records with archaeological survey allows us to compare a reliable estimate of rural population levels to those of other periods in the same landscape. For Boeotia (Bintliff 2005) the Ottoman peak is only a quarter of that for the late Classical era, if well above any estimates for Medieval times. As Dertilis (1992) comments significantly, in post-Roman Greece labor was effectively scarcer than land till the Modern era, which forced state and wealthier landowners to rely on direct cultivation by peasant families rather than create vast estates with waged or slave labor. This dependence on family plots served to sustain the family farm, whether freehold, or as part of, in later Ottoman times, the estate of a magnate, into becoming a building-block of traditional post-Ottoman Greek agriculture.

Panaya Ottoman-era Village

Intensive archaeological survey at Ottoman villages such as Panaya in the Valley of the Muses (Bintliff 1996) gives closer detailed confirmation of the tax records, when we observe the dramatic expansion of the site, between its modest scale in the Frankish thirteenth and fourteenth century, then a village called Zaratova (see Chapter 19), and its heyday at some 12 ha and hence some 1100 inhabitants in the sixteenth century, based on the dispersal of dated surface ceramics across the gridded site-area (Figure 20.2). Its size is remarkably close to that of its forerunner, ancient Askra, nearby in the Valley floor, at its Classical or Late Roman peak, which we had already estimated at over 1000 inhabitants. The defters for the sixteenth century AD give site VM4, listed as "Panaya" village, approximately the same population.

The detailed economic breakdown of Panaya's production shows a steady rise in agricultural and pastoral yields with some interesting changes in the balance of products (Table 20.1). Moreover further details enrich this impression of prosperity: imports of fine, highly decorated tablewares from both Italy and Anatolia at this and other contemporary early Ottoman villages (Vroom 1999) go with our archaeological mapping of several of the 10 watermills listed in the village's tax records, as well as our work at the two monasteries in the Valley founded by the village itself at this time.

Site Vm4 (If-et)

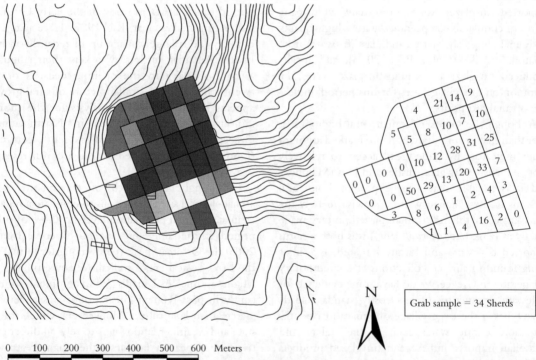

0   100   200   300   400   500   600   Meters

N

Grab sample = 34 Sherds

Figure 20.2   Maximum expansion of the deserted village of Zaratova (Frankish era)/Panaya (Ottoman era), occurs in the fifteenth to sixteenth centuries AD or Early Ottoman phase. The spread of dated finds covers some 11 ha. J. L. Bintliff, "Reconstructing the Byzantine countryside: New approaches from landscape archaeology." In K. Blelke *et al.* (eds.), *Byzanz als Raum.* Wien 2000, 37–63, Figure 16. Table source: ibid., Figure 17.

Table 20.1 Economic and demographic records from the Ottoman defters for the village of Panaya (site VM4).

THE DEMOGRAPHIC AND ECONOMIC DEVELOPMENT OF THE VILLAGE OF PANAYA 1466–1570

	Households	Unmarried young men	
1466	79	18	
1506	213	9	(in 1506 and 1506 explicitly mentioned as
1521	190	20	a GREEK Village)
1540	189	56	
1570	220	59	

SOURCE DATA					INTERPRETATION		

Name of product and year of registration		Tithe expressed in load (himl) 1 load = 166, 764 kilogr.	value of 1 load in akçe	Total production in kilogr.	total value in akçe	kg. per household	value in akçe per household
WHEAT	1506	200	35	256560	53846	1204	253
	1540	153	36	196268	42369	1117	224
	1570	250	46	320700	88462	1458	402
BARLEY	1506	135	15	173178	15577	813	73
	1540	59	16	75685	7262	392	38
	1570	80	25	102624	15385	466	70

SHEEP	tax amount	price per head in akçe	total sheep	Total value in akçe	number of sheep per household	akçe per household
1506	15	18	30	540	0.14	2
1540	124	22	248	5456	1.31	29
1570	1900	28	3800			

WINE	tithe in medre (lm. 71 liter)	price per medre	total prod. in liters	total value in akçe	liters per household	akçe per household
1506	700	10	497000	70000	2333	329
1540	325	20	230750	65000	1221	344
1570	222	23	157620	51060	716	232

COTTON	tithe in bales	price per bale	total production in bales	total value in akçe	akçe per household
1506	250	2	1923	3846	18
1540	173	5	1331	6654	35
1570	160	6	1231	7386	34

Source: M. Kiel, "The rise and decline of Turkish Boeotia, 15th–19th century." In J. L. Bintliff (ed.), *Recent Developments in the History and Archaeology of Central Greece*. Oxford 1997, 315–358.

The Valley of the Muses is a good example of a "settlement-chamber," where (as we have observed several times already) there seems always to have been just one central village from early farming times onwards. The coincidence of a maximal village population of similar scale in Greco-Roman times in Askra, in the Valley floor, and at VM4-Zaratova-Panaya above it on a defensive ridge, raises interesting questions about the close links between demographic climaxes and the capacity of a confined landscape to support them (its "carrying capacity") (Bintliff 2005). The majority, Albanian villages remain far below ancient population levels for their districts.

Other Monuments of the Early Ottoman Era

Islamic societies wherever they expanded brought a wider range of crops and great skill in water management (Watson 1974). When the Aegean entered this sphere of agricultural innovation through incorporation into the Ottoman Empire, it is clear that a remarkable expansion of such practices occurred. Sadly very little has been done to explore the Ottoman impact on agriculture, although the Aegean countryside is littered with ruined watermills and overgrown irrigation channels. Once again Kiel has been a pioneer, this time on urban water management (1992). Mouzakis (2008) illustrates the potential of water- and wind-power studies in the post-Medieval era. In the Valley of the Muses (see Box) the Ottoman defters list 10 watermills belonging to the village of Panaya in the sixteenth century, yet another symptom of flourishing local community investment in land management.

Urban Life in Early Ottoman Times

In Boeotia, the two regional urban centers of Livadheia and Thebes expand at the same time as rural villages during the first two centuries after the Ottoman conquest (compare Figures 19.6 and 20.1). At their peak in 1570 they have some 8000 and 4000 occupants respectively, large centers by contemporary provincial standards. Mackenzie's (1992) portrayal of Ottoman Athens in a short and uncritical book, which does unfortunately continue to circulate in that city today, perpetuates the historical limitations and cultural bias of the Travelers on whom it is based. The only serious account is Machiel Kiel's (1987) pioneer study of the town and its Attic countryside as recorded in the Ottoman tax archives. Kiel's access to the contemporary archives shows Athens, at some 18,600 occupants in 1570, as one of the major towns of the Early Ottoman Balkans. Ottoman policy was to repopulate or restore towns, and often populations were transported to Aegean cities from elsewhere in the empire: in 50 years the population of the Thessalian centers Trikkala and Larissa jumped by 60 percent for

this reason, essentially through Turkish immigration (Lawless 1977).

From archival research, also primarily by Kiel (1990, 1996), we can tell that every town in Greece at this period would have seen the construction of major architectural works: mosques, seminaries, covered markets, bathhouses, as well as water installations (Kiel 1992) and bridges. These seem to have been almost entirely destroyed, or if surviving are only now receiving sporadic protection and conservation. The modern cities of Chalcis and Thessaloniki are notable pioneers in the restoration and display of their Ottoman monumental heritage.

It is salutary to note that Kiel estimates (1996) that only 1 percent of the named major Ottoman buildings mentioned in sources for the city of Larissa in Thessaly, survive today. What is left in most Greek towns are also often fragments of structures which are not protected from decay or destruction, and frequently misinterpreted, since just a few cities have an active policy of conserving Ottoman monuments. Kiel has also introduced us to an even more unimagined world which has become lost to Greek consciousness, the flourishing activity of Ottoman literature, scholarship, and artists which once characterized the major and minor towns of Greece. He has given hints of this in his discussions of the vanished city of Giannisa in Western Macedonia (1990), and also of Thessalian Larissa.

The Crisis of the Middle Ottoman Era

From the late sixteenth century, and more markedly during the seventeenth, the Ottoman Empire suffered a series of crises, during which its nature changed fundamentally. It remained a large state, even till the end of the seventeenth century not to be taken lightly militarily by its Christian enemies in Western Europe, but it was weakened by demographic decline, loss of power at the center in favor of regional elites, and an impoverishment of the peasantry who should have provided a firm basis in tax surpluses and manpower. Additionally, the rising financial and commercial power of Western European states began to subvert the traditional economic system within the Ottoman world, whilst a flood of cheap Spanish silver caused devaluation of the currencies of Europe. Finally, climatic conditions during the same period, the "Little Ice Age," affected Europe as a whole through reducing crop predictability and yields, and in the Aegean may well have encouraged the expansion of marshland in the lowlands. This negative environmental development was assisted by a weakened state unable to keep such areas dry. Apart from declining crop yields, worsening drainage encouraged marsh sicknesses and malaria.

As with the flourishing sixteenth century, some of these symptoms are common to the European Christian world, where the "Seventeenth Century Crisis" has long been under active discussion (Rabb 1975). Factors which might be shared are firstly of course the climatic downturn, but secondly the theory of the French historian Le Roy Ladurie of neo-Malthusian cycles. In studies of France and the wider European scene (Ladurie 1966, Ladurie and Goy 1982), he has suggested that pre-industrial populations tended to expand beyond sustainable levels for agriculture, falling victim to crises, from which only depopulation (whether directly driven by food deficits or wars and revolts tied to food shortages) could save them. Indeed for the Ottoman world it has also been argued by historians (Kiel 1997) that agricultural production did not keep pace with population and thus food prices rose, this being one of the causes of the stagnation and then decline widely visible from the late sixteenth century. As we have seen, however, although this may well apply to the larger villages such as Panaya, it does not to the commoner Albanian foundations and the overall level of population.

A more specific symptom of decay was the inexorable shift of ownership from the hands of free peasant communities paying low taxes to the central authorities, toward a class of provincial landowning elite (the *ayan*), who milked the peasant surpluses for themselves, as well as taking over much of the tax formerly boosting state finances. The tied estates resulting from this shift in the countryside became known as *çiftliks*, although the term literally refers to a farm or plot. Especially in the eighteenth century, çiftliks expanded, with the aim of producing cash crops in wheat, maize, cotton, wool, and tobacco for urban markets within the empire and for exchange with Western merchants beyond it (Sigalos 2004).

Currently there is much discussion on the increased development of çiftliks during the troubled seventeenth century, stimulated by the thoroughly negative judgment on them passed by eighteenth- and nineteenth-century Western Travelers. More recently they have played a prominent role in historical debates about the wider context for some of the economic and social changes observed in the middle to later Ottoman Empire. Immanuel Wallerstein pioneered the concept that the Empire was increasingly drawn into a dependent relationship with the West European states, deploying terms such as core–periphery or world system (for these ideas see earlier, Chapter 5) (Wallerstein 1974, 1979). The subservience of formerly free peasants as a result of increasingly commercial agriculture has, as also for contemporary countries of Central and Eastern Europe, been described as a "secondary feudalism," with the çiftliks as a symptom.

However, some Ottoman historians (such as Çizakça 1985), suggest that the impact of Western commercialism and capitalism, and industrial incursions, on Ottoman society, was marked from the seventeenth century but not terminally crippling till the end of the eighteenth and in the nineteenth centuries. But in any case, from the latter sixteenth century, more and more state lands became privatized and this trend increased in the following centuries, tied to new forms of production. On the one hand, peasant payments did not alter significantly, heading to a higher authority for the rights of land use, and on the other hand, the rise of plantation production was very rare at first. Indeed with population decline, the state was encouraging privatization of its untilled lands to recover production shortfalls. Nonetheless, although the initial scale of çiftliks was small, just two to three households each, by the late seventeenth century large estates had become common and magnate rights grown hereditary. The great Ottoman scholar Inalcik (1972) drew attention to this as a central symptom of the increasing loss of control over the provinces by central government, as land surpluses and tax-raising were becoming the family right of the class of *ayan*, provincial landed elites. Before the end of the eighteenth century, a member of each regional *ayan* was chosen to represent the area politically. The most powerful provincial magnates maintained

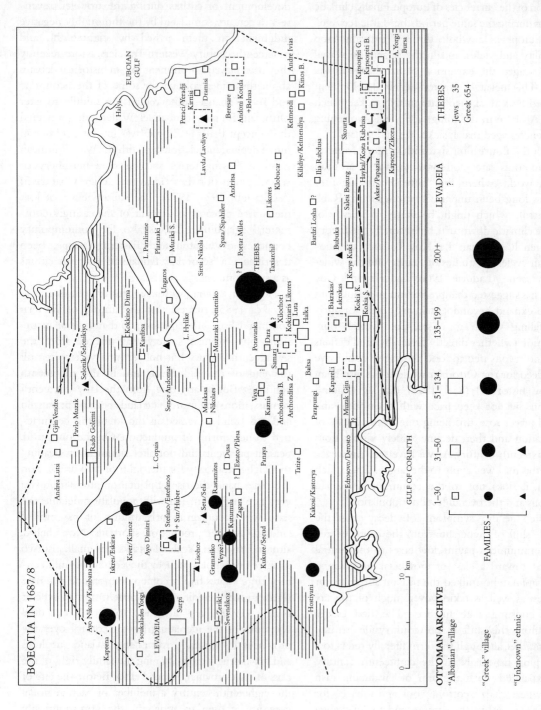

Figure 20.3 The decline of Boeotia between 1570 and 1687 is vividly revealed by the shrinking number and size of settlements by the latter tax date (Ottoman archives translated by Prof. M. Kiel).
J.L. Bintliff, "Reconstructing the Byzantine countryside: New approaches from landscape archaeology." In K. Belke *et al.* (eds.), *Byzanz als Raum.* Wien 2000, 37–63, Figure 13.

mercenary militias, ostensibly to combat the rising forces of banditry, but as often to oppress the peasantry.

The significance of çiftliks goes beyond the incorporation of formerly free peasant plots into large estates. Increasingly these bigger estates were specializing in cash crops for an international market, including the demands for raw materials by the West European commercial powers. Cheap food but also cotton and animal fibers were in great demand in the West, and this would only increase in the eighteenth century with the rise of industrialized production there. The weakness of the Ottoman state in not encouraging an independent entrepreneurial merchant class laid the Ottoman Empire open to Western traders. The *ayan* class saw increasing advantages in reorienting production on their larger and more market-effective specialist estates toward agents of Western countries. The growth of such a core–periphery economics can be seen as at least one of the elements disempowering the Ottoman state from its former military and economic strength.

We noted in Chapter 17 John Haldon's (1992) pertinent parallel between the cyclical rise and fall of the Byzantine and the Ottoman Empires: both Empires began with a traditional tax extraction to support a rigidly centralized fiscal and military system, run by a new service elite. But the latter developed rather into a service aristocracy and diverted state resources to its personal fortunes. The rise of the seventeenth-century *ayan* is paralleled by the tenth-century expansion of the Byzantine regional landed elite, occupying land of the peasants who should have been the free backbone for the army and its economic support. Further parallels involve the tax advantages (capitulations) offered to Western merchants by both Empires, which subverted the strength of the state's economy. Haldon intriguingly suggests an additional partial parallel, that is attested in the Byzantine case, and seems likely to agree with aspects of the Early Ottoman-era rural community, where the early phase sees a free peasantry in villages only partially integrated into the market, cultivating land offered by the state.

A further element in the Ottoman decline was the rising cost of warfare. Competing with the Christian armies required a larger standing army and rifle regiments. The manpower was increasingly that of mercenaries, owing to the declining status and freedom of the peasantry, whilst the professional Janissary regiments were allowed to supplement their income, becoming a hereditary elite of city traders and artisans (Lawless 1977). At the same time, from the late sixteenth century, the Empire's expansion was stalled by powerful states on various sides, so that it had to invest heavily in profitless wars to maintain its borders to both East and West. The necessary tax rises compounded the state's losses to provincial magnates in surpluses and tax.

The seventeenth-century Ottoman tax records show all too clearly the swift reversal of the prosperity and dense populations of the preceding century. In the Peloponnese for example, when the Venetians briefly reconquered the region from the Ottomans in 1685, they recorded a mere 125,000 people. Although we must allow for deaths and emigration consequent on the war itself, this may well represent the loss of one half of the sixteenth-century Ottoman census figure, and we can reasonably argue that most of the loss was due to long-term demographic decline over the preceding century. For comparison, the 1687 Ottoman tax record for the province of Boeotia (Figure 20.3) serves as a good parallel, when we match it to the map shown earlier for 1570. In a map highly reminiscent of the inferred settlement pattern produced by the fourteenth-century collapse, we see many settlements abandoned, and those which survive reduced dramatically in size, whilst the tax census informs us that most have been converted from semi-autonomous communities paying taxes to support the Ottoman military elite, into çiftliks. The great village of Panaya-VM4, for example, loses two-thirds of its population and is fragmented into a dozen serf-estates. The surface survey of the village appears even more startling: only a handful of sherds were collected in our large sample which were datable to the later Turkish era.

A contemporary Western Traveler, however, Wheler, writes that by the later seventeenth century the main focus of the Panaya village had been transferred a mere kilometer away to the east, to where its direct successor the modern village of Askra-Panaghia is to be found. The timespan of "Late Turkish" VM4 is thus likely to be very short, as befits its scanty surface record. Nonetheless, as the tax record for this village makes clear, a population collapse and reduction to serfdom are associated with the abandonment of the VM4 site.

In any case we are fortunate to have for archaeological study three clear examples of deserted Boeotian çiftliks: at the settlement site of Harmena; a much smaller example of just four longhouses, end-to-end, within the ancient city of Tanagra; and the nearby deserted village of Guinosati. Most remarkable was the chance discovery by Kiel of a rare late tax record for the Harmena community, an eighteenth-century assessment. Here it is described as a "great çiftlik," and indeed its population is considerable for its era, some 200–300 inhabitants. We were interested to see exactly what material conditions were like in such a serf-estate. The ceramic finds from the surface of Harmena are very common and mostly well-made bright glazed wares, rather than cheap homemade coarseware which one might have expected from such a community. On the other hand, none of the more expensive Anatolian or Italian fine wares were found, agreeing with Blake's theory on the declining wealth of the South European peasantry in the seventeenth and eighteenth centuries (see earlier). On the positive side, however, is the mention in the eighteenth-century tax record of a group of people living in the çiftlik who were there voluntarily, as additional workers, which might hint at conditions which were not entirely unprofitable to the workforce. Even in Boeotia, where the stereotype seventeenth-century decline does appear to be the rule, there were still major achievements, symbolized by the joint discovery by myself and Kiel of a lost great mosque in Thebes (see Chapter 21). Nonetheless, Thebes had shrunk from 8000 to 4000 inhabitants between 1570 and 1642.

The picture we have been building up so far for trends in the Middle Ottoman Mainland should not, nonetheless, be seen as a simple reflection of the rest of the Ottoman Aegean, let alone all the imperial provinces. As both Ottoman history and the beginnings of a regional Ottoman archaeology grow in data and sophistication, we can see that although the general picture portrayed so far holds for large swathes of the Empire, there is significant local variation. Thus in the Near East, some areas had only a limited Early Ottoman florescence, whilst in contrast, in Thessaly Kiel has shown (1996) that in the seventeenth to eighteenth centuries the towns and some village areas remained prosperous and populous.

Vionis' research on the Cyclades in Frankish and Ottoman times, focusing on settlement history, vernacular architecture, and material culture, has also argued that there was an equally flourishing period for most islands in the seventeenth to eighteenth centuries (2005a–b, 2009). Ottoman rule had remained at a distance and Venetian-origin aristocrats and their Greek *archontes* equivalents retained control over the island peasantry from nucleated towns. The rise of European commerce, chiefly with the West but also with parts of the Ottoman world beyond Greece, stimulated the emergence of a flourishing upper and middle class of merchants and businessmen, drawn both from traditional landed elites and mixed-marriage middle-class townsmen. Cycladic trade and shipping ranged increasingly widely from the seventeenth into the nineteenth centuries and brought prosperity and demographic buoyancy. Davis' (1991) pioneer linking of field survey and late Ottoman-era sources has shown interesting economic and other differences between the inhabitants of nucleated and dispersed settlements in this and the subsequent Early Modern period on the Cyclades.

Venice's control over Crete till the late seventeenth century and of the Ionian Islands till the end of the eighteenth saw a rather similar regime: land control was dominated by major landowners of Venetian and Greek stock. But here the Venetian state took a far greater interest in its colonies through regular interference in the economy, at times to the advantage or disadvantage of its Greek possessions (Stallsmith 2007). Greek merchants however benefited from the Venetian empire to expand their networks from Crete and the Ionian Islands into the Western world (Braude 1985). The strong state control and meticulous management of Venetian conquests can also be seen, with its archaeological and landscape evidence, in the recent analysis of the administration of the Navarino district of Messenia during the short-lived Venetian occupation (ca. 1685–1715) of the Peloponnese (Davies 2004).

The Late Turkish Era

Despite these many symptoms of crisis, the Ottoman Empire was weakened but not broken by these successive problems, experiencing a modest recovery during the eighteenth century. Thus there are signs in the Ottoman world of a revival of population and economy, together with evidence of some new directions. In the Peloponnese, for example, the demographic low point of 125,000 inhabitants after the Venetian conquest was made up progressively during the subsequent Ottoman reoccupation, reaching by the Greek War of Independence in 1821 an impressive figure of 400,000 people. Once again, though, the general trend is shared with the rest of Europe, and indeed some of the economic developments are a response to Western stimuli. A famous Mainland Greek example of regional prosperity in this period is presented by the cotton and silk textile villages of the Thessalian hill and mountain periphery (Lawless 1977, Petmezas 1990, Kizis 1994), which showed remarkable growth between 1750 and 1815 (see Chapter 21). To avoid the general temptation to attribute this solely to inbuilt ethnic Greek talent we can note that similar foci of productivity are also active in Anatolia and other Ottoman provinces at the same time. These are symptoms of wider growth and investment. Moreover, as Petmezas shows, the decline and collapse of the Thessalian textile centers and other foci elsewhere in the Empire owe most to the growing effectiveness of Western European competition, and the lack of technological development within these industries themselves in the late eighteenth and early nineteenth centuries, rather than to the dead hand of Ottoman control. Elsewhere however, it has been argued that Ottoman trade and industry *could* adapt to encroaching globalization through modifications to their existing practices, with positive long-term effects, as in Syria.

The development of later Ottoman industry has been discussed in the framework of proto-industrialization. This is a concept characterizing the expansion of domestic industries producing goods for non-local markets which took place in many European regions between the sixteenth and nineteenth centuries (Ogilvie 1993), was often rural, and lacked advanced technology or centralized factories. Although some see this phenomenon as laying the basis for widespread true industrialization, critics comment that most such experiments rarely succeeded in competing with dominant Western industrial towns. The Greek version appears to fit this scenario.

The long-term effects of such negative internal developments laid the seeds of the ultimate break-up and then demise of the Ottoman Empire. The weakness of the central government increased, in parallel to the rising dominance of the local provincial elites – the regional governors (*pashas*) and the landowning elite (*ayan*). These regional magnates, who dominated provincial administration and controlled most of the surplus production, exercised increasingly arbitrary power. By the mid-eighteenth century the *ayans* were formally charged by the state with regional administration and security, town-provisioning, tax-collection, and the dispatch of troops (Sigalos 2004). Feeding the lucrative demand from Western Europe for agricultural products and raw material for textile production, the larger landowners exported major amounts of regional surpluses illegally, weakening internal supplies and industry. Stimulated by the growing importance of international trade, Balkan merchants likewise sidestepped the moribund and non-entrepreneurial control systems of guilds maintained by the Ottoman state. They obtained rights to deal with foreigners through *berats* or official permits: these were issued to consuls and ambassadors of foreign powers and then distributed to clients amongst indigenous Christian communities. In any case scholars suggest that a considerable amount of production eluded taxation altogether.

This increase in the "core–periphery" economy, in which the Ottoman world supplied cheap materials in return for expensive manufactures and luxuries from the West, was partly encouraged by the state in order to appease Western Christian nations, who now had the military advantage over their Islamic neighbor. Yet there were some positive signs during this period. Local manufactures could sometimes compete with Western factory products, at least within the Empire, due to cheaper labor and traditional quality skills, as well as through meeting specific local cultural needs. The arrival of maize from the New World during the seventeenth century boosted crop production, being a hardy and flexible plant which expanded the food base. Other novel crops such as cotton, tobacco, and sugar were now being grown widely in the Ottoman provinces and were in high demand in more temperate countries unsuitable for their growth. A vigorous land trade developed between the Balkans and Western and Central Europe in the eighteenth and early nineteenth centuries, primarily for wool and cotton, and it was communities in the upland regions of North and Central Greece who came to control much of this (Lawless 1977). The historic mountain-town of Arachova near Delphi, a popular tourist venue today, preserves something of the character of these boom-towns and villages.

The positive picture which is emerging for this era has a downside, because it raised new challenges to the previously beneficial, official mentality of tolerant multiculturalism in the Ottoman world. The Early Empire produced a widely prosperous and satisfied society in town and country over most of Greece. The undoing of this system in almost every respect began to encourage two developments of historical importance, but which must be kept separate.

On the one hand, the rising economic and political power of regional elites encouraged them to demand and take a greater political role versus the central government, using the official support of the agents of foreign powers as protection. This led to the development of a prosperous middle and upper class throughout the Aegean region (Lawless 1977). For others, the entire Ottoman system was brought into question, especially as it was magnates and traders within ethnic networks who were asserting their new power and wealth, encouraging them toward concepts of nationalism, inspired by the model of Western nation-state formation. In the case of Greece, the very limited inroads of Islam and a selective adoption of Ottoman culture, taken with the never-extinguished continuity of Greek language and the Orthodox Faith, created a natural stimulus for a revival of Hellenism ("Greekness"), as a focus for a potential struggle for ethnic independence. This Hellenic concept was especially cultivated abroad, amongst émigrés and Greek commercial networks, where foreign intellectuals and politicians with a Classical education were receptive to the concept of a great nation from Antiquity, now held in chains by an alien and non-Christian power.

Yet the situation on the ground was much more complicated: in the area of the modern state of Greece a bewildering mix of populations existed well into the nineteenth century, with major survivals even today. Orthodox Greeks were matched in most regions by other communities: not just by a minority of genuine Turkish immigrants, but other groups such as the Albanians who had colonized vast areas of the countryside in the fourteenth to sixteenth centuries, the Slav communities of the north of the country both resident and immigrating from the sixth century through Ottoman times, and the Romanian-speaking Vlachs. There were also other more specialized groups, for example Armenian and Jewish commercial settlers, the latter forming the dominant community in the great city of Thessaloniki. One virtue of the Ottoman system was the deliberate cultivation of multicultural coexistence. European nationalism brought with it many advantages, but with it came an intolerance of groups seen as not belonging to "the nation," a recipe for oppression, expulsion, and even ethnic cleansing. Both Greece and the Balkans, as well as Anatolia, were to experience these forces when the Ottoman Empire eventually broke up into competing and aggressive nationalisms fighting for a share of its territory.

The implications of these historical trends at the local and regional level, would be that we might expect signs of demographic and economic recovery in the eighteenth-century tax records for Boeotia and other Greek provinces, and in the archaeological record. However, as a result of the decay of administrative structures, later Ottoman tax archives are less plentiful and more summary, with correction factors required for inadequate recording and tax evasion. Nonetheless the limited records for Boeotia, supplemented by Ottoman figures reported by Western Travelers, do indeed suggest a rise in village populations above the seventeenth-century nadir. A clearer sign of a growing prosperity amongst the middle and upper class comes from the study of domestic housing in Aegean towns, and to a lesser extent in the country, as Sigalos' recent overview (2004) reveals.

Inexorable outside forces were nonetheless undermining the Ottoman Empire's capability of holding together as the Modern World began to form: the long rise of capitalism and global trade, industrialization and commercial farming, radical changes in the administration of states, in education and citizenship, all were impacting into the provinces and major cities of the Empire out of its ever-increasing interactions with Western European countries. A state-within-a-state had already developed with the nexus of magnates and merchants in close contact with this wider world, economically, socially, and often politically. The constraints of Ottoman regulations and its obviously declining competitiveness in every sphere forced government programs of internal reform, with varying degrees of success.

Modernizing the army, experiments in parliamentary democracy, radical overhauling of the education system, and increased opening-up of markets to global trade, were carried out by the Ottoman Empire, but the results were imbalanced (McCarthy 1997). The wide support for Westernization in sociopolitical and economic affairs was contrasted with a related feeling of growing nationalism amongst the ethnic and religious communities whose continued existence and self-awareness had formerly been one of the sustaining strengths holding the Empire together. Would the Ottoman State modernize to its citizens' satisfaction, before the alternative road to self-improvement offered by its fragmentation into independent nations won through? Western powers were likewise in two minds about these options. A pliant, weak Ottoman state provided optimal conditions for profitable exploitation by Western traders, bankers, and factory-owners, whilst a mosaic of struggling new nation-states might provoke wars amongst themselves and between the Great Powers. The Napoleonic conquests with their superficial yet effective promotion of freedom from tyranny, and the wide appeal amongst European Enlightenment and then Romantic writers and intellectuals for human rights and ethnic traditions, had energized large sectors of Aegean and Balkan society into a desire to attain greater freedoms. For most, it seems, change was certainly long-needed and desirable, but to be sought through radical reform of the Ottoman state. It was probably still only a minority who envisaged change through revolutionary uprising and the creation of new nation-states.

The Greek Revolution of 1821–1830 was a victory for the nationalists, followed through the rest of that century and into the first two decades of the twentieth by the break-up into new nation-states of the rest of the Ottoman world. Even the Turkish populations in the heartlands of Anatolia and the hinterland regions of the capital Istanbul were led to turn their backs on everything Ottoman political and social culture had stood for, being refocused by their charismatic leader Kemal Ataturk into a newly-created Turkish nationalist and secular state. However it was merely Southern Greece (without Crete and the Ionian Islands) which formed the new Greek state in 1832: other parts of the country only gradually left Ottoman control (Color Plate 22.1) over the nineteenth and early twentieth centuries.

Late Ottoman Rural Life

The increasingly detailed reports of Western Travelers, from the late seventeenth century onwards, matched by maps and pictures appended to their travelogues, and enhanced from the late nineteenth century through photographic records (such as those preserved in the "photothèques" of the French and German Schools in Athens), can be combined with the Ottoman archives to build up an overall picture of town and village life during the Late Ottoman era and the first few generations of the independent Greek state. In fact the quality of historical geographical information reaches an unsurpassed peak during the early to late nineteenth century, when teams such as the French scientific expeditions to South and Central Greece record not only the characteristics of contemporary settlement, but also document deserted village locations. The latter are extremely valuable for locating settlements mentioned in Ottoman tax records and the Travelers.

Machiel Kiel's rich presentation (1996) of the detailed archival evidence for Thessaly finds no support for the idea that the lowlands were largely abandoned in later Ottoman times by Greek peasants fleeing oppression; instead he suggests that there is rather a trend for Greek upland inhabitants to migrate to the lowlands, where Muslim villages had low birth rates compared to neighboring Christian villages. The new archival and topographical researches in Messenia by the PRAP Project, coordinated by Jack Davis, are also beginning to document the rural realities behind the rather black and white picture offered by Western Travelers, providing already significant corrections to the scenario they indicate (Bennet et al. 2000, Zarinebaf et al. 2005). Boeotia, after the significant population

decline and relocation phase of the seventeenth century, discussed earlier, sees stability in surviving inland
villages till the next phase of disruption caused by the
early nineteenth-century War of Independence. But in
coastal areas piracy appears to have led villages to
adopt inland locations or more hidden, defensive plans
(Forbes 2000), and certainly Eastern Boeotia becomes
noticeably depopulated due to piracy and banditry in
Late Ottoman into Early Modern times. However it
appears that a more important change occurred in the
later nineteenth century, when rural insecurity in the
early Greek state caused nucleation of many villages
and a final phase of abandonments. Finally, as already
noted, the often oppressive çiftlik estates of this era
were concentrated in the major plains of Greece, contrasted with more prosperous independent village
societies in the uplands (particularly where textile
industries were focused), and with commercial communities on the coasts and on key communication
routes inland where a new economic boom was visible
(Sigalos 2004, Vionis 2005a).

I have elsewhere argued (Bintliff 1995, 2000) that
for South-Central Mainland Greece we can now
identify at least three major transitions in rural village
dynamics. The first is that great decline and recolonization documented for Late Frankish and Early
Ottoman times, which leads into a flourishing period
of very numerous and populous rural settlements
during the sixteenth-century Pax Ottomanica. The
second is a more drawn-out process in which village
numbers and village size generally decline, over the
seventeenth to later nineteenth centuries (with localized recovery in the eighteenth century), the result of
military and socio-economic problems (probably also
climatic), resulting in a thinner spread of villages. But
villages then blossom into substantial size in the last
third of the nineteenth century and the first half of
the twentieth. We do know that other regions of
Greece and indeed of the wider Ottoman Empire
vary considerably in the timing of their cycles of
growth, stagnation or decline, and although many do
follow this broad pattern, many clearly have out-of-
phase cycles to this scheme. Such variability offers
essential material for clarifying the historical processes
at work in regional trajectories, as I have suggested for
regional diversity in the Greco-Roman Aegean
(Bintliff 1997). Comparisons and contrasts with parts

of the Aegean under Venetian rule, especially those
passing from Ottoman to Venetian rule and vice-versa,
given the often fine detail given by Venetian archival
sources, are already revealing fascinating insights into
such processes (Davies and Davis 2007).

Nonetheless the archaeological evidence for lowland Mainland Greece matches the evidence of
Western Travelers and sporadic archival sources, to
offer a picture of a poor and downtrodden peasantry
largely trapped within a tied-tenant or share-cropping
system, contrasted to wealthy landowners and merchants exploiting their labor (Lawless 1977).

Late Ottoman Town Life

We have seen the evidence for localized urban growth
in the coastal towns and upland regions of Greece for
this era. Noting the rise of a more independent, indigenous species of middle-class merchants, shippers,
financiers, and proto-industrialists in such towns and
large villages, we can add that the decentralization of
power and wealth from the capital to the provinces
further stimulated the flourishing of such lesser
centers. The proliferation of urban mansions, imitating Ottoman styles inside and out, as well as Western
fashions in interior house design and personal dress,
merged together to emphasize the internationaliza-
tion of the rising Greek bourgeoisie (Sigalos 2004,
Vionis 2005a, 2009). Owing to the early rise in the
Southern Mainland of the independent Greek state
and its understandable rejection of all things Ottoman
in the aftermath of the bloody Revolutionary War,
little remains there to reflect this phase of Greek town
life, whereas in the North of the Mainland the later
incorporation into the Greek state allowed much
more to survive till today (Sigalos 2004).

Nonetheless Athens, the goal of numerous Travelers
and Western artists during this period, is sufficiently
recorded to allow us a view of the later Ottoman
town (Camp 2001). Increasing insecurity from both
pirates and foreign invaders led the governor to rewall
the lower town in 1778, Hadrian's Arch becoming
one of its gates. Hadrian's Library was used as the basis
for the governor's residence. The Acropolis had a garrison and an associated upper town covered its surface
(see this book's cover). The Parthenon's mosque was

Figure 20.4 Eighteenth-century Ottoman complex behind the Tower of the Winds, Athens, in the early nineteenth century.
Painting from Theodore de Moncel, *Vues pittoresques des monuments d'Athènes*. Paris 1845. © 2011 The British Library Board. All rights reserved. 648.a.28.

Figure 20.5 Eighteenth-century Ottoman complex behind the Tower of the Winds, Athens, today. Author.

rebuilt after its predecessor had been destroyed with much of the ancient temple during the seventeenth-century Venetian bombardment. A sad reflection of the modern city's continuing failure to come to terms with all its rich past is the following encounter made by the author in 2010: if you visit the fine Hellenistic Tower of the Winds in the Roman Agora, a solid fence and an entrance ticket lead you to a well-conserved and presented ancient monument. But stand outside that fence and turn around 180 degrees and across the road stands a fragmentary ruined eighteenth-century Ottoman gateway of considerable refinement, and associated ruins: bushes grow from it, it is unfenced and unmarked and its days are surely numbered. It has long been identified as an Islamic religious school (*medrese*) from 1721 (Travlos 1993) (Figures 20.4 and 20.5).

A much more sensitive attitude appears in an article by Pallis (2006) on the Athenian rural suburb Kifisia and its Ottoman monuments. He describes its use as a summer retreat for Athenian Turks, with mosques, a religious school, bathhouse, travelers' hostel, country residences, and other features, while regretting the late nineteenth-century atmosphere of ultra-Hellenism in which all these buildings were demolished.

Ceramics of the Ottoman-Venetian Era

John Hayes has been the crucial pathfinder in the development of a detailed study of complete Ottoman ceramic assemblages, in the Bodrum Camii and Saraçane excavation reports (Hayes 1981, 1992), updating pioneer studies of decorated tablewares from urban excavations in Athens (Waagé 1933, Frantz 1942). Inspired by Hayes' subsequent work for a number of Greek survey projects are recent studies by Vroom (1998, 2003, 2007) and Vionis (2005a–b, 2006b, 2009). Venetian-dominated regions have not had such attention, so that MacKay (1996) remarks in a study of a small group of Italian majolica imports from Crete that even publishing such poorly-provenanced finds marks an innovation.

Domestic and coarse wares do not change so dramatically between Medieval and post-Medieval times in Greece until the nineteenth century, although current research is identifying trends through the Ottoman era, and regional variants. We confine ourselves here to the decorated wares, which now become a steadily growing percentage of the assemblage. We already noted a steady rise in Byzantine to Frankish times in glazed ware representation, but Hayes pinpointed a later enhancement in Istanbul Ottoman-era assemblages: they comprise 35–40 percent for Early Ottoman, but 60–80 percent for Late Ottoman. In rural Greece however, the percentage of glazed wares remains at 30 percent in both eras (Vionis 2006b). Glazing, usually directly onto the clay except for tablewares, was now being applied to almost all kinds of household pots. This had functional value, creating impermeability and easier cleaning, but may have equally served to imitate metal vessels, thus to enhance the pottery's attractiveness. However some containers become less visible: after the recognizable amphorae series of Byzantine times, it appears that much of the transport containers from Frankish through Ottoman times were shifting to wooden barrels. Finally, in Europe and the Islamic world, there is a widespread shift to metalware for the kitchen, tableware, and work assemblages, which for the vast bulk of the population meant ironware and pewter (very rarely surviving till today in archaeological contexts, but common in Folklore Museums). The imbalance of ceramic assemblages in terms of quantity and forms may be a guide to these missing elements, and a good start can be made as with earlier eras through study of contemporary art (icons and travelers' illustrations), where both contemporary and biblical scenes are portrayed with current household items (Vroom 2003, Vionis 2005a, 2009). An icon from Zakynthos shows that by the seventeenth century pewter tableware was a major replacement item for ceramics (Mylonas 1998, figure 22).

Pottery styles as often do not change with key historical events, and the first relevant, widespread Aegean assemblage is characterized as Late Frankish-Early Turkish (fourteenth to sixteenth centuries). The three commonest styles are:

1. Brown and Green Sgraffito late thirteenth to seventeenth century, wide careless incised decoration, especially with brown and green splashes (Color Plate 20.3b).
2. Proto-Majolica, tin-glazed polychrome, Southern Italian product, late twelfth to early fifteenth century.
3. Archaic Majolica, tin-glazed painted and sgraffito-decorated, Northern Italian product, thirteenth to seventeenth century.

At the late Frankish-Venetian town of Kephalos on Paros (Vionis 2006a), distributional studies suggest that the Lower Town and its peasants possessed local Late Sgraffito wares, whilst the elite of the Upper Town were owners of more expensive Italian majolica imports.

In the following but also overlapping Early to Middle Ottoman era the major tablewares are:

1. Local Majolica, Italian influenced, especially blue and white, also polychrome, associated with the appearance of distinctive trefoil-mouth jugs, fifteenth to eighteenth century (Color Plate 20.3b).
2. Late Sgraffito, includes trefoil jugs, with blue and green splashes, fifteenth to eighteenth century.
3. A high-quality blue and white, or polychrome, painted white paste ware from Iznik in Northwest Turkey, sixteenth to seventeenth century (Color Plate 20.2a).

For the Late Ottoman eighteenth century, cheaper and less elaborate painted earthenware tableware from Kütahya, also in Northwest Turkey (Color Plate 20.2b), is accompanied by finer majolica tablewares from Italy, for example Pesaro (Color Plate 20.3a), which seem made specifically for the Aegean markets (including some with Greek inscriptions). As just noted, over time more and more non-tableware vessels are monochrome-glazed.

Coffee-drinking spread from Ethiopia to Yemen and then took off in popularity throughout the Ottoman empire from the sixteenth century, with its typical drinking-cups (Lewis 1995). Another typefossil of Ottoman times is the clay tobacco pipe with a molded clay bowl (*chibouk-style*), likewise spreading through the empire from the end of the sixteenth century; its typology has been analyzed to allow pipes to form a significant dating tool (Robinson 1985, Humphrey 2009).

Following Blake (1980), Italian rural impoverishment for the sixteenth to early eighteenth centuries, a consequence of economic decline and political stagnation, was marked by cheap slip-coated wares being the best quality obtained. In the later eighteenth and nineteenth centuries this improved (renewed penetration in quantity of exotic glazed wares but from Western and regional factories), culminating in what has generally been recognized as a Mediterraneanwide boom for rural society in the final decades of the nineteenth century, within the framework of an increasingly integrated capitalist and commercial, export-oriented agricultural economy in which Greek rural society plays its part. In Greece Blake's first era contrasts the rising wealth of the merchant and landowning class in towns and proto-industrial villages, against the continuing poverty of peasant life in the lowland farming settlements till the demise of the tied-labor system and other major improvements over the course of the nineteenth century. Only initial evidence for peasant villages is available, such as that from deserted later Ottoman çiftliks in Boeotia (Vionis 2006b), but the cheap glazed wares normal till the later nineteenth century suit the continuing use of traditional longhouses and the literary accounts for peasant impoverishment (as predicted by Blake's (1980) model). On the Cyclades, however, the rise of a prosperous international town-based Greek merchant class with continued cultural links to Italy results in a different picture, with the widespread dispersal of late majolicas and other Italian tablewares from the seventeenth century onwards.

References

Angelomatis-Tsougarakis, H. (1990). *The Eve of the Greek Revival.* London: Routledge.

Atasoy, N., J. Raby, and Y. Petsopoulos (1994). *Iznik: The Pottery of Ottoman Turkey.* London: Alexandria Press/ Laurence King.

Bennet, J., J. L. Davis, and F. Zarinebaf-Shahr (2000). "Pylos Regional Archaeological Project, Part III: Sir William Gell's itinerary in the Pylia and regional landscapes in the Morea in the second Ottoman period." *Hesperia* 69(3), 343–380.

Bintliff, J. L. (1995). "The two transitions: Current research on the origins of the traditional village in Central Greece." In J. L. Bintliff and H. Hamerow (eds.), *Europe Between Late Antiquity and the Middle Ages. Recent Archaeological and Historical Research in Western and Southern Europe.* Oxford: BAR Int. Series 617, 111–130.

Bintliff, J. L. (1996). "The archaeological survey of the Valley of the Muses and its significance for Boeotian history." In A. Hurst and A. Schachter (eds.), *La Montagne des Muses.* Geneva: Librairie Droz, 193–224.

Bintliff, J. L. (1997). "Regional survey, demography, and the rise of complex societies in the ancient Aegean: Core–periphery, neo-Malthusian, and other interpretive models." *Journal of Field Archaeology* 24, 1–38.

Bintliff, J. (2000). "Reconstructing the Byzantine country-side: New approaches from landscape archaeology." In K. Belke et al. (eds.), *Byzanz als Raum.* Wien: Österreichische Akademie der Wissenschaften, 37–63.

Bintliff, J. L. (2005). "Explorations in Boeotian population history." In P. L. Smith (ed.), *Studies in Honor of John M. Fossey I. The Ancient World* 36(1), 5–17.

Bintliff, J. L. (2007). "Considerations for creating an Ottoman archaeology in Greece." In S. Davies and J. L. Davis (eds.), *Between Venice and Istanbul: Colonial Landscapes in Early Modern Greece.* Athens: American School of Classical Studies at Athens, Hesperia Supplement 40, 222–236.

Blake, H. (1980). "Technology, supply or demand?" *Medieval Ceramics* 4, 3–12.

Braude, B. (1985). "Venture and faith in the commercial life of the Ottoman Balkans, 1500–1650." *International History Review* 7, 519–542.

Bryer, A. and H. Lowry (eds.) (1986). *Continuity and Change in Late Byzantine and Early Ottoman Society.* Birmingham: University of Birmingham/Washington, DC: Dumbarton Oaks Research Library.

Camp, J. M. (2001). *The Archaeology of Athens.* New Haven: Yale University Press.

Çizakça, M. (1985). "Incorporation of the Middle East into the European world economy." *Review* 8, 353–377.

Davies, S. (2004). "Pylos Regional Archaeological Project, Part VI. Administration and settlement in Venetian Navarino." *Hesperia* 73(1), 59–120.

Davies, S. and J. L. Davis (eds.) (2007). *Between Venice and Istanbul. Colonial Landscapes in Early Modern Greece.* Athens: American School of Classical Studies, Hesperia Supplement 40.

Davis, J. C. (1991). "Contributions to a Mediterranean rural archaeology: Historical case study from the Ottoman Cyclades." *Journal of Mediterranean Archaeology* 4, 131–215.

Dertilis, G. (1992). "Terre, paysans et pouvoir économique (Grèce, xviiie–xxe siècle)." *Annales. Histoire, Sciences Sociales* 47(2), 273–291.

Dokos, K. and G. Panagopoulos (1993). *To venetiko ktimatologio tis Vostitsas.* Athens: Morphotiko Institouto Agrotikis Trapezas.

Doorn, P. K. (1989). "Population and settlements in Central Greece: Computer analysis of Ottoman registers of the fifteenth and sixteenth centuries." In P. Denley et al. (eds.), *History and Computing II.* Manchester: Manchester University Press, 193–208.

Forbes, H. (2000). "Security and settlement in the Mediaeval and post-Mediaeval Peloponnese, Greece, 'Hard' History versus Oral History." *Journal of Mediterranean Archaeology* 13, 204–224.

Frantz, M. A. (1942). "Turkish pottery from the Agora." *Hesperia* 11, 1–28.

Goodwin, G. (1971). *A History of Ottoman Architecture.* Baltimore: Johns Hopkins University Press.

Haldon, J. F. (1992). "The Ottoman state and the question of state autonomy: Comparative perspectives." In H. Berktay and S. Faroqhi (eds.), *New Approaches to State and Peasant in Ottoman History*. London: Frank Cass, 18–108.

Hayes, J. W. (1981). "The excavated pottery from the Bodrum Camii." In C. L. Striker (ed.), *The Myrelaion (Bodrum Camii) in Istanbul*. Princeton: Princeton University Press, 36–41.

Hayes, J. W. (1992). *Excavations at Sarachane in Istanbul 2: The Pottery*. Princeton: Princeton University Press.

Humphrey, J. H. (2009). "The Ottoman clay smoking pipes from Mytilene." In J. Bintliff and H. Stöger (eds.), *Medieval and Post-Medieval Greece. The Corfu Papers*. Oxford: BAR Int. Series 2023, 121–131.

Inalcik, H. (1972). "The Ottoman decline and its effect upon the Reaya." In H. Birnbaum and S. Vryonis (eds.), *Aspects of the Balkans, Continuity and Change*. The Hague: Mouton, 338–354.

Inalcik, H. *et al.* (1997). *An Economic and Social History of the Ottoman Empire, 1300–1914*. Cambridge: Cambridge University Press.

Jardine, L. (1996). *Worldly Goods. A New History of the Renaissance*. London: Macmillan.

Karidis, D. N. and M. Kiel (2002). *Mitilinis astigraphia ke Lesvou chorographia*. Athens: Olkos.

Kasdagli, A. (2007). "Notarial documents for agrarian history." In S. Davies and J. L. Davis (eds.), *Between Venice and Istanbul. Colonial Landscapes in Early Modern Greece*. Athens: American School of Classical Studies, Hesperia Supplement 40, 55–70.

Keydar, C. (1983). "Small peasant ownership in Turkey: Historical formation and present structure." *Review* 7, 53–107.

Kiel, M. (1987). "Population growth and food production in 16th century Athens and Attica according to the Ottoman Tahrir Defters." In J.-L. Bacque-Grammont and E. van Donzel (eds.), *Proceedings of the VIth Cambridge CIEPO Symposium*. Istanbul-Paris-Leiden: Divit Press, 115–133.

Kiel, M. (1990). *Studies on the Ottoman Architecture of the Balkans*. Aldershot: Variorum.

Kiel, M. (1992). "Remarks on some Ottoman-Turkish aqueducts and water supply systems in the Balkans – Kavalla, Chalkis, Aleksinac, Levkas and Ferai/Ferecik." *Utrecht Turcological Series* 3, 105–139.

Kiel, M. (1996). "Das türkische Thessalien." In R. Lauer and P. Schreiner (eds.), *Die Kultur Griechenlands in Mittelalter und Neuzeit*. Abhandlungen der Akademie der Wissenschaften in Göttingen. Philologisch-historische Klasse, Dritte Folge 212, 109–196.

Kiel, M. (1997). "The rise and decline of Turkish Boeotia, 15th–19th century." In J. L. Bintliff (ed.), *Recent Developments in the History and Archaeology of Central Greece*. Oxford: BAR Int. Series 666, 315–358.

Kizis, G. (1994). *Pilioreitiki oikodomia*. Athens: Politistiko Technologiko Idrima ETBA.

Ladurie, E. L. R. (1966). *Les Paysans de Languedoc*. Paris: École Pratique des Hautes Études.

Ladurie, E. L. R. and J. Goy (1982). *Tithe and Agrarian History from the Fourteenth to the Nineteenth Century*. Cambridge and Paris: Cambridge University Press / Éditions de la Maison des Sciences de l'Homme.

Lawless, R. I. (1977). "The economy and landscapes of Thessaly during Ottoman rule." In F. Carter (ed.), *An Historical Geography of the Balkans*. London: Academic Press, 501–532.

Lewis, B. (1995). *The Middle East*. London: Weidenfeld & Nicolson.

McCarthy, J. (1997). *The Ottoman Turks*. London: Addison Wesley Longman.

MacKay, T. S. (1996). "A group of Renaissance pottery from Heraklion, Crete: Notes and questions." In P. Lock and G.D.R. Sanders (eds.), *The Archaeology of Medieval Greece*. Oxford: Oxbow, 127–137.

McKee, S. (2000). *Uncommon Dominion: Venetian Crete and the Myth of Ethnic Purity*. Philadelphia: University of Pennsylvania Press.

Mackenzie, M. (1992). *Turkish Athens*. Reading: Ithaca Press.

Malliaris, A. (2007). "Population exchange and integration, 1687–1715." In S. Davies and J. L. Davis (eds.), *Between Venice and Istanbul. Colonial Landscapes in Early Modern Greece*. Athens: American School of Classical Studies, Hesperia Supplement 40, 97–109.

Mouzakis, S. A. (2008). *Myloi ke diamorphosi pheoudarchikou dikaiou sti ditiki, byzantini ke othomaniki oikonomia ke koinonia*. Athens: Epimeleia Epistimonike Etaireia Attikon Meleton.

Mylonas, Z. A. (1998). *Mouseio Zakynthou*. Athens: Ministry of Culture.

Ogilvie, S. C. (1993). "Proto-industrialization in Europe." *Continuity and Change* 8, 159–179.

Pallis, G. (2006). "Ta othomanika mnimia tis Kiphisias." *Athens Annals in Art and Archaeology* 39, 229–240.

Petmezas, S. D. (1990). "Patterns of protoindustrialization in the Ottoman Empire. The case of Eastern Thessaly, ca. 1750–1860." *Journal of European Economic History* 19, 575–603.

Rabb, T. K. (1975). *The Struggle for Stability in Early Modern Europe*. Oxford: Oxford University Press.

Robinson, R. C. W. (1985). "Tobacco pipes of Corinth and of the Athenian Agora." *Hesperia* 54, 149–203.

Sigalos, E. (2004). *Housing in Medieval and Post-Medieval Greece*. Oxford: BAR Int. Series 1291.

Sphiroeras, V., A. Avramea, and S. Asdrachas (1985). *Chartes ke chartographoi tou Aigaiou pelagous*. Athens: Olkos.

Stallsmith, A. B. (2007). "One colony, two mother cities: Cretan agriculture under Venetian and Ottoman rule." In S. Davies and J. L. Davis (eds.), *Between Venice and Istanbul. Colonial Landscapes in Early Modern Greece*. Athens: American School of Classical Studies, Hesperia Supplement 40, 151–171.

Tolias, G. (1999). *The Greek Portolan Charts*. Athens: Olkos.

Travlos, J. (1993). *Poleodomiki exelixis ton Athinon*. Athens: Ekdoseis Kapon ke Angeliki Kokkou.

Triposkoufi, A. and A. Tsitouri (eds.) (2002). *Venetians and Knights Hospitallers. Military Architecture Networks*. Athens: Hellenic Ministry of Culture.

Tsigakou, F. M. (1981). *The Rediscovery of Greece*. London: Thames & Hudson.

Vionis, A. K. (2004–2005). "The Medieval and post-Medieval pottery and Tanagra village-history." In Bintliff, J. L. et al., "The Tanagra project: investigations at an ancient city and its countryside (2000–2002)." *Bulletin de Correspondance Hellénique* 128–129, 541–606.

Vionis, A. K. (2005a). " 'Crusader' and 'Ottoman' material life: Built environment and domestic material culture in the Medieval and post-Medieval Cyclades Islands, Greece (c.13th–20th [centuries] AD)." University of Leiden, PhD thesis, Faculty of Archaeology.

Vionis, A. K. (2005b). "Domestic material culture and post-Medieval archaeology in Greece: A case-study of the Cyclades Islands." *Journal of the Society for Post-Medieval Archaeology* 39, 172–185.

Vionis, A. (2006a). "The thirteenth–sixteenth-century *kastro* of Kephalos: A contribution to the archaeological study of Medieval Paros and the Cyclades." *Annual of the British School at Athens* 101, 459–492.

Vionis, A. (2006b). "The archaeology of Ottoman villages in central Greece: Ceramics, housing and everyday life in post-medieval Boeotia." In A. Erkanal-Öktu et al. (eds.), *Studies in Honor of Hayat Erkanal: Cultural Reflections*. Istanbul: Homer Kitabevi, 784–800.

Vionis, A. (2009). "Material culture studies: The case of the Medieval and post-Medieval Cyclades, Greece (c. AD 1200–1800)." In J. Bintliff and H. Stöger (eds.), *Medieval and Post-Medieval Greece. The Corfu Papers*. Oxford: BAR Int. Series 2023, 177–197.

Vroom, J. (1998). "Early Modern archaeology in Central Greece: The contrast of artefact-rich and sherdless sites." *Journal of Mediterranean Archaeology* 11, 131–164.

Vroom, J. (1999). "Medieval and post-Medieval pottery from a site in Boeotia: A case-study example of post-Classical archaeology in Greece." *Annual of the British School at Athens* 92, 513–546.

Vroom, J. (2003). *After Antiquity. Ceramics and Society in the Aegean from the 7th to the 20th Century A.C.* Leiden: Leiden University Archaeological Studies 10.

Vroom, J. (2007). "Kütahya between the lines: Post-Medieval ceramics as historical information." In S. Davies and J. L. Davis (eds.), *Between Venice and Istanbul: Colonial Landscapes in Early Modern Greece*. Athens: American School of Classical Studies at Athens, Hesperia Supplement 40, 70–93.

Waagé, F. O. (1933). "Excavations in the Athenian Agora: The Roman and Byzantine pottery." *Hesperia* 2, 279–328.

Wallerstein, I. (1974). *The Modern World-System. Capitalist Agriculture and the Origins of the European World Economy in the Sixteenth Century*. London: Academic Press.

Wallerstein, I. (1979). "The Ottoman Empire and the capitalist world economy: Some questions for research." *Review* 2(3), 389–398.

Watson, A. M. (1974). "The Arab agricultural revolution and its diffusion, 700–1100." *Journal of Economic History* 34, 8–35.

Zarinebaf, F., J. Bennet, and J. L. Davis (2005). *A Historical and Economic Geography of Ottoman Greece. The Southwestern Morea in the 18th Century*. Athens: American School of Classical Studies, Hesperia Supplement 34.

Further Reading

Athanassopoulos, E. F. (1997). "Landscape archaeology of Medieval and pre-Modern Greece: The case of Nemea." In P. N. Kardulias and M. T. Shutes (eds.), *Aegean Strategies*. Lanham: Rowman & Littlefield, 79–105.

Aymard, M. (1982). "From feudalism to capitalism in Italy: The case that doesn't fit." *Review* 6(2), 131–208.

Baram, U. and L. Carroll (eds.) (2000). *A Historical Archaeology of the Ottoman Empire. Breaking New Ground*. New York: Kluwer Academic/Plenum.

Berktay, H. and S. Faroqhi (eds.) (1991). *New Approaches to State and Peasant in Ottoman History. Journal of Peasant Studies* 18(3–4) special issue.

Bintliff, J. L. (1997). "The archaeological investigation of deserted medieval villages in Greece." In G. de Boe and F. Verhaege (eds.), *Rural Settlements in Medieval Europe*. Zellik: Archaeological Institute for the Heritage, 21–34.

Bintliff, J. L. and A. M. Snodgrass (1988). "Mediterranean survey and the city." *Antiquity* 62, 57–71.

Bintliff, J. L. et al. (2000). "Deconstructing 'the sense of place'? Settlement systems, field survey and the historic record: A case-study from Central Greece." *Proceedings of the Prehistoric Society* 66, 123–149.

Bintliff, J. L. *et al.* (2001). "The Leiden Ancient Cities of Boeotia Project: Preliminary report on the 2001 season." *Pharos. Journal of the Netherlands Institute in Athens* 9, 33–74.

Bommeljé, Y. and P. Doorn (1996). "The long and winding road: Land routes in Aetolia (Greece) since Byzantine times." In H. Kamermans and K. Fennema (eds.), *Interfacing the Past*. Leiden: Analecta Praehistorica Leidensia 28, 343–351.

Cherry, J. F., J. C. Davis, and E. Mantzourani (1991). *Landscape Archaeology as Long-Term History*. Los Angeles: Cotsen Institute of Archaeology, University of California.

Dunn, A. (2009). "Byzantine and Ottoman maritime traffic in the estuary of the Strymon." In J. Bintliff and H. Stöger (eds.), *Medieval and Post-Medieval Greece. The Corfu Papers*. Oxford: BAR Int. Series 2023, 15–31.

Harrison, P. (1993). "Castles and fortresses of the Peloponnese." *Fortress* 17, 2–20.

Hütteroth, W. (1975). "The pattern of settlement in Palestine in the sixteenth century." In M. Maoz (ed.), *Studies on Palestine during the Ottoman Period*. Jerusalem: Magnes Press, 3–10.

Jochalas, T. (1971). "Über die Einwanderung der Albaner in Griechenland." *Beiträge zur Kenntnis Südosteuropas und des Nahen Orients* 13, 89–106.

Mazower, M. (2004). *Salonika, City of Ghosts: Christians, Muslims and Jews 1430–1950*. London: Harper Collins.

Rackham, O. and J. Moody (1996). *The Making of the Cretan Landscape*. Manchester: Manchester University Press.

Stedman, N. (1996). "Land-use and settlement in post-medieval central Greece: An interim discussion." In P. Lock and G. D. R. Sanders (eds.), *The Archaeology of Medieval Greece*. Oxford: Oxbow, 179–192.

Vionis, A. K. (2001). "Post-Roman pottery unearthed: Medieval ceramics and pottery research in Greece." *Medieval Ceramics* 25, 84–98.

21

Material Culture, the Built Environment, and Society in Ottoman and Venetian Greece

Domestic Housing in the Post-Medieval Era

The study of standing buildings, still in use, ruined or preserved in paintings, drawings, and photographs from the last few centuries, offers the student of material culture an immensely insightful resource for understanding the nature and dynamics of past societies. Archaeology is by definition the analysis of past material culture, so it is not necessary to confine our attention to private houses and public buildings excavated by "archaeologists"; we can and should make use of these other rich resources evidencing the built environment. In the Aegean, this is all the more important because Post-Medieval Archaeology does not yet exist as a defined discipline in the region. Till the last few years, most excavations in Greece by Greek and foreign teams did not treat Ottoman and nineteenth- and early twentieth-century AD levels as worthy of detailed recording, so we have precious few dig reports and finds catalogs to draw on for reconstructing domestic life and major pre-Modern monuments. In this and the following chapter I shall make no further excuses for bringing in many forms of material culture which come from much wider contexts than pure archaeology. Most buildings have been studied by architects, whilst movable material culture has been mainly approached through Folklore and

Rural Heritage scholarship. However there is one more vital source of information which can only increase, probably logarithmically, and that is the steady growth of regional survey projects, whose directors are now well aware of the necessity of treating the period 1400–1900 AD as seriously and as carefully as any previous era.

In the development of domestic life, the house plays as central a role to archaeologists as it did for past societies themselves, thus archaeologists can benefit greatly from the mature development of its study ("Vernacular Architecture)" by architects, art historians, anthropologists, and folklorists (Sigalos 2004).

In his famous geographical survey of the Balkans, Cvijic (1918) recognized regional house and settlement types, and tied these mainly to ethno-historic communities or "cultures." Thus for Greece the "Greek-Mediterranean" settlement predominated, characterized by nucleated villages whose houses consisted of an upper floor for humans above ground floors for farm and transport animals. Pockets of Turkish Muslims were associated with the Turkish-Oriental house, which had a stone foundation and overhanging upper stories of mudbrick and timber (*sahnisi*). Finally, çiftlik settlements housed Greek laborers on estates, especially on the arable plains of Eastern Greece; here there were simple low peasant houses in a square dominated by the "*konak*" tower of the landlord (*bey*). Megas (1951) was a folklorist who

The Complete Archaeology of Greece: From Hunter-Gatherers to the 20th Century AD, First Edition. John Bintliff.
© 2012 John Bintliff. Published 2012 by Blackwell Publishing Ltd.

pioneered the classification of Greek house types, but linked these with a Greek nationalist aim to derive them from ancient times. Moutsopoulos (1982) summarized major Greek house forms, but similarly saw these as indigenous, originating via Byzantine domestic architecture from Classical and prehistoric traditions. Wagstaff (1965) rather emphasized environment; for example, a dominance of limestone creates the typical Greek house, whilst mudbrick logically replaces this on the great plains. Likewise the arid climate favored flat roofs on the Aegean islands and East Greek littoral, contrasted to pitched roofs inland with more rain and snow. Furthermore the inland hilly and mountainous parts of Greece encouraged the rise of two-story houses adapting to sloping settlement surfaces. A cultural element was allowed, so that there could be, as with Cvijic, a Turco-Oriental house, although Wagstaff considered that separate female quarters were confined to Muslims. Towerhouses were seen as ethnic Albanian or Maniot (the Mani is a remote rocky peninsula in the far south of the Peloponnese famous for its feuding clans and independence from outside government). Aalen (1987) also summarized the main vernacular (private house) types, but was innovative in including temporary rural field-huts (*kalyves*) and sheepfolds (*mandres*). The greatest contribution has been the multi-authored series of "Greek Traditional Architecture" (Philippides 1983–1990), organized region by region. These volumes give an excellent overview of the typology and plan of homes, and occasionally village plans. One weakness is that the historical development of houses is not researched in depth, and internal fittings are little explored, nor the social arrangements which changing home designs reflected.

However within the Greek vernacular architecture tradition there are other studies which do make up for these omissions, amongst which the fine thesis of Kizis (1994) on the houses of the Pelion peninsula stands out. The pioneer regional archaeological survey of the University of Minnesota in Messenia already included an anthropological study of several villages (notably Karpofora) by Aschenbrenner (1972), and it is one of that team, Fred Cooper, who has led an international project to record the traditional houses of the Western Peloponnese before their heritage is replaced by modern homes (Cooper 2002, Coulton 2009). The archaeologist Guy Sanders has produced important evidence for the settlement plans of the Venetian colonies on the Cyclades (1996), followed by Ince and Ballantyne for Venetian Kythera (2007), whilst Rackham and Moody included traditional homes in their volume on the historical ecology of Crete (1996), where there exists a long tradition of recording elite public and private Venetian architecture (Stallsmith 2007). The Kea Survey produced a fine study of Early Modern "landscape architecture" by Todd Whitelaw (1991), which linked agricultural terracing to field houses and other rural built features of the island. Recently the PRAP survey in the Pylos region of Messenia has been studying traditional villages (Lee 2001) and Venetian-Ottoman military architecture (Davies 2004), and the latter topic with an overview of major Greek sites is well presented in Triposkoufi and Tsitouri (2002). Our own Boeotia Project made early progress with town, village, and house plans (Stedman 1996, Bintliff *et al.* 1999), which led to large-scale planning of deserted Medieval and post-medieval villages (Sigalos 2004). This work continues with the current Leiden-Ljubljana Boeotia survey (Bintliff *et al.* 2007, 2009).

In his overview of published pre-Modern domestic housing in Greece, Sigalos (2004) comments on the resultant map of different house types (Color Plate 21.1a) that no simple trend appears. Nonetheless in Northern Greece, incorporated late into the Greek State, the rising commercial wealth of town and country over the period from the eighteenth to early twentieth centuries allowed the Late Ottoman International Style to flourish. In contrast Southern Greece from the early nineteenth century increasingly rejected that Oriental influence in favor of Western architectural styles: Renaissance-Baroque influences and more recent "Neoclassical" forms associated with the "Greek Revival" or rediscovery of Classical Greek architecture. Moreover, much of the urban fabric of Southern towns had been demolished during the War of Independence. On Crete the long Venetian occupation has left a uniquely rich architectural environment (Venetian-Aegean style), notably from the seventeenth century, whilst the Frankish-era conquest of the Cyclades and other Aegean islands was followed by only limited intrusions of later building styles, allowing settlement plans and house types to survive on a large scale in former Venetian colonial townships and rural villas (Aegean style).

We earlier noted that many architectural studies of traditional Greek houses focus on the structure of the domestic unit, but do not give equal detail to internal furnishings (mobile or fixed), and the use of space in functional but also social terms. Additionally in the Greek climate, much of daily life, even in the winter months, takes place outdoors, adding workspace, light, air, and often warmth, to everyday activities. Thus courtyards (*aulí*), outside benches, storehouses and stables, ovens, and wine or olive presses, are just as much part of the built environment of traditional Greek home life as the major domestic roofed spaces.

Domestic Housing in the Ottoman Period

During the eighteenth and nineteenth centuries the indigenous elites of the Ottoman provinces such as the Balkans looked to Ottoman house styles, furnishings, and even domestic arrangements for gender, as bearing the cachet of class. Ottoman-style houses were predominantly used by the middle and upper classes of Greek and other ethnic communities in the Aegean, who had both the wealth and desire to emulate the styles of the wider Empire. As Vionis (2003) shows, this applies to some extent even in regions such as the Cyclades where there was a very low Turkish presence. However the survival pattern of buildings occupied by different social groups is very uneven in time and space (Sigalos 2004).

An issue of contemporary interest is that of gender in spatial terms (Sigalos 2004). Although sectors of Aegean society were affected by Islamic culture with its prohibitions on female sociability and dress, practices were variable. Our sources point to areas of the home reserved for women of the house, the *haremlik*, as well as to the building of small mezzanine (half-story) levels or expanded cupboards with screens to allow females to listen and observe whilst remaining invisible to non-family male visitors. These also survive in significant numbers in standing buildings. What fits with our earlier observations on the emulation of Ottoman behavior is the fact that such customs were widespread amongst the wealthier Christian urban populations, along with other Oriental customs relating to dress and general house design. On the other hand, the large-scale participation of women in working-class craft, trade, and agriculture, meant that most of the urban and almost all rural households must have practiced everyday mixing of genders in work and leisure. However, as was normal till living memory in Modern Greece, unmarried girls would always have family chaperones with them.

Another general aspect of settlements in the Ottoman Greek landscape is internal organization. Rural villages were often sectored into neighborhood house-clusters on the basis of kinship; our most detailed mapping of this comes from the Mani peninsula in the Peloponnese (Saitas 2009).

Urban Planning and House Forms in Ottoman Times

Ottoman towns in the Balkans were typified by their division into ethnic or religious quarters (*machalades/mahalle*) centered around their own foci of worship and the mansions of their community leaders (Braude 1985) and were taxed and administered as such by the Ottoman authorities. Towns had usually developed organically rather than to a formal plan, with small winding streets, some cobbled, mostly not, little wheeled traffic, and goods generally brought into town by donkey or on foot (Lawless 1977). They had few open spaces, their social centers being the bathhouses (*hamam*), open markets (*suq-bazaar*), covered markets (*bedestan*), merchant hostels (*khan*), churches, synagogues, and mosques. A castle often serves for the town's Ottoman garrison and governor. On the Greek Mainland it was common that only public secular and religious buildings were usually of stone or brick, the rest were of wood and mudbrick (but usually on stone foundations). Lawless suggests for Mainland towns of the Early Ottoman era, but especially in the lowland plains, that most town houses differed little from rural village habitations, single-story cottages of mudbrick, a style still observable into the early nineteenth century for the poorer occupants of Trikkala.

Venetian colonial towns also had quarters focused on churches and elite mansions, and added to garrison-forts elaborate city walls in earth faced with stone. In keeping with Italian practice, large and small squares were frequent as were wider streets, and the main square might be faced by the town hall, governor's residence, cathedral, and bishop's palace. A far greater use of stone was in evidence.

In the fifteenth to seventeenth centuries neither Ottoman Greek nor Venetian towns were normally major industrial centers. The Ottoman towns were usually market-towns for their regions, residences of the provincial elite and of more specialized trades and services. The importance of fairs seems to indicate too that Ottoman towns were inadequate in meeting their regional needs in objects of commerce (Lawless 1977). But Venetian towns, typically maritime, were in contrast usually nodes for international trade in and out of their regions and in transit traffic passing through them.

Although there arose widespread rural peasant impoverishment and an associated decline in urban populations in Mainland Greece, from the seventeenth century onwards, there were localized signs of recovery by the eighteenth to early nineteenth centuries, both in urban centers and some country regions, connected often to a growing commercial and proto-industrial prosperity (especially from the production of textiles). Both towns and villages participating in this wide trend exhibit the contemporary construction of large mansions for the leading families profiting from these developments. Sigalos (2004) notes how in this era in the Ottoman Balkans, areas on major land and sea routes and those with cotton and wool textile industries witness economic growth, stimulating elaborate houses for a prosperous community, of which a very large number still survive in the towns and villages of Thrace, Macedonia, Epirus, and Thessaly. Lawless (1977) describes how the wealthier inhabitants constructed grand houses in stone and wood to replace simpler dwellings, as well as investing in richly-decorated churches and schools, while developing an interest in intellectual life and thereby cultivating a sense of national consciousness. He contrasts this with the continuing

simplicity and poverty of the çiftlik estates in the lowland plains.

Two- to three-story town houses appear in the seventeenth and spread rapidly in the eighteenth and nineteenth centuries as the result of the rising wealth of the urban landowning and commercial classes, and in the countryside, estate-centers linked to commercialization might feature large multi-story tower-houses, or more extensive country mansions (archontika). The cachet of class led to the diffusion through these new urban and rural mansions of Oriental house designs, internal furnishings, and associated lifestyles. Although in general the Aegean Islands, Crete included, stayed rather in their "Frankish-Venetian" building traditions, peripheral areas which became networked into these economic developments adopted the International Ottoman style, such as on Thasos and Lesbos in the North Aegean. However although Modern Crete preserves a large number of Italian-inspired urban and rural mansions for both Greek and Venetian wealthy families dating from the Venetian occupation (1204–1669), once under Ottoman rule, there eventually developed a tendency to adopt the International Ottoman style of architecture, so that examples of eighteenth-century date fit the wider Aegean trend. A similar late development occurred in the Cyclades.

According to Sigalos (2004) key aspects of Ottoman fashions in Aegean town houses and the rural residences of wealthy landowners include: (1) a clear vertical division with ground floors possessing attached yards/gardens, combining leisure and open-air work- and storage-space, while the upper floors are for domestic and social life; (2) the upper floors are articulated around a key access space, the iliakos-hagiati, either an open veranda opening to the garden/yard or at least to the outside world, or an enclosed corridor or gallery, the former suited to domestic and social life in the warmer months; (3) opening off (2) are a series of modular rooms of ondas type (see 'Textile Villages of Mount Pelion' Box in next section), square units for flexible use usually with built-in benches/beds (sofas) round the walls; (4) especially on the uppermost floor ondas rooms can project out from the house (sahnisia) to allow airflow and light from different directions into the house, and via grilled shutters allow the occupants to observe the townscape without reciprocal visibility; (5) the upper floors may contain a cosmopolitan mix of Oriental furnishings – textiles, carved and painted wall and ceiling designs, and portable objects of metal and ceramic, as well as imports and imitation of the same from Christian Europe. The *ondas* module is suited to flexible use of space at different times of the day, or the year. A reception room can become a bedroom, since built-in cupboards (*mousandres*) and the interior of the *sofas* are used for the storage of bedding and other household materials. Wealthier homes can designate rooms for winter or summer use, for private and semi-public or reception space, and for the seclusion of women. Sigalos emphasizes that the flexibility of the *ondas* concept marks a distinction of importance to the Western-originating development in Early Modern Greece of invariable, set functions for rooms: being a flexible rectangular space which can be multiplied and ranged either along a veranda or round an internal reception space, allowing functional, gender, and social separation.

The town of Ioannina in Northwest Mainland Greece (Loukakis 1960) preserves many fine houses of the wealthier class from later Ottoman times. Archontika, or the mansions of the elite of the town, are large multi-story complexes focused on an internal garden. The ground-floor rooms as usual are for work and storage, whilst the upper-floor chambers are ranged behind a veranda opening onto the garden (extended *hagiati*). As often in pre-Modern traditional houses, the upper floor(s) are reached directly from the ground by a staircase, here a monumental one. There is a generic similarity to the plans of merchants' hostels or *khans*. Lesser in scale yet still impressive are the town houses of the middle class (Figure 21.1): two to three storys high, the ground floor (d) has stores and a yard. The first floor (c) has a living suite suited for winter (*cheimoniatiko*) opening off a reception space (*metzopatoma*), whilst the second floor (b) has a formal reception room, also suited for winter months, a family living room of *ondas* type, and a long gallery-room, which may be an open or enclosed veranda (*hagiati-iliakos*), but suited for domestic and social life in the warmer months. Interestingly, in some wealthy houses there may be a small space reserved for females to retreat on the arrival of male visitors, illustrating the adoption of Islamic standards of domestic modesty amongst the wealthier Christian households. In Ioannina and another regional town of Epiros, Metsovo, such houses of the richer classes combine International Ottoman architectural styles with much internal decoration deriving in fashion but also directly via import from West and Central Europe; wonderful Western carved and painted wall and ceiling art and stained glass mixes easily with other furnishings and objects of Oriental type. The extensive commercial and social contacts of such flourishing towns of eighteenth- and early nineteenth-century Greece are clearly emphasized in such cosmopolitan reflections within the domestic built environment (Philippides 1999, Sigalos 2004).

In the historic town of Kavala in Northeast Mainland Greece, the Greek archaeologist Bakirtzis has pioneered the study of post-Medieval urbanism, with recording and conservation of houses threatened by modern development during the 1970s. In many articles in the journal *Archaiologikon Deltion* he has outlined the distinctive homes with Ottoman features from the eighteenth and nineteenth centuries (cf. listing in Sigalos 2004). Architectural styles compare with those already discussed, and likewise here the display rooms were highly embellished with paintings and carved wall and ceiling ornaments, where the attractive merging of Western and Oriental fashion results in the so-called "Turco-Baroque" style.

In the Peloponnese the significant port-town of Pylos consisted of a castle, a walled lower town, and an extramural settlement (Sigalos 2004, Davies 2004). The seventeenth-century traveler Evliya Celebi claimed the following houses for each of these units: 33, 600, and 200. Muslims dominated in such walled settlements, which seem to have been made up of closely-packed houses, with at least the ground floor of stone, some at least with yards, contrasted to the more dispersed extramural settlements with gardens attached to the houses. Another fortified port-town was Kiparissia (Sigalos 2004), likewise in Messenia province. Still today the road to the castle is lined with derelict terraced townhouses of Ottoman style, constructed of stone ground floors with the traditional wood-structure upper domestic rooms overhanging the street.

Study of Ottoman houses has tended to focus on the outstanding mansions of the upper classes and neglected those of the remaining population, due to

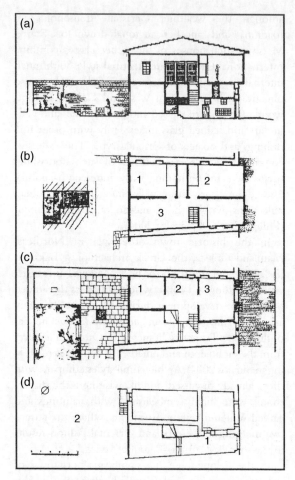

Figure 21.1   Town house in Ioannina.
E. Sigalos, *Housing in Medieval and Post-Medieval Greece.*
Oxford 2004, Figure 60.

their lesser architectural pretensions. In addition to the case of Ioannina cited earlier, where less prestige homes were analyzed, we might also mention the town of Verroia in Northeastern Greece, where Chrysopoulos (1960) combines analysis of the *archontika* of the wealthy with homes of at least the middle class, belonging to the *laika* or non-elite families. They appear to reflect scaled-down versions of grander houses, consisting of terraced homes, with a ground floor garden and storage area, then from the garden an exterior stair leads to a first floor veranda-corridor space suited to much social and domestic life in the warmer months. This latter reception space opens

onto two rooms of *ondas* form allowing domestic life in the cooler months and potential privacy. In the *archontika* we may note once more that some possess built spaces for temporary female seclusion. The poorer urban families appear to have used the form of the rural longhouse, giving a rustic appearance to the less central zones of Ottoman towns, away from the houses of merchants, manufacturers, the professions, and wealthier landowners. Evidence for this comes from Livadheia (see Text Box) and Argos.

In general, after mosques, little survives of communal buildings from Ottoman towns, but we can admire the modern initiative of the city of Thessaloniki in conserving its fifteenth-century covered market (*Bedestan*), still in use, and its restoration of a splendid contemporary bath-house (the *Bey Hamami*) (Kourkoutidou-Nikolaidou and Tourta 1997).

The towns of the Cyclades and most other Aegean Islands remained largely within the Frankish architectural and planning traditions introduced in the thirteenth century, apart from the more traditional Greek vernacular suburbs which lay outside the formally planned colonial central areas, the rural villages, and as seen some local Late Ottoman architectural emulation (Sanders 1996, Vionis 2001, 2005, 2009). The largest collection of pre-nineteenth-century West European-inspired public and private buildings in Greece lie on Crete and the Ionian Islands. Crete remained in Venetian hands to 1669, and contains a rich legacy of fortresses and the urban and rural mansions of the wealthier classes (colonial and indigenous). Study of this heritage has been long underway by architects and historians (Gerola 1905–1932), although till recently integration with archaeological material culture studies has been limited. The elite of the island naturally followed Italian stylistic fashions in the display architecture of their residences, so that Renaissance and Baroque façades and ground plans are widespread (Figure 21.3). The isolation of Crete, after the Ottoman conquest of the rest of the Aegean and of Cyprus, forced the Venetian Republic to invest in urban fortifications of immense scale and sophistication, such as can be admired in Herakleion and Rethimnon, as well as in coastal forts such as Frangokastello. After Ottoman capture however, the island's elite shifted housing fashions to the International Ottoman style (Sigalos 2004). Just as with the (neglected) flourishing literary and musical

Ottoman Livadheia

The Boeotian town of Livadheia, now the regional capital, provides a useful case study of the problems and potentials of studying Ottoman towns in much of Modern Greece (Bintliff *et al.* 1999, Sigalos 2004). The Old Town lay alongside the River Herkyna, largely overlying the small ancient city. Medieval and Ottoman Livadheia was a small community, consisting of three zones. The Castle was divided into a military-administrative Acropolis, below which was built a walled lower town. Beyond this lay an extramural quarter, on both sides of the river, associated with the Middle Byzantine church of Panayia. The town appears to have developed into a significant community under later Frankish rule, then prospered in later Ottoman times as the center of a *Kaza* or administrative unit for Western Boeotia, trading local production of textile dyes, wool, cereals, tobacco, and rice on an international scale. It was drawn and described by many early nineteenth-century Travelers (Tsigakou 1981). Apart from the Medieval Castle, little survives, although Western visitors such as Leake noted the urban mansions with "spacious chambers and galleries in the Turkish manner." From the late nineteenth century onwards, the town has abandoned its historic core, to spread on a vastly greater scale both to the north and east (where lies the modern administrative and commercial heart).

In the Southwest quarter of modern Livadheia, the core of the Old Town is the former extramural district on the left bank of the river. Sources identify the main street as running parallel and west of the river, along which we know of at least three mosques. One lies beneath the modern cathedral (Metropolis), another has been recorded in remnants within later buildings at a small square called *Tabachna*. Both were associated with a small widening of the street to create market areas. A third mosque miraculously survives between them as a shell above a small shop.

Descriptions of the town indicate its plan was of narrow winding streets, and even today the old Main Street (Odos Stratigou Ioannou), still possesses this character. This street was fronted by two- to three-story houses with overhanging upper floors, whilst to their rear the riverside houses displayed a similar profile attractively overlooking the Herkyna. Some of these were genuine mansions, but just one has been preserved as a national monument, the house belonging to the most notable of the leading local Greek families (*archontes*), that of Logothetis. Travelers met a warm welcome from various members of this clan, and the house today shows a typical combination of International Ottoman style architecture and lavishly decorated internal reception rooms combining Western and Oriental designs. Sources remark on the emulation amongst the Livadheia elite of Ottoman lifestyles, for which a famous picture of one of the Logothetis family is an eloquent witness. His Islamic dress, the sofa, hookah pipe, and Oriental fireplace are striking.

The Main Street and the banks of the river were thus faced with several mosques, two- to three-story homes for the landowning, mercantile, and administrative elite of the town, as well as the owners of small shops which opened onto the road. Just one further house in original style (if rebuilt in post-Ottoman times) survived till our own architectural survey, of interest as it represents a less prestigious town house with shop below. Sadly it appears today on the verge of demolition (Figure 21.2). The ground-floor shop and storage area was not connected to the upper residential floor, which was accessed from outside stairs on the slope at the back of the house. This upper floor retains its *sahnisi* overhang which once would have been largely a veranda with shutters opening onto the street, behind which two rooms would have provided a more private family room and a semi-public reception room or *saloni*. Leake in the early nineteenth century describes homes in the town as commonly formed of sets of rooms ranged along a veranda.

As one moved away from the Main Street, an extensive suburb stretched uphill to the west, with a smaller one across the river and also uphill to the east. Further mosques and Christian churches formed small neighborhood foci in a warren of

Figure 21.2 A ruined overhang-house, main street, Ottoman Livadheia.

E. Sigalos, *Housing in Medieval and Post-Medieval Greece*. Oxford 2004, Figure 167.

tiny alleys and dense house-blocks. In these outer districts it seems likely that "urban" forms of two-story homes were increasingly matched by simpler,

more "rural" house forms occupied by poorer families employed in the town or working the countryside around. Their homes would have been of the agricultural longhouse variety, modified often to one-and-a-half-story structures, to take advantage of the typical sloping terrain. In an architectural survey undertaken by our Boeotia project (Bintliff *et al.* 1999, Sigalos 2004), a surprising number of these homes were recorded, although most were in ruinous condition and since then have mostly been demolished. One fine one-and-a-half-story house we recorded is very rural in all respects but for its urban location. A large yard with a gated wall and ancillary structures for crop-processing, leads to a house with ground-floor storage and stabling. Direct stair access from the yard takes one first to a veranda *hagiati*, behind which lie the formal and informal domestic spaces.

In the first Ottoman tax record of 1466 (Bintliff 1995, Kiel 1987), some 1000 inhabitants are listed for Livadheia, 30 percent being Muslim. In Boeotia as widely through the Balkans, Islamic and other immigrants (such as Jews), were clustered into towns and fortresses, partly for protection, but also to reflect their dominant role in commerce and as rentier landowners. Hardly any Muslims are recorded in Boeotian villages. Under the positive influence of the Early Ottoman Empire, the town's population had by 1570 quadrupled, whilst a seventeenth-century source mentions half a dozen mosques and a similar number of churches, which provided the administrative and social subdistricts (*mahalles*) of the town.

culture of Ottoman Greece, Venetian Crete gave rise to a lively production of the arts, including literature and painting: the star product was Domenikos Theotokopoulos or El Greco (1541–1614), who combined Byzantine traditions with Western artistic styles (Holton 1991).

Even more Italian is the planning and architecture of the Ionian Islands off the west coast of Greece. They were under Venetian rule between 1363 and 1797, after which French then British administration

retained them within a Western political and cultural sphere of influence. Apart from the major public buildings for local administration and the great defense works (such as Corfu Castle), a wide range of housing types represents the long centuries of Western rule and all classes of the population living within the towns (Figure 21.4). Zivas (1974) underlines the close links between Italian architecture and the development of local schools of literature and the other arts, but perhaps stresses too much the military element in suggesting

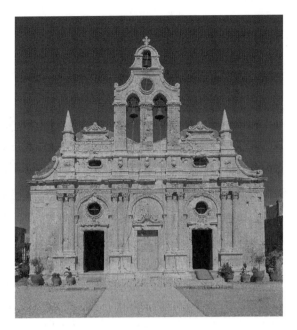

Figure 21.3 The Venetian-era monastic church at Arcadi, Crete.
Shutterstock Images/Paul Cowan.

Figure 21.4 Seventeenth-century Venetian palace in Corfu (The Nobles' Lounge).
Author.

that the prevalence of multi-story terraced house-blocks, reminiscent of modern apartments, was affected by restrictions of space within town defenses. Such designs were characteristic of non-elite housing in Italian cities from the Middle Ages (Sabelberg 1985).

On Mainland Greece several key port-towns central to Venetian maritime power, although lost to the Ottomans in the sixteenth century, and briefly recaptured during the Venetian occupation of the Peloponnese from 1685 to 1715, contain notable Italian-style public and private architecture, including Methoni, Koroni, and Navplion (cf. Triposkoufi and Tsitouri 2002, with references). On the island of Kythera off the southern Peloponnese, the main Venetian town at Chora follows the Cycladic model of a fortified town of two-story houses, with an inner *Kastro* for the governor and defense forces, and an outer *Bourgo* for the elite citizens of the island. In the countryside however the abolition of serfdom by Venice allowed new village foundations for local peasants during the sixteenth century; these follow the Cycladic island model of concentric houses to defend the community from pirate attack. Interestingly their two-story homes show a rise in peasant status, allowing a spatial division between storage and stock, and domestic space (Ince and Ballantyne 2007), and perhaps emulation of colonial town-dwellings.

Vernacular Housing in the Countryside

For Ottoman Greece, if the houses of the wealthier in towns, and their estate-centers in the countryside, have largely been destroyed and replaced by post-Ottoman styles, a far greater survival can now be postulated for Ottoman-era peasant houses, either in their original fabric, or retaining their design although rebuilt in the post-Ottoman period. It is well known in Vernacular Architecture studies, that peasant homes show greater stylistic stability than those of the richer classes, a result of lower disposable income and decreased desire to alter houses to suit fashion and the demands of social aspiration. The most prominent Mainland form of rural peasant home, already observed also in towns, is the single-story or one-and-a-half-story longhouse (Stedman 1996, Sigalos 2004) (Color Plate 21.1b: the Agricultural Style). This formerly sheltered both the family and some domestic animals, and is a form that survived widely till very recently in remote districts of the Mainland country-side (notably in the Skourta Plain, Dimitsantou-Kremezi

1996), and which we have been able to demonstrate reaching back in deserted Boeotian villages to the seventeenth or eighteenth century if not earlier. The social and symbolic meanings of such longhouses have been explored on Cyprus by Sant Cassia (1982).

At the early Ottoman deserted village of Panaya-VM4 there are traces of house outlines which may point to such longhouses being already typical for rural settlements in the fifteenth and sixteenth centuries. Stedman (1996) noted that the oldest longhouses in traditional Boeotian villages usually lay with a similar alignment, often north to south to allow one long face to gain maximum morning sun, but were separated by a notable distance from one another.

This recalls our observations from Medieval Greece, where we saw that typical non-elite dwellings possessed an open workspace, rarely enclosed, around them. Life would have been lived very publicly in these settlements. The surviving longhouses often have outside bread ovens and sheds for storage, as well as less commonly a press for oil or wine. It is unclear how elaborate pre-Modern farm complexes of this type were, since deserted Ottoman and early nineteenth-century villages with such houses can both lack and possess ancillary structures to the longhouse. It seems likely that one half of the single-story house was typically occupied by the family, the other by essential domestic animals for transport, milk, and plowing (Figure 21.9). In one-and-a-half-story houses it was possible to separate the stock by level. The creation of two-story houses in rural contexts, the estate owners and managers apart, and excluding "proto-industrial" villages (see below), is considered to be a development almost exclusively within the Early Modern era of changed village economics.

The rise of serf-estates in the Middle Ottoman period, during the seventeenth century, began with small scale çiftliks consisting of a few families, but these were increasingly replaced by large communities which could include towerhouses of the landowner or estate manager. The small hamlet on the acropolis of the ancient city of Tanagra in Boeotia, discovered during our surface survey of the site, is almost certainly a çiftlik, consisting of four longhouses end-to-end associated with a restricted scatter of domestic ceramics of seventeenth- to eighteenth-century age (Bintliff et al. 2004–2005). No controlling

Figure 21.5 Ottoman-period painting of a çiftlik with peasant houses, towerhouse, and church.
E. Sigalos, *Housing in Medieval and Post-Medieval Greece.* Oxford 2004, Figure 137.

larger structure was found, suiting the early form of estate.

Another deserted Boeotian village, Mavrommati Harmena, is a "great çiftlik" from an eighteenth-century Ottoman tax record, with several hundred inhabitants (Kiel 1997, Sigalos 2004). At the top of the sloping site we found a small but impressive complex centered on a well-built, multi-story house. Stretching below this focus was a much more extensive, dispersed scatter of unpretentious, single-story longhouses. It is not difficult to compare this housing stratification with the standard layout and style of Ottoman çiftliks discussed in later nineteenth- and early twentieth-century human geography studies of the Balkans (cf. Cvijic 1918, 246) (Figure 21.5). The large number of rather primitive rubble foundation longhouses and one much more pretentious, multi-story (*konak*) house, must represent peasant families and the estate owner or supervisor respectively.

The wide spaces separating longhouses in sites such as Harmena also allow family expansion to be accommodated, either by extending the longhouse or adding a second house to one end of an existing home. Some of the Harmena longhouses cleared of vegetation for study showed yards with low walls, and one possible external oven. The dominant multi-story structure (*konak*) at the top of the settlement, close to a threshing-floor, has a group of auxiliary rooms, probably for storage of the estate's produce. At another deserted Boeotia çiftlik, Guinosati, a likely controlling tower has also been identified amid dispersed long-houses (Vionis 2006, 2008).

A further çiftlik studied archaeologically is the deserted village of Baklaki in North-Central Greece (Haagsma *et al.* 1993), whose use continued into the Early Modern period. As usual the houses were constructed across the sloping contours, allowing a one-and-a-half-story plan, with the basement for storage and stabling, the upper floor for domestic accommodation. A useful overview of the physical form of rural villages in Thessaly, especially the common çiftliks, is provided by Lawless (1977). In Epirus the pre-Ottoman fortress of Ragion appears to have been resettled as a çiftlik (Preka-Alexandri 1988), with a series of single-story houses associated with a towerhouse (*konak*).

The estate-centers of the Middle to Late Ottoman era, whether owned by ethnic Turks or Greeks, generally show Ottoman architectural features. Figure 21.6a shows a towerhouse from Lesbos. Figure 21.6b is the other common rural estate-center, the *archontiko*, which can include a tower in its more complex forms, and is reminiscent of urban mansions (also termed *archontika*). This example (Triantaphyllopoulos 1976) was built in the usual style of stone lower and wood-frame upper floors, found also in urban mansions, with three storys around a yard.

On the one hand, it is reasonable to note a possible ancestry for these towers in the Frankish feudal tower, unsurprising since the economic and locational context are very similar. Indeed in Boeotia we have been able to demonstrate that Frankish towers continued in use through Ottoman times in several cases. The sturdy entrance door and grilled lower windows show that protection from robbers and bandits was a requirement, but the front door is on the ground floor, pointing to an absence of serious military threat. Also in contrast is the residential uppermost floor. Here we see a typical Ottoman feature, the use of square room modules (*ondas*), which radiate around the center of the structure, and may project on cantilevers outwards from the tower (*sahnisia*).

As befitting a totally different cultural tradition, the Venetian countryside on Crete till the seventeenth century and that of the Ionian Islands and Kythera till the eighteenth saw elaborate rural estate-centers in

Figure 21.6a Ottoman-period rural elite mansion: towerhouse type, Lesbos.
E. Sigalos, *Housing in Medieval and Post-Medieval Greece.* Oxford 2004, Figure 18.

Figure 21.6b Rural elite mansion: *archontiko* type, Epiros. Historic photograph.
E. Sigalos, *Housing in Medieval and Post-Medieval Greece.* Oxford 2004, Figure 58.

Italianate Renaissance-Baroque styles, comparable to contemporary Venetian colonial townhouses (Sigalos 2004, Ince and Ballantyne 2007).

Apart from estate-centers and rural mansions of the wealthy, rural peasant settlement in the Aegean islands and on the Mainland remains clustered into hamlets or villages for the most part, until the changing political and economic climate of the late nineteenth century. Texts inform us that in many Aegean landscapes the cultivation of distant fields and pastures might involve the use of seasonal dispersed huts and animal-folds, although it was also often the case that large numbers if not the whole community might shift to a seasonal second village for these purposes (*kalyvia*).

Although traditional Greek villages were till recently dominated by a central square (*plateia*) and the main church, around which clustered coffee-houses and shops, there is good reason to doubt that this characterized most Ottoman and Medieval rural settlement plans. A more irregular open dispersed pattern linked to agricultural paths, interspersed with churches, fountains, and small open spaces at road junctions, may have been typical. Groups of houses might be tied by kinship into small neighborhoods. The communal public space and a wider street network seem at present to be late nineteenth-century innovations connected to the introduction of more "urban" infrastructure into the countryside (Stedman 1996, Sigalos 2004).

Aalen in a pioneering study of rural architecture on the island of Kephallenia (1984), suggested a chronological development for peasant housing (Figure 21.7). The oldest form was a one-story longhouse shared by the stock and the family. Using slope differences a one-and-a-half-story version could develop, but since this was associated in surviving examples with a more complex division of rooms, he considered this to be a later form, associated with a rising status for small-scale farmers from the mid-nineteenth century. The two-story farmhouse with yet further horizontal and vertical subdivisions he also dated from the mid-nineteenth century onwards, reflecting for him the accommodation of wealthier farmers as well as rural professions such as lawyers, doctors, and merchants. As we have already noted, the archaeological data from deserted Ottoman villages rather suggests that the one-and-a-half-story longhouses are typical from Medieval times onwards, although the internal divisions in Aalen's plans *are* probably later modifications, indeed of nineteenth- to twentieth-century age, when undivided rooms or minimal divisions were replaced by more elaborate internal house divisions.

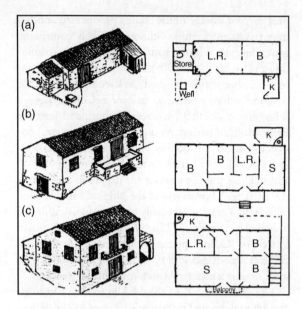

Figure 21.7   Aalen's model for rural farm evolution on Kephallenia, developing through phases A to C.
E. Sigalos, *Housing in Medieval and Post-Medieval Greece.* Oxford 2004, Figure 31.

The spread of two-story houses seems to demonstrate the very belated general diffusion of the styles of 'town life' to the countryside.

Interestingly, the general long-term trend for simple peasant houses from Medieval through post-Medieval times, till improving social and economic conditions encouraged multi-story, more elaborate rural homes in the twentieth century, is not universal. On Kythera the Medieval peasants lived in simple homes, but in the sixteenth century they could occupy two-story village houses; significantly however the return to single and one-and-a-half-story houses in the eighteenth-century villages may mark downscaling of social aspiration and perhaps wealth (Ince and Ballantyne 2007).

Other exceptions are formed by rural settlements which played a major role in the regional and interregional upsurge of manufacturing and commerce of the eighteenth and early nineteenth centuries. In such cases the controlling families may build "urban-style" mansions in rural settlements, or if the whole community is prospering, multi-story expansive residences can become more widespread in a village. Thus in the central Peloponnese in the Gortynia district (Benechtsou 1960) a flourishing pastoral and manufacturing production is associated with Late Ottoman substantial, multi-story houses (up to even five levels), using the steep slopes to assist construction. The domestic accommodation lay in the upper floor(s), whilst the lower were deployed for storage, stabling, and textile production. The well-conserved hillside textile village of Arachova in Central Greece has a similar development in its impressive architecture.

As a result of wider commercial entanglement, many of these elaborate homes exhibit the influence of the International Ottoman style, but also, since Western European partners were actively integrated into such trade, architectural and furnishing styles from Italy and further afield. In general however, the appearance of multi-story houses in Greek villages is a late nineteenth-century phenomenon marking the gradual spread of improved incomes in post-Ottoman Greece (Stedman 1996).

One famous case study is that of the textile villages of the Pelion Peninsula in Thessaly (see Text Box).

A very different case study is that of the largely infertile, remote maritime peninsula of Mani in the Peloponnese (Saitas 1990, 2009). Isolated from easy contact with the wider world and with limited resources, its inhabitants developed specific adaptations to such conditions. Competition for scarce agro-pastoral land and the threat of pirates encouraged a culture of endemic intercommunity feuding and heavily-fortified settlements and houses. A proliferation of defensive towers marks the skyline of surviving traditional community architecture.

There is growing interest in one of the commonest rural building types recorded in the Travelers for the Ottoman to Early Modern Balkans, the *Khans* or

Textile Villages of Mount Pelion

The surviving traces of these settlements' Late Ottoman prosperity are their wonderful multi-story, finely decorated houses (Kizis 1994).

Kizis divides the larger houses, belonging to leading families in the textile and other commercial businesses, into three chronological groups. The Early Period has fortified stone towerhouses, with overhanging upper floors which can be partly open loggias or entirely enclosed. The similarity to rural towerhouses is clear (see earlier Lesbos example). The basic module is one square room per floor, appended with externally-projecting wings of modular form (*ondas*). If the tower with its hierarchical functional spaces (storage to domestic to formal reception and leisure) reflects the older Medieval feudal tower tradition, the overhanging floor and *ondas* are visibly influenced by Ottoman upper-class fashion. In Kizis' Middle Period rising wealth brings a further influence from the grander multi-story town-house tradition (Figure 21.8). The multiplication of internal spaces and their increasingly elaborate decoration and furnishings are further signs of "bourgeois" prestige display

Figure 21.8 Middle Period (Late Ottoman) wealthy house in Mount Pelion.
E. Sigalos, *Housing in Medieval and Post-Medieval Greece.* Oxford 2004, Figure 50.

culture, although variant arrangements of *ondas* around a focal communication space are at the base of the design. The third period is final Ottoman to Early Greek state and shows a reorientation to Western architecture in the form of Neoclassicism.

wayside travelers' hostels. They have recently been mapped by the Dutch Aetolia Project in the rugged uplands of Aetolia (North-Central Greece) (Bommeljé and Doorn 1996) in relation to an historical-geographical analysis of communication systems in the long term within that region. Further structural and functional study of this class of monument should be undertaken to link the sparse surviving traces of these building complexes to their frequent depiction in nineteenth-century Travelers' books. A case-study architectural recording of a nineteenth-century ruined khan features in the recent Asea Survey in the Peloponnese (Forsen and Forsen 2003). In Ottoman Greece and the wider Balkans, this era also saw a great expansion of cobbled roads (*kalderimis*) whose construction was promoted by the state with the aid of local communities, along with associated bridges. Western Travelers note their heavy use with long goods caravans of pack-animals, camels, and ox-carts (Reinders and Prummel 2003).

Religious, Military, and Other Public Architecture

We already noted the rare survival of Ottoman mosques in much of Greece. But there is much to be done in researching written and pictorial records of lost examples, where often it is possible to discover Ottoman records referring to their foundation or maintenance (Kiel 2002). One such example I discovered in the background of an icon of Saint John the Baptist from Thebes. Our Boeotia Project Ottoman archivist, Machiel Kiel, also specializes in architecture and has published this lost monument (Kiel 1999), based on this image, attributing it to the 1660s and classing it, with a very similar mosque in Athens, as a major provincial imitation of the great imperial mosques of Istanbul.

The prosperity of the Ottoman Aegean in the fifteenth and sixteenth centuries, and the more restricted wealth of parts of the Greek population in the seventeenth to early nineteenth centuries, are manifested not merely in mansions in town and country, but also in the patronage of Orthodox churches and monasteries. It has sometimes been claimed that "Byzantine Art," relying as it did on Byzantine imperial and elite

patronage, would have virtually disappeared with the takeover of the Ottomans. A small proportion of churches were indeed taken over and converted to mosques by the Ottomans, in part to meet the urgent need for places of Islamic worship for the conquerors, as well as (in the case of prestige churches such as Aghia Sophia in Constantinople) to demonstrate the victory of Islam. However in keeping with traditional Islamic tolerance of other ethnic and religious communities, most were not just allowed to continue as places for Christian worship, but could be rebuilt or founded throughout the Ottoman era (cf. Vocotopoulos 1984). In a few cases we know that Ottoman financial support was provided for church repair or construction, whilst religious institutions of all faiths were given tax privileges. It can also be shown that at the major churches and monasteries there can be found impressive works of art from the Ottoman centuries. Thus on Mount Athos (Cormack 2000) the sixteenth century witnessed great buildings and art and many of the most accomplished Greek artists went to work there.

Bouras (2006) argues however that there is a contrast between the Early to Middle, and then Late, Ottoman eras. In the former the tax-privileged rural monasteries erected large well-decorated churches in traditional Middle Byzantine styles (although paintings can be in contemporary fashion, such as the Cretan School), whilst Mainland towns see small monuments inhibited by the dominant Islamic atmosphere. Additionally the countryside sees a proliferation of small public churches donated by local Greek elites, who may be commemorated in the paintings (notably in Epirus and the Pindos uplands), doubtless a reflection of the wide level of rural prosperity. In the Venetian possessions in Greece, Renaissance and later Baroque church architecture entirely displaces Byzantine traditions and reflects a wider Italianization in lifestyle. The standard design for Venetian areas is an aisled basilica with prominent façades, highly ornamented in carved stone and plaster (Figure 21.3). For the Cyclades, a more hybrid culture creates churches where older Italian Gothic styles mix with Byzantine and Italian Renaissance influences. Nonetheless a unitary trend in both Ottoman- and Venetian-controlled regions is for great attention to be given to grand wooden altar screens with inset icons.

For Late Ottoman times, from 1700 into the nineteenth century, Bouras argues for Ottoman Greece that monasteries continue to be well endowed by wealthy Orthodox elites and retain traditional Byzantine architectural traditions. For Mount Athos notable sponsors are the Greek elite in Istanbul (the *Phanariots*) and in the Ottoman Danubian provinces. Very different is an explosion of new rural churches which almost completely abandon Byzantine forms and combine influences from popular architecture, Venetian design, Ottoman "Baroque" ornament, and a perhaps conscious revival of Early Christian plans. The standard design is a large three-aisled, wood-roofed basilica and is particularly to be found in the proliferation of substantial village churches which replace the often small domed monuments preceding them. The taste for carved and painted wood shows clear influences from the contemporary mansions of local elites (*archontika*), who usually funded such new communal foci (wealthy merchants, shippers, and landowners). Naturally some of the finest examples are found in the most flourishing economic foci such as eighteenth-century Mount Pelion and the island of Lesbos.

Till very recently, the military architecture of the Ottoman Aegean has been barely researched. It had long been clear that many castles and towers, and in some cases urban walls, of Byzantine-Frankish-Venetian foundation continued in use and were modified during Ottoman times. Ottoman archives are full of details of the maintenance of such installations. Much valuable work could be done on the Ottoman constructional evidence at Greek fortifications, although one has to admit that little has been published to modern recording standards for earlier phases of these monuments, with the standard books and articles on Greek castles remaining remarkably vague on questions of phasing (Andrews 2006 [1953]). Promising developments can now be show-cased: the recent detailed tower- and castle-recording of Frankish fortifications in Greece (Lock 1986, Gregory 1996), study of the Ottoman phase of the castle at Mytilene (Karidis and Kiel 2002, Williams 2009), the Messenian PRAP Project's textual and architectural analysis of Navarino castle (Zarinebaf *et al.* 2005), and initiatives such as the Archi-Med Pilot Action (Triposkoufi and Tsitouri 2002).

Finally port facilities have been approached innovatively by the Strymon Valley Survey in Macedonia (Dunn 2009). As has also been shown in Thessaly (Reinders and Prummel 2003), an Ottoman-era decline in port-towns occurred to the advantage of land routes, but nonetheless coastal warehouse facilities existed of major importance for the imperial grain supply and for the private export of çiftlik commercial products in the later Ottoman era.

Material Culture in the Middle to Late Ottoman Era

The artifactual reflection of the table manners of Ottoman Greece are part of a wider transformation of material culture in the seventeenth to early nineteenth centuries. They seem in many ways to parallel the rise of Ottoman styles of domestic houses and interior furnishings amongst the middle classes. In Frankish times and still in the "Golden Age" of the Early Ottoman sixteenth century, table manners and table vessels show a common culture between Western and Eastern Europe, enhanced by the actual import and export of some wares between the Italian cities and the Ottoman provinces. At some stage in the Middle to Late Ottoman period, most of Greece seems to have shifted toward more Near Eastern forms of tableware and table customs, with the general abandonment of chairs or benches, and high tables, and a proliferation of dishes shared by several people, in favor of low tables, very low stools or floor seating, and single large dishes shared by many diners (Figure 21.9) (Vroom 2003, Vionis 2008). The iconographic evidence is neatly matched by pottery assemblages from later Ottoman-era deserted villages (Vionis 2006).

For the Mainland longhouse societies, illustrations, descriptions, and archaeology stress the poverty of material culture but a balancing concern with cleanliness even of earth floors (Stedman 1996, Vionis 2006). The contrastingly expansive homes of the wealthy recall similar Early Modern class divisions in rural and urban housing elsewhere in Europe (Symonds 2001). On the Ottoman Mainland the wealthy constructed elaborate houses in the Ottoman International style, but their interiors, especially in the eighteenth and nineteen centuries, combined Islamic

Figure 21.9   Interior of a peasant single-story longhouse (*makrinari*) in early nineteenth-century Attica (by Stackelberg). The house form is a longhouse variant with a central semi-division wall along its length *(kamara)*. Note the limited possessions and the dining mode of low table and central large shared dish, and the absence of high chairs or benches. A. Dimitsantou-Kremezi, *Attiki. Elliniki paradosiaki architektoniki.* Athens 1984, Figure 49.

domestic furnishings (divans, sofas, carpets) with Western décor (paintings, stucco) (Philippides 1999). Many such houses survive in Northern Greece, whilst transported interiors are well displayed in the Benaki Museum.

In contrast, from the late fifteenth century in Italy, the rise of individualism can be traced in the retention of high tables and chairs and the introduction of personal place-settings, in the context of emergent capitalist society in the North and Center of that country. We can observe imitation of these table manners and equipment in the Italianized Ionian Islands during the eighteenth century: a contemporary icon from mid-eighteenth-century Zakynthos (Mylonas 1998, figure 22), despite a Biblical scene as its theme, shows a meal with high dining chairs, a richly-ornamented marble table, and wall décor, all associated with a fine majolica dish and table-settings for individual diners. In the contemporary Cyclades Athanasios Vionis finds a fascinating opportunistic eclecticism of fashions amongst the leading families (of Italian and Greek origin) regarding table manners

and also dress codes, reflecting their international connections (2003, 2009).

An Annales Perspective

As we noted earlier, scholars such as Haldon (1992) have noted the parallelism between the Byzantine and Ottoman empires, whose flourishing then decline in the *medium term* can be linked to weakening of the central state and devolution to self-aggrandizing local elites. A further parallel to the fate of the Byzantine state can be found in the increasing role of capitalist intervention emanating from Western Europe, reducing the self-sufficiency of Ottoman commerce and industry. The rise and fall of a prosperous peasantry is also matched. The *short term* is most striking in the unexpected Ottoman conquest of Crete in the seventeenth century, placing the island on a very different trajectory to that of the Ionian Islands which remained in the West European developmental mode.

In contrast, the short-lived contemporary Venetian occupation of the Peloponnese seems to have had few long-lasting effects. On the *longer term*, the favorable environment for ethnic entrepreneurship within the Ottoman Empire led by the seventeenth and eighteenth centuries to a widespread class of Greek businessmen, with networks in both East and West. Greeks played a key role in international finance and religious culture throughout Christian Europe and the Ottoman Balkans and Middle East, through their cultural influence and personal *diaspora* (migration). Ironically, the price that the Greek people were to pay for the birth of their independent state in the nineteenth century, was a drastic and permanent shrinkage of this commercial and cultural world (Kamusella 2009).

A Personal View

The Ottoman era in Greece is a long period, for which the archaeological evidence now appears to be abundant, at least in the countryside. More willing hands are needed to exploit the innumerable deserted villages with their surface pottery scatters and ruined houses. In the towns, continual redevelopment should offer many opportunities to study houses and everyday life (recent examples include rescue excavations in Thebes and research excavation in Ancient Corinth), even though specialists in the material are still just a handful of scholars. With a growing, if unsteady, rapprochement between the modern Greek and Turkish states, scholarly interest within Greece amongst historians and archaeologists is progressing. One looks forward to the day when the sherds and walls of the Ottoman period are integrated into a full respect for the entire multi-ethnic and multi-faith societies that it included, and in which the texts consulted are not just the tax records but the poetry and personal writings of the Ottoman intellectuals and (multicultural) ruling elites.

References

Aalen, F. (1984). "Vernacular buildings in Cephalonia, Ionian Islands, Greece." *Journal of Cultural Geography* 4, 56–72.

Aalen, F. (1987). "Review article: Greek vernacular architecture." *Vernacular Architecture* 18, 41–50.

Andrews, K. (2006 [1953]). *Castles of the Morea*. Princeton: American School of Classical Studies at Athens.

Aschenbrenner, S. (1972). "A contemporary community." In W. A. McDonald and G. R. Rapp (eds.), *The Minnesota Messenia Expedition. Reconstructing a Bronze Age Regional Environment*. Minneapolis: University of Minnesota Press, 47–63.

Benechtsou, I. (1960). "Spitia Gortynias." In P. A. Michelis (ed.), *To elliniki laiko spiti*. Athens: Ethniko Metsovio Polytechneio, 159–193.

Bintliff, J. L. (1995). "The two transitions: Current research on the origins of the traditional village in Central Greece." In J. L. Bintliff and H. Hamerow (eds.), *Europe Between Late Antiquity and the Middle Ages. Recent Archaeological and Historical Research in Western and Southern Europe*. Oxford: BAR Int. Series 617, 111–130.

Bintliff, J. L. *et al.* (1999). "The traditional vernacular architecture of Livadhia." In *Livadhia: Past, Present and Future*. Livadhia: Municipality of Livadhia, 85–99. (In modern Greek.)

Bintliff, J. L. *et al.* (2004–2005). "The Tanagra Project: Investigations at an ancient city and its countryside (2000–2002)." *Bulletin de Correspondance Hellénique* 128–129, 541–606.

Bintliff, J. L. *et al.* (2007). "The Leiden-Ljubljana Ancient Cities of Boeotia Project. Summer 2007–Spring 2008." *Pharos. Journal of the Netherlands Institute in Athens* 15, 18–42.

Bintliff, J. L. *et al.* (2009). "The Leiden-Ljubljana Ancient Cities of Boeotia Project. 2009 season." *Pharos. Journal of the Netherlands Institute in Athens* 17 (in press).

Bommeljé, Y. and Doorn, P. (1996). "The long and winding road: Land routes in Aetolia (Greece) since Byzantine times." In H. Kamermans and K. Fennema (eds.), *Interfacing the Past*. Leiden: Analecta Praehistorica Leidensia 28, 343–351.

Bouras, C. (2006). *Byzantine and Post-Byzantine Architecture in Greece*. Athens: Melissa.

Braude, B. (1985). "Venture and faith in the commercial life of the Ottoman Balkans, 1500–1650." *International History Review* 7, 519–542.

Chrysopoulos, N. (1960). "Ta laika spitia tis Verroias." In P. A. Michelis (ed.), *To elliniko laiko spiti*. Athens: Ethniko Metsovio Polytechnio, 286–299.

Cooper, F. (2002). *Houses of the Morea: Vernacular Architecture of the Northwest Peloponnesos (1205–1955)*. Athens: Melissa Press.

Cormack, R. (2000). *Byzantine Art*. Oxford: Oxford University Press.

Coulton, M. B. (2009). "The Morea Vernacular Architecture Project." In J. Bintliff and H. Stöger (eds.), *Medieval and Post-Medieval Greece*. Oxford: BAR Int. Series 2023, 153–156.

Cvijic, J. (1918). *La Péninsule balkanique*. Paris: Armand Colin.

Davies, S. (2004). "Pylos Regional Archaeological Project, Part VI. Administration and settlement in Venetian Navarino." *Hesperia* 73(1), 59–120.

Dimitsantou-Kremezi, A. (1996). *Attiki. Elliniki paradosiaki architektoniki*. Athens: Melissa.

Dunn, A. (2009). "Byzantine and Ottoman maritime traffic in the estuary of the Strymon." In J. Bintliff and H. Stöger (eds.), *Medieval and Post-Medieval Greece. The Corfu Papers*. Oxford: BAR Int. Series 2023, 15–31.

Edwards, C. (1993). "Dayr Hanna: An eighteenth century fortified village in Galilee." *Levant* 25, 63–92.

Forsen, J. and B. Forsen (eds.) (2003). *The Asea Valley Survey. An Arcadian Mountain Valley from the Paleolithic Period until Modern Times*. Stockholm: Swedish Institute in Athens.

Gerola, G. (1905–1932). *Monumenti veneti nell'isola di Creta*, Vols. I–IV. Venice: Istituto Veneto di Scienze, Lettere, ed Arti.

Gregory, T. E. (1996). "The medieval site on Mt Tsalika near Sophiko." In P. Lock and G.D.R. Sanders (eds.), *The Archaeology of Medieval Greece*. Oxford: Oxbow, 61–76.

Haagsma, B. J. *et al.* (1993). "Between Karatsadagli and Baklali." *Pharos* 1, 147–164.

Haldon, J. F. (1992). "The Ottoman state and the question of state autonomy: Comparative perspectives." In H. Berktay and S. Faroqhi (eds.), *New Approaches to State and Peasant in Ottoman History*. London: Frank Cass, 18–108.

Holton, D. (1991). *Literature and Society in Renaissance Crete*. Cambridge: Cambridge University Press.

Ince, G. E. and A. Ballantyne (2007). *Paliochora on Kythera: Survey and Interpretation*. Oxford: BAR Int. Series 1704.

Kamusella, T. (2009). *The Politics of Language and Nationalism in Modern Central Europe*. London: Palgrave Macmillan.

Karidis, D. N. and M. Kiel (2002). *Mitilinis astigraphia ke Lesvou chorographia*. Athens: Olkos.

Kiel, M. (1987). "Population growth and food production in 16th century Athens and Attica according to the Ottoman Tahrir Defters." In J.-L. Bacque-Grammont and E. van Donzel (eds.), *Proceedings of the VIth Cambridge CIEPO Symposium*. Istanbul-Paris-Leiden: Divit Press, 115–133.

Kiel, M. (1997). "The rise and decline of Turkish Boeotia, 15th–19th century." In J. L. Bintliff (ed.), *Recent Developments in the History and Archaeology of Central Greece*. Oxford: BAR Int. Series 666, 315–358.

Kiel, M. (1999.) "The icon and the mosque: Orthodox Christian art as a source to retrieve the lost monuments of Ottoman architecture of Southern Greece. The case of Istife/Thebes." In *Festschrift for Aptullah Kuran*. Istanbul: Yapı Kredı Yaynları, 223–232.

Kiel, M. (2002). "Die Rolle des Kadi und der Ulema als Förderer der Baukunst in den Provinzzentren des Osmanischen Reiches." In S. Prätor and C.K. Neumann (eds.), *Frauen, Bilder und Gelehrte. Festschrift Hans Georg Majer*. Istanbul: Simurg, 569–601.

Kizis, G. (1994). *Pilioreitiki oikodomia*. Athens: Politistiko Technologiko Idrima ETBA.

Kourkoutidou-Nicolaidou, E. and A. Tourta (1997). *Wandering in Byzantine Thessaloniki*. Athens: Kapon Editions.

Lawless, R. I. (1977). "The economy and landscapes of Thessaly during Ottoman rule." In F. Carter (ed.), *An Historical Geography of the Balkans*. London: Academic Press, 501–532.

Lee, W. E. (2001). "Pylos Regional Archaeological Project, Part IV. Change and the human landscape in a modern Greek village in Messenia." *Hesperia* 70, 49–98.

Lock, P. (1986). "The Frankish towers of Central Greece." *Annual of the British School at Athens* 81, 101–123.

Loukakis, P. (1960). "To gianniotiko spiti." In P. A. Michelis (ed.), *To elliniko laiko spiti*. Athens: Ethniko Metsovio Polytechnio, 194–228.

Megas, G. (1951). *The Greek House: Its Evolution and Its Relation to the Houses of the Other Balkan Peoples*. Athens: Ministry of Coordination.

Moutsopoulos, N. K. (1982). *I rizes tis parasodiakis mas architektonikis*. Athens: Akademia Athinon.

Mylonas, Z. A. (1998). *Mouseio Zakynthou*. Athens: Ministry of Culture.

Philippides, D. (1999). *Greek Design and Decoration*. Athens: Melissa Press.

Philippides, D. (ed.) (1983–1990). *Elliniki paradosiaki architektoniki*. Athens: Melissa Press.

Preka-Alexandri, K. (1988). "Anaskaphikes ergasies: Thesprotia – Pyrgos Ragiou." *Archaiologikon Deltion* 43B1, 353–356.

Rackham, O. and J. Moody (1996). *The Making of the Cretan Landscape*. Manchester: Manchester University Press.

Reinders, H. R. and W. Prummel (eds.) (2003). *Housing in New Halos. A Hellenistic Town in Thessaly, Greece*. Lisse: Balkema.

Sabelberg, E. (1985). "Die 'Süditalienische Stadt'." *Erdkunde* 39, 19–31.

Saitas, Y. (1990). *Mani*. Athens: Melissa Press.

Saitas, Y. (2009). "Social and spatial organisation in the peninsula of the Mani." In J. Bintliff and H. Stöger (eds.), *Medieval and Post-Medieval Greece*. Oxford: BAR Int. Series 2023, 133–152.

Sanders, G. D. R. (1996). "Two kastra on Melos and their relations in the Archipelago." In P. Lock and G.D.R. Sanders (eds.), *The Archaeology of Medieval Greece*. Oxford: Oxbow, 147–177.

Sant Cassia, P. (1982). "Some implications of the changes to the house and social space in rural Cyprus." In Y. de Sike (ed.), *Chypre. La Vie quotidienne de l'antiquité à nos jours*. Paris: Maison de l'Homme, 175–186.

Sigalos, E. (2004). *Housing in Medieval and Post-Medieval Greece*. Oxford: BAR Int. Series 1291.

Stallsmith, A. B. (2007). "One colony, two mother cities: Cretan agriculture under Venetian and Ottoman rule." In S. Davies and J. L. Davis (eds.), *Between Venice and Istanbul. Colonial Landscapes in Early Modern Greece*. Athens: American School of Classical Studies, Hesperia Supplement 40, 151–171.

Stedman, N. (1996). "Land-use and settlement in post-medieval central Greece: An interim discussion." In P. Lock and G.D.R. Sanders (eds.), *The Archaeology of Medieval Greece*. Oxford: Oxbow, 179–192.

Symonds, J. (2001). "South Uist: An island story." *Current Archaeology* 15(7), 276–280.

Triantaphyllopoulos, D. D. (1976). "Nomos Ioanninon: Konitsa: Archontiko Sisko Konitsa." *Archaiologikon Deltion* 31B2, 219–220.

Triposkoufi, A. and A. Tsitouri (eds.) (2002). *Venetians and Knights Hospitallers. Military Architecture Networks*. Athens: Hellenic Ministry of Culture.

Tsigakou, F. M. (1981). *The Rediscovery of Greece*. London: Thames & Hudson.

Vionis, A. K. (2001). "The meaning of domestic cubic forms: Interpreting Cycladic housing and settlements of the period of foreign domination (ca. 1207–1821 AD)." *Pharos* 9, 111–131.

Vionis, A. K. (2003). "Much Ado About … a red cap and a cap of velvet. In search of social and cultural identity in Medieval and post-Medieval insular Greece." In H. Hokwerda (ed.), *Constructions of Greek Past. Identity and Historical Consciousness from Antiquity to the Present*. Groningen: Egbert Forsten, 193–216.

Vionis, A. K. (2005). "'Crusader' and 'Ottoman' material life: Built environment and domestic material culture in the Medieval and post-Medieval Cyclades Islands, Greece (c.13th–20th [century] AD). University of Leiden, Faculty of Archaeology, PhD thesis.

Vionis, A. (2006). "The archaeology of Ottoman villages in central Greece: Ceramics, housing and everyday life in post-Medieval Boeotia." In A. Erkanal-Öktu *et al.* (eds.), *Studies in Honor of Hayat Erkanal: Cultural Reflections*. Istanbul: Homer Kitabevi, 784–800.

Vionis, A. (2008). "Current archaeological research on settlement and provincial life in the Byzantine and Ottoman Aegean." *Medieval Settlement Research* 23, 28–41.

Vionis, A. (2009). "Material culture studies: The case of the Medieval and post-Medieval Cyclades, Greece (c.AD 1200–1800)." In. J. Bintliff and H. Stöger (eds.), *Medieval and Post-Medieval Greece. The Corfu Papers*: Oxford: BAR Int. Series 2023, 177–197.

Vocotopoulos, P. L. (1984). "Three cross-shaped churches in the region of Vonitsa." *Athens Annals of Archaeology* 17, 100–115.

Vroom, J. (2003). *After Antiquity. Ceramics and Society in the Aegean from the 7th to the 20th Century A.C.* Leiden: Leiden University Archaeological Studies 10.

Wagstaff, M. (1965). "Traditional houses in Modern Greece." *Geography* 50, 58–64.

Whitelaw, T. M. (1991). "The ethnoarchaeology of recent rural settlement and land use in Northwest Keos." In J. F. Cherry, J. C. Davis, and E. Mantzourani (eds.), *Landscape Archaeology as Long-Term History*. Los Angeles: Cotsen Institute of Archaeology, University of California, 403–454.

Williams, H. (2009). "Medieval and Ottoman Mytilene." In J. Bintliff and H. Stöger (eds.), *Medieval and Post-Medieval Greece*. Oxford: BAR Int. Series 2023, 107–114.

Zarinebaf, F., J. Bennet, and J. L. Davis (2005). *A Historical and Economic Geography of Ottoman Greece. The Southwestern Morea in the 18th Century*. Athens: American School of Classical Studies, Hesperia Supplement 34.

Zivas, D. A. (1974). "The private house in the Ionian Islands." In N. Doumanis and P. Oliver (eds.), *Shelter in Greece*. Athens: Architecture in Greece Press, 98–114.

Further Reading

Bintliff, J. L. (2000). "Reconstructing the Byzantine countryside: New approaches from landscape archaeology." In K. Blelke *et al.* (eds.), *Byzanz als Raum*. Wien: Österreichische Akademie der Wissenschaften, 37–63.

Blake, H. (1980). "Technology, supply or demand?" *Medieval Ceramics* 4, 3–12.

Harper, R. P. and D. Pringle (eds.) (2000). *Belmont Castle. The Excavation of a Crusader Stronghold in the Kingdom of Jerusalem*. Oxford: Oxford University Press.

Jardine, L. (1996). *Worldly Goods. A New History of the Renaissance*. London: Macmillan.

Kezer, Z. (1996). "The making of a nationalist capital: Socio-spatial practices in early Republican Ankara." *Built Environment* 22, 124–137.

Kiel, M. (1990). *Studies on the Ottoman Architecture of the Balkans*. Aldershot: Variorum.

Kiel, M. (1996). "Das türkische Thessalien." In R. Lauer and P. Schreiner (eds.), *Die Kultur Griechenlands in Mittelalter und Neuzeit*. Abhandlungen der Akademie der Wissenschaften in Göttingen. Philologisch-historische Klasse, Dritte Folge 212, 109–196.

Lee, M. *et al.* (1992). "Mamluk caravanserais in Galilee." *Levant* 24, 55–94.

Marzolff, P. (2006). "Lechonia. Ein mediterranes Schicksal." In *Doron. Timitikos tomos ston Kathiyiti Niko Nikonano*. Thessaloniki: 10th Ephoreia of Byzantine Antiquities, 89–99.

Petersen, A. (1998). "Qalat Ras al-Ayn: A sixteenth century Ottoman fortress." *Levant* 30, 97–112.

Vroom, J. (1996). "Coffee and archaeology. A note on a Kutahya Ware find in Boeotia, Greece." *Pharos. Journal of the Netherlands Institute at Athens* 4, 5–19.

22

The Archaeology of Early Modern Greece

Introduction

The chronological start to this period is the end of Turkish domination and the foundation of the Greek state in 1830. The end is a matter of opinion, and brings us to the nature of Early Modern Archaeology in a global sense. If Medieval Archaeology has now had a healthy grounding as a formal field for some 50 years, and Post-Medieval Archaeology for at least 40 years, the archaeology of the nineteenth and twentieth centuries is less clearly defined and not so established academically. Its boundaries with Cultural Studies, Art History, Anthropology, Sociology, and Folklore are neither clear nor, might one say, would benefit from any attempt to clarify. Indeed Marc Dion, a modern artist working with material culture found through "beachcombing" on the shores of the Thames in London, is as much exploring the cultural value of recent debris as archaeologists who are called to excavate the same areas in the context of redevelopment projects (Mouliou 2009).

The situation in Greece is less developed than in Northwest Europe or America, not only as we have already seen in the fields of Medieval and Post-Medieval Archaeology, but also in that of the Modern Age. The almost unparalleled richness of the Greco-Roman eras in Greece are enough to preoccupy almost all professional archaeologists, both Greek and foreign. Furthermore the needs of the enormous tourist industry and public interest in the periods when Greece shone brightest in cultural terms (Hamilakis and Yalouris 1996, Hamilakis 2007, Mouliou 2009), have all served to prevent major work on the material culture of the recent eras of Greek history. Nonetheless a research initiative for Industrial Archaeology within the Greek Ministry of Culture (Ministry of Culture 1989), and the recent Antiquities Law protecting monuments and finds up to 100 years ago, point to promising developments. One becomes increasingly aware of the growing collections of clothes and domestic artifacts (including ceramics, photographs, etc.), which represent the life of most people in Greece from the late Ottoman era to the immediate postwar (WWII) period. Admittedly this is generally within the context of folklore museums or Modern Greek history and heritage organizations, but nonetheless these are of immense value for an archaeological and material culture approach to the last few hundred years.

As is well known, the nineteenth to early twentieth century witnessed the final subversion of the Ottoman Empire by Western military, political, economic, and social pressures (insights into these processes can be seen in three excellent studies of their impact, at the imperial capital of Istanbul by Çelik (1986) and Mansel (1995), and at the city of Thessaloniki by Mazower (2004)). The Empire's dismemberment was associated with its replacement by many nationalisms,

The Complete Archaeology of Greece: From Hunter-Gatherers to the 20th Century AD, First Edition. John Bintliff.
© 2012 John Bintliff. Published 2012 by Blackwell Publishing Ltd.

as strong in Greece as in the survival capsule created by Ataturk in the form of a created rather than rediscovered Turkish nationalism. In Southern Mainland Greece, rejection of the Ottoman past meant rebuilding middle-class homes, and erecting new public buildings, in Neoclassical style. Rural life however was far less radically transformed, except by prolonged decay and stagnation. In many parts of the countryside there were severe economic problems till the last quarter of the nineteenth century, which held back the remodeling of peasant life, whether we look at houses, portable material culture or lifeways in general. Travelers of the period are frequently struck by poverty and underdevelopment (Tsigakou 1981). However the last three decades of the nineteenth century began to bring more dramatic changes in the Greek countryside, with improved transport and the rise of national and international trade both impacting progressively in rural areas (Aschenbrenner 1972). In many landscapes rural population by the end of the nineteenth century at last returned to the level of the late sixteenth-century Ottoman climax, but for most of Southern Greece it seems well below the levels reached in Classical Greek times (Bintliff 1997, 2005).

The Historical Context

During the Greek War of Independence (1821–1830) urban life and economic prosperity was, in the south of the country, crippled by the prolonged and destructive struggle. The final Ottoman era had in any case been very negative for the development of Greek life, due to corruption amongst imperial and local officials and the failings of the Ottoman economy to adapt to and take advantage of commercial and industrial modernization (in no small part due to its undermining by Western bankers and entrepreneurs for their own financial advantage). On the other hand there had developed an indigenous response amongst Balkan middle- and upper-class society to the waves of economic and cultural change emanating from Western Europe from the late eighteenth century, and the additional Napoleonic stimulus to political emancipation and nationalism. As a formally multicultural empire, the later Ottoman Empire offered scope for ethnic and religious communities to develop networks

of trade and production, and unintentionally to encourage such groups to affirm and strengthen their identity. In such changing international circumstances this served as a potential springboard for aspirations to achieve a greater degree of self-government or even for some, independence. (For good modern historical backgrounds see McNeil 1978, Clogg 1992, Koliopoulos and Veremi 2004.)

But the successful Greek Revolution of the 1820s created a small state (Color Plate 22.1), comprising Southern and Central Greece. The incorporation of Northern Greece and Crete, together with the Ionian and Dodecanese Islands, had to await the late nineteenth and early twentieth centuries. Thus the creation of the modern Greek territorial state was not just a matter of a few revolutionary years of struggle, but a long drawn-out process of irregular large increments. Moreover in order to comprehend the history of the young independent Greek kingdom, even up to the present day, we need to set the new state into its preceding era of final Ottoman control.

The weakened central administration had progressively allowed local indigenous elites (ayan) as well as imperial officials to assume wide-ranging powers in town and country outside of the capital Istanbul. Greater contact with Western merchants provided many opportunities for enrichment, while the dependence of large sectors of the peasant farming and urban artisan communities on regional elite families encouraged clientelism (informal dependence of the poor on rich patrons). The achievement of independence from Ottoman rule was thus seen in divergent ways by the people of Southern Greece. Established elites envisaged their political and economic bases to be threatened by any development of "democratic" reforms, believing the lower classes to be incapable of participating in public affairs. In contrast, the Greek intelligentsia and especially those living as expatriates in Western Europe were more inclined to plan for the creation of a modern, educated citizenry and a stronger state bureaucracy, in which traditional patrons would be subordinated. There was also a third constituency to be included, not numerically large, but whose power was nonetheless real: this was the widespread phenomenon of armed bands (armatoloi), whose origin lay in the weakness of the official Ottoman army and provincial militia, allowing local bosses to make use of such irregulars to police their spheres of influence. They also had arisen as bandits where neither state nor local bosses were able to assert total control. During the Revolution these bands had often earned credit in the cause of Independence, but their existence now clashed with the intended creation of a civil society policed by the state. There was yet a fourth element to upset the steady flourishing of the young state, and that was the imposition by the Great Powers of an alien concept, kingship, and its first incumbent, a Bavarian prince, on the nascent nation-state.

These historical pressures burdened Greece with a constant threat of political disorder, diverting energies from pressing action to promote the economy and welfare of the rural and urban population. Until the last quarter of the nineteenth century population was depressed and land use limited, whilst health, education, and living conditions for the bulk of the population remained poor. The condition of the rural peasantry only began to improve at the end of the nineteenth century, before which their life remained remote from the limited points of commercial development centering on the key ports of the kingdom and their immediate hinterlands. Industrialization was also highly localized and small-scale into the early twentieth century, allowing a minute working class to arise around Athens and in small pockets in other larger urban centers. The lack of technological innovation had long plagued craft and industry in later Ottoman times and it continued throughout the early decades of the new Greek state. Efforts to revive cotton manufacture in Livadheia town in Boeotia during the 1830s, for example, failed, only succeeding during the 1860s, by which time the city acquired a virtual monopoly of processed cotton production for the kingdom (Sigalos 2004). During the latter nineteenth century Greece saw a slow expansion in the scale and spread of local industrial processing of its agricultural cash crops such as cotton, silk, tobacco, and currants. However a population boom outstripped wealth accumulation, whilst highly unstable markets for these cash crops could impact severely on peasant fortunes, with the result that this era and the first half of the twentieth century saw massive emigration into distant parts of the world,

notably North America and Australia, to seek a faster and securer path to enrichment.

At the start of the twentieth century living conditions improved, communications became more efficient, and over the following decades the kingdom expanded to incorporate large landscapes in the North and on Crete. Meanwhile the Greek economy as a whole began to interact more vigorously with that of the wider commercial world. Population gradually moved toward levels only achieved in many regions previously during the climax of Classical Greek civilization, 2500 years earlier. Yet Greece remained a land with limited resources in raw materials to promote heavy industry or international exchange, and a traditional small-scale agriculture little suited to compete with global commercial-estate farm produce. Moreover during the largest part of the twentieth century Greek politics suffered from violent see-saws from left to right, a dictator, a Civil War hard on the heels of a devastating Nazi occupation, and a military junta. Nonetheless renewed modernization and growth in every aspect except political stability marks the postwar era, whilst entry into the EEC in 1981 seemed to promise well for a very different twenty-first century to the uneven development of its predecessor. As I write however (2011) the consequences of an incomplete modernization process in the workings of the state and in the relationship between private and public economics have brought the country into a debilitating crisis. One must hope that Greece will emerge from this with a more lasting and robust form of civil society.

The Material Culture of the Early Modern Era

We can approach this period of almost two centuries along a series of archaeological dimensions: movable material culture found in very good condition largely in Folk Museums, but in far greater numbers as artifacts at deserted villages or in exposures in and around contemporary settlements; standing buildings such as houses still occupied, or at least in some kind of use, and also as ruined foundations; and Early Modern field systems.

Early Modern ceramics

It must be admitted that no archaeological textbook or large-scale case study exists for the ceramics in use over the Aegean, if we mean a total assemblage for each region. On the other hand the decorated wares have been brought together by Greek specialists in attractive volumes (Kyriazopoulos 1984, Korre-Zographou 1995), and some classes of widely-sold pithoi and other specialist pots have also been studied (Hampe and Winter 1962, Blitzer 1990). The basic work of establishing a series of assemblages of coarse wares, domestic wares, and tablewares for each region of Greece is only just beginning. Ceramic assemblages from individual villages are an important resource, as with our Boeotia Project finds from the village surface survey of modern Mavromati in Boeotia (Vroom 1998), where the continuing flourishing of that village required us to collective surface finds from garden zones between the houses and in the peripheral sectors of traditional rubbish disposal. For the last two centuries we could illustrate the participation of such an inland, agricultural community in new networks of ceramic exchange including distant Greek and Anatolian centers of production, as well as Italian and Western European factories. Significantly these new orientations include the arrival of cheap industrial tablewares for individual table settings (see below).

The dramatic takeoff in rural population and agricultural production in the late nineteenth century, in both Italy and Greece, could be expected to be reflected in a new variety and richness of decorated and imported ceramics found at rural surface sites. This is indeed argued for the eighteenth- and nineteenth-century survey finds in North-Central Italy by Blake (1980), with rural improvement marked by renewed penetration in quantity of exotic glazed wares. In Greece the last quarter of the nineteenth century witnessed a phenomenal population boom focused on generally larger villages, one paralleled in almost all the rural zones of the Mediterranean lands. More secure conditions and the impact of commercial agriculture, a rise in rural industrial production (proto-industrialization), and improvements in maritime and overland communications, are amongst the critical factors. One material symptom is the arrival in quantity during this period either side of 1900 of relatively inexpensive factory-produced ceramics into rural villages, including imports from Western Europe.

The rise of such factory-products led to imports to Greece during the nineteenth century from a wide range of distinctive centers making true porcelain tablewares or fine ware imitations in other fabrics (Color Plate 22.2b left). Surface finds in the Aegean include sherds from England, France, Germany, and Austria, with a particular popularity from the later nineteenth into the early twentieth century of the cheap but well-made glazed earthenware tablewares from Grottaglie in the Italian province of Apulia (Colour Plate 22.2b right). Production within Greece concentrated on traditional storage jars (pithoi), including giant versions from a small number of well-known centers of production, and competent glazed earthenwares for heavier-duty household use.

By this time the orientation of rural life was once again facing toward Western Europe, so that rapidly we see the adoption of modern styles of individual eating as required by the ceramic sets being supplied. As in later Ottoman times however, a major part of household assemblages was now met through copper and iron (and increasingly from the mid-twentieth century, plastic) containers, most of the first two now recycled, although fortunately these are well represented in folklore museums. As a warning however to regional surveyors, remoter parts of Greece without good local clays may have relied almost entirely on metal, wood, and other organic containers and implements till well into the twentieth century, leaving little ceramic debris to mark settlements (Vroom 1998).

The following descriptions of Early Modern ceramics (Color Plates 22.2a–b) are based on the research of A. Vionis (unpublished lectures).

Late Sgraffito wares

Epirus and Macedonia saw a tremendous production of polychrome sgraffito wares (jugs and flasks) (Color Plate 22.2a left) during the eighteenth and nineteenth centuries as a result of cultural influences stemming from economic growth and trade with the Ionian Islands and Italy. They are widely distributed throughout Greece and into Northwestern Turkey. The sgraffito decoration is incised whilst green and brown paint splashes enrich the decoration under a clear or yellow lead glaze. Motifs include flowers, animals, and people.

Çanakkale ware

Production center, Çanakkale (Northwestern Turkey) (Color Plate 22.2a right). Flourishing from the mid eighteenth to the late nineteenth century. Coarse fabric, white slip, then designs painted in brown, blue, orange, yellow, and white, and covered with a creamy lead glaze. Motifs: boats, mosques, animals, flowers.

Transfer-printed wares

Technique used in England since the later eighteenth century and fashionable in Greece after 1860 (Color Plate 22.2b left). Decoration is engraved onto a bronze plaque, the surface of which is then inked, and the design transferred onto thin paper and from that to the ceramic object, where it is sealed under a transparent glaze. Produced in Western Europe, with a white fine clay or porcelain body. Also known as *Syriana*, since the Greek merchants who placed the orders for these dinner wares were established on the island of Syros. Ubiquitous in Greece.

Grottaglie or Corfu wares

Originally produced in Apulia (Southeast Italy), then local production arose on Corfu and Kythera (Color Plate 22.2b right). Mainly plates. Medium hard fabric, painted decoration in blue, yellow, and brown over a lead-tin opaque glaze resembling earlier Majolica. Motifs: flowers, animals. Ubiquitous.

Siphnos cookware

Siphnos in the Cyclades was known since the early eighteenth century for quality cooking-pots, due to the good quality lead glaze and high heat-resistant local clay. Distributed throughout Greece till being replaced from the 1970s by metal and plastic wares.

Rural houses and housing culture

Excavations have not yet focused on buildings of the Modern Greek state, not least because it is only as a result of a very recent update to antiquities legislation that material culture of all kinds after the Medieval period has been protected formally. Even

so, the limit is still set at over 100 years ago, although one imagines that growing interest in Industrial Archaeology in Greece may allow study also of major twentieth-century installations. Despite these limitations, the enthusiasm of Greek and foreign architects for recording traditional buildings, notably the remarkable series of volumes in several languages published by the Melissa Press (Kartas 1982, Philippides 1983–1990), has allowed a considerable record of Early Modern vernacular (local domestic) architecture in the Greek Aegean. House and village studies associated with regional archaeological projects have been published, amongst others by Aschenbrenner (1972), Lee (2001) and Cooper (2002). We now possess in the monograph by Sigalos (2004) a synthesis and analysis of all the chief publications in this field. He has further demonstrated how an archaeological perspective on the evidence now available, taken in its historical context, can yield major insights into popular life from Ottoman into Modern times. I shall lean heavily on this major work in the following discussion of Early Modern developments in housing.

We noted earlier that the Mainland rural peasantry till the late nineteenth century dwelt for the most part in nucleated settlements, lacking regular plans and even the "traditional" infrastructure of a main square ringed by public buildings. Houses were generally one-story, of rectangular or longhouse style (Figure 22.1a and Color Plate 22.3a), but in sloping terrain a one-and-a-half-story house was common. In the single-story form, domestic animals shared the home, with limited division of the two halves of the roofed space. A yard was a major feature, usually on the side of the house where most light and warmth through the year was available. Ancillary facilities such as a bread oven, presses for oil and wine, and storage sheds, could be found around the house and yard, but an enclosure wall round the property was rare and usually not a high barrier. Life was lived in the public eye and was as much as possible carried out in the open air. In contrast, the wealthier landowners and professional classes owned larger rural homes or estate-centers. They might be towerhouses or more extensive multi-story mansions (*archontika*), and be built as imposing monuments within the low-rise villagescape,

Figure 22.1a Historic photograph of Thespies-Erimokastro longhouse-village, Boeotia, ca. 1890.
© EFA/P. Jamot.

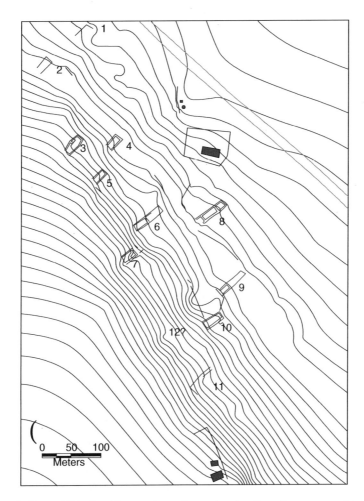

Figure 22.1b Deserted village of Rhadon. House ruins and two churches. Late Ottoman to mid-nineteenth century.
E. Sigalos, *Housing in Medieval and Post-Medieval Greece*. Oxford 2004, Figure 43.

or as independent entities in the open country, but mostly they conformed to variants of the International Ottoman style.

A good example of a ruined village abandoned due to late nineteenth-century banditry is the site of Rhadon in the rocky hinterland of the Boeotian town of Orchomenos (Figure 22.1b). The Ottoman archives inform us that Rhadon was founded as an Albanian colony by Early Turkish times, whilst recent records show it was abandoned for the larger neighboring village of Pavlo in the late nineteenth century. The surface ceramic finds are the expected mixture of sixteenth- to nineteenth-century wares. Planning of the ruined settlement by the Boeotia Project showed a characteristic settlement design for Mainland lowland settlements. Associated with two churches (shown within their enclosures), still maintained by descendants of the villagers, we see a line of (12?) discrete longhouses, of typical single- or occasionally one-and-a-half-story form, ranged across a gentle slope and with a north–south aspect, so as to allow one long side of the home to receive maximum sun in the winter months. The wide space between each identical house and the absence of elaborate enclosures conveys a sense of the communal openness of rural life in such Early Modern hamlets, whilst the absence of a public square and non-religious public buildings is noteworthy.

A rather different sort of deserted site is the once very common outlying estate-center belonging to a monastery (*metochi*). The surviving nineteenth-century ruins at Sta Dendra not far from Rhadon consist of a small cluster of at least four longhouses and one smaller rectangular house, as at Rhadon loosely spread across the site but with a common north–south alignment. On the eastern edge of the ruins stands a more complex building made up of eight chambers. This seems to have been a storehouse or stable. In the south of the hamlet is a still-maintained church.

In the final quarter of the nineteenth century conditions for Aegean countryfolk began to improve. Rural insecurity was dealt with, vast areas of state land were finally distributed to local communities, communication by land and sea improved, and the Greek agricultural economy saw a piecemeal incorporation into international commerce, all of which led to a dramatic general transformation of the Greek village and its territory. A desire to improve production encouraged farmers to invest more effort in their land (Davis 1991, Whitelaw 1991) through increased terracing, the improvement of rural paths, and the building of field-houses for storage, temporary residence or crop-processing. In some regions dispersed settlement reappeared, if still within the sphere of a village boundary and rarely far from a nucleation, but also a symptom of increased investment in land use.

At the same time rising wealth and social aspirations introduced "urban" forms of housing to the rising class of farmers of "middling status" in the Aegean countryside and local professionals (doctor, teacher, lawyer) (Stedman 1996, Sigalos 2004). This meant not only two-story homes, with a clear separation of stock (below) and humans (above), but an increase in the number of internal family spaces associated with a West European "bourgeois" concept of defining rooms for distinct functions. This departed from the previously-dominant Ottoman concept in complex houses of accumulations of flexible domestic spaces (*ondas*). A formal reception room, or *saloni*, was a parallel to the Victorian "parlor," and contained displays of the more expensive pottery and metal objects owned by the household, together with photographs of family members as a "dynasty" proud of its generational development. Kitchens could be set apart from a general family room, and eventually private bedrooms were normal, not just for the family but for parents, grandparents, and children.

Also diffusing from towns into villages was the concept of a village square with a prominent church, coffee-houses, shops, and an administrative building: a small-scale imitation of a town center. This seems to be developing largely in the late nineteenth and early twentieth centuries.

In the towns the new Greek state had rapidly and formally rejected maintenance of Ottoman-era street plans and house styles. It encouraged the adoption of architectural styles for public and private use which glorified both the Greek ancient past, and the order and regularity of Western European designs, which were themselves rooted in Greco-Roman traditions filtered through Renaissance and Baroque elaborations. The new tradition was Neoclassicism (Kardamitsi-Adami and Biris 2005). Beginning in the larger urban centers, where it had been encouraged by the Bavarian royal court, it spread more slowly,

Figure 22.2 Neoclassical village house in Messenia.
Courtesy E. Sigalos.

during the late nineteenth and early twentieth
centuries, into the smaller towns and then the villages,
being adopted first by the "leading sectors" of
wealthier landowners and the professions. Now the
villagers saw fine four-square multi-story homes arising in their midst, with neat cut stone at the corners
(*quoins*) and around doors and windows (Figure 22.2).
The tiled roofs imitated ancient models, with
decorative terracotta affixes. House façades were
marked by symmetry. Even in Northern Greece,
which remained under Ottoman control into the
early twentieth century, "Westernization" of the
Empire resulted in a widespread adoption of
Neoclassical architecture in public and wealthy private construction (Sigalos 2004).

The house transformation was accomplished with
an easy modification of the former one- or one-and-
a-half-story longhouse, through erecting a second
story within the same scheme (Sigalos 2004). Often
the dimensions of the older house were retained and
its two-room plan. Separate access to the upper floor
from outside underlined the conceptual division, having already existed as we have seen in Ottoman-era
town houses.

However the traditional pre-Modern homes
remained in the majority till the 1960s. Today they are
heading toward an almost universal extinction. Case
studies seem to indicate that multi-story houses of
"Modern" Neoclassical type were widespread but in a
minority, as rural wealth was confined to a small middle and upper class by recurrent problems of Greek

politics and economics, till the last third of the twentieth century, when the Aegean went through a new
burst of economic growth. When wealth finally began
to spread to the majority of rural inhabitants, from the
1960s onwards, yet newer styles were emulated, with
an emphasis on domestic versions of concrete
Modernism, decorated with new forms of
Internationalism copied from America and even with
small-scale versions of "tourist hotel" architecture.
The pace of change can be illustrated through my
own case studies from Boeotia (see Text Box).

In a classic anthropological monograph, Friedl
(1962) captured a phase of major change in the
Central Greek village of Vasilika, looking back to life
in previous generations as well as observing recent
and ongoing transformations toward a wealthier and
in material terms far more complex "modern" lifestyle. She argued that the basic Early Modern home
had been single-story and windowless, animals and
humans cohabiting. As a result of external influences
we might term "urban" or "bourgeois," it had gradually become common to create physical and conceptual boundaries. She noted the combination of
pre-Modern alongside "Western" Modern stylistic
importations. Often three rooms resulted: a traditional
earth-floored one remained as the kitchen, two others
with wooden floors served as a bedroom and a combined living and reception room. At the time of study
Vasilika had very few grander homes but they
conformed to diffusing urban models: two storys, the
ground floor with a storage/stock room and a second
area for living, cooking, and sleeping, whilst the upper
floor, separately accessed from an outside staircase,
contained an alternative domestic space and a more
public guest reception room (the *saloni*). At the top of
the stairs a veranda (*hagiati*) offered a suitable
semi-open space for summer family life, including
sleeping. In the *saloni* a display of family valuables, fine
furniture, and family photographs gave a sense of
status and generational stability. The alternative family
rooms allowed a choice of location dependent on
season, and scope also for different generations and
events to be accommodated.

In Macedonia another study conveniently placed
in time is that of Common and Prentice (1956),
who found rural settlements still made up of dispersed, rather randomly-placed houses, without a

Domestic Housing Changes in Boeotia

In the village of Aghios Georgios near ancient Koroneia in Boeotia (Bintliff *et al.* 2007) house survey found hardly any houses predating the late twentieth century. It was urgent to record those surviving before their demolition. The reasons for traditional homes remaining till now are closely tied to the survival of the oldest family members, who remain physically and emotionally attached to the residences of their younger years. Often the old, simple house exists as a partly-occupied home for the oldest generation, or may be used by animals or for storage and processing, or is already in ruins awaiting final destruction and replacement by a modern luxury bungalow or multi-story concrete structure. One house we recorded in 2007 was T-shaped, with each limb a single-story structure on different levels to fit a steep slope. One limb was a roofless ruin, the other continued to contain storage space and a family room. The surviving grandmother had come to the old house in the 1930s as a bride, and gave us detailed memories of how the extended family used the home. Just as in our discussion of Ottoman-era domestic life, she recalled the eating of meals seated on low stools around a low table, and was able to produce the latter for us.

Now grandmother and her children's family live in a large concrete three-story house in an adjacent part of the house-plot, where previously part of the yard and a kitchen garden had been situated.

Another Boeotian village, Aghios Thomas, clearly less wealthy, contains a larger number of traditional homes, all it seems of longhouse type. They appear now to be out of normal residential use, but their appearance along the main street adjacent to their replacements, Modernist villas and multi-story homes, is a striking witness to the extraordinary rate of change in the last two generations (Color Plates 22.3a–b).

In the Boeotian village of Chaeroneia the decaying remains of the traditional longhouses are dwarfed by recent concrete two-story replacements, whilst a more traditional form of local family dominance can be shown by the nineteenth-century towerhouse of the Rangavé family, even today rising prominently from the villagescape. This elite family had formerly been active in Ottoman service in the Northern Balkans but emigrated to the new Greek state after its foundation (Sigalos 2004). The style is reminiscent of Ottoman-era elaborations of Medieval towers and predates the diffusion of Neoclassical forms to the Greek countryside.

clear street infrastructure, although by now a village focus had crystallized around a square, onto which faced the main church, shops, and coffee-houses. Most families still occupied one-story earth-floored houses with almost no furniture; in adjacent yards lay ancillary structures for farm-use. A minority of wealthier homes were two-story. In the Ionian Islands Aalen (1984) documented the late nineteenth-century transformation of rural peasant homes into two-story residences, with urban Neoclassical influences and associated new lifestyles (see Figure 21.7). Likewise, the study by Kizis (1994) of the mansions of the Mount Pelion villages identified a third house style (for preceding styles see Chapter 21) from the nineteenth century onwards,

when Neoclassicism is adopted in the grand family residences.

Field systems and land use

What should attract far more attention from archaeologists is the remarkable potential of the nineteenth and twentieth centuries in Greece for deeply insightful links between artifacts, houses, the very full historical and ethnographic records, and built landscapes. Rapidly disappearing is the last category of material evidence, what geographers call "landscape architecture," the accumulating human modifications to the countryside in the shape of field divisions, terracing, stream diversions, built paths, threshing-floors, temporary field-huts, and many other physical impacts. We already have a fine pioneer study with Todd Whitelaw's (1991, 1994) analysis of the field systems and rural structures for storage or residence on the island of Kea. Combining aerial photos, field mapping, and historic records, a valuable understanding was achieved of the radical restructuring of the island's countryside during the late nineteenth and early twentieth century. Whitelaw suggested that the Late Ottoman peasantry had no clear rights to land or its profit, this being in the hands of the Church or powerful landowners, who invested little in its infrastructure. When the new Greek state finally redistributed land as freehold to the peasantry, at the same time as opportunities for commercial agricultural marketing increased, farmers responded by a major building campaign in the landscape, improving the layout and drainage of fields, access routes, and facilities for working their estates. Hamish Forbes (2007) has also reminded us of the temporary use of rural landscapes through the year in Ottoman and Early Modern Greece, and the difficulty of detecting this archaeologically, as well as showing the complexities of relating archives to oral history and surface archaeology for the recent development of settlements on the Peloponnesian peninsula of Methana (Forbes 2009).

Changes in the Countryside

The same nineteenth-century and early twentieth-century Travelers' reports and pictures (paintings, sketches, and increasingly photographs; Tsigakou 1981), which assist the identification of deserted villages and offer details of lifestyles for the Late Ottoman era, are equally significant for our understanding of the history and archaeology of town and country during the early generations of the young Greek state after the Revolution (from the 1830s well into the twentieth century). Major resources include the "photothèques" or collections of historic views of Greece in the French and German Archaeological Schools in Athens, and the extremely detailed maps prepared by the French Army Geographical Service immediately after the creation of the new kingdom, in the Peloponnese (Bory de St. Vincent 1836), and Central Greece (never published but the basis for the

excellent cover of that area in the *Atlas de la Grèce* of 1852). Since the 1980s there has been a growing interest in historic photographs of Greece (cf. Figure 22.1a), shown in a series of books (for example Louvrou 1999, Koumarianou 2005) and a center for photographic archiving in Athens (Stathatos 1999).

The field investigation of the archaeology of Early Modern villages can take two obvious forms. They can be found identified as deserted villages or as still-occupied historic villages. Both can be approached through the collection of surface pottery (for the former), and for the latter from ceramics found on their outskirts and between houses or in yards and gardens. Frequently house ruins survive on abandoned village-sites, or in neglected older quarters of contemporary settlements, and these can date back through the last 180 years of the modern Greek state, and even back into the Ottoman period.

It remains to be shown whether the signs of demographic growth in eighteenth-century Greece and the well-known historic evidence for a rising middle class of urban merchants were associated with any improvement in the living conditions of rural communities. Subsequently, the endemic violence of the Greek Revolution precipitated large-scale village abandonments and relocations in the South. This was followed by difficult decades from the 1830s to 1870s. Firstly many country districts were terrorized by bandits (Jenkins 1961, Slaughter and Kasimis 1986). Indeed a final phase of changes to the village network took place during the nineteenth century, as insecurity continuing as late as the 1870s caused many settlements to become deserted as communities clustered into larger villages against rural banditry. These usually remain as communities today. Secondly, land reforms remained urgent but neglected. All of this prevented a rapid recovery of the Greek countryside after the establishment of the Modern Greek state until the 1880s.

A working hypothesis would be that most Mainland village communities were generally impoverished longhouse dwellers for the intermediate period, with few ceramic vessels and those of mediocre quality (even the occasional imports which are attested are of cheap "peasant porcelain" such as Çanakkale ware). The early nineteenth-century painting illustrated in the previous chapter (Figure 21.9) of a family within their longhouse may be representative of the poor living standards of the nineteenth-century peasantry: animals at one end of the house, the human family at the other, with a small collection of household utensils kept below the rafters – the odd earthenware vessel, some metal containers, wood and leather often used in place of ceramics. Small wonder that Western Travelers visiting Greece to glory in its Classical monuments considered its surviving inhabitants a sadly fallen race, best left in the background of their sketches and travelogues (Tsigakou 1981).

The last quarter of the nineteenth century witnessed a phenomenal population boom focused on generally larger villages, one paralleled in almost all the rural zones of the Mediterranean lands. More secure conditions and the impact of commercial agriculture, a rise in rural industrial production (proto-industrialization), and improvements in maritime and overland communications, are amongst the critical factors. Land reclamation, especially drainage of the extensive lowland marshes of Greece, opened up highly fertile land and reduced endemic wetland diseases (Fels 1944).

The massive population exchanges following the Greco-Turkish war of the early 1920s led to almost all parts of modern Greece being affected either by the emigration or immigration of populations. Since the Second World War, further large-scale changes to the rural settlement system have seen contrasted developments. On the one hand, agricultural villages in remoter, more rugged terrain have declined in favor of those in or near plains suitable for irrigated cash crops. On the other, we witness the often uncontrolled creation of new tourist or weekend and second-home settlement concentrations; if many houses or apartment blocks arise in natural resort locations by the sea, in some regions almost as many second homes can be found inland in rocky, scrubby terrain, inexpensive to purchase and easily accessible from the largest centers of population such as Athens.

The more prosperous and educated small farmers typical for twentieth-century Greece became for foreign archaeologists, historians, and anthropologists a supposed element of continuity to the admired Classical (or even Bronze Age) past, studied to understand the lifestyles and attitudes of their heroic predecessors (Fotiadis 1995), despite the remarkable changes in rural society that were occurring in the second half

of that century (Slaughter and Kasimis 1986, Forbes 2007, 2009).

Urban Change

After the creation of the independent Greek state in 1830, towns changed at varying rates from their Ottoman form. One of the faster transformations was in what scholars refer to as "polite architecture." The wealthier classes, who had previously emulated the Ottoman International style in their town houses and rural mansions, turned their heads "Westwards" and also "backwards in time" by adopting Neoclassical designs. These could result in entirely new constructions, but also might be applied as new façades to existing homes. For a while in the nineteenth century, the port of Ermoupolis on the island of Syros was a key commercial port, and it was a flourishing center for Neoclassical commissions from its prosperous merchant class (Kartas 1982, Agriantoni et al. 1999).

On a piecemeal basis, town plans were altered, also to conform to "Western" and "Classical" logic (Yerolympos 1996). The Greek government formally announced that straight, grid-plan communication lines were to be preferred to the twisting, narrow lanes of Ottoman towns, the latter to be removed as they "so explicitly reflected the character of their former rulers" (quoted in Sigalos 2004). Towns such as Navplion, Kalamata, Tripolis, Patras, and Athens were in part redesigned, or expanded, according to regular Western urban planning principles. In the expanding Early Modern town of Livadheia, the Old Town retained its cramped and picturesque character well into the late twentieth century, but to the north and east vast new suburbs arose on a grid-plan, with large open spaces at major intersections. Lining these new prestige streets arose ranks of Neoclassical mansions for the prospering middle classes (Bintliff et al. 1999, Sigalos 2004). In contrast the other major town of Boeotia, Thebes, had its original center replanned along gridline streets during the nineteenth century, destroying a more multifocal plan of winding small lanes linking religious foci which had characterized the Ottoman town.

When, after some experimentation and debate on alternatives, Athens was chosen in 1833 as the

Figure 22.3   Neoclassical Main Building of Athens University, late nineteenth century. Wikipedia image.

permanent capital of the new Kingdom of Greece, the Bavarian rulers brought in foreign architects to ornament the city with appropriate public buildings for its role. Naturally the Neoclassical style was adopted, reflecting the intention of reconnecting the new state with the finest moments of its past. Today along Panepistimiou Street, the central complex of the Academy, the University, and the National Library are impressive achievements in this style of the 1850s to 1880s (Figure 22.3), and still attract attention within their surrounding modern concrete higher-rise shopping and apartment blocks. It was a natural counterpoise that Kapodistrias, the first President of Greece, ordered the demolition of traditional over-hang rooms (*sahnisia*) as reminiscent of the hated Turks (Sigalos 2004). Fortunately for everyone, a scheme by the German Neoclassical architect Schinkel to construct a new royal palace-citadel-museum on the Acropolis for the imported Bavarian King Otto, was not approved (Étienne and Étienne 1992, Hamilakis and Yalouris 1996).

The pace of regular planning but also increasingly, unplanned expansive urban sprawl, increased considerably with the arrival in the 1920s of a vast army of refugees and population exchange communities, resulting from the disastrous outcome of the war with Turkey. These incomers were accommodated all over the Greek towns and also in new rural settlements, since they included town-dwellers and villagers from what is today European and Anatolian Turkey. A classic analysis of the effect of this on the city of Athens has been made by Bastea (1999). For the rise of Athens from 1833 and its escape from an early attempt at formal planning by the Bavarians see Ante (1988).

But we should not exaggerate the scale of change. There was indeed a proliferation throughout the Aegean of new street plans, Neoclassical and later "Modernist" homes for the wealthy, and "worker cottages" for a small proletariat. But there was also, perhaps still dominant, the continuing survival alongside these new forms of life of traditional narrow winding streets and Ottoman-style house plans in towns for the lower middle classes, and agricultural-style single- and one-and-a-half-story longhouses for the poorer classes both in urban suburbs and in rural settlements. Descriptions and photographs till the mid-twentieth century and the widespread survival of such architecture even today (if ruined or *en route* to demolition in the near future) confirm this picture. In provincial towns with a few thousand inhabitants, the norm till the mid-twentieth century, life was very internalized, and out-marriage was atypical (Caftanzoglou 1994), whilst such market-centers were not strongly interconnected so as to create an integrated urban system for Greece (Dertilis 1992, Katochianou 1992). As for the appearance of the townscapes, the town of Argos for example, was largely destroyed in the War of Independence, which led to a new town plan which expanded on the old irregular settlement with new regular suburbs. Yet it remained essentially a low-rise townscape until the first tower-block appeared in 1962, followed in the 1970s by hundreds more for apartments and stores (Piérart and Touchais 1996).

All this gives a material basis to the view often expressed that Modern Greeks have a strong sense of identity, but in two contrasted senses (Leigh Fermor 1966). One is to their recreated Classical Greek past, of which they are rightly proud, the other however is to the qualities of Greek life and sensibility inherited from Greek mentalities common in Medieval and Ottoman times (*Romaiosyne*). As we saw above, in contemporary villages three generations of a single family can view a discordant time-perspective on their own property. This can include three-story Modernist or even Postmodernist luxury concrete housing, with all the latest furniture and electronic fixtures, surviving alongside a single-story longhouse with minimal furniture and retaining simple fittings from the early twentieth or even late nineteenth century, and a plan which may descend from several centuries earlier.

However, as noted for rural settlements, the owners of both traditional and modernizing houses became keen to follow Western bourgeois patterns in the internal definition of space. A multiplication of rooms and their subdivisions became typical, to mark out spaces for distinct activities, whether functional or social.

Industrial Archaeology

This is a growing field in Aegean historical research (Ministry of Culture 1989; *Monumenta* electronic journal). Published studies include the changing fates and functions of commercial and manufacturing premises and public transport facilities (e.g.,

Papanicolaou-Christensen 1986), and analysis of specific installations (e.g., for water- and wind-mills, Mouzakis 2008). Much rich material survives from the last 150 years, since Greece developed large-scale complexes for these purposes. Real industrialization only properly arose in Greece from the end of the nineteenth century and was largely confined to Athens and small pockets at the other major urban centers, a situation still observable at the end of the twentieth century (Katochianou 1992). In the provincial Boeotian town of Livadheia for example (Sigalos 2004) a local dispersed proto-industrial tradition of textile manufacture (see Chapter 21), encouraged the subsequent establishment of a series of factories in the town, chiefly for cotton, utilizing the strong water-power from the river Herkyna. Today some of these installations have been refurbished to provide the modern town in the public areas of its old quarter (now largely a leisure zone) with cultural halls, restaurants, and a pleasant place to promenade. Dating back to such industrializing suburbs, small homes for non-farming workers occasionally survive in the rapidly-modernizing urban fabric in cities like Livadheia.

The late nineteenth-century expansion of the Greek economy and its international commercialization can also be followed in the rural agricultural sector through new forms of building construction. In this period a British venture, the Lake Copais Company, succeeded in draining a perennial body of freshwater and marshland in Boeotia (Slaughter and Kasimis 1986, Papadopoulos 1993), some 200 km^2 of reclamation. The Company was poorly managed, and made no significant dividends for its international shareholders. The drained land was let out on short-term contracts to the surrounding villagers, who were treated badly. There were riots and conditions were sufficiently unattractive to leave much of the reclaimed "polders" uncultivated. The Company was finally forced to hand over its rights to the Greek government in the 1950s. Life for the "colonial" managers and foreign staff of the Company had nonetheless been rather luxurious. We hear about this from time to time in outside accounts (e.g., Levi 1971 concerning Haliartos).

For an archaeologist the surviving complex is still vast and impressive. Beside the lake at Haliartos, an

Early Ottoman village was in ruins by the nineteenth century, when the Lake Copais Company established its base there. With a large staff of expatriate managerial and clerical officials, supported by numerous Greek service personnel, a veritable town was called into existence. Being in a natural half-way location between the two major towns of East and West Boeotia, Thebes and Livadheia, and far enough to attract its own clientele for small businesses, shops, and professions, the "colonial" enterprise gradually grew into a local market town. When the Company was expropriated in the early 1950s it was converted into a nationalized company commissioned to maintain the drainage system, although the land was shared out amongst 16 local villages, which have prospered as a result ever since.

What remains of the "Company Village" is a very extensive and striking heritage. A minor part of the offices and barns for the produce of the drained lake has been converted into a cultural center (Figure 22.4a), whereas most of these facilities are locked ruins. Set back from the former main road can still be found the "bungalow villas" for the clerical-supervisor class of expatriates (Figure 22.4b). They were clearly designed to recall the suburban villas of outer London, with neat front and back gardens and many ornamental trees and shrubs. For the top management, substantial mansions in extensive woodland continue to excite visions of garden parties and the associated games of cricket and tennis that we know were popular with this expatriate community.

Symbolic Material Culture

Although the rich and diverse non-ceramic material culture of nineteenth- and twentieth- century Greece deserves fuller attention than we here have space for, there is a variety of topics which a future Early Modern Archaeology of Greece should include. Dress and furniture are increasingly well represented in museums such as the refurbished Benaki in Athens and we are able to study these topics further in well-illustrated books. For *dress*, see Papantoniou (1996), Anon. (2006), Broufas and Raftis (1993). These studies inform us on the one hand of the trend known throughout Southern Europe and the Eastern Mediterranean of the "Westernization" of clothes, and the trickle-down effect as first the wealthy and more educated emulate bourgeois lifestyles of Western and Central Europe, before they reach all classes. On the other hand, they also show the persistence of distinct local folk costumes in the Greek provinces, recognizable down to village level (Color Plate 22.4). Originally regional folk costumes included both everyday and special occasion clothes, but increasingly they became confined to the latter, and most recently they tend to appear for "cultural events" which have lost their real identity as celebrations of living local traditions. For archaeologists, these relations between material culture and society are of great importance, not only for an Archaeology of the Recent Past, but to illuminate comparable changes in much earlier periods. The mixing of materials and cultural influences on the very distinctive formal dress of each Greek village opens up major insights into concepts of identity, population contacts, and the globalization of textile fabrics. Of special interest is the mixture of Western and Eastern dress in recent centuries in the Cyclades, marked by strong influences from Venice and the Ottoman world (Vionis 2003) and the much longer wearing of Italian and other West European clothes (at least amongst the middle and upper classes) on the Venetian Ionian Islands (Theotoky 1998).

An overlap between dress and furnishings comes with the study of *embroideries* and *jewelry* to be worn on the body or for the latter also placed on house furniture, also rich in social and economic meanings. For studies of the post-Medieval and Early Modern period see Zora (1981), Trilling (1983), and Vionis (2005).

Dress of course offers one of several pathways into the study of the construction of the modern Greek nation, in which many ethnic or religious minorities have been absorbed into a culture centering on Greek Orthodox populations (Bintliff 2003, Karakasidou 1997). A prominent example is the wearing of a short kilt by the Greek National Guard, which is actually derived from Greek Albanian male dress (Biris 1998). For the archaeologist tracing village histories, a relevant and striking observation is the policy within the new Greek state, frequently solicited by these communities themselves, to "ethnically cleanse" place-names denoting non-Greek settlers, for example of Albanian or Slav origin,

Figure 22.4a   Surviving remains from the late nineteenth and early twentieth centuries of the Lake Copais Company's establishment, Haliartos. Offices and barns for the produce of the drained lake.
Author.

Figure 22.4b   Surviving remains from the late nineteenth and early twentieth centuries of the Lake Copais Company's establishment, Haliartos. The "bungalow villas" for the clerical-supervisor class of expatriates.
Author.

replacing them with a Classical toponym from the neighborhood (Alexandri 2002).

Furniture and *fixed house furnishings* are also a fruitful area to combine existing folklore analyses with an archaeological approach. Mobile furniture is introduced by Darzenta-Gorgia (2000) and fixed furnishings in Kizis (1994) and Philippides (1999).

Early Modern Greek *burial traditions* have been studied in a pioneer ethnoarchaeological study (Tzortzopoulou-Gregory 2008), sensitive to historical processes. From a database of more than 2000 graves in Corinthia and Kythera it is argued that current village cemeteries are essentially new foundations since the founding of the Greek state, when relocations outside communities were enforced from earlier graveyards within villages. Early simple graves were replaced in the twentieth century by stone monuments usually of some sophistication, reflecting rising incomes and Western influence to commemorate family members. The author significantly links the monumentalization of graves (Color Plate 22.5b) with the equivalent rise in sophistication of houses over the same period.

The study of *mobile art* can also be incorporated. One published example could be mentioned. Mykoniatis (1986) in a thoughtful study of plaster busts and statues of the period 1833–1862 suggests that the cheapness and flexibility of plaster sculpture (compared to marble) ideally suited the needs of contemporary patrons. There was an enthusiasm for reviving ancient Greek art and a desire for affordable new works in Neoclassical styles which this material could match. Important individuals in Early Modern Greek life, as well as Neoclassical compositions of an historicist nature, celebrated the "rebirth of Greece" through expressing in art its favored identity as the inheritor of ancient glory. There is also a striking link between the purity of white nineteenth-century plaster casts and new marble statues and the contemporary enthusiasm for seeing Classical temples and sculpture as equally idealized in their lack of naturalistic colors. This was despite clear evidence by this time for the high degree of color in ancient Greek artworks (Lowenthal 1988).

A mansion filled with Early Modern artworks with a unique origin lies today on the rural fringes of the town of Corfu: the Achilleion (Dierichs 2004). The wife of the Austrian Emperor Franz Joseph, Elisabeth (popularly called Sissi) had it constructed as a summer retreat in 1891. By this late date, the mixture of styles associated with a retrospective Romanticism had replaced pure Neoclassicism as a favored architecture for the upper and middle classes. The design of the villa and its décor are thus harmonious but culturally mixed. The mansion exterior mixes Baroque and Renaissance with wings like a Greco-Roman villa, while inside there are walls with imitation Pompeian wall-paintings and others with contemporary Romantic realist art depicting Classical subjects. The halls and gardens are filled with imitation Greco-Roman art and nineteenth-century heroic fantasy figures of Sissi's favorite myth-hero Achilles (Color Plate 22.5a). After Sissi's assassination in 1898 it was bought by the German Emperor Wilhelm. The German court was conveyed here for periods of holiday residence by boat from the head of the Adriatic, while from this mansion many of the dramatic affairs of the final years of the German Empire were played out. The building and its fascinating display of imagination concretized for foreign philhellenes (admirers of Greece), marks the steady rise in Greece's function as a potential "Disneyland" where the idealized "Other" could be encountered or resurrected in the original soil of myth.

This amputation of the intervening millennia between Classical and Modern Greece is a central aspect of the use of "symbolic capital" to homogenize the young nation around an inspiring image of its former greatness. Thus might Greece's greatness be revived after the intervening periods of foreign domination (Lowenthal 1988, Mouliou 1994, 2009). Seemingly essential to this aim was the permanent destruction of intervening material culture: between 1836 and the end of the nineteenth century the Athens Acropolis was "cleansed" not only of its Ottoman and Frankish but also its Byzantine and Early Christian monuments (Hurwit 1999). Doukellis (2004) underlines how the very recent pedestrian precinct around the Acropolis creates the townscape as a picture, movement through which signposts key monuments in the city's Classical cultural identity. Bastea (2003) recalls growing up in Thessaloniki with an instinctive admiration for its mosques and traditional houses in the Upper Town, yet her formal education counter-intuitively allowed her to feel that the homogeneous Greek city had always been essentially the same since its foundation in the fourth century BC. The rich multicultural world of the pre-Second World War city had effectively been erased from the collective memory of most of its inhabitants.

In a parallel fashion, ethnographer Hamish Forbes (2009) explains how most inhabitants in traditional Greek rural farming villages still possess a limited historical perspective, in which the detailed past ends with their grandparents' generation, after which local legend merges every other era. Indeed for them, the "Acropolis-focused" history of schoolbooks and national culture is a remote object divorced from their landscape and their communities' history. Such provincial communities instead increasingly identify with local historical or even legendary events that can be celebrated within their own localities.

An Annaliste Perspective

In the *medium term* the slow recovery of Greek rural and urban life after the traumas of the Late Ottoman era has culminated in population levels and lifestyles without previous parallel. Advances in production (for example chemical fertilizers, tractors, bank loans) and Greece's position in the EU and international markets, have enabled the country to achieve a relatively high degree of prosperity. The massive promotion of tourism ensures a steady year-round income to many parts of the land. In these respects Greece has shared in European-wide innovations and initiatives. In parallel, Early Modern Greece has also shared in the rise of the nation-state, the globalization and commercialization of agricultural and industrial production, and the convergence of political and social values within Western societies. More unique are *short-term* events, which have hindered Greece's advance: the nineteenth-century failings of its politicians to solve the land question, a twentieth-century dictatorship and military junta, and a society plagued by an infrastructure of clientelism inherited from late Ottoman times. And yet here especially Braudel's own preference for the longer term seems to offer a positive viewpoint for Greece's future. Improvements in standards of living and education, the modernization of the still important

rural farming sector, and the steady support of EU partners are vital features of Modern Greece which are the result of Greeks enthusiastically and energetically seizing on advances and opportunities arising across Europe as a whole over the last two centuries.

A Personal View

Having begun my own research in Greece as a landscape archaeologist in the early 1970s, daily contact with rural farmers, their villages, and small towns has been an annual part of my life for almost 40 years. I naturally followed the accepted scholarly view that the "direct historical approach" allowed one to see many surviving traditions of work, social organization, and mentalities in contemporary rural society, that emanated from medieval, ancient, and even prehistoric life. This view was challenged through working firstly with our Boeotia Project sociologist Cliff Slaughter (Slaughter and Kasimis 1986), and later with our Ottomanist Machiel Kiel (Kiel 1997), with post-Medieval ceramic specialists Joanita Vroom (2003) and Nasos Vionis (2005), and finally with our housing and settlement specialist Lef Sigalos (2004). I gradually realized how dynamic the last three centuries of Greek life have been. The possible similarities between society, religion, and mentalities in Early Modern Greece, Antiquity, and late Prehistory are not to be rejected out of hand (Forbes 2009), but are largely convergences due to similar socio-economic and ecological conditions. On the other hand, one major result of our own and other regional projects' researches has been to demonstrate genuine continuities in many practical aspects of rural life since the Frankish period, in housing and other aspects of lifestyle. The rapid disappearance of these links to the recent past bring urgency to the task of recording their still-visible remains in town and country, work which will require the promotion of post-Medieval archaeology and local history throughout Greece, especially through schools (Papagiannopoulos 2004). This is, encouragingly, a rapidly growing field of interest.

Greece has a wonderful Classical heritage to be proud of and its inspiration has always survived during the last 2500 years amongst the peoples of the Aegean and in the wider world. But the Greek landscape and people also have a fascinating and inspirational past from the millennia before Classical times and for the millennia since then to the very recent past. I hope this volume will contribute to a wider awareness of the rich history of this beautiful country in every century of its remarkable past.

References

Aalen, F. (1984). "Vernacular buildings in Cephalonia, Ionian Islands, Greece." *Journal of Cultural Geography* 4, 56–72.

Agriantoni, C. *et al.* (1999). *Ermoupoli – Syros.* Athens: Olkos.

Alexandri, A. (2002). "Names and emblems: Greek archaeology, regional identities and national narratives at the turn of the 20th century." *Antiquity* 76, 191–199.

Anon. (2006). *Greek Costume.* Athens: Benaki Museum.

Ante, U. (1988). "Zur Entwicklung des Grossraumes Athen." *Geographisches Rundschau* 40, 20–26.

Aschenbrenner, S. (1972). "A contemporary community." In W. A. McDonald and G. R. Rapp (eds.), *The Minnesota Messenia Expedition. Reconstructing a Bronze Age Regional Environment.* Minneapolis: University of Minnesota Press, 47–63.

Atlas de la Grèce (1852). Paris: Geographical Service of the French Army.

Bastea, E. (1999). *The Creation of Modern Athens: Planning the Myth.* Cambridge: Cambridge University Press.

Bastea, E. (2003). "Dimitris Pikionis and Sedad Eldem: Parallel reflections of vernacular and national architecture." In K. S. Brown and Y. Hamilakis (eds.), *The Usable Past. Greek Metahistories.* Lanham/Boulder: Lexington Books, 147–169.

Bintliff, J. L. (1997). "Further considerations on the population of ancient Boeotia." In J. L. Bintliff (ed.), *Recent Developments in the History and Archaeology of Central Greece.* Oxford: BAR Int. Series 666, 231–252.

Bintliff, J. (2003). "The ethnoarchaeology of a 'passive' ethnicity: The Arvanites of Central Greece." In K. S. Brown and Y. Hamilakis (eds.), *The Usable Past. Greek Metahistories.* Lanham/Boulder: Lexington Books, 129–144.

Bintliff, J. L. (2005). "Explorations in Boeotian population history." In P. L. Smith (ed.), *Studies in Honor of John M. Fossey I. The Ancient World* 36(1), 5–17.

Bintliff, J. L. *et al.* (1999). "The traditional vernacular architecture of Livadhia." In *Livadhia: Past, Present and Future.* Livadhia: Municipality of Livadhia, 85–99.

Bintliff, J. L. *et al.* (2007). "The Leiden-Ljubljana Ancient Cities of Boeotia Project. Summer 2007–Spring 2008." *Pharos. Journal of the Netherlands Institute in Athens* 15, 18–42.

Biris, K. (1998). *Arvanites. I dorieis tou neoterou ellinismou.* 3rd edn. Athens: Melissa.

Blake, H. (1980). "Technology, supply or demand?" *Medieval Ceramics* 4, 3–12.

Blitzer, H. (1990). "KOPONEIKA: Storage-jar production and trade in the traditional Aegean." *Hesperia* 59, 675–711.

Bory de St. Vincent, J. G. B. M. (ed.) (1836). *Expédition Scientifique de Morée.* Paris/Strasbourg: F. G. Levrault.

Broufas, C. and A. Raftis (1993). *40 Greek Costumes from the Dora Stratou Theatre Collection.* Athens: Dora Stratou Theatre.

Caftanzoglou, R. (1994). "The household formation pattern of a Vlach mountain community of Greece: Syrrako 1898–1929." *Journal of Family History* 19(1), 79–98.

Çelik, Z. (1986). *The Remaking of Istanbul: Portrait of an Ottoman City in the Nineteenth Century.* Seattle: University of Washington Press.

Clogg, R. (1992). *A Concise History of Greece.* Cambridge: Cambridge University Press.

Common, R. and A. Prentice (1956). "Some observations of the lowland Macedonian village." *Tijdschrift voor Economische en Sociale Geografie* 47, 223–227.

Cooper, F. (2002). *Houses of the Morea: Vernacular Architecture of the Northwest Peloponnesos (1205–1955).* Athens: Melissa Press.

Darzenta-Gorgia, E. (2000). *To epiplo.* Vol. 1, *To elliniko epiplo.* Athens: Ekdoseis Philippoti.

Davis, J. L. (1991). "Contributions to a Mediterranean rural archaeology: Historical case study from the Ottoman Cyclades." *Journal of Mediterranean Archaeology* 4, 131–215.

Dertilis, G. (1992). "Terre, paysans et pouvoir économique (Grèce, xviiie–xxe siècle)." *Annales. Histoire, Sciences Sociales* 47(2), 273–291.

Dierichs, A. (2004). "Das Achilleion auf Korfu." *Antike Welt* 35(2), 47–53.

Doukellis, P. (2004). "From the territory to the landscape and back again." In P. Doukellis and L. Mendoni (eds.), *Perception and Evaluation of Cultural Landscapes.* Athens: National Research Centre, 249–261.

Étienne, R. and F. Étienne (1992). *The Search for Ancient Greece.* London: Thames & Hudson.

Fels, E. (1944). *Landgewinnung in Griechenland.* Gotha: J. Perthes, Petermanns Geographische Mitteilungen 242.

Forbes, H. (2007). "Liquid landscape and fluid populations." In S. Davies and J. L. Davis (eds.), *Between Venice and Istanbul. Colonial Landscapes in Early Modern Greece.* Athens: American School of Classical Studies, Hesperia Supplement 40, 111–135.

Forbes, H. (2009). "Researching ekina ta khronia (times past) in a rural Greek community." *Public Archaeology* 8, 88–107.

Fotiadis, M. (1995). "Modernity and the past-still-present: Politics of time in the birth of regional archaeological projects in Greece." *American Journal of Archaeology* 99, 59–78.

Friedl, E. (1962). *Vasilika. A Village in Modern Greece.* Orlando: Holt, Rinehart & Wilson.

Hamilakis, Y. (2007). *The Nation and Its Ruins. Antiquity, Archaeology, and National Imagination in Greece.* Oxford: Oxford University Press.

Hamilakis, Y. and E. Yalouris (1996). "Antiquities as symbolic capital in modern Greek society." *Antiquity* 70, 117–129.

Hampe, R. and A. Winter (1962). *Bei Töpfern und Töpferinnen in Kreta, Messenien, und Zypern.* Mainz: Habelt Verlag.

Hurwit, J. M. (1999). *The Athenian Acropolis.* Cambridge: Cambridge University Press.

Jenkins, R. (1961). *The Dilessi Murders.* London: Longman.

Karakasidou, A. (1997). *Fields of Wheat, Hills of Blood. Passages to Nationhood in Greek Macedonia, 1870–1990.* Chicago: University of Chicago Press.

Kardamitsi-Adami, M. and M. Biris (2005). *Neoclassical Architecture in Greece.* Los Angeles: J. Paul Getty Museum, Getty Trust Publications.

Kartas, A. (1982). *Syros. Elliniki paradosiaki architektoniki.* Athens: Melissa.

Katochianou, D. (1992). "The Greek system of cities." *Ekistics* 59, 56–60.

Kiel, M. (1997). "The rise and decline of Turkish Boeotia, 15th–19th century." In J. L. Bintliff (ed.), *Recent Developments in the History and Archaeology of Central Greece.* Oxford: BAR Int. Series 666, 315–358.

Kizis, G. (1994). *Pilioreitiki oikodomia.* Athens: Politistiko Technologiko Idrima ETBA.

Koliopoulos, J. S. and T. M. Veremi (2004). *Greece. The Modern Sequel. From 1821 to the Present.* London: Hurst & Co.

Korre-Zographou, K. (1995). *Ta kerameika tou ellinikou chorou.* Athens: Melissa.

Koumarianou, A. (2005). *Athina. I poli – I anthropi.* Athens: Potamos.

Kyriazopoulos, V. D. (1984). *Ellinika paradosiaka keramika.* Athens: Eommex.

Lee, W. E. (2001). "Pylos Regional Archaeological Project, Part IV. Change and the human landscape in a modern Greek village in Messenia." *Hesperia* 70, 49–98.

Leigh Fermor, P. (1966). *Roumeli: Travels in Northern Greece.* London: John Murray.

Levi, P. (ed.) (1971). *Pausanias. Travels in Greece.* London: Penguin Books.

Louvrou, I. (ed.) (1999). *Thessalonique 1913 & 1918. Les Autochromes du Musée Albert-Kahn.* Athens: Olkos.

Lowenthal, D. (1988). "Classical antiquities as national and global heritage." *Antiquity* 62, 726–735.

McNeil, W. H. (1978). *The Metamorphosis of Greece since World War II.* Oxford: Blackwell.

Mansel, P. (1995). *Constantinople. City of the World's Desire, 1453–1924.* London: John Murray.

Mazower, M. (2004). *Salonika, City of Ghosts. Christians, Muslims and Jews 1430–1950.* London: Harper Collins.

Ministry of Culture, Greece (1989). *Biomichaniki archaiologia.* Athens: Archaeological Receipts Fund.

Monumenta. Magazine for the protection of the natural and architectural heritage in Greece and Cyprus, http://www.monumenta.org (electronic journal).

Mouliou, M. (1994). "The Classical past, the Modern Greeks and their national self. Projecting identity through museum exhibitions." *Museological Review* 1, 70–88.

Mouliou, M. (2009). "The concept of diachronia in the Greek archaeological museum: Reflections on current challenges." In J. Bintliff and H. Stöger (eds.) *Medieval and Post-Medieval Greece. The Corfu Papers.* Oxford: BAR Int. Series 2023, 233–241.

Mouzakis, S. A. (2008). *Myloi ke diamorphosi pheoudarchikou dikaiou sti ditiki, byzantini ke othomaniki oikonomia ke koinonia.* Athens: Epimeleia Epistimonike Etaireia Attikon Meleton.

Mykoniatis, E. (1986). "Original plasters of the Othonic period." *Athens Annals in Art and Archaeology* 19, 185–225.

Papadopoulos, A. K. (1993). "The drainage and exploitation of Lake Copais (1908–1938). Socio-economic implications of the exploitation of Lake Copais, Greece." University of Bradford, School of Social and Economic Studies, PhD thesis.

Papagiannopoulos, K. (2004). "Teaching local history and archaeology in Greek schools." In P. N. Doukellis and L. G. Mendoni (eds.), *Perception and Evaluation of Cultural Landscapes. Proceedings of an International Symposium, Zakynthos, December 1997.* Athens: Research Centre for Greek and Roman Antiquity, National Hellenic Research Foundation, Meletimata 38, 223–231.

Papanicolaou-Christensen, A. (1986). "Christian Hansen et l'établissement de filature en soie." *Athens Annals in Art and Archaeology* 19, 139–152.

Papantoniou, I. (1996). *Ellinikes topikes endymasies / Greek Regional Costumes.* Nafplion: Peloponnesian Folklore Foundation.

Philippides, D. (1999). *Greek Design and Decoration.* Athens: Melissa Press.

Philippides, D. (ed.) (1983–1990). *Elliniki paradosiaki architektoniki.* Athens: Melissa Press.

Piérart, M. and G. Touchais (1996). *Argos. Une ville grecque de 6000 ans.* Paris: CNRS.

Sigalos, E. (2004). *Housing in Medieval and Post-Medieval Greece.* Oxford: BAR Int. Series 1291.

Slaughter, C. and C. Kasimis (1986). "Some social-anthropological aspects of Boeotian rural society: A field report." *Byzantine and Modern Greek Studies* 10, 103–159.

Stathatos, J. (1999). "Pioneers of national pride." *Times Literary Supplement* (16 July), 18–19.

Stedman, N. (1996). "Land use and settlement in post-Medieval central Greece: An interim discussion." In P. Lock and G. Sanders (eds.), *The Archaeology of Medieval Greece*. Oxford: Oxbow, 179–92.

Theotoky, E.-L. I. (1998). *I kerkiraikes endymasies tis polis / Corfu Town Costumes*. Athens: Epsilon.

Trilling, J. (ed.) (1983). *Aegean Crossroads. Greek Island Embroideries in the Textile Museum*. Washington: The Textile Museum.

Tsigakou, F. M. (1981). *The Rediscovery of Greece*. London: Thames & Hudson.

Tzortzopoulou-Gregory, L. (2008). "Cemeteries in the countryside: An archaeological investigation of the Modern mortuary landscape in the Eastern Corinthia and Northern Kythera." In W. R. Caraher, L. J. Hall, and R. S. Moore (eds.), *Archaeology and History in Roman, Medieval and Post-Medieval Greece*. Aldershot: Ashgate, 307–344.

Vionis, A. K. (2003). "Much Ado About … a red cap and a cap of velvet. In search of social and cultural identity in Medieval and post-Medieval insular Greece." In H. Hokwerda (ed.), *Constructions of Greek Past. Identity and Historical Consciousness from Antiquity to the Present*. Groningen: Egbert Forsten, 193–216.

Vionis, A. K. (2005). "'Crusader' and 'Ottoman' material life: Built environment and domestic material culture in the Medieval and post-Medieval Cyclades Islands, Greece (c.13th–20th [century] AD)." University of Leiden, Faculty of Archaeology, PhD thesis.

Vroom, J. (1998). "Early Modern archaeology in Central Greece: The contrast of artefact-rich and sherdless sites." *Journal of Mediterranean Archaeology* 11, 131–64.

Vroom, J. (2003). *After Antiquity: Ceramics and Society in the Aegean from the 7th to the 20th Century A.C.* Leiden: Leiden University Archaeological Studies 10.

Whitelaw, T. M. (1991). "The ethnoarchaeology of recent rural settlement and land use in Northwest Keos." In J. F. Cherry, J. C. Davis, and E. Mantzourani (eds.), *Landscape Archaeology as Long-Term History*. Los Angeles: Cotsen Institute of Archaeology, University of California, 403–454.

Whitelaw, T. M. (1994). "An ethnoarchaeological study of rural land-use in North-West Keos." In P. N. Doukellis and L.G. Mendoni (eds.), *Structures rurales et sociétés antiques*. Paris: Les Belles Lettres, Annales Littéraires de l'Université de Besançon 508, 163–186.

Yerolympos, A. (1996). *Urban Transformations in the Balkans (1820–1920)*. Thessaloniki: University Studio Press.

Zora, P. (1981). *Embroideries and Jewellery of Greek National Costumes*. Athens: Museum of Greek Folk Art.

Further Reading

Bintliff, J. (2000). "Deconstructing 'the sense of place'? Settlement systems, field survey, and the historic record: A case-study from Central Greece." *Proceedings of the Prehistoric Society* 66, 123–149.

Kezer, Z. (1996). "The making of a nationalist capital: Socio-spatial practices in early Republican Ankara." *Built Environment* 22, 124–137.

Index

Printed and bound by CPI Group (UK) Ltd, Croydon, CR0 4YY